CANADIAN ISSUES

IN

ENVIRONMENTAL ETHICS

CANADIAN ISSUES

IN

ENVIRONMENTAL ETHICS

edited by

Alex Wellington, Allan Greenbaum
and Wesley Cragg

broadview press

Cataloguing in Publication Data

Main entry under title:

Canadian issues in environmental ethics

ISBN 1-55111-128-4

1. Environmental ethics - Canada.   I. Wellington, Alex, 1958-
II. Greenbaum, Allan.   III. Cragg, Wesley.

GR42.C352 1997   179'.1'0971   C97-930207-2

Broadview Press Ltd. is an independent, international publishing house, incorporated in 1985.

North America:

PO Box 1243, Peterborough Ontario, Canada K9J 7H5

3576 California Road, Orchard Park NY USA 14127

phone, fax and e-mail addresses for North America: (705) 743-8990 (phone); (705) 743-8353 (fax); 75322.44@COMPUSERVE.COM

UK and Europe:

BRAD (Book Representation and Distribution Ltd.)

244a London Rd., Hadleigh, Essex UK   SS7 2DE (1702) 552912

Australia:

St. Clair Press, PO Box 287, Rozelle NSW 2039 (02)818 1942

elsewhere:

Please order through local wholesalers or direct from North America.

Broadview Press Ltd. gratefully acknowledges the support of the Ontario Arts Council and the Ministry of Canadian Heritage.

PRINTED IN CANADA

Contents

ACKNOWLEDGEMENTS

Thanks to Don LePan and the rest of the team at Broadview Press for taking this project on in the first place and for sticking by it during the evolution of this book, which was fraught with the usual delays and difficulties (and then some). We would also like to thank Cole Dudley for her commitment and perseverance throughout the long and demanding process of typesetting and preparing the book for production. Special thanks to Peter Shepherd for his help in proofreading and his suggestions for the introduction.

Alex would like to acknowledge the inspiration of her students in Environmental Philosophy and Ethics at Ryerson Polytechnic University. Allan would like to thank Lilian Nattel for moral support and editorial advice. Wes would like to thank the Social Sciences and Humanities Research Council of Canada (SSHRC) Strategic Grant Program (Applied Ethics) for funding the research for two of the papers in this volume (Chapters 5 and 19).

HOW THIS BOOK CAME INTO BEING

Several years ago, Alex Wellington was asked to design a course in Environmental Philosophy and Ethics.* She knew that the course had to be applied, and that it should have as much of a Canadian focus as possible. The difficulty was to find materials that were applied and were predominantly Canadian. There were few Canadian books on environmental ethics available at that time, and most of those were predominantly theoretical in focus. There was a two volume collection on Environmental Ethics put out by the Institute for the Humanities at Simon Fraser University.[1] That collection contained thorough coverage of the theoretical issues in environmental ethics, and some articles which were applied in focus, but it did not provide a systematic review of the crucial issues that were of relevance to the Canadian scene. Another problem with those books was the striking lack of adequate gender representation - Volume One had no articles by women and Volume Two had only one, written by a non-Canadian. The only books which were very comprehensive in the range and scope of application and issues covered were either American or British. It occurred to her then that there was a need for a book which surveyed the field of applied environmental ethics with specific application to the Canadian context. The experience of having to use a package of materials to supplement a text which was not Canadian inspired Alex to think about initiating a book project to fill the need she perceived.

Soon after that, Allan Greenbaum and Alex began the planning for this book by creating a title, developing a proposal, and setting out a call for papers. Then Wesley Cragg came onto the

project when the call for papers was being distributed, and brought his wealth of experience to it. Wes had been motivated by similar concerns – to provide applied ethics materials on issues of relevance to Canadians – in the development of his Contemporary Moral Issues series (now in Fourth Edition). For those books, he endeavoured to find papers which were either written by Canadians, or which addressed their topics from a perspective or angle which had particular relevance to the Canadian context.

We designed the book around a thematic approach, one which could allow for the widest possible coverage of distinct topics and issues which were most germane to contemporary Canadian society. Yet, we also wanted to have the presentation of the thematic treatments organized around a structural framework. That framework has been outlined in the introduction which follows this preface. The three main sections we envisaged for the book were: Resource Use, Nature Preservation and Environmental Justice. We felt that these cluster categories reflected common trends and represented prominent focal points within the literature, both in Canada and elsewhere. We hope we have provided a book which could be used in a variety of different courses, from Canadian studies to philosophy, including political science, anthropology, sociology, cultural geography, religious studies, and of course environmental studies.

Our first priority in selecting papers for inclusion was regional representation. It was our intention all along that the book should provide reasonable regional representation, both in terms of the issues addressed and where authors are located. We had hoped to have articles which would deal with topics that were of particular relevance for the various regions of Canada. The book does include treatments of the following: fishing in the Atlantic region, forestry in British Columbia and Quebec, ranching and farming in the Prairies, hydroelectric power in Quebec and British Columbia, nuclear power in Ontario, mining in western and northern Canada, and agriculture across Canada. It was also clearly imperative to have extensive coverage of issues that were of significance to First Nations peoples. We also wanted to ensure that the book had good gender representation. To this end, just over a third of the pieces in this book were written (or in one case, co-written) by women, although we had hoped for even more.

Another objective was to include papers that presented a combination of conceptual analysis and factual information. We interpreted conceptual analysis fairly broadly, to include traditional philosophical argument and policy analysis along with general social theory. We thought that papers would be enhanced by the inclusion of specific details attained by the application of methods of the social and natural sciences. We did not expect that the papers themselves would be the product of primary research in the social or natural sciences, but we did expect that authors would have some familiarity with the findings of the social and natural sciences that are relevant to the issue or topic in question. Some of the papers are specifically oriented around case studies, other papers take an inherently theoretical approach. This collection is made up, for the most part, with original contributions. Only a few have been previously published elsewhere.

The book is not organized around the central theoretical debates, including anthropocentrism vs. bio/ecocentrism, preservation vs. conservation, deep ecology, social ecology, and so on. These debates, along with discussions of animal rights,

ecofeminism, the criticisms of anti-environmentalists and advocates of "wise use" approaches, and the role of economic analysis do arise throughout the papers in this book. If the intent was to provide a rigorous and comprehensive treatment of the theoretical issues, the book would have been better designed as an explicitly and inherently theoretical rather than applied project. Such a book, with a Canadian focus, would be well worth producing, but it would be another book, a different book, and awaits someone to undertake it.

To do both in the same book – to rigorously cover the theoretical debates and comprehensively survey the practical issues – would be an enormous undertaking. There are some recent collections of environmental ethics that attempt to do both; however, many suffer from one of two problems. Either there is insufficient theoretical material, or more commonly a fairly limited range of issues is covered. When a book does contain adequate coverage of both theoretical and practical issues, it tends to be huge.[2] Moreover, in all of the books that we are aware of, when there is discussion of practical issues the emphasis is on material of relevance to an American or British audience.

Our book is certainly not meant to be the last word on the subject, or the only one of its kind. There were many people working in the field in Canada whose work we had hoped to be able to include, but could not, for various reasons including time constraints and conflicting commitments. There would easily be enough material for several other books of the sort we have produced – a thematic, issue oriented approach – or for subsequent volumes of papers, in a series, for instance. This book is just one contribution to the continuing development of a distinctively Canadian tradition of environmental ethics.

We look forward to hearing from our readers and from the users of this book.

This request came from Ron Pushchak, the director of the Environmental Management Certificate Program for Continuing Studies at Ryerson Polytechnic University.

ENDNOTES

[1] Volume One was edited by Philip Hanson and Volume Two was edited by Raymond Bradley and Stephen Duguid.

[2] For example, Environmental Ethics: Readings in Theory and Application, edited by Louis Pojman, contains 72 pieces (three times the number in this book), of which all but five are reprinted from elsewhere. Even then, there is at least one glaring omission in that book. It includes a section on Non-Western Perspectives on Environmental Ethics which covers Hinduism, Buddhism, and Islamic, African and Third World perspectives. Yet, that section does not include any material on Native American perspectives, nor do the perspectives of First Nations or issues of interest to aboriginal people appear to be covered elsewhere in the book. It is hard, even for a huge book, to cover everything. Another example of a thorough and comprehensive collection which is also huge, is The Environmental Ethics and Policy Book, edited by Donald VanDeVeer and Christine Pierce.

CONTRIBUTIONS AND LINKAGES

THEMES IN CANADIAN APPLIED ENVIRONMENTAL ETHICS

by Alex Wellington, Allan Greenbaum and Wesley Cragg

APPLIED ENVIRONMENTAL ETHICS

The Field of Environmental Ethics

THIS IS AN EXCITING TIME TO BE INVOLVED IN THE DE-velopment of the field of environmental ethics. From its roots in the early 1970s, when the first courses in environmental ethics began to be offered in North American colleges and universities, the field has expanded into a rich and diverse arena exemplifying interdisciplinary trends, focus on global issues, and an increasingly multicultural emphasis.[1] There is now quite a vibrant and substantial body of literature in normative, or theoretical and applied, or practical environmental ethics. The current flourishing of the field of environmental ethics can be seen in the proliferation of journals. The journal *Environmental Ethics*, edited by Eugene Hargrove, began publication in 1979; since that time it has been joined by several other journals including *Environmental Values*, edited by Alan Holland, *Ethics and the Environment*, edited by Victoria Davion, and *Worldviews: Environment, Culture and Religion,* edited by Clare Palmer. There are now so many collections of readings in environmental ethics that one could easily fill a bookshelf with them alone.

In the past twenty plus years, Canadian writing in environmental ethics has found a place in the pages of *Alternatives* (currently edited by Robert Gibson at the University of Waterloo) and the *Trumpeter* (edited by Alan Drengson formerly at the University of Victoria), and more recently, the *Journal of Agricultural and Environmental Ethics* (edited by Frank Hurnik and Hugh Lehman at the University of Guelph) in addition to the journals mentioned above.[2] Many Canadian colleges and universities have developed courses and streams of programs in environmental ethics. The development of the field in Canada, as elsewhere, has been shaped by the interaction of scholars working in a remarkable range of areas, including administrative studies or business programs, aesthetics, biology or ecology, cultural studies or media studies, economics, education, engineering, geography, history, law or legal studies, literary studies, politics, religious studies, sociology and women's studies or gender studies. People working in all of these areas have joined with philosophers to discuss the finer points of environmental discourse and the implications of their applications. There are now debates within debates. Moreover, academics working and writing in environmental ethics have created connections between the humanities and the social sciences.

Environmental ethics ultimately represents a rethinking of ethics necessitated by the identification, recognition and acceptance of environmental values. Wesley Cragg has previously discussed the kind of reflections which generate the interest in, and perceived need for, the field of environmental ethics. As he has put it elsewhere:

Most of us are aware of the importance of the environment for our own well-being. Much of our life is spent coping with it, enjoying it, or escaping from it. Until recently, however, we have not asked about the impact of our behaviour on the environment. It seems that we have been content to assume that the environment could and would look after itself. The negative impact of our lifestyles on the world around us could therefore be safely ignored or, if not ignored, escaped by simply moving on. The

1

shortsighted character of this approach is now becoming inescapably obvious. Acid rain is now understood to have a devastating impact on forests, agriculture, and water resources. The Great Lakes basin has become a repository for many of the deadliest chemicals known. Our energy resources are being depleted. Nuclear power, once seen as a future source of unlimited, inexpensive energy, has become a source of serious concern on a number of counts: the threats of leaks and accidents, the as-yet-unsolved problem of storing nuclear wastes, the long-term hazards of uranium mine tailings, and so on. Our forests and soils, too, are being severely depleted. Many species of animal life are extinct or endangered, and our treatment of animals generally has come under increasing critical scrutiny. The list can be extended indefinitely.[3]

A crucial component of the inspiration for environmental ethics is the awareness of the "environmental crisis". The contours and dimensions and level of seriousness of the "crisis" are still hotly debated. Anti-environmentalists tend to contest the assertion of a crisis, and they decry the doomsday rhetoric and apocalyptic warnings publicized by environmentalists.[4] There are few in the general public, however, who would dispute the claim that there is a crisis of some sort, a crisis precipitated by a lack of fit between human beings and the natural environment. The evidence for that crisis consists of a number of "problems" in contemporary society: ecological disasters (such as drought, desertification, flooding or soil loss), excessive pollution of water and air, global warming and the greenhouse effect, ozone depletion, the extinction of species, the threat to natural areas posed by development, the depletion of natural resources (caused by overfishing and deforestation, etc.), the difficulty of dealing with waste (whether toxic or not) and so on. The series, State of the World reports edited by Lester Brown and others at the Worldwatch Institute, provide useful surveys of the global situation.

The Development of Applied Environmental Ethics

There is a story which could be told about the development of the field of environmental ethics. This story can be found throughout the introductions to collections; the story told here is a composite picture. The story has three phases, episodes, or stages. The first phase consists of conventional applied environmental ethics. The second phase consists of several related but distinguishable challenges to conventional applied ethics, which attempt to redress the shortcomings identified in that whole approach. There is an explicitly normative, an explicitly cosmological, and an explicitly political element of the second phase. There is, nevertheless, overlap between these three streams. The third phase consists of a turn to "practical ethics" away from both applied philosophy and normative theorizing, influenced by pragmatism and postmodernism.

Phase I: Conventional Ethics Applied to the Environment

Prior to the development of environmental ethics, modern moral philosophy was dominated by the two traditions – utilitarianism and deontological theories. The latter consists of various versions of social contract theory, respect for persons theory, and other rights and duty based theories. Applied philosophy began by taking the insights, conceptual apparatus, and methodologies of philosophy and applying them to a range of practical, real world problems and everyday activities.[5] Applied or practical ethics developed as an attempt to make philosophy relevant to pressing contemporary social issues. The field rests upon the assumption that conceptual analysis and philosophical argument along with philosophical theorizing can fruitfully be brought to bear on areas of social life which are the subject of controversy and debate.

The 1989 McDonald Report, *Towards a Ca-*

nadian Research Strategy in Applied Ethics, characterized applied ethics in terms of three features: "(1) the linkage of theory and practice; (2) interdisciplinary methodology; and (3) user-orientation".[6] As McDonald and others have pointed out, the term "applied ethics" and its characterization have been the subject of debate and controversy. The initial formulations of applied ethics tended to be quite simple, even crude, or so critics thought. The simplified approach to doing applied ethics likened it to following a recipe: Take a Principle (say the Principle of Utility or the Principle of Respect for Persons). Take a Fact Situation (a real world moral problem). Apply the Principle to the Fact Situation, and presto, you get a response to the situation or, better yet, a solution to the problem. This conception of applied ethics, which has been called the "engineering model of ethics" has been subject to extensive and sustained criticism.[7]

The earliest environmental applications of ethics tended to consist of "ordinary ethics" applied to "situations in which facts about the environment" were important.[8] Thus, they defined the environment "in terms of the opportunities (resources) it presents to human beings and the obstacles (pollution) human beings create to the satisfaction of their wants and needs".[9] The theoretical frameworks used were often those inspired by or taken from theories of distributive justice or economic analysis. The problems examined tended to be ones that arose from industrial and commercial activities, and the criteria for evaluating activities were all derived from notions of human rights or human welfare.[10] The conventional approach to environmental ethics, the critics charged, rested on attitudes that lead people to "treat nature as nothing but raw material for satisfying human desires".[11] These treatments of environmental issues which presumed the view that humans are the origin and the measure of all values elicited complaints about their pervasive "resourcism".

Many philosophers continued, and still continue, to write conventional applied environmental ethics, much of which became increasingly sophisticated, especially the treatment of issues concerning future generations.[12] Most prominent and influential has been the application of economic analysis to environmental problems. Many policy analysts, decision makers and politicians have argued that the resolution of environmental problems should be determined by the application of a cost-benefit analysis, which derives from the ethical perspective of economic analysis. Economic analysis was initially applied to pollution problems, but since then has been extended into a huge range of environmental issues, including workplace safety, consumer safety, land use, nature preservation, and species preservation.[13] The increasing influence of economic analysis has been resisted by environmentalists, for reasons which are discussed in the papers by Anne Bell (Chapter 13), Allan Greenbaum (Chapter 16) and Alex Wellington (Chapter 12) in this book. Economic analysis is also discussed by Andrew Brook (Chapter 7) and Lionel Rubinoff (Chapter 8) and by Wesley Cragg and Mark Schwartz (Chapter 19).

The ethical perspective of economic analysis is clearly human-centred, and as such is subject to criticism on those grounds. It has also been criticized by the adherents of a different, but still human-centred, perspective – that of social justice. The easiest way to characterize the contrast between the two perspectives is to say that an economic analysis is based on the fundamental, or core, value of utility, interpreted in terms of economic efficiency and that a social justice approach is based on the fundamental, or core value of equality. The social goal which is the priority for the economic analysis approach is the maximization of overall utility, measured in terms of wealth maximization. Social justice, on the other hand, rests upon the social goal of an egalitarian distribution of social resources, which entails a fair allocation of benefits and burdens resulting from social policies.

The work of John Rawls is one of the most influential philosophical articulations of a theory of justice. His concept of the "difference principle" in particular, has become axiomatic. That principle stipulates that any inequalities in the distribution of social resources are justifiable only if they are part of a system which works overall to the benefit of the least well-off members of society.[14] Many environmental philosophers have taken the ideas of Rawls and applied them to environmental issues.[15] Peter Penz's paper (Chapter 24) on international environmental justice addresses the relevance of Rawls' theory to global issues.

A profusion of articles and books in the United States have been articulated and elaborated of an environmental justice perspective. This work has looked at evidence for the disparate impact of environmental laws, and has provided evidence that many laws and policies tend to have the effect of advantaging the already advantaged and further disadvantaging the already disadvantaged.[16] The proponents of an environmental justice approach have also been critical of the concerns of preservationist environmentalism for paying insufficient attention to issues of class, race, gender, ability and other bases of discrimination.[17]

The relationship between social justice and environmental concern has sometimes been cast in terms of the opposition exemplified by the simple formula "social justice versus environmental protection". Yet, as Robert Paehlke and Pauline Vaillancourt Rosenau argue, there is actually much more basis for "common purpose" between social justice movements and environmental movements than may be perceived.[18] They point out that environmentalist concerns with human health and economic sustainability, in particular, have the potential to coincide with social justice concerns. Contemporary philosophers and sociologists have undertaken the formulation of a social justice perspective which is premised upon

the importance of equal environmental protection.[19]

The general approach of conventional applied ethics considers existing moral categories and conceptions of value to be adequate.[20] Philip Elder's work is an example of the conventional approach.[21] He reports that he feels "great personal distress" about the "diminishing wilderness or impending extinction" of animal and plant species.[22] Yet, he finds that ordinary ethics provides sufficient resources for rigorous environmental protection. Many, many philosophers disagree with that claim.

Phase II: Environmental Ethics and Beyond
There are a few concepts and distinctions which need to be clarified in order to make sense of the story of environmental ethics. The distinction between anthropocentric, or human-centred theories and nonanthropocentric theories is a crucial one. The assimilationist theories were content to retain human beings as the source and locus for value; the challengers dispute this limitation. They argue instead that beings other than humans should be recognized to have moral importance. A related distinction is that between instrumental value – the value something has as a means to an end – and intrinsic value – the value something has in itself. Anthropocentric moral theories insist that non-human nature has only instrumental value, whereas the nonanthropocentric alternatives assert the existence of intrinsic value, or inherent worth, in non-human nature. Nature has moral significance independent of human use, or even of human valuing, for some philosophers. These concepts are discussed in the papers by Jerry Valen DeMarco (Chapter 14), Allan Greenbaum (Chapter 16) and Alex Wellington (Chapter 12).

Nonanthropocentric environmental ethics draws upon the conceptual tools and resources provided by moral philosophy in order to assess the moral worth and moral status of non-human nature. It makes use of the style of argumentation of conventional moral philosophy.[23] A series of candidates for ethical theories have been developed to address the question which beings are deserving of moral consideration and thus have moral significance. These theoretical approaches explore the possibility that an "enhanced understanding of ecosystems" and other ecological knowledge will lead to the "transformation of fundamental ethical principles" and not just to new types of applications.[24] Many observers of the field mark its origins with the publication of seminal papers in the areas of animal liberation, deep ecology, ecofeminism, and non-anthropocentric ethics.[25] Deep ecology and ecofeminism and other so-called radical environmental philosophies are discussed below. Here we focus on the challenges to conventional applied ethics presented by nonanthropocentric normative philosophy, also sometimes called ecological ethics.[26]

Philosophers contend that there are certain properties or characteristics, the possession of which is necessary for an entity to be entitled to moral consideration.[27] The disagreement is about which criteria have to be satisfied in order for a being to be deemed worthy of moral standing.[28] The brief account of the development of the reconstructionist critique goes as follows: First philosophers required that an entity or being had to satisfy the requirements of rationality or language use in order to merit moral consideration. Moral consideration in this sense would include either utilitarian conceptions of welfare or rights or deontological conceptions of rights and related duties. Thus, on the rationality or language criteria, only human beings would satisfy the criteria stipulated, only humans are entitled to respect and to have their interests counted. However, the critics pointed out that not all humans could satisfy the criteria, and therefore not all humans would be worthy of equal consideration.

Once it has been pointed out that not all humans would meet the conditions for moral standing, the space opens up to argue that if one wants to have all humans covered, different and more inclusive criteria must be substituted. The charge is that the conventional, anthropocentric positions are speciesist, that they exemplify human chauvinism.[29] Peter Singer suggested that sentience should be the criteria, such that any and all entities, organisms or beings which are sentient (capable of experiencing pleasure and pain) deserve moral standing. He proposed the Principle of Equality of Interests in order to argue that vertebrates at least should be included within the scope of beings whose interests are counted in utilitarian calculations.[30] Tom Regan, on the other hand, proposed that entities which are "subjects of a life", should be deemed to be rights-holders.[31] These entities, mainly mammals, should be considered to have rights to existence which would block actions detrimental to their flourishing.

The next step in the argument was to move from justification for animal liberation or animal rights to justification for the moral standing of all nonhuman living beings. The shift was from sentientist approaches to ethics to biocentric approaches. Starting with Kenneth Goodpaster (influenced by Albert Schweitzer) and continuing with Paul Taylor, philosophers proposed that all living beings should be deemed to have moral standing and that moral consideration should be extended to all forms of life.[32] The claim was that all things that are living have interests, interests in continued life at the least.[33] Human beings would be subject to duties in regard to nonhuman life forms, including duties of noninterference. Humans would be required to curtail their activities to avoid doing harm to other nonhuman beings in order to act morally. At this stage in the argument, we are still talking about individual entities.

The development of ecocentric ethics marked a further expansion in the circle of beings who were put forth as candidates for moral standing. Now the proposal was to extend moral consideration to ecosystems, to include all of nature in the category of things that have non-instrumental, or intrinsic value. Living and non-living nature, including animals, birds, insects, plants, trees, rivers, lakes, rocks, soil, mountains, and so on, is all morally significant, on this position. Much of the work in this vein was initially inspired by the work of Aldo Leopold, a non-philosopher who worked as an ecologist and wildlife manager. His essay, "The Land Ethic", has probably been the most cited and most influential piece in the whole field.[34]

Leopold presented his ethic as but the latest development in an organic evolution of moral consciousness. Leopold was instrumental for introducing aesthetic and ecological concepts into the discourse of environmental ethics and environmental advocacy – concepts such as beauty, harmony, stability, integrity and diversity. Contemporary environmental philosophers, such as J. Baird Callicott and Holmes Rolston have taken his ideas and turned them into systematic and comprehensive philosophical positions.[35] Some have labelled the approaches that come out of Leopold's work with the term "ecological sensibility".[36] This latest move, from organisms to ecosystems is said to represent a shift from atomistic to holistic ethical approaches.[37] Atomism, or individualism, in ethics, refers to the belief that the individual organism or person is the locus of value, as well as the source of value. Holism enables one to discuss entities or systems such as species or ecosystems as being morally significant as wholes. The general claim made is that the whole itself has intrinsic value.[38] The issue of holism versus individualism and the relative balance between them as dual aspects of an environmental ethic has been much debated in the literature.[39]

One of the most pervasive tensions in the literature has been the divide between preservationist environmentalists and adherents of animal rights and animal liberation theories.[40] This divergence has tracked in many instances, although not all, the division between atomistic and holistic

ethical theories. The conflict has been most marked in instances where domestic or feral (now wild, previously domesticated) animals pose a threat to delicate ecosystems, and to endangered plants, birds, and animals.[41] Environmentalists are concerned with the flourishing of populations and species, and the relative balance of native to non-native species. Animal rights advocates defend the interests of individual animals against the holistic interests of the ecosystem championed by preservationist environmentalists. Conflicts between the interests of wildlife preservationists and animal protection interests have frequently clashed in the United States and lawsuits have resulted.[42] In Canada, domestic animals are less significant in terms of threats to imperilled species, but are still a problem.[43] Thus, the philosophical ideas and distinctions have fed into, and spiralled out of, the activities of activists and policy makers.

We come to just about the end of the story of the normative element of the second phase. The story as told is but one interpretation of the development of the field, but it is the common one and it is thematic rather than strictly chronological.[44] The story has been schematized by a series of concentric circles by Roderick Nash, representing the ever-widening scope of moral concern.[45] Yet, it has to be recognized that there is no consensus on the linear model presented above.[46]

It is possible to list examples endlessly of ongoing points of disagreement in environmental ethics: for many, the only value nature has is instrumental value, but for others, the value of nature is intrinsic, and for others still it is inherent.[47] For some, the threshold of moral considerability is species membership (ie. the human species), but for others the threshold of moral considerability is sentience, and then for still others it is life or perhaps simply existence. Even where there is agreement on what counts for moral standing, there are disagreements about the level of moral significance. Some think all beings or species have equal significance, whereas others favour a graded or differential scale.[48] For some ethics must be atomistic, but for others it can or even must be holistic. For some, ethics must be monistic; yet, for others, it has to be pluralistic. We will return to the latter issue in the discussion of the third phase.

One last point that bears mentioning is that the choice of theory, or rather the choice of criteria for moral standing has elicited significant attention from other philosophers and has generated an enormous amount of controversy. Contributions made by normative environmental ethicists to the broader realism of environmental thought and advocacy include the following: reappraisals of notions of self and individual, reflections on "the relationship between humans and nature", and the addition of "new dimensions to thinking about appropriate political arrangements".[49] This is in addition to the emphasis placed upon the connections between ecology and ethics.[50] Many of the issues that have been raised by the normative philosophers have inspired others to develop different theories which will be discussed below.

As mentioned above, non-anthropocentric normative moral theory was not the only stream of thought that characterized the second episode in the development of environmental ethics. Other streams of environmental thought took shape around the same time (which is to say the 1970s and 1980s). The umbrella term "environmental thought" has been used to distinguish those streams of writing which disclaim the label "environmental ethics". These other streams also reject the anthropocentrism of traditional Western moral philosophy, but they do not locate the fundamental problem in a faulty theory of value or obligation. Rather, they regard anthropocentric moral views as symptomatic of some more fundamental cultural ills.

According to one stream of environmental thought, these ills are fundamentally ones of consciousness and metaphysical belief. This stream

of thought has had considerable influence on popular environmentalism.[51] Cosmological environmental thought (variants of which also go by such names as "ecosophy", "ecophilosophy", and "transpersonal ecology"[52]) has also provided much of the philosophical inspiration of the radical deep ecology movement.[53] Deep ecology was initially coined by Arne Naess, and contrasted with "shallow environmentalism"; the contrasting positions are outlined in Alan Drengson's piece (Chapter 1). Jerry Valen DeMarco (Chapter 14) and Annie Booth (Chapter 21) provide elaboration on the development of ideas in deep ecology. Peter Miller (Chapter 2) also draws on the contrast between shallow and deep ecology and presents a range of positions from informed humanism to ecocentrism. Other radical tendencies in environmental thought – ecofeminism and social ecology – will briefly be discussed below.

Cosmology is concerned with the nature of reality and the universe. The cosmological stream of environmental thought is marked by the view that, in John Livingston's words "the environmental problem is not a technical, legal or moral problem, it is a metaphysical one":[54]

[T]he issue is essentially cosmological .... The problem is metaphysical – not ethical, not aesthetic. The problem is the traditional western humanistic vision of man and his cosmological role.[55]

Proponents of cosmological environmental thought have dismissed normative environmental ethics as "prosthetics", as being simply "not enough".[56] According to Alan Drengson, "something is fundamentally wrong with the cultural adaptations characteristic of modern society. These shortcomings cannot be corrected merely by extending the value systems inherent in that society".[57] What is needed, rather, is "a dramatic and fundamental shift in the way human beings and human institutions are able to perceive and receive the world around them".[58] One author explained her reasons for "not talking about environmental ethics anymore" as follows: ethics is "a human construct which makes reference only to human interests; it is applied by humans, based on values determined and articulated by humans... and extends only to those things we value".[59] The general charge is that the environmentalist ethos, the love and concern for the natural world which motivates many environmentalists, is not translatable into "something as formalized and defined as a code of ethics".[60]

The suggestion is that the environmentalist ethos is not a matter of do's and don'ts, but is rooted in a set of beliefs and perceptions regarding the nature of Nature and the nature of the human Self. That is, the environmentalist ethos is at odds with the prevailing "dominant paradigm" and presages a shift to a new "ecological paradigm". A "paradigm" is way of thinking that encompasses much more than definitions; it includes models, metaphors, and conceptual gestalts.[61] The "dominant paradigm" which informs Western industrial culture, according to this view, is one that sees all of nature, organic and inorganic alike, as a fundamentally lifeless machine – wholly separate from, inferior to, and at the disposal of, the human species. The job of environmental thought is to help accomplish a "paradigm shift" by exposing and questioning this deeply rooted and largely unconscious set of beliefs and perceptions. It seeks to articulate an alternative worldview in which non-human beings are conceived and perceived to be kin, or all of nature is conceived and perceived as part of one's own extended Self.[62] Proponents suggest that such a worldview, once internalized, will spontaneously generate the kind of ecologically benign conduct that normative environmental ethics seeks to prescribe.

As things have developed, some environmental thinkers who once dismissed the field of environmental ethics now have their work regularly included in environmental ethics anthologies.[63] The explanation for the apparent turnaround may

have a lot to do with the organic evolution of the field, which has expanded and been transformed by the successive waves of criticism and reconstruction. Indeed, the dichotomy as we have presented it here may be too stark, since there has been a considerable amount of cross-fertilization between environmental thought and environmental ethics.[64]

The cosmological stream of environmental thought was established early in Canada, and it has secured a prominent niche in the Canadian environmental theory scene. John Livingston's *One Cosmic Instant* was published in the same year that "environmental ethics" appeared as a distinct field of academic inquiry and the expression "deep ecology" first appeared in the environmental lexicon.[65] Alan Drengson of the University of Victoria is a pre-eminent figure in what might be called the Pacific Rim ecosophy tradition; Neil Evernden (who with Livingston cultivated a hotbed of environmental theorizing at Toronto's York University) has created a unique and influential brand of phenomenological environmental thought which has many affinities with the cosmological stream.[66]

Ecofeminism and social ecology differ from both normative environmental ethics and the cosmological streams within this second phase of environmentalist reflection. Adherents of the explicitly political approaches attribute the abuse of non-human nature neither to faulty ethical norms nor to faulty cosmological paradigms, but to relations of domination and exploitation among humans, and to the ideological structures that have grown up around these relations. Social ecologists and ecofeminists also engage in practices of ethical and cosmological critique and reconstruction, but they insist that these practices must be rooted in an analysis of hierarchy and oppression among humans.[67]

Ecofeminism is difficult to situate in any definitive way, since there are such diverse strands and approaches that fall under the rubric of ecofeminism. Ecofeminism, as a social movement, is also extremely diverse. Ecofeminists emphasize the relationship between gender hierarchy – that is, androcentrism and patriarchy – and the anthropocentric project of dominating non-human beings and natural processes.[68] There are feminists who work within the conventional applied ethics model, and address environmental issues but they are not usually considered to be ecofeminists. Among the range of positions that are included as ecofeminist, there are care ethic perspectives, cosmological perspectives, and also virtue ethic perspectives in addition to the radical political and specifically anti-domination versions commonly associated with the term ecofeminism.[69] Some ecofeminists have taken great pains to distinguish themselves from deep ecology, in particular, and to present a critique of the masculinist bias of the writing found under that heading.[70] Some ecofeminists have associated themselves with the social ecology banner, others have distanced themselves from it. The topic of ecofeminism is dealt with at length in the paper by Annie Booth in Chapter 21 and also in the paper by Karen Krug in Chapter 22.

Social ecology is a philosophical and political movement that draws on anarchist thought (especially that of Kropotkin), elements of the Frankfurt School's neo-Marxist theorizing regarding the relationship between the domination of nature and the domination of humans, and various green-decentralist, bioregionalist and non-anthropocentrist currents within the broader ecology movement.[71] Social ecology has been very influential among some Canadian activist circles, though it has played less of a role in Canadian theorizing. In Canada, social ecology perhaps has its highest profile in Montreal, where it has influenced people involved in municipal level ecopolitics, and where Dmitri Rossopoulous and other anarchist intellectuals have established publishing venues (Black Rose Books and the jour-

nal *Our Generation*) for radical environmental and political thought.

There have been several rifts among and between adherents of the various radical perspectives, as was mentioned above. Deep ecologists have been subjected to sustained criticism from both social ecologists and ecofeminists, for paying insufficient attention to the "logic of domination" and hierarchy, and for seeming to neglect the political relations among humans in the social sphere in their theories.[72] Social ecologists have likewise been criticized by ecofeminists for not according sufficient weight to gender, in either the explanations of hierarchy and domination or in the recipes for overcoming them. Certain environmentalists have made valiant efforts to try to create linkages and connections between the various strands of radical ecophilosophy.[73] Many other theorists and activists have urged that environmental philosophers abandon attempts at unification in the spirit of multivocality and diversity.

Phase III: Practical Ethics, Pragmatism and Postmodern Environmental Ethics

If the first episode in our story involved the application of traditional moral theories to environmental problems and the second episode involved efforts to rethink, expand or radically revise moral and political theory in the light of the environmental crisis, the third episode involves a movement away from abstract theorizing and a reemphasis on the concrete texture of particular problems, practices and perspectives. The impetus for this shift, which figures increasingly in the environmental ethics literature of the 1990s, is multifaceted.

Many commentators have noted that disagreements at the level of moral theory or philosophical doctrine do not always map onto disagreements at the level of practical positions or policy recommendations (and vice versa). Armstrong and Botzler emphasize the striking divergence of approaches to environmental ethics along with an apparent convergence on policy recommenda-tions.[74] Similarly, Lisa Newton and Catherine Dillingham say that: "it matters very little whether we approach ... problems from the perspective of ecofeminism or deep ecology, or ... from Kantian or utilitarian perspectives".[75] What does matter, they and others argue, is to examine and reexamine social practices relating to choice of technologies, energy use and resource consumption patterns, settlement patterns, land use and ownership, and so on.

This pragmatic approach is contrasted with such theory-laden rivals as (on the one hand) eco-nomic analysis, which reduces all values to con-sumer preferences, and (on the other hand) ecocentric and holistic versions of the land ethic which grant moral standing to non-human nature. Proponents of pragmatism especially resist the calls for monism; they insist that real life situa-tions are too complex to be captured by any set of principles.[76] The rivals are charged with attempt-ing to fit all environmental questions into a Procrustean bed of preconceived moral considera-tions, while being at best out of touch with the real world of environmental policy and activism, and at worst exacerbating environmental conflicts by giving the antagonists lofty-sounding names for their prejudices.[77]

Pragmatists have been inspired by critiques of foundational theories. Contemporary social theo-rists have characterized the "postmodern condi-tion" in terms of suspicion of "metanarratives". In the environmental field, such metanarratives or master theories might include grand, single-principle anthropocentric, biocentric or ecocentric normative theories, cosmological "paradigms", or social theories that attempt to account for all harm and subordination in terms of a single dynamic.[78] Environmental pragmatists champion "practical ethics", as distinct from both "applied ethics" and ethical theorizing. "Environmental pragmatism" is defined as "the open-ended inquiry into the spe-cific real-life problems of humanity's relationship

with the environment".[79]

The environmental pragmatism, practical eth-ics approach is opposed not only to the grand theo-rizing of phase II environmental thought and eth-ics, but even more so to the conception of applied ethics that, in our account, characterized phase I (regardless of whether the ethical theories so ap-plied are of the phase I or the phase II variety). Summarizing the arguments of Bryan Norton, its leading exponent, Don Marietta concisely captures the flavour of the "practical ethics" approach:

Norton speaks of principles being generated from practice....[P]hilosophers should join nonphilosophers in efforts to solve problems. Formation of theory and work on concrete cases should...be alternated so that theory is checked against our moral intuitions...Norton's approach makes environmental philosophy and ethics in-teractive, with feedback loops between a devel-oping philosophy and the actual situations in which decisions must be made.[80]

Contemporary research in practical ethics and environmental policy studies departs from the conception of "application" that characterizes (our caricature of) phase I not only in what it says about the relationship between theory and practice but also in respect of what it finds about the relation-ship between facts and values. As Wesley Cragg has written elsewhere, previous work in applied ethics has already indicated that:

facts always play an important role in moral argument. It is true that simply assembling facts cannot in itself resolve a moral issue. Yet, in the absence of a sound factual base, moral argument is even more problematic, and ultimately perhaps more contested. Environmental issues pose seri-ous problems in this respect. The relevant facts are usually assembled by scientists and are usu-ally communicated in technical language. Obtain-ing and assembling facts in an understandable way is a major task on the road to the moral evalu-ation of environmental issues...[Further,] and relatedly, because we depend so heavily on sci-entific experts to provide the facts needed for moral evaluation, we also have a tendency to as-sume that environmental ethics is a field in which only experts are competent to pass judgement.[81]

The conventional approach to applied ethics meshes well with a particular model of public policy formation. This model is associated with a theoretical framework identified as "sequential assessment". In the common model for policy for-mation, facts and values are distinguished and treated separately. The assumption is that an ob-jective technical problem can be addressed, in the first instance, by science, and that ethics and poli-tics subsequently provide the subjective policy component. A policy is ultimately inherently nor-mative. One cannot deduce an ethical conclusion through a description of facts alone, and thus, eth-ics must be part of the policy process. This model characterizes the different contributions of science and ethics in terms of the distinction between de-scription and prescription. Science is the source of descriptive statements about the nature of real-ity through analysis of facts and experience. Eth-ics is the domain of inquiry that attempts to an-swer normative questions, and provide prescrip-tive statements.

In this "classical" conception of applied ethics and policy theory, the processes of fact-finding and value deliberation were notionally divorced. Scientists produced value-neutral (if value-rel-evant) facts, while philosophers (or the political process, in the case of policy formation) deter-mined the empirically neutral value principles to apply to those facts. One consequence of this view is that it renders the fact disputes that pervade environmental issues philosophically uninterest-ing. By contrast, a significant area of contempo-rary research in applied environmental philoso-phy (and also in social scientific examinations of environmental decision-making) concerns the extent to which value issues play an irreducible role in the construction of environmental facts,

particularly where value issues intersect with ar-eas of scientific uncertainty.[82] Factual uncertainty is discussed in Alex Wellington's paper (Chapter 12); the value-ladenness of facts is touched on in the papers by David Oppenheim and Robert Gibson (Chapter 6), Ingrid Leman Stefanovic (Chapter 15) and Wesley Cragg and Mark Schwartz (Chapter 19).

Contemporary practitioners of applied ethics are drawn to theorizing the relationship between environmental ethics and environmental activism. The development of the field of environmental ethics in Canadian universities and colleges, as in the United States, followed after the development of environmentalism as a social movement. Many early researchers were originally inspired by the environmental movement outside the university and many more continue to draw inspiration from the movement to this day. As is noted in the McDonald Report on Applied Ethics, environmen-tal ethics is an area of applied ethics in which there has historically been the most political activity but which has been the least developed academi-cally.[83] Two findings of the report are significant for present purposes. One is the later development of courses in environmental ethics relative to other areas of applied ethics.[84] The other is the finding that environmental activists were reported to be "deeply suspicious of fundamental ethical enquir-ies concerning the environment".[85] Both of these factors may help account for the state of the field in Canada at the time the report was written.

The pragmatic account of practical ethics dis-cussed above corresponds almost exactly to the conception of "applied ethics" described in the McDonald Report which referred to the interdis-ciplinary, user-focused nature of applied ethics and the role of "reflective equilibrium" between theo-retic coherence and concrete insight. For this rea-son, we have no hesitation in using the term "ap-plied environmental ethics" in the title of this vol-ume to refer to a field whose ambit includes the literature characteristic of phase III environmental ethics as well as the other two phases. For the purposes of the present project, we have adopted an inclusive and all-encompassing notion of "applied ethics". We consider the term to be interchangeable with the term "practical ethics". We use the term in such a way as to cover the narrower conceptions of conventional normative ethics as well as the broader conceptions of policy analysis and environmental thought.

CANADIAN ISSUES

It is our contention that the specifics of the Canadian situation are sufficiently different (from those of other countries) and interesting to warrant treatment in their own right. This book is divided into three sections, which we think would map nicely onto theme areas or areas of emphasis within the general field of Canadian Studies. Those three sections are: Resource Use, Nature Preservation and Environmental Justice. We discuss them in a slightly different order below, as we deal with Resource Use and then Environmental Justice before we come to Nature Preservation.

Resource Use and
the Canadian Political Economy

The distinctive nature of Canadian environmental issues reflects the nature and history of the Canadian economy.[86] On the one hand, Canada is an affluent industrialized country. Issues concerning distinctive obligations of rich countries, such as Canada, are addressed by Peter Penz in Chapter 24. On the other hand, like many Third-World nations, Canada's economy has traditionally been based on the export of natural resources. The influential Canadian economic historian and social theorist Harold Innis has described the central role of what he called "staple commodity" production in the history of Canada.

Over the course of much of its history, Canada has functioned as a "hinterland" providing one or another raw material to a more populous "metropolis" (first France and Britain and then the United States). Fish from the Atlantic coast and furs from the interior were the first of these staples. In quantitative terms, the fur trade is no longer of much economic significance to the country as a whole, but it remains important to the economies of many First Nations and remote rural non-Native communities. The fur trade generates controversy around the animal welfare issue, and in recent decades, animal activists have campaigned in Europe in an effort to dry up the market for Canadian furs.[87] Aspects of the fur controversy are explored in Wendy Donner's essay in this book (chapter 9).

Commercial fishing, although a bigger industry than the fur trade, is now also a modest component of the total Canadian economy. The fishery contributes about a billion dollars yearly to the Canadian economy, less than 1 percent of the entire goods-producing sector. Nevertheless, it is of great importance to some regions. In the 1980s, the fishery contributed about 10 percent of the value of the goods producing sector in the Atlantic provinces, and in Nova Scotia, for example, every 1 percent change in fishery production gives rise to a 1.4 percent change in the total provincial income.[88] The collapse of the Atlantic ground fishery, discussed by Ray Rogers (chapter 4), is perhaps the most economically significant of the ecological catastrophes Canada has experienced.[89]

Canada's premier food resource industry in no longer fishing but agriculture. A variety of ethical and environmental issues arise from agriculture, and are discussed in Karen Krug's paper (Chapter 22). The papers by Michael Allen Fox and Roger Cohen (Chapters 10 and 11) deal with the relative environmental impacts of livestock and crop production. Agriculture has also been the dominant force that has shaped the landscape and ecology several parts of Canada, such as the lower mainland of British Columbia, the southern parts of Alberta, Saskatchewan and Manitoba, and southern Ontario. Nature protection issues that arise in such landscapes, quite different from those to do with wilderness, are discussed by Allan Greenbaum in chapter 16.

The forest industry is Canada's largest.[90] In the 1980s, the forest industry provided an annual net contribution of $12 billion to Canada's balance of trade, and directly contributed $4 billion per year to government revenues through taxes, timber sales and export duties. After fish and furs, timber was among the earliest export staples on which the Canadian economy was built. The timber industry, based on the extraction of sawlogs, is still an important part of the Canadian economy, especially in those regions (like coastal British Columbia and central Ontario) where big trees grow. Conflict between the preservation of old-growth forests and the production of saw timber continues to generate some of the most contentious and high-profile environmental issues in Canada, such as those over the logging of Clayoquot Sound on Vancouver Island and the Temagami region of Ontario. The papers by Peter Miller (Chapter 2) and Alan Drengson and Duncan Taylor (Chapter 1) both address the disputes concerning logging practices generally, and the situation at Clayoquot Sound specifically.

Economically speaking, by far the biggest segment of the forestry industry is based on the production not of timber but of pulp and paper. Paper manufacturing in Canada began in 1805, but paper was then not yet a wood product. The process of producing paper from wood pulp was invented in the 1840s, and the first Canadian pulp and paper mills were built in Quebec in the 1860s. The $14 billion a year pulp and paper industry is the largest in Canada. It accounts for 3 percent of Canada's GDP and 9 percent of its exports. The industry expanded rapidly in the 1920s in Ontario and Quebec, and again in the 1960s in BC; it is also a mainstay of the economy of Atlantic Canada. Most recently, pulp mills have been developed in northern Alberta. Because pulp mills can utilize trees that are too small to be of much value as sawlogs, the paper industry can make economic use of Canada's vast slow-growing northern forest. The industry can cut at relatively short intervals by making use of small trees.

The forest industry produces a range of environmental impacts. Extensive areas of forest are clear-cut to provide wood for the mills. The mills themselves are significant sources of air and water pollution. In the past decade or so, bleached kraft mills have attracted much attention from environmentalists and regulators, because it has been discovered that the chlorine used to bleach the pulp in these mills reacts with organic effluents to produce toxic organochlorine compounds including dioxins and furans. The three essays in the forestry section of this book do not address the pollution problems, but examine the ethical issues raised by forest management and logging practices.

Mining is another important component of Canada's resource economy. Canada's first major mineral export was phosphate, a fertilizer, the extraction of which began in the 1870s. In the 1880s, the vast nickel and copper deposits of the Sudbury basin in central Ontario were discovered, and the famous Klondike gold rush occurred in the Yukon in the period 1896-1905. In the 1980s, Canada's 400 mines and quarries produced about 60 different kinds of mineral commodities, worth some $34 billion per year.

Mining directly and indirectly accounts for about 5 percent of employment in Canada. Employment in mining (as in forestry) has declined in recent decades due to technological changes, but wages in mining remain higher than those in any other major industry. All mining produces environmental impacts in the form of tailings and so on; surface mining in particular has conspicuous impacts on the face of the land. Chapter 5 of this book, by Wesley Cragg, David Pearson and James Cooney on surface mining, and Chapter 13 by Anne Bell on the Tatshenshini controversy (involving the proposed Windy Craggy surface mine) address mining issues.

The energy sector overlaps with mining, in that it involves fossil fuel and uranium production.

Coal is mined in Nova Scotia, and oil has been produced in southwestern Ontario, but the major deposits of fossil fuels occur in the geological formation which underlies the Great Plains and extends north to the Beaufort Sea. Uranium is mined in northern Ontario and northern Saskatchewan, and used to fuel nuclear reactors that supply much of Ontario's electricity needs. Andrew Brook, in Chapter 7, examines the ethical issues connected with the nuclear fuel cycle. Historically, the most important source of electricity in Canada has been hydro. Between 1920 and 1950, hydro supplied 90 percent of Canada's electricity needs; it presently supplies about 55-60 percent.

Energy is also part of Canada's resource export economy. Canada is not only an exporter of fossil fuels and uranium, but also of hydro-electricity. Here again we see the characteristic pattern of environmentally disruptive "frontier" or hinterland development undertaken for the sake of urban industrial consumption and export. Such development has often brought private or government-organized energy industry projects into conflict with First Nations people inhabiting the hinterland regions in which the projects are to take place. Wesley Cragg and Mark Schwartz (Chapter 19) discuss historical injustices arising from a hydro-electric project in northern Ontario which was originally developed to power a pulp mill that supplied paper for the New York Times. In several well-known cases, First Nations opponents succeeded in stopping proposed frontier energy developments, such as the McKenzie Valley gas pipeline[91] and the second phase of the massive James Bay hydro-electric project in northern Quebec (intended to export electricity to New York), which is mentioned (along with a proposed B.C. hydro-for-export proposal) by Lionel Rubinoff in Chapter 8.

Although traditionally Canada has been a staples based economy, there are indications that it is also following global trends towards developing high technology industries. Many predictions have been proffered by the advocates of biotechnology industry about the potentially lucrative and laudable benefits to be gotten from biotechnology research and development. These have been countered by criticisms from public interest groups that biotechnology is unlikely to be as beneficial as promised, or may in fact be quite pernicious in its overall effects. At the present time, there is insufficient evidence about the role that the industry will play in the Canadian economy.

There is perhaps more to say, though, on the question of public attitudes towards the industry. Regarding biotechnology, one commentator had this to say: "The simplest thing to say about public awareness of biotechnology in Canada is that there isn't much".[92] The Canadian Institute of Biotechnology commissioned a survey of public attitudes on biotechnology in 1993. That study found the following: "67 percent of the public believes that biotechnology poses 'some' or 'a lot' of danger to society. Conversely, and in response to a different question, 67 percent said that they believed that biotechnology offers either 'some' or 'a lot' of benefit to society".[93]

Generally, people preferred biotechnology to conventional technologies, "especially when it replaces the use of chemicals in the environment in such applications as crop protection and environmental cleanup".[94] Yet, people were still concerned about the potential environmental impacts of genetic research, particularly of research that "goes awry". These results tend to suggest that the Canadian public is at present quite uncertain about potential environmental risks posed by biotechnology. This underlines the argument presented by David Oppenheim and Robert Gibson in Chapter 6 about the crucial importance of regulatory oversight.

Environmental Justice

The topic of justice is relevant to the themes discussed in this introduction in at least two related but distinct respects. First, a social justice ethical perspective counters and corrects the potential biases created by the pervasive influence of economic analysis in environmental policy circles. That topic has already been discussed above. Environmental justice also provides an ethical framework for discussing the particularities of the socio-economic and political cultures of different regions or localities. Concern for justice is not distinctively Canadian. Yet, the circumstances that give rise to environmental justice concerns in Canada are distinctly shaped by the historical pattern of development discussed above.

The burgeoning American environmental justice literature has focused on issues such as the disproportionate exposure of poor communities of colour to industrial wastes, agricultural pesticides and other toxic products of industrial society. This reflects the history and political economy of United States.[95] The Canadian manifestation of an environmental justice perspective has focused instead on the disparate impacts of Canada's hinterland resource exploitation economy. Canadian treatments have evidenced a concern with the outcomes of resource extraction and industrial development generally, and resource development megaprojects specifically for rural people – especially First Nations people.

Gender and class inequality are clearly issues of relevance to contemporary Canadian society; the topic of gender and justice has been dealt with above. It turns out that the issue of class has not played a prominent role in the Canadian environmental ethics literature to date, except for the work of Ted Schrecker and Karen Messing.[96] Regional inequality is the dimension of systematic inequality that has been explored most extensively in Canadian social science literature. Resource development and management issues can be characterized as questions of control – who gets to control the use of a resource, who gets to benefit from the use of a resource, and who suffers the negative effects from the use of a resource. These are the crucial issues of distributive justice. There is often a geographical dimension to environmental conflicts over resource use. These conflicts sometimes pit urban versus rural dwellers, province versus province, region versus region, and so on.

These issues arise in the case studies dealt with by Elisa Shenkier and Thomas Meredith in Chapter 3 (involving the Algonquin Indians at Barriére Lake) and Lionel Rubinoff in Chapter 8. Laura Westra's paper in Chapter 17 examines the Oka Crisis within the framework of an environmental justice perspective, and specifically makes use of an environmental racism analysis. The concern with unrectified injustices, in particular, is the theme of Wesley Cragg and Mark Schwartz's paper in Chapter 19, and of Ron Pushchak's paper in Chapter 18. As Ron Puschak makes clear, the very "emptiness" of Canada's "empty spaces" is a resource in itself, exploited at the expense of those for whom these spaces are not empty at all, but home.

Tensions between the aspirations of aboriginal peoples and those of environmentalists, including animal rights advocates is another recognizable theme.[97] The potential for conflict and the pernicious role played by non-native stereotypes of natives is addressed in Deborah McGregor's paper in this book (Chapter 20). The tensions are also briefly discussed by Jerry Valen DeMarco (Chapter 14). George Wenzel's book, *Animal Rights Human Rights: Ecology, Economy and Ideology in the Canadian Arctic*, explores the effects of the campaign to ban seal hunting on the Inuit of Arctic Canada.[98] Wenzel's book is the focus of Wendy Donner's paper in this book (Chapter 9). The issue of animal rights and environmentalist campaigns to boycott products obtained by sealing or trapping has been a recurring source of conflict in Canada and elsewhere. The topic of the negative impacts of these campaigns on native traditional lifestyle is dealt with by Rebecca Aird.[99]

Nature Preservation
and Canadian Cultural Identity

The "wild" hinterland has not only structured Canadian history and economy, but has played a well known part in shaping the culture and consciousness of Canadians. The formative role that wild nature has played in the development of Canadian identity is a commonly told story. As current federal Environment Minister Sergio Marchi has said: "Our incredible richness and diversity of plants and wildlife provide us with one of the abiding symbols that define our sense of identity and bind us together, whatever our origins, from coast to coast to coast. Wilderness has been a major source of inspiration for Canadian artists and authors; it offers spiritual renewal to aboriginal peoples and gives all Canadians a sense of pride and belonging".[100]

Canadian self-conception, whether for domestic consumption or for export, has rested on representations of wild nature in art and literature. One has only to think of the Group of Seven collection at the McMichael Gallery,[101] the Woodland School of native artists,[102] the photography of Freeman Patterson or John and Janet Foster, the films of Bill Mason, the poetry of Al Purdy and Earl Birney, or the writings of Ernest Thompson Seton to recognize the crucial importance of nature imagery.[103] Certain prominent novels, such as Margaret Atwood's *Surfacing*, Wayland Drew's *The Wabeno Feast*, Marian Engel's *Bear*,[104] and Graeme Gibson's *Perpetual Motion*, deal centrally with human relationships with nature.[105] Another example is provided by one of Margaret Atwood's short stories, "Wilderness Tips", which has a character who exemplifies the romantic stereotyping of native people. That character illustrates the role of the "imaginary Indian" that is discussed by Deborah McGregor in Chapter 20.

George Woodcock has said that the literature of experience of wilderness has given special shape to Canadian literature.[106] Wilderness, he says, is both physical immediacy and state of mind. Although the vast majority of Canadians are urban dwellers, nature has continued to play a crucial role in their lives culturally and recreationally. The significance of wilderness values and the public policy aspects of nature preservation, including species preservation are addressed by Anne Bell, Allan Greenbaum, Jerry Valen DeMarco and Alex Wellington in Chapters 13, 16, 14 and 12 (respectively). The thematic threads of the complex relations between humans and nature in Canadian culture have been taken up and examined in the work of cultural and literary critics such as Northrop Frye, Gaile McGregor, John Wadland, and Alexander Wilson.[107]

The self-representation of Canadian culture outlined above has been problematized by many contemporary critics who emphasize that the "common story" has its origins in white, middle-class society. The critics note that mainstream society has exhibited an allegiance to "stubborn notions of the hinterland as white, explorer space". As one commentator has put it: "Indeed wilderness has been integral to Canadians' sense of themselves and it has most often been determined by art: books movies and the like... [N]ature, in the canonical imaginary, has been almost unanimously underpopulated ... This sort of desertion is what gives the [hinterland] ... such a deeply apolitical and ahistorical feel".[108] Much of the recent writing in cultural studies which adopts a postmodern perspective, attempts to contextualize notions of "nature", to politicize and historicize it.[109]

Have these forces produced a distinctively Canadian environmental problematic, or a distinctly Canadian environmental consciousness? It is difficult to answer such a question definitively. At least one study has found that, among both activists and the general public, Canadians are more environmentally concerned, less anthropocentric in their value system, less materialistic, and more supportive of public participation and government regulation than are Americans.[110] On the other hand, differences between Canadians and Americans are notoriously elusive. Much of the popular wisdom among social scientists about the differences between Canadian and American values on a range of issues has been called into question by recent research.[111] Comparative studies of the environmental policy process have found consistent differences in approach, reflecting different political cultures, but they have not found consistent differences in outcomes.[112]

Nevertheless, if the topics and approaches covered in the present volume are any indication, it is possible to discern a distinctive Canadian flavour. Urban pollution problems are not unknown in Canada – the toxic tar ponds in Sydney, Nova Scotia, the lead contamination from the Canada Smelter operation in Toronto, and the smog problems of Toronto and Vancouver come to mind at once. Yet, the environmental issues that dominate Canadian thinking remain those related to nature and to the resource extraction industries of the hinterlands, including the impact of those industries on native peoples.

The role of nature in the Canadian imagination, mentioned above, has helped to shape a body of environmental thought and advocacy that emerges from the Canadian natural history tradition. It is refracted through the experiences of generations who have grown up experiencing the Rockies or expanses of the prairies, or taking canoe trips through the mazes of lakes and rivers in Algonquin , La Vérendrye or Quetico provincial parks, hiking along the Niagara Escarpment, or even walking in the wooded ravines of Toronto. For many Canadian environmentalists, their love of nature has been formed and strengthened through nature hikes and trips to the semi-wild but still ecologically significant local parks and conservation areas scattered across the country. Ingrid Leman Stefanovic's paper, in Chapter 15, deals with a project designed to develop a code of ethics for a such a park (Short Hills Park in south-ern Ontario).

These experiences, cultivated by local and regional natural history and wilderness advocacy groups, resonate with the work of thinkers such as John Livingston and Neil Evernden. These latter figures have been enormously influential in shaping the working environmental ethic of Canadian environmental advocates and activists, yet they identify not with the world of academic moral philosophy (from which they distance themselves quite explicitly) but with the Canadian branch of the North American natural history tradition.

Philosophy and Activism

The development of environmental ethics has been driven by the realization of the urgency and pervasiveness of the problems which constitute the environmental crisis. Philosophers have been led to the consideration of environmental issues by their concern for making philosophy relevant to real life problems. They have come to recognize that there is much to be gained from listening to the experiences of those who are closest to the manifestations of those problems, whether as participants in the processes or as activists demonstrating and lobbying for change. This has meant that there has been a fertile and stimulating conversation between environmental activists and environmental philosophers.

Bryan Norton and Eugene Hargrove have made the points that environmental philosophers need to become more practical and environmental practitioners need to become more philosophical.[113] Others have argued that divorcing theory from practice is not only undesirable, but it is probably not feasible either. There is, they would say, no such thing as pure theory, since to theorize is to practice, in effect. When we theorize we do so from within worldviews, which in turn both generate and endorse particular practices. Moreover, to explore the significance of practices and actions one must acknowledge that the way people treat each other and the way they treat the environment are "both parts of comprehensive worldviews".[114] Action is the instantiation of the results of theorizing and understanding.[115] It is important to recognize the power of ideas to orient individual action, to alter social values, and to transform social practices.[116] It is thus necessary to examine the roots of action in ideas, and to evaluate both the actions and the ideas.

Don Marietta points out that "living environmentally can be every philosopher's daily activism".[117] He discusses an expansive notion of environmental activism which includes teaching and writing, and campus activism in addition to commonly recognized political activism such as taking part in marches and demonstrations and chaining oneself to trees. Examples of possible campus activism abound: starting recycling and composting programs, setting up a nature preserve on campus, lobbying for energy conservation measures, replacing lawns with naturalized gardens. Pamela Courtenay Hall's work deals with current innovations in Canadian environmental education programs. Some of that work is included in Chapter 23 of this book.

We would end on this note: there is lots for everyone to do, so philosophers should engage in the forms of activism for which they have a talent and an opportunity.[118]

ENDNOTES

[1] These same points are made by Susan Armstrong and Richard Botzler in the Introduction to their edited collection, *Environmental Ethics: Divergence and Convergence*. That collection contains a section called "Multicultural Perspectives" and the collection edited by Louis Pojman, titled *Environmental Ethics: Readings in Theory and Application* includes a section called "Non-Western Perspectives on Environmental Ethics".

[2] During 1995-96 the following articles by Canadians appeared in the pages of *Environmental Ethics* and *Environmental Values*: A. Dionys de Leeuw, "Contemplating the Interests of Fish"; Andrew Kernohan, "Rights Against Polluters"; Andrew Light and Eric Higgs, "The Politics of Ecological Restoration"; Bruce Morito, "Value, Metaphysics and Anthropocentrism"; Rebecca Raglan and Marian Scholtmeijer, "Shifting Ground: Metanarratives, Epistemol-

ogy and the Stories of Nature"; David Rapport, "Ecosystem Health: More Than a Metaphor?"; Catriona Sandilands, "From Natural Identity to Radical Democracy".

[3] Introduction to Chapter Six of *Contemporary Moral Issues*, Third Edition, by Wesley Cragg, page 315. McGraw-Hall Ryerson, 1983.

[4] Examples of anti-environmentalist writing include: Ronald Bailey, *Ecoscam: The False Prophets of Ecological Apocalypse*; Ben Bolch and Harold Lyons, *Apocalypse Not: Science, Economics and Environmentalism*; Dixy Lee Ray, *Trashing the Planet* and *Environmental Overkill*.

[5] The area of applied ethics is now so established and so voluminous that it would take a book length treatment almost just to provide a bibliography for it. For a good overview of the field see the papers collected in the "Methodology, Critical Potential, and Skeptical Doubts" section of *Applied Ethics: A Reader*, edited by Earl Winkler and Jerrold Coombs.

[6] The McDonald Report, *Towards a Canadian Research Strategy for Applied Ethics*, consists of the Report by the Canadian Federation for the Humanities To the Social Sciences and Humanities Research Council, for which Michael McDonald was the Principal Investigator, Marie-Hélène Parizeau was the Senior Researcher and Daryl Pullman was the Research Assistant. That report has played an invaluable role in stimulating interest and identifying opportunities in applied ethics in addition to presenting an overview of the field at the time. (page 11)

[7] See Arthur Caplan, "Ethical Engineers Need Not Apply: The State of Applied Ethics Today". See the papers in J. DeMarco and R. Fox, eds., *New Directions in Ethics* for more on the model and its alternatives.

[8] Donald Scherer and Thomas Attig, "Introduction" to *Ethics and the Environment*, page 2.

[9] *Supra*

[10] See for example the following papers in *Ethics and Problems of the 21st Century*, edited by K. Goodpaster and K. Sayre: "Contrasting Methods of Environmental Planning" by R. M. Hare and "Starvation and Human Rights" by Alan Gewirth. There are exceptions in that collection, such as the papers by Kenneth Goodpaster, Peter Singer, and Richard and Val Routley.

[11] Michael Zimmerman, "General Introduction" to *Environmental Philosophy: From Animal Rights to Radical Ecology*, page vii.

[12] See the papers in *Responsibilities to Future Generations*, edited by Ernest Partridge and *Obligations to Future Generations*, edited by R.I. Sikora and Brian Barry. Canadians have made significant contributions to this literature; examples include Jan Narveson, "Future Generations and Us" and Wayne Sumner's "Classical Utilitarianism", both published in *Obligations to Future Generations*.

[13] For an accessible and forceful treatment of the topic, see William Baxter's *People or Penguins: The Case for Optimal Pollution*. See the Editors' Notes to Section One, Volume One of *Social Conflict and Environmental Law*, edited by Greenbaum, Wellington and Baar, for a discussion of the interlocking assumptions which constitute the ethical framework of economic analysis, and the criticisms of those assumptions which have been raised by environmentalists.

[14] See John Rawls, *A Theory of Justice* and *Political Liberalism*. For an introduction to Rawls' work and further references to the voluminous literature which discusses Rawls' ideas, see Lesley Jacobs, *An Introduction to Modern Political Philosophy*.

[15] See for example: Robert Elliot, "Rawlsian Justice and Non-Human Animals"; Russ Manning, "Environmental Ethics and Rawls' Theory of Justice"; Brent Singer, "An Extension of Rawls' Theory of Justice to Environmental Ethics"; Daniel Thereo, "Rawls and Environmental Ethics: A Critical Examination of the Literature". Donald VanDeVeer, "Of Beasts, Persons, and the Original Position". Also see *Policy for Land: Law and Ethics* by L.K. Caldwell and Kristin Shrader-Frechette.

[16] See the article by Lavelle and Coyle, "Unequal Protection: The Racial Divide in Environmental Law", which reports on the results of a National Law Foundation study documenting disparate impact of environmental protection laws. The article is found in *Toxic Struggles*, edited by R. Hofrichter.

[17] Including, but not limited to, ability, sexual orientation, religion, age, etc. See the articles collected in *Confronting Environmental Racism: Voices From the Grassroots*, edited by Robert Bullard. See also Troy Hartley's piece, "Environmental Justice: An Environmental Civil Rights Value Acceptable to All World Views".

[18] See Robert Paelhke and Pauline Rosenau, "Environment/ Equity: Tensions in North American Politics".

[19] See the papers collected in *Faces of Environmental Racism*, edited by Westra and Wenz. The work of the American sociologist Robert Bullard - whose paper, "Decision Making" is included in that book - has played a crucial role in the development of an environmental justice perspective.

[20] Andrew Brennan uses the term "assimilationist" in his "Introduction" to *Ethics and the Environment*, page xv.

[21] See his "Legal Rights for Nature - The Wrong Answer to the Right(s) Question".

[22] *Supra*, page 290.

[23] Commentators have called this approach the Method of Argument from Analogy and Anomaly.

[24] Scherer and Attig, "Introduction", *Ethics and the Environment*, page 2.

[25] Those papers were: Peter Singer, "Animal Liberation", published in the *New York Review of Books*; Arne Naess,

"The Shallow and the Deep, Long Range Ecology Movement: A Summary", published in the journal *Inquiry*; Francoise d'Eaubonne, "Feminism or Death" (later published in several anthologies); Rosemary Radford Reuther, "Motherearth and Megamachine: A Theology of Liberation in a Feminine Somatic and Ecological Perspective", published in her collection, *Liberation Theology*; and Richard Sylvan (then Routley), "Is There a Need for a New, an Environmental Ethic", given as an address to the Fifteenth World Congress of Philosophy. The pieces by Naess, Singer, and Sylvan (then Routley) all appeared in 1973; the d'Eaubonne piece in 1974 and the Reuther piece in 1972. Interestingly enough, a significant forerunner to contemporary anti-environmentalist writing, Ayn Rand's *The New Left: The Anti-Industrial Revolution* also appeared around the same time (1971).

[26] Andrew Brennan, in the introduction to *Ethics and the Environment*, emphasizes the notion of challenge in contrast to assimilation.

[27] For elaboration on these issues and on the development of the line of reasoning presented in the following passages, see the introduction to *Environmental Ethics* by Robert Elliot and the introduction by J. Baird Callicott to *Environmental Philosophy* (edited by Zimmerman et al.).

[28] Moral Standing has to do with the recognition of interests in moral deliberation. If a being, organism or entity is deemed to have moral standing, then the interest or well-being of that entity must be counted or considered in deciding what it is permissable to do. The harm which would be suffered by any entity with moral standing counts against the moral worth of any action or policy which would cause the harm (that harm must then be justified or else avoided). It is important to distinguish moral standing from legal standing, which has to do with the recognition by a court of an entitlement. If a person or legal entity is determined to have suffered a legally recognizable wrong (violation of rights, a harm covered under a cause of action), that person or entity has standing to sue. Christopher Stone, in *Should Trees Have Standing?* proposed not only that nonhuman "natural objects" were deserving of moral standing, but that they should be granted legal standing as well.

[29] It is interesting to note, as J. Baird Callicott does in the Introduction to *Environmental Philosophy*, edited by Zimmerman et al., that these terms were drawn from the critiques of discourse developed by feminists and other social critics, who identified problems of human chauvinism, sexism, and racism. There is, to this day, controversy in some circles over whether it is appropriate to extend the anti-discrimination critique beyond the species barrier. No self-respecting political philosopher would argue in favour of sexism or racism today, but many still feel justified in the presumption of speciesism.

[30] See Singer, "Not for Humans Only: The Place of

Nonhumans in Environmental Issues" and *Animal Liberation*.

[31] See Tom Regan, *The Case for Animal Rights*.

[32] Albert Schweitzer was a theologian and medical missionary who wrote *The Philosophy of Civilization*. See Kenneth Goodpaster, "On Being Morally Considerable" and Paul Taylor, *Respect for Nature*.

[33] This is a very contentious issue in the philosophical literature. The claim is that interests can consist in "some set of loosely specifiable biological goals in terms of which a being might be characterized as flourishing". Further, the notion of harm involved here is one in which acting so as to impede the flourishing of an entity, say a plant for example, or to frustrate its biologically determined goals, is to harm that entity. See Robert Elliot, "Introduction" to *Environmental Ethics*, page 10. Some philosophers insist, however, that in order to be deemed to have interests an entity or organism must have desires, or else be capable of "forming preferences about their own future states". Elliot, page 9. See Joel Feinberg, "The Rights of Animals and Unborn Generations". Debates over these kinds of claims have themselves flourished in the pages of the journal *Environmental Ethics*.

[34] Bruce Littlejohn draws on the inspiration of Leopold's ideas in "Wilderness and the Canadian Psyche", page 20.

[35] In an essay entitled "Four Forms of Ecological Consciousness", John Rodman distinguishes between four stages of environmental philosophy: conservation, preservation, moral extension and then ecological sensibility. The latter includes a concern for the liberation of nature.

[36] See *In Defence of the Land Ethic* by J. Baird Callicott and *Philosophy Gone Wild* by Holmes Rolston. Christopher Stone has also made interesting use of Leopold's work in *Should Trees Have Standing*.

[37] There is some debate over whether it necessarily requires such a shift. See Elliot, "Introduction" to *Environmental Ethics*, page 10-11.

[38] Robert Elliot, in the introduction to *Environmental Ethics*, provides elaboration of the claims made on behalf of ethical holism and their contested status philosophically.

[39] There is quite a large literature on this topic alone: See, for example, J. Baird Callicott's collected essays, *In Defense of the Land Ethic*. Also see "Ethical Holism and Individualism and Individualism" by Don Marietta. For the opposing view, see for example, Harley Cahen, "Against the Moral Considerability of Ecosystems".

[40] See the papers collected in *The Animal Rights/ Environmental Ethics Debate*, edited by E. Hargrove. See also Gary Varner, "Can Animal Rights Activists Be Environmentalists?" Michael Allen Fox has addressed these issues as well; see, for example, "Environmental Ethics and the Ideology of Meat Eating".

[41] The problem is most acute in Australia, where a major cause of endangerment for native fauna and flora is predation and land degradation by introduced, feral and domestic species. Predation by the European red fox and feral cats, along with competition and land degradation by feral rabbits and goats are some of the main processes which threaten native species in Australia.

[42] Lawsuits have resulted in the United States when measures were proposed to remove or eliminate feral sheep and goat populations in order to protect endangered species of birds, plants, and a lizard.

[43] See the article by Jack Hanna, "Deer Dilemma" for an account of the situation at Rondeau Provincial Park in southern Ontario.

[44] For instance, Aldo Leopold wrote the essay, "A Land Ethic", which inspired so many environmental philosophers in 1949. Thus, a crucial piece of the holistic, ecocentric ethical story occurred long before most of the writing in the stages said to lead up to it. Further, Jeremy Bentham wrote the work in which the passage, "The question is not, Can they *reason*? nor Can they *talk*? but, Can they *suffer*?" appears in 1789 (*The Principles of Morals and Legislation*).

[45] See Roderick Nash, *The Rights of Nature*. The diagram is reproduced in Jerry Valen DeMarco's paper, Chapter 14, in this book. J. Baird Callicott provides a cogent and succinct account of the development of environmental ethics in his introduction to *Environmental Philosophy*, edited by Zimmerman et al.

[46] There is, in fact, not even a consensus on whether or not there is supposed to be a consensus.

[47] See the work of Paul Taylor, *Respect for Nature* and in his articles in the journal *Environmental Ethics* for elaboration on the distinction between intrinsic value and inherent worth. His work, and that distinction, is discussed in Chapter 3 of this book.

[48] Holmes Rolston takes this approach throughout his writings.

[49] Robert Elliot makes these points in the introduction to *Environmental Ethics*, pages 8-9. Also, J. Baird Callicott, in "Environmental Philosphy is Environmental Activism", points out that Dave Foreman identified the following four forces that shaped the environmental movement of the 1990s: first, "academic philosophy", second, "conservation biology", third, "independent local groups", and fourth, "Earth First!". Callicott comments: "That's right, 'academic philosophy' heads the list". See Callicott's article for further discussion. (page 33)

[50] See William Blackstone, "Ethics and Ecology"; Holmes Rolston, "Is There an Ecological Ethic"; Andrew Brennan, *Thinking About Nature: An Investigation into Nature, Value, and Ecology*.

[51] See, eg., Gordon and Suzuki, *It's a Matter of Survival*.

[52] See Warwick Fox, *Toward A Transpersonal Ecology: New Foundations for Environmentalism*. Also see *The Deep Ecology Movement*, edited by Alan Drengson and Yuichi Inoue and *Deep Ecology for the 21st Century*, edited by George Sessions.

[53] See: Naess, "The Shallow and the Deep, Long-Range Ecology Movements"; Devall and Sessions, *Deep Ecology: Living as if Nature Mattered*; Drengson and Inoue, *The Deep Ecology Movement: An Introductory Anthology*; Merchant, *Radical Ecology;* and Sessions, *Deep Ecology for the Twenty-first Century*.

[54] Livingston, "Rightness or Rights" p. 309.

[55] Livingston, *The Fallacy of Wildlife Conservation* p. 50.

[56] See John Livingston's piece, "Ethics as Prosthetics" and Alan Drengson's editorial "Why Environmental Ethics is Not Enough" in *The Trumpeter*.

[57] Alan Drengson, "Why Environmental Ethics is Not Enough", editorial, *The Trumpeter*, page 122.

[58] John Livingston, "Nature for the Sake of Nature", page 246.

[59] Annie Booth, "Why I Don't Talk About Environmental Ethics Anymore", page 134.

[60] *Ibid*.

[61] Scherer and Attig discuss the notion of paradigm shift in the introduction to *Ethics and the Environment*, page 2. For a discussion of the origins of the notion of "paradigm shift" in the history of science and its adoption by environmental thought, see Drengson, *Beyond Environmental Crisis*.

[62] See, for example, Freya Mathews, *The Ecological Self*; Warwick Fox, *Toward a Transpersonal Ecology*.

[63] For instance, Annie Booth and Alan Drengson both have papers in this book, and both, along with John Livingston, have had their work included in other environmental ethics collections as well.

[64] Some approaches, such as those influenced by A.N.Whitehead's process philosophy, seem to straddle the ethical and the cosmological. See, for example, Birch and Cobb, *The Liberation of Life*, Susan Armstrong-Buck, "Whiteheads Metaphysical System as a Foundation for Environmental Ethics", and John Haught, "The Emergent Environment and the Problem of Cosmic Purpose."

[65] It was subtitled *Man's Fleeting Supremacy* and was published in 1973. That book was followed in 1981 by *The Fallacy of Wildlife Conservation*. Livingston's 1994 book, *The Rogue Primate*, won the Governor General's Award.

[66] See Alan Drengson's *Beyond Environmental Crisis: From Technocrat to Planetary Person* and Neil Evernden's *The Natural Alien* and *The Social Creation of Nature*.

[67] To cite just one example, Carolyn Merchant in her book *The Death of Nature* takes up a theme of central importance to cosmological environmental thought, namely the mechanization, devitalization and disenchantment of the Western conception of nature during the early modern age, but examines how this process reflected shifts in the symbolic means by which the subordination of women was represented and accomplished.

[68] Important anthologies include Diamond and Ornstein, eds., *Reweaving the World*; Plant ed.,, *Healing the Wounds*; and Gaard, ed., *Ecofeminism*.

[69] See the following: Catriona Sandilands, "Political Animals: The Paradox of Ecofeminist Politics"; Val Plumwood, *Feminism and the Mastery of Nature*, Elizabeth Dodgson Gray, *Green Paradise Lost*; Karen Warren, "The Power and Promise of Ecological Feminism"; Alex Wellington, "Feminist Positions on Vegetarianism: Arguments For and Against and Otherwise"; Charlene Spretnak, ed., *The Politics of Women's Spirituality: Essays on the Rise of Spiritual Power Within the Feminist Movement*. Robert Elliot suggests that ecofeminism could be considered a variant of a virtue ethic, in his introduction to *Environmental Ethics*, page 5.

[70] See Ariel Salleh, "Deeper Than Deep Ecology: The Eco-Feminist Connection" and "The Ecofeminism/Deep Ecology Debate"; Deborah Slicer, "Is There an Ecofeminism-Deep Ecology "Debate"?". See also "The Deep Ecology - Ecofeminism Debate And Its Parallels" by Warwick Fox.

[71] The leading social ecology theorist is Murray Bookchin. See: Bookchin, "Freedom and Necessity in Nature", "Thinking Ecologically: A Dialectical Approach" and *The Ecology of Freedom*. On anarchism and ecology, see also John Clark, *The Anarchist Moment*. On the Frankfurt School's analysis of domination, see Leiss, *The Domination of Nature*. On this same topic, and on the relationship between the thought of the Frankfurt School and that of social ecology, see Eckersley, *Environmentalism and Political Theory* chapters 5 and 7. For a sympathetic critique of some approaches to bioregionalism, by a Canadian influenced by social ecology, see Don Alexander, "Bioregionalism: Science or Sensibility".

[72] The most cogent and friendly critique of deep ecology by a social ecologist is provided by George Bradford, "Toward a Deep Social Ecology", found in Zimmerman et al., *Environmental Philosophy*.

[73] See for instance the general introduction to Zimmerman et al., *Environmental Philosophy: From Animal Rights to Radical Ecology*, written by Michael Zimmerman, which includes references to further work of his along the same lines.

[74] See the introduction to Susan Armstrong and Richard Botzler, eds., *Environmental Ethics: Divergence and Convergence*, page xvii. Conversely, a range of environmental positions may be compatible with a given philosophical or cosmological view, as Allan Greenbaum suggests in "Environmental Thought as Cosmological Intervention".

[75] Newton and Dillingham, "Introduction" to *Watersheds: Classic Cases in Environmental Ethics*, page 4. They go on to say that what is needed is "sound policy", policy which "will have to go deeper than the immediate surface causes of the incident that has focused our attention, to examine the political and economic practices that made it inevitable". (page 4)

[76] On suspicion of "metanarratives": J.-F. Lyotard, *The Postmodern Condition*. Examples of "postmodern" environmental thought might include M. Oelschlager, ed., *Postmodern Environmental Ethics*, Donna Haraway, *Simians, Cyborgs and Women*, and Bennett and Chaloupka, eds., *In the Nature of Things*. Moral pluralists are also sceptical of attempts at grand unified theories in moral philosophy; see Christopher Stone, *Earth and Other Ethics: The Case for Moral Pluralism.*

[77] Light and Katz, *Environmental Pragmatism* p. 2.

[78] Brennan, "Introduction", *Ethics and the Environment*. See the introduction to *Environmental Pragmatism*, edited by Andrew Light and Eric Katz, for an overview of the debate.

[79] See the papers by Bryan Norton and Paul Thompson in Light and Katz, eds.,, *Environmental Pragmatism*. This view is, of course, not uncontested by those whom it targets. J. Baird Callicott, a leading proponent of the ecocentric ethical theory camp with some affinities to the cosmological stream, defends his position vigorously against the pragmatists and pluralists; he insists that his work is influential in environmental policy circles and suggests that Norton—one of his chief critics—is ultimately an apologist for old-fashioned human-centred nature-exploiting attitudes. See Callicott, "On Norton and the Failure of Monistic Inherentism"; also see Callicott's essay "Environmental Philosophy is Environmental Activism: The Most Radical and Effective Kind", in Marietta and Embree, *Environmental Philosophy and Environmental Activism*.

[80] Don Marietta, Introduction, in Marietta and Embree, *Environmental Philosophy and Environmental Activism*, pp. 4-5.

[81] Wesley Cragg, Introduction to Chapter Six, *Contemporary Moral Issues*, page 316.

[82] Important Canadian contributions to this literature include: Brunk, Haworth and Lee, *Value Assumptions in Risk Assessment*; Harrison and Hoberg, *Risk, Science and Politics;* Leiss and Chociolko, *Risk and Responsibility;* Salter, *Mandated Science*; Savan, *Science Under Siege*; Richardson, Sherman and Gismonti, *Winning Back the Words*. See also Shrader-Frechette, *Science Policy, Ethics and Economics* and *Risk and Rationality*.

[83] See McDonald, *Towards a Canadian Research Strategy for Applied Ethics*, page 58.

[84] At the time the report was written (1989), there were only half as many courses in environmental ethics as in bioethics

or professional and business ethics. *Supra*, page 58.

[85] As the report goes on to say: activists were so suspicious that "they viewed reflection on the grounds of human responsibility of the environment as itself an environmentally subversive activity". *Supra*, page 63.

[86] Much of the information in the following paragraphs comes from various articles in *The Canadian Encyclopedia*, Second Edition, 1988.

[87] See, eg., Herscovici, *Second Nature*; Lynge, *Arctic Wars: Animal Rights, Endangered People*; and Wenzel, *Animal Rights, Human Rights.*

[88] See the following: Alan Finlayson, *Fishing for Truth*; Terry Glavin, *Dead Reckoning*; Patricia Marchak et al., eds., *Uncommon Property*; and Evelyn Pinkerton, ed., *Co-operative Management of Local Fisheries.*

[89] See *The Oceans Are Emptying*, also by Ray Rogers.

[90] For treatment of the international dimensions of the forestry industry, Canadian and other, see Patricia Marchak's *Logging the Globe*.

[91] See Thomas Berger, *Northern Frontier, Northern Homeland*.

[92] Rick Walters says this in a piece found in the journal *Bio/Technology*, Volume 13, March 1995, page 216.

[93] The study was undertaken by Decima Research and "included focus groups and a national telephone survey of 1,500 Canadians". Rick Walter, "We Must Boost Public Acceptance of Biotech", *Bio/Technology*, Volume 13, March 1995, 216.

[94] Rick Walter, *supra*, page 217.

[95] See the articles contained in *Environmental Justice: Issues, Policies, Solutions*, edited by Bunyan Bryant; *Toxic Struggles: The Theory and Practice of Environmental Justice*, edited by Richard Hofrichter; *Confronting Environmental Racism: Voices From the Grassroots*, edited by Robert Bullard. Also see *Forcing the Spring: The Transformation of the American Environmental Movement* by Robert Gottlieb.

[96] See Ted Schrecker, "Risks Versus Rights: Economic Power and Economic Analysis in Environmental Politics"; "Environmentalism and the Politics of Invisibility"; "Ethics and Institutions: How We Think About Policy Decisions"; "The Political Content and Context of Environmental Law"; *The Political Economy of Environmental Hazards*. See also Karen Messing, "Union-Initiated Research in Genetic Effects of Workplace Agents: A Case Study" for a discussion of systemic bias against science initiated on behalf of working class people.

[97] It is an unfortunate fact that most collections of environmental ethics contain numerous treatments of issues involving First Nations peoples written by non-natives without a sufficient balance of papers written by members of First Nations. The present book is no exception.

[98] See also Finn Lynge, *Arctic Wars: Animal Rights Endangered Peoples*.

[99] Rebecca Aird, "Animal Rights and Environmentalism".

[100] Sergio Marchi, Minister's Forward, Bill C-64 (*Canadian Endangered Species Act*), 1996.

[101] The "Oh! Canada Project" exhibition, held at the Art Gallery of Ontario during 1996, attests to the enduring importance of the work of the Group of Seven, and to the myriad ways their work has influenced, and continues to influence, the development of Canadian culture.

[102] This group includes Norval Morrisseau and Carl Ray, among others.

[103] Ernest Thompson Seton, 1860-1946, has been credited with originating the genre of the realistic animal story - a genre whose other distinguished Canadian practitioners include Fred Bosworth and R.D. Lawrence. He was also one of the founders of the Boy Scout movement, but split with its British and American founders over what he perceived as their militaristic tendencies. See John Wadland's book, *Ernest Thompson Seton: Man in Nature and the Progressive Era*.

[104] The Governor General Award Winning novel *Bear* has its own entry in the Canadian Encyclopedia.

[105] See also the story, "Death By Landscape" by Margaret Atwood (included in the collection titled *Wilderness Tips*).

[106] See Bruce Littlejohn's discussion and the references for Woodcock's work in "Wilderness and the Canadian Psyche". For examples of this literature, see the collection *Treasures of Place: Three Centuries of Nature Writing in Canada*, edited by Wayne Grady.

[107] See Northrop Frye's *The Bush Garden*, Gaile McGregor's *The Wacousta Syndrome: Explorations in the Canadian Landscape* and *The Noble Savage in the New World Garden: Notes Towards a Syntactics of Place*, and John Wadland's essay "Wilderness and Culture" in Gaffield and Gaffield, eds., *Consuming Canada*; and Alexander Wilson, *The Culture of Nature: North American Landscape From Disney to the Exxon Valdez*.

[108] Kyo Mclear, "Plots of Land: Rural Asian Writing is Giving the Hinterland a Facelight" (pages 32-33).

[109] See the papers found in the collection, *In the Nature of Things: Language, Politics, and the Environment*, edited by Jane Bennett and William Chaloupka. See also Margot LaRocque, "Speaking Animals" and Catriona Sandilands, "From Natural Identity to Radical Democracy".

[110] See M.A. Steger, J. Pierce, B. Steel and N. Lovrich, "Political Culture, Postmaterial Values and the New Environmental Paradigm: a Comparative Analysis of Canada and the United States".

[111] See, for example, Baer, Grabb and Johnson, "Reassessing Differences in Canadian and American Values", in Curtis

and Tepperman, eds., *Images of Canada*.

[112] See Harrison and Hoberg, *Risk, Science and Politics*; George Hoberg, "Comparing Canadian Environmental Performance in Environmental Policy" and "Environmental Policy: Alternative Styles".

[113] They make these points, respectively, in "Where Do We Go From Here?", in Ferré and Hartel, eds., *Environmental Ethics and Environmental Policy*.

[114] Victoria Davion makes these points in the introduction to *Ethics and Environmental Policy: Theory Meets Practice*, edited by Ferré and Hartel. See "Introduction: Where Are We Headed", page 2.

[115] Richard Hart, "Introduction", *Ethics and the Environment*.

[116] J. Baird Callicott makes points along these lines in his "Introduction" to the co-edited collection, *Environmental Philosophy: From Animal Rights to Radical Ecology* (edited by Zimmerman et al.).

[117] In the introduction to Marietta and Embree, eds., *Environmental Philosophy and Environmental Activism*, page 15.

[118] Don Marietta says this, modifying slightly something that Peter Wenz has said. See "Introduction" to *Environmental Philosophy and Environmental Activism*, page 15. See especially the passage on "Teaching as Environmental Activism", on page 12.

References and Selected Bibliography

We have prepared an extensive bibliography, which attempts to canvas the significant trends and developments in the field of environmental ethics, with special emphasis on highlighting and providing context for Canadian material. In addition to the non-fiction works referred to in the Introduction, this bibliography includes the following: major collections, readers and other important or seminal treatments in the field of environmental ethics, selected recent Canadian writings in environmental ethics, significant Canadian contributions in the area of environmental thought and advocacy, and some other Canadian writing on topics relevant to environmental issues and policy. Items by Canadians or with a Canadian focus are identified with an asterisk (*).

One of the factors emphasized by the McDonald Report *(Toward a Canadian Research Strategy for Applied Ethics)* to account for the incomplete state of the field of environmental ethics relative to others in applied ethics was the lack of elaborate bibliographical efforts. We hope that our efforts in this regard will go some way to correcting the situation, and we apologize to anyone whose work we may have inadvertently overlooked.

Aird, Rebecca. "Animal Rights and Environmentalism". In C. Gaffield and P. Gaffield, eds., *Consuming Canada*, 1995.*

Alexander, Don. "Bioregionalism: Science or Sensibility". *Environmental Ethics*, Volume 12:2 (1990) 161-174.*

Allen, Robert. *How to Save the World: Strategy for World Conservation*. Prentice-Hall, 1980.

Armstrong-Buck, Susan. "Whitehead's Metaphysical System as a Foundation for Environmental Ethics". *Environmental Ethics*, Volume 8: 3 (Fall 1986), 241-259.

Armstrong, Susan J. and Richard G. Botzler, editors. *Environmental Ethics: Divergence and Convergence*. McGraw-Hill, 1993.

Atkinson, Michael, editor. *Governing Canada: Institutions and Public Policy*. Harcourt Brace and Company, 1993.*

Attfield, Robin. *The Ethics of Environmental Concern*. Second Edition. University of Georgia Press, 1991.

Attfield, Robin. *Environmental Philosophy: Principles and Prospects*. Avebury, 1994.

Attfield, Robin and Andrew Belsey, editors. *Philosophy and the Natural Environment*. Cambridge University Press, 1994.

Baer, Douglas, Edward Grabb and William Johnson, "Reassessing Differences in Canadian and American Values". In J. Curtis and L. Tepperman, eds., *Images of Canada: The Sociological Tradition* Prentice-Hall, 1990.*

Bailey, Ronald. *Ecoscam: The False Prophets of Ecological Apocalypse*. St. Martin's Press, 1993.

Barbour, Ian, editor. *Western Man and Environmental Ethics*. Addison-Wesley, 1973.

Baxter, William. *People or Penguins: The Case for Optimal Pollution*. Columbia University Press, 1974.

Bell, Anne. "Cost-Benefit Analysis: A Conservation Caveat". *The Trumpeter: Journal of Ecosophy*,

Volume 11:2 (Spring 1994), 93-94.*

Bennett, Jane and William Chaloupka, editors. *In the Nature of Things: Language, Politics and the Environment*. University of Minnesota Press, 1993.

Berger, Thomas. *Northern Frontier, Northern Homeland: The Report of the Mackenzie Valley Pipeline Inquiry* (1977). Douglas and McIntyre, 1988.*

Berry, R.J, editor. *Environmental Dilemmas: Ethics and Decisions*. Chapman and Hall, 1993.

Birch, Charles and John Cobb. *The Liberation of Life*. Cambridge University Press, 1981.

Blackstone, William T. "Ethics and Ecology". In W. Blackstone, ed., *Philosophy and Environmental Crisis*.

Blackstone, William T., editor. *Philosophy and Environmental Crisis*. University of Georgia Press, 1974.

Boardman, Robert, editor. *Canadian Environmental Policy: Ecosystems, Politics and Process*. Oxford University Press, 1992.*

Bolch, Ben and Harold Lyons. *Apocalypse Not: Science, Economics and Environmentalism*. Cato Institute, 1993.

Bookchin, Murray. "Freedom and Necessity in Nature: A Problem in Ecological Ethics." *Alternatives* 13:4 (1986) 29-35.

Bookchin, Murray. "Thinking Ecologically: A Dialectical Approach." *Our Generation* 18:3 (1987) 3-19.

Bookchin, Murray. *The Ecology of Freedom*, revised edition. Black Rose Books, 1991.

Booth, Annie. "Why I Don't Talk About Environmental Ethics Anymore." *The Trumpeter: Journal of Ecosophy* Volume 6(4), Fall 1989, 132-34.*

Bradley, Raymond and Stephen Duguid, editors. *Environmental Ethics: Volume II*. Institute for the Humanities, Simon Fraser University, 1989.*

Brennan, Andrew. *Thinking About Nature: An Investigation of Nature, Value and Ecology*. University of Georgia Press, 1988.

Brennan, Andrew, editor. *The Ethics of the Environment*. Dartmouth Publishing Company, 1995.

Brooks, Stephen. *Public Policy in Canada: An Introduction*. Second Edition. McClelland and

Stewart, 1993.*

Brubaker, Elizabeth. *Property Rights in Defense of Nature.* Earthscan, 1995.*

Brunk, Conrad, Lawrence Haworth and Brenda Lee. *Value Assumptions in Risk Assessment: A Case Study of the Alachlor Controversy.* Wilfred Laurier University Press, 1991.*

Bruntland, Gro Harlem (Chairman). World Commission on Environment and Development. *Our Common Future.* Oxford University Press, 1987.

Bryant, Bunyan, editor. *Environmental Justice: Issues, Policies and Solutions.* Island Press, 1995.

Bullard, Robert, editor. *Confronting Environmental Racism: Voices from the Grassroots.* South End Press, 1993.

Burningham, Kate. "Environmental Values as Discursive Resources." In Guerrier et al., *Values and the Environment.*

Butala, Sharon. *The Perfection of the Morning: An Apprenticeship in Nature.* Harper Collins, 1994.*

Cahen, Harley. "Against the Moral Considerability of Ecosystems". *Environmental Ethics*, Volume 10:3 (Fall 1988), 195-216.

Caldwell, L. K., and Kristin Shrader-Frechette. *Policy for Land: Law and Ethics.* Rowman and Littlefield, 1993.

Callicott, J. Baird, editor. *Companion to A Sand County Almanac: Interpretive and Critical Essays.* University of Wisconsin Press, 1987.

Callicott, J. Baird. *In Defense of the Land Ethic: Essays in Environmental Philosophy.* State University of New York Press, 1989.

Callicott, J. Baird. "The Case Against Moral Pluralism". *Environmental Ethics*, Volume 12:2 (Summer 1990), 99-124.

Callicott, J. Baird. "On Norton and the Failure of Monistic Inherentism." *Environmental Ethics* 18:2 (Summer 1996) 219-21.

Campbell, Mora. "Time Waits for No Beast: Temporality and the Dis-integration of Nature". *Alternatives*, Volume 19:4 (August/ September 1993), 22-27.*

Campbell, Mora. "Beyond the Terms of the Contract: Mothers and Farmers". *Journal of Agricultural and Environmental Ethics*, Volume 7:2 (1994),

205-220.*

Caplan, Arthur M. "Ethical Engineers Need Not Apply: The State of Applied Ethics Today". *Science, Technology and Human Values*, Volume 6, Fall 1980, 24-32.

Caputo, Tullio, Mark Kennedy, Charles E. Reasons and Augustine Branigan, editors. *Law and Society: A Critical Perspective.* Harcourt Brace Jovanovich, 1989.*

Carlson, Allen. "Nature and Positive Aesthetics." *Environmental Ethics* 6:1 (1984) 5-34.*

Cheney, Jim. "Postmodern Environmental Ethics: Ethics as Bioregional Narrative". In Oelschlaeger, ed., *Postmodern Environmental Ethics.*

Clark, John. *The Anarchist Moment: Reflections on Culture, Nature and Power.* Black Rose, 1984.

Clark, Judy. "Corncrakes and Cornflakes: The Question of Valuing Nature." In Guerrier et al., editors, *Values and the Environment.*

Coward, Harold and Thomas Hurka, editors. *Ethics and Climate Change: The Greenhouse Effect.* Wilfrid Laurier University Press/ Calgary Institute for the Humanities, 1993.*

Cragg, Wesley, editor. *Contemporary Moral Issues.* Third Edition. McGraw-Hill Ryerson, 1992. [Fourth Edition co-edited with Christine Koggel forthcoming in 1997]*

Curtis, James and Lorne Tepperman, editors, *Images of Canada: The Sociological Tradition.* Prentice-Hall, 1990.*

Danielson, Peter. "Morality, Rationality and Politics: The Greenhouse Dilemma." In E. Winkler and J. Coombs, editors, *Applied Ethics: A Reader.*

Darier, Éric. "Environmental Studies in Context: Knowledge, Language, History and the Self". In M. Mehta and E. Ouellet, eds., *Environmental Sociology*, 1995.*

D'Eaubonne, Francoise. "Feminism or Death". In E. Marks and I. de Courtivron, eds., *New French Feminisms: An Anthology.* University of Massachusetts Press, 1980.

De Leeuw, A. Dionys. "Contemplating the Interests of Fish". *Environmental Ethics*, Volume 18(4), 1996, 391-410.*

DeMarco, Joseph and Richard M. Fox, editors. *New Directions in Ethics: The Challenge of Applied Ethics*. Routledge and Kegan Paul, 1986.

Dene Cultural Institute. "Traditional Ecological Knowledge and Environmental Assessment". In C. Gaffield and P. Gaffield, eds., *Consuming Canada*, 1995.*

Des Jardins, Joseph. *Environmental Ethics: An Introduction to Environmental Philosophy*. Wadsworth, 1993.

Devall, Bill and George Sessions. *Deep Ecology: Living As If Nature Mattered*. Peregrine Smith Books, 1985.

Diamond, Irene and Gloria Feman Orenstein, editors. *Reweaving the World: the Emergence of Ecofeminism*. Sierra Club Books, 1990.

Doern, G. Bruce and Richard W. Phidd. *Canadian Public Policy: Ideas, Structure, Process*. Second Edition. Nelson Canada, 1992.*

Dotto, Lydia. *Ethical Choices and Global Greenhouse Warming*. Wilfrid Laurier University Press/ Calgary Institute for the Humanities, 1993.*

Drengson, Alan. *The Practice of Technology*. State University of New York Press, 1985.*

Drengson, Alan. *Beyond Environmental Crisis: From Technocrat to Planetary Person*. Peter Lang, 1989.*

Drengson, Alan. "Why Environmental Ethics is Not Enough", *The Trumpeter: Journal of Ecosophy* 6:4 (Fall 1989) 121-22.*

Drengson, Alan. "Protecting the Environment, Protecting Ourselves: Reflections on the Philosophical Dimension". In R. Bradley and S. Duguid, eds., *Environmental Ethics*, Volume II, 1989.*

Drengson, Alan and Yuichi Inoue, editors. *The Deep Ecology Movement: An Introductory Anthology*. North Atlantic Books, 1995.*

Drengson, Alan and Duncan Taylor. *Ecoforestry: The Art and Science of Sustainable Forest Use*. New Society Publishers, 1997.*

Dryzek, John S. *Rational Ecology: Environment and Political Economy*. Basil Blackwell, 1987.

Dryzek, John. "Green Reason: Communicative Ethics for the Biosphere". In Oelschlaeger, ed., *Postmodern Environmental Ethics*.

Eckersley, Robin. *Environmentalism and Political Theory: Toward an Ecocentric Approach*. State University of New York Press, 1992.

Ehrenfeld, David. *The Arrogance of Humanism*. Oxford University Press, 1978.

Elder, Philip S. "Legal Rights for Nature: The Wrong Answer to the Right(s) Question". *Osgoode Hall Law Journal*, Volume 22:2 (Summer 1984), 285-295.*

Elliot, Robert. "Rawlsian Justice and Non-Human Animals". *Journal of Applied Philosophy*, Volume 1 (1984), 95-106.

Elliot, Robert, editor. *Environmental Ethics*. Oxford University Press, 1995.

Elliot, Robert and Arran Gare, editors. *Environmental Philosophy: A Collection of Readings*. Pennsylvania State University Press, 1983.

Evernden, Neil. *The Paradox of Environmentalism*. Symposium Proceedings, Faculty of Environmental Studies, York University, June 1984.*

Evernden, Neil. "The Environmentalists' Dilemma". In N. Evernden, ed., *The Paradox of Environmentalism*, 1984.*

Evernden, Neil. *The Natural Alien: Humankind and Environment*. University of Toronto Press, 1985.*

Evernden, Neil. *The Social Creation of Nature*. Johns Hopkins Press, 1992.*

Feinberg, Joel. "The Rights of Animals and Unborn Generations". In Blackstone, ed., *Philosophy and Environmental Crisis*, 1974.

Ferré, Frederick and Peter Hartel, editors. *Ethics and Environmental Policy: Theory Meets Practice*. University of Georgia Press, 1994.

Finlayson, Alan C. *Fishing for Truth: A Sociological Analysis of Northern Cod Stock Assessments from 1977-1990*. ISER Books, 1994.*

Fitzharris, Tim, and John Livingston. *Canada: A Natural History*. Viking Studio/Penguin Books, 1988.*

Foster, Janet. *Working for Wildlife: The Beginning of Preservation in Canada*. University of Toronto Press, 1978.*

Fox, Michael Allen. "Animal Experimentation: A Philosopher's Changing Views". *Between the Species*, Volume 3:2, Spring 1987, 55.*

Fox, Michael Allen. "Environmental Ethics and the Ideology of Meat Eating." *Between the Species* Volume 9 (1993) 121-32.*

Fox, Warwick. *Towards a Transpersonal Ecology: Developing New Foundations for Environmentalism.* Shambhala, 1990.

Fox, Warwick. "The Deep Ecology - Ecofeminism Debate And Its Parallels". In Zimmerman, et. al., eds., *Environmental Philosophy*, 1995.

Freeman, Milton. "The Nature and Utility of Traditional Ecological Knowledge". In C. Gaffield and P. Gaffield, eds., *Consuming Canada*, 1995.

Frye, Northrop. *The Bush Garden: Essays on the Canadian Imagination.* Anansi, 1971.*

Frye, Northrop. "Canada: New World Without Revolution". In *Divisions on a Ground: Essays on Canadian Culture.* Anansi, 1982.*

Gaard, Greta, editor. *Ecofeminism: Women, Animals, Nature.* Temple University Press, 1993.

Gaffield, Chad and Pam Gaffield, editors. *Consuming Canada: Readings in Environmental History*, Copp Clark, 1995.*

Gayton, Don. *The Wheatgrass Mechanism: Science and Imagination in the Western Canadian Landscape.* Fifth House, 1990.*

Gayton, Don. *Landscapes of the Interior: Re-Explorations of Nature and the Human Spirit.* New Society Publishers, 1996.*

Geist, Valerius and Ian McTaggart-Cowan, editors. *Wildlife Conservation Policy.* Oetselig Enterprises, 1995.*

Girard, Michel F. "The Oka Crisis From an Environmental History Perspective, 1870-1990". In C. Gaffield and P. Gaffield, eds., 1995.*

Glaven, Terry. *Dead Reckoning: Confronting the Crisis in Pacific Fisheries.* Greystone Books/Douglas and McIntyre, 1996.*

Godyer, John. *Essentials of Canadian Society.* McClelland and Stewart, 1990.*

Goodpaster, Kenneth E. "On Being Morally Considerable". *Journal of Philosophy*, Volume 75(6), 1978, 306-25.

Goodpaster, K.E. "From Egoism to Environmentalism". In K. Goodpaster and K. Sayre, eds., *Ethics and Problems of the 21st Century*, 1979.

Goodpaster, K.E. and K.M. Sayre, editors. *Ethics and Problems of the 21st Century.* University of Notre Dame Press, 1979.

Gordon, Anita and David Suzuki. *Its a Matter of Survival.* Stoddart, 1990.*

Gottlieb, Robert. *Forcing the Spring: The Transformation of the American Environmental Movement.* Island Press, 1993.

Grady, Wayne, editor. *Treasures of the Place: Three Centuries of Nature Writing in Canada.* Douglas and McIntyre, 1992.*

Grant, George. *Technology and Empire: Perspectives on North America.* Anansi, 1969.*

Gray, Elizabeth Dodson. *Green Paradise Lost.* Roundtable Press, 1981.

Greenbaum, Allan. "Taking Stock of Two Decades of Research on the Social Bases of Environmental Concern". In M. Mehta and E. Ouellet, eds., *Environmental Sociology: Theory and Practice*, 1995.*

Greenbaum, Allan. "Environmental Thought as Cosmological Intervention". Forthcoming in *The Trumpeter*, 1997.*

Gruen, Lori and Dale Jamieson, editors. *Reflecting on Nature: Readings in Environmental Philosophy.* Oxford University Press, 1994.

Guerrier, Yvonne, Nicholas Alexander, Jonathan Chase and Martin O'Brien, editors. *Values and the Environment: A Social Science Perspective.* John Wiley and Sons, 1995.

Hamilton, Lawrence S., editor. *Ethics, Religion and Biodiversity: Relations Between Conservation and Cultural Values.* The White Horse Press, 1993.

Hanna, Jack. "Deer Dilemma." *Seasons* Volume 29:3 (Autumn 1989) 20-23.*

Hanson, Lorelei. "Turning Rivals into Allies: Understanding the Wise Use Movement. *Alternatives*, Volume 21:3 (July/Aug. 1995) 26-31.*

Hanson, Philip, editor. *Environmental Ethics: Philosophical and Policy Perspectives, Volume I.* Institute for the Humanities, Simon Fraser University, 1986.*

Hanson, Philip P. "Morality, Posterity and Nature". In P. Hanson, ed., *Environmental Ethics: Philosophical and Policy Perspectives*, 1986.*

Hanson, Philip P. "What Environmental Ethics Can Do For You". In R. Bradley and S. Duguid, eds., *Environmental Ethics*, Volume II, 1989.*

Haraway, Donna. *Simians, Cyborgs and Women: The Reinvention of Nature*. Routledge, 1991.

Hargrove, Eugene C. *Foundations of Environmental Ethics*. Prentice-Hall, 1989.

Hargrove, Eugene, editor. *The Animal Rights/ Environmental Ethics Debate: The Environmental Perspective*. State University of New York Press, 1992.

Harlow, Elizabeth. "The Human Face of Nature: Environmental Values and the Limits of Nonanthropocentrism". *Environmental Ethics*, Volume 14:1, Spring 1992, 27-42.*

Harrison, Kathryn and George Hoberg. *Risk, Science and Politics: Rgulating Toxic Substances in Canada and the United States*. McGill-Queen's University Press, 1994.*

Hart, Richard E., editor. *Ethics and the Environment*. University Press of America, 1992.

Hartley, Troy. "Environmental Justice: An Environmental Civil Rights Value Acceptable to All World Views." *Environmental Ethics* Volume 17:3 (1995) 277-290.

Haught, John F. "The Emergent Environment and the Problem of Cosmic Purpose". *Environmental Ethics*, Volume 8:2 (Summer 1986), 139-150.

Herscovici, Alan. *Second Nature: The Animal Rights Controversy*. CBC Enterprises, 1985.*

Hessing, Melody. "The Sociology of Sustainability: Feminist Eco/Nomic Approaches to Survival". In M. Mehta and E. Ouellet, eds., *Environmental Sociology*, 1995.

Hoberg, George. "Comparing Canadian Performance in Environmental Policy." In, R. Boardman, ed. *Canadian Environmental Policy: Ecosystems, Politics, and Process*. Toronto: Oxford University Press, 1992.*

Hoberg, George. "Environmental Policy: Alternative Styles." In Atkinson, ed., *Governing Canada: Institutions and Public Policy*. Harcourt, Brace and Company, 1993.*

Hofrichter, Richard, editor. *Toxic Struggles: The Theory and Practice of Environmental Justice*. New Society, 1993.

Howlett, Michael and M. Ramesh. *Studying Public Policy: Policy Cycles and Policy Subsystems*. Oxford University Press, 1995.*

Hughes, Elaine, Alastair Lucas and William Tilleman II. *Environmental Law and Policy*. Emond-Montgomery, 1993.*

Hummel, Monte, editor. *Endangered Spaces: The Future for Canada's Wilderness*. Key Porter Books, 1989.*

Hummel, Monte, editor. *Protecting Canada's Endangered Spaces: An Owner's Manual*. Key Porter, 1995.*

Jacobs, Lesley A. *An Introduction to Modern Political Philosophy: The Democratic Vision of Politics*. Prentice Hall, 1997.*

Jacobs, Michael. *The Green Economy: Environment, Sustainable Development and the Politics of the Future*. University of British Columbia Press, 1993.

Johnson, Lawrence E. *A Morally Deep World: An Essay on Moral Significance and Environmental Ethics*. Cambridge University Press, 1991.

Kernohan, Andrew. "Rights Against Polluters." *Environmental Ethics*, Volume 17:3 (1995) 245-257.*

LaDuke, Winona. "A Society Based on Conquest Cannot Be Sustained: Native Peoples and the Environmental Crisis". In R. Hofrichter, ed., *Toxic Struggles*, 1993.

LaRocque, Margot. "Speaking Animals: Notes on the Human Voiceover in Wildlife Documentaries." *Undercurrents: A Journal of Critical Environmental Studies*, Volume 2, 1990.*

Lavelle, Marianne and Marcia A. Coyle. "Unequal Protection: The Racial Divide in Environmental Law". In R. Hofrichter, ed., *Toxic Struggles*, 1993.

Lee, Dennis. *Savage Fields: An Essay in Literature and Cosmology*. Anansi, 1977.*

Leopold, Aldo. *A Sand County Almanac And Sketches Here and There*. Oxford University Press, 1949.

Lester, James P., editor. *Environmental Politics and Policy: Theories and Evidence*. Second Edition. Duke University Press, 1995.

Leiss, William. *The Domination of Nature*. Beacon Press, 1974.*

Leiss, William, editor. *Ecology Versus Politics in Canada*. University of Toronto Press, 1979.*

Leiss, William and Christina Chociolko. *Risk and Responsibility*. McGill-Queen's University Press, 1994.*

Light, Andrew and Eric Higgs. "The Politics of Ecological Restoration." *Environmental Ethics*, Volume 18:3 (1996) 227-248.*

Light, Andrew and Eric Katz, editors. *Environmental Pragmatism*. Routledge, 1996.

List, Peter, editor. *Radical Environmentalism: Philosophy and Tactics*. Wadsworth, 1993.

Littlejohn, Bruce. "Wilderness and the Canadian Psyche". In Hummel, ed., *Endangered Spaces*, 1989.*

Livingston, John A. *One Cosmic Instant: A Natural History of Human Arrogance*. McClelland and Stewart, 1973.*

Livingston, John A. *The Fallacy of Wildlife Conservation*. McLelland and Stewart, 1981.*

Livingston, John. "The Dilemma of the Deep Ecologist". In N. Evernden, ed., *The Paradox of Environmentalism*, 1984.*

Livingston, John A. "Rightness or Rights?" *Osgoode Hall Law Journal* Volume 22:2 (1984) 309-21.*

Livingston, John. "Moral Concern and the Ecosphere". *Alternatives*, Volume 12:2 (Winter 1985), 3-9.*

Livingston, John A. "Ethics as Prosthetics." In P. Hanson, ed., *Environmental Ethics: Philosophical and Policy Perspectives*, 1986.*

Livingston, John A. "The Ecological Imperative". In R. Bradley and S. Duguid, eds., *Environmental Ethics*, Volume II, 1989.*

Livingston, John A. "Nature for the Sake of Nature". In Hummel, ed., *Endangered Spaces*, 1989.*

Livingston, John A. *Rogue Primate: An Exploration of Human Domestication*. Key Porter, 1994.*

Lynge, Finn. *Arctic Wars: Animal Rights, Endangered Peoples*. University Press of New England, 1992.

Lyotard, Jean-Francoise. *The Postmodern Condition: A Report on Knowledge*, translated by Geoff Bennington and Brian Massumi. University of Minnesota Press, 1984.

Manning, Russ. "Environmental Ethics and Rawls' Theory of Justice". *Environmental Ethics*, Volume 3:2 (Summer 1981), 155-165.

Mannison, D.S., M.A. McRobbie, and R. Routley, editors. *Environmental Philosophy*. Monograph Series, No. 2. Department of Philosophy, Research School of the Social Sciences, Australian National University, 1980.

Marchak, Patricia. *Logging the Globe*. McGill-Queen's University Press, 1995.*

Marchak, Patricia, Neil Guppy, John McMullin, editors. *Uncommon Property: The Fishing and Fish Processing Industries in British Columbia*. Methuen, 1987.*

Marchi, Sergio. Minister's Forward, Bill C-64 (*Canadian Endangered Species Act*), 1996.*

Marietta, Don E. Jr. "Ethical Holism and Individualism". *Environmental Ethics*, Volume 10:3 (Fall 1988), 251-258.

Marietta, Don E. Jr. and Lester Embree, editors. *Environmental Philosophy and Environmental Activism*. Rowman and Littlefield, 1995.

Mathews, Freya. *The Ecological Self*. Routledge, 1991.

Mathews, Freya. "Relating to Nature: Deep Ecology or Ecofeminism?" *The Trumpeter: Journal of Ecosophy*, Volume 11:4 (Fall 1994), 159-166.

Matthews, Ralph. *Controlling Common Property: Regulating Canada's East Coast Fishery*. University of Toronto Press, 1993.*

McDonald, Michael (principal investigator). *Towards A Canadian Research Strategy for Applied Ethics*. A Report by the Canadian Federation for the Humanities To the Social Sciences and Humanities Research Council. Ottawa, May 1989.*

McGregor, Gaile. *The Wacousta Syndrome: Explorations in the Canadian Landscape* University of

Toronto Press, 1985.*

McGregor, Gaile. *The Noble Savage in the New World Garden: Notes Towards a Syntactics of Place.* University of Toronto Press, 1988.*

McLaughlin, Andrew. *Regarding Nature: Industrialism and Deep Ecology.* State University of New York Press, 1993.

Mclear, Kyo. "Plots of Land: Rural Asian Writing is Giving the Hinterland a Facelift." *This Magazine* Volume 30:3 (Nov./Dec. 1996) 32-37.*

Mehta, Michael and Éric Ouellet, editors. *Environmental Sociology: Theory and Practice.* Captus Press, 1995.*

Merchant, Carolyn. *The Death of Nature: Women, Ecology and the Scientific Revolution.* Harper and Row, 1980.

Merchant, Carolyn. *Radical Ecology: The Search for a Livable World.* Routledge, 1992.

Messing, Karen. "Union-Initiated Research in Genetic Effects of Workplace Agents: A Case Study." *Alternatives*, Volume 15:1 (1988) 14-18.*

Miller, Harlan B. and William H. Williams, editors. *Ethics and Animals.* Humana Press, 1983.

Miller, Peter. "Values as Richness; Toward a Value Theory for the Expanded Naturalism in Environmental Ethics". *Environmental Ethics*, Volume 4:2, Summer 1982, 101-114.*

Miller, Peter. "Do Animals Have Interests Worthy of Our Moral Interest?" *Environmental Ethics*, Volume 5:4, Winter 1983, 319-333.*

Morito, Bruce. "Value, Metaphysics and Anthropocentrism". *Environmental Values*, Volume 4:1 (1995) 31-47.*

Mowat, Farley. *Sea of Slaughter.* McClelland and Stewart, 1984.*

Murphy, Raymond. *Rationality and Nature: A Sociological Inquiry into a Changing Relationship.* Westview Press, 1994.*

Naess, Arne. "The Shallow and the Deep, Long-Range Ecology Movements." *Inquiry*, Volume 16 (1973) 95-100.

Narveson, Jan. "Future People and Us." In R. Sikora and B. Barry, *Obligations to Future Generations.*

Narveson, Jan. "Against Animal Rights". In P. Hanson, ed., *Environmental Ethics: Philosophical and Policy Perspectives*, 1986.*

Narveson, Jan. "On A Case for Animal Rights". *Monist*, Volume 70:1, January 1987, 31-49.*

Narveson, Jan. "Moral Philosophy - What It Is and Why It Matters!" In W. Cragg, ed., *Contemporary Moral Issues*, 1992.*

Narveson, Jan. *Moral Matters.* Broadview Press, 1993.*

Narveson, Jan. "Is There Really a Risk of Overpopulation?" *Risk Abstracts* 9:1 (1992) 1-9.*

Nash, Roderick. *The Rights of Nature: A History of Environmental Ethics.* University of Wisconsin Press, 1989.

Newton, Lisa H. and Catherine K. Dillingham. *Watersheds: Classic Cases in Environmental Ethics.* Wadsworth, 1994.

Norton, Bryan G. *The Preservation of Species: The Value of Biological Diversity.* Princeton University Press, 1986.

Norton, Bryan G. *Why Preserve Natural Variety?* Princeton University Press, 1987.

Norton, Bryan G. *Toward Unity Among Environmentalists.* Oxford University Press, 1991.

Norton, Bryan G. "Economists' Preferences and the Preferences of Economists". *Environmental Values*, Volume 3:4 (1994), 311-332.

Norton, Bryan G. "Applied Philosophy vs. Practical Philosophy: Toward an Environmental Policy Integrated According to Scale". In D. Marietta and L. Embree, eds., *Environmental Philosophy and Environmental Activism*, 1995.

Norton, Bryan G. "Integration or Reduction: Two Approaches to Environmental Ethics". In A. Light and E. Katz, eds., *Environmental Pragmatism*, 1996.

Noske, Barbara. *Beyond Boundaries: Humans and Animals.* Black Rose, 1997.*

Oelschlaeger, Max, editor. *Postmodern Environmental Ethics.* State University of New York Press, 1995.

Paehlke, Robert. *Environmentalism and the Future of Progressive Politics.* Yale University Press, 1989.*

Paehlke, Robert, editor. *Conservation and Environ-*

mentalism: An Encyclopedia. Garland Publishing, 1995.*

Paelhke, Robert and Douglas Torgerson, editors. Managing Leviathan: Environmental Politics and the Administrative State. Broadview, 1990.*

Paelhke, Robert and Pauline Vaillancourt Rosenau. "Environment/ Equity: Tensions in North American Politics". Policy Studies Journal, Volume 21:4 (1993), 672-686.*

Partridge, Ernest, editor. Responsibilities to Future Generations. Prometheus Books, 1981.

Partridge, Ernest. "Values in Nature: Is Anybody There?" Philosophical Inquiry, Volume 7 (1986), 96-110.

Passmore, John. Man's Responsibility for Nature. Duckworth, 1974.

Pinkerton, Evelyn. editor. Co-operative Management of Local Fisheries: New Directions for Improved Management and Community Development. University of British Columbia Press, 1989.*

Plant, Judith, editor. Healing the Wounds: The Promise of Ecofeminism. Between the Lines, 1989.*

Plumwood, Val. Ecofeminism and the Mastery of Nature. Routledge, 1993.

Poff, Deborah and Wilfrid Waluchow, editors. Business Ethics in Canada. Second Edition. Prentice-Hall Canada, 1991.*

Pojman, Louis P., editor. Environmental Ethics: Readings in Theory and Application. Jones and Bartlett Publishers, 1994.

Preece, Rod and Lorna Chamberlain. Animal Welfare and Human Values. Wilfrid Laurier University Press, 1993.*

Raglon, Rebecca and Marian Scholtmeijer. "Shifting Ground: Metanarratives, Epistemology, and the Stories of Nature." Environmental Ethics, Volume 18:1 (1996) 19-38.*

Rapport, David. "Ecosystem Health: More Than a Metaphor?" Environmental Values, Volume 4:4 (1995) 287-309.*

Rawls, John. A Theory of Justice. Harvard University Press, 1971.

Rawls, John. Political Liberalism. Columbia University Press, 1993.

Ray, Dixy Lee with Lou Guzzo. Trashing the Planet: How Science Can Help Us Deal with Acid Rain, Depletion of the Ozone, and Nuclear Waste (Among Other Things). Harper Collins, 1990.

Ray, Dixy Lee with Lou Guzzo. Environmental Overkill: Whatever Happened to Common Sense? Harper Collins, 1993.

Regan, Tom. "The Nature and Possibility of an Environmental Ethic." Environmental Ethics, Volume 3:1 (Spring 1981).

Regan, Tom. The Case for Animal Rights. University of California Press, 1983.

Regan, Tom, editor. Earthbound: New Introductory Essays in Environmental Ethics. Random House, 1984.

Regan, Tom. "Honey Dribbles Down Your Fur". In P. Hanson, ed., Environmental Ethics: Philosophical and Policy Perspectives, 1986.

Regan, Tom. "Does Environmental Ethics Rest on a Mistake?", Monist, Volume 75 (1992), 161-182.

Regan, Tom and Peter Singer, editors. Animal Rights and Human Obligations. Prentice-Hall, 1976.

Reuther, Rosemary Radford. "Motherearth and Megamachine: A Theology of Liberation in a Feminine, Somatic and Ecological Perspective". In Reuther, Liberation Theology. Paulist Press, 1972.

Richardson, Mary, Joan Sherman and Michael Gismondi. Winning Back the Words: Confronting Experts in an Environmental Public Hearing. Garamond Press, 1993.*

Rodman, John. "The Liberation of Nature?" Inquiry, Volume 29 (1977), 83-131.

Rodman, John. "Four Forms of Ecological Consciousness Reconsidered". In Scherer and Attig, eds., Ethics and the Environment.

Rogers, Ray. Nature and the Crisis of Modernity. Black Rose Books, 1994.*

Rogers, Ray. The Oceans are Emptying: Fish Wars and Sustainability. Black Rose Books, 1995.*

Rolston, Holmes III. "Is There an Ecological Ethic?" Ethics, Volume 85 (1974-75), 93-109.

Rolston, Holmes III. Environmental Ethics: Duties to and Values in the Natural World. Temple University Press, 1988.

Rolston, Holmes III. *Philosophy Gone Wild: Environmental Ethics*. Prometheus Books, 1989.

Rolston, Holmes III. *Conserving Natural Value*. Columbia University Press, 1994.

Routley, Richard. "Is There a Need for a New, an Environmental, Ethic". *Proceedings of the Fifteenth World Congress of Philosophy*, Volume 1, (1973) 205-210.

Routley, Richard (now Richard Sylvan) and Routley, Val (now Val Plumwood). "Against the Inevitability of Human Chauvinism". In K. Goodpaster and K. Sayre, eds, *Ethics and Problems of the 21st Century*, 1979.

Rowe, J. Stan. "Crimes Against the Ecosphere". In R. Bradley and S. Duguid, eds., *Environmental Ethics*, Volume II, 1989.*

Rowe, J. Stan. *Home Place: Essays on Ecology*. NeWest Books, 1990.*

Rubinoff, Lionel. "Beyond the Domination of Nature: Moral Foundations of a Conserver Society". *Alternatives*, Volume 12:2 (Winter 1985), 37-48.*

Sadler, Barry and Allen Carlson. *Environmental Aesthetics: Essays in Interpretation*. University of Victoria Press, 1982.*

Sagoff, Mark. "Animal Liberation and Environmental Ethics: Bad Marriage, Quick Divorce". *Osgoode Hall Law Journal*, Volume 22:2 (Summer 1984), 297-307.

Sagoff, Mark. *The Economy of the Earth: Philosophy, Law, and the Environment*. Cambridge University Press, 1988.

Sagoff, Mark. "Four Dogmas of Environmental Economics". *Environmental Values*, Volume 3:4 (1994), 285-310.

Salleh, Ariel. "Deeper Than Deep Ecology: The Eco-Feminist Connection". *Environmental Ethics*, Volume 6:4 (1984), 335-341.

Salleh, Ariel. "The Ecofeminism/Deep Ecology Debate". *Environmental Ethics*, Volume 14:3 (1992), 195-216.

Salter, Liora. *Mandated Science: Science and Scientists in the Making of Standards*. Kluwer Academic Publishers, 1988.*

Sandilands, Catriona. "Political Animals: The Para-dox of Ecofeminist Politics". *The Trumpeter: Journal of Ecosophy*, Volume 11:4 (Fall 1994), 167-172.*

Sandilands, Catriona. "From Natural Identity to Radical Democracy." *Environmental Ethics*, Volume 17:1 (1995) 75-91.*

Savan, Beth. "Sleazy Science". *Alternatives*, Volume 13:2 (April 1986), 11-17.*

Savan, Beth. *Science Under Siege: The Myth of Objectivity in Scientific Research*. CBC Enterprises, 1988.*

Scherer, Donald, editor. *Upstream/ Downstream: Issues in Environmental Ethics*. Temple University Press, 1990.

Scherer, Donald and Thomas Attig, editors. *Ethics and the Environment*. Prentice-Hall, 1983.

Schrecker, Ted. *The Political Economy of Environmental Hazards*. Law Reform Commission of Canada, 1984.*

Schrecker, Ted. "The Political Content and Context of Environmental Law". In T. Caputo et. al., *Law and Society: A Critical Perspective*, 1989.*

Schrecker, Ted. "Ethics and Institutions: How We Think About Policy Decisions". In R. Bradley and S. Duguid, eds., *Environmental Ethics*, Volume II, 1989.*

Schrecker, Ted. "Risks versus Rights: Economic Power and Economic Analysis in Environmental Politics". In D. Poff and W. Waluchow, eds., *Business Ethics in Canada*.*

Schrecker, Ted. "Environmentalism and the Politics of Invisibility." In M. Mehta and E. Ouellet, eds., *Environmental Sociology: Theory and Practice*. [original version published in *Alternatives*, Volume 20:2 (1994) 32-37].*

Sessions, George, editor. *Deep Ecology for the 21st Century: Readings on the Philosophy and Practice of the New Environmentalism*. Shambhala, 1995.

Shrader-Frechette, Kristin. *Science Policy, Ethics and Economic Methodology*. D. Reidel, 1985.

Shrader-Frechette, Kristin. *Risk and Rationality: Philosophical Foundations for Populist Reforms*. University of California Press, 1991.

Sikora, R.I. and Brian Barry, editors. *Obligations*

to *Future Generations*. Temple University Press, 1978.*

Singer, Brent. "An Extension of Rawls' Theory of Justice to Environmental Ethics". *Environmental Ethics*, Volume 10:3 (Fall 1988), 217-231.

Singer, Peter. "Not For Humans Only: The Place of Nonhumans in Environmental Issues". In K. Goodpaster and K. Sayre, eds., *Ethics and Problems of the 21st Century*, 1979.

Singer, Peter. *Animal Liberation: New Ethics for Our Treatment of Animals*. Second Edition. New York Review of Books/ Random House, 1990.

Skolimowski, Henryk. *Ecophilosophy: Designing New Tactics for Living*. Marion Boyars, 1981.

Slicer, Deborah. "Is There an Ecofeminism-Deep Ecology "Debate"?" *Environmental Ethics*, Volume 17:2 (Summer 1995), 151-169.

Spretnak, Charlene, editor. *The Politics of Women's Spirituality: Essays on the Rise of Spiritual Power Within the Feminist Movement*. Doubleday, 1982.

Sprigge, T.L.S. "Some Recent Positions in Environmental Ethics Examined". *Inquiry*, Volume 34 (1991), 107-128.

Steger, M.A., J. Pierce, B. Steel and N. Lovrich. "Political Culture, Postmaterial Values and the New Environmental Paradigm: A Comparative Analysis of Canada and the United States." *Political Behavior* Volume 11 (1989) 233-54.*

Sterba, James. "Reconciling Anthropocentric and Nonanthropocentric Ethics". *Environmental Values*, Volume 3:2 (1994), 229-244.

Sterba, James, editor. *Earth Ethics: Environmental Ethics, Animal Rights, and Practical Applications*. Prentice-Hall, 1995.

Steverson, Brian K. "Contextualism and Norton's Convergence Hypothesis". *Environmental Ethics*, Volume 17:2 (Summer 1995), 135-150.

Steverson, Brian K. "On the Reconciliation of Anthropocentric and Nonanthropocentric Environmental Ethics". *Environmental Values*, Volume 5:4 (1996), 349-361.

Stone, Christopher. "Should Trees Have Standing?: Toward Legal Rights for Natural Objects". *South-ern California Law Review*, Volume 45 (1972), 450-501.

Stone, Christopher. *"Should Trees Have Standing? Revisited: How Far Will Law and Morals Reach? A Pluralist Perspective"*. *University of Southern California Law Review*, Volume 59 (1985), 1-154.

Stone, Christopher. *Earth and Other Ethics: The Case for Moral Pluralism*. Harper and Row, 1987.

Sumner, L.W. "Classical Utilitarianism". In R. Sikora and B. Barry, eds., *Obligations to Future Generations*.*

Sumner, L.W. "The Canadian Harp Seal Hunt: A Moral Issue". *Alternatives*, Volume 12:2 (Winter 1985), 15-22.*

Sumner, L. Wayne. "Welfare, Sentience, and Moral Standing". In P. Hanson, ed., *Environmental Ethics: Philosophical and Policy Perspectives*, 1986.*

Sumner, L. W. "How to Do Applied Ethics." Keynote address to the Ontario Philosophical Society, York University, Toronto, Ontario, November 4 1994.*

Suzuki, David. *Inventing the Future: Reflections on Science, Technology and Nature*. Stoddart, 1989.*

Swift, Jamie. *Cut and Run: The Assault on Canada's Forests*. Between the Lines, 1983.*

Sylvan, Richard and David Bennett. *The Greening of Ethics: From Anthropocentrism to Deep-Green Theory*. White Horse Press/ University of Arizona Press, 1994.

Taylor, Paul. *Respect for Nature: A Theory of Environmental Ethics*. Princeton University Press, 1986.

Thereo, Daniel P. "Rawls and Environmental Ethics: A Critical Examination of the Literature". *Environmental Ethics*, Volume 17:1 (Spring 1995), 93-106.

Thompson, Paul B. *The Spirit of the Soil: Agriculture and Environmental Ethics*. Routledge, 1995.

Torgerson, Douglas. "The Paradox of Environmental Ethics". *Alternatives*, Volume 12:2 (Winter 1985), 26-36.*

Tribe, Laurence. "Ways Not to Think About Plastic Trees: New Foundations for Environmental Law". *Yale Law Journal*, Volume 83 (1974), 1315-1348.

VanDeVeer, Donald. "Of Beasts, Persons, and the

Original Position". *Monist*, Volume 62 (July 1979), 368-377.

VanDeVeer, Donald and Christine Pierce, editors. *People, Penguins, and Plastic Trees: Basic Issues in Environmental Ethics*. Wadsworth, 1986.

VanDeVeer, Donald and Christine Pierce, editors. *The Environmental Ethics and Policy Book: Philosophy, Ecology, Economics*. Wadsworth, 1994.

Varner, Gary E. "Can Animal Rights Activists Be Environmentalists?" In D. Marietta and L. Embree, eds., *Environmental Philosophy and Environmental Activism*, 1995.

Wadland, John. *Ernest Thompson Seton: Man in Nature and the Progressive Era 1880-1915*. Arno Press, 1978.*

Wadland, John. "Wilderness and Culture". In C. Gaffield and P. Gaffield, editors, *Consuming Canada*, 1995.*

Warren, Karen J. "The Power and Promise of Ecological Feminism". In S. Armstrong and R. Botzler, eds., *Environmental Ethics: Divergence and Convergence*.

Wellington, Alex. "Feminist Positions on Vegetarianism: Arguments For and Against and Otherwise". *Between the Species: A Journal of Ethics*, Volume 11: 3/4, Summer and Fall 1995.*

Wenz, Peter. *Environmental Justice*. State University of New York Press, 1988.

Wenzel, George. *Animal Rights, Human Rights: Ecology, Economy and Ideology in the Canadian Artic*. University of Toronto Press, 1992.*

Weston, Anthony. *Back to Earth: Tomorrow's Environmentalism*. Temple University Press, 1994.

Westphal, Dale and Fred Westphal, editors. *Planet in Peril: Essays in Environmental Ethics*. Harcourt, Brace and Company/ Holt, Rinehart and Winston, 1994.

Westra, Laura. *An Environmental Proposal for Ethics: The Principle of Integrity*. Rowman and Littlefield, 1994.*

Westra, Laura and Peter Wenz, editors. *Faces of Environmental Racism: Confronting Issues of Global Justice*. Rowman and Littlefield, 1995.*

Wilson, Alexander. *The Culture of Nature: North American Landscape from Disney to the Exxon Valdez*. Between the Lines, 1991.*

Winkler, Earl and Jerrold Coombs, editors. *Applied Ethics: A Reader* Blackwell, 1993.*

Zimmerman, Michael E., general editor; J. Baird Callicott, George Sessions, Karen J. Warren and John Clark, editors. *Environmental Philosophy: From Animal Rights to Radical Ecology*. Prentice-Hall, 1993.

SHIFTING VALUES
SEEING FORESTS AND NOT JUST TREE$

1

by Alan Drengson and Duncan Taylor

EARLY IN THE MORNING ON AUGUST 9, 1993 NEARLY 300 men, women, and children, many of them chanting and singing, were arrested and hauled away by the RCMP for protesting clearcut logging in British Columbia's Clayoquot Sound. The morning's confrontation constituted the largest single mass arrest in BC history. By the end of the summer the number charged with obstructing the logging bridge across Clayoquot Sound's Kennedy River totaled 800. Many of the protesters arrested that morning had been camped in a clearcut that had become known throughout the province as the "Black Hole". The slashed, burned, blackened and eroded hills surrounding the protest camp looks down on that part of Highway 4 which divides in opposite directions at the point where it reaches the west coast of Vancouver Island: to the southeast the road ends at the town of Ucluelet, to the northwest it ends at the community of Tofino. The fact that these communities lie geographically at opposite ends of Pacific Rim National Park merely underscores the polarization that has arisen between the residents of Ucluelet and Tofino regarding the future of the 350,000 hectares of coastal temperate old growth forest in this region.[1]

Since the early 1970s the town of Tofino has become home to an increasing number of people who openly espouse a "pro-environmental" position with respect to how the forests of this region should be used. Once almost solely dependent on logging and fishing, Tofino now boasts that most of its revenue is derived from purely sustainable forms of wilderness recreation tourism such as kayaking, backpacking, and whale watching, that is utterly dependent on maintaining the integrity of the Sound's forests, rivers, and inlets. In turn, the native bands belonging to the Nuu-Chah-Nulth Tribal Council, that live on many of the islands outside Tofino, have laid claim to the Clayoquot Sound Region and have let it be known that *status quo* resource extraction will no longer be tolerated.

In contrast, on the other side of Pacific Rim National Park, the majority of the residents of Ucluelet have remained almost solely dependent on the forest industry for their employment and livelihood. Indeed, in the past decade they have witnessed thousands of forestry workers on Vancouver Island laid off due to pressure on the forest industry to maintain its international competitiveness. This has led to rapid changes in equipment and mechanization procedures resulting in a downsizing of the labour force. And when uncertainty regarding forest policy and access to harvestable timber in Clayoquot Sound is also factored in, tensions have tended to be projected in terms of simplistic arguments of "jobs" versus "preservation." However, this dichotomy is not new.

People active in environmental issues over the last two decades have witnessed the polarization of debates raging over the protection of wilderness values by preservation of ancient West Coast forests, versus the economic values of logging. In the United States, particularly in the states of Washington and Oregon, this crystallization has been evident in the "owls versus jobs" phrases used to describe the way the issues are seen. Here the owls are used to represent the environment, and jobs the workers and business. The polarization between the residents of Tofino and Ucluelet may be seen to characterize the rift that exists between environmentalists and those who are stridently anti-environmentalist and claim that environmentalism undermines human and economic well-being. But while this portrait is true to some extent it fails to take account of the "conservationist" stance held by many proforestry advocates. Consequently, the debate between these towns also reflects a more scholarly debate between supporters of what has been termed the deep ecology movement" and proponents of "reformist environmentalism." For some time now, spokespeople from Ucluelet and other forestry-dependent communities have claimed that they are the "real" conservationists – but conservationists that are realistic enough to respect the human benefits that accrue from one of Canada's largest and most economically important industries.

The impression one sometimes gets from these debates is that we must choose between ecologically sound practices and human economic and social welfare needs. In our view, the jobs versus environment account is a caricature of our situation and options with respect to resolving current conflicts. As long as attention is focussed on this narrow account, resolution seems impossible: Either we sacrifice the environment for jobs (economic values) in the short term – to meet the demands of social justice and human needs, or we sacrifice jobs – to save the environment for our long-term interests. This is a no-win situation. However, we believe that there is a win-win solution. This solution is predicated on the recognition that sustainable communities and economies are subsystems of healthy biophysical systems and not the other way around.

Since the rise of modernity in the seventeenth century, we have been rapidly converting natural capital to financial capital and changing our ecological systems to meet the imperatives of an ever-expanding consumptive economic system. This has to change. Indeed, for the long-term survival of our own species as well as the many other life forms with whom we share this planet, we now need to recognize that our economic system is a subsystem of the larger biophysical ecology and that it has to be transformed to meet the imperatives of the latter. In this way we can reach a win-win situation. In this way we can have long-term forestry jobs, healthy communities and a healthy natural ecosystem. The road into Clayoquot goes in opposite directions – indeed, it symbolically points to the choice between two very different world views and sets of values.

In the current conflict over forest preservation and logging we can see that there are definitely two different orientations or approaches at issue. One is the dominant, mainstream, expansionist model of modernism, the other is an emerging ecological paradigm. The *first* is based on a human "exemptionalist" model of our relation to nature – humans exist apart from and outside of nature; it accepts a utilitarian value system. In the expansionist paradigm, nature is regarded essentially as a storehouse of resources to be utilized for the meeting of ever-increasing material needs by an ever-increasing human population. Consequently, this position equates growth with the progress of development which, in turn, is regarded as a prerequisite for human happiness and prosperity, claiming that any drop in this growth rate must inevitably result in stagnation, mass unemployment and distress. Those who argue for this position claim that new technological advances can be relied upon to increase global standards of living, harness renewable and more environmentally "friendly" sources of energy, and increase food production and the availability of other biological products through breakthroughs in biotechnology. In turn, more efficient technologies are seen to be able to solve the problems created by previous technologies, to create substitutes for depleted resources and to replace damaged ecosystems.

On the other hand, the ecological paradigm is based on humans as participants in nature; it accepts an ethic based upon respect for diversity and ecocentric values. The two views in question differ in their sense of values which are intrinsic to nature and to human life. Intrinsic or inherent values are cherished for their own sake. We consider them to be good in themselves; they are ends. Instrumental values are pursued as a means to other things and states which are themselves valued. In the case of valuing the natural world, people holding the intrinsic nature view (the deep ecology movement for example) cherish other beings for their own sake, quite independent of their usefulness or economic value to humans. The instrumentalist nature view (the shallow ecology movement) sees all intrinsic value as vested solely in humans.

The result is that the world is valued only as means; its value is as resource to be used for human consumption and enjoyment. The *intrinsic-nature* view sees a world rich in inherent values, beings have value in themselves, quite independently of human interests. In the *instrumentalist nature* view we have an obligation to manage and control the world to meet human needs and desires, insofar as this is consistent with our interests and those of future generations. In the *intrinsic nature* view we have an obligation to manage ourselves so as to preserve the beauty and integrity of the planet's ecological processes and functions. *All* beings count; their vital needs must be respected when we design our practices.

Some of the characteristics of this emerging ecological paradigm may be summarized as follows:

* The universe is an interrelated totality, with all of its parts interconnected and interlocked. A corollary to this is the rejection of those dualistic and atomistic categories inherent within the Newtonian mechanistic perspective on which the expansionist paradigm is founded – for example, the epistemological separation of the subjective knower from the objective known, and the radical separation of facts from values.

* Nature is intrinsically valuable; animals, trees or rocks all have worth and value in themselves regardless of what value they may have for human beings. This is essentially an ecocentric and non-anthropocentric perspective and a rejection of the typically quantitative approach to nature with its emphasis on viewing the natural world primarily in economic and utilitarian terms.

* Nature is both a physical and a symbolic forum from which to stand back from modern society. In nature – and especially in the more wild areas – humans are afforded an opportunity to actualize their own inner spiritual, aesthetic and moral sensibilities. Moreover, physical nature – especially wilderness – is a benchmark against which the state of human society may be judged. Consequently, large areas of the natural world should be preserved and protected from human interference.

Throughout the twentieth century environmental debates have been polarized in terms of these two dominant perspectives. For example, the same type of polarization that continues to occur over the ancient forests has also been evident in disputes over industrial fishing and agriculture and their ecological viability. The first famous articulation of the polarized views referred to above surfaced in debates between John Muir (naturalist and essayist and founder of the Sierra Club in 1892) and Gifford Pinchot (U.S. Chief Forester who largely determined President Theodore Roosevelt's conservation program) early in this century.[2]

Anticipating the later work of Aldo Leopold, Muir argued for the adoption of an environmental land ethic, but one that would recognize the inherent value of natural entities and their right to pursue their own destiny, to continue to evolve. He believed we should preserve large areas of wilderness so that it can evolve independent of human manipulation – even if no human ever visits such areas. In doing so, he was rejecting a basic tenet of modernity which had come to view nature primarily in utilitarian and economic terms. Moreover, it was to put him increasingly at odds with his contemporary Gifford Pinchot as well as the values that dominated North American society at the turn of the twentieth century.

Conservation as championed by Pinchot, on the other hand, was to be an ally of the expansionist paradigm. In many respects, it was for this that it had gained a certain legitimacy by 1908 when President Theodore Roosevelt held the first National Conference on Conservation at the White House. And not surprisingly, John Muir was not invited. By 1909 the Canadian government had established its own Commission of Conservation.[3] Indeed, the "wise use" school of Pinchot in the United Sates and Clifford Sifton in Canada equated conservation with "sustainable exploitation." For both men, conservation should work against the wastefulness and environmentally disruptive excesses of a developing society, but not against development *per se.* For land to be protected or "alienated" from resource development and extraction was seen to be politically and economically naive. Indeed, conservationists argued that land must be utilized in the interests of a growing industrial economy thereby providing jobs and wealth to the larger society. Ideally, conservation would require that wise "scientific" management procedures be adopted in the utilization of all resources, including forests, soils, waters and wildlife. Moreover, wherever possible, these resources would be harvested in terms of a renewable crop. In this way, Pinchot and others believed that nature's resources could be "used" and "saved" simultaneously and thereby conserved for future human generations.

Pinchot's legacy lives on with those who champion the sustainability of the existing expansionist paradigm. In other words, conservation was to reinforce the dominant industrial expansionist world view by ideally protecting the ability of the land to provide a limitless supply of resources — hence, *sustainable economic development.* On the other hand, John Muir's position is favoured by those proponents of an emerging ecological perspective who believe that we must recognize ecological limits to growth and transform our economies to meet its imperatives — not the other way around. Moreover, it is argued that the products of ecological and evolutionary processes can only be sustained by protecting the integrity of the ecological processes that give rise to them. This necessitates the preservation of large areas of wilderness for the ongoing protection of biodiversity as well as aesthetic and spiritual values.

In other words, we must ultimately reject the expansionist paradigm and learn to live off of the "interest or abundance" of nature while protecting its "biological capital." Current wise-use strategies consume natural capital and diversity. Hence, the need to go from the current emphasis on models for sustainable economic development to strategies *for developing environmental sustainability.* The stress would then place our priorities on maintaining biodiversity and ecological processes.

While there is some uncertainty about exact details and specific timetables, people who have knowledge of Earth's ecosystems agree that the large scale industrial practices, as imposed today upon the biological processes of the planet, are not sustainable. On the other hand, in the modern period most Westerners accept without question modernism's definition of progress, that through science and technology we can have unlimited growth (certainly an unscientific belief), greater and greater wealth, more and more power, more and more speed, and so on.

We have partially realized these aims, except for the last several years when the standard of living has not been going up, debt has been increasing, and social problems have multiplied beyond our capacity to find solutions. We tend to look at each of these problems on its own so as to find individual and even individualistic solutions. But the problems, like the debt, have become intractable.

Our apparent solutions often create more problems than real solutions. Even as we increase efficiency, cost effectiveness and competitiveness in forestry (and fishing and farming) and have been cutting greater and greater volumes of timber with fewer workers, at the same time communities based on forestry have had increasingly hard economic times and decreasing employment. The same things have happened in fishing and farming communities. The application of the industrial paradigms of modernism to these resource based economies has been disastrous, not only for the humans involved, but also for future generations and the ecosystems that produce the needed resources.

Forest ecosystems, for example, produce trees and a great diversity of other organisms and processes beneficial to us. Remove the whole forest by extensive clearcutting and this great productive power is reduced to nearly zero. That area of land will now be recovering for a long time. Recent industrial methods try to turn forests into monocultured agricultural products, and the result of such methods is a dramatic reduction in ecological diversity. This is reflected in the human communities in reduction of economic diversity to single industry towns. The methods, scale and economy of industrial forestry leads to depopulation of forest-based communities and to reduced biological, economic and cultural diversity. Ecoforestry maintains and gives rise to greater diversity. It is based on the recognition that sustainable communities depend on sustainable forest ecosystems.

The expansionist worldview upon which modernism is based reduces all values to a common monetary measure – for example, dollars. If dollars are the only measure widely accepted for evaluating courses of action, then the demands of modern progress (as defined above) will be to use all resources to our maximum ability so as to generate the largest short-term gains. The creation of wealth in this way is often illusory, for it is based not only on increasing public and private debt, but also on increasing social and ecological debts. Even if we took all human interests into account, strove for economic and social justice, and considered the interests and needs of future generations, we would still not be able to resolve our current dilemmas without embracing a larger system of values, a broader, more inclusive understanding of how we participate in local, regional and global ecosystems.

Broader perspectives such as these help us to better understand our whole heritage and the debt we owe to the natural processes which provide us with a rich accumulation of ecological wealth. This accumulation, we can then appreciate, is part of larger sustaining processes which allow abundance to be continually produced. When we look at our problems with a narrower focus, as suggested by the dominant paradigm, we can be led to think that we must sacrifice either jobs or healthy ecosystems. Nothing could be further from the truth, they are interdependent. Thus, if we work within the limits of local ecosystems, but add diversity to our economies, we can produce many levels of value-added activity. The end result will be greater prosperity for all but the few megacorporations that have no stake in preserving local communities or ecosystems.

A solution then, might be to redefine the wise-use philosophy of Gifford Pinchot. If we consider the needs of future generations of humans over several hundred years, can we not then design practices that take conservation seriously? The crux then will be seen to be how to build conservation costs into the system's economics. This approach could buy time. However, in our view it cannot resolve our *fundamental* problems. We cannot design sustainable practices without a deeper understanding of the relevant values and costs. Any values lost must be figured as costs. In addition, just as a person who is egocentric often fails to perceive community values, so a person who is anthropocentric (believes that only humans have inherent value) can have difficulty understanding and perceiving the diversity of ecological values inherent in the forests and Earth. It is not just a matter of short-term versus long-term perspectives, although looking at our situation with a broader temporal perspective certainly helps. It is a matter of a different frame of reference.

The dispute that erupted in the forests of British Columbia in the summer of 1993 over the government-industry decision to clearcut much of the forests of Clayoquot Sound exemplifies the nature of the debate we have been describing. In 1995 the British Columbia government legislated its Forest Practices Code that promised that forestry would be conducted in an environmentally sound way.

To the critics, however, the Forest Practices Code was a band-aid solution that would merely help to prolong the lifespan of a dying industrial forestry status quo. It was still very mainstream, and mainstream thinking is still steeped in ideas of sustained yield and cosmetic cuts, for example, those which follow natural contours and boundaries, rather than on understanding whole, natural, forest ecosystems with their multitudes of functions, values, beings and processes.

Sustaining a steady flow of raw material to be turned into commodities by means of longer rotations and smaller clearcuts could ultimately lead to the same results as the large-scale conversion of diverse natural forests into just a few commercially profitable species and single age monocultures. This thinking is based on attempting to control and redesign the forest, by removing the old forests and replacing them with "superior" desired species, which are managed "intensively" – meaning by the same methods of industrial agriculture, based on machines and external subsidies such as fertilizers, pesticides and petrochemicals.

Our description of the conflicts so far, should make it evident that one way to break the impasse would be to change our forest practices so that they are consistent with the ways in which natural forests sustain themselves through diversity, recycling of woody debris and natural succession and regeneration. If an economy is based on a natural resource and its use, than clearly the elimination of that resource will destroy the economy over time. This has been dramatically shown in the case of much of the Newfoundland fishing industry with the virtual elimination of the northern cod stock.

Considerable clarity in this situation can be gained by considering the conflicting views as representing the clash between the shallow or reform ecology movement and the long-range, deep ecology movement. (With respect to the terminology we have already employed – shallow ecology is very much part of the expansionist perspective and deep ecology is virtually identical to the emerging ecological perspective).

Arne Naess of Norway introduced this terminology in the early 1970s to characterize the two main trends in environmentalism as a worldwide, grassroots movement. It was clear to Naess that people in different cultures argued for an approach to the natural world that took diversity as central. Since the environmental crisis requires fundamental changes in values and attitudes, we cannot go on with business as usual. We must question deeply our fundamental values. People in different cultures have different ultimate philosophies: They could be Buddhists, Christians or philosophical pantheists, and yet they all share the same Earth. In his travels Naess found that people in quite different places support certain general principles which he articulated as the platform principles of the deep ecology movement.

The platform principles of the deep ecology movement as stated by Naess and Sessions (1985) are:

ALAN DRENGSON AND DUNCAN TAYLOR

1. The well-being and flourishing of human and nonhuman Life on Earth have value in themselves (synonyms: intrinsic value, inherent value). These values are independent of the usefulness of the nonhuman world for human purposes.

2. Richness and diversity of life forms contribute to the realizations of these values and are also values in themselves.

3. Humans have no right to reduce this richness and diversity except to satisfy *vital* human needs.

4. The flourishing of human life and cultures is compatible with a substantial decrease of human population. The flourishing of nonhuman life requires such a decrease.

5. Present human interference with the nonhuman world is excessive, and the situation is rapidly worsening.

6. Policies must therefore be changed. These policies affect basic economic, technological, and ideological structures. The resulting state of affairs will be deeply different from the present.

7. The ideological change is mainly that of appreciating *life quality* (dwelling in situations of inherent value) rather than adhering to an increasingly higher standard of living. There will be a profound awareness of the difference between big and great.

8. Those who subscribe to the foregoing points have an obligation to directly or indirectly try to implement the necessary changes.

(Quoted from Deep Ecology by Bill Devall and George Sessions, Gibb Smith, Salt Lake City, 1985.)

In contrast, the platform principles of the shallow or reform ecology movement are as follows (synthesized by us):

1. Humans and their communities are the only beings which have intrinsic worth.

2. Progress involves applying scientific knowledge to increase technological power so as to satisfy human needs and wants.

3. No developments should be pursued if they seriously damage human interests and the rights of future generations of humans to fulfill themselves.

4. We and our descendants depend upon the resources of the Earth.

5. These resources should be used wisely so that human interests now and in the future are not jeopardized.

6. Pollution and resource waste are in conflict with human well- being and future interests.

7. We should fight pollution and resource depletion.

8. Anyone who agrees with the need to preserve environmental integrity for human benefit should support reforms (higher gas mileage, greater efficiency, etc.) which end environmental degradation and resource abuse.

As the debate has worn on, public perceptions and policies related to forests have been also changing. For an increasing number of people, it has become clear that the mere reform of conventional practices will not preserve the integrity of natural forests in terms of sustaining biodiversity, the ability of forest ecosystems to adapt to new and changing environmental conditions, and to protect the full range of forest values.

Consequently, advocates of the ecological paradigm argue that our practices must be redesigned from the ground up so that they recognize the intrinsic value of biological diversity. We cannot develop ecologically sound and responsible practices unless we do take account of and respect both biodiversity and diversity of values – both in natural systems and in the human cultural systems whose whole long-term viability is predicated upon them.

Let us consider, then, how such a redesign might take place.

Here is a chart outlining the industrial philosophy of imposing machine structures on nature in contrast to the ecological paradigm:

Industrial philosophy	Ecological paradigms
1. Business as usual	1. Need new practices
2. Technical fixes for environmental problems	2. Design approaches which prevent problems
3. Nature as raw material, only instrumental value	3. Nature is intrinsically valuable
4. Mechanistic models	4. Whole systems models – community ordered organic ecosystems
5. Isolated objects, subject/object dualisms	5. Fields, processes, interrelationships, interdependent dualities
6. Technical knowledge suffices	6. Need understanding, wisdom
7. Reductionistic	7. Holistic
8. Progress defined economically	8. Progress defined by all values, moral, spiritual, aesthetic, etc.
9. Consumptive lifestyles	9. New low impact lifestyles

Next let us consider how this approach applied to agriculture contrasts to the emerging ecoagricultural approach:

Industrial Agriculture and Ecoagriculture

1. Capital intensive/Knowledge and labour intensive

2. Large-scale monocultures/Small-scale, mixed crops, etc.

3. Simplifies ecosystem/Increases cropland diversity and complexity

4. Imposes management on Nature/Lets nature "manage"

5. Uses chemicals, fire, etc./Uses no biocides and uses fire sparingly

6. Ignores biological communities/Enhances soil communities

7. High input costs/Low input costs

8. Large agribusiness farms/Small, family sized farms

9. Elimination of rural communities/Regeneration of communities

Finally, let us consider the main contrasts between conventional industrial forestry and ecologically-based forestry. Indeed, it may be observed that while the goals of ecologically-based forestry are largely in keeping with the principles of a deep ecology approach at times they overlap with some of the "wise use management" conservation principles of shallow ecology and Gifford Pinchot. In light of current Canadian economic and political realities, this should be expected.

Industrial Forestry/Ecoforestry

1. Trees are seen as products/Forests are ecological communities

2. Short-term production goals/Long-term sustainability

3. Agricultural production model/Forest ecosystem model

4. Trees are the only cash crop/Diverse forest products and services

5. Trees' survival dependent on humans/Self-sustaining, self-maintaining, and self-renewing

6. Chemicals/No chemicals

7. Clear-cuts/Harvesting surplus wood and selective removal

8. Same age stands of trees/All ages of trees

9. Monoculture of single or few species/All species of trees

10. Simplified ecosystem/Natural biodiversity and complexity

11. Capital intensive-Corporate based/Labour intensive and locally based

12. Redesigning nature/Accepting nature's design

13. Life span, 60-100 years/Life span, millennia

14. Loss of the sacred/Sense of the sacred and mysterious

15. Older traditions, Aboriginal knowledge outdated/Older traditions and aboriginal knowledge are sources of wisdom

Methods for attaining these ecoforestry goals are the following:

Principles of Ecoforestry:

1 Retention must be the first consideration in any planned remval of trees from a stand. Emphasize what must be left to esure the protection of such things as rare spcies, sites of native cultural significance, iparian zones (that is water courses, lakeshores, etc.).

2 Leave ripaian zones intact, no tree removal should take place in the most sensitive areas. Protect water quality by minimizing alterations to natural drainage patterns.

3 Maintain composition and structures to support fully functioning forests. Important forest structures such as large old trees, snags and large fallen trees are maintained by letting a minimum of 20 to 30 percent of overstory trees (well distributed spatially and by species) grow old and die in any timber extraction area.

4 Use the lowest impact removal methods possible. Avoid building roads and compacting forest soils as much as possible – all roads should be small scale, contour, low grade roads requiring a minimum of blasting.

5 Plan in terms of the needs of the larger watershed – even if owner does not control or own the watershed. A watershed zone plan must designate areas where tree removal is not permitted and those where different levels and types of removal are possible.

6 Prohibit clearcutting as currently practiced and utilize ecologically appropriate partial cutting methods that maintain the canopy structure, age distribution and species mixtures found in healthy natural forests in a particular ecosystem type.

7 Select trees as candidates for removal by considering how abundant and redundant their structures and functions are to the rest of the forest as a whole, leaving potential wildlife trees (to become snags and large woody debris).

8 Allow the forest to regenerate trees through seeds from trees in the logged area. Tree planting will generally not be required because a diverse, fully functioning forest is always maintained, assuring natural regeneration.

9 Maintain ecological succession to protect biological diversity. The process of brush control will be avoided. Over time, all forest phases must occupy every forest site, even on sites managed solely for timber.

10 Prohibit slashburning. However, fire is an acceptable tool in landscapes which have a history of naturally occurring fires – but use with caution.

11 Prohibit pesticide use. Disease, insects and shrub/herb vegetation are essential parts of a fully functioning forest.

12 Maintain and restore topsoil quality by leaving sufficient, large and small debris.

13 Maintain beauty and other natural aesthetic qualities in the visual, sound, and odour landscapes.

14 Always look to the forest as a whole and how each part contributes to the needs and health of the larger whole in which it resides.

15 Rely as much as possible on local people and markets. Engage in full cost accounting.

16 Remember that wisdom begins with recognizing our limitations and ignorance. When in doubt, don't![4]

While this form of "ecoforestry" is not yet the norm, there are current indications that there is a trend in this direction. In the wake of the Clayoquot Sound protests and arrests in 1993 the British Columbia Government agreed to commission a panel of experts in forest ecology and native cultural concerns to investigate the best way that logging could proceed in Clayoquot Sound. In the spring of 1995 the Scientific Panel for Sustainable Forest Practices in Clayoquot Sound released its final report entitled *Sustainable Ecosystem Management in Clayoquot Sound: Planning and Practices*. To the delight of some and the shock of others, the findings of the panel, if fully implemented, would turn BC forest practices on their head. In short, the report, in terms of its values and practices, not only is a scathing critique of industrial forestry, but it is a major endorsement of ecologically-based forms of forestry. It emphasizes that we must first consider what must be left in the forest to maintain fully functioning forest ecosystems, rather than asking how much we can take out for maximum profit. The Scientific Panel starts with a whole systems view of forest communities:

"The world is interconnected at all levels; attempts to understand it entail analyzing its components and considering the whole system....In developing guiding principles, the Panel has tried to maintain a holistic view of forest ecosystems, to recognize connections across the landscape, and to draw on both scientific knowledge and the Nuu-Chah-Nulth 'lived experience.' Current forest management standards will be assessed, and new standards developed, in this context." (Report 4, p. 25)

Rejecting the traditional emphasis on purely economic and utilitarian values from the forest the Panel has advocated the need to protect all forest values and all forestry components – regardless of the value humans may place on them. For example:

"Human activities must respect the land, the sea, and all the life and life systems they support. Living organisms have a place in nature that must be sustained to maintain the health of the system in which they exist. The necessity to maintain natural ecological systems – including the land and sea themselves – supersedes the value that society may place on any individual component of those systems." (Ibid., p. 25)

The Panel has also recognized that the long-term viability of a culture and its economy is utterly dependent on the long-term viability of the ecosystems in which they reside. In other words, the economy is a subsystem of the biophysical system and must meet its imperatives – not the other way around:

"Long-term ecological and economic sustainability are essential to long-term harmony. The Panel views harmony as a stable and healthy relationship between people and the ecosystems that support them. Maintaining harmony is the responsibility of each generation to those that follow. Stand-

ards guiding land use and resource management should ensure ecological, cultural, and long-term economic sustainability. Current rates of population growth and resource extraction may not be sustainable or permit the desired harmony." (Ibid., p. 25).

"The Panel recommended that an ecosystem approach to planning be adopted, one in which "the primary planning objective is to sustain the productivity and natural diversity of the Clayoquot Sound region. The flow of forest products must be determined in a manner consistent with objectives for ecosystem sustainability." (Report 5, p. 153).

The Report rejects traditional clearcut logging in favour of a "variable-retention" silvicultural system that attempts to mimic the characteristics of natural forests. It states:

"The variable-retention system provides for the permanent retention after harvest of various forest 'structures' or habitat elements such as large decadent trees or groups of trees, snags, logs, and downed wood from the original stand that provide habitat for forest biota." (Report 5, p. 83).

In short, the variable-retention technique would:

i) "maintain watershed integrity; maintain the stability and productivity of forest soils; maintain waterflows and critical elements of water quality within the range of natural variability and within natural waterways";

ii) "maintain biological diversity; create managed forests that retain near-natural levels of biological diversity, structural diversity, and ecological function; maintain viable populations of all indigenous species; sustain the species, populations, and the processes associated with the late-successional forest stands and structures;"

iii) "maintain cultural values; protect areas and sites significant to First Nations people;"

iv) "maintain scenic, recreational, and tourism values" and,

v) "be sustainable – provide for a sustainable flow of products from the managed forests of Clayoquot Sound." (Report 5, p. 151).

The Panel also emphasizes the need to take the cultural and spiritual needs of the native people of Clayoquot Sound into account. It notes that "indigenous people live within the landscape from which they and the rest of society extract resources. Because of their longer, often closer connections to nature, the cultural and spiritual relationships of First Nations peoples with their environment are different from those of other cultures. Such cultural and spiritual needs must be accommodated in standards governing land use and resource management." (Report 4, p. 25). The panel also specifically recognizes the ecological knowledge of First Nations in Report #3.

The systemic approach to the forests of Clayoquot Sound, taken by the Clayoquot Sound Scientific Panel, emphasizes the close interdependencies that exist among community, cultural, economic and biophysical sustainability. All too often forest-based communities feel out of control, the decisions for the land being made elsewhere driven purely by economics of scale. Increasingly, representatives of forest communities have argued for the need to have more control and say over what takes place in their watersheds. This has certainly been the case in regard to the native people of Clayoquot Sound as well as with respect to the communities of Tofino and Ucluelet. Indeed, there are compelling arguments to be made for increased levels of local control so long as regional and national standards of forest management are maintained.

Current arguments include the following:

1. Community dependence on exports of a single resource leave the local economy vulnerable to external market variations. Long-term

stability requires diversification and investment in the local economy. Such development is best accomplished through local initiatives and planning.

2. Outside control of the local resource base often results in surplus revenues being redirected elsewhere. Companies tend to be reluctant to purchase from local suppliers, invest in local manufacturing, or locate head offices and research facilities in the community. Alternatively, it is argued that a community-based forestry would more readily be able to keep revenues within the region.

3. Small-scale forms of ecoforestry can best protect the wide rage of economic and environmental values. For example, community-based enterprises are more apt to be sensitive to the protection of water supplies and wildlife habitat, while providing opportunities for tourist and recreational revenue. It is argued that small-scale forestry may be less wasteful and better able to produce a wider variety of specialized wood products through intensive management. Small-scale is "site-specific," using a variety of harvesting procedures and is better suited to the practice of a more environmentally sustainable "holistic" and ecoforestry based form of management and technology practices.

4. Locally controlled resources are responsive to the changing needs, values, and life-styles of the local population. Control over one's resources gives a feeling of a greater sense of control over one's life.

Canadians are now at a juncture in their history when they are finally beginning to realize that they are living far beyond their economic and environmental means. We have become a wealthy country because we have been recklessly converting natural wealth into financial capital – but at a cost which is unsustainable. Like the road into Clayoquot Sound that bifurcates in two directions,

we have now reached a similar fork in terms of how we live and interact with the larger biophysical world upon which we are utterly dependent. The Clayoquot Sound Scientific Panel's Report points in the direction of an emerging ecological paradigm (or some would say world view). It argues for a systemic approach to the management of forest ecosystems and to the recognition that sustainable forestry must take into account the full range of values within a given ecosystem as well as respect the cultural values of those who reside within this ecosystem. The BC Government has promised to abide by the Panel's recommendations. If it does, it will be the beginning of a radical shift in the way that forestry is conducted in Canada's most economically important forest province. The proverbial horse will have been let out of the barn and forest policies elsewhere in the province will eventually have to come in line with practices that the Panel claims are "not only the best in the province, but the best in the world." (Report 4, p. 8). The gauntlet has been thrown down. Do we have the foresight and the political will to make the transition to ecoforestry – i.e. to ecologically responsible forest use?

ENDNOTES

[1] i) Phil Carter, "The Summer of Clayoquot," *Borealis*, Vol. 5, NO. 1, Issue 15, Spring, 1994, Edmonton, pp. 8-17;

ii) Ron MacIssaac and Anne Champagne, eds., *Clayoquot Mass Trial*, New Society Publishers, Gabriola Island, B.C., 1994;

iii) Tzeborah Berman, Maurice Gibbons, et al., *Clayoquot and Dissent*, Ronsdale Press Ltd., Vancouver, 1994;

iv) Howard Breen-Needham, Sandy Francis Duncan, eds. *Witness to Wilderness: The Clayoquot Sound Anthology*, Arsenal Pulp Press, Vancouver, 1994.

[2] Some good discussion of Muir and Pinchot are found in: i) Roderick Nash, *Wilderness and the American Mind*, Yale University Press, New Haven, 1979;

ii) Carolyn Merchant, ed., *Major Problems in American Environmental History*, D.C. Heath and Company, Lexington, Massachusetts, 1993; iii) Stewart Udall, *The Quiet Crisis*, Avon Books, New York, 1963.

[3] Thomas L. Burton, *Natural Resource Policy in Canada: Issues and Perspectives*, McClelland and Stewart, Toronto, 1977.

[4] These points are a synthesis of principles found in ecoforestry literature, see such writers as Merv Wilkinson, Orville Camp, Chris Maser, and Herb Hammond in the bibliography.

References

I. Philosophical Context

Bowers, C.A.; *Education, Cultural Myths, and the Ecological Crisis;* SUNY Press, Albany, NY; 1993.

Devall, B.; *Simple in Means, Rich in Ends: Practicing Deep Ecology;* Gibb Smith, Salt Lake City UT; 1988.

Devall, B. & Sessions, G.; *Deep Ecology: Living as If Nature Mattered*; Gibb Smith, Salt Lake City UT; 1985.

Drengson, A.; *Beyond Environmental Crisis: From Technocrat to Planetary Person*; Peter Lang, NY, 1989.

Drengson, A. & Yuichi Inoue, Editors; *The Deep Ecology Movement: An Introductory Anthology;* North Atlantic Books, Berkeley; 1995.

Fox, W.; *Toward a Transpersonal Ecology: Developing New Foundations for Environmentalism;* Shambala, Boston; 1990.

Mathews, F.; *The Ecological Self;* Barnes & Noble, Savage Md; 1991.

McLaughlin, A.; *Regarding Nature: Industrialism and Deep Ecology;* SUNY, Albany, NY; 1993.

Naess, A.; *Ecology, Community, and Lifestyle;* Cambridge University Press, London; 1991.

Snyder, G.; *The Practice of the Wild*; North Point, San Francisco; 1990.

II. The Theory and Practice of Ecoforestry

Camp, O.; *The Forest Farmer's Handbook: A Guide to Natural Selection Management*; Sky River, Ashland; 1984.

Hammond, H.; *Seeing the Forest Among the Trees: The Case for Wholistic Forest Use*; PoleStar Press, Vancouver; 1991.

Head, S. & Heinzman, R. (eds.); *Lessons of the Rainforest*; Sierra Club Books, San Francisco; 1990.

Kaza, S.; *The Attentive Heart: Conversations With Trees;* Fawcett-Columbine of Balantine Books, NY; 1993.

Maser, C.; *The Forest Primeval;* Sierra Books, San Francisco; 1990.

Maser, C. & Sedell J; *The Forest to the Sea: The Ecology of Wood in Streams, Rivers, Estuaries and Oceans;* St. Lucie Press, Delray FL; 1994.

Pilarski, M., editor; *Restoration Forestry: An International Guide to Sustainable Forestry Practices;* Kivaki Press, Durango Co.; 1994.

Robinson, G.; *The Forest and the Trees: A Guide to Excellent Forestry*; Island Press, Covelo CA; 1988.

Wilkinson, M. & Loomis R.; *Wildwood: A Forest for the Future*; Reflections, Gabriola BC; 1990.

III. Critiques of Industrial Forestry and Related Topics

Banuri, T. & Marglin F.A. (eds.); *Living With the Forests: Knowledge, Power and Environmental Destruction;* Zed Books, London; 1993.

Devall, B., (ed.); *Clearcut: The Tragedy of Industrial Forestry;* Sierra Club Books & Earth Island Press, San Francisco; 1994.

Drushka, K., Nixon, B., Travers, R., et al.; *Touch Wood: BC Forests at the Crossroads;* Harbour Books, Madeira, BC; 1993.

Ervin, K.; *Fragile Majesty: The Battle for North America's Last Great Forest*; Mountaineers, Seattle; 1989.

Maser, C.; *The Redesigned Forest*; R. & E. Miles, San Diego CA; 1988.

M'Gonigle, M. & Parfitt, B.; *Forestopia: An Urgent Guide to the Economic Transition of the BC Forest Industry*; Institute for New Economics, Vancouver, BC; forth-coming 1994.

O'Toole, R.; *Reforming the Forest Service*; Island Press, Covelo CA; 1988.

Perlin, J.; *A Forest Journey: The Role of Wood in the Development of Civilization;* Norton, NY; 1989.

Raphael, R.; *Tree Talk: The People and Politics of Timber;* Island Press, Covelo CA; 1981.

IV. The Larger Environmental and Cultural Context

Berger, J.; *Restoring the Earth;* Knopf, NY; 1985.

Berger, John (ed.); *Environmental Restoration*; Island Press, Covelo CA; 1990.

Berry, W.; *The Unsettling of America: Culture and Agriculture;* Avon, NY; 1977.

Blackburn, T. & Anderson, K.; *Before Wilderness: Environmental Management by Native Californians;* Ballena Press, Menlo Park CA; 1993.

Boone, A.; *The Language of Silence;* Harper and Row, NY; 1970.

Bowers, C.A.; *The Cultural Dimensions of Educational Computing: Understanding the Non-Neutrality of Technology*; Teachers College Press, New York; 1988.

Boyd, D.; *Rolling Thunder;* Delta, NY; 1974.

Brown, L. et al.; *State of the World 1993*; Norton, NY; 1993.

Bruntland, G.; *Our Common Future;* Oxford University Press, London and NY; 1988.

Cairns, J. (ed.); *The Recovery Process in Damaged Ecosystems;* Ann Arbor Science Publications, Ann Arbor MI; 1980.

Cajete, G.; *Look to the Mountains: An Ecology of Indigenous Education*; Kivaki Press, Durango CO; 1994.

Commoner, B.; *The Closing Circle*; Bantam Books, NY; 1972.

Carter, V. & Dale T.; *Civilization and Soil;* University of Oklahoma Press, Norman; 1974.

Daly, H. & Cobb J.; *For the Common Good: Redirecting the Economy Toward Community, the Environment and a Sustainable Future*; Beacon, Boston; 1989.

Drengson, Alan; *Doc Forest and Blue Mountain Ecostery*; Ecostery House, Victoria, BC, Canada; 1993.

Drengson, Alan; *The Practice of Technology;* SUNY Press, Albany, NY; 1995.

Duncan, D.; *The River Why?*; Bantam, NY; 1983.

Ehrlich, P. & A.; *Extinction: The Causes and Consequences of the Disappearance of Species;* Random House, NY; 1981.

Goldsmith, E.; *The Way: An Ecological Worldview*; Shambala, Boston; 1993.

Gore, A.; *Earth in the Balance: Ecology and the Human Spirit;* Houghton Mifflin, NY; 1992.

Gradwohl, J. & Greenburg, R.; *Saving the Tropical Forests;* Smithsonian Institute, Washington D.C.; 1978.

Harrison, H.P.; *Forests: Shadow of Civilization;* Univ. of Chicago Press, Chicago; 1992.

Harker, D. & K., & Evans, S. & M. (eds.); *Landscape Restoration Handbook;* Lewis Publications, Boca Ratton FL; 1992.

Harner, M.; *The Way of the Shaman;* Bantam, NY; 1986.

Henderson, H.; *Creating Alternative Futures: The End of Economics;* Harper and Row, NY; 1978.

Hughes, D.; *American Indian Ecology*; Texas Western Press, El Paso; 1983.

Hyams, E.; *Soil and Civilization*; Harper and Row, NY; 1976.

Jackson, W., Berry, W., & Colman, B.; *Meeting the Expectations of the Land: Essays in Sustainable Agriculture;* North Point, San Francisco; 1984.

Jordon, W.R., Gilpin,M.E. & Abers, J.D. (eds.); *Restoration Ecology: A Synthetic Approach to Ecological Research*; Cambridge, London & NY; 1987.

Kusler, J. & Kentula M. (eds.); *Wetlands Creation and Restoration*; Island Press, Covelo CA; 1990.

Leopold, A.; *Sand County Almanac;* Oxford, NY & London; 1949.

Macy, J.; *World as Lover, World as Self;* Parallex Press, Berkeley; 1991.

Mander, J.; *In the Absence of the Sacred: The Failure of Technology and the Survival of the Indian Nations*; Sierra Books, San Francisco; 1991.

McRobbie, G.; *Small is Possible*; Abacas, London; 1989.

Meadows, D. & R.; *The Limits to Growth;* A Club of Rome Study, Universe, NY; 1972.

Naess, A.; *Gandhi and Group Conflict: An Exploration of Satyragraha, Theoretical Background*; Universitetsforlaget, Oslo; 1974.

Norberg-Hodge, H.; *Ancient Futures: Learning from Ladakh*; Sierra Books, San Francisco; 1991.

Orr, D.; *Ecological Literacy: Education and the Transition to a Post Modern World*; SUNY Press, NY; 1992.

Pianka, E.; *Evolutionary Ecology;* Harper and Row, NY; 1978.

Ponting, C. A; *Green History of the World;* Penguin, New York and London; 1993.

Quinn, D.; Ishmael, Bantam, New York; 1993.

Savory, A.; *Holistic Resource Management;* Island Press, Covelo CA; 1988.

Scherer, D. & Attig, T.; *Ethics and the Environment*; Prentice Hall, Englewood Cliffs NJ; 1983.

Schumacher, E.F.; *Small is Beautiful: Economics as if People Mattered*; Harper and Row, NY; 1973.

Schumacher, E.G.; *Good Work*; Harper and Row, NY; 1979.

Shepard, P. & McKinley, D.; *The Subversive Science: Essays Toward an Ecology of Man*; Houghton Mifflin, NY; 1967.

Shiva, V.; *Monocultures of the Mind: Biodiversity, Biotechnology and the Third World*; Third World Network, Penang, Malaysia; 1993.

Soulé, M. & Wilcox, M., *Conservation Biology Vol 1*; Sinauer, NY; 1980.

Soulé, M.; *Conservation Biology Vol 2*; Sinauer, NY; 1986.

Smith, J.R.; *Tree Crops: A Permanent Agriculture*; Island Press, Covelo CA; 1950.

Wilson, E.O.; *The Diversity of Life*; Harvard Press, Cambridge MA; 1992.

FROM LOCKE TO GAIA

ENVIRONMENTAL ETHICS AND CANADIAN FOREST POLICY

2

by Peter Miller

War in the Woods: World Views in Conflict

"Grannies convicted in log war"

"B.C. court finds first 44

of Clayoquot 700 guilty"

- Winnipeg Free Press, October 7, 1993

FOR OVER A DECADE, CANADIAN FORESTS HAVE BEEN a war zone of contesting peoples and contested territories. Moreover, behind the conflicts on the ground, in a metaphysical dimension, lie clashing values and world views. In this chapter, I wish to characterize some philosophical aspects of the conflict and then draw upon lessons from environmental ethics to explore the prospects for peace. While the battles have made the headlines, emerging peace initiatives, including an emergent revolution in Canadian forest policy, have been much less visible to public view.

The headlined arrests at Clayoquot Sound in British Columbia signal a much broader state of forest conflict in Canada. During 1987 to 1989, "The Great Forest Sell-Off " of northern Alberta, Saskatchewan and Manitoba triggered broad protests and fierce opposition (Nikiforuk and Struzik 1989). Environmental coalitions formed rapidly to defend forests and rivers from harm by the invasion of giant pulp and paper mills with their extensive timber licenses (e.g., Repap Manitoba received harvest and management rights to 20 percent of the province).[1] First Nation protesters in Meadow Lake, Saskatchewan blockaded roads, while Lubicon Cree in Alberta employed picketing and boycott tactics to oppose the leasing of their traditional lands (SLDF 1995). Police arrested Ontario NDP leader Bob Rae defending the

Temagami old growth forest alongside protesters locked to tractors (Appleby and Mackie 1989).

Although most combatants in this "war in the woods" are committed to non-violent means, in other respects, the war analogy holds. A permanent state of hostility and distrust obtains between opposing parties and breaks out in skirmishes over territory to be won or lost. Battles are fought in the courts through injunctions and suits; in the legislature and government through lobbying and debates between politicians; in the market place through boycotts; and in the hearts of the public through public relations campaigns. Stereotypes of loggers and tree-huggers abound.

Conflict and confrontation, together with strategic planning and maneuvering to outflank the other side, make exciting drama and headline news. But what is the "shooting about"? And what are the prospects for a peace that is honorable for all? In the simplest terms, the battle lines are drawn between those who want to cut down a part of the forest and others who would "Let it Be!" Behind these simple, stark and apparently incompatible alternatives lie very different conceptions and valuations of the forest, which mark yet another set of fissures in our troubled country. Unresolved aboriginal land claims are a significant part of this struggle, but not the whole. The lines of division run through the heart of non-aboriginal society as well. In many ways, for better and for worse, how we relate to one another depends on how we relate to the land. Humanistic ethics require environmental ethics.

In order to understand the need for a new departure in ethics and forest policy, we shall first visit John Locke's legacy: a classical point of departure that has, with ruinous effect, informed much of our political and economic thought about how we ought to relate to the land and value it. Some of the Lockean deficiencies are manifest from perspectives informed by biological science. Other deficiencies we "know" as a part of our cultural identity and experience as Canadians. Together these perspectives demand new and different depictions of nature, and of our place in it, than Locke could provide. "Mother Earth" and "Gaia" are two symbolic alternatives that nicely summarize some of the features that Locke left out. But a policy cannot be based on symbols alone. Environmental philosophy helps to spell out the alternatives, relate them to scientific and psycho-social perspectives, and formulate emergent ethical concerns and norms. Recent initiatives in Canadian forest policy and practice express intentions to manage activities on the forest landscape in terms of these new understandings.

Locke's Legacy and the Valuation of Forests

In ideological terms, the war in the woods might be described as a battle of world views that value our forests in profoundly different ways. One, which I call Locke's Legacy after the 17th century philosopher John Locke, is a purely industrial world view which sees the forest primarily as a material resource that has little or no value unless exploited.[2] An alternative view, popular among environmentalists and traditional aboriginal communities (but considered suspect by some feminists), sees the forest, and nature as a whole, as an intrinsically valuable nurturing object of love - Mother Earth or Mother Nature.

We begin with Locke, who wrote:

> Land that is left wholly to Nature, that hath no improvement of Pasturage, Tillage, or Planting, is called, as indeed it is, **waste**, and we shall find the benefit of it amount to little more than nothing.

Furthermore Locke calculated that improved land derives 99 to 99.9 percent of its value from the labour of cultivation rather than from the land resource itself (Locke 1947).

Under these assumptions, to leave land unexploited when someone is willing to mix with it labour and capital to provide jobs that produce useful and saleable products is a wasteful, and perhaps immoral, extravagance. The products of the land only *become* valuable once we mine it, harvest it or farm it. Hence, governments have presumed that they have a strong mandate to lure new investors to unexploited forest lands, as the provinces of Alberta, Saskatchewan and Manitoba have done in recent years.[3]

It is important, I think, to see how wrong Locke is; because so many of the traditional socio-economic assumptions that have guided the Industrial Revolution to the present, and continue to influence our resource ministries and forest industry, are derived from his outlook. Even if we restrict our attention to the utilitarian values Locke apparently had in mind, his proportions are quite preposterous and value-blind.

The fact that people are willing to pay for timber and mineral rights and undeveloped land indicates that even in an economic sense the land has some value prior to the mixing of labour with it. But market prices for land and resource use are poor indicators of the absolute value of the materials nature provides for us. On Crown lands, government policies to subsidize forest industries may depress resource prices, while in free markets, a plentiful current supply to market has the same depressing effect even for finite non-renewable resources (as is evident in price wars for fossil fuels).[4] Our present market system fails to assign full value to our endowments of natural capital, such as the limited supply of concentrated and accessible deposits of oil in the ground or long-evolved diverse and complex forest ecosystems, and to reflect the true economic costs of their depletion or destruction.

But some of the most valuable goods we have are not produced by human toil nor found in any market. Indeed, the most plentiful resource of all that we draw on continuously with least admixture of our own labour is also the most vital to our survival, the free air we breathe. Is it accurate to say that the more bountiful nature is to us the less valuable her gifts? That is poor thanks. It is also poor theory, since it confuses value in the form the price of an incremental unit of a resource that is widely, easily and freely available in the short term (e.g., the money you would be willing to pay for a jug of air) with the absolute value of unpolluted healthy natural systems that continue to maintain and generate a plentiful supply of fresh air and many other resources. But that is one way we have traditionally undervalued the "free" goods of the commons.

Suppose, generalizing from Locke, we were to take as our measure of value the extent of the production processes that yield the goods that sustain us. A lot of work goes into the production of the bread that feeds us, for example. The farmer, miller, baker, and shopkeeper all do their part. But consider what else was required: the complex chemical processes within the wheat plant that utilize solar energy to convert elements from soil and air into foodstuffs; the workings of weather, worms, plants and microorganisms needed to produce the soil in which the grain grows; the ancient plant life and subsequent geological processes that formed the fossil fuels that propel the farmer's tractor; the evolutionary course of life that produced the complex machinery of the wheat plant and indeed of the human labourers themselves producing grain and bread.

Locke's ninety-nine-to-one ratio could well be reversed. The labours of farmer, miller and baker, great as they are, are but a tiny fraction of the processes that created the bread. The natural resources we work with, including our own selves, are themselves products of complex processes from all time, most of which we have little hope of duplicating. Moreover, most of these processes are, as far as we know, confined to the one small planet in the universe known to have permitted the evolution of life: planet Earth, a.k.a. Gaia.[5]

I have argued at some length that, even within his limited framework of anthropocentric, utilitarian commodity production, Locke grossly undervalued the contributions of natural resources and processes. Also ignored were life-support values apart from commodity production; non-an-

---

Table 1
Locke's Mistakes

ℛ The value of nature lies exclusively in its utility to humans (thus ignoring values inherent in natural entities themselves).

ℛ The utility of nature to humans lies exclusively in its function as a material resource (thus ignoring nature's "psycho-spiritual" utilities engaging thought and feeling).

ℛ Nature has utility only when transformed through human production processes (thus ignoring nature's ability to create finished goods with little or no effort on our part, e.g., oxygenated air, clean water, natural edibles, and solar warmth).

ℛ The utility of nature as a material resource approaches zero apart from human production processes (thus ignoring or devaluing nature's own extensive, complex production processes which (a) include human productivity as part of themselves and (b) make all human production to be essentially a co-production with other natural processes using complex natural ingredients such as fibre, wood, soil, seed germ, and myriad physical, chemical, and biological processes).

---

thropocentric values inherent in other living things; and the intellectual, aesthetic, moral and spiritual contributions of nature to human well-being over and above bare subsistence. These tremendous gaps in Locke's valuation of nature are summarized in Table 1 and elaborated in the remainder of this chapter.

The moral consequences of such value-blindness can be catastrophic, because anyone believing Locke's assessment would think that if the land and natural systems on it are virtually worthless, there is nothing there to harm. Even the most conscientious and upright person intent upon avoiding every harm could do terrible things out of such value-blindness, and that, I think, is an important part of the story of our environmental crisis. It is not just the work of moral monsters. Moreover, I believe these criticisms of Locke apply equally to Marxist versions of the labour theory of value and to various other attempts to root all value in market preferences, humanly assembled capital, intellect, labour, and the like. It is a wholesale western bias that transcends parochial sub-divisions such as, for example, the differences between communism and capitalism.

An alternative to the purely industrial resource view of our forests is the injunction to love and respect our Mother Earth. A variant of the view has recently been given a scientific cachet by James Lovelock, who called it the Gaia hypothesis - viewing earth as a single, multiple-organed living entity, in which forests, rivers, oceans, estuaries, ice-caps and atmosphere have their distinctive roles in maintaining the whole evolving, self-creating system of living nature (Lovelock 1987). "Mother Nature" or "Mother Earth" bore us (i.e., provided the conditions for the emergence of human life). She nurtures us physically in some ways that are virtually effortless on our part (e.g., providing the air we breathe) and others that require extensive work on our part to utilize (e.g., providing trees that we turn into paper and houses). But she also nurtures us intellectually, aestheti-

cally and spiritually as we experience her intricacies and beauty and explore her riches through science, art and worshipful contemplation. As well, Mother Nature provides us with kin or siblings in the form of myriad fellow creatures who have emerged from the same evolutionary womb as ourselves.

Ecofeminists are divided on the appropriateness of the Mother Earth symbolism. Under patriarchal society, both nature and women have been devalued. One feminist response is to reject the linkage between the two as a limitation on women. Another response is to welcome the ascendency of matriarchal symbols displacing oppressive patriarchal ones. I side with the latter because of the power, history and currency of Mother Earth symbolism in both aboriginal and non-aboriginal cultures. The Mother Earth symbol permits explicit exposition in terms of human origins and nurturance, the kinship between living things, an appreciative love of nature, and the systemic character of the biosphere noted by James Lovelock in his Gaia hypothesis. Of course the symbolism is not to be taken literally and no symbol works without numerous qualifications. The reader may reflect on whether "Parent Earth" might not be a better symbolic substitute, as proposed once to me by Karen Warren.

Note that the Mother Nature view does not prohibit all resource extraction, but it does prescribe that as we suck at her breast, we not devour or destroy our Mother and her health, beauty and many reproductive and nurturant functions. In direct contrast to the Lockean type of industrial resource view, subscribers to the Mother Earth outlook agree that we don't have to transform forests into paper or lumber through industrial processes before they begin to have value. Because industrial processes often threaten these original values of natural forests, protection and preservation are frequently the order of the day. But a prescription to preserve some forest lands and leave them unexploited, to "let it be!", grates against the value system of the Lockean industrial economic tradition, which is still active in many ways in our practices, institutions and thought. That is what the shooting is about in this war in the woods. MacMillan Bloedel was issued a license to log two-thirds of the centuries-and millennia-old trees of Clayoquot Sound in the next eighty years. Hundreds of protestors blocked those efforts, with 700 of them arrested, to prevent that from happening.

Forests and Canadian Identity

Relations to our forests divide Canadians, as was dramatically evident at Clayoquot Sound, but even more fundamentally our forests unite us because of the dominant place they have in our landscape, our psyche and our economy. Forests are perhaps the most significant shared geographical feature of our identity as Canadians; they cover almost half of the Canadian landscape and stretch from sea to sea. Moreover, in Canada, 94 percent of our forests are on publicly owned Crown land. The forests we hold in common, our natural heritage, are both a prime industrial resource and places for adventure, exploration, delight, wonder and love. A successful Canadian forest policy must respond to this full spectrum of significance.

Canada's forests are "green gold" (Marchak 1983). Forest products are the commodities that provide the country's greatest export earnings, producing billions of dollars in foreign exchange and supporting communities and economies across the nation. In 1993, forest product exports earned $26.7 billion to create a favourable balance of trade of $22.3 billion. Almost as much again was earned from sales within Canada. One in every fifteen jobs in Canada in 1994 was due to direct and indirect forest sector employment (CFS 1995). But the forest industry has also historically achieved the reputation (partly exaggerated, partly deserved) of being an environmental disaster as well - polluting waterways, contributing massively to the garbage glut through its throw-away paper products, and destroying natural ecosystems and old growth forests (Maser 1988, Hammond 1991, Sinclair 1988). Both the economic and environmental stakes are high and, on the face of it, in sharp opposition.

Besides their importance as a source of fibre and timber, our forests provide numerous ecological services, such as soil stabilization, climate moderation, carbon storage, nutrient storage and cycling, water storage and cycling, and habitat for many living things. Forests also provide a prime space for recreation and tourism, aesthetic inspiration and spiritual renewal, and they are viewed with respect and reverence by many Canadians, both aboriginal and others. Favourite artists and photographers interpret Canadian landscapes and wildlife.

The importance of the non-timber values of forests is well-documented. F.L. Filion, et al (1993) report:

In 1991, 18.9 million Canadians (90.2 percent of the population) took part in one or more wildlife-related activities, devoting a total of 1.3 billion days and $5.6 billion to these activities.

Monte Hummel (1989) informs us that:

. . . in a 1987 national Gallup poll, over 95 percent of Canadians voiced their approval of government spending to preserve our wilderness areas. This high level of support extended across all regions of Canada, and among all socio-economic groups. * * * These kind of data are further buttressed by powerful Canadian opinion in favour of protecting the environment in general. For example, 93 percent of us say we shouldn't relax environmental laws to achieve economic growth; 88 percent say protecting the environment is more important than keeping prices down; 87 percent are upset about the lack of action taken to protect the environment; 84 percent participate in wildlife-

*related activities; 82 percent express
concern about saving endangered species;
70 percent say we should do more to protect
the environment even if it means jobs must be
lost in the process; and 70 percent believe
that major spending on the environment
would in fact have a positive effect on the
economy.*

Comments Hummel:

*In light of such overwhelming support, it is
downright deceitful for decision-makers to
be cautious about providing conservation
leadership, using the excuse that "public
opinion hasn't caught up yet."*

While a prolonged economic recession might affect such statistics, it is evident that our forests have a very high value not just in their potential for harvest but even left untouched, as-is. When industrial forestry operations are perceived to be destructive of the many other values forests sustain, the battles ensue.

Locke's Legacy in Forest Management

The Canadian experience encompasses forests as industrial resource and as life-sustaining, beautiful Gaia. While the Gaia hypothesis can encompass the extraction of timber as a material resource, it cannot encompass a Lockean view which reduces or subordinates all forest values to timber values that are realized only when the forest is harvested. In this section, I shall selectively emphasize the Lockean elements in recent forest resource management, while acknowledging that some very promising transformations of forest policy are underway, to be discussed later.

Although forestry in Canada is currently in transition along the path from Locke towards Gaia, examples of the Lockean mentality in resource management abound in recent literature and practice. To former Quebec Premier Robert Bourassa, undammed water running freely to the sea in northern Quebec is a waste, because the opportunity for extracting electrical energy is missed (Bourassa 1985). Manitoba's Forestry Branch defines the "wood fibre supply" as "the total volume of standing trees in Manitoba" (SDCU 1990, p. 25). That is akin to defining Manitoba's "meat supply" as "the total volume of flesh of all animal life in Manitoba" (including pets and humans). Every tree in the Province is viewed through a single lens: its theoretical potential as a source of wood fibre. This singular lens is found elsewhere in forestry policies and language. For example, Manitoba's Forestry Branch has adopted a mission statement that subordinates every other forest value for the land under its jurisdiction (which includes Manitoba's provincial parks) to the value of the fibre supply. One of the roles the Branch must fulfill is "to allow other resource opportunities within designated forestry land, so long as such opportunities complement and do not conflict with existing or future forest harvesting operations" (MNR 1994). The Forestry Branch has a new marketing wing, whose mission it is to find enterprises to harvest whatever portion of the Annual Allowable Cut is not being utilized. According to this mind-set, although other forest values are acknowledged (which is a step beyond John Locke), they are strictly secondary to the supreme value of timber extraction.

Manitoba recently completed hearings on a Forest Management Plan for Louisiana-Pacific that illustrate these points. Manitoba's Director of Forestry confirmed that his branch, which manages Manitoba's forest landscapes, markets only fibre for harvest, not wilderness experiences nor any forest goods or services other than timber. (That is the job of the Tourism, which is not a part of Natural Resources.) Moreover, the agreement signed with Louisiana Pacific (which is renewable forever!) guarantees the company 900,000 cubic metres of wood a year and permits the Province to withdraw a maximum of 0.5 percent of the area within the next ten years, despite the fact that there are unsettled aboriginal land claims and unfulfilled commitments to establishing representative protected areas large enough to sustain ecological integrity. If the company cannot meet its wood supply needs or incurs greater costs from an alternate supply or from more costly harvesting regulations, the Province must compensate the company.

Despite the fact that Manitoba's Round Table on Environment and Economy chaired by Premier Filmon issues documents promising informed public participation in decision-making as cornerstones of sustainable development, the terms of this agreement were never subject to public review. Needless to say, environmentalists and First Nations are either cynically resigned or furious at this betrayal of the principles of the Canada Forest Accord, treaty claims and the Province's own sustainable development principles. They wonder, does it take a Clayoquot Sound protest in every province to get our governments to pay heed to their commitments?!

Under such a regime, nothing counts as multiple-use forestry unless one of those uses is a wood fibre harvest, and the Forestry Branch is the guardian of this potential in a way in which they are not guardians of forest cathedrals for religious experiences or unfragmented forest tracts for caribou and neo-tropical migrant birds. Forest lands are said to be wastefully "locked up" for "single use" purposes if ever they are preserved from harvest, despite the multiple functions, values and utilities that forests sustain quite apart from their role as a fibre source. Trees beyond their preferred harvest age are called "overmature," i.e., their rates of growth have slowed and they verge on becoming wasted as a fibre resource from the ravages of disease and fire. Never mind that they host birds, nitrogen-fixing lichens and woodland caribou!

Once the central value of a forest is identified as its supply of wood fibre, there develops a powerful incentive to redesign the forest to enhance this value. Forests then become subsumed under the agricultural model, as indicated by the title of a Canadian Pulp and Paper Association booklet *Farming Canada's Forests* (CPPA 1989).

The conversion process from forest to tree farm is described by Chris Maser (1988):

As we liquidate the ancient forests, we are redesigning the forests of the future. In fact we are redesigning the entire world, and we are simultaneously throwing away nature's blueprint. Nature designed a forest as an experiment in unpredictability; we are trying to design a regulated forest. Nature designed a forest over a landscape; we are trying to design a forest on each hectare. Nature designed a forest with diversity; we are trying to design a forest with simplistic uniformity. Nature designed a forest of interrelated processes; we are trying to design a forest based on isolated products. Nature designed a forest in which all elements are neutral; we are trying to design a forest in which we perceive some elements to be good and others bad. Nature designed a forest to be a flexible, timeless, continuum of species; we are trying to design a forest to be a rigid time-constrained monoculture. Nature designed a forest of long-term trends; we are trying to design a forest of short-term absolutes. Nature designed a forest to be self-sustaining and self-repairing; we are designing a forest to require increasing external subsidies - fertilizers, herbicides and pesticides.

Note that in Canada, at least in the West, we are, for the most part, still planting and tending our first "crop" of trees. The ones we cut are still in original natural forests, but in ever more remote locations. This has two consequences: (1) the replacement process described by Maser is spreading ever farther afield into the interior of B.C. and the more northerly boreal forests of the so-called "prairie" provinces with an ever-extending network of roads and a consequent steady loss of forest wilderness; (2) a process of "highgrading" at the landscape level is occurring, whereby the stands that are most valuable because of their accessibility, the quality of their fibre, and the volume of wood per hectare are harvested first leaving the commercially less valuable natural stands for the future (Hammond 1991). In Canadian forestry we are still engaged in a mining operation, but with agricultural aspirations. At least in the coastal areas of B.C., there is no hope or intention of ever again replacing the volumes and quality of wood of the original ancient forests that have been harvested, much less their climax ecosystems. I know of no forest management plan that intends to institute a 1000-year rotation, or even one of centuries.

Once we have cut as much of the ancient forests of B.C. as we are willing to cut, a massive "falldown" in quality and quantity of harvestable timber resource will occur. The consequences of our biologically unsustainable cutting rates are soil degradation, loss of biodiversity, macro and micro climate change, poor regeneration and the like. We shall be left with much impoverished and diminished younger plantations that cannot yield the same high grade products as the original forests could. For example, according to an analysis by Forintek, second growth Douglas Fir has problems with structural strength, warping and workability. In order to be able to mill high grade lumber from it, the trees require pruning during growth and an extension of rotation age from sixty to ninety years. Because such cultivation requirements appear to be uneconomic, the industry's future is projected to lie increasingly in the production of chips that can be pressed into boards and structural materials and pulped for paper (Hammond 1991, Kellog 1989).

The picture that I have tried to paint so far is of a forest industry built on the Lockean assumption that until it is able to mix capital and labour with nature's resources, those resources have little or no value and what value they might have should be subordinated in such a way as to provide little hindrance to the extraction of the resource. To be sure, there is a version of an ethic of stewardship built into forestry practices insofar as they uphold the principle of sustained yield forestry (i.e., not cutting in a year more than the annual replacement growth), but we have seen that in coastal B.C., at least, with the expectation of a "falldown", that is not interpreted to mean that the current quantity and quality of timber cut can be sustained in perpetuity. Trees having centuries of growth will be replaced by plantations in which only sixty to eighty years of growth will be the norm. The first cut is recognized to be the richest one.[6]

In other locations, however, where less massive and ancient trees are being cut, there is held out the hope that "intensive forest management" may in fact yield greater volumes of marketable fibre per hectare than nature produces. The previous quotation from Maser indicates some of the objectives of intensive forest management. These are achieved by such practices as eliminating competition from non-commercial species by applying chemical herbicides or other means; thinning trees to optimize their growth; protecting plantations from insects and fire; planting preferred commercial species in place of those that might naturally regenerate; and planting genetically "superior" stock or "plus" trees. The crucial questions raised by such practices are: 1) Can they in fact increase yields of quality wood or fibre in the long run?, and 2)With what other forest values are they compatible and which values are being sacrificed?

No wonder that the forest products industries and government regulators have found themselves so frequently in conflict with many citizens who love their forests and with aboriginal bands on whose ancestral lands they operate. Even if foresters as individuals may share the more multifaceted vision and diverse values symbolized by Gaia (and many of my acquaintance do), their organizational and economic mandates, and the very language they use to characterize the forest inventory, display the heavy hand of Locke. The industry has been permitted by its regulators to operate on a massive scale using methods that bring tremendous short-term and often long-term changes to our forests. They continue to penetrate with roads and encroach upon and diminish remaining wilderness areas including irreplaceable ancient forests. And they have regularly subscribed to the Lockean bias of subordinating all other forest values to the extraction of timber and fibre for industry.

New Directions from Environmental Ethics

In the last section I claimed that, although current forest policy is undergoing a transformation from Locke towards Gaia, examples of the Lockean bias abound even now. Philosophy can play an important role in this social transformation by a) criticizing inadequate theoretical views, b) constructing and interpreting alternative visions, c) analysing the implications of critically examined theories for policy, and d) encouraging a constructive dialogue amongst participants with diverse views. In this section I shall summarize theoretical alternatives that have emerged in the young field of Environmental Ethics as a background for describing new departures in forest policy in the next section.

What are the implications for ethics of the displacement of Locke's legacy by revised understandings of the natural world and our place in it? I shall answer by means of a quite simple - perhaps simplistic sketch of environmental ethics.

The most inclusive ethical principle that I can think of is, as St. Thomas Aquinas noted, to do good and avoid evil (Aquinas 1944, I-II, Q. 8). Ethics, as I understand it, has the job of reflecting on human practice - on the many activities we engage in individually and collectively. It does so in order to identify some of the most egregious harms we are prone to commit and the most basic goods we should strive to protect or realize, so

that we may better fulfill the broad mandate to do good and avoid evil. Environmental ethics, in turn, specializes the broad mandate of ethics by trying to identify harms and benefits rooted in features of our natural environment. Such features may be identified and evaluated within a variety of frameworks distinguished by the kinds of values of concern and whether the benefits and harms are thought to belong exclusively to humans or not. I shall single out four such frameworks: an *informed* environmental humanism, an *enriched* environmental humanism, organismic biocentrism, and ecocentrism.

I call an ethical view humanistic if the goods and evils that it prescribes for us to do or avoid happen only to human beings. In contrast, biocentric and ecocentric views count goods and evils occurring to other forms of life than the human and to ecosystems as ethically important too. These views are summarized in Table 2. It is interesting to note that a cornerstone for the new forest policy, the *Canada Forest Accord,* adopted in March, 1992 by Canada's forest ministers, industry leaders and others, takes an ecocentric and biocentric stance when it declares that "our goal is to maintain and enhance the long-term health of our forest ecosystems, for the benefit of all living things both nationally and globally..." (CCFM 1992a).

The further contrast between informed and enriched environmental humanism I draw as follows. *Informed* humanism, as such, need make no new departures in identifying what is intrinsically good and evil in human affairs. Generally speaking, life, health, the development of our faculties, fulfilling and just human relationships, happiness and other positive values are good; death, sickness, incapacitation, social isolation and destructive or unjust relationships, suffering and despair are bad. Doing good means we should try to promote these human goods and to avoid, mitigate or alleviate the evils.

Within the framework of informed humanism, as we become more knowledgeable about the causal processes in nature, we learn of new pathways by which human activities cause harm to other humans. Lead in our gasoline incapacitates by causing neurological damage; carcinogens kill. Thus on traditional humanistic ethical grounds, taking into account new scientific information, the activities which generate these environmentally mediated harms should be proscribed, other things being equal. We should also protect the fundamental "ecological services", such as soil stabilization, climate moderation, carbon storage, nutrient storage and cycling, water storage and cycling, the preservation of genetic resources, and, in general, the multiplicity of life-support functions that nature provides in order to sustain human life, health and material well-being.

Enriched humanism goes beyond informed humanism in recognizing new ranges of value, of goods that might be enjoyed or destroyed by humans. For example, the *Canada Forest Accord* includes the recognition that "our forest heritage is part of our past, our present and our future identity as a nation," and that "the spiritual qualities and the inherent beauty of our forests are essential to our physical and our mental well-being." These summary claims can be elaborated in a multitude of ways as the religious, cultural, emotional, aesthetic, recreational, educational, and scientific dimensions of our interactions with the natural world in general, and forests in particular, are explored. We need to take account of a vast range of "psycho-socio-spiritual utilities"[7] that forests provide in addition to the

---

Table 2
Developments in Environmental Ethics

1. Informed humanistic ethics - Traditional assumptions about ethics for the sake of humans are retained, but new behavior is prescribed because of a shift in knowledge or circumstances. "Thou shalt not kill" implies "Thou shalt control toxic emissions."

2. Enriched humanistic ethics - Humans are still the beneficiaries, but new environmental values are recognized. For example, the Canada Forest Accord recognizes that "the spiritual qualities and the inherent beauty of our forests are essential to our physical and our mental well-being." Enlightened humanism is both informed and enriched.

3. Animal liberation or "faunaism" - The range of potential beneficiaries is extended to include sentient animals, particularly the more complex and intelligent, i.e. those that are more like us. The relevant moral values are traditional ones - like avoidance of suffering and loss of freedom - but now applied to non-human animals.

4. Organismic biocentrism - Potential beneficiaries are further extended into the plant world. Because plants are not conscious, other values than sufferings and pleasures must be used to characterize the benefits and harms to which plants are prone, such as health, sickness, injury and flourishing.

5. Ecocentrism - This position recognizes ecosystems and the biosphere, i.e. the "land", as the ultimate beneficiaries towards which we should be responsible. The Canada Forest Accord combines biocentric and ecocentric stances when it declares that "our goal is to maintain and enhance the long-term health of our forest ecosystems, for the benefit of all living things both nationally and globally...."

---

fundamental "environmental services" of sustaining the biophysical conditions of life, such as moderating climate, water cycling, nutrient cycling, atmospheric composition, wildlife habitat, and further evolutionary development of species.

Finally, let us call a humanism that is at once informed and enriched an *enlightened* humanism.

Nor can one ignore the interplay of newly appreciated environmental values and the issues of aboriginal well-being, culture, sovereignty and land claims. The implications for the aboriginal inhabitants of Canada of each of the new value frameworks that I have identified are still being drawn.

Thus the new directions from environmental philosophy consist of drawing the ethical implications of our more recently informed, enriched and less humanly arrogant understandings of our place in the natural world. Both western science and a revision of our values in the direction of aboriginal outlooks have combined to elicit a new respect for the workings of nature. To read certain passages in the *Canada Forest Accord* one might think that we had all become "deep ecologists" who personally identify with and respect the intrinsic values of the natural world.[8] I believe that at some level this may be true; there is indeed a new sensibility abroad in the land. But clearly it is still locked in combat with much more destructive and exploitative outlooks that are rooted deeply in our consciousness, our lifestyles, our economy, our government regulatory regimes and our forest industries. Only quite recently has a new synthesis begun to emerge.

From Ethics to Policy
The Canada Forest Accord

The ethical injunction to do good and avoid evil requires for its observance a recognition of values, i.e. the various kinds of goods and evils that one is to pursue or avoid. Several value perspectives pertinent to our relations with nature are summarized in Table 2 above. Most of these can be found in two companion documents: the Canada Forest Accord and Sustainable Forests: A Canadian Commitment, which were adopted in March 1992 by all of Canada's forest ministers, forest industry representatives and a variety of other stakeholder groups (CCFM 1992a,b).

The *Canada Forest Accord* is a declaration that affirms the importance of forests for Canada's national identity, for wildlife, for their spiritual qualities and inherent beauty, for the health of all life on earth and for socio-economic benefits, particularly benefits to forest-dependent communities. The *Accord* also pledges its subscribers to intelligent and sensitive stewardship and declares the entitlement of Canadians to a say in forest management. The summary goal of the *Accord* "is to maintain and enhance the long-term health of our forest ecosystems for the benefit of all living things both nationally and globally, while providing environmental, economic, social and cultural opportunities for the benefit of present and future generations" (CCFM 1992a).

This *Accord* is obviously written against the backdrop of forest discord with which we began. One article of the Accord's vision for the future proclaims:

> *There will be clear and harmonious relationships for all those involved with forests . . . bringing about agreement on approaches to forest management through consultation, mutual respect and the sharing of information (CCFM 1992a).*

The *Canada Forest Accord* expresses agreement on, and commitment to, a broad vision. A companion document, *Sustainable Forests: A Canadian Commitment,* articulates a National Forest Strategy for realizing that commitment (CCFM 1992b). The Strategy comprises nine strategic directions containing ninety-six specific commitments (with deadlines) to be accomplished by governments, industry and segments of the public. Moreover, performance in the fulfillment of these commitments is to be assessed by independent audits, the first of which was completed in September 1994 (Baskerville, et al 1994).

The ninety-six commitments encompass forest stewardship measures that respect forest ecosystems and biodiversity and undertake initiatives to improve forest management, to expand public participation in management, to develop diversified economic opportunities consonant with forest protection, to coordinate and intensify forest research, to educate and train forest workers, to foster enlightened private woodlot management, to pursue special opportunities for aboriginals in forestry, and to develop a prominent role for Canada in global forest initiatives. On the latter point, Canada has taken leadership positions in promoting the forest-related international Conventions on Biodiversity and Climate Change adopted at the Earth Summit held in Rio de Janeiro in June, 1992. As well, it has promoted more recent negotiations to establish international conventions on principles, criteria and indicators of sustainable forestry (UNEP 1992, BSAT 1994, BWG 1995, CCFM 1995).

Model Forests

Among the many commitments of the new National Forest Strategy was the development of a network of Model Forests - ten in Canada and a growing number in other countries, such as Russia, Mexico, Malaysia and the United States. This inspired creation of Canada's (now defunct) "Green Plan" committed federal funds as a lure and a resource for the formation of a number of partnerships of diverse stakeholders, who were to establish "working models of sustainable forestry in each of the major forest regions of Canada" (Forestry Canada, 1991).

There were a number of shared expectations for all the Model Forests in the program:

- Each Model Forest had to be managed for a multiplicity of diverse forest values and interests.

- Each had to be a "working forest" that included industrial harvests, but other interests and values also had to be included, and portions of the forest might consist of protected, unharvested areas.

- Direction for each Model Forest was to lie with a Partnership Committee or Board of stakeholders including industry, governments, environmental organizations, aboriginal peoples, universities, etc.

- Together the Model Forests would form a network for the exchange of ideas, research and experience and to link with a growing number of international Model Forest partners.

The goal of the Model Forest Network was to accelerate the implementation of sustainable development through integrated management for diverse values supported by:

- new approaches and concepts,

- research and technological innovation,

- developing forest information systems and databases,

- testing and demonstrating best forestry practices, and,

- training, education, communications and technical transfer.

Each Model Forest had to create its own vision, goals and workplan within this broad framework. For example, Manitoba Model Forest pledged to create "an operationally-viable, ecologically-sustainable model of forest management and use" achieved by creating "a harmonious partnership" which rests on four basic principles: (1) respect and care for the community of life, (2) respect for human diversity, (3) open and respectful problem-solving, and (4) working creatively with nature for human and environmental benefits (MAMFPP 1992).

Model Forests are as much a social experiment as they are spurs to forest research, technology and improved practices, due to the fact that they are governed by partnerships of diverse stakeholders, who frequently have been at odds. Moreover, they introduce a new scale and type of organization, since they operate at a regional level that encompasses different communities, institutions and individuals having quite diverse backgrounds and interests in the forest. In other words, the "top-down" federal initiative of providing broad criteria, funding and network support was designed to encourage in response a series of "bottom-up" local initiatives to build organizations, each of which would be a diverse partnership united by two things: (1)various interests in a shared forest land-base, and (2) a commitment to principles of sustainable development (Miller 1995b).

A Wildlife Policy for Canada

Finally I would like to cite a remarkable document, *A Wildlife Policy for Canada*, signed in September 1990 by Canada's ministers responsible for wildlife (WMCC 1990). Many of the same ministers later signed the *Canada Forest Accord*. Foreshadowing the *Accord*, the Wildlife Policy's goal "is to maintain and enhance the health and diversity of Canada's wildlife, for its own sake and for the benefit of present and future generations of Canadians."

A fundamental novelty of the policy is the broadening of the definition of wildlife to include:

all wild organisms and their habitats - including wild plants, invertebrates, and microorganisms, as well as fishes, amphibians, reptiles, and the birds and mammals traditionally regarded as wildlife.

Thus our forests are not only habitats for wildlife but themselves wildlife and subject to this policy in their own right.

The policy establishes at least one clear principle of priority that reflects an ecocentric ethic: "The maintenance of viable natural populations of wildlife always takes precedence over their use by people." Moreover, it supports and elaborates the objectives of what is popularly known as the "Endangered Spaces" campaign for ecosystem preservation:

Governments will complete and maintain comprehensive systems of protected areas, through legislation and/or policy, that include representative ecological types and give priority to the protection of endangered or limited habitats. To allow species to change their local and regional distributions in response to climate change and other factors, the protected area systems must be designed to:

- Protect the diversity of Canada's physical environments

- Contain a range of environments within each protected area

- Link protected areas by corridors of suitable habitat

Remember that the wildlife here discussed are natural indigenous organisms of every kind. What emerges as an ideal is a reverse image of the policies of the past, which countenanced a few islands of protection in a sea of development. Instead it envisages pockets of development surrounded and buffered by a connected network of wild lands, a Swiss cheese landscape.

So many of the statements of principle in recent federal policy sound very attractive and responsive to the strengthening recognition of environmental values. But there are other agendas afoot as well in some tension with these. *Sustainable Forests: A Canadian Commitment* also includes the objective "to improve the quantity, quality and continuity of supply of forest resources" and intensive silvicultural practices are a part of that program (CCFM 1992b).

The natural Swiss cheese vision of the Canadian national wildlife policy, it is fair to say, is partially countered by another interpretation by the forest industry of how to protect ecological integrity, sustainability and biodiversity (Booth 1993). Industry is prepared to manage forests for diverse values on an integrated basis by treading more lightly in their forest operations and thus reducing the need for extensive protected areas to maintain integrity and biodiversity. Whether this can be done or not is a matter for research, but that research itself will require more natural and humanly undisturbed areas as a baseline for comparison. Thus on either scenario, there is a case to be made both for protected areas and for softened impacts from forest operations. Although some research has been done in support of the agenda of identifying representative natural areas for protection, the lion's share has gone to the development of knowledge and tools to protect biodiversity and ecological integrity on harvested landscapes.

Reflections on Ethics: Practice and Theory

These are exciting times for Canadian forest policy as we attempt to integrate social and environmental idealism, economics, ecological science and the practical concerns of forest management and operations. There is plenty of work for all citizens who have a stake in the forests, including applied philosophers willing to get their hands dirty in real world issues requiring, in cooperation with others, programs and actions having uncertain outcomes. As suggested earlier, philosophers can play an important Socratic role by facilitating a better quality of dialogue than is usually found in the polarized "war in the woods," beginning with simple human decency and respect. Some of my logging friends say, "Hey, we're environmentalists too," even as they must respond to the economic imperative of securing an affordable fibre supply. And those of us outside the forest industries must recognize our own dependence on their products and economic returns. Reflections like these can temper a "holier-than-thou" attitude and incline us to pitch in to help in the greening of government and industry and ourselves. But such participation is no substitute for the critical and evaluative functions of ethical reflection.

Philosophers have a professional role to play

in the recognition, articulation, criticism, synthesis and justification of significant values that give direction and importance to our policies and practices. Having done so, they can engage in advocacy and critique in various forums to identify where forest policy and practice diverge from espoused or well-founded principles and expose inadequate or obstructive administrative, planning and assessment processes. There is a big gap between the idealistic declarations to which governments subscribe and their ability or willingness to act, which is a source of a good deal of cynicism about government intentions. As described earlier, major decisions that are binding in perpetuity are still being made on the basis of the old Lockean principles and without consulting Canadian citizens. Deals are done as though the *Canada Forest Accord* had never been signed, and we have an obligation to point that out and protest.

However, to the extent that forest policy and planning processes open up and the shared values of the Accord are acknowledged (as is the intent, for example, of the Model Forest program), a different role becomes possible for the practical philosopher. When espoused environmental and social ideals are given real power and authority through conscientious public participation in planning, we can work alongside officials and fellow-citizens more as problem-solvers than as critics. We can help to draw the implications of shared principles in relation to local circumstances, accumulating knowledge and recognized concerns and constraints, and design new ways of operating on the land. We have a lot to learn in such multi-disciplinary settings in which diverse perspectives and interests criss-cross. But as Socratic figures with some facility in the realm of concepts and productive dialogue, we also have a lot to offer in this voyage of co-discovery of how best to realize our ideals in practice under real-world constraints.

Immersion in such practical concerns can in turn breathe new life into a broad array of the most fundamental theoretical issues that philosophers face. What are values and how can they be identified, understood, legitimated and criticized? What kinds of entities, if any, have intrinsic value? How shall we characterize such ecosystemic norms as integrity, health and richness? What are the relations between biological and value categories? What are the scope and kinds of human responsibilities? What are the implications of our place in nature for human society and human selfhood, caring and responsibility? What are the wellsprings of motivation and the grounds of justification to which one can appeal in making moral claims? What are the criteria for recognizing more and less adequate scientific claims? How can priorities be established and decisions made in cases of conflict?

The issues of environmental philosophy have invited investigations into historical, religious, and cultural perspectives and comparisons; the foundations of society, law, economics and politics; the philosophy of nature and science; systems theory and ethical theory; and conceptions of the self, gender, power and relationships.

In short, applied environmental ethics is one path to responsible citizenship and to the renewal of philosophy.

ENDNOTES

[1] The Repap development in Manitoba marked my own baptism as a philosopher-activist with the rapid invention of an environmental coalition T.R.E.E. (Time to Respect Earth's Ecosystems) to promote environmental advocacy and dialogue on forests issues.

[2] The discussion of Locke's Legacy is adapted from Miller 1995a.

[3] Dr. Kenneth O. Higginbotham, former Assistant Deputy Minister of Alberta Land and Forest Services, reports the response in Alberta to these new timber allocations: *"What surprised government, and many other observers, was that this expansion of industrial activity into provincial Crown land was not welcomed universally. Significant public concern was raised about clean air and clean water. Concern was also raised about the fact that the land-use planning process had not been applied to much of the forested area of the province. In addition the public was concerned that*

fish, wildlife, and other forest values were not considered in forestry management" (Stelfox 1995, Preface).

[4] In Canada, low government stumpage fees on timber have prompted a series of countervail measures by the U.S. government, "alleging that provincial stumpage and log-export policies provided a subsidy to Canadian producers" CFS (1994, p. 14).

[5] Given a long and complex network of production processes, one can ask, where does the value begin and how far does it extend? The chain of value can be either lengthened (as I have proposed) or shortened. Could one not argue that the farmer's efforts are worthless, because we don't eat unhusked grain, and so are the miller's, because we don't eat raw flour? Perhaps only the baker or cook is able to turn material waste into a beneficial commodity ready for consumption. On the other hand, even the loaf of bread on the table falls short of value, since if we did not engage in the labour of chewing and swallowing, we would starve to death; the bread might as well still be the part of the untilled wasteland. Then again, chewing and swallowing contribute nothing to our subsistence unless our gastric and intestinal processes are functioning, so it seems that the value-creating activity lies deep in our bowels. On the other hand, if it is sheer productivity in general (of which human labour is a special case) which is the criterion of value, then value begins and extends throughout the system, even to uninhabited stars and planets, wherever the universe generates anything.

Another thought experiment, proposed by Robert Nozick (1974), sources value not in subsistence needs but in appropriating activities which mix human labour with natural resources. The tilling of the land has the double function of endowing the land with value and making it owned by the farmer. Since the farmer owns her labour, she owns the laboured upon land. But, asks Nozick, could she own the ocean by squeezing an orange and throwing the juice into the ocean for dispersal? There was a time when the act of planting a flag was thought to create ownership of a continent, and we are still living with the consequences of such acts of appropriation.

[6] Indeed the area-based Annual Allowable Cut (AAC) in B.C., which contemplates declining volumes as old growth forests are liquidated until an equilibrium is reached in volumes harvested in rotations of 100 years or less, recently survived a court challenge in "Sierra Club of Western Canada vs. Chief Forester, Appeal Board" B.C.S.C. [1993].

[7] J. Baird Callicott (1985) distinguishes "material-economic" and "psycho-spiritual" utility (p. 262).

[8] Norwegian Philosopher Arne Naess (1973) coined the phrase "Deep Ecology" in "The Shallow and the Deep, Long-Range Ecology Movements: A Summary." Shallow ecology corresponds to the position of Informed Humanistic Ethics identified in Table 2; nature is viewed as devoid

of intrinsic value and is instrumentally valued primarily as a natural resource for exclusively human ends. In a later article, Naess (1986) summarized Deep Ecology in eight points:

1. The well-being and flourishing of human and non-human life on Earth have value in themselves. These values are independent of the usefulness of the non-human world for human purposes.

2. Richness and diversity of life forms contribute to the realization of these values and are also values in themselves.

3. Humans have no right to reduce this richness and diversity except to satisfy vital needs.

4. The flourishing of human life and cultures is compatible with a substantially smaller human population. The flourishing of non-human life requires a smaller human population.

5. Present human interference with the non-human world is excessive, and the situation is rapidly worsening.

6. Policies must therefore be changed. These policies affect basic economic, technological, and ideological structures. The resulting state of affairs will be deeply different from the present.

7. The ideological change will be mainly that of appreciating life quality (dwelling in situations of inherent value) rather than adhering to an increasingly higher standard of living. There will be a profound awareness of the difference between bigness and greatness.

8. Those who subscribe to the foregoing points have an obligation directly or indirectly to try to implement the necessary changes.

References

Appleby, Timothy and Mackie, Richard; 1989; "Ontario NDP Leader Among 16 Arrested at Anti-Logging Protest"; *The Globe and Mail;* September 19: A11.

Aquinas, St. Thomas; "Summa Theologica"; In *The Basic Writings of Saint Thomas Aquinas*; Ed. A. C. Pegis. Random House, New York, N.Y.; 1944

Baskerville, G., et al; *National Forest Strategy - Sustainable Forests: A Canadian Commitment - Mid-Term Evaluation Report. National Forest Strategy Coalition*; Hull, Québec; 1994.

Booth, D., et al; . "Natural Forest Landscape Management in Canada: Setting a Global Standard for Implementing Sustainable Development"; *Forestry Chronicle*; 1993; 69: pp.141-145.

Bourassa, R.; *Power from the North*; Prentice-Hall Canada, Scarborough, Ontario; 1985.

(BSAT) Biodiversity Science Assessment Team; *Biodiversity in Canada: A Science Assessment for Environment Canada*; Environment Canada, Ottawa; 1994.

(BWG) Biodiversity Working Group; *Canadian Biodiversity Strategy: Canada's Response to the Convention on Biological Diversity*; Biodiversity Convention Office, Environment Canada, Hull, Québec; 1995

Callicott, J.B.; . "Intrinsic Value, Quantum Theory, and Environmental Ethics"; In *Environmental Ethics*; 7(3): pp. 257-270; 1985

(CCFM) Canadian Council of Forest Ministers; *Canada Forest Accord;* Hull, Québec; 1992a.

(CCFM) Canadian Council of Forest Ministers; *Sustainable Forests: A Canadian Commitment*; Hull, Québec; 1992b.

(CCFM) Canadian Council of Forest Ministers; *Defining Sustainable Forest Management: A Canadian Approach to Criteria and Indicators*; Natural Resources Canada, Hull, Québec;1995

(CFS) Canadian Forest Service; *The State of Canada's Forests 1993*; Natural Resources Canada, Hull, Québec; 1994.

(CFS) Canadian Forest Service; *The State of Canada's Forests 1994;* Natural Resources Canada, Hull, Québec;1995.

(CPPA) Canadian Pulp and Paper Association; 1989; *Farming Canada's Forests: Forest Management and Silvaculture*; Montreal.

Filion, F.L., et al; *The Importance of Wildlife to Canadians: Highlights of the 1991 Survey*; Canadian Wildlife Service, Environment Canada, Ottawa, Ontario; 1993.

Forestry Canada; *Model Forests: Background Information and Guidelines for Applicants*; Hull, Québec; 1991

Hammond, H.; *Seeing the Forest Among the Trees: The Case for Wholistic Forest Use*; Polestar Press, Vancouver, B.C.; 1991.

Hargrove, E. . "Anglo-American Land Use Attitudes"; In *Ethics and the Environment;* D. Scherer and T. Attig, eds.; Prentice-Hall, Englewood Cliffs, N.J.; 1993; pp. 96-113.

Hummel, M.; "The Upshot" In, M. Hummel, ed., *Endangered Spaces: The Future for Canada's Wilderness;* Key Porter Books, Toronto, Ontario; 1989

Kellog, R.M. ed.; 1989. *Second Growth Douglas-fir: Its Management and Conversion for Value*; A report of the Douglas-fir Task Force, Forintek Canada Corp., Vancouver, B.C., Special Pub. No. SP-32. pp.173; cited in Hammond (1991).

Locke, J., 1947. "Second Treatise". In, *Two Treatises of Government,* ed. T.I. Cook; Hafner Press, New York and London, sec.42-43; cited in Hargrove 1983; p. 109.

Lovelock, J.E.; *Gaia: A New Look at Life On Earth;* Oxford University Press, Oxford and New York; 1987.

(MAMFPP) Manitou Abi Model Forest Project Partnership; *Manitou Abi Model Forest Proposal;* Pine Falls, Manitoba; 1992.

Maser, C.; *The Redesigned Forest*; E. Miles, San Pedro, CA; 1988.

Miller, P.; "Towards a Forest Policy for Canada: New Directions from Environmental Ethics"; In Philippe Crabbé, ed., *An Environmental Ethics Perspective on Canadian Policy for Sustainable Development;* Institute for Research on Environment and Economy (IREE), University of Ottawa, Ottawa, Ontario; 1995a; pp. 235-247.

Miller, P. 1995b. "Sustainable Livelihoods and the Manitoba Model Forest: A Top-Down Initiative to Foster Bottom-Up Sustainable Resource Management at the Regional Level"; In N. Singh & L. Ham, eds., *Community-Based Resources Management and Sustainable Livelihoods: The Grass-Roots of Sustainable Development*; International Institute for Sustainable Development, Winnipeg; 1995; pp. 38-60.

Miller, P.; "Integrity, Sustainability, Biodiversity and Forestry". In L. Westra and J. Lemons, eds., *Ethical and Scientific Perspectives on Integrity*; Kluwer Academic Publishers, Dordrecht, The Netherlands; 1995c.

Miller, P., 1996; "On Doing Good and Avoiding Evil in Nature: Foundational Reflections on Environmental Ethics". In Marrietta, D. & Embree,L., eds., *Environmental Ethics and Metaphysics,* (Forthcoming).

(MNR) Manitoba Natural Resources; "Mission and Roles of the Forestry Branch" ; In *The Forestry Branch Eleventh Annual Report 1993-1994*; Winnipeg, Manitoba; 1994.

Naess, Arne; *Inquiry*; 16: pp.95-100; 1973.

Naess, Arne; *Philosophical Inquiry*; VIII, No. 1-2: pp.10-31; 1986.

Nikiforuk, A. & Struzik, Ed; . "The Great Forest Sell-Off", In, *Report on Business Magazine;* November, 1989; pp.57-71.

Nozick, Robert; *Anarchy, State and Utopia;* Basic Books, New York; 1974.

(SDCU) Sustainable Development Coordination Unit; *Sustainable Development Land & Water Strategy: Workbook on Forests*; Winnipeg, Manitoba; 1990.

Sinclair, W.F.; *Controlling Pollution from Canadian Pulp and Paper Manufacturers: A Federal Perspective*; Environment Canada, Ottawa; 1988.

(SLDF) Sierra Legal Defence Fund Newsletter; "Pickets vs. Profits: Daishowa SLAPPs Friends of Lubicon"; October, 1995.

Stelfox, J.B., ed.; *Relationships Between Stand Age, Stand Structure, and Biodiversity in Aspen Mixedwood Forests in Alberta;* Jointly published by Alberta Environmental Centre (AECV95-R1, Vegreville, AB, and Canadian Forest Service (Project No. 0001A), Edmonton, AB; 1995.

(UNEP) United Nations Environment Program; *Convention on Biological Diversity*; No. 92-7807, Nairobi, Kenya; June 5,1992.

(WMCC) Wildlife Ministers' Council of Canada; *A Wildlife Policy for Canada*; Canadian Wildlife Service, Ottawa; 1990.

THE FORESTS AT BARRIÈRE LAKE

EURO-AMERICAN AND INDIGENOUS PERCEPTIONS OF THE NATURAL ENVIRONMENT

3

by Elisa Shenkier and Thomas Meredith

Introduction

ENVIRONMENTAL ETHICS, BY DEFINITION, INFLUENCE THE behaviour of humans towards the the non-human environment. Consequently, the current global environmental crisis has precipitated a critical reexamination of environmental ethics. In the discussion of solutions to the crisis, two requisites have emerged: the first is sustainability – that is, the degree to which actions do not destroy the environmental systems on which they depend. The second is equity – that is, the degree to which actions promote social relations that will be accepted by the people or groups involved. In fact, because no environmental relationship can be sustainable if it builds reactive pressure from people or groups involved, and no social relationships can be equitable if required resources are being depleted, these requisites are inextricably linked. Neither is attainable without the other, and as the World Commission on Environment and Development[1] reported, solving the global environmental problems requires addressing questions of inter-cultural inequity.

This paper examines the questions of sustainability and equity by focusing on a case study of conflict up to 1991, between two cultural groups over a single environmental resource. The cultural groups are the Algonquin of Barrière Lake, Quebec, and the Euro-American culture of the industrial south of Quebec. The resource is the forest land in the ancestral home of the Algonquin. The paper explores the significance of environmental ethics and the role of ethical analysis in achieving environmentally sustainable and socially equitable solutions to the resource conflict. It does so by examining the relationship between ethics and value and by considering the significance of differences in environmental ethics between the two cultures. Paul W. Taylor's six distinct categories of value[2] are used to explore how the Algonquin and Euro-American assessment of ecological resources differ. In his book, *Respect for Nature*, he has delineated these concepts: 1) instrumental value, 2) commercial value, 3) merit or excellence, 4) intrinsic value (also known as the immediately good), 5) the intrinsically valued, and 6) inherent worth.[3] In order to facilitate a comprehensible analysis, the value concepts are applied to the perceived value and worth of the forest resources. These may serve to clarify criteria for conflict resolution and resource management. We attempt to show that the Algonquins of Barrière Lake have a larger sense of moral community, that is a broader realm of moral consideration, than Euro-Americans. If this is true it implies that, in this case and perhaps in others, the discussions arising from resource conflict should not be sought through strictly market analysis (or worse, power politics), but rather through moral assessment.

Re-examining Environmental Ethics

The need to reassess or even restructure presently held notions about interactions with, as well as rights of and obligations to, the natural world has led to the creation of an extensive body of literature. The roots of our environmental crisis have been attributed to a variety of causes, but questions of attitude or perception have provided common ground for inquiry. The gamut of expression regarding the foundations of modern environmental attitudes ranges from the theory of human domination, to the influence of Judeo-Christian thought, to the movement from "tribal" to "civilized" society, and on to the democratization of society and the consequential elimination of the barrier between science and the technology of daily life.

The concern for environmental protection is, however, relatively new to the industrial world and it challenges both the will and the ability of individuals and social organizations to adapt. It defines humans as ecological players in a vulnerable landscape rather than as independent masters of an indestructable environment. This shift requires not simply a superficial re-examination of routine practices, but a deeper assessment of the moral basis of our relationship to the earth. Understanding the human relationship to the environment implies a study of the basis of that relationship. Many of the new theories in environmental philosophy centre around Aldo Leopold's Land Ethic, "A thing is right when it tends to preserve the integrity, stability, and beauty of the biotic community. It is wrong when it sdoes otherwise."[4] Arne Naess (1973), in advocating what he calls Deep Ecology, suggests that the environmental problems of the modern age are the consequences of degraded attitudes and perceptions. The goal of Deep Ecology is to transform the attitudes which lead to environmental degradation. Deep Ecology is contrasted with Shallow Ecology which is said to provide short-term remedies while neglecting the cause of the problems. The tradition of human domination melded with a world view which is fueled by a technological habit and implicit faith in science create the backdrop for extensive degradation. Deep Ecology criticizes Shallow Ecology, asserting that attitudes and perceptions, not simply policies or activities, must be transformed. Ecologically responsible policies must look beyond pollution and resource depletion into the degradative nature of currently and widely held perceptions.[5]

According to Taylor, "obligations have no meaning without conscience, and the problem we face is the extension of the social conscience from people to the land."[6] A moral code defines appropriate relationships among members of a moral community.[7] It provides the rules of engagement for any interaction of members of the moral community and so, if one is to understand the nature of interaction, it is necessary to understand the nature of the moral code. Characterising a moral code requires answers to two sets of questions: one about the prescribed rights and duties of acceptable relationships, the other about the membership of the community to whom the rights and duties apply. Leopold's consideration of the land ethic continues:

All ethics so far evolved rest upon a single premise: that the individual is a member of a community of interdependent parts. His instincts prompt him to compete for his place in that community, but his ethics prompt him also to co-operate (perhaps in order that there may be a place to compete for).

The land ethic simply enlarges the boundaries of the community to include soils, waters, plants, and animals, or collectively, the land.[8]

Taylor also rejects a strictly human standpoint "in which our own well-being is tacitly assumed as the standard for living a good and worthwhile life"[9]. His view is biocentric in that it concentrates on the individual biological organism and that individual is seen as the focal point of moral considerability. J. Baird Callicott agrees with the need for a non-anthropocentric viewpoint but proposes an ecocentric perspective which focuses moral attention on the ecosytem as a whole. "The ecocentric land ethic, conceived by Leopold and elaborated by Callicott, is thus a holistic ethic ..."[10] in which right and wrong are determined by their impact on the "integrity, stability and beauty of the biotic community"[11].

These moral viewpoints of biocentrism and ecocentrism offer useful guidelines for the development of a living environmental ethic. Their differences are perhaps more theoretical than practical for both lead toward respectful treatment of the natural environment, be it by virtue of its individual elements or the whole.

However, in cases where two cultures interact, differences in moral codes, or incongruencies in the extent of moral communities, may influence how interactions transpire. Environmental decisions that are based on the narrower perspective of environmental value and restrictive membership in the moral community are less likely than decisions based on the broader view to produce results that are environmentally sustainable or socially equitable. It is therefore necessary to recognize these differences as possible determinants of negotiation in cases where cultural groups do interact. Within the context of discussions of reconciling human impacts with environmental responsiveness, cultural groups do need to interact and negotiate – implicitly or explicitly – on the matter of managing interconnected ecological resource systems. It is therefore essential that some understanding of the implications of moral codes and the extension of moral communities be developed and recognized. In the case where resource conflicts appear to be based in differences in perception of value, in part due to differences in the extension of membership in the moral community, environmental ethics become essential elements of resource negotiations.

Negotiations on conflicting uses of the forests of Barrière Lake have to date been primarily on the basis of monetary concerns. Fundamental differences in the moral codes of the two cultural groups – and in the extent of their moral communities – profoundly affect the nature of the negotiations. These differences need to be made clear for the negotiating process to be successful.

Failure to recognize differences in the limits of moral communities may involve a violation of moral codes, specifically in cases where the extent of the moral community of a politically dominant group is narrower than that of the subdominant group. If the politically dominant group's moral community does putatively extend to humans in subdominant groups, then it can be argued that decisions compatible with both moral codes can only be assured by accepting the broader definition of moral community. This assertion has implications for the discussion of environmental protection.

A Land Ethic or Respect for Life: Native American and Euro-American Perspectives

There is no one unified Native American belief system, there is diversity and varity amongst the First Nation cultures, but this "should not obscure a complementary unity to be found among them".[12] This common ground is perceived to lie in their world views which, although varied, have all typically included and supported an environmental ethic.

Environmental awareness and knowledge are integral to traditional native culture. They are perpetuated through active application in daily life – survival requires accurate knowledge and response. Myth and ritual connect the material and spiritual world. They present the means by which "individuals are trained to study the resource potential of their environment and bring their own lives into life-sustaining relationships with the world of nature."[13] Myths represent guidelines for appropriate behaviour and interaction with the natural world.

The Native American conception is that human and nonhuman communities interconnect. Such an inclusive and intersecting perception of the world appears to engender a more balanced relationship with the natural environment. Their social structure encompasses the natural world. Native culture can be said to entail: 1) a need to sustain the environment, 2) myth and ritual that support sustainable behaviour, 3) both a social structure and moral community that encompass the natural world.[14]

Tribal cultures that extend moral standing to non-human elements are inevitable impediments to those who assume a strictly material view of nature. This generates conflict as the native culture is viewed as an obstacle to progress – something to be overcome. Where the Euro-Americans have had dominance, native people and their ecosystems have joined the ranks of the dominated.

The quest for a path to "sustainable development" may, however, change the way in which such conflicts are evaluated and resolved. The situation at Barrière Lake, Quebec is one in which commercial logging interests (and the governments that support them) have come into conflict with the traditional users of the forests. What distinguishes this case from the countless preceding cases is that an attempt has been made to articulate the opposing views and resolve conflicts through a formal agreement rather than through force or attrition. This provides an opportunity to assess the respective positions and to determine the extent to which an ethical analysis of the case may contribute to a sustainable resolution.

The Community at Barrière Lake

The Algonquins of Barrière Lake live within the boundaries of the La Vérendrye Wildlife Reserve and depend upon their natural surroundings for their subsistence activities which are presently threatened by the impacts of forestry operations. This paper concentrates on forestry issues although other forms of development and exploitation, such as hydro-electric projects, mining activities, recreational hunting and fishing, exaggerate environmental stresses such as acid rain, and are also contributing to the destruction of the Barrière Lake resource base.

The Location

Barrière Lake is situated about 250 kilometres north of Ottawa and 100 kilometres northwest of Montreal. The Algonquins of Barrière Lake have an interest in lands in the areas identified as Forestry Management Units (UGs = unités de

gestions) seventy-three and seven. These units lie within the boundaries of the La Vérendrye Wildlife Reserve and extend into the Grand Lac Victoria Beaver Preserve. Their dependence upon the lands within UGs seventy-three and seven is significant because their land based economy includes hunting, fishing, and trapping.

The History

The Barrière Lake Algonquin have occupied the land in question since time immemorial. An archaeological study by the Quebec government confirms Algonquin occupation of the Barrière Lake region, dating back 6,000 years.[15] These traditional inhabitants call themselves "Mitchikanibikonginik", meaning "People of the Stone Weir". The name refers to a particular site, called Mitchikanibinik, where "a natural stone ridge once ran across a shallow narrow at Barrière Lake."[16]

The Mitchikanibikonginik are but one of ten communities known together as the Algonquin Nation. This nation claims as its collective ancestral territory all land and water within the Ottawa River watershed, straddling the border between the provinces now known as Quebec and Ontario. Chief Matchewan asserts that Parliment Hill is part of the traditional hunting grounds of the Algonquin Nation, that is unsurrendered Algonquin land.

Algonquin bands whose territory was more accessible than that of the Mitchikanibinikonginik were adversely affected by settler encroachments. The Mitchikanibikonginik were amongst the last to be affected due to the relative inaccessibility of their land. Two large reserves were eventually established for the dislocated people but the fact remains that none of the territory claimed as traditional Algonquin land has ever been surrendered or ceded to the Crown. In addition, the pre-existing rights of the Algonquin people to these lands were specifically recognized by the Royal Proclamation of 1763.

The pre-existing rights of the Algonquins, addressed in the Royal Proclamation, were also recorded in the "Three-Figure Wampum Belt."[17] In eastern North America, before the arrival of European explorers and settlers, the Indian nations used to record their agreements and laws on wampum belts. A wampum is a cylindrical bead of either white or purple colour, derived from the hard shell of a clam. The beads are woven together to "form designs that symbolize actual events. It takes years to make a wampum belt and once made it is handed down from generation to generation, along with the memory of what it records."[18]

According to the Algonquin viewpoint, their contemporary relations with the federal and provincial governments stem from the Three-Figure Wampum Belt Agreement made with the English and the French. As their descendants, the governmental representatives of both Canada and Quebec are legally bound by this agreement. The memory and power of the agreement are still alive for the Algonquin people who presented it to the First Ministers of Canada during the final constitutional conference on aboriginal matters held in Ottawa in 1987. The agreement asserted the recognition of the First Nations by the English-speaking and French-speaking nations and also stipulated the involvement of the First Nations i any questions regarding land. "This historic agreement also provided that the matter of jurisdiction was to be based on mutual respect and equality."[19]

The sanctity of the agreement is marked by the fact that it was "blessed by a representative from the Vatican who would [supposedly] see [to] its fulfillment."[20] A cross on the belt symbolizes that involvement and commitment.

The People
The Algonquins of Barrière Lake have a strong traditional land-based economy and are committed to its continued viability. They compose the only permanent community in the area relying heavily upon the land for physical subsistence and cultural survival. Their environment provides their livelihood and defines their way of life. Their community, presently composed of 50 people, has traditionally occupied the Lake Barrière region. Some members of the community live on the Rapid Lake Reserve where they are surrounded by forestry operations, while many others prefer to live in separate settlements in the bush. Despite their long-term residence and continued dependence upon the land base, the Algonquins of Barrière Lake have not historically been consulted about the way in which the area is managed, but have been excluded from both decision-making and planning processes.

The area is essential to the Algonquin peoples' continued existence, both physically/materially and culturally/spiritually, the forest and its resources being central to the Algonquin way of life. Material subsistence is not the only issue as the lands are also used by the members of the Barrière Lake band for the practice and pursuit of their non-material culture. Long-term occupation of the land around Barrière Lake has given rise to a special relationship based upon an intimate knowledge of the forest. The forest's spiritual significance is essential to the band's culture for the land at Barrière is considered sacred.

Jean-Maurice Matchewan, traditional chief of the Algonquins of Barrière Lake, believes that a continued or increased level of lumbering and tree planting activities in the area used and occupied by his band would lead to the virtual destruction of their culture and jeopardize their existence as a distinct and organized society. Chief Matchewan states that he and the members of his community are not opposed to forestry operations per se, but to the present methods of planning, exploitation, and management.[21]

Forestry and Barrière Lake
The province of Quebec has allotted virtually all productive forest to commercial forestry. A series of new management agreements has recently

been negotiated across the province. These have proceeded without adequate notice, thus negating the possibility of meaningful public participation. Despite the significant impact on the province's indigenous peoples, they have been neither consulted nor included in either the negotiations for, or the formation of, new agreements.

A historical overview
of forestry operations in La Veréndrye
Forestry operations began in what is now the east-central portion of the La Veréndrye Wildlife Reserve in the mid to late 1880s. By the 1870s the coastal regions had been virtually cleared of pine, although the interior was logged selectively and only the best quality pine was harvested. All timber rights were leased by the 1890s. From that point on, forestry and associated activities escalated. As the mid 1890s approached, logging roads were extended into previously inaccessible regions of La Veréndrye, and the cumulative effects of logging activities were evidenced by habitat destruction and increased poaching. During this period a significant number of men from the Barrière Lake community were employed at the lumber camps. Mechanical methods of harvesting began to replace hand logging in the latter half of the 1960s, marking the onset of clearcutting and a subsequent loss of jobs.

The present state of forestry in La Veréndrye
Long-term forestry agreements (contrats d'approvisionnement et d'aménagement forestier = **CAAFs**) lock the Barrière Lake lands into "priority forest production" for the next twenty-five years, after which time they may be renewed at five year intervals. The CAAFs are supposed to demonstrate the sharing of responsibilities between the government and the forest industry. Under this agreement, a wood processing plant is granted the right to harvest a given volume of one or two species on a specified territory each year. This apparently ensures the stability of the timber supply, that is trees.

The stability of the resource is essential to the company, but maintenence of a viable resource base is also contingent upon the company fulfilling certain commitments. A company that enters into a timber supply and forest management agreement undertakes to carry out, at its own expense, its own silviculture, the reforestation of the harvested area. The siliviculture treatments must reach the production objectives stipulated by the agreement – the company must prepare a twenty-five year general management plan, as well as a five year plan, and an annual forest management plan. These plans are filed so that the general public may be informed before the plans are approved by the Minister of Forests. In addition, companies are required to pay government royalties corresponding to the true stumpage value of standing timber – this value is determined by the Quebec Minister of Energy and Resource – but part of these royalties may be paid in reforestation procedures.

Despite the fact that the La Vérendyre is a designated Wildlife Reserve, approximately fifty percent of its area has already been clear or partially cut. The designation of the entire Reserve for priority forest production displays a complete disregard of the Algonquin way of life. No recognition is given to the Algonquin's subsistence needs, nor those of the region's wildlife and plantlife. The Algonquins of Barrière Lake want to develop a land use regime that includes and respects activities other than logging. They do not want to exclude logging from the area but want to ensure the integrity of the land for future generations and multiple uses.[22]

The principle of "sustainable development" put forth by the World Commission of he Environment and Development in its report entitled *Our Common Future*, provides guidelines in the pursuit of integrated resource management.[23] The Algonquins of Barrière Lake have proposed a special trilateral process designed to acknowledge and incorporate the concerns of the three interested parties; the Algonquins themselves, the provinicial government, and the federal government. The proposal seeks to integrate a conservation strategy with an economic plan for the area. Both the federal and provincial governments have agreed to participate in this process. The band had also requested a postponement in the signing of the twenty-five year Forestry Management Agreements (CAAFs) in an attempt to ensure that no constraints would be placed upon the development and implementation of a sustainable development conservation strategy but this request was denied. Quebec's Forests Minister Albert Côté has signed three new CAAFs.

The signing of the CAAFs places severe restrictions upon future conservation strategies and ignores the recommendations of the Bruntland Report, which suggests that the traditional rights of tribal and indigenous peoples be recognized and that "they should be given a decisive voice in formulating policies about resource development in their areas."[24] The Algonquins of Barrière Lake believe that any determination about the sufficiency of forest production should entail an analysis of the full potential of the forest, not simply potential lumber production. The forest produces many things. Its non-timber value is quite vast, ranging from wildlife to food and medicinal plants and the variety of activities that it sustains, such as hunting and fishing, trapping, traditional arts and crafts. Chief Matchewan suspects that the provincial government will be reluctant to change the legally binding cutting agreements for fear of being sued by the logging companies for breach of contract.[25]

Barrière Lake Alqonguin and the Impacts of Forestry Operations

Negative impacts resulting from forestry operations abound and will only escalate as the new CAAFs are put into effect. The repercussions include habitat degradation and destruction, disruption of traplines, and reductions in wildlife populations. These are the direct and consequen-

tial results of logging operations – because logging itself increases accessibility for recreational hunters – and the aftermath of herbicide and pesticide use. Although the range of impact has not been fully assessed, the damage caused by logging and related activities adversely affects people, animals and plantlife.

These impacts have been noted by the Algonquins of Barrière Lake and studied by environmental consultants and trained foresters engaged by the band. The detailed affidavits of Chief Matchewan and other members of the Barrière Lake community, as well as those of environmental research consultant Rebecca Aird and registered professional forester Peter E. Higgelke, document changes in the natural environment which is adversely affecting the human and non-human inhabitants in the region.[26]

Much of the land that has been clearcut is not regenerating into the original forest composition, if at all. A major factor concerning the success or failure of natural regeneration is soil quality. The soil quality of the region is poor and has been damaged by logging operations. Although some regeneration occurs it rarely approximates the original forest composition. It appears that the growth of any merchantable timber is considered sufficient and hat no consideration has been given to the animals and people who depended upon the original forest for their material well- being; that is their needs for food, shelter, medicinal plants and so forth.

In 1985, the Quebec Minister of Energy and Resources (MER = Ministère de l'Energie et des Resources) began intensive reforestation operations. These operations include the use of herbicides and pesticides which have an adverse effect on the resource base of the Barrière Lake Algonquins. Reforestation also creates a habitat-poor monoculture. These tree farms are more contentious than the regenerated forests for they in no way resemble the composition or bio-diversity of the original forest.

Value and Worth:
Criteria Applied to the Case Study

Paul W. Taylor presents a biocentric paradigm in which respect for nature provides the foundation for an environmental ethic in much the same manner as respect for humans provides the basis for ordinary interpersonal relations. Recognition of the non-instrumental worth of the various individual living organisms is central to his argument. He presents six distinctive value concepts:

1) Instrumental value is the value accorded to something in recognition of its usefulness as the means to a desired end.

2) Commercial value is the economic worth of something as measured by its market value.

3) Merit or excellence refers to the fulfillment of certain standards.

4) The immediately good refers to the experience or activity of a conscious being during which it feels enjoyment, satisfaction, or pleasure in and of itself. The experience is deemed worthwhile simply because the conscious participant feels it to be so. This is also sometimes referred to as "intrinsic value."

5) The intrinsically valued is always employed in reference to a human valuer. An entity is valued when a person deems it "worthy of being preserved and protected because it is the particular thing it is."[27] The types of entities which fall into this category range from persons to members of the biotic community on to physical objects and then even to social practices. "From a moral point of view, correlative with intrinsically valuing something is the recognition of a negative duty not to destroy it ... and a positive duty to protect it from being destroyed ... by others."[28]

6) Inherent worth is the value something possesses simply because it has a good of its own. If an entity has inherent worth then its welfare is deserving of recognition. Its good becomes the concern of all moral agents who are thus obligated to promote or protect its well-being "as an end in itself and for the sake of the being whose good it is."[29] This category is applied to living things (humans, animals, and plants) for, according to Taylor, only they can have goods capable of being promoted or destroyed. These criteria are intended to expand notions of value and worth, as well as the standards by which they are assessed.

Taylor's six value concept criteria can be used to to explore the differences between the Algonquins of Barrière Lake and the Euro-Americans that pertain to resource use and moral considerability. The viewpoints which will be explained and assessed are based upon the positions taken by those involved in the negotiations. Cultural values are reflected in the planning documents of the respective groups, providing some distillation of what people think and believe. The range of variation that exists within the communities is not the issue. This is not an attempt to describe general cultural norms but to understand the negotiation process and the official viewpoints of the parties involved. The forest resource, and its perceived worth or value, will be reviewed according to Taylor's model.

Instrumental value deals with the means to desired ends. The forest could be valued in this way by both of the cultural groups, though their interpretations of this type of valuing would be different. The Euro-American may find the instrumental value of a tree lying in its prospective end use as lumber perhaps in a house or furniture, or its potential to be transformed into pulp and paper. These are valid ascriptions of instrumental value. Lena Nottaway[30] presents the traditional Algonquin perspective on the forest and its instrumental value, showing that the forest provides a variety of special trees which serve a variety of purposes. Certain trees are used in the preparation of medicinal ointments and tinctures. The roots and the bark serve different functions. Some members of the band still partake in the traditional arts and crafts, such as threading birch bark baskets, which requires the availability of the appropriate tree species. Accordingly, Toby Decoursay suggests that the instrumental value of the forest is vast. The forest provides:

many kinds of animals, moose, ducks, beaver, owl, partridge, bear, muskrat, geese, sturgeon, white fish and others. [In addition, the forest provides trees that are used] for different things; spruce for log houses, poplar for smoking hides, [and] birch for canoes. Many of the smaller plants like blueberries, raspberries, and wild cherries [are good to] eat. There are also many medicines [made] from plants. Cedar makes a good medicine for colds and chest problems.[31]

Decoursay lives in the bush with his wife and their six children for most of the year, only occasionally visiting the reserve at Rapid Lake. He asserts that the forest provides all the essentials for survival and believes that his children are healthier because of their dependence upon bush food. According to the traditional Algonquin viewpoint, the instrumental value of the forest cannot be overestimated for it carries the potential to satisfy all life-sustaining needs.

Hence, for the first criteria both cultural groups perceive some instrumental value in the forest. The difference lies in the diversity of the experience for the Algonquins appear to have a wider range of potential uses for the various resources found within the forest. In reference to the forest's vast instrumental value, Chief Maurice Matchewan asserts that:

...a determination on the sufficiency of forest production should entail an analysis of the full potential of the forest, and not only potential lumber production ... a forest produces many things besides trees, notably wildlife, foods, herbal medicines, and plants ... a forest also provides us with a basis for a whole range of services, notably professional trapping, hunting and fishing, tourist activities, sport hunting and fishing, outfitting, camping, hiking and other recreational activities.[32]

Another member of the Algonquin community, elder Lena Jerome, also addresses the issue of instrumental value. She offers a critique of logging practices, showing how the methods employed are adversely affecting the forest and its resources:

... timber cutting ... [is] killing all the herb medicines, the animals and the medicines that the animals eat. Also, they shouldn't hurt the trees that the animals eat. They're going to hurt the plants growing on the ground from the machines they use now. This is worse, it's like bringing a monster over here to ruin everything ... they are cutting all kinds of trees now ... When they used to use a buck saw a long time ago, they didn't hurt the other trees. They just took the ones they wanted. That machine, it's just ruining the country ... there's no jobs for people, the machine is doing all the work. They used to cut just what they wanted. It used to be better, the other trees were there, the animals had something to eat. Now its clearcutting. There's nothing for them there, they don't go there, you don't see them ... That's why we can't find any good birch bark in the country here; the trees have been hurt. We have to go to the big island to find the good bark. Its so hard to find ... We use bark for lots of things.[33]

Commercial value is the second of Taylor's concepts. The economic worth of something is evaluated according to its market price or by the amount of money that one can sell it for. Commercial value is high on the priority list of the Euro-American, for this is the major issue of conflict in the Barrière Lake region. The Quebec Minister of Energy and Resources (MER = Ministère de l'Energie et des Resources) controls the management of resources in the La Vérendrye

Wildlife Reserve and advocates the extraction of its natural resources, most specifically via hunting, fishing, and logging activities. In addition, the Quebec government has signed timber supply and forest management agreements (CAAF 's) with different logging companies and is thus legally and financially bound to respect them. The commercial value of the forest for the government is intensified by the threat of a potential financial penalty if the agreements are broken or altered in any way. The logging companies are quite obviously attuned to the commercial value of the forest. The Algonquins are undoubtedly aware of the commercial value of their forest but do not appear to be preoccupied by this notion of value. A quote from the band's economic development advisor, Hector Jerome, clarifies the two divergent viewpoints. Reflecting on a clearcut he wonders at how different the native view is from that of governments and logging companies. "They only see money when they look at a tree."[34]

Merit or excellence, the "good - making" properties by which something fulfills a certain grading or ranking standard is apprehended by both cultural groups, yet once again with variant manifestations. From the Algonquin perspective, certain trees are goo for certain specific uses, be they medicinal or artisanal. The native traditions dictate which trees should be used for what purposes, and experience tells the individual which is a meritorious or excellent example. Knowledge of the diversity of the forest and the variety of uses marks the Algonquin perception of merit or excellence. Clearcut logging, which is often justified as a quick and efficient means of extracting the forest's commercial resources, is viewed by Patrick Wambamoose as both wasteful and inefficient for it ignores the merit of the forest's individual elements. He claims that "it wastes so much ... Loggers knock down all the trees in one area but don't use them all [and] motor oil from their machines runs in slicks until it reaches the water."[35]

Questions of merit or excellence and issues of diversity in cultural perspectives are addressed in the *Affidavit* of Lena Jerome. An elder who is nearly eighty years old, Jerome offers great insight into traditional Algonquin attitudes and values as regards the forest. She discusses the perceived value of the forest, showing how it extends beyond mere instrumental worth into the realm of merit and excellence. In describing the different uses, Jerome expands upon what constitutes a meritorious example of birch bark or an excellent specimen of medicinal herb. The diversity of perceived value once again marks the divergent attitudes of the two cultural groups in question.

Intrinsic value, what Taylor also calls the "immediately good", refers to any experience or activity that a conscious being finds enjoyable, pleasurable, satisfying, or worthwhile in itself. Members of both cultural groups could apprehend and experience this type of value. A walk in the forest, hearing bird songs, or the discovery of a blueberry bush are all candidates for the immediately good. The discrepancy lies in actual human proximity. The governmental and industrial decision-makers do not live in the bush, are not familiar with the forest. There are two consequences of this: 1) the obvious which suggests that if the decision-makers are not there to see or appreciate the forest, then its presence, deterioration, or loss will mean little to them, and 2) their capacity for appreciation is unlikely to match that of the local residents for, in residing in the city, they do not acquire the sensitivity to nuance that prolonged exposure brings, just as one who has had limited exposure to classical music can hardly be expected to be an informed judge or critic of a performance. The entity which is the object of the human valuer's attention may be a person, animal, or plant, a physical object, a place, or even a social practice. This value is independent of whatever instrumental or commercial value it might have. Something is intrinsically valued in so far as someone cherishes, loves, and admires it, and thereby places intrinsic value on its existence and deems it worthy of being preserved and protected simply because of the particular thing that it is. This type of value represents the sentiments of the Barrière Lake Algonquin toward their forest.

The last of Taylor's value categories is inherent worth. This is illustrated by Jacques Bugnicourt's description of forest values in India: "It is in those trees that our Gods frolic." [36] This implies a value that is totally independent of humans. In describing North American native perspectives, Callicott asserts "the Western tradition pictures nature as material, mechanical and devoid of spirit (reserving that exclusively for humans), while the American Indian tradition pictures nature throughout as an extended family or society of living ensouled beings." [37] Toby Decoursay, in his affidavit to the Trilateral Agreement process, said "The old people used to tell me that the land at Barrière is sacred."[38] Lena Jerome, an elder in the Algonquin band, said "We don't want timber cutting. It is killing all the herb medicines, the animals and the medicine that the animals eat. lso, they shouldn't hurt the trees that the animals eat. They are going to hurt the plants growing on the ground ..." [39] The notion of "hurt" extended to animals, trees and plants demonstrates moral consideration. And in this case the organisms listed are not being cited for their utility to humans but rather as entities in their own right. Louise Ratt , a member of the band, said "The feast had to be made to thank nature ..." [40] This implies moral considerability. There is even evidence of volition on the part of nature. In Lena Jerome's *affidavit* is the report that, at the time commercial logging began, the Chief said "one day [the loggers] will be stepped on by the timbers."[41] This evidence is not merely anecdotal or idiosyncratic but is embedded in the principles of the Algonquin Task Force of Special Representatives. Item three asserts that humans are a part of nature and not separate from it. That implies equality of standing of humans

and non-humans. Item eight is "Recognition of the importance of living species other than humans, and of generations other than our own." [42] This makes no exclusive mention of the subset of species useful to humans. It is absolute and inclusive.

The Euro-American simply does not display the same sentiment of spiritual connectedness to the land which extends the notion and experience of intrinsic valuing into the realm of respect and duty – protecting the valued entity from misuse. As suggested throughout this inquiry, the native conception of the land base fosters respectful treatment and sustainable use. The cooperative spirit is shown to extend to other humans as well as the natural world and its "other than human" inhabitants. The maintenance of the land base is contingent upon its protection and intertwined with both cultural and environmental perpetuation . This fundamental difference in perception between the Barrière Lake community and the southern industrial community is of immeasurable importance in considering the implications for environmental sustainability.

The final variety of value is inherent worth. This final criterion displays a certain purity of purpose. It states that an entity is to be valued simply because it has a good of its own, which is deserving of the moral consideration or concern of all moral agents. Taylor suggests that since the criterion only makes sense with reference to living things, then "the class of entities having inherent worth is extensionally equivalent to the class of living things."[43] Humans, animals. and plants are placed within the same domain of importance. This notion conforms to the Algonquin perspective. For urban bureaucrats, literally disconnected from nature in their daily lives, the natural world cannot help but be "Other", perhaps alien, and therefore difficult to appreciate for its inherent value. Conversely, for people organically connected to nature in their daily lives the separation will be less.

Concluding Remarks
on the Application of Theory

This study has verified that: 1) cultural differences in the perception of, and attitudes toward, the forest resource do exist, 2) these cultural differences extend into the moral realm, determining membership in the moral community, 3) the difference in cultural attitudes has been the cause of misunderstandings and has thus inhibited a clear exchange of knowledge and the just resolution of resource conflicts. Specifically, it substantiated that: 4) the Algonquins of Barrièr Lake function within a more broadly extended realm of moral consideration than the Euro-American, the native sense of community being shown to encompass the natural world and its "other than human" inhabitants. Moreover, 5) the management plans of the Algonquin reflect a deeper commitment to both environmental and cultural sustainability than those of the proponents of the commercial forestry industry.

The consideration of Taylor's value concept criteria led to questions of attitudinal and perceptual differences which necessarily reflected upon the cultures' values and ascriptions of worth. Each of Taylor's categories of value addresses a different aspect of knowledge and perception, including both the personal and the cultural. Respect is ascribed to certain entities, human or otherwise, which enter into the realm of consideration. MER has to date focused primarily upon resource extraction, displaying an inclination towards a limited or contained perception of value, most specifically linked to instrumental and commercial usefulness. The more subtle, or spiritually connected, value concepts are seemingly ignored. Merit or excellence may enter the realm of consideration though only superficially, while intrinsic value, the intrinsically valued, and inherent worth are seemingly disregarded.

This lack of consideration, respect, and understanding was made obvious through the denial of interactive co-management. No serious considera-

tion had been given to the possibility of designating traditional use areas with special co-management arrangements and environmental standards. What may *possibly* be reversible within the time frame of forest ecology may be devastatingly irreversible in socio-economic and cultural terms. "Certainly this is the case for a community such as Barrière Lake, whose continuity of land use is critical to the maintenance of land-based skills and the related social organization."[44]

The connection between a culture and the particular environment in which it developed is great. Remove the land base from which knowledge has been constructed and perpetuated through tradition, and the culture itself will crumble. Subsistence economies are most clearly linked to the land. Their cultural survival is contingent upon the maintenance of a known, sound, natural environment. Although the subsistence based group may themselves regulate resource use and consumption, they cannot implement regulations which are binding for members of other cultural groups.

This was the case before the signing of a Trilateral Agreement which was intended to open doors which had previously been barred. The proposed Agreement offered encouragement after a long period of disempowerment. It appeared that the Algonquins were to play an active role in the planning and management of their forest. It seems, however, that they were unduly optimistic for several elements of the Agreement have already been ignored or reneged upon.

As the industrial world continues to extend its influence and increase its unsustainable environmental impact, it is inevitable that both the pressure on non-industrial, resource-based cultures and the search for a sound environmental ethic will intensify. Ironically, the conflicts that arise in the industrial world may be tempered by the application of knowledge from non-industrial, resource-based cultures and, at the same time, advances in the application of traditional knowledge may best be made by studying the conflicts that arise in industrialized society. The Algonquin culture is threatened by the commercial resource industries of the south, but in examining the conflicts arising from the Trilateral Agreement process, it is possible to see how a broader spectrum of criteria for value, extended to a larger moral community, can produce an environmental ethic that is compatible with both environmental and culturl sustainability.

Intercultural resource negotiations that fail to recognize differences in the spectrum of criteria of value or membership in a moral community will lead to conflict. If the narrower or more restrictive view is sanctioned by the dominant cultural group, the conflict can be resolved through force – economic, political, or armed. If sustainability is the objective, force must be avoided and conflicts must be resolved in accordance with an appropriate environmental ethic. Logically, the broader definition of value and the greater extension of moral community are more likely to include, and therefore be compatible with, the narrower. Hence, a reasonable first approach to analysing conflict is to begin by defining these parameters. One criterion for resolving conflicts, to optimise sustainability, would then be the extent to which these parameters conform to the ideals of a recognized system of environmental ethics.

The conflict between the Algonquin and the commercial forest interests appears to be based in differences in perception of value, in part due to differences in the extension of membership in the moral community. Thus, dimensions of environmental ethics become essential elements of resource negotiations. Negotiations that do not recognize this cannot likely produce a harmonious resolution. Negotiations that do recognize it will determine that the Algonquin perception of environment has more in common with the core tenets of environmental ethics than do the perceptions of the forest industry interests. Decisions that base desire to realize instrumental and commercial value within the context of the need to protect other values will serve to reduce conflict and thus promote cultural sustainability. To the extent that these decisions do protect other values, they will also promote environmental sustainability. [45]

ENDNOTES

[1] World Commission on Environment and Development, *Our Common Future*, (Oxford: Oxford University Press, 1987).

[2] Paul W. Taylor, *Respect for Nature*, (Princeton, New York: Princeton University Press, 1986).

[3] Paul W. Taylor, *Respect for Nature*, p. 73.

[4] Aldo Leopold, *A Sand County Almanac*, p. 219.

[5] Arne Naess, "The Shallow and the Deep, Long-Range Ecology Movement: a Summary", *Inquiry* (1973) 16, pp. 95-100.

[6] Paul W. Taylor, "Are Humans Superior to Animals and Plants?", *Environmental Ethics* (1984) 6, p. 151.

[7] Questions of behaviour, community, and appropriateness are explored by both Aldo Leopold in *A Sand Country Almanac*, and James Rachel, *The Elements of Moral Philosophy*, (New York: Random House, 1986).

[8] Aldo Leopold, *A Sand Country Almanac*, (New York: Oxford University Press, 1966), p. 219.

[9] Paul W. Taylor, "Are Humans Superior to Animals and Plants", *Environmental Ethics*, 6 (1984), p. 159.

[10] Ibid.

[11] Ibid.

[12] J. Baird Callicot, "Traditional American Indian and Western European Attitudes Toward Nature: An Overview", *Environmental Ethics*, (1982), p. 29.

[13] Robin Ridington, "Technology, Worldview and Adaptive Strategy", *Canadian Review of Sociology and Anthropology*, 19 (4), (1982), p. 80.

[14] R. Dasmann, *Environmental Conservation*, 4th edition, (New York: Wiley, 1976), p. 1.

[15] Two consulted sources made reference to an archaeological study conducted by the Quebec government which substantiates Algonquin long-term occupancy of the Barrière Lake region: Chief Jean-Maurice Matchewan, "Mitchikanibikonginik Algonquins of Barrière Lake: Our Long Battle to Create a Sustainable Future", in Boyce Richardson, ed., *Drumbeat: Anger and Renewal in Indian Country*, (Toronto: Summerhill Press, 1989), p. 11 and Eileen Frere, "The Algonquins of Barrière Lake", *Borealis*, 2 (2), p. 23.

[16] Chief Jean-Maurice Matchewan, "Mitchikanibikonginik Algonquins of Barrière Lake: Our Long Battle to Create a Sustainable Future", p. 10.

[17] The Three-Figure Wampum Belt is discussed by Chief Matchewan, ibid, pp. 11-12, and by a community elder, Lena Jerome, *Affidavit*, (March 20, 1990), p. 5.

[18] Chief Matchewan, ibid, p. 11.

[19] Ibid, p. 11.

[20] Ibid, p. 23.

[21] Ibid, p. 161.

[22] Ibid.

[23] World Commission on Environment and Development, *Our Common Future*, (Oxford:Oxford University Press, 1987).

[24] Ibid, p. 12.

[25] Ibid, p. 160.

[26] Rebecca Aird, *Affidavit* (Sworn to the Commissioner of Oaths for the District of Ottawa-Carleton on March 27, 1990) and *Alienation of the Traditional Lands Through Conflicting Use,* (Unpublished Report prepared for the Algonquins of Barrière Lake, 1990), and Peter E. Higgelke, *Affidavit*, (Sworn to the Commissioner of Oaths for the District of Ottawa-Carleton on March 29, 1990).

[27] Paul W. Taylor, "Are Humans Superior to Animals and Plants", *Environmental Ethics,* 6 (198), p. 151.

[28] Ibid.

[29] Ibid.

[30] George Kalogerakis, "Saving the Old Ways", *The Ottawa Citizen*, July 21, 1991.

[31] Toby Decoursay, *Affidavit,* (March 29, 1990), p. 1.

[32] Jean-Maurice Matchewan, *Affidavit,* (March 30, 1990), p. 1.

[33] Lena Jerome, *Affidavit*, (March 20, 1990), p. 3.

[34] George Kalogerakis, "Saving the Old Ways", *The Ottawa Citizen*, July 21, 1991.

[35] Ibid.

[36] Jacques Bugnicourt, Cultures and Environments. In *Conservation with Equity*. P. Jacobs and D. Munro (eds.), (Cambridge: IUCN, 1987), 101.

[37] J. Baird Callicott, "Traditional American Indian and Western European Attitudes Toward Nature: An Overview", *Environmental Ethics* (1982)4, p. 294.

[38] Toby Decoursay, *Affidavit*, (March 29, 1990), p. 1.

[39] Lena Jerome, *Affidavit*, (March 20, 1990), p. 3.

[40] Louise Ratt, *Affidavit*, (March 29, 1990), p. 2.

[41] Lena Jerome, *Affidavit*, (March 20, 1990), p. 3.

[42] Terms of Reference for a Task Force of the Special Representatives Pursuant to Article 5, September 1991, p. 2.

[43] Paul W. Taylor, "Are Humans Superior to Animals and Plants", *Environmental Ethics*, 6 198), pp. 150-151.

[44] Rebecca Aird, *Alienation of Traditional Lands Through Conflicting Uses*, (unpublished report for the Algonquins of Barrière Lake, 1990), p. 56.

[45] We thank Russell Diabo, Policy Analyst for the Algonguins of Barrière Lake, for his generous assistance. His time and knowledge were invaluable in this undertaking. The second author acknowledges with gratitude support from the SSHRC. Lastly, we would like to thank the reviewers of this paper and the editors of the text for their incisive and insightful comments.

THE AFTERMATH OF COLLAPSE
ETHICAL ASPECTS IN THE REGULATORY FAILURE OF CANADA'S EAST COAST FISHERY

4

by Raymond A. Rogers

THIS PAPER ARGUES THAT THE PROFOUND FAILURE IN the regulation of Canada's East Coast fishery requires a form of analysis which goes beyond the concerns for policy delivery and resource efficiency, and instead requires an ethical consideration which would contextualize and historicize the dominant realities in the fishery so as to "find a frame of reference to which the market itself is referrable." The paper makes this case by claiming that current economic and technological realities do not provide a viable social context for conservation to manifest itself, and that this failure in viability can be linked to the expanding forces of economic globalization generally. In order to create a viable social context for conservation, Atlantic coastal communities may have to engage in a sea claim of the fish in order to create a system of community-based management. A case is made that conservation requires the solving of history, rather than just the solving of problems.

The collapse of Canada's East Coast fishery in the early 1990s has been referred to as a "great destruction" of biblical proportions.[1] This failure in viability in the relationships between human communities and natural communities in the East Coast fishery is profoundly at odds with the prescribed goals of Canadian resource management frameworks, which were focused on creating ecological and economic stability in the fishery. An analysis of the divergence between the theory of resource management, centred on ecological and economic stability, and the practice of management, which has led to depletion and dependence, points to the inability of resource management frameworks to control destructive fishing prac-

tices, the realities of which are connected to economic and technological realities that are present in modern society generally. As an example of relationships between human and natural communities, therefore, the fishery may be a useful case study for examining the possibility that conservation may require a more antagonistic relationship between its self-described goals and modern economic and technological realities.

Conservation initiatives operating at the level of the nation state and making use of the structures and processes of modern society have been unable to ensure a viable relationship between human communities and natural communities. An ethical perspective on conservation– which takes as its starting point the implicit recognition of membership in community and is linked to local community management – may provide a perspective which is more challenging to the increasing homelessness of economic relations in the context of globalization.

An approach which links human community and natural community aligns critiques of modern economy with social conceptions of nature. This kind of analysis leads to a view of natural communities and non-capitalist human societies in terms of what Marshall Sahlins and Dominique Temple refer to as the generalized embeddedness of relations where there is no economic activity separate from social ends.[2] Karl Polanyi conveys this embeddedness in terms of forms of integration based on reciprocity and redistribution.

The undermining of generalized embeddedness occurs most dramatically in the context of an ascendant expansive capital, (beginning in 17th

Century England) and this is a defining aspect of social transformation in modernity. For Polanyi, this transformation leads to the "fictitious" commodification of land and labour as they become disembedded objects for sale in the market. The representation of embedded sociality in other human communities highlights the current disembedded relations which dominate the world. This embedded sociality can be linked with a social conception of natural communities in which, as naturalist John Livingston states, "all participants are subjects." Contrary to the views of nature in most resource management and sustainability discussions, Livingston represents a natural community in this way:

> *At the level of the community, "other" is bereft of whatever abstract meaning or utility it may have had up to this point. In the functioning multispecies community, all participants are subjects . . . . There need be no other; the community is a whole unto itself.[3]*

It is this relational and participatory sense of community – in which no individual or group dominates and no "other" is exploited or objectified – which can be linked with an embedded conception of human community so as to provide a basis for a social analysis of modern relations in which, increasingly, all participants are objects. By allowing for the appearance of "subjects" in human and natural communities, Livingston counters the materiality of the "object" being "put out of sight" by commodity relations. By doing so, this analysis presents conceptions of humans and nature in resource management and sustainability as a social failure which can be located in a wider crisis of modernity. What I mean by social failure is that human identity and nature have become increasingly defined as disenfranchised objects which increasingly serve commodity relations. In other words, humans and nature have become the "means" and not the ends of so-

cial relations. This can be seen in the terms "human resources" and "natural resources," where "resource" signifies a means which facilitates commodity production. By contrast, the participation of subjects implies that social relations can be ends in themselves and not serve a dominant economic purpose. An example is family relations. When one exchanges gifts in the family, the first thing one does is remove the price tag, because the exchange is not an economic transaction, but one which promotes the social solidarity of the family (subjects). Alternately, to say "time is money" is to convey a sense of human identity which is dominated by economic relations (objects).

Livingston's social conception of nature allows for a recognition that, in the terms defined here, there may be no difference between nature and "the social" in providing an analysis of current regulatory failures. Livingston's perspective also makes problematic the appearance of "the other" by recognizing that there may be forms of relations in which all participants are subjects.

An egalitarian conception of human community, with an emphasis on social responsibility and symmetrical relations, provides the opportunity for the acceptance of an egalitarian and social sense of natural communities as well. This perspective – which re-embeds humans in community and allows for the recognition of nature as community, rather than only as a resource – provides the significant ethical challenge to modern economic and technological realities which current resource management frameworks do not possess.

This socially-embedded perspective is in sharp contrast to current conservation initiatives in Canada's East Coast fishery which are focused around the privatization of shares of the annual quota. These initiatives will lead to a concentration of ownership of the fish – if there are any left to catch – in fewer and fewer hands, and to a marginalization of the inshore fleet which is closely connected to coastal communities.

As well as creating hierarchical divisions between humans, these realities of privatization and deregulation make the fish even more vulnerable to increasingly globalized economic forces. This movement towards privatization and deregulation in the aftermath of the collapse of large portions of the fishery reflects the fact that the Canadian government has misunderstood the causes of overexploitation, and as a result of this misunderstanding, it engages in policy creation that does not solve conservation-related problems, but exacerbates them instead.

The East Coast fishery provides a valuable case study for examining sustainability issues generally because there are close similarities between the resource management theory used in that fishery and the current sustainability initiatives in global management such as *World Conservation Strategy, Our Common Future, Managing Planet Earth*, and *Caring for the Earth*. In fact, the goals and strategies set forth to integrate conservation and development in the fishery are all but identical to those outlined in global management tracts aimed at sustainability. When we consider that the sustainability debate is a recent, and largely theoretical discussion, the situation arises where the profound failure in the practice of conservation in the fishery may also shed light on certain aspects of the theory of sustainability. The depth of the failure in the fishery necessarily raises ethical issues which have not usually been considered central issues for those involved in the regulation of living natural resources.[4]

Rather than analyze the relationships and processes which have caused the collapse of the fishery, most relevant fishery discussions have demonized the foreigner, the seal, and changing climatic conditions which allegedly caused the cod to freeze to death off the coast of Labrador. There has also been much finger pointing by the various sectors within the fishing industry: the inshore blames the offshore, the long-liners blame the draggers, the small companies blame the multinationals, and everyone blames the government. This kind of scapegoating is indicative of the contentiousness that pervades the world of unsustainability after ecological collapse has occurred, and inhibits a worthwhile discussion which might get at some of the broader ethical aspects of conservation strategies.

The "Turbot War" between Canada and Spain in the spring of 1995 highlights in more dramatic terms the fact that, in the aftermath of ecological collapse, conservation can at times only be implemented through conflict and confrontation. In fact, the strife of the "Turbot War" would be unthinkable if it had not been preceded by the ecological collapse of the northern cod in Canadian waters.

Ecological breakdown can become a precondition which can lead to social and political breakdown, and therefore raises the possibility that – once we enter the world of unsustainability – there may not be any easy road back to the world of social and ecological stability. Lester Brown makes the case that when "sustainable yield thresholds are crossed, the traditional responses proposed by economists no longer work."[5] In a world that is more and more often operating in the aftermath of collapse, there is the possibility that a great deal of the sustainability debate – as it relates to pollution permits, effluent taxes, voluntary guidelines, etc. – has already been eclipsed in many parts of the world by the realities of social and political instability. We are therefore confronted with the situation where conservation measures are insufficiently challenging to modern economic and technological realities before ecological collapse occurs and, in the aftermath of collapse, conservation initiatives are very difficult to institute because of social and political instability.

It may be far more worthwhile and far more

beneficial, therefore, to challenge the destructive realities which cause environmental problems before ecological collapse occurs, rather than attempting to do so in its wake. This challenge may require a broader ethical consideration of both the nature of the forces which cause environmental problems, and the decisions we make as a society about how to regulate and prevent those problems from occurring. Discussions of conservation of nature, therefore, may be inseparable from the discussions and analysis of the broader social and political context in which conservation initiatives are manifested. Central to this perspective is the consideration that viable conceptions of human communities and natural communities are markedly different from the way humans and nature are represented within late capitalism.

This kind of analysis leads in two directions, and relates in general terms to first, defining the problem and second, strategizing in the context of current historical realities with initiatives which might bring forth solutions to those problems. I will attempt to relate this process to a brief discussion of the problem of overexploitation in Canada's East Coast fishery, and what kind of strategizing toward solutions can arise out of this kind of analysis.

Defining the Problem:
Background to Ecological
and Economic Collapse in the Fishery

Throughout most of the British Colonial period after the discovery of the "New World," the Northwest Atlantic was a source of salt cod which fed the labourers on plantations in the Caribbean. Ships would leave London, bringing supplies to the colonies of what is now Atlantic Canada. After loading up with salt cod, the ships would sail to the tropical plantations in the Caribbean, where they would drop off the fish and load up with sugar and molasses from the plantations, before sailing back to England.

During the twentieth century, changes in tech-

nology and international relations led to a transformation of these receding colonial relationships as well as the fishing practices which were associated with them, especially following World War Two. Along with the surplus of war ships which were converted to fishing vessels, technological developments such as radar, sonar, diesel engines, hydraulics, synthetic material for nets, and refrigeration, transformed the realities that shaped the exploitation of the fish in the Northwest Atlantic in the 1950s and 1960s. For example, the development of refrigerated distribution networks over continental areas, as well as aboard fishing vessels, transformed the salted product sought after by predominantly rural societies into a fresh-frozen product in demand in the most prosperous countries in the world. At the same time, the rapid expansion of fast food outlets created the need for feedlots which produced the beef, pork, and chicken for these new industries, and it was fish meal that provided the high-protein food for this industry.

The expansion of high-technology fishing by an international distant water fleet after World War II – which was made up of twenty or so of the world's most industrialized countries – led to a collapse in the fish communities off Canada's East Coast during the early 1970s, as well as in several other ocean fisheries around the world. Until that time there was no regulation of this increasingly powerful international fleet of ships beyond voluntary membership in the International Commission for the Northwest Atlantic Fishery (ICNAF), set up in 1949. The ecological collapse of the fish, combined with the inability of international agencies to implement regulations in the aftermath of the crisis, because they lacked the regulatory capability to do so, led directly to the declaration of the 200-mile Exclusive Economic Zones by coastal states in 1977. As the Canadian government stated in a discussion paper for the Law of the Sea Conference in 1974, "the Canadian government considers customary international law inadequate to protect Canada's interest in the protection of the marine environment and its renewable resources."[6]

It was hoped that nationalizing the fish inside the 200-mile limit would enable coastal states to provide a more stable economic return for domestic fishing fleets and, at the same time, put in place the regulatory infrastructure and biological information base needed to insure long-term conservation of the fish. This was the self-proclaimed mandate of the Canadian government, as one of the leaders of the call for a 200-mile coastal zone at the United Nations in the mid-1970s.

In order to justify its claim to international waters, Canada developed its first comprehensive approach to fisheries regulation. Management goals were clearly laid out in *Policy For Canada's Commercial Fisheries* (1976):

- Institute a coordinated research and administrative capability to control fishery resource use on an ecological basis and in accordance with the best interests (economic and social) of Canadian society.

- Develop a fully effective capability for the monitoring of information on resource and oceanic conditions, for the surveillance of fleet activity, and for the enforcement of management regulations.[7]

This attempt at comprehensive regulation was expanded into the early 1980s through a complex framework based on limited-entry, licensing, gear and vessel restrictions, and trip quotas. Despite these attempts to control exploitation, the fishery expanded rapidly – in large part aided by government subsidies – so that in four years the Canadian domestic fleet was larger than the international fleet which had collapsed fish communities in the early 1970s. This rapid expansion led to serious overcapacity, especially in the offshore fleet, which caused economic problems examined by the Kirby Task Force (1983). The task force report recommended the creation of large verti-cally-integrated fish companies like Fisheries Products International and National Sea Products. This emphasis on the priorities of large-scale industry had dramatic effects on fisheries policy. Comprehensive regulation of a commonly-held national resource was gradually replaced by privatization and deregulation as a basis for management because they were perceived to be more efficient and less costly to Canadian taxpayers, and more suited to the business strategies of the newly-created large Canadian fishing corporations.

But why has this program which was directed toward economic and ecological stability failed so miserably in Canada? I believe the most important thing to understand about Canada's East Coast fishery is that the fish were exploited to the point of collapse before it was thought that this exploitation should be regulated in any way. This practice of resource exploitation to the point of collapse is profoundly at odds with resource management theory. The goals of resource management as laid out, for example, in Mitchell's normative model of how resources should be assessed and regulated[8] are usually defined as follows: 1) resource analysis assesses the quality and quantity of the resource in question; 2) resource management establishes the regulatory framework which will control exploitation on an ongoing basis; and 3) resource development converts the resource to a commodity or service available to society. In other words, first the generative capacities of the natural communities which are to be exploited are ascertained, and then management frameworks are established which will limit exploitation so as to preserve these natural processes over the long-term.

When exploitation to the point of collapse precedes conservation measures, the opposite of the goals of management occurs. First, scant biological analysis precedes the collapse, and after the collapse it is all but impossible to understand the interactions of the pre-collapse natural community. Second, a fully-developed exploitation sector is already in place and resists any downsizing by regulators.

This underlying reality – that development precedes conservation – caused both the strife among participants in the fishery as well as the economic and ecological uncertainty which has pervaded the industry. Mitchell describes how the policy process usually occurs in resource management:

1. Identification of a significant problem for which either there is no policy or else present policies are inadequate.

2. Formulation of a policy which attempts to solve the problem.

3. Implementation of the policy.

4. Monitoring the effects of the policy.[9]

This sequence reverses the stages of Mitchell's normative model, because the "significant problem" identified is usually the overexploitation of the resource. Rather than study and policy development preceding exploitation, exploitation has given rise to a "significant problem." This "problem-centred" approach has characterized the development of new versions of fishery policy. It is also reflected in a great many other policy initiatives related to the environment which attempt to overcome past difficulties in regulating exploitation of the natural world.

What is clear in the case of the fishery, and resource management and sustainability literature generally, is that conservation initiatives instituted in the aftermath of collapse, and which make use of the structures and processes of modern institutional and legal frameworks, have a difficult time ensuring either economic or ecological viability. This kind of resource management is, in reality, crisis management.

Almost all fishery policy that now exists has come about from inquiries into breakdowns in the industry. Because the policies that arose from these inquiries were implemented in the aftermath

of a crisis, they cannot fulfil the twin mandates of biological conservation and economic stability. Rather, their purpose was to assuage the cries for more fish from an industry that wanted to fish its way out of trouble and government policy makers who were more interested in economic development than they were in conservation.

These problems are not unique to the Canadian fishery. For example, the globalization of the fishing industry that occurred in the late 1960s and early 1970s with the expansion of the international distant water fleets, is now being experienced by many Southern countries in terms of other resources and other sectors of their economies. And once again, it is clear that conserving natural or human communities is not considered a high priority by resource developers. In fact, the patterns of crisis management and brinkmanship that have occurred in the fishery are being repeated across a wide range of activities which global sustainability initiatives are attempting to address.

Arthur McEvoy describes similar problems in the California fishery. He associates these problems with the structures and processes of modern economic relationships:

Throughout most of its history, U.S. law worked in service to the private economy to dissolve whatever barriers either the ecology of the resources themselves or the efforts of some fishers to stabilize their relations with the fish might place in the way of sustained expansion. The fundamental autonomy and irresponsibility of market actors, which lay at the core of the fisherman's problem, was an article of constitutional faith, the perceived foundation of liberty and opportunity for harvesters. When they did attempt to curtail fishery use, lawmakers had to depend on the political favour of the industry for whatever power they had to influence the course of events. The fisherman's problem thus reproduced itself in the very structure of policy processes which were supposed to correct it.[10]

Adding to this statement, McEvoy comments further ". . . the fisherman's problem consists as much of people stealing from each other as it does of people stealing collectively from nature."[11] This idea of people stealing from each other forms the basis of Garret Hardin's famous metaphor of "the tragedy of the commons," where individuals escalate their use of the commons because, while the benefits accrue to individuals, the costs of increased exploitation are shared by the group. This race to expand exploitation eventually brings ruin to all because, in the absence of restrictions, no one is rewarded for conserving and those who do participate only experience a temporary increase in benefits before over-exploitation causes collapse and everyone loses.

It is this set of relations which McEvoy attributes to modern market relations. The history of regulation in Canada's East Coast fishery has been defined by the attempt to overcome the initial "tragedy of the commons" which occurred in the international context in the early 1970s. The literature on the common property problem sets out two alternate solutions: the "unified directing power" of the nation state to implement comprehensive regulation, or the privatization of shares of the commons among participants. National regulation only repeated the tragedy because resource managers misunderstood the cause of ongoing theft. They blamed it on common property – where the "free" resources of the high seas are not fully internalized into the market system and therefore cannot be taken into account – rather than on modern economic and technological realities, and therefore the Canadian government merely internalized within the national context the same realities which caused collapse in the international arena.

This dispute over whether common property is the cause of the problems in the fishery, or whether common property is the solution to these problems, goes right to the heart of the ethical debate with regard to many environmental problems. In other words, do we assume that market behaviour in the context of modern economic and technological realities is a given, and then set about finding the best way to make use of these realities in the name of efficiency and utility? Or do we make problematic the historical expansion of these realities because we claim that it is the kinds of relationships that have been created by these modern realities which are the problem, and that we can't change these relations without challenging the dominant economic and technological realities in our world? I would argue that the profound crisis in Canada's East Coast fishery goes beyond the goal of increased efficiency, and requires the addressing of the way humans relate to each other and to nature.

The central issue raised by regulatory failure in the fishery involves finding a way to set out viable conceptions of human communities and natural communities which are not the captive of the economic realities in which – to use McEvoy's terms – people steal from each other and from nature. In a world that is increasingly defined by the goals of privatization, deregulation, free trade, and economic globalization, this becomes an ever more difficult problem, in Canada's East Coast fishery and elsewhere. In fact, privatization, deregulation and free trade represent the institutionalization of the very structures and processes which promote the tragedy of the commons.

The connection between environmental problems and modern economic structures suggests that it is very difficult to solve the problems of conservation by using these same structures, as Canada has attempted to do in the East Coast fishery. Conservation initiatives are inseparable from the political and economic realities in which they manifest themselves, and this raises the issue of whether globalization is a viable context for successful conservation of the natural world. Beyond that, what is certainly clear is that it is all but impossible to create viable conservation initiatives in the aftermath of ecological collapse. Indeed, it may be difficult to insure civil stability in increasingly volatile and strife-ridden political situations which follow environmental crisis.

Conservation Strategies: *Community-Based Resistance to Globalization*

A modern theory of resource management should recognize that relations between humans and their environments are complex, involving many aspects of sociocultural systems, and that a definition of resource management that stresses rationality with the coercive backing of the state as the only kind of management is shallow indeed.[12]

In attempting to define the problems related to why resource management theory and practice are so at odds with each other in the case of Canada's East Coast fishery, I have argued that, as Anthony Stocks states in the above quotation, conservation was conceived of in "shallow" terms and was unable to mitigate the predatory realities of the wider "sociocultural system" related to modern economic and technological realities. The reason that conservation initiatives only begin to be developed in the aftermath of ecological collapse is that those living in modern society have a hard time accepting that standard practice in a modern economy is, many times, destroying the web of the natural world. What could be more normal than buying a fish or a piece of beef or a loaf of bread in a supermarket? But when you trace where those products came from, it becomes clear that there are very destructive economic processes at work to produce the food we take for granted. In order to have a viable discussion about conservation of the natural world, it may be necessary to challenge these modern relations and to find a way to talk about viable communities – both human and natural – which can provide the context for genuine conservation.

This kind of recognition returns us to my earlier statement that there are two main aspects to environmental issues: the analysis of the causes of the problem, and the strategizing toward some kind of resolution of those problems. If, as in the case of the fishery, analysis of the problem points to the recognition that the structures of everyday life and the structures that cause environmental problems are the same, we are confronted with a difficulty. It may be all but impossible to separate what is causing environmental problems from the texture of a whole society. For example, if analysis leads to the conclusion that it may not be viable for large corporations to expect a profit from exploiting natural communities such as cod within the increasingly competitive global economy, concerns are raised about solving this problem within the context of that current global economy, where the nation state increasingly perceives its role as one which centres on dismantling regulatory frameworks in the name of promoting a global economy. Ethical considerations do not universalize the present as the only context within which to consider these issues, and can lead to wide-ranging considerations of perspectives that are not usually part of the normal discussions of the regulation of a resource.

Polanyi outlined a social approach to the discussion of economics when he stated that "the market cannot be superseded as a general frame of reference unless the social sciences succeed in developing a wider frame of reference to which the market itself is referable."[13] From Polanyi's statement we can derive a sense of the "social" that subverts the domination of present realities by recognizing that those current depictions of reality are the expression of a particular group within a particular set of relations at a particular time in history, and are not to be universalized as the only frame of reference in which to understand an issue. To set forth a form of social analysis that superseded neoclassical economic models was very important to Polanyi because he saw the workings of the market as very destructive to forms of human and natural community.

This historical contextualization of current realities can lead to very useful analysis, but a difficulty arises when we attempt to apply this analysis to resolving current problems such as those in the fishery because – although wide-ranging perspectives have been considered in the analysis – when we return to the issue at hand, those involved in the issue have their vested interests and may not be willing to consider anything but what appears to be to their own short-term advantage. Most of the time those short-term interests are directly linked to one's place within current historical realities, which remain as they were, despite one's analysis.

Economic globalization may not be a social context that offers much hope for conservation, given that it is driven by privatization, deregulation, and free trade as well as the parallel diminishing of the role of the national civic society. If there is to be any future for conservation of biotic communities, what may be required is the creation of a viable social context. This can only be done by resisting the current forces of economic and technological expansion.

Conservation is not an on/off switch for destructive behaviour imposed by an external authority, at some upper level of exploitation, at the last minute, as it has operated in the quota system in the fishery. By contrast, conservation may only begin in the implicit recognition of one's place in human community and natural community. In large part then conservation is an ethical and cultural issue, not a regulatory problem amenable to current political-economic approaches. This recognition is antithetical to many of the realities current in modern life, and therefore it must also be linked with socio-political resistance to the dominant structures of late modernity.

In setting up this contrast in social contexts, and linking conservation to social context gener-

ally, I put myself in the position of having to solve history in order to solve problems in the world's ocean fishery, especially when it is considered that at present history is moving concertedly in the direction which makes conservation of the natural world increasingly difficult.

Resistance to the colonizing forces of modern economy have appeared in various parts of the world. The resistance of the Kanak people to French colonization in what is known as New Caledonia in the South Pacific is especially noteworthy. In a letter to the Kanak entitled "The Policy of the Severed Flower", in which he discusses their liberation document, Dominique Temple outlines what he perceives as the contrast between Kanak culture and the one based on modern economic production: ". . . the principle according to which power is in proportion to giving [in Kanak culture], which is the inverse of Western society's principle, wherein power is in proportion to accumulation."[14] Temple relates the centrality of gifts generally to societies based on reciprocity and redistribution, or what Karl Polanyi described as embedded social relations as opposed to the disembedded relations of modern economy. The circulation of goods in the Kanak culture has nothing to do with the accumulation of goods, but rather, circulation is defined by giving, not taking.

Therefore, for Temple the universalization of modern market relations leads to the erasure of the basis of Kanak reciprocity and masks the fact that one system is not reducible to the other and that these systems are in fact "antagonistic and do not even beget the same concepts, the same ideologies, the same notion of value. . . and are two different systems of civilization."[15] Central to this difference is the presence of the sacred within reciprocity. This is not the sacredness of a transcendent god, but is a sacredness that is "rigorously and specifically human."[16] In the context of discussions of conservation, this animated sense of being can be more broadly located in all sentient beings, not just in humans. This links human communities with the whole of the life world.

It may seem like quite a leap from the colonial history of the Northwest Atlantic fishery to a discussion of Kanak resistance to French colonization in the South Pacific. What I am trying to point out is that the first step toward a viable discussion of conservation of the natural world requires a challenge to the universalizing categories of modern economy so as to begin to question the intellectual ruin called economic development. This is precisely what Temple is doing in his discussion of the Kanak and the French colonizers. The Kanak base their resistance on a conception of themselves which is of an entirely different order than modern economy. Extricating human communities and natural communities from this production model is central to the conservation project.

Like Aboriginal people in Canada who in full recognition of their cultural difference have set about reclaiming their sense of community from the Canadian Department of Indian Affairs, or like local communities in the Southern hemisphere who struggle against the edicts of international financial institutions, Atlantic coastal communities may have to set about reclaiming control of nearby natural communities on which they have depended. Such a "sea-claim" would be based upon a radically-democratic conception of interrelationships.

In contrast to the regulatory basis of Canada's declaration of the 200-mile limit based on the recognition of predatory international fishing practices – which were then only replicated internally within national boundaries – coastal communities require a more viable ethical and cultural basis for conservation of community which can begin to challenge the causes of ecological instability. This approach then links a broader ethical analysis which does not universalize present historical realities to a cultural strategy for resolving the problem. This strategy attempts to "solve history" by challenging those current realities which it regards as destructive to the viability of human and natural communities.

In a book entitled *Natural Connections: Perspectives in Community-based Conservation*, Marshall Murphree states that community-based conservation has three aspects: a clear "claim" of ownership of the resources in question by the community; a clear definition of the community in question; and democratically-created regulation within the community.[17] It is this social and cultural project of defining community linked to a "sea claim" which can form the viable basis for conservation. Similarly, David Ralph Matthews argues with regard to the Newfoundland fishery that this project involves "reconstructions of meaning" related to the "link between commons and community" that focuses on "the identification with and commitment to community. . ."[18]

There is the added conundrum in this project – as witnessed in the strife between traditionalists and militants in native communities concerned with cultural survival – that in order to resist and challenge in the name of community, there is a risk in becoming your enemy, as it were. Even the more moderate situations related to the negotiation of land claims requires – if we are to accept Temple's contrast between donor cultures and those based on accumulation – that donor cultures stop being themselves in order to "drive a hard bargain." Temple sets out the cultural context of negotiation in this way:

If one puts together a system of reciprocity and an exchange system where both know no other law but their own, so that exchangers think they are dealing with exchangers, and donors dealing with other donors, an accretion takes place between the two systems, but they accrete in favour of the exchange system and its triumph.[19]

This "historical misunderstanding" explains why systems of reciprocity were so readily disorganized by exchange all over the world during the colonial period. It also remains as a serious disadvantage for cultures who are forced to resist and challenge in the name of the gift. Therefore, acts of self-preservation in the modern world can be at odds with the values of these cultures. In these terms the negotiating table can be seen as a site of cultural violence. To save yourself, you have to stop being who you are. After all, gifts are those things in life which can be conspired against, but, most times, cannot be made to happen.

ENDNOTES

[1] Richard Cashin.1993. *Charting a New Course: Toward the Fishery of the Future*. Ottawa: Minister of Supply and Services, pp.vi-vii.

[2] Marshall Sahlins. 1972. *Stone Age Economics*. Chicago: Aldine, p. 182-83, and Dominique Temple. 1988. "The Policy of the Severed Flower" in *INTERculture*, Vol. 21 (1). pp.10-35.

[3] John Livingston. 1994. *Rogue Primate: An Exploration of Human Domestication*. Toronto: Key Porter, p.111.

[4] I discuss this issue at length in *The Oceans are Emptying: Fish Wars and Sustainability*. Montreal:Black Rose Books. 1995.

[5] Lester Brown. 1995. *State of the World.* New York: Norton, p.15.

[6] Canada. 1974. *Law of the Sea Discussion Paper*. Ottawa: Department of External Affairs, p.3.

[7] Fisheries and Marine Science. 1976. *Policy for Canada's Commercial Fisheries*. Ottawa: Dept. of Environment, pp. 63-64.

[8] Bruce Mitchell. 1989. *Geography and Resource Analysis*. London: Longman-Wiley, pp.2-5.

[9] Mitchell (1989:6).

[10] Arthur McEvoy. 1986. *The Fisherman's Problem: Ecology and Law in the California Fisheries, 1850-1980.* New York: Cambridge-University Press. pp. 253-254.

[11] McEvoy. (1986:257)

[12] Anthony Stocks. 1987. "Resource Management in an Amazon Varzea Lake Ecosystem: The Cocamilla Case." *The Question of the Commons*. (Bonnie McCay & James Acheson, eds.) Tuscon: University of Arizona Press, p. 110.

[13] Karl Polanyi. 1968. *Primitive, Archaic and Modern Economics*. (George Dalton, ed.) New York: Doubleday Anchor, p. 174.

[14] Temple (1988: 12).

[15] Temple (1988: 17).

[16] Temple (1988: 24).

[17] David Western and R. Michael Wright, eds. 1995. *Natural Connections: Perspectives in Community-Based Conservation*. Washington: Island Press.

[18] David Ralph Matthews. 1993. *Controlling Common Property: Regulating Canada's East Coast Fishery*. Toronto: University of Toronto Press, p. 94.

[19] Temple (1988: 28).

ETHICS, SURFACE MINING AND THE ENVIRONMENT

(First published in Resource Policy *Vol. 17, No. 10, December 1996. Republished in* Contemporary Moral Issues *— 4th edition (Toronto: McGraw Hill Ryerson, 1997.)*

5
by Wesley Cragg, David Pearson and James Cooney

THIS PAPER DESCRIBES WHAT IS INVOLVED IN BUILDING an ethical component into mine planning, development, operations, closure and site rehabilitation. How best corporate practice measures up to ethical criteria is examined. Finally, reasons for adopting an ethical stance in mining are set out and evaluated.

The Social and Environmental Parameters of Surface Mining

Human endeavour moves more material on the surface of the Earth each year than the ice sheets of the last ice age (Hooke, 1995). Not all of it results from mining but that is the prime reason for such prodigious effort. The Syncrude operation in the Athabasca Tar Sands moves 300,000 tons of bituminous sand a day, while the operation of the Goldstrike mine in Nevada produces 50 kg of gold per day from 325,000 tons of ore. The Bingham Canyon copper mine in Utah is the largest human excavation in the world involving the removal of more than seven times the amount of material excavated to create the Panama Canal (Young, 1992).

The impact of surface mining goes beyond the sheer size of its excavations. The purpose of this paper is to review the variety and scope of those impacts and to present an ethical perspective that in our view ought to shape decisions relating to the planning, development, operation and closure of surface mines.

From a corporate perspective, surface mining has many economic advantages including low production costs, high productivity, low capital investment and short development time. One spe-

cific result is that deposits which would otherwise be uneconomical to mine, can be profitably exploited. On the other hand, it is an extraction process that has a much larger environmental footprint than a normal underground operation, partly because of the excavation itself, but also because of the very large volume of waste rock produced. An open pit can be expected to generate about fifty times more rock waste than an underground mine (Ripley et al., 1978). In the case of many base metal and coal mines, the waste rock frequently contains sulphide minerals that react with rain water and produce acidified run-off, contaminating both surface and ground water.

The excavation itself can be expected to have a significant influence on the flow regime of the ground water in the area especially while it is kept dry during operations of the mine. After closure and rehabilitation of the site, interference with ground water may be due to much more subtle factors such as altered rainwater infiltration rates caused by a disturbed soil profile.

Some aspects of surface mining are similar to those of underground operations. Tailing storage and infra-structure development such as roads, rail lines, housing, and power plants pose the same challenges. All in all, however, there is no doubt that the impact on the "mine site" itself and the off-site or what Marshall (1982) called "shadow" effects are more far reaching than for underground mining particularly with regard to potential conflict with competing land uses, both current and future. A good example is the Falconbridge Thayer Lindsley Mine located about 5 kms from the centre of Sudbury, an underground operation which is barely visible from the nearby road. The issues raised by its development would have been very different had a pit mine been proposed.

Normally, the life of a surface mine will be relatively short. Mining companies are faced, therefore, with the issue of how their use of land as a mine is to be integrated with both prior and subsequent uses and the values associated with each. Is treatment of the excavation and the waste materials generated simply a matter of landscape engineering? Should the goal be to protect the ecosystem of the area from long term damage? Or should mine site rehabilitation have more complex goals such as reintegrating the site with the natural environment of the area?

What this brief overview indicates is that mining companies must decide what values should guide the decisions they make with regard to mine development, mine operations, mine closure and finally the rehabilitation of mine sites when the value of the land for mining purposes has been exhausted. More specifically, what role should be given to ethical considerations in this process?

Ethics and Surface Mining

Surface mining brings with it both costs and benefits. Let us define those who stand to gain or lose from a specific mining development as a mine's stakeholders.[1] What ethics requires is that a company not ignore or externalize stakeholder impacts for which it has a primary responsibility.[2] How then does a company determine what its responsibilities are? The answer has five parts:

1. To begin with, every mining venture requires the voluntary participation and cooperation of a wide range of individuals, groups, organizations and institutions; employees, investors, governments and government departments are examples. For the most part, the relationships that develop with thesestakeholders will be contractual in nature. Adopting an ethical stance requires that a company bargain fairly

in building contractual relationships with voluntary stakeholders. Genuinely voluntary involvement requires informed choice. And informed choice requires in turn, that a company disclose information available to it which could reasonably be expected to affect in a material way a stakeholder's decision to become involved.[3]

2. Adopting an ethical stance also requires a conscientious effort to identify involuntary stakeholders and to identify carefully the nature of their stake in a project. An involuntary stake is created whenever a decision-making process exposes people to direct and significant risks which they would not willingly assume or about which they have no knowledge. When significant risks or impacts are treated as externalities and ignored unless otherwise required by law, the result with few exceptions is the creation of involuntary stakeholders. Externalizing risks and costs transfers them to involuntary stakeholders who may have little to gain by way of benefits in return. Failure by a mine's owners to accept responsibility for cleanup and land reclamation following mine closure is a good example of this process.[4]

3. Adopting an ethical stance requires that a mining company carefully distinguish voluntary and involuntary stakeholder relationships. This is important because of the unbalanced bargaining power, research capability and privileged access to information that mining companies normally have. A community facing depressed economic conditions, or individuals faced with a loss of traditional subsistence harvesting, are not voluntary stakeholders simply because they acquiesce in a mining development. Indeed one of the implications of taking an ethical stance is a willingness to see the voluntary/involuntary distinction as a continuum rather than a dichotomy.

4. Adopting an ethical stance requires that a com-

pany seek and support a fair distribution of costs and benefits for all stakeholders. Fair distribution has three dimensions. The first is mitigation. Industrial activity by its very nature creates risks. Surface mining is obviously no exception. Mitigating risk is a primary moral obligation that will have significant and complex social and environmental dimensions affecting planning, operations, mine closure and site reclamation. Furthermore, it is an obligation which management has to both involuntary and voluntary stakeholders. Hence it will include such things as: environmental protection; sensitivity to cultural, social, economic, religious and subsist-ence impacts; and health and safety issues.

A second dimension is fair compensation for costs or impacts that cannot be mitigated. Typically this will require that mining projects internalize all costs directly attributable to their operations for both voluntary and involuntary stakeholders. Those costs may be the result of environmental damage or pollution, economic or social dislocation (for aboriginal stakeholders, for example), unavoidable health and safety risks to employees and so on. How to determine fair compensation will be one of the most challenging elements in this process.

A third dimension is a fair distribution of benefits from mining operations. This will include: fair wages and benefits; healthy and safe working conditions; a fair return to supporting communities in the form of taxation; corporate and financial involvement in social and environmental projects; a fair return to stockholders; sensitivity to special needs on the part of various stakeholders, for example, disadvantaged minorities, people unable to compete for jobs created by a mining project because of inadequate access to training opportunities, indigenous people and cultures; and so on.

5. Finally, an ethical company has an obligation to avoid harmful impacts on stakeholders from which recovery is likely to be difficult or onerous or perhaps impossible. This will require a willingness not to initiate projects that are likely to impose unacceptable human or environmental risks or costs.

This account with its five components gives rise to three questions. First, is the environment itself a stakeholder? Do mining companies have obligations to protect the environment independently of the costs which environmental impacts might carry for human beings or human communities? This is, of course, a highly contentious issue. Some will argue that the environment should be respected for its own sake and that significant environmental harm should be avoided for its own sake, whether or not the welfare of human beings is either directly or indirectly at risk.

Not surprisingly, environmentalists who argue that the environment should be accorded the status of an independent stakeholder generate deep suspicion and scepticism on the part of resource industries in general and the mining industry in particular. The reason is not hard to find. How, it might be asked, are we to determine whether the disturbance to the environmental status quo inflicted by a mining operation is environmentally harmful? There are answers to this question, of course. Harm occurs, as we have already noted when human beings are adversely impacted. We might extend this to sentient creatures capable of experiencing pain or suffering. At this level mitigation is a plausible response and also clearly achievable in most circumstances. It is hard to see any place in this context, however, for the concept of compensation. Equally, activity that threatens the viability of species is relatively easily described as harmful. Here once again because the notion of harm has a reasonably uncontroversial or at least arguable application, so too does talk of mitigation, and curtailment.

Objections are justified, however, when any activity that visibly disturbs the land is described as damaging or harmful in ways requiring a response involving mitigation, compensation or curtailment. For in most of these cases, curtailment or avoidance will be the only available response since both mitigating all impacts or compensating for impacts that cannot be mitigated will not be possible. And where this is true, it would seem that the only point in identifying the environment as a stakeholder is to provide a rhetorical or ideological platform from which to attack mining and similar extractive activities. The charge would be that these activities are by their nature morally unacceptable or at the least morally suspect.

There is a significant practical sense, however, in which very little turns on the outcome of the theoretical debate about the ethical status of the environment as a stakeholder except for those who believe that mining should be prohibited in principle because of the environmental impacts it unavoidably has. This is because the nature of surface mining and the environmental risks and costs associated with it are increasingly well known. Combined with this is increasing recognition on the part of leading mining companies with a commitment to respecting "best practice" standards as well as the environmentally concerned public of the interconnected nature of environmental and human well-being. Finally, protecting the environment has an unavoidably social dimension since what we are seeking is protection from *human* activity.[5]

What this implies, we suggest, is that there is very little practical justification for treating environmental and social issues in isolation. Anyone seriously concerned about human well-being must also be concerned about environmental protection and well-being. Equally, though perhaps more controversially, anyone seriously concerned about the environment must take human well-being into account, since finding and implementing solutions will require human cooperation. Our position, then, is that in practice it is not necessary to treat the environment as a stakeholder in order to ensure that environmental values are carefully weighed and protected in the planning and operation of surface mines. What would appear to be required, however, is a willingness to incorporate an ethical perspective into all aspects of mining activity.

There is a second question that also needs to be addressed. The framework just sketched is essentially open in structure. It does not and cannot generate algorithms leading in advance to a hard edged set of universal rules for mining. If the approach suggested is correct, what ethics requires is commitment to a process of evaluation that cannot be achieved in practice without honest and open stakeholder involvement and assessment. But is this adequate? Does it not leave too much room for individual interpretation and application?

This kind of worry about our ethically oriented model, though understandable, is not justified. In practice, the process we have described will lead to explicit, concrete, project-specific rules and principles. These rules and principles will have clear implications for projects to which they apply. It is true that the principles that emerge for one case will not necessarily apply to the next one. This is a strength, however, and not a weakness. What is required in an advanced country with developed educational institutions and a sophisticated modern economy will not parallel ethical requirements for developments in non-cash economy contexts, to take just one example.

At its most basic, ethics requires sensitivity to the impacts of one's activities on others. Evaluating projects from the perspective of all stakeholders ensures this kind of sensitivity.

Finally, our ethical model gives rise to a third set of questions. Is our proposal practical? Would adopting an ethical stance as we describe it make any difference to companies that are already comany difference to companies that are already committed to "best practice" standards in their mining operations? Equally important, what can we learn from a study of current best practice about the need or justifiability of building ethics into the planning, development, operation and closure of surface mines? The remainder of our discussion will focus on these questions.

Current Best Practice

As a practical matter, mining companies, like all large industrial organizations, have a natural tendency to define "ethics" narrowly. What this means is that ethics will be defined in terms of the obligations employees owe the company and the obligations the company owes to employees. Individuals working in a company are likely therefore to be subject to a code of conduct (e.g. honesty in financial transactions, respect for company property, avoidance of conflict of interest, etc.), infractions of which may result in company imposed sanctions if they are detected. Most companies will assume that any wider ethical obligations, to society at large for example, will generally be set out in law (e.g. full and fair disclosure of material information to all shareholders, possession of valid operating permits for all activities requiring regulatory approval, maintenance of health and safety standards for all employees, honest and transparent accounting practices, etc.). Infractions by a company of norms of this kind may well incur legal sanctions.

Companies and individuals in companies are also guided by values that go beyond the norms established in codes of conduct and legal regulations, values like teamwork, recognition of individual and group achievement, responsiveness to community and environmental concerns, and so on. Finally, there are the patterns of thinking that shape how a company learns from and about the world around it and how it makes decisions. For mining companies, reflecting as they do an engineering mentality, the process of acquiring infor-

mation is likely to invoke descriptors such as sensory, concrete, analytical and solution oriented (as opposed to intuitive, abstract, theoretical and process oriented). Information for mining companies consists essentially of facts (e.g. ore grades, environmental baseline conditions, measured public opinion) on which strategy is based, rather than relationships within which objectives are pursued. The decision-making style of mining companies can be described as traditionally having been command and control, or top-down management. The conventional management/union divide further accentuates this traditional decision-making style.

However, at the cutting edge of innovation (strategic planning, community relations, etc.), mining companies are less readily characterized by their traditional information-acquisition processes and decision-making practices. The external world within which mining companies must formulate their strategies is a complex interaction of dynamic systems (governments, communities, special interest groups, markets, investors, etc.). Mining companies themselves are dynamic systems, learning organizations whose value orientations, information acquisition processes and decision-making practices evolve in response to the lessons of experience. Successful interaction of a mining company with these other dynamic systems, its key stakeholder groups, requires the use of intuitive, open-minded information-acquisition processes and of consensus-building, bottom-up decision-making practices.

Success for most mining companies will consist of wealth maximization from projects for shareholders through efficient long-term operations. That is to say, mining companies are intentional communities formed for the purpose of wealth maximization. To abandon this goal in pursuit of other objectives is likely to be considered unethical. In this respect, companies resemble other intentional communities, such as environmental special interest groups, and can be distinguished from organic communities, such as indigenous or local communities. This difference has a bearing on the sort of negotiations a mining company engages in with different sorts of stakeholders.

Projects which are generally supported by governments, communities and significant special interest groups are less likely to be subject to conflicts capable of creating inefficiency (perhaps in the extreme even personal risks for employees) and of eroding returns to shareholders. Minimizing conflict, therefore, is the main motivitator for dealing with stakeholders. Long-term support, however, is not simply a matter of decisions reached through consultation and negotiation, no matter how involved and protracted, but of carefully nursed on-going relationships.

Large mining companies, by virtue of the resources at their command, have the ability to influence the direction in which thinking and even values evolve in various stakeholder groups. Exerting such influence is a legitimate part of the mutual education process; however, the message must be credible, with an objective and balanced description of costs as well as benefits. Stakeholder groups must feel that they have arrived at conclusions about projects on their own without being manipulated. Otherwise, their support once achieved may not be sustainable in the long term. The most successful relational strategy for a mining company will be, therefore, to put as much (or more) emphasis on receiving and adjusting to messages as on getting messages out. In circumstances where a stakeholder group does not have the ability or resources to reach constructive decisions about a project (i.e. in their own best interest in light of their particular values and objectives), it is in the interest of the mining company to provide appropriate assistance, generally not directly but through a third party whose primary loyalty will be to the stakeholder group, but who will be neutral with respect to the issues at stake.

Generally speaking, the direct cost of consultation and consensus building with stakeholder groups, while involving considerable time and effort on the part of staff people, is marginal in the overall economics of most mining projects. Mitigation and compensation costs which may be agreed to as necessary because of environmental or social disturbance are also likely to be affordable by most projects, as long as the decisions fairly reflect reality. Building consensus around realistic expectations may not be easily achieved, however. Many stakeholder groups understandably will see a major mining project as an opportunity to press their wish list on the project proponent, inflating all and any costs associated with the project while making little reference to project benefits. For example, a municipal government may stress a project's impact on physical and social infrastructure (roads, schools, etc.) without calculating the increased direct and indirect cash flow to the municipal treasury from new residences and businesses. Similarly, an indigenous community may stress a project's impact on traditional culture and lifestyle without reference to the benefits of up-graded education and industrial skill training for its members.

Sustaining broad-based support by stakeholders over the long-term ultimately requires that the benefits anticipated are realistic, that realistic expectations materialize and that commitments are respected. It also requires that conditions surrounding the project be reviewed periodically and agreements between the mining company and stakeholders be adjusted if appropriate. For example, sometimes in the case of communities with little experience of mining, employment expectations will be unrealistic. The number of long-term jobs likely to be created by a projected may be exaggerated. Equally, a company may underestimate the capacity of a community to provide trained and motivated employees. In both cases, employment targets may need to be revised over time to better reflect reality. The same may also be true of profits earned and how they are shared, environmental impacts and what is needed to deal with them adequately and so on.

In summary, mining companies have good pragmatic reasons for consulting effectively with all stakeholders and adapting projects to reflect legitimate concerns and interests just because minimizing conflict and building public support is in a company's own long term best interest. Pursuing these goals, therefore, does not seem to require an ethical justification for a company with an intelligent, far-sighted understanding of its own interests.

Ethics and Best Practice Compared

What our account to this point suggests is that a mining company committed to best practice will treat its stakeholders in much the same way whether guided by explicitly ethical commitments as we have described them on the one hand or by long-term profit maximization on the other. Why is this so? The reason, we suggest, lies with the law. In the developed world, voluntary stakeholders are protected by human rights laws, laws establishing health and safety standards, collective bargaining rights and so on. Environmental protection acts and their various relatives protect involuntary stakeholders. The courts are available to test contracts built on inaccurate or misleading information or unfair bargaining based on significant power imbalances thus ensuring that the involvement of voluntary stakeholders is genuinely voluntary. Increasingly, the law places a high cost on a failure to mitigate harmful environmental impacts, requires fair compensation for the harmful impacts that cannot be mitigated, and ensures a fair (though arguably only a minimally fair) distribution of benefits through taxation, minimum wages, paid holidays, universal health coverage, pensions and so on. Finally the risk of court imposed liability for corporate activity that seriously harms either people or the environment is now so severe that the temptation to cut corners has been significantly reduced. In short, it would

appear that, in the developed world, risk averse, consensus-oriented strategic planning makes ethics redundant.

It might be objected that ethics and intelligent, pragmatic, profit maximization are likely to have parallel results only in industrially advanced democracies with fully developed legal systems. Proponents of a pragmatic rather than an ethical model of strategic planning will have a short answer to this worry, however. The world, they are likely to point out, has become a global village. Electronic communications have brought various parts of the world much closer together. A company that meets only local legal standards in its world wide operations risks exposure and censure by an aggressive media and a concerned public. It follows that, if a company's goal is to minimize conflict and maintain good public relations, it will set high standards for its operations in all parts of the world whether required to do so by law or not.

Should we be concerned that the social good that comes from enlightened mining practices is not motivated by ethical considerations? Some will answer yes to this questions. But if we understand the focus of ethics to be the quality of life of the people and communities in which business transactions are conducted, the motivation of those contributing to the achievement of this goal seems less significant. If environmental protection is our goal, does it matter why a mining company sets out to achieve high environmental standards in its operation?

Let us accept for the limited purposes of this discussion that having the "right" motivation is less important than achieving good results. Can we then set aside explicitly ethical considerations in favour of intelligent pragmatic strategies for pursuing mining company objectives, as this line of argument suggests?

Ethics and Surface Mining

The pragmatic, profit maximizing alternative to ethics builds on three things: a narrow interpretation of corporate ethical responsibilities, respect for prevailing cultural norms and laws, and good public relations aimed at minimizing conflict. Is this an adequate "ethics substitute"? Let us conclude with four reasons for scepticism in this regard and an observation. These observations may help to explain why in practice genuinely enlightened mining is so rare.

1. A company that seeks to maximize profits for its shareholders and interprets its ethical responsibilities narrowly will find it hard to resist narrow interpretations of its legal responsibilities. Note that modern (e.g. common law) legal traditions are confrontational and not consensus-building in character. As a consequence, narrow interpretations of legal responsibility almost always militate against honestly, frankly and openly engaging in the kind of stakeholder dialogue that we have argued ethics (as we describe it) requires and is designed to facilitate.

2. Interpreting both law and ethics narrowly will impact on how legal, political and community relations risks are identified and interpreted and to whom a company assigns the burden of proof in identifying risks that need to be addressed. Risk assessment is not value free. How a company weighs risks will be shaped ultimately by how it defines its responsibilities. A company that takes the view that its primary (ethical) responsibility is to maximize shareholder value will evaluate risks to other stakeholders quite differently from a company that believes that its ethical obligations require that it balance the interests of all its stakeholders in making decisions.[6]

3. As we point out above, mining companies are themselves significant players in shaping public attitudes through public relations initiatives, lobbying and public education. Guided by a desire to maximize profit, a narrow interpretation of its ethical responsibilities and the goal of minimizing conflict, a mining company will have little reason to identify culturally invisible, or disliked stakeholders, carefully evaluate their stake and give them project status. What is more, such a company will have little reason to try to persuade the influential public to take a broad rather than a narrow view of either the public's or its own responsibilities toward such individuals or groups, particularly since doing so might well generate risks to profit maximization that would otherwise be avoided.

4. Finally, a company that does not build an ethical dimension into its strategic planning may thereby lose a key tool for anticipating and leading developments in public attitudes. In other words, consciously adopting an ethical stance may be important to understanding and participating effectively in public debate and the development of public policy. This is because considerations of fairness are influential in public debate. Ethics also plays a key role in building respect and trust, both of which are vital to open and cooperative dialogue and good community relations. As a consequence, ethics provides a reliable foundation for building good community relations.

It is worth noting, however, that arguments of the sort just canvassed have a certain ironic quality. They imply that in their own long term interests, mining companies have good pragmatic reasons for putting ethics ahead of profit maximization. An ethical company will balance profit maximization with a commitment to respect the interests of all its stakeholders as important in their own right. Furthermore, an ethical company will seek to balance the interests of all its stakeholders whether it has identified a financial benefit in so doing or not.

There is a final industry-based consideration that also points to the need for articulated ethical guidelines. Clearly, some mining companies are committed to best practice standards with their implications (as we have described them above) for sound social and environmental policies. These companies are industry leaders. However, if the standards of the industry as a whole are to be brought to best practice standards, each company's own judgement of what is in its long-term interests is unlikely to have the effect of raising standards to a uniformly high level. There are therefore powerful pragmatic reasons for the industry as a whole to define the social and environmental obligations of mining companies in terms of ethical principles.

To conclude, adopting an ethical stance requires that a company balance a variety of stakeholder values as important in their own right. We have not explored in this paper how that balancing is to be achieved. Nevertheless, we can say that in our view adopting an ethical perspective does not require that the interests of all stakeholders be given the same weight in all decisions. How to balance stakeholder interests however, must await development at another time.

What our discussion does show however is that enlightened environmental and social practices guided either explicitly or implicitly by ethical considerations should have a central role in surface mining.

ENDNOTES

[1] A stake is defined by the Oxford English Dictionary as an interest, something to be gained or lost or something at risk. A stakeholder is someone who stands to gain or lose directly from a mining operation, or someone who is put at risk by decisions having to do with a mining development or its closure.

[2] For a more detailed articulation of stakeholder theory which sets out the parameters of the view assumed in our analysis see "A Risk Based Model of Stakeholder Theory" (Max Clarkson, Director, The Centre from Corporate Social Performance and Ethics, The School of Management, The University of Toronto, unpublished).

[3] This is a widely accepted requirement for establishing the existence of a contract in law. It is also a recognized requirement in investment regulations and other areas of business where ensuring informed choice is a recognized obligation.

[4] The decision of Galactic Resources to declare bankruptcy and thus avoid costs resulting from a leak from an ore leaching pad that poisoned 27 km of the Alamoso River in Colorado as well as adjacent farms and ranches is an illustration. (Discussed in *The Corporate Ethics Monitor*, Vol 6, Issue 4, July-August 1994.)

[5] For an interesting recent discussion on this theme see "Uncertainty, Resource Exploitation, and Conservation: Lessons from History" by Donald Ludwig, Ray Hilborn, and Carl Walters in *Science*, 2 April 1993, Vol. 260 pp. 17 & 36. The authors of the article conclude: "Resource problems are not really environmental problems: They are human problems that we have created at many times and in many places, under a variety of political, social and economic systems."

[6] For a discussion of the role of values in risk assessment see *Value Assumptions in Risk Assessment: A Case Study of the Alachlor Controversy* by Conrad Brunk, Lawrence Haworth and Brenda Lee (Waterloo: Wilfred Laurier Press, 1991).

References

Ripley, E.A., R.E. Redman & J. Maxwell 1978. *Environmental Impact of Mining in Canada*. In National Impact of Mining #7. Centre for Resource Studies, Queen's University, Kingston, Canada.

Hooke, R. 1995. "Humans Outdo Nature in Moving Earth". American Association for the Advancement of Science Annual Meeting.

Marshall, I.G. 1982. *Mining, Land Use, and The Environment*. Lands Directorate, Environment Canada, Ottawa.

Young, J.E. 1992. Mining the Earth. In L.R. Brown (ed.) *The State of the World* 1992. New York: W.W. Norton.

The authors wish to acknowledge Social Science and Humanities Research Council (Applied Ethics) funding assistance for this project.

ETHICS FOR NEW LIFE FORMS

APPLYING THE PRECAUTIONARY PRINCIPLE TO THE REGULATION OF BIOTECHNOLOGY[1]

6

by David Oppenheim & Robert Gibson

UNTIL RECENTLY, HUMANITY'S ABILITY TO CONTROL living things was limited to manipulating the external environment. While we could change the observed characteristics of things through careful breeding, determine where organisms lived and what they ate, we were forced to respect the barriers imposed by biology. This changed when the advent of recombinant DNA (rDNA) technologies in the 1970's enabled scientists to begin treating genetic codes as interchangeable building blocks. Now, scientists are able to engineer life, to change the environment and ourselves from within by extracting desired traits from one species and inserting them into another. This fusion of biology and technology has propelled us to a biotechnological age which includes crops resistant to pesticides, cows which produce more milk, and fish which grow faster and larger than normal. Other products that are in the research and development stage and expected soon to appear in the marketplace include gene-therapies to fight genetically-triggered diseases and crops that produce compounds used to make plastic.

Biotechnology's promoters say the industry is growing swiftly and will be our economic salvation. A 1994 advertising supplement in the Toronto *Globe and Mail* asserted that biotechnology is not only "essential to the future" but also "an engine for the economy."[2] Some experts believe biotechnology will play a role in up to 70 percent of Canada's GNP by the year 2010.[3]

At the same time, biotechnology raises considerable fears. The main immediate concerns centre on the potential effects of open-environment (outside the laboratory) use of new, genetically-engineered life forms. Critics have argued that such products could have negative effects on human health, endanger natural species, including commercially important ones, and disrupt associated ecological systems and communities. Some have gone further, suggesting that biotechnology could undermine the security of basic attitudes about human identity and what is natural.

While there are disagreements about the likelihood and significance of the possible problems, the need for an effective system of regulation is recognized. In Canada, the federal government's response has generally followed the conventional approach to environmental regulation, which assumes the basic desirability of the technology because of anticipated economic benefits and seeks to avoid or mitigate associated problems of particular processes, products or applications. Market demand is seen as an effective and sufficient indicator of overall product desirability, and regulatory action is seen as a vehicle for ensuring safeguards are in place to address potential negative effects in specific cases.

The conventional regulatory approach here is risk-based environmental assessment. This requires the case by case assessment of proposed applications, with technical evaluation of threats to human health and safety and environmental quality, and expert determination of the acceptability of these risks to affected parties.

Critics of this approach to the regulation of biotechnology point to a number of problems with risk assessment and the case specific focus. They argue that while the market system may be good at identifying possible benefits of new products and applications, it provides inadequate incentives and mechanisms for identifying negative effects of biotechnologies and other such innovations. This is true especially where the negative effects include the cumulative, interrelated effects of many products and applications and where the negative effects are imposed on public goods or on individuals who do not have enough political and economic ability to protect their interest. In response to the market's inadequacy, the critics propose careful regulatory control. They insist, however, that simple case-by-case assessments and permit requirements would be insufficient. The limited predictability of biotechnology's effects, and the need to face its cumulative or overall implications for ecological and socio-economic systems and for basic attitudes to humanity and nature, make biotechnology regulation a larger and unavoidably value-laden challenge. Consequently, the regulatory regime for biotechnology should be designed to include processes for making broad, explicitly ethical judgements in the face of uncertainties and difficult trade-offs. Furthermore, given the risks and uncertainties of biotechnology, the regulation of its products and processes must be approached with cautious anticipation and avoidance of potential problems. Such an approach, emphasizing precaution and requiring a democratic process for making collective, anticipatory decisions on what values to apply in the guidance as well as regulation of biotechnology development, would stand in sharp contrast to the conventional favouring of technical, information-based, case-specific decision making.

Our culture has seldom been inclined to confront the profound changes that accompany technological innovation. As Langdon Winner has observed, "the interesting puzzle in our times is that we so willingly sleepwalk through the process of reconstituting the conditions of human existence."[4] Deliberations on biotechnology so far offer a good case in point. Most official attention to the subject has focused on how to drive the

bandwagon faster, to attain the leading edge, enhance competitiveness and reap the lion's share of benefits. When regulatory matters have been raised, the discussions rarely have included serious attention to the broader and deeper issues concerning the future it may bring and the desirability of guiding this powerful vehicle for change along a more responsible path toward a more attractive end.

As a contribution to consideration of a more ambitious approach, this paper reviews the regulatory challenge of biotechnology and outlines a mechanism for selecting and using ecological, social, and economic principles and criteria to guide biotechnology development and approvals. The proposed "precautionary screening process" – an elaboration of a notion already raised by researchers with the Canadian Institute for Environmental Law and Policy[5] – would provide for open, explicitly value-laden decision making that recognizes ethical questions beyond immediate and case-specific issues of risk to human health and the environment. Its conclusions would be used to direct biotechnology research into areas of social importance.

The first section of the paper briefly examines the issues surrounding biotechnology and the need for its regulation. This is followed by a critique of the existing regulatory approach, highlighting its main deficiencies with respect to biotechnology. The final portion of the paper sets out the "precautionary screening process" as a possible response to the identified deficiencies of the existing approach.

We do not make large claims for our work here. The analysis and proposal are general and preliminary; much more careful deliberations are needed to design a workable regulatory regime that incorporates a precautionary screen or its equivalent. We do hope, however, that the idea will spur discussion not only concerning application to biotechnology regulation, but also concerning the larger set of broadly technological developments that promise to reconstitute the conditions of human existence.

Promises and Fears of Biotechnology

Biotechnology can be broadly defined to refer to "the use of living organisms, or parts thereof, for the production of goods and services."[6] Under this definition, any product or process derived from living organisms, including commercially used bacteria, fungi, yeasts and plants, would be classified as biotechnology. Techniques considered conventional by today's standards, such as selective breeding and the use of bacteria to make cheese, are examples of the historic use of biotechnology for human benefit. Indeed, proponents of biotechnology point to these techniques to illustrate the existence of a "safe" precedent for today's biotechnologies. For them, the new genetic engineering techniques are merely an extension of age-old practices.

In the last twenty years, the development of recombinant DNA techniques (rDNA) and cell fusion has enabled scientists to transfer desired traits (genetic material) from one species to another, eradicating previous biological barriers. While the process is complex, the essential innovation is the ability of scientists to bypass the sexual compatibility limits of traditional cross-breeding. Genes from fish, tomatoes, humans, indeed any living organism, can now be interchanged to produce new life forms. The products or processes of this genetic engineering define modern biotechnology.

Innovator canola, developed by the agrochemical company AgroEvo for tolerance to their herbicide Liberty has been approved by Agriculture Canada for commercial use. The Flavr Savr, a slower ripening tomato, and milk from cows given recombinant Bovine Growth Hormone (rBGH), a genetically engineered hormone designed to increase a cow's milk production by up to 20 percent, are two products in use in the United States and which may soon appear on the shelves of Canadian consumers. Soon to follow will be porcine growth hormone which produces leaner pigs, plants which produce a variety of chemicals and possibly even vaccines, and numerous other products with applications in the fields of human health, agriculture, forestry, fisheries, mining, petrochemicals, even waste water treatment and other aspects of environmental protection.[7]

Although biotechnology is only in its formative stages, its rapid growth has inspired intense debate. Along with the perceived benefits of biotechnology, citizen, labour and agricultural groups have identified concerns ranging from biodiversity losses resulting from increased focus on genetically-engineered monocultures,[8] to social justice effects of patenting genetically-engineered versions of seeds developed freely by generations of third-world farmers.[9] Other concerns include ecological disruptions from escaped self-replicating organisms,[10] environmental and economic implications of herbicide-resistant crops that favour more chemically-intensive agriculture and greater dependence on a few multinational corporations,[11] and the broader philosophical implications for our sense of human identity once rDNA techniques are applied generally to correct human abnormalities and meet prevailing standards of beauty and appearance.[12]

Such changes are not entirely unprecedented. Human technological evolution has already brought enormous change to human and ecological systems. While biotechnology will likely bring new social behaviours, economic and political arrangements, ecological systems, attitudes to nature and even definitions of humanity, it can also be seen as merely another step along an established path of evolution.

The issue is whether it is a step too far. A central fear is that genetic engineering applications will take us from manipulating nature in the human interest to severing our link with what is natural, both in ourselves and in life around us. Biotechnology's critics argue that we must at least assess the implications of altering the basic building blocks of life,[13] and consider whether we should limit biotechnology on the basis of an ethical judgement that exerting so much control over the biological commons would take us beyond our proper role in the ecosystem. If we view our relationship to the surrounding world as being within rather than apart from the ecosystem, then perhaps we are ethically bound to observe a degree of restraint.

Proponents of biotechnology argue that since we are already at point D in controlling life then point E is both inevitable and justified. In the case of rBGH, advocates argue that it is "just another tool"; since we already control much of a cow's life (how it is raised, what it eats, what sire it is bred with, etc.), rBGH is not a significant departure from our present practices. It is just the next logical development.[14] This is not entirely reassuring, however. Like a carrot prompting a cart horse, technology entices us forward in a way that keeps us from noticing much about the road ahead. Each offering results in such a slight movement that by the time we realize we are far from home, no serious re-examination of our fate seems possible. Gradual evolutionary steps in the technological manipulation of nature have moved us ever closer to the point of no return where we will have essentially disconnected ourselves from our environment. Developing and using genetic engineering techniques to reinvent all species, including ourselves, could be the step that passes this point.

The tendency towards a redefinition of what is human or what is natural rests on the reductionist view of living organisms as packages of interchangeable parts. Abby Lippman, a genetic epidemiologist, refers to this process in the biotechnological age as geneticization. As applied to humans, geneticization is

the ongoing process by which differences

between individuals are reduced to their DNA codes, with most disorders, behaviours and physiological variations defined, at least in part, as genetic in origin. It refers as well to the process by which interventions employing genetic technologies are adopted to manage problems of health. Through this process, human biology is incorrectly equated with human genetics, implying that the latter acts alone to make us each the organism she or he is.[15]

Biotechnology is not the only force at work in the reduction of humans to replaceable parts. Plastic surgery, new reproductive technologies and virtual reality are also contributors to the practice of treating human individuals essentially as collections of components to be saved, manipulated and recreated. The result, according to Jeffrey Deitch, is a redefinition of what it means to be human:

Social and scientific trends are converging to shape a new conception of self, a new construction of what it means to be a human being. The matter of fact acceptance of one's "natural" looks and one's "natural" personality is being replaced by a growing sense that it is normal to reinvent oneself."[16]

The Human Genome Project intends to map and sequence all the genetic information characteristics of human beings. Its proponents expect it to enable development of genetic screening tests for numerous genetic defects and disorders. It could also facilitate selecting among human fetuses, job applicants and future spouses.[17] An associated $23-35 million project is collecting and storing DNA from hundreds of "endangered" indigenous human communities or "isolates of historic interest" worldwide, in the expectation that identified differences in genetic make-up might prove scientifically and medically useful in the future.[18]

As with genetic engineering itself, these and other such initiatives both promise considerable benefits and provide openings for serious abuses. They raise a host of specific philosophical, ethical and legal questions (for example about genetic privacy, discrimination, abortion, liability and eugenics). But their most profound effects may be on our understanding "what it means to be a human being."

David Jennex argues that genetic engineering, by reducing life to its component parts (DNA), threatens to undermine our sense of self and our capacity to view living things as subjective entities which embody a sense of purpose.[19] In a brave new world of genetically engineered life and virtual nature we will have lost much of our usual grounds for establishing meaning. The implications for how we will then see and treat ourselves, our fellow humans and our environment are unknown, but could easily be destructive to community, ecology and individual mental health.

Worries about such effects will, for some, provide grounds for arguing that biotechnologies should simply be banned. But a good case can also be made that biotechnology could bring important benefits for humans and even for ecosystems. Achieving the benefits while avoiding the negative effects and facing the surrounding ethical issues, is the challenge for biotechnology regulation.[20]

The Conventional Regulatory Approach and its Deficiencies

Canada does not yet have a specific regulatory framework devoted to biotechnology products and processes. A variety of existing laws and guidelines apply to certain aspects of biotechnology research and application. For example, studies and applications in contained laboratory conditions may be generally subject to provincial occupational health and safety laws, and good practice in medical research involving genetic manipulation is encouraged by guidelines developed by the federal government's Medical Research Council.[21] Specific releases of genetically-engineered organ-

isms into the environment may be covered by sectorally focused legislation including federal and provincial laws regulating pesticide products and uses, food and drug laws, the federal *Fisheries Act,* and agricultural legislation concerning seeds, plants and fertilizers.[22] In so far as certain biotechnology products may be classified as "toxic" substances, they may also be covered by the *Canadian Environmental Protection Act,* [23] and it is possible that some biotechnology "projects" or "physical activities" might be included under the new *Canadian Environmental Assessment Act.* [24]

This patchwork approach, relying on legislation that for the most part was not designed to address the particular challenges of biotechnology regulation, has long been recognised as unsatisfactory.[25] In partial response, the federal government's 1990 *Green Plan* included a commitment to establish a more coherent national regulatory regime for biotechnology.[26] The promised new regime, still under development, was to include national standards and codes of practices for certain biotechnology activities, supported by new regulatory initiatives under the *Canadian Environmental Protection Act.* [27] But the expected result will still rely on a multiplicity of existing and new laws, and critics argue that it will fall short of providing a comprehensive regime for biotechnology regulation.[28]

In the anticipated regulatory approach, the focus is still to be on case-specific evaluation and, where necessary, control of specific products, processes and applications.[29] Most regulatory deliberations and actions will be initiated only after proponents have completed their research and development work and have sought permits for new products or activities (e.g. importing, manufacturing, testing or using new genetically-engineered products).[30] This fragmentation of biotechnology control into a multitude of decisions increases the likelihood of regulatory gaps and inconsistencies. In particular, it discourages attention to cumulative effects and other larger issues surrounding biotechnology and its regulation. The reactive focusing of regulatory action on permit applications also discourages anticipatory attention to larger issues. Even consideration of case-specific concerns tends to be more difficult if regulatory involvement is left to the end of the proposal development process when proponents of planned products and activities have already made substantial investments.

Finally, there are doubts about risk assessment, the main evaluatory methodology to be used in the case by case permit application reviews. If the traditional approach to risk assessment is followed, the regulatory deliberations will involve first assessing the product's potential risk or threat to environmental quality and to human health and safety, and then attempting to calculate the acceptability of the identified risks to the potentially affected parties.[31] Challenges to the appropriateness and adequacy of the risk-based approach for biotechnology regulation[32] centre on five main concerns:

(i) there is inadequate information for risk calculation

Conventional risk-assessment relies on reasonable confidence in information base and analytical methods used for predicting and evaluating effects. Especially in the first phase of the risk-assessment process – calculating the potential risk of a technological product or process – the task is seen as a scientific and technical matter. This is reasonable enough where there is reliable and comprehensive information about the nature and severity of possible effects, but is problematic where the information base is weak.

In the case of biotechnology, some methodologies exist for laboratory and field tests and proponents express confidence that the results are reliable. Biotechnology, however, is devoted to producing new life forms. Its products are alive and ecologically alien; the current research base is limited and the variety of possible products, applications and routes along which these life forms and

their effects can move is enormous. The potential effects are therefore likely to be extraordinarily difficult to predict with confidence.

Because even the most thorough and comprehensive assessments of a proposed biotechnology will be incomplete, regulatory decisions will necessarily involve choices concerning how to evaluate the importance of uncertain and unknown factors. Regulators must, for example, decide whether and how far to err on the side of caution. Such choices are inevitably value-laden; they reflect the preferences of the decision makers. Who decides and what preferences prevail are therefore crucial issues in regulatory process design. Simple reliance on risk assessment methods applied by experts is not satisfactory. The processes must be designed to face – openly, explicitly and democratically – the need to make choices among possible responses to uncertainties.

(ii) risk acceptability cannot be determined scientifically

Traditional risk-based assessment, which often fails to recognize the value-laden aspects of scientific or technical work in defining risks, tends also to underplay the political and moral questions surrounding determination of what levels and kinds of risks are socially acceptable level. As Mausberg *et al* note, this aspect of the risk-benefit model is problematic because it "attempts to use science to resolve political and moral questions, something which science itself insists it cannot do."[33]

Here too it is evident that the necessary corrective involves explicitly recognizing that value-laden choices must be made, and ensuring that the regulatory regime includes an appropriate process for making these choices.[34]

(iii) the product-specific focus of risk-based assessment misses overall and cumulative effects concerns

Conventional technology regulation typically uses risk-based assessments in decisions about individual product approvals. Sometimes, for the sake of streamlining approvals, the assessments are scoped somewhat more broadly to review defined families of closely-related products.[35] But only questions of risk and safety are addressed. More comprehensive concerns are ignored or treated as matters outside the regulatory sphere that must be addressed, if at all, as matters of policy.

Where there are no serious concerns beyond the individual product level, or where such concerns have been addressed and resolved through public debate on the policy issues, narrowly-focused regulatory assessments may be adequate. In the case of biotechnology, however, it is clear that there are broad scale concerns about potential effects and ethical implications of biotechnology applications, and that these have not yet been addressed through an open assessment of biotechnology policy.[36] Many of the major concerns raised by critics of biotechnology centre on cumulative risks and overall effects that cannot be assessed comprehensively or efficiently at the individual product or even family-of-products level.[37] While a product-specific assessment could be expected to address the risk that a particular genetically engineered crop variety might transfer its traits to wild varieties, it would not be well-suited to address issues of patenting equity, cumulative effects on genetic diversity and overall socio-economic implications for family farms. As Jennex has observed,

> ... raising piecemeal issues concerning the likely consequences of our being exposed to specific commodities will not prevent the gradual integration of recombinant products into our daily lives, with the result that we will one day forget that we had felt a deeper unease regarding how genetic engineering might impact on the status of life itself.[38]

An adequate biotechnology regulation process would have to include or be integrated with a process for assessing the relevant policy-level issues

concerning overall and cumulative effects.

(iv) risk-assessments of products ready for approval come too late in the decision making process

Regulatory decision making initiated at the product approval stage is naturally biased in favour of approvals. By this time the proponent has already devoted substantial resources to product research and development; expectations have been raised and important investments may hang in the balance. Facing these realities, most regulatory authorities are understandably loath to issue rejections.

Environmentalists and others have frequently decried regulatory bias in late-stage project and product approvals, and have lobbied for corrective action to strengthen the voice of intervenors and increase the accountability of decision making. Where such reforms have been made, a variety of important improvements have resulted. Nonetheless, late rejections remain rare and costly. All sides have reason to seek a solution that would be more effective, efficient and fair.

The most promising possibilities lie in clear *a priori* definition of the criteria for judgement and early determination of what is and what is not likely to be worthy of approval. This could include early product-specific decision making - for example, screening product ideas at the conceptual stage. But the setting of criteria would also involve addressing broader policy-level issues. And success of both the criteria setting and the screening would depend on application of a fair and credible decision-making process.

(v) the risk-based approach is traditionally weak in considering risks and distributional effects

Generally, the desired benefits of proposed new technologies are more likely to be anticipated, described and evaluated than potentially negative side-effects and other problems.[39] The benefits always have proponents, who are often well-organized, well-funded and capable in the technical work of supplying appropriate arguments for formal assessments. The task of ensuring adequate attention to the less predictable risks often falls largely to the potential victims or their representatives. Where the anticipated benefits are great, those who expect to receive the benefits are naturally inclined to demand firm evidence in support of any claims about significant risks or other reasons for hesitation and restriction. The combination of a heavy burden of "proof" placed on the potential victims of risks, and the relative difficulty of identifying and evaluating these risks, tends to favour to the benefits over the risks and the proponents over the victims.[40] This effect is exacerbated when the assessment and decision making process is not designed to facilitate the participation of public intervenors.[41]

An associated weakness of most risk-benefit work is inattention to the distribution of benefits and risks or costs.[42] The objective in the end is usually to weigh the former against the latter to reach an overall conclusion. The general global experience with economic and technological innovations in recent decades, however, suggests that the benefits typically accrue to those who are already advantaged while the negative effects fall disproportionately to the already disadvantaged. "Net gains" that disregard increasing disparities are morally questionable and, in the long run, contribute to misery, division and insecurity that are destructive for everyone.

Some of these problems could be addressed through revision of the prevailing approach to risk assessment. Certainly risk-assessment methodologies could pay more attention to questions of distribution and include more sophisticated compensatory mechanisms to account for information limitations, but the necessary decision making for these and other such steps is as much ethical as technical. How the necessary choices are made, and by whom, are central issues and establishment of a credible public process for making the choices

would have to be included in risk-assessment revisions.

Such revisions to risk assessment at the case-specific level would not be enough by themselves, however. They would not, for example, address the evident needs for comprehensive assessment of the overall and cumulative effects issues or provide earlier indication of what kinds of biotechnology processes, products and risks are or are not likely to be worthy of approval. What appears to be needed is an additional mechanism that would provide both comprehensive assessment and early guidance for the industry. Such a mechanism could be provided in a precautionary screening process.

Addressing the Deficiencies – Instituting a Precautionary Screen

The rationale for precaution in biotechnology regulation rests on recognition of uncertainty. The risks of biotechnology applications cannot be predicted with confidence and unanticipated effects, both specific and cumulative, could be deeply regrettable. Consequently, we must always presume there is some likelihood of negative results, even where no serious, immediate hazards can be identified. Given the uncertainties and the significance of potential consequences, biotechnology must be approached with precaution.

The essential question that underlies the precautionary approach is, "What purposes are so important to us that to obtain them we would be willing to accept the risk of unknown but potentially significant damages?" It may be that, after careful, comprehensive assessment of the overall prospects for biotechnology, we would conclude that there are no such purposes and that genetic engineering is something that we would be wise not to pursue at all. If, instead, we conclude that for some purposes the uncertain risks may be acceptable, we then need a means of making the more specific decisions on what purposes and possible biotechnology applications qualify. This is the role for a precautionary screen.

As a mechanism for applied precaution, the screen would be used to evaluate anticipated biotechnology applications. It would centre on a public process using carefully considered criteria to evaluate the ecological, socio-economic and ethical importance of possible benefits in areas where biotechnology research is beginning or expected.[43] The criteria themselves would be the product of a public process that considered the promises and uncertainties of biotechnology and its possible overall and cumulative effects in light of broader ecological, socio-economic and ethical objectives.

The screen's use would restrict biotechnology where, for example, its promised benefits would be merely cosmetic. In so far as concerns about human identity and links with nature are confirmed in the comprehensive assessment, the screen might be used to keep certain areas of ecology and human reproduction free from genetic manipulation. But in so far as a credible overall assessment has revealed at least some biotechnology applications to be desirable, the central purposes of the screen would be positive - to direct investment and research to areas of recognized importance, and ensure more efficient, effective and fair evaluation of individual proposals.

A Three-Part Regulatory Process
In rough outline, a biotechnology regulation process including a precautionary screen would have three main parts: an initial comprehensive assessment to develop the screen and other elements of biotechnology policy, the screen itself, and a revised risk assessment mechanism for case by case approval decisions.

The initial comprehensive assessment would amount to a generic environmental assessment of biotechnology policy and regulation. Its scope and responsibilities would include the following activities:

· examining the needs for (anticipated benefits of)

biotechnology applications and alternative ways of satisfying these needs;

· identifying and evaluating the full range of concerns about the predicted and possible effects of biotechnology applications, overall and in particular sectors (e.g. agriculture);

· assessing alternative means of encouraging, directing and controlling research, development and application of biotechnology initiatives;

· identifying and proposing the set of principles and criteria to be used in making regulatory decisions for biotechnology.

Such assessments at the policy level in Canada have rarely been open to public scrutiny, much less effective public participation. Here, however, the credibility and potential effectiveness of the process depend heavily on the evident legitimacy of the process, especially in identifying the principles and criteria to be used in subsequent decision making.

The screen would apply the principles and criteria developed through the comprehensive assessment. Its design could loosely follow the coarse/fine filter models often seen in ecological research. The coarse filter, which would apply the general precautionary principle and the basic value principles that emerge from public discussion, would be used to identify categories of potential products and uses that clearly would not serve the prevailing social objectives. The fine filter would involve closer examination of certain questionable products and uses in light of a more detailed set of social, ecological and economic principles and criteria.

Identification of a working set of basic value principles and more detailed social, ecological and economic principles would be a central task in the initial comprehensive assessment of biotechnology policy and regulation. Like any other set of principles these would reflect the effective participants' understanding of their world and their views about what is to be valued and feared. We do not assume that there is any one set of proper principles or any ideal political process for identifying the set that best expresses current understanding and broadly accepted preferences. The proposed process merely recognizes the importance of value-based judgements in biotechnology regulation and seeks to provide an open and democratic means of identifying the principles to be used.

Ordinarily, the filtering would be done at the conceptual stage, before significant resources had been devoted to product research and development. In this way, further work on products or processes that failed to meet the principles, and criteria would be discouraged before they reached the stage of field testing or risk assessment. Again, much would depend on the credibility of the process, including its success in ensuring effective involvement of all interested parties.

Finally, the revised risk-assessment process would be used at the same point that conventional risk-assessment is now used, when approvals are sought for specific products and uses. While the precautionary screen would be expected to provide clear early guidance about which applications are and are not likely to merit approvals, careful assessment of individual proposals would still be necessary to identify specific risks (e.g. to human health and ecological processes) and means of avoiding or mitigating them. If the specific risk assessment revealed unexpectedly serious dangers, the final decision still could be to refuse approval of an application. More often the case-specific assessment would assist in determining appropriate conditions of approval.

Principles of Process
At each step in this three-part process effective public involvement is crucial. The emphasis throughout is on directing biotechnology along a socially desirable path, reflecting the preferences, desires and concerns of society. If biotechnology's advocates are right, the industry and its products are likely to affect the lives of most citizens, and if history is any guide, the most negative effects are likely to be felt by the traditionally most vulnerable – those with the least power and fewest resources.

The relevant deliberations and decision making at each stage should therefore be open and accessible to the broadest possible range of participants. To compensate for existing political and economic inequities, special efforts to facilitate broad public participation (for example through some form of participant funding) would be appropriate.[44] The burden of proof that a proposed product or application satisfies the screening principles and criteria should be borne by the proponents, who stand to be among the chief beneficiaries of the anticipated approval. And careful attention to the distribution of effects, both positive and negative, should be mandatory in assessment at each step in the process.

Achieving a broad-based consensus on the questions at hand here will no doubt be difficult and the problem is exacerbated by the scale of the biotechnology's applications and potential effects. Because biotechnology is now treated as a matter of national importance with effects that are not constrained by provincial borders, the likely driving force behind the regulation of biotechnology in Canada will be the federal government.[45] Biotechnology is, however, an international pursuit. While individual nations can take independent regulatory courses, effective control in the global interest will require international co-operation. The principles of open and participative decision making do not fit well with the need for national and international responses. Nevertheless the principles are crucial and we have in recent years begun to learn much about facilitation of broader involvement through multi-stakeholder bodies, roundtable processes and a host of related initiatives.

Furthermore, it is not intended that this process produce the definitive judgement of what constitutes a socially desirable technology. Values and understanding will change over time, and the process will have to be flexible and dynamic to account for this. For example, the process should include a monitoring mechanism for comparing the actual with the predicted effects of approved technologies and reviewing evidence of overall effects. As well the policy assessment conclusions, especially the screening principles and criteria, should be subject to mandatory re-evaluation, perhaps every seven years.

Illustrative Principles and Criteria

The proposed process rests on the precautionary principle, which, in the context of accepted social and ecological realities, can be used as a basis for elaborating subsidiary principles. For example, valuing of precaution in view of concerns about unknown social and ecological effects suggests a valuing of social and ecological integrity and a concern for the future, including the interests of future generations. However, this exercise has limited potential. Selecting and specifying the basic value principles for the screen's coarse filter and the more detailed ecological, social and economic principles for the fine filter is a larger task that must be done through open public deliberations in the comprehensive assessment. They cannot be pre-defined. For illustrative purposes, however, we can outline some possibilities.

One source of illustrative principles and criteria is the Sustainable Society Project. Initiated at the University of Waterloo and now based at the University of British Columbia, the Project has adopted a "backcasting approach" to defining and seeking routes to a sustainable society. The idea, essentially, has been to decide where we would like to go (i.e. what qualities we would want a future Canadian society to express); evaluate the practical feasibility of various scenarios for such a society in light of such constraints as likely resource availability, energy efficiency expectations, etc.; adjust the vision as necessary, and finally attempt to chart a path to get there. An initial step

was to outline a set of characteristics that would define a desirable, sustainable society for Canada.[46]

The coarse filter basic value principles set out in Table 1 are drawn from the definitional work of the Sustainable Society Project.

Table 1

Illustrative Basic Value Principles

❖ The continued existence of the natural world is inherently good. The natural world and its component life forms, and the ability of the natural world to regenerate itself through its own natural evolution have intrinsic value.

❖ Cultural sustainability depends on the ability of a society to claim the loyalty of its adherents through the propagation of a set of values that are acceptable to the populace and through the provision of socio-political institutions that make realization of those values possible.

❖ A sustainable society requires an open, accessible political process that puts effective decision-making power at the level of government closest to the situation and lives of the people affected by a decision.

❖ All persons should have freedom from extreme want and from vulnerability to economic coercion as well as the positive ability to participate creatively and self-directedly in the political and economic system.

For the fine filter ecological and socio-economic principles and criteria, it is necessary to consider more specifically the hopes and fears surrounding biotechnology. Table 2 provides illustrative examples of principles and criteria which reflect recurring issues raised in the literature and public debates concerning biotechnology in general and specific applications such as rBGH. The lists are not complete; the statements are more general than would be desirable for a workable screening mechanism and no attempt is made to suggest an order of priorities. Moreover, most of the positions favoured are debatable. The lists in Table 2 nonetheless indicate the kinds of considerations that would be addressed.

Table 2-a
Illustrative Ecological Principles/Criteria

❖ Life support systems must be protected. Genetic engineering applications that promise to assist decontamination of air, water and soils and reduce waste flows should be favoured.

❖ Biotic diversity must be protected and enhanced.

❖ The integrity of ecosystems must be maintained or enhanced, for example through careful management of soils and nutrient cycles.

❖ The state of the earth's genetic material affects all life forms and therefore should be "owned" and "controlled" by the public.

❖ The product or process should address the causes rather than the symptom of environmental problems.

❖ Significant new environmental threats to human health must be avoided.

❖ Efficiency gains won at the expense of the health and welfare of animals should not be accepted.

❖ Introduction of new products and processes must not undermine the stability and resiliency of ecological systems.

❖ New products or processes must not require more inputs (resources/capital), or result in more wastes than available or feasible alternatives.

Table 2-b
Socio-Economic Principles/Criteria

❖ Genetically engineered products **and processes** must serve recognized needs, for example, needs for basic health and security.

❖ The distribution of expected benefits and risks must reduce current disparities.

❖ The diversity, flexibility and sustainability of industries must be maintained and enhanced.

❖ Innovations must provide meaningful employment and opportunities for individuals to contribute to society.

❖ Application of genetically engineered products and processes should enhance self-reliance at all levels of society and reduce individual and community dependence on outside powers over which they have little or no control.

❖ The ability of small producers/businesses to survive should not be compromised.

❖ Introduction of new products or processes is not acceptable where there are viable alternatives that offer equivalent benefits and pose fewer and more certain risks.

❖ The calculation of benefits and risks must cover the "cradle to grave" existence and implications of the product or process, including factors traditionally externalized as public costs.

Inevitably, both at the screening and later approvals stages, decision makers will face conflicts between competing criteria. For example, a product offering significant human health benefits may raise serious animal welfare issues. To some extent this problem may be reduced through efforts to set priorities among criteria. But even with priorities, conflicts will remain. Moreover, there is usually a considerable distance between abstract principles and practical application. In the end, it will fall to the immediate decision-making process and the relevant decision makers to choose. This again underlines the importance of ensuring a fair and open process for decision making at each stage and for giving careful attention to the matter of determining who the final decision makers are, and how they can be kept accountable to the public they serve.

Directing and Restricting Research and Development

Introduction of an anticipatory precautionary screen for biotechnology is from some perspectives a modest proposal. Despite concerns that uncontrolled genetic engineering will remove the last links between humanity and nature and undermine the foundations of our own identity, the screening idea accepts that genetic engineering is to be pursued, even encouraged in some fields. It also offers to reduce approval process inefficiencies by pre-screening research areas and identifying those most likely to merit regulatory approval. But at the same time it is clearly meant to restrict and direct scientific and economic innovation. It is therefore bound to be contentious.

The conclusions of precautionary screening would be merely indicative. They would not explicitly restrict research by making certain research illegal.[47] Instead they would identify those areas where the expected products and processes appear unlikely to satisfy the criteria for regulatory approval. Investors might reasonably conclude that their resources might be more judiciously directed elsewhere, but proponents convinced that greater understanding will lead to different conclusions might choose nonetheless to continue. Positively stated, the intent is to direct research into socially desirable areas. Applications in areas which do not meet the agreed principles would, by virtue of having been screened out by a cred-

ible and authoritative process or previously rejected at the approval stage, be identified by industry as socially "undesirable" and not worth pursuing. The hope is that after a certain adjustment period the screen will become increasingly pre-emptive, influencing the industry earlier in the technology development process, and perhaps ultimately fostering a biotechnology industry that is self-directed to socially desirable ends.

Still, research would in effect be restricted and this does raise some legitimate discomforts. A flexible, innovative and healthy society depends on letting its scientists and researchers pursue their work; the same can be said of writers and artists. The most useful and ground-breaking work is often that which may be at odds with convention and majority opinion. However, scientific research in biotechnology is already directed and restricted, chiefly by research funding decisions which reflect corporate perceptions about what will in the end prove profitable. For biotechnological research the question is not whether restriction and direction should occur but what criteria should be applied and by whom.

The unfortunate reality of the purely economic considerations driving individual decision making in the market place (competitive maximization of profit and efficiency, etc.) is that they do not include larger social and ecological objectives and cannot reasonably be expected to ensure that these objectives are served. Regulatory compensations are therefore required. In the case of biotechnology, however, the conventional regulatory response of case-specific review and permit requirements is ill-equipped to address these larger concerns. The proposed regulatory screen approach merely recognizes that the economic market and conventional permitting controls are focused on an unacceptably narrow set of priorities and limited to case-by-case decision making. They do not provide adequate direction for an area of research whose most serious effects are likely to be cumulative and are in any event beyond confident prediction.

Conclusion

The May 1994 advertising supplement to the Toronto *Globe and Mail* that we mentioned at the beginning trumpeted biotechnology as something that "touches our lives in myriad ways we don't think about" and that is essential to what defines Canada - forests, a pristine environment, a breadbasket for the world, and a first-rate health care system.[48] While a helping of advertising hyperbole may be involved here, it seems likely the industry will eventually deliver significant effects for our lives and environment, including important benefits in areas we care about. At the same time, however, serious concerns have been raised about risks and potential negative effects, including ones that we cannot now predict.

The currently favoured approach to regulating biotechnology is not well equipped to address concerns about cumulative and overall effects, or respond adequately to the imperative for precaution in the face of significant risks and uncertainties. But we are still in the early days of biotechnology. It is not too late to focus our collective attention on the emerging biotechnology industry, assess its implications for humanity and the natural environment and consider how we wish to direct its evolution. By applying the precautionary principle and an explicit set of commonly developed ecological and socio-economic criteria, we may yet guide this new technology to ends we choose.

ENDNOTES

[1] An earlier version of this paper was included in an Appendix to the *Report of the Biotechnology Council of Ontario* published by the Canadian Institute for Environmental Law and Policy.

[2] Toronto *Globe and Mail,* Report on Business, advertising supplement, "Biotechnology, the future of science, today," May 24, 1994, p.C1.

[3] McIntyre, T. C., *Asleep at the Switch - The Federal Government and Planning for High Technology: The National Biotechnology Strategy 1983-1989* Ph.D. thesis, School of Urban and Regional Planning, University of Waterloo, 1991, p.181.

[4] Langdon Winner, *The Whale and the Reactor* (Chicago: University of Chicago Press, 1986), p.10.

[5] Marcia A. Valiante and Paul R. Muldoon, "Biotechnology and the environment: a regulatory proposal," *Osgoode Hall Law Journal* 23 (Summer 1985), pp. 349-394.

[6] National Biotechnology Advisory Committee, *National Biotechnology Business Strategy: Capturing Competitive Advantage for Canada* (Ottawa: Department of Industry, Science and Technology, 1991), p. 11.

[7] For an outline of commercial opportunities identified by Canadian promoters of biotechnology advancement see National Biotechnology Advisory Committee, *National Biotechnology Business Strategy: Capturing Competitive Advantage for Canada* (Ottawa: Supply and Services Canada, 1991), pp. 29-38.

[8] Vandana Shiva, *Monocultures of the Mind: Biodiversity, Biotechnology and the Third World* (Penang, Malaysia: Third World Network, 1993); and Ernst Ulrich von Weizsacker, *Earth Politics* (London: Zed Books, 1994), pp. 110-111.

[9] Mary Pickering and Rural Advancement Foundation International, "Broad patents on basic crops cause alarm," *Alternatives* 21:1 (1995), pp 10-11.

[10] A summary list of possibilities is provided in Paul Muldoon and Burkhard Mausberg, "The regulation of biotechnology, " in David Estrin and John Swaigen, eds., *Environment on Trial: A Guide to Ontario Environmental Law and Policy* third edition (Toronto: Emond Montgomery, 1993), pp. 240-241.

[11] See Roger Wrubel, "The promise and problems of herbicide-resistant crops," *Technology Review* 97:4 (May/June 1994), pp.57-61.

[12] David Jennex, *Genetic Engineering and Our Sense of Self*, Ph.D. thesis, Department of Philosophy, University of Waterloo, 1994.

[13] See, for example, Jeremy Rifkin *Algeny* (New York: Penguin Books, 1984); and papers by Michael Fox and others in Peter Wheale and Ruth McNally, eds., *The BioRevolution - Cornupopia or Pandora's Box?* (London: Pluto Press, 1990).

[14] See for example, Howard A. Schneiderman and Will D. Carpenter, "Planetary patriotism: sustainable agriculture for the future," *Environmental Science and Technology* 24:4 (April 1990), pp. 466-473. Schneiderman and Carpenter, who are senior officials of Monsanto, a leading chemical company and commercial biotechnology pioneer, assert, "Gene transfer is just a natural extension and acceleration of plant breeding."

[15] Abby Lippman, quoted in Ruth Hubbard and Elijah Wald, *Exploding the Gene Myth: How Genetic Information is Produced and Manipulated by Scientists, Physicians, Employ-*

ers, Insurance Companies, Educators and Law Enforcers (Boston: Beacon Press, 1993), p.2

16 Jeffrey Deitch, "Post-human," *Adbusters Quarterly - Journal of the Mental Environment* 3:1 (1994), p. 21.

17 Erik Lindala, "Renewed debate surfaces around Human Genome Project" and "Genetic screening poses social impact concerns," *Alternatives* 20:4 (1994), pp. 12-13.

18 Rural Advancement Foundation International, "Patenting indigenous peoples," *Earth Island Journal* (Fall 1993), p. 13.

19 Jennex (note 11).

20 For a survey of anticipated beneficial applications and accompanying concerns see Muldoon and Mausberg, (note 9), pp. 238-241.

21 Muldoon and Mausberg (note 9), pp. 236-237.

22 Muldoon and Mausberg (note 9), pp. 245-252. See also Mark S. Winfield and Burkhard Mausberg, "CEPA, chemical new substances and biotechnology, " in Burkhard Mausberg, Paul Muldoon and Mark Winfield, *Reforming the Canadian Environmental Protection Act,* a submission to the Standing Committee on Environment and Sustainable Development (Toxics Caucus of the Canadian Environmental Network, September 1994), p.23.

23 *Winfield and Mausberg (note 21), pp. 19-22.*

24 *Biotechnology projects that involve "physical works" will be covered by the Canadian Environmental Assessment Act* if the federal government is doing the project, or if federal lands or money are used, or if certain specified federal regulatory requirements under other laws apply. As well certain "physical activities" or classes of physical activities may be specified as projects subject to the assessment requirements of the Act.

25 Multistakeholder agreement on the need for a clear and effective regulatory regime for biotechnology in Canada was reported in 1985 by Valiante and Muldoon (note 4), p.369. For a more recent call for regulatory coherence, including standard minimum requirements for notice and assessment, see Canada, House of Commons Standing Committee on Environment and Sustainable Development, *It's about our Health: Towards Pollution Prevention* (Ottawa: House of Commons, 1995), pp.121-124.

26 Environment Canada, *Canada's Green Plan for a Healthy Environment* (Ottawa: Supply and Services Canada, 1990), p. 50.

27 *Initial proposals for Canadian Environmental Protection Act* initiatives were set out in Environment Canada, Biotechnology Section, Commercial Chemicals Branch, *Proposed Notification Regulations for Biotechnology Products under the Canadian Environmental Protection Act* (Hull: Environment Canada, September 1990). The proposed overall federal approach is set out in Government of

Canada, "News Release: Federal government agrees on new regulatory framework for biotechnology," (Ottawa, 11 January 1993), 3pp., which is accompanied by "Backgrounder: A federal regulatory framework for biotechnology," 3pp.

28 Muldoon and Mausberg (note 9), pp.256-257.

29 See, for example Agriculture and Agri-Food Canada, "Biotechnology, agriculture and regulation," in *BioInfo: Regulation of Agricultural Products* 1:1 (1995), pp.1-3.

30 According to Dr. Des Mahon of Environment Canada, "through this process, all biotechnology products will be subject to appropriate notification and assessment processes, either under the new regulations [under the *Canadian Environmental Protection Act*] or through regulations under other acts" - quoted in Greg Cento, "Coalition claims biotechnology regulations are inadequate," *Alternatives* 20:2 (1994), p.6. In 1991, the National Biotechnology Advisory Committee, representing business and academic interests, recommended reduction of case-by-case regulatory burdens by initially ranking biotechnology products by "category of risk" to humans and the environment and not assuming "that every biologically-based product or process automatically poses a risk." See National Biotechnology Advisory Committee (note 6), p.21. The federal approach, however, still assumes notification and assessment for all individual cases covered by the various laws.

31 For a useful summary of the traditional approach to risk assessment see Conrad Brunk, Lawrence Haworth and Brenda Lee, *Value Assumptions in Risk Assessment: A Case Study of the Alachlor Controversy* (Waterloo: Wilfrid Laurier University Press, 1991).

32 For other listings of the main concerns see Cento (note 29), p. 8; and Burkhard Mausberg, Mark Winfield, Jacqueline Munroe and Brewster Kneen, "Growing safely? concerns about biotechnology and the regulatory process: a report to Agriculture Canada, " December 15, 1993, pp. 6-7.

33 Mausberg et al (note 31), p.7.

34 See Conrad Brunk, Lawrence Haworth and Brenda Lee (note 30) and, same authors, "Is a scientific assessment of risk possible? value assumptions in the Canadian Alachlor controversy," in *Dialogue* 30, pp.235-247.

35 This seems to be the intent of the National Biotechnology Advisory Committee's recommendation. See note 26, above.

36 See McIntyre (note 2).

37 Indeed some experts argue that proper assessments ought to go beyond the cumulative effects even of whole categories of biotechnologies and their applications. The US Environmental Protection Agency's Science Advisory Board, for example, has included negative biotechnology effects in a long list of current and anticipated environmental

stressors and has urged more comprehensive attention to their interactive, cumulative implications for human and ecological wellbeing. See USEPA, Science Advisory Board, *Beyond the Horizon: Using Foresight to Protect the Environmental Future* (Washington, D.C.: EPA, January 1995), esp. pp. 13-17.

[38] Jennex (note 11), p. 229.

[39] See, for example, Tony Hiss, "How now drugged cow? biotechnology comes to rural Vermont," *Harper's Magazine* 289:1733 (October 1994), pp. 80-90.

[40] Langdon Winner, "On not hitting the Tar Baby," in *The Whale and the Reactor* (note 3), pp. 138-154.

[41] On the need for a public role in biotechnology regulation, see Muldoon and Mausberg (note 9), pp. 257-258.

[42] T. F. Schrecker, "Ecology as if people (and power) mattered," a paper presented at the *Symposium on Ecological Risk Assessment Uses, Abuses and Alternatives,* Center for the Analysis of Environmental Change, Oregon State University, Corvallis, Oregon, November 1994 , forthcoming in *Human and Ecological Risk Assessment* 1:3 (1995).

[43] The screening would also recognize that somewhat different biotechnologies and associated risks would be involved in different areas of biotechnology application.

[44] On the importance of participant funding in such regulatory decision making see, for example, Canada, House of Commons Standing Committee on Environment and Sustainable Development (note 24), pp.233-234.

[45] At present, those provinces in the process of considering biotechnology regulations appear to concede primary responsibility on the question of assessment and approval to the federal government. See Winfield and Mausberg (note 21), p.20.

[46] John Robinson, George Francis, Russel Legge and Sally Lerner, "Defining a sustainable society: values, principles and definitions," *Alternatives* 17:2 (1990), pp.36-46.

[47] Such restrictions are likely to be necessary in some specific areas, but that is not what we are addressing here.

[48] Toronto *Globe and Mail* (note 1).

ETHICS OF WASTES
THE CASE OF THE NUCLEAR FUEL CYCLE

7

by Andrew Brook

IN CANADA AND THE UNITED STATES, WE CONSUME A huge amount of energy and other goods relative to other parts of the world and are totally dependent on large industries. Among the problems created by this way of life, the vast quantity of often dangerous wastes we produce is among the more difficult. A particularly interesting case study for the ethics of wastes and their management is the nuclear power industry. It presents some major waste management problems, problems that will require enormous amounts of money and labour to solve.

What to do about nuclear wastes is a policy question; policy questions always have moral questions at their heart. Those posed by nuclear energy tax the full resources of modern moral philosophy. In a classic study of two decades ago, Arthur Porter put it this way:

> *... an assessment of the value of nuclear power ... ultimately requires an examination of the acceptability to society of the risk and benefits of the technology, relative to other options. This process is, by definition, extremely difficult since value judgments of a particularly complex kind, transcending nuclear power per se, are clearly involved. Indeed, whose values are to be judged worthy and how this assessment is to be accomplished with justice are pertinent questions.[1]*

All this is just as true today as it was when Porter wrote it. Of the wide range of cost/risk/benefit issues to which Porter alludes, we will concentrate on those resulting from the wastes created by nuclear power. The major wastes in the

nuclear industry are the wastes from the mining and milling process used to create uranium fuel and the wastes left behind when this fuel is used to generate electricity in a reactor. We will focus on what are called high level wastes, the wastes created by burning fuel in a reactor. Our aim is to determine the values that should govern policy questions about these wastes and how to apply these values in a variety of contexts. The most central ethical question concerns our obligations to future generations.[2]

Ethical decisions always underlie policy decisions.[3] The former are often made in an analytic vacuum that we would not begin to accept for making design decisions or investment decisions. Similarly, cost/benefit assessments are often carried out with very narrow notions of what can properly be classed as costs or benefits. Here is how an ideal method for settling ethical issues in policy contexts might work. First we would collect the relevant facts: what are the problems, what are the possible solutions? We would next identify basic ethical principles such as fairness in the distribution of costs, risks and benefits over populations and times, liberty for the people concerned, and so on. Then we would lay out criteria for setting costs against costs, benefits against benefits, etc., both considered broadly enough to include full social costs and benefits, direct and indirect. Finally, we would apply the principles and criteria to the facts. We will carry this method out as fully as a short paper allows. We will sketch the relevant facts about the nuclear fuel cycle, identify relevant values, and lay out some of the relevant costs and benefits.

High Level Reactor Wastes

In Canada, all nuclear reactors are CANDU (*Canadian Deuterium Uranium*) reactors. Unlike virtually all reactors everywhere else in the world, the uranium in the fuel they use is not enriched; the ratio of the various uranium isotopes is the same as the one that occurs naturally.[4] Nuclear reactors are concentrated in Ontario, where they generate about 50 percent of the province's electricity, though there are also a few in Quebec and New Brunswick. Nuclear reactors generate electricity by setting up a controlled chain reaction in the radioactive component of uranium fuel, uranium 235. This fuel is manufactured into pellets held in tubes tied together into circular bundles; these bundles are inserted into long tubes inside the reactor. The chain reaction in this fuel generates an enormous amount of heat. The heat is used to superheat steam, which then powers turbines connected to electrical generators. When the uranium is 'burned', the industry term for the chain reaction, a number of highly radioactive materials come into existence inside the fuel bundles – radioactive strontium, cesium, americium, and so on – and the metal holding the pellets also becomes radioactive.

One important new mineral is plutonium, which is dangerous both radiologically and chemically – the radiation from a minute amount on the inside of the lungs can cause lung cancer and plutonium is chemically more toxic than almost any other material. Plutonium also poses a security risk; it can be refined into bomb grade material. Of the two atomic bombs exploded over Japan by the United States, one used refined plutonium, the other heavily enriched uranium 235.

The radioactivity in uranium fuel increases many orders of magnitude when the uranium 235 is burned.[5] Natural processes of radioactive decay restore the spent fuel to something like the radioactivity it once had but that takes 300 to 800 years (after about 500 years, the radioactivity of the fuel has decreased 200,000 times[6]). Different radioactive materials decay at rates that vary by orders of magnitude. Plutonium, for example, has a halflife of about 24,000 years, which make wastes in which it occurs particularly long lived.[7]

Compared to the amounts of wastes produced by other industrial processes, the volume of high level wastes produced by a reactor is quite small, however. A pellet of fuel roughly the size of a large marble produces enough electricity to power an average house for a year. By comparison, it would take *tons* of coal producing *tons* of CO_2 and a large amount of fly ash to produce the same amount of electricity. All the high level wastes ever produced in Canada weigh less than 25,000 tons. In fact, all the high level waste produced by Canadian reactors in a history that is now about forty five years long is still stored onsite, in large pools of water for the first six years or so, then in thick concrete containers as the fuel becomes less active. This form of storage is adequate to ensure that there is almost no release of radioactivity to the atmosphere so long as nothing goes wrong. However, the proviso, 'so long as nothing goes wrong', is important. These methods need constant monitoring and maintenance. They are thus the very opposite of being a passive, permanent solution requiring no further human intervention.

Mine/Mill Wastes

To make the fuel burned in reactors, uranium ore is mined and milled to extract the uranium and then fabricated into fuel. This process produces large quantities of low level wastes. The amounts of these wastes are huge – well over 150 million tons of these wastes now exist in Canada alone – and they may lead to more exposure to radiation than any other part of the fuel cycle.[8] Because the volumes are so huge, and also because much of the waste is fluid, these 'low level' wastes may well be a more intractable problem than high level wastes. No good scheme for managing them has ever been devised. Thus they eminently deserve to be studied from the ethical point of view. In this paper, however, we will focus on high level wastes. One reason is that a promising scheme has been devised for dealing with these wastes and it is in need of careful ethical assessment.[9]

Long Term Management of High Level Wastes

High level wastes are stored in highly corrosion-resistant structures. Thus they will not disperse for a long period of time, though still well before the radioactive materials in them decay to insignificant levels. Release via a massive uncontained explosion or fire on the model of the Chernobyl disaster is unlikely in Canada or the United States. What exploded in Chernobyl was active fuel with a full scale chain reaction going on in it. The reactor had no provision for containing such an eruption. However, all reactors outside the former Soviet countries have massive reinforced concrete shells around them for precisely that purpose.

By the time fuel is removed from the reactor, it is spent; there is no longer a chain reaction going on in it. The dangers in this material are heat and extremely high levels of radioactivity, and the major risk is over the long term. Over time, there is an increasing risk that the active monitoring of water tanks and concrete containers needed to ensure safety will decrease or even cease altogether. If the monitoring and necessary repairs ceased, living beings could spend dangerous amounts of time around the pools and concrete containers in the medium term; and in the long term these pools and containers themselves would deteriorate, allowing the spent fuel within to dissipate.

A method for permanent disposal of spent fuel has been undergoing research and development in Canada for a couple of decades now. The method involves sinking shafts deep into stable, generally unfissured structures of plutonic rock in the Canadian Shield; the relative absence of fissures means that the water in them essentially does not flow. Over one thousand possibly suitable structures have been identified.[10] The spent fuel,

which is itself highly resistant to corrosion, would be put into containers (probably either copper or titanium). These containers would be placed in clay-lined cavities in vaults running off a main shaft (clay-lined to prevent moisture penetration). The vaults and shafts would then be backfilled and sealed, effectively isolating the wastes from the environment and making any contact between them and living beings highly unlikely. The aim is to achieve a level of isolation such that there would not be more than one chance in a million per year that a maximally exposed creature would develop a fatal cancer or serious genetic defect, and that this isolation be assured for at least 10,000 years without active intervention. We receive much more radiation than this every year from the radium found in all rock, concrete and soil, from X-rays, from air travel, and so on.

Everything to do with nuclear power is contentious but nuclear wastes have one feature that distinguishes them from other nuclear issues: they are already with us. Thus there is no longer any question about whether to bring them into existence. This means that many of the ethical issues that are central to decisions about nuclear power, issues arising from such questions as whether to build more reactors or phase out the ones we already have, do not arise. The question of whether to create more wastes by building new reactors remains open, of course, but even if no further reactors were ever built the 25,000 tons of high level wastes that we have already created would still be with us. The principal ethical issue that remains is this: are we obliged to assume the costs of disposing of these wastes, and as permanently as possible, or is it permissible for us to pass at least some of the costs of dealing with them on to future generations? This issue breaks into two questions:

1. What are our obligations? and,

2. To what beings: just human beings, or all creatures, ecosystems, and the biosphere as a whole?

Values for the Facts

Our task now is to identify values appropriate to the facts about wastes from the nuclear fuel cycle. Nuclear wastes have two useful features as a test case for ethical issues of waste management:

1. Nobody currently alive and nobody for a number of generations is going to benefit much from finding a more permanent solution to them; the current solution will protect us and a number of generations to come. (Spent fuel does have one possible near benefit, but exploiting it is actually made more difficult by long term disposal, a point to which we will return.) Thus managing them does not give rise to difficult questions about distribution of benefits: who should get, or be allowed to use, how much of what, when and how?, and similar questions of distributive justice. Wastes raise primarily cost questions: given that they have to be managed for many thousands of years, who is obliged to assume the costs of doing so? This simplifies the ethical situation.

2. Because nobody alive now or for some time is going to benefit much from finding a more permanent solution than the one already in place, finding a more permanent solution will not be motivated by self-interest. Thus, the arguments in its favour have to be moral ones alone.

What are our obligations with respect to nuclear wastes? A number of issues need to be distinguished:

1. Principles. What are the general principles that should guide our ethical thinking about the disposal of nuclear wastes?

2. Scope. Are our obligations restricted to humans or do they extend to other creatures? To the environment? To the biosphere as a whole? To future generations as well as to the current one? Only to people, animals and ecological systems close to us or over the whole surface of the planet?

1. and 2. cover the two issues identified at the end of the last subsection. Other partly moral, partly conceptual issues are also highly relevant:

3. Discounting. Are creatures of other kinds or far distant future generations of our own kind worth less morally than people existing now?

4. Cost/risk/benefit. Given that better solutions to a waste management problem tend to cost more money, what, all aspects of risk, cost and benefit considered, is the optimal expenditure on this problem versus other social problems and demands?

5. Moral assessment and risk assessment. How should risk assessments shape our moral assessment?

6. Uncertainty. Given that we can never be certain about any outcome in a complex industrial system and given that the further we project into the future, the more uncertain we become, how can we reach ethical conclusions in the face of such uncertainty?

7. Reducing risk vs. retaining benefits. What is the appropriate balance between reducing the risks contained in high level wastes and leaving open the possibility of exploiting the very considerable economic potential that the fuel rods still contain?

8. Procedural issues. What procedures would allow us to arrive at fair and democratic decisions and who should have what roles in them?

1. Principles. What principles should govern our ethical thinking about deep disposal?[11] One is a principle of distributional equity: costs, risks and benefits must be distributed equitably, at a time and across time. A second is that liberty is a particularly central good (benefit), at least for members of the human species, and any reduction of liberty requires particularly powerful justification. We need to narrow both notions down.

The part of the principle of distributional equity of relevance here is this:

A. Fairness. Those who benefit should bear the costs.

It follows from this principle that, since the people now alive have reaped most of the benefits of the activities that have created the high level wastes we are considering, we have an obligation to bear the costs of disposing of them, and disposing of them permanently. I do not think that there is any way around this.

That may appear to settle the matter and so far as identifying our obligations on *this* issue, it does. But obligations can be overridden if there are conflicting obligations that are even stronger. We will take up this issue in 4. below. Furthermore, even if A. settles our intergenerational obligations, there is also a tricky interregional issue. Most of the beneficiaries of nuclear power live in or near large centres; people in the outlying regions have reaped few benefits. Yet any long term solution to the wastes will inevitably be constructed in some outlying region; that's where the appropriate rock structures are found and there is room to build a large complex boring into them.

To see our way to the most ethical solution here, I think the word 'inevitably' is important: if any long term disposal facility must be built in the hinterland, then there are only two choices: construction in the hinterland or forego a long term solution and continue the short term procedures now in place. If so, then disposal in the hinterland is the fair*est* long term solution possible, even if it is not entirely fair. Were we to adopt it, we would still be obliged, of course, to ensure that the costs to present and future beings in the area selected are kept as low as feasible, that benefits be maximized, and that any differential in costs is accompanied by fair compensation. The secure, well paid jobs that go with a waste disposal facility would be one compensatory benefit.

The aspect of the ethics of liberty of relevance to nuclear wastes is this:

B. *Liberty.*   Our actions must infringe on the lives of other beings to the smallest extent reasonably possible.

This principle applies particularly obviously to human beings but it may well apply to many other beings, too, as we will see below. Here are some of the ways in which the management, or perhaps more accurately *mis*management, of high level wastes could restrict liberty: causing pain; damaging bodies; harming abilities; imposing significant protection costs; spoiling ecosystems; reducing opportunities; and so on. Some of the examples I just gave concerned freedom *from* (freedom from unnecessary pain, unnecessary costs, etc.) and some concerned freedom *to* (not harming the field of available opportunities). With this distinction, we can spell out the demand of liberty this way:

B^1. *Liberty.*   We must choose the solution to the disposal of high level wastes that will impose costs and harms on them and limit their freedom to pursue their life as they would live it to the minimum extent reasonably possible.

Note that even this longer version of the principle of liberty is weaker than some would argue it should be. It says nothing about *enhancing* freedom from or freedom to.

Of course, protecting the liberty of future beings requires that we restrict our own liberty in certain ways. In particular, the liberty to spend the resources needed to dispose of nuclear wastes permanently on things of immediate benefit to us must go. Thus the demands of fairness and the liberty of future beings are in conflict with enhancing our own liberty. To resolve this conflict, we have to look deeper.

Here is a principle that can start to resolve the conflict:

C. *Equal worth.*   Prior to considerations of morally relevant distinguishing qualities, each person has the same value as any other.

The argument for it is a general principle of rationality: unless we treat similar things as similar, it would be impossible to make general, comparative judgments about them at all. If so, it would be irrational to assign two relevantly similar people different moral value. This argument grounds the ethical principle of equal *prima facie* worth on a general consideration about what is required for rationality as a whole.

To be sure, discriminatory assignments of value can be justified – so long as there is a morally relevant difference. And we could be quite generous about what such differences might be.[12] Other kinds of partiality might also be allowable. For example, only a few people (including myself) are within my control; partiality toward these people will increase the chances of my doing what I can to procure and distribute things of value in this world. Similarly, special bonds of affection may justify special concern if the loss of those bonds would seriously undermine my life having any point or purpose in my eyes, seriously undercut my self-confidence, and so on. All these would reduce my chances of doing something of value. (Williams has explored arguments for partiality to some people and also for partiality to humans over other beings, an issue directly related to Scope below.[13])

Some differences are not morally relevant, however. Self-interest, maximizing (or a desire to maximize) one's own benefits and minimizing one's costs simply because the benefits and costs would accrue to me, is not, for example. Here there is no relevant difference between me and anyone else; as the nineteenth century philosopher Henry Sidgwick put it, mere numerical difference makes no moral difference. Similarly, the collective self-interest of one's own generation is not by itself a morally relevant difference between one's own generation and future generations. In general, no one person (even if he is me) and no one generation (even if it is mine) have features that justify giving that person or generation preferential treatment in the distribution of costs and benefits.

Since we are the ones enjoying the benefits of nuclear energy, any passing on of the costs of the activities involved would constitute just such a discriminatory assignment of costs and benefits. From this we can conclude that we have a moral obligation to find a permanent, passive solution to the problem of nuclear wastes. If we were passing on additional benefits as large as the benefits we are enjoying and if we were also assuming half the costs of these benefits, the conclusion would not hold. But it seems unlikely that we are doing so. Of course, the principle of fairness, Principle A, may well be just an instantiation of Principle C, the equal worth principle: to treat someone according to A, to make costs assumed proportional to benefits received, may just be one way of treating everyone equally. However, it is possible to argue for C in ways not available with A.

Finally, let me say a brief word about an objection to my use of liberty that will have occurred to some people: liberty is a distinctively human good. Therefore any analysis appealing to it will apply only to humans, not to beings of other kinds. I will consider the general issue of obligations to the nonhuman in the next section but on this specific issue, I think we can say the following: (i.) Animals do care about their own liberty; think of how animals suffer when caged. (ii.) Disease, radioactive poisoning, etc., limit the liberty of animals just as much as of humans.

2. Scope. Questions of scope come in a number of dimensions. To how many kinds of creatures do our obligations extend, just to humans or also to other creatures, the various ecological systems, and the biosphere as a whole? Over what space – to people, animals and ecologies close to us or across the whole planet? And over what span of time – just to us or to future generations, too? We are most apt to reach ethical judgments that can be defended if we take the widest possible scope: All beings, not just humans; everywhere on the planet, not just in our own communities; and at all times, not just now and in the immediate future. If something has the capacity to be harmed, it has interests, and if it has interests, the principle of equal worth can be applied, *mutatis mutandis,* to argue that it would be unfair to load a discriminatory mix of costs and benefits on it.

Quantifying 'discriminatory' over members of various species, the species themselves, their ecosystems, etc., will be a difficult task but it will be an unavoidable one if we wish our waste management decisions to be ethical over the scope of the whole biosphere.[14]

3. Discounting. Even if we do consider everything everywhere and at all times, does it all have to be given *equal* consideration? This is the difficult issue of discounting. In economics, discounting is clearly justified. An economic benefit in the distant future is worth less to me now than one immediately available to me. Is there anything comparable in ethics? Is it ever ethical to value far distant beings, beings far in the future, beings very different from us (earth worms, say, or bacteria) less than we value ourselves and the human beings immediately around us?

This issue tends to break down into two subissues. One concerns *human* beings far distant from us in space or time, the other concerns *all other* beings. In connection with the first, I cannot see any ethical justification for valuing one human being less than another, no matter where or when that human being may live. By contrast, we might be able to make a case for valuing some forms of life less than others: even if we want to keep plentiful *examples* of each kind of life, even down to bacteria, etc., it is far less clear that each *individual* in many lifeforms deserves the same concern as we extend to human individuals.

All this raises a number of difficulties for the principles enunciated earlier. For beings where preservation of genetic material may be more important than protection of the wellbeing or even the existence of individuals, liberty is at most a far smaller concern. Likewise, with such beings we switch from the worth of individuals to the worth of types, something anathema to the ethics of human beings. When one combines these complications with the uncertainties that still infect the notion of discounting for the future in general, I think we rapidly find ourselves completely at

sea. For these reasons, I will restrict my discussion of discounting to human beings.

For distant human beings, especially human beings distant in time, we might try to use the economist's notion of discounting to justify extending less concern to them than we extend to human beings living now. It would argue that future generations, like other things in the future, are worth less than the equivalent things right now. This is the principle that a bird in the hand is worth two in the bush. In financial contexts it can be argued for on a number of bases: uncertainties or probabilities, rates of return on present wealth, and so on. The economist's notion probably has no relevance to moral questions. One discounts the economic value of the future on the basis of its value for us (now); one considers the moral worth of future generations on the basis of their value, period – their value for anyone, including themselves.

There are, however, other discounting principles. Some people might argue that far distant people, just by being so far distant, are worth less per head than people currently alive. While this does not seem a morally relevant difference, being mere location in time, two other discounting principles are perhaps more plausible.

1. Nature of future persons. The farther we move into the future, the greater the probability that persons alive then will be different from us in one or another of a number of relevant ways: they may be immune to radiological damage and chemical poisoning; though still at risk, such risks may no longer affect their interests; their forms of social life may be so different from ours that their moral worth is reduced; they may be such moral monsters that they would not merit our moral concern. These all seem to be very remote possibilities.

2. Existence of future persons. The farther we move into the future, the greater the probability that no persons will exist at all. This claim is sound but ignores the fact (as does the first) that significant damage from nuclear wastes could occur within a few hundred years if nothing more is done, a period short enough to reduce the probability considerably.

To see the real moral force of these discounting principles, it is essential to distinguish between *epistemic* possibility ('It may, I just don't know') and *real probability* ('It may; reliable calculation reveals a chance of . . . , which is more than insignificant'). If we just don't know, we can ensure that we have met our obligations (though we don't, of course, know that we have them either) only by acting as though there will be people in the future, and people relevantly like us. And even if we do know that there is some real probability that there won't be, this probability must, I think, be fairly high before our obligation to act as though there will be is significantly reduced – though this point is controversial. So long as there is any significant probability that there will be relevantly similar people, there is a probability that we have obligations. Thus any discounting principle of which I am aware seems to have only a negligible effect on our obligations to future generations.

In addition to the question of temporal scope and discounting, there is an important ethical issue that arises with spatial scope and consideration of beings elsewhere on the planet. Canada is not the only country with nuclear waste disposal problems. Indeed, compared to the problems faced by the United States, Russia or any other bomb producing country, our problems are pretty small. Both the United States and Russia have literally hundreds of times as much high level waste in storage as we do. If we can find a passive, permanent solution to our own high level wastes, do we have an obligation to use it to help other countries deal with theirs?

The issues here are practical and political as well as ethical. On the practical side, there is the issue of transportation and the dangers inherent in moving highly toxic wastes such long distances.

On the political side, there is the fact that both the United States and Russia have been massively less responsible in their management of high level wastes than Canadians have been, Russia in particular. Nevertheless, a question does arise about whether we have obligations to peoples in other parts of the world as they face their nuclear waste problems.

4. Cost/risk/benefit. Earlier we looked at the implications of principles of fairness and protection of liberty for the management of nuclear wastes. Another principle is also important, indeed can overrule the demands of fairness and liberty in some contexts. It is the broadly utilitarian principle that we should strive to get the maximum benefit, that is to say, to do the greatest good, for each expenditure of resources and incurring of risk. The argument for this principle is very simple: anything else wastes resources. The mechanism for applying it is cost/risk/benefit analysis.

Cost/risk/benefit analysis is the activity of assessing the benefits of a proposal, the costs of achieving those benefits, and the risks involved. More precisely, it consists of analyzing financial risks – financial costs times probability of incurring them; nonfinancial risks – harms times probably of incurring them and costs of rectifying them; and both the probability and the size of the benefits that would accrue.

Sometimes benefits are so great or costs relative to a benefit so high that neither an analysis nor additional moral judgment is needed to decide what should be done. For example, no competent cost/risk/benefit analysis of hospitals is going to question whether we should keep them – though there can certainly be disagreement about how many we need, what kind, and where, as we are seeing! We view health as a benefit that can be traded off against other things only down to a certain level (though that level may be falling right now). At the other extreme, no competent public authority would allocate $1m to fix a few potholes.

But benefits and/or costs are often not so clear.

In particular, better management of wastes is a benefit that we have historically viewed as readily tradeable for other benefits, lower debt loads for example. For this reason, we tend to make decisions about waste management on a comparative basis: for a given expenditure, what is the greatest benefit we can attain and at what overall cost of resources and harms? I think that this is the right approach and that we should do it on the widest possible basis.[15] In considering radiological wastes, we should take into account, for example, the fact that nonradiological toxins have no halflife. In considering an expenditure of resources to dispose of radioactive wastes, we should consider what else we could accomplish for the same money. And not just for us; also for people elsewhere and well into the future, and for beings of other kinds. (Canadians are part of the five percent of the population of the world that uses forty percent of the world's resources; we can afford to be generous.)

Here is one central issue: for a given cost, at a given probability or risk level, what is the greatest obtainable benefit? To meet our obligations to future generations with respect to the hazards in radioactive wastes would cost a lot. Would the benefit conferred on living things as a whole from expending resources on these wastes be as great as the benefits we could confer by expending the resources in some other way?

Some answers to this question might well cancel obligations arising from application of the principles of fairness and liberty. Suppose that the answer to the above question is no, that achieving a permanent solution to nuclear wastes would not be a benefit as great as we could achieve by expending the same resources in other ways. Suppose further that the greater benefit can be secured with as much fairness and protection of liberty across species, space, and time as would be true of a permanent disposition of nuclear wastes. In this situation, our obligations with respect to nuclear wastes would either be cancelled or greatly reduced. Resources can be expended only once, and we can obtain a greater benefit with as much fairness, etc., by expending them another way. Therefore, we are obliged to expend them the other way. If we have spent them some other way, then we cannot expend them on nuclear wastes. But ought implies can: if we cannot do something, then we have no obligation to do it. Therefore, our obligation to expend the resources on nuclear wastes is either cancelled or at least greatly reduced.

Whether the answer is no is a complicated, partly philosophical, partly factual question: philosophical to the extent that we would need criteria for comparing costs and ranking benefits; factual for reasons that are obvious. A couple of examples of possible alternative expenditures of the relevant resources may serve to highlight not only the complexity but also the practical reality of both the philosophical and the factual issues. There is increasing evidence that one unhappy byproduct of modern medicine is damage to the human gene pool. The exponential increase and spread of diabetes is one example. Certainly passing on a sound gene pool would be a great benefit to future generations, so long as it could be done fairly and with respect for individual liberty. An even simpler example is CO_2 and other 'greenhouse gas' emissions; all fossil fuel power generation releases vast quantities of CO_2 and also SO_2, as well as fly ash, particulate carbon and even radiation. (Some authorities suggest that the radon and other radioactive materials released when some coal is burned in a normal operation exceed the amount of radioactivity likely to be released from a nuclear power plant during the most seriously likely breakdown or accident.) Or what about the benefits of winding 'big energy' options such as nuclear, fossil and hydro generation down and substituting 'small' options such as conservation and solar and wind generation?

Would the benefit of improvements in the gene pool or in levels of greenhouse gas and other emissions or in conversion to small energy options be as great as the benefit of freedom from the dangers of radioactive poisoning from reactor wastes or uranium tailings? And could they be secured for a similar expenditure of resources? I doubt that anyone knows the answer to these questions. But the questions must be asked. As Bodde has put it, "our duty is to create solutions to the disposal of radioactive wastes in the context of other threats to human existence, rather than in isolation" – and not just to human existence![16] Rational public policy requires answers to thousands of similar questions. Ask yourself: What *would* the balance be if the comparison were with renewable energy? And what would it be if the comparison were with heavy metal contamination? (Heavy metals have no halflife and retain their toxicity forever.)

These hypothetical cost/benefit questions are still artificially simplistic. The real cost/benefit questions (and hence the real moral questions) also include:

i. When we allocate resources to create a new benefit, how should the new benefits in turn be used? For example, should we use it to expand wealth or to enhance health, safety or make other gains in liberty?

ii. Then distributional questions arise: additional wealth or liberty for what beings, over what space and what time? We are clearly permitted to consume some benefits but it is equally clear that if we are to honour the principles of the equal worth of every person and the worth of all that lives, we cannot consume as much as we like unless we can leave others with the same largesse. Within these parameters, however, lies an enormous range of options, both with respect to us and others alive now, us and future generations, and us and other kinds of being.

iii. Technical questions, such as whether the

principle of equal worth can be realized in equal cost/benefit *ratios,* or whether equal cost/benefit *distributions* (so that everyone gets the same amount of each, and not just the same ratio) are required. This question too needs to be asked for nonhuman as well as human beings.[17]

. . . . And so on, almost without limit. Public policy that is rational from the cost/benefit point of view (and therefore public policy that meets even the necessary conditions of moral soundness) is extraordinarily complicated – something that will come as no surprise to those familiar with the deep and sometimes unavoidable vacuum in which many policy decisions are taken.[18]

It is perhaps worth noting, before we leave this topic, that cost/benefit issues may also be relevant to our previous discussion of probability and obligations. There I argued that the probability of there not being relevantly similar people, or people at all, must be determinate and fairly high before our obligations are significantly reduced. This argument may have to be modified in the following way. If the costs of meeting these obligations are high enough that great benefits could otherwise be achieved, our obligations may fall faster than would otherwise be the case. The same might be argued, *mutatis mutandis,* for other creatures, ecological systems, etc.

5. Moral assessment and risk assessment. Costs and benefits and other aspects of resource utilization always have risks attached: there is a risk that expending resources will not achieve the targeted benefit, that something in the process will have unintended side effects, and so on. How should assessment of risks guide our ethical assessments? In my view, no matter how well technological risk assessment based in probability calculations is done, it is never settles the ethical questions. Of course, this does not imply that risk assessments have no role to play. Even if we should always do a separate ethical assessment, we must also ground it in the best knowledge of the facts available. This is what the regime of risk assessment can provide. Nevertheless, after all the facts are in, we still have to apply our ethical principles and make an independent determination of what we ought to do.

Here is an easy example to demonstrate that level of risk and level of ethical seriousness are not the same thing. Consider the spate of children run over by school buses every year. With these accidents, increased moral acceptability is not linear with decreasing risk. Reducing the frequency of such accidents would not be enough to make the ones that remain morally acceptable. No such accidents are acceptable. That implies that the only acceptable level of risk in this case is the lowest level attainable or perhaps no risk at all. In short, risk and moral acceptability are not in a linear relationship.

Here is another way in which risk assessment does not settle the ethical questions. In Canada we generate electricity primarily in three ways: nuclear fission, burning fossil fuels (coal, oil or natural gas), and hydro power. Compare nuclear to fossil fuel generation. These technologies clearly have very different harm/probability profiles. The harms that nuclear power can inflict are catastrophically large, as Chernobyl demonstrated, but the probability of incurring them is generally thought to be quite low, at least in Canada. By contrast, with fossil fuel we are virtually certain to incur the harms they can produce, harms such as the CO_2 and SO_2 emissions and release of radium and other radioactive and/or toxic elements already mentioned and also depletion of a nonrenewable resource. However, these harms are generally considered less significant than those that a nuclear disaster can inflict. Whether we are right to consider the harms inflicted by burning fossil fuels relatively less significant might be debated but the point I want to make here is this. Only by a separate ethical assessment in the light of our various visions of the good life for ourselves and other kinds of beings can one assess the high harm/low probability risks of nuclear power

against low harm/high probability risks such as we find with fossil fuels.

Other philosophically difficult questions arise about costs and risks, too. For example, how does diminishing level of risk work, or rather, how should it work, as a discounter of costs? It is quite clear that it does do so: in connection with the nuclear industry we have been able to accept some potential costs that would be quite horrendous because we have been able to convince ourselves that the risk of having to pay them is quite low. Since we cannot avoid running some low risks of high costs in whatever we do, it seems clear that some discount factor must be morally acceptable. But how much a cost can be discounted as the probability of risk moves to very small figures is totally unclear. It is an important question in connection with the nuclear industry generally and in connection with our relation to future generations in particular. The principle of equal worth is unlikely to be able to help us with it.

Second, is there such a thing as an absolutely unacceptable cost, however low the risk and whatever the benefit? Given the Doomsday aura that surrounds certain aspects of the nuclear industry, this is a question that some people have asked. Even the principles, let alone the criteria and facts, for an adequate answer probably do not exist.

A third difficult question about costs starts from the idea that the depletion of nonrenewable resources is itself a cost being imposed on future generations. Classical economic cost/benefit analysis does not seem well suited to thinking about this kind of cost, there being no possible benefit that could compensate for it. Criteria for assigning cost values to questions of depletion are needed and might be difficult to find.

6. Uncertainty. We can never be certain about any outcome in a complex industrial system and the further we move into the future, the more uncertain we become. How can we reach ethical conclusions in the face of such uncertainty?

One of the most ethically vexing aspects of the nuclear industry or any other big, technologically complex system flows from the limits of knowledge. Though I have spoken about many factual issues above as though the relevant facts are known with a high degree of certainty, in fact that is not always the case. It would have taken many detailed qualifications to identify even the most important limits to certainty but that does not mean that they do not exist. This compounds the problem of risk assessment: not only must we try to assess the level of risk in each relevant context, risk being a matter of the size of a danger times the probability of it occurring, we must also recognize that there are uncertainties built into these calculations so large that our conclusions could be seriously in error.

There is probably no good ethical way to take account of this limitation. The best we can do from the moral point of view is to err on the side of caution. Where we are dealing with the health and safety of large numbers of humans and other living things over large ecological systems and geological periods of time, we can be sure that we have met our obligations in the face of uncertainty only if we build the worst outcomes that are at all likely into our analyses at all relevant points.

7. Reducing risk vs. retaining benefits. As well as posing very serious risks of radiological and chemical poisoning, spent nuclear fuel also houses a huge potential benefit. As was noted earlier, one of the results of fissioning uranium is an even heavier and more fissionable metal, plutonium. Plutonium does not exist in nature but substantial amounts of it are contained in spent reactor fuel. Since it is just as good a reactor fuel as uranium, it would generate enormous amounts of additional energy if it were to be 'burned' in its own controlled chain reaction. This gives rise to a tricky ethical question.

On the one hand, we want to protect future generations from the risks posed by the plutonium in spent fuel – unprotected contact and diversion for weapons. On the other hand, we do not want to cut them off from a potentially huge benefit. What is the optimal balance between reducing these hazards over a geological time frame and leaving this potential benefit available to future generations? In the light of the diversion risk, should we make it impossible for future generations to use this resource at all? After all, it does have potential to be used to make bombs.

8. Procedural issues. My comments on procedural ethics will be very sketchy; the topic requires a paper of its own. In connection with the management of nuclear wastes, a number of important ethical issues arise that have to do with procedures. Who should make the decisions? What procedures will allow all stakeholders to have a fair say? What procedures will generate the best decisions? (These are not necessarily the same.) How can we prevent the majority from tyrannizing minorities; should communities have veto power, for example, over the location of a facility in their area? (This is a basic problem in all democratic decision making.) Can compensation justify overruling a community's or an individual's objections? And how should the wishes of people with views very different from ourselves be taken into account?

This last question is pressing with respect to the geological deep disposal proposal. The facility is likely to be built in northern Ontario. If it is, aboriginal people will be far more affected by the facility than by any other aspect of the nuclear fuel cycle. Yet, not only have they not received many benefits from the power thus generated, they tend to view the world and our place in it in a way that is quite antithetical to big power or any other system that imposes heavy environmental demands. How should these people enter the decision making process, in particular the process of choosing a site?

The Current Proposal
We have now discussed the eight considerations introduced earlier: principles; scope; discounting;

cost/risk/benefit; moral assessment and risk assessment; uncertainty; reducing risk vs. retaining benefits; and procedures. It seems to me that the conclusion is clear: we have an ethical obligation to find a permanent, passive solution to the problem of radioactive waste management. A true ethical skeptic or someone with a strong interest in ignoring the problem of nuclear wastes might still try to wiggle out, but to refuse to accept such arguments as ethically binding would be pretty much to get out of the business of justifying courses of action, finding good and sufficient reasons for what we do, altogether. Moreover, we do care about these principles – they are deeply embedded in our view of how interpersonal relations ought to be governed and therefore in our notions of self-respect and sense of decency.

How does the current proposal to bury spent fuel in plutonic rock in the Canadian Shield fare when assessed against these desiderata?

1. Deep geological disposal of high level wastes probably achieves fairness and protects future liberty better than any other proposal.

2. Compared to other options, deep disposal seems likely to provide protection of the widest scope in all three dimensions, that is, kind of being, time, and place.

3. Because of its long time frame, deep disposal discounts future generations of people and other living things less than any other disposal option being considered.

4. Concerning costs and benefit, deep disposal would clearly force those who benefit to assume the costs. On the issue of achieving the greatest benefit for a given cost, however, I wonder if the deep disposal concept may not be less than optimal. I suspect that greater social and ecological goods could be attained by building a less secure facility and expending some of the funds in other ways. I have in mind things such as other protections for ecosystems, population control, and of course the perennial demands of feeding the hun-

gry, helping people find sustainable ways to provide for themselves, and achieving a fairer distribution of resources.

5. Because deep disposal reduces risk as far as is reasonably achievable, given current knowledge, it does as well at satisfying our moral demands for risk reduction as any disposal method is likely to do.

6. At least half a billion dollars worth of research has been done in connection with the deep disposal option. Thus the uncertainties in our knowledge have probably been reduced more than is true of any other option being considered.[19]

7. Recovering the plutonium contained in spent fuel buried in plutonic rock would be expensive but not impossible. So a balance is struck between minimization of harm and retrievability of possible benefits, though one favouring minimization of harm.

8. Since most of the important procedural issues will arise as the proposal is considered in the public arena and decisions are made about commencement, site, etc., it is too early to say how the proposal stacks up procedurally.

Application to Other Issues
The methodology we have used for determining our obligations in connection with nuclear wastes could be applied to many other issues, too. Within the nuclear industry, some nonenvironmental issues to which it could be applied include: uranium mining and an economy based on exploitation of natural resources; marketing nuclear technology; terrorism and the weapons risk; consumption vs. conservation in industrial economies; the creation of a technological 'priesthood' having esoteric knowledge and a lot of resulting power; and other industrial and social structure issues.[20]

The moral analysis offered above can be applied to other social and environmental issues, land use policy for example. The issues that arise in connection with policy for the use of land (such as soil depletion, biomass depletion, and diversion of land from agriculture to housing, transportation and industry) have essentially the same moral structure as the issue of nuclear wastes.[21] They are all situations in which gaining a benefit for ourselves now will impose large costs on future generations of humans and other beings with little by way of compensating benefits unless we do something. Yet the costs of doing anything effective would be quite high and yield little if any direct benefit to us. The moral issue is also the same: Do we have an obligation to assume the costs of our current activities, thus saving future generations from having to do so?

More analysis is needed before definitive moral conclusions can be reached about nuclear energy and the environment, both factual and criterial analysis. Much has been done – a number of fairly well founded standards now exist, for example, and a promising proposal for a high level waste disposal facility is under consideration. But more remains to be done and we still do not have an integrated ethical framework within which to think about the industry and what surrounds it as a whole.

The biggest problem may not be the lack of a clear ethical framework, however. In many areas of social policy, what we are obliged to do is actually quite clear. The problem is to muster the personal and political will and the resources to do it. I think that we know what we should do about nuclear wastes: find the most permanent, passive solution to them that comes at a reasonable cost, given the costs of other potential benefits, and that will not make future exploitation of the fuel impossible. How do we marshall the will and the resources to do it?[22]

ENDNOTES

[1] Royal Commission on Electric Power Planning, *A Race Against Time* (known as the Porter Commission Report after the Chair of the Commission, Arthur Porter). Toronto: Queen's Printer, 1978, p. 153.

[2] The best collection of papers on obligations to future generations is still Partridge, E. ed. *Responsibilities to Future Generations*. Buffalo NY: Prometheus, 1981.

[3] There is now an extensive literature exploring the relationship between ethics and issues in public policy. For some examples, see:

Brown, Donald. Ethics, Science, and Environmental Regulation. *Environmental Ethics* 9(4), Winter 1987, 331-349.

Kelman, Steven. Cost Benefit Analysis: An Ethical Critique. *Regulation* January/February 1981, 74-82.

Leonard, Herman B. and Richard J. Zeckhauser. Cost-Benefit Analysis Defended. *Report of the Centre for Philosophy and Public Policy* 3(3), 1983.

Sagoff, Mark. Fact and Value in Ecological Science. *Environmental Ethics* Volume 7(2), Summer 1985, 99-116.

Shrader-Frechette, Kristin. Environmental Impact Assessment and the Fallacy of Unfinished Business. *Environmental Ethics* 4(1), Spring 1982, 37-47.

(All these articles are reproduced in A. Greenbaum, A. Wellington, and E. Baar, editors, *Social Conflict and Environmental Law.* Captus Press, 1995.)

Some interesting longer studies are:

Salter, Liora. *Mandated Science: Science and Scientists in the Making of Standards.* Dordrecht: Kluwer Academic Publishers, 1988.

Schrecker, Ted F. *Political Economy of Environmental Hazards.* Ottawa: Law Reform Commission of Canada, 1984.

Brunk, Conrad, Lawrence Haworth, and Brenda Lee. *Value Assumptions in Risk Assessment: A Case Study of the Alachlor Controversy.* Waterloo: Wilfred Laurier University Press, 1991.

Shrader-Frechette, Kristin. *Risk and Rationality.* Berkeley: University of California Press, 1991.

[4] Here is what is meant by saying that uranium is enriched. In nature, more than 99 percent of uranium is of the isotope 238, less than 1 percent is 235, the fissionable material. In bombs, enough of the 238 is removed to raise the portion of 235 to roughly 70 percent of the total. The fuel in most reactors is enriched, too, but the ratio of 235 is increased only to about 7 percent, not to 70 percent or more as in bombs. In CANDU reactors the fissionable 235 is in the same proportion as in nature, about .7 percent of the total. Among other things, this makes CANDU fuel more difficult to use as raw material for bombs.

[5] An order of magnitude is ten times larger or smaller than the initial amount. So if X is two orders of magnitude larger than Y, then X is 100 times (10x10) larger than Y.

[6] '300 to 800 years': see the report of the Advisory Panel on Tailings of the Atomic Energy Control Board, *An Appraisal*

of Current Practices for the Management of Uranium Mill Tailings (AECB 1156). '200,000 times less': Environmental Impact Statement on the Concept for the Disposal of Canada's Nuclear Fuel Wastes. Atomic Energy of Canada Ltd 10721, COG-93-11, 1994. Unless otherwise noted, facts cited concerning high level wastes are taken from this document.

[7] A halflife is the time it takes the radioactivity in a material to diminish by one half. Thus plutonium is half as radioactive after 24,000 years, one quarter as radioactive after 48,000 years, one eighth as radioactive after 72,000 years, and so on.

[8] American Physical Society, Report to the American Physical Society by the Study Croup on Nuclear Fuel Cycles and Waste Management, Review of Modern Physics 50 (January 1978), pp. 1-186.

[9] For more on the ethics of managing low level uranium mine/mill waste, see A. Brook, Obligations to Future Generations: A Case Study Contemporary Moral Issues, 3rd edition. Ed. A. W. Cragg. Toronto: McGraw-Hill Ryerson, 1992.

[10] Similar proposals are under investigation in the United States, Sweden, and other parts of the world.

[11] At this point, some ethicists would introduce the leading metaethical positions such as libertarianism, contractarianism, utilitarianism, and various egalitarian and deontological approaches. An interesting example is contained in Ch. 6 of the first reference document for Environmental Impact Statement on the Concept for the Disposal of Canada's Nuclear Fuel Wastes. Atomic Energy of Canada Ltd 10721, COG-93-11, 1994. The reference document is M. Greber et al., The Disposal of Canada's Nuclear Fuel Waste: Public Involvement and Social Aspects. AECL 10712, COG-93-2, 1994. Some of this moral background can also be found in R. Gaizauskas, A Philosophical Examination of Our Responsibility to Future Generations. Project for the AECB (AECB: Ottawa, 1977). I have adopted a different strategy.

[12] We could even go so far as to weigh personal attributes differentially without violating the principle, though many would consider these morally irrelevant: for some people and in some contexts, having Beethoven's powers may make him more valuable than John Smith. Likewise for other kinds of genius, sensitivity, and maybe even personal beauty, grace or charm.

[13] Williams, B. Ethics and the Limits of Philosophy. Cambridge, MA: Harvard University Press 1985, see esp. Ch. 6.

[14] Holmes Rolston mounts an argument along these lines connecting interests to moral worth in Environmental Ethics. Temple University Press 1988.

An argument diametrically opposed to the thrust of his and my analysis has enjoyed some currency in libertarian and contractarian circles. It urges that we have no obligations to future generations, to other creatures, or even to many contemporary persons, as follows:

1. We have obligations only where someone has rights; rights are conferred by explicit or implicit agreement of others.

2. Only actual, not possible, persons can enter into agreements and thereby gain rights. Very few even of them have entered any such agreements with me or people with whom I share rights.

3. In particular, no future person could enter agreements or have rights; to contract, you have to be alive.

4. Hence no future person can have rights now.

5. Hence we have no obligation now to future persons.

6. Likewise, mutatis mutandis, for other species, most other people alive now, and so on. Even if we accept 1. to 3., however, 4. does not follow. First, a person's rights may extend further in time than the person does. Thus any actual person, no matter at what time he or she is actual, may well have rights now. Second, the argument as a whole assumes that we have no obligations to people and other beings that are not conferred by agreement. Against this view, a powerful argument can be mounted that people and other beings have intrinsic value, value that does not depend on whether others acknowledge it or bind themselves by agreement to respect it.

[15] People, Penguins, and Plastic Trees, Pt. IV. Ed. D. VanDeVeer and C. Pierce (Belmont CA: Wadsworth, 1986) contains a useful collection of papers on various aspects of cost/risk/benefit analysis.

[16] Bodde, D. L. Radioactive wastes: pragmatic strategies and ethical perspectives. In D. Maclean and P. G. Brown, eds. Energy and the Future. Totawa NJ: Rowman and Littlefield 1983, p. 121.

[17] To some extent, this is merely an academic question. Some level of cost is unavoidable to any being who has to service a body, so any strict adherence even to the ratio interpretation will achieve at least some measure of distributional equity.

[18] In some contexts, at least three further cost/benefit questions would have to be addressed. Fortunately, they do not affect our obligations with respect to nuclear wastes. (i) Are total benefits of an activity greater than minimum total costs? With respect to nuclear wastes, the answer is almost certainly yes. (ii) Are sufficient total resources available at all? The answer is again yes, though the real question here is whether sufficient resources can reasonably be made available; and were the answer not yes, we would have to go into that very difficult question in a serious way. (iii) Will future generations be able to secure the same benefits for themselves much more cheaply than we can? Although the answer is probably no, the whole question can be rejected,

if my earlier argument is sound, because it is we who are reaping the benefits of nuclear power and so there is no sound moral reason in general that future generations should be made to assume any of the costs.

[19] For a full discussion of the issue, see Shrader-Frechette, Kristin. *Burying Uncertainty: Risk and the Case against Geological Disposal.* Berkely CA: University of California Press, 1993. She arrives at a conclusion somewhat different from mine.

[20] For a good, though somewhat dated introduction to these broader issues in the ethics of nuclear power, see Shrader-Frechette, Kristin. *Nuclear Power and Public Policy.* Dordrecht, Holland: Reidel, 1980.

[21] See Shrader-Frechette, K. and L. K. Caldwell *Policy for Land ; Law and Ethics.* Lanham MD: Rowman, 1993.

[22] I would like to thank Christine Koggel, Wesley Cragg, Ann Wiles and Alex Wellington for many helpful comments and suggestions.

* Editor's Note: The AECB studies may be obtained by writing to: Atomic Energy Control Board, 280 Slater St., P.O. Box 1046, Ottawa K1P 5S9. Atomic Energy of Canada Ltd. documents can be obtained from: AECL Research, Whiteshell Laboratories, Pinawa, Manitoba R0E 1L0. The material you wish to obtain should be identified by name and date or number as indicated above.

POLITICS, ETHICS, AND ECOLOGY
CONFRONTING THE TRAGEDY OF THE COMMONS

8

by Lionel Rubinoff

CRITICS OF THE GROWTH ECONOMY HAVE PERSISTENTLY raised questions about the equation of welfare with affluence and the life-style of progressive consumption which, although it has been promoted as the path to peace and prosperity, has fostered instead conditions which have led to a tragedy of the commons.[1] One of the characteristic features of the growth ethic is a generally misguided faith in the magic of the "technological fix" which encourages and facilitates, almost without reservation, the implementation of policies that permit the substitution of an artificial for a natural environment.[2] In a society whose institutions and values have been shaped by such attitudes citizens in search of consumer satisfaction will often turn a blind eye to the willingness of politicians to compromise environmental and ethical standards for the purpose of protecting their political agendas. Such compromises are often rationalized in the name of the so-called public "interest" and carry the promise of substantial economic benefits for the citizenry at large. In truth, however, the economic benefits are more likely to be enjoyed by the corporate elites (upon whom the politicians rely for their hold on power); and usually at the expense of the citizenry who are consistently misled by their political leaders into believing that the GNP is the ultimate index of economic health and public welfare.[3]

For the sake of holding onto the power which is the reward for their support of the corporate agenda, politicians are prepared not only to suppress any information that does not support their policies but to discredit those who speak out against the corporate agenda. Since the reinvention of the natural environment by technological means has served the corporate agenda well this technological assault on the environment in the name of progress has become a characteristic feature of capitalism. Environmentalists who wish to preserve nature and protect its "rights" are thus demonized and unfairly represented as as "luddites" and "enemies" of the so-called "public interest." The corporations meanwhile have cleverly conscripted the public into supporting their contempt for the agenda of environmentalists by sponsoring and helping to promote such pressure groups as "The Wise Use Movement" in the U.S. and the "Share Movement" in B.C. – both of which have been inspired by the leadership of Ron Arnold, who has portrayed environmentalism as a conspiracy to "kill jobs" and "trash the economy."[4]

In Ibsen's play, *An Enemy of the People*, we have a classic case of the deliberate use of deception by public officials for the purpose of protecting those invested economic interests which provide the basis for their conception of the public good. The problem arises when the public health officer Dr. Thomas Stockman, who is a civil servant, issues a report to his brother the Mayor, indicating that the public baths which are the chief source of the community's economy are poisonous and a threat to public health. Rather than risk economic ruin, the Mayor and the directors of the baths conspire to suppress this information until such time as they can afford to correct the problem. For the present, however they are simply not willing to pay the price necessary to meet the required environmental and public health standards that would ensure the safety of the tourists who frequent the baths.

This leads to a heated debate between the mayor and his brother and forces the public officials and local "free press" to take a stand in support of either the medical officer or the so-called "public interest" as interpreted by the Mayor. At first the press corps and some of the public officials are inclined to support Dr. Stockman, but they soon realize that if the report is made public the authorities will be forced to close down the baths until such time as the necessary renovations have been completed. When it is made clear that the cost of these alterations will have to be supported by the taxpayers at large, and not the directorate of the baths, they are easily persuaded that Dr. Stockman's report is merely an unverified hypothesis, and no doubt exaggerated at that. It would thus, in their view, be premature to release it.

It is not that they have decided to tell a deliberate lie. They have rather readjusted their values, priorities and moral principles in order to accommodate their shift of allegiance from Dr. Stockman to the Mayor and the so-called "public interest." They have adopted a crude, if not corrupt, interpretation of utilitarianism which enables them to determine that the greatest happiness of the greatest number, or the greatest balance of good over evil, will be achieved by suppressing rather than releasing the report, thus ignoring J.S. Mill's admonition that "truth is part of the meaning of utility."[5] In the process it is Dr. Stockman who now stands against the "public interest," and is therefore "an enemy of the people." In the end he finds himself totally outcast and alone in his crusade to speak the truth.To make matters worse, the very people on whose behalf Dr. Stockman imagines himself to speak turn against him because even they do not want to hear what he feels obliged to tell them. They will thus refuse to listen to him and will regard him as an irresponsible subversive; thereby safeguarding their own invested interests and protecting the jobs upon which they depend for their livelihood.

The plot of Ibsen's play is not something foreign to contemporary life in Canada. Recent Canadian history contains many examples of public policy decisions and industrial projects that compromise even the most modestly conceived environmental standards required by Canadian legislation, let alone what ought to be the standards governing our economic activities. These case studies illustrate how science, law and the democratic right of public participation (and even in some cases the economic interests of the public) are all sacrificed if they are perceived to stand in the way of mega-projects that have a privileged place in the government and corporate agendas. Rather than the political agenda of governments in power being shaped by a genuine vision of the public good, the public good is determined by a political agenda that has been shaped by an overriding corporate influence. For the sake of these interests, information regarding the environmental impact of mega-projects is suppressed, and not only people working on behalf of community-based and public interest environmental organizations, but even scientists employed by government agencies, are consistently frustrated in their attempts to present the truth as they know it.

The practice of compromising environmental standards for the sake of the corporate agenda, which includes bestowing the privileges of power upon those who play along, is made easier by the technocratic attitude that seems to have taken possession of industry and government. The foundation of this attitude is a seemingly uncritical faith in the magic of the technological fix combined with the conviction that there is nothing special about the natural environment that requires keeping it intact in its existing form.[6] In short, according to this dogma, "plastic trees" are as good as "natural ones." Indeed, as Martin Kreiger has argued, "much more can be done with plastic trees and the like to give most people the feeling they are experiencing nature." "We have to realize," he continues, "that the way in which we experience nature is conditioned by our society – which more and more seems to be receptive to responsible interventions."[7] That these interventions are more and more taking the form of a technological fix does not for Kreiger seem to be a matter of moral concern.

The Great Whale Project:
Science Vs Politics

In our first case study, the Great Whale Hydro Project, we have a graphic example of the use of political pressure to silence scientific criticism of a mega-project whose completion was high on the political agendas of both the federal and the Quebec governments. Once completed this project would consist of huge Hydro electric dams across the Great Whale River which would flood an area of 44,000 square kilometres, thus creating a water filled reservoir the size of Prince Edward Island. The flooding not only threatens the traditional hunting and trapping grounds of the Cree, but a federal government scientist, Dr. John Rudd, has recently assembled some data that might implicate the project in global warming by the greenhouse effect.[8] In September 1992 Dr Rudd was invited to give testimony about his research to a group of scientists meeting in New York City for the purpose of reviewing the Quebec Hydro Project. However, at the last minute his superiors in the federal Department of Fisheries and Oceans told him that he would not be allowed to go. The excuse they gave was that his research was still in a preliminary stage of development and had not yet gone through the usual process of peer review. It was thus deemed premature for Dr. Rudd to publicize his speculations on the matter. It was Dr. Rudd's conviction, however, that scientists, as scientists, have a moral as well as a professional obligation to offer expert opinion on the implications of hypotheses formulated on the basis of their research data without having to worry about the possible political implications of doing so. Society, he believes, depends upon scientists offering their opinions on the ethical and public health implications of their research in an unbi-

ased manner. He would agree, in other words, with the stance taken by Dr. Stockman in Ibsen's play, *An Enemy of the People*.

The hypothesis that Dr. Rudd and his colleagues had developed at the Fresh Water Institute in Winnipeg, and about which he was prepared to speak, was that hydro-electric reservoirs created as a result of the flooding of peat moss may be producing greenhouse gases that will exacerbate the already serious enough global warming phenomenon. In such cases of massive flooding of peat lands, the water level rises above the level of the plants causing the plants to die. Instead of absorbing carbon dioxide from the atmosphere and storing that carbon as peat, they begin to decompose, and the decomposition of the organic material, as is very well established, results in the production of methane and carbon dioxide. The concern is that because of the scale of the Great Whale Project, this phenomenon may be occurring at a substantial rate. Data in support of this hypothesis has already been made available by the results of research conducted in other parts of the country, where the production of large quantities of carbon dioxide and methane have been observed to occur in both naturally occurring wetlands and artificially created pools. The creation of additional artificial pools on top of naturally occurring wetlands will only decrease the capacity of peatlands to store carbon dioxide and increase the production of gasses. And this may occur on a scale similar to what might be expected to result from a coal-fired electrical generating plant.

These speculations, according to Dr. Rudd, tend to undermine the myth that hydro-electric power is the cleanest form of power in the world. Accordingly, what he wanted to tell his colleagues in New York was that the electricity generated by the Great Whale project in Quebec could be as damaging to the environment as if it had been generated by the burning of coal. His advice was to have been a recommendation that there be a moratorium on the construction of the project until scientists were able to assess the results of experiments already underway, the conclusions of which would have a significant bearing on the Great Whale Project. In other words, until there was clear evidence that the project was environmentally safe, it was Dr. Rudd's considered opinion that we would be well advised to proceed with caution. Other prominent research scientists in this field agreed with him.

Why then was he forbidden to attend the meeting in New York? The suspicion is that the claim of Dr. Rudd's superiors that his research was at too preliminary a stage to be made public was just an excuse to hide another agenda. Other scientists have testified that there is sufficient experimental data to warrant Dr. Rudd's advice on the matter. The real reason was more likely a concern by the federal government that the release of such information, and a recommendation by one of their own scientists to delay the completion of the Great Whale Project, could embarrass the federal government at a sensitive time in their negotiations with Quebec over constitutional issues. Hence Dr. Rudd was ordered not to attend the meeting in New York. If so, then we have a blatant example of a deliberate attempt to suppress scientific information about a government supported mega-project – that frankly places the entire world community at risk – for the sake of a political agenda of importance to Canadian politicians. Even though it might be true that Dr. Rudd's research could take another three years to complete, it should be obvious that if his hypothesis is confirmed, and there has not been a moratorium on the construction of Great Whale, the damage that would result could be irreversible. The observations of the distinguished environmental scientist Dr. David Schindler on this matter confirm this evaluation:

With respect to being in the preliminary stages, Rudd is in the preliminary stages of one critical experiment, but he has seventeen years of experience with other sorts of experiments that are of direct relevance to flooding of wetlands and other situations of that type that relate to the Great Whale project. In particular, he's probably the world's foremost expert on processes controlling the methylation of mercury and the release of mercury from flooded wetlands and uptake by fish. My opinion is that he has plenty to say to that panel about the effects of the Great Whale project on fisheries and wetlands and other components and on the release of methane to the atmosphere. I view this as just the usual excuse of government bureaucrats to keep scientists from giving scientific information in forms that might interfere with the Canadian political agenda. It's infuriating that we have some of the best scientific experts in the world in the federal Government and the public does not have access to what they know because they are used as political tools.[9]

There are other ethical issues at stake, such as the impact the Great Whale has had on the culture of the Cree. The question raised here is whether – quite apart from the greenhouse effect – there is any moral justification for the disruption of the natural ecosystem, and the Cree way of life that depends upon this eco-system, for the sake of the economic gains that are promised by the Project? In this and other examples of conflicts between the environment and the economy, policy decisions are sometimes legitimized by an appeal to disagreement among scientists; as in the controversy over global warming. But while policy decisions that use scientific uncertainty as an excuse for inaction may pretend to have the support of science, they are in truth the outcome of value judgments in which importance is assigned to short term economic and political considerations rather than to environmental concerns and the welfare of posterity. In cases where science is unable to provide conclusive evidence concerning the potential risks to ecosystems of mega-projects, it becomes the responsibility of public policy to decide when there is enough evidence and whether to require further studies before approval is granted.

In the case of the Great Whale, as in the play by Ibsen, economic and political considerations have, throughout most of the history of this project, taken precedence over ethical concerns for the welfare of the Cree and scientific concerns over ecosystem-integrity. For politicians, mega-projects like the Great Whale are deemed defensible on the grounds that the economic benefits that accrue for the corporate proponents will "trickle-down" to the general public. Contrary to what politicians may argue, however, mega projects are usually not justifiable on simply economic grounds, as the citizens of Ontario have learned painfully over the many years of subsidizing the debts incurred by Ontario Hydro's massive investment in nuclear energy production, and as Donald Dewees of the University of Toronto has indicated concerning the Ontario Hydro Supply Demand Hearings.[10] In any case, considering what is at stake for both the environment and the culture of the Cree, the news that the Quebec government has decided to halt all construction on this project can only be greeted with jubilation by environmentalists and concerned citizens.

Alcan and The Kimano-Completion Project
Another mega-project with profound implications for the environment is the massive Alcan Kitimat-Kimano hydro project on the Nechako river in British Columbia. The story behind this project offers a prime example of how transnationals like Alcan have succeeded in creating a separate ethic for themselves that exempts them from the constraints that we have traditionally come to expect will be imposed by government officials in a democracy, acting in their capacity as trustees of the public interest. And once again we have an example of invested interests overriding the advice of senior scientists concerned about the impact of a

mega-project on the environment.[11]

The background to this issue may be described briefly as follows. Following the end of World War Two in 1945, many of the Canadian industries that had sustained considerable growth during the war because of their role in supporting the Allied efforts continued to expand as the post-war world introduced the prospect of a bright new economic future. One of these companies, the Aluminium Company of Canada, or Alcan, expanded westward from Ontario and Quebec to British Columbia. In 1950, in an effort to provide themselves with an inexpensive source of Hydro-electric power, Alcan initiated the development of the Kitimat-Kimano project, made possible by a set of agreements with the provincial government of British Columbia. In an effort to encourage Alcan's expansion into B.C., premier Byron Johnson introduced special legislation authorizing his cabinet, "notwithstanding any law to the contrary," to do what it thought necessary to help establish a new aluminum industry in the Province.[12] The agreement of 1950, observes John Goddard, "reads like an expression of gratitude to Alcan for taking a chunk of wilderness off the government's hands."[13] As a result of these agreements Alcan took possession of the Nechako River watershed, the Nechako being the third largest tributary of the Fraser River.

The Alcan project required the creation of large reservoirs of water. This was made possible by the building of the Kenny dam on the headwaters of the Nechako which caused the flooding of 80,000 acres of the watershed. The dam, which was completed in 1952, reversed the natural easterly flow of the headwaters of the Nechako westward into a chain of lakes that became a large reservoir. From this artificially created reservoir the water was then piped through a 16 km tunnel to a power house inside the Coast Mountains at Kimano, where a 900 mega watt generating station consisting of eight hydroelectric generators was installed. An 82-Km transmission line was then built from Kimano to Kitimat, where Alcan erected a townsite and one of the world's largest aluminium smelters, employing 2200 workers and supporting a community of 11,000 people.[14] By constructing its own dam and generating facilities Alcan became virtually energy self-sufficient and thus protected itself from the expense of increasing utility rates. Alcan is currently one of the world's most powerful trans-nationals, employing 50,000 employees in 25 countries throughout the world, with annual revenues of approximately 8 billion dollars.[15] It has bauxite mines in five countries, smelting facilities in five countries, factories for semifinished products in 12 countries and sales outlets worldwide.[16] It has been the most profitable company in Canadian history. In 1988, for example, it made a $901 million (U.S.) profit, more than any other Canadian company to that point.[17]

Although the environmental damage caused by the Kitimat/Kimano project has never been fully assessed, the obvious effects include flooding, habitat loss, displacement of indigenous peoples, and a 33 percent reduction in water flow in the Nechako River, resulting in what now appear to be serious negative consequences for the salmon fisheries which depend upon the Fraser River. Indeed, from the very beginning, the damage to the environment and the communities of the Native Peoples living in the flooded areas was devastating. In 1952, for example, the Carrier Indians of Cheslatta Lake were forced to abandon their homes with only a few days notice. Then, in one of the more sordid episodes in the history of Canada, Indian Affairs officials forged signatures of the exiled Natives on legal documents that surrendered their Native lands to Alcan. Company officials then ordered the homes of the Natives burned to the ground. The Natives themselves were relocated to a windy plateau outside their traditional territory, where diseases like tuberculosis and alcoholism have taken their toll.[18] To this day, changing water levels continue to flood

their burial grounds. Not until March, 1993 were the claims of the Carrier-Cheslatta Indians finally addressed by a multi-million dollar out-of-court settlement with the federal government.

Despite these impacts, Alcan proposed an expansion of its Kimano and Kitimat facilities which called for the building of a second tunnel from the reservoirs at the Kenny Dam to Kimano where four more generators would be installed. This would make it possible for Alcan to build additional smelters. To accomplish this purpose the company intended to make full use of its water rights on the Nechako and Nanika Rivers. This expansion, known as the Kimano Completion Project (KCP), would, when completed, reduce the flow of the Nechako to an estimated 12 percent of its former rate, thereby creating even more serious problems for both the migrating and spawning salmon and the resident communities.

Alcan's intent to pursue the completion of the project was announced in the late 1970's. The company did not need the extra generating capacity at that time but was prompted into action by the realization that in order to achieve its most profitable position it would be necessary to complete the project by the year 2000. When the original agreements were entered into, Alcan was granted a conditional licence which would become a permanent licence at the end of 1999, based on whatever facilities existed at that time, and applying the cheap 1950 rate formula to all completed installations. The company was therefore under pressure to complete the project by the year 2000.

Accordingly, in 1978 Alcan decided to proceed with the project and sell its excess electrical power to B.C. Hydro, which would in turn sell its excess on the American market. Nechako Valley residents now firmly believe that from the beginning Alcan never had any intention of constructing another smelter in British Columbia but was planning instead to become an unregulated, privately-owned power utility.[19]

From the very beginning, Alcan's proposals for the KCP were met with expressions of concern by residents, environmentalists, and senior scientists employed by the Department of Fisheries and Oceans (DFO). The basis of concern was related not only to the quantity of water to be diverted, and the ensuing flooding that would result, but to the flow rates and fluctuating temperatures of the water ways through which the salmon travelled on their way to their spawning grounds. The responsibility for the welfare of the salmon and other fish affected by the project rests with the DFO. In keeping with this responsibility, upon learning of Alcan's intent to proceed with the completion project, the DFO undertook a series of studies to determine the impact of the project on the fish. Because the DFO is also invested with the authority to stop the project, Alcan wisely waited for the DFO to reach some conclusions before investing heavily in the project. By 1985, however, Alcan had lost patience with the DFO and was prepared to take the issue to court. The DFO thus prepared itself for a court battle and instructed the task-force of scientists engaged in the study to prepare its evidence against Alcan for publication and presentation to the courts.

Needless to say, Alcan officials opposed publication of the findings of either their own scientists or the DFO task-force and, thanks to the newly elected pro-business government of Brian Mulroney, the matter was never brought before the courts. Towards the end of August, 1987, after failing to persuade senior scientists to reinterpret the data in ways that would support a compromise proposal favouring Alcan, and before the DFO had a chance to present its case against Alcan before the courts, a four-day closed door meeting took place at Alcan's Vancouver headquarters between Alcan and top government officials – but excluding scientists assigned to the task-force – which resulted in the Minister, Tom Siddon, agreeing to an out-of-court compromise settlement. Instead of scientists assigned to the original task-

force, Siddon invited to the meeting representatives of a different working group led by UBC President Dr. David Strangway. The terms of reference for the Strangway committee included a provision that the Nechako water flows be "equivalent to" the level sought by Alcan.[20] According to the terms of the Settlement Agreement, Alcan would eventually be permitted to divert 88 percent of the water and would also assume responsibility for the management and monitoring of the fish stocks based on its own mitigation procedures. In what appeared to be an astonishing reversal of department policy Alcan thus achieved most of what it wanted.[21]

Tom Siddon has consistently and publicly maintained that his decision was made on the strength of advice he had received to the effect that Alcan's own 22 volume impact report detailing their proposed mitigation procedures was scientifically sound. He firmly believed, he told the CBC's *The Fifth Estate*, that not only would there be no net habitat loss but that the long-range future of the fisheries industries met all of the conditions necessary to ensure sustainable development. However, government scientists who were part of the original task force have a different story to tell. When interviewed by *The Fifth Estate* the consensus among the scientists was not only that Siddons' decision was taken in complete disregard of their advice, but that their exclusion from the 1987 closed-door meeting at which the Agreement was signed was a deliberate attempt to suppress scientific evidence that conflicted with Alcan's interests.

The senior scientists who were excluded from the closed door session in August 1987 disagreed both with Alcan's original proposals and with the DFO's compromise proposals eventually incorporated into the Agreement. According to Don Alderice, a retired senior scientist with the DFO and a member of the task force, pressure was applied to the task force scientists to support the Minister's compromise position while adhering to the scientific evidence. As reported by John Goddard, Alderice claims that they were told "not to fight with Alcan" but to "compromise" and "come to a gentleman's agreement." "At one point," Alderice explained,

> we as a task force put in our preliminary report to Ottawa. Soon after that... Tom Siddon visited the personnel in Vancouver. He said: 'I will not accept this paper. That is my policy, and if you don't like it, shut up or get out.' He indicated that the report was not acceptable because it didn't allow Alcan to do what it wanted. What the feds were trying to do was produce a body of research information that said to Alcan, 'This is okay, go ahead.'[22]

In short, it appears that there was a blatant attempt on the part of DFO officials to co-opt scientists into supporting the political agenda of the federal Cabinet, thus tempting them to compromise their scientific integrity. When they refused, the Strangway working committee was assembled; apparently with instructions to be more co-operative. Evidence supporting this allegation became public on October 14, 1992, when the NDP MP from British Columbia, Brian Gardiner, unveiled a package of confidential letters and memos written by federal scientists which documented the internal struggle over the water flows that occurred within the DFO both prior to and after the signing of the agreement. Many of the details concerning the contents of this package have been reported by Bev Christensen in her recently published book, *Too Good to be True*.[23] The following text taken directly from Christensen's book unfolds a scenario reminiscent of the plot of Ibsen's *An Enemy of the People*.

> In this package was a memo written July 18, 1986, by H. Mundie, of the department's fisheries research branch in Nanaimo, to Rod Bell-Irving, of the department's fisheries research branch in Vancouver. The memo

begins: "Howard Smith has asked me (June 26) to make changes in my expert witness statement of June 3 and to send a revision to you and a copy to him." Mundie goes on to say Smith criticized his statement for being too adversarial and negative. He expresses concern about changing evidence he claims clearly indicates reducing the river flows further would reduce the salmon-production capacity of the Netchako River.

> ....my statement consists mainly of fact, not of opinion. Of 29 cases of regulated [river] flow, 26 resulted in reduced salmon stocks. This outcome has a likelihood of one in 200 of occurring by chance. This hardly leaves room for subjective views.

> He alleged that the department appeared to be asking him to make the argument that, since the department's proposed flows were higher than Alcan's, they were more acceptable.

> The lesson of the case histories is that one cannot remove 69 per cent of the water from a river and expect to maintain salmon runs. There is, therefore, no relative merit in the DFO flows over those of Alcan; both are insufficient.[24]

> Near the conclusion of the letter Mundie says Howard Smith told him those members of the department's technical staff who do not support the minister (for which read "change their expert witness statement") "must take their game and play elsewhere."

> Mundie informs Bell-Irving he sought legal advice to help him resolve his dilemma over whether he should obey orders or tell the truth.

> The answer was unequivocal; my obligation was to tell the truth under oath. I was informed that I would be in a far graver

predicament if I signed an affidavit that I did not wholly believe in. I am left with no choice, therefore, but to give my first priority to the acquisition and presentation of the best possible information.

Gardiner charged, based on the information he had obtained, that it was apparently politics, not science, that motivated the federal government first to seek an out-of-court settlement, and then to exempt Alcan's project from its environmental review process. Both moves, he claimed, were made because the government was afraid of the damning evidence its own fisheries biologists would give at the trial or during environmental hearings.[25]

William Schouwenburg, the senior biologist in the DFO's program-planning and economics branch, was equally troubled by the pressure exerted on federal fisheries scientists to change their testimony. Schouwenburg was also the man who wrote the 380-page report of the Kimano task-force which until that point had not been made public. The following excerpt from a memo by Schouwenburg, dated October 25, 1990, documents his growing frustration about efforts being made within the DFO to present Alcan's proposals in a favourable light. In this memo Schouwenberg writes:

I fully appreciate that anyone that is given the task of justifying the technical merits of the agreement under any circumstances will be stressed to the limit. As far as I am concerned it would be like trying to keep clean while following closely behind an operating manure spreader.[26]

Gardiner had also obtained a copy of the Kimano task-force report which he made available to the media. It concludes with eight recommendations about the conditions that should be maintained in the river to protect the salmon.[27] They are clearly at odds with the concessions

granted to Alcan in the 1987 Settlement Agreement approved by Tom Sidden and his Deputy Minister.

Christensen cites another memo written by Schouwenburg and forwarded to the members of the task-force in November, 1990, together with a final version of the still-secret task-force report.

I have attached copies of the exchange of correspondence I had with the Director General [Pat Chamut] which clearly demonstrates the desperate lengths to which he is prepared to go to hide the fact that the Nechako Agreement was a political and not a technical resolution to the problem. He did, however, leave me an "out" so that I could finalize the report and that I have done. Do not assume that any request from the public to see this document will be honoured. In the recent flare up over the wonderfulness of the assessment process and the lack of public input to the final Agreement, Mr. Chamut refused to provide this document to [Dr.] Gordon Hartman [a DFO fisheries biologist]. It appears that the words "Alcan," "Nechako" and "Kimano" as well as any knowledge pertaining to those words are to [be] wiped from the minds of anyone employed in DFO other than those officially designated as spokespersons.

Before I retire next March, it is my intention to write a memo to the Director General on how the suppression of technical information affects the morale of the professional staff involved as well as raising ethical questions. Perhaps it will help us regain a clear separation between science/technology and politics that is essential for us to maintain our professional credibility.[28]

Christensen's narrative account of events associated with Schouwenburg's retirement make reference to a rather interesting turn of events. It seems that on April 1, 1991, after he had retired,

Schouwenburg returned a commendation he had received from the DFO for his contribution to the Kimano Task Force. In a letter accompanying the returned commendation, which was also included in the package of information released by Gardiner during his 1992 press conference, Schouwenburg explains and defends his actions on the grounds that, in his estimation, the way in which the 1987 Settlement Agreement was being defended by the Minister and federal bureaucrats compromised and tainted the scientific integrity and professional reputations of the members of the task force who had dedicated so much of their careers to it. The following excerpt from that letter speaks for itself and, together with the other remarks by Schouwenburg, tends to support the previously cited accusations made by Dr. David Schindler in his comments on the difficulties experienced by Dr. John Rudd with his superiors in the DFO because of his concerns about the Great Whale project.

While I remained in the Department, I kept this award posted on the wall as a reminder of how much the politicization of the public service combined with bureaucratic cynicism is responsible for the very low morale of the Department's staff. Every time I saw such a similar award posted elsewhere, I wondered to what degree that person's reputation had been sacrificed by some self-serving politician or bureaucrat. Now that I have resigned from the public service I no longer need such painful reminders.

...Many of the terms of the Settlement Agreement run contrary to the advice given in the Kimano Task Force by the best minds the Department could muster from its ranks. Many issues are not addressed by the Agreement. This is largely because the Minister of the day and my Member of Parliament, Tom Sidden, did as he is empowered to do and made a political

decision on the project.

The terms of the Nechako [Settlement] Agreement flowed from the deliberations of the Strangway Working Group. The DFO members of that working group were in essence instructed (intimidated?) by your predecessor, Dr. Peter Meyboom, to ensure they came up with a resolution of the problems which were consistent or compatible with Alcan's objectives. This of course meant that the positions taken by the Kimano Task Force and the team of experts involved in the preparation of our court case were to be abandoned.[29]

Christensen reports that in October 1990 the staff of the DFO had been advised that only their boss, Director-General Pat Chamut, was to speak publicly about the Settlement Agreement. Federal scientists still employed by the DFO had also been ordered not to talk to anyone about the KCP prior to the start of the court case – allegedly in an effort to prevent information from being inadvertently released to Alcan. The ban was continued even after the Settlement Agreement was signed so that nothing was known of those discussions until after fisheries biologists who had worked on the task force had either retired or left the department, and were therefore free to begin talking publicly about their concerns. "The muzzling of federal fisheries biologists," writes Christensen, "was just one of the obstacles facing researchers looking for the rationale behind the agreement. Non-government researchers and reporters, including myself, found their efforts to uncover the truth – hidden by the documents, deals, deceptions, allegations and controversy that had piled up around the 1987 Settlement Agreement – were being stifled by government regulations."[30]

With the authority of the 1987 Settlement Agreement behind them, Alcan began construction on the completion project in 1988. But on October 9, 1990, opponents of the project, under the leadership of the Rivers Defence Coalition and the Sekani Tribal Council, filed documents asking the Federal Court to require the federal government to subject the KCP to its new Environmental Assessment Review Process, commonly referred to as EARP. Three days later the federal Cabinet responded by approving an order exempting the KCP and the 1987 Settlement Agreement from the EARP process. With this order Alcan appears to have been given an exemption from Law.[31]

Federal fisheries minister, Bernard Valcourt, defended this action on the grounds that the environmental concerns of the federal government had been answered by the studies already completed on the project by Environcon, Alcan's environmental consultant.[32] Commenting on this decision, former federal biologist Don Alderice, who opposed the project before the agreement was signed, characterized it as a deliberate attempt to suppress information which supported the opponents of the project and undermined the credibility of Alcan's mitigation procedures—which he and other scientists interviewed by the CBC's *The Fifth Estate* referred to as "laughable." The scientists, interviewed by both *The Fifth Estate* and by David Suzuki, in the course of preparing his *The Nature of Things* program "Trading Futures", emphasized the fact that Alcan's proposals had been rejected by all the federal scientists assigned to the Kimano Task Force which had been evaluating Environcon's environmental studies at the time the 1987 agreement was signed. They were also extremely annoyed, if not downright incensed, by the attempt to silence their objections by excluding them from the Strangway working group appointed by the DFO. The Strangway group had been instructed to find ways to protect the fish within the water flows Alcan was demanding, and their advice, rather than that of the federal scientists, was apparently given favourable consideration at the closed-door meeting in 1987 from which the federal scientists had been excluded.

Faced with the Cabinet's exemption order the coalition of opponents was forced to change its tactics once again, this time challenging the validity of the exemption order. The Carrier Sekani Tribal Council had already launched a separate action, claiming the exemption order was beyond the authority of the Cabinet and that it was also unconstitutional as it would adversely affect the Carrier people's aboriginal right to fish. Opponents of the project were thus jubilant when on May 16th, 1991 federal court Justice Allison Walsh ruled in their favour, declaring the federal Cabinet's exemption order "a failure to undertake a legal obligation." In a wide-ranging decision Justice Walsh dismissed Alcan's procedural objections, quashed the 1987 Settlement Agreement and ordered that the project be subjected to the federal EARP process. Unfortunately for the opponents, however, on May 8, 1992, following an appeal by Alcan and the federal government, Justice Walsh's decision was overturned by a three-person appeal panel, thus allowing the company to proceed with the project. Both the Carrier Sekani Tribal Chiefs and the Rivers Defence Coalition announced their intention to appeal this decision to the Supreme Court of Canada. Regrettably, this plan was frustrated, however, when the Supreme Court refused without comment their application to appeal the decision.

The refusal of the Supreme Court to even consider their appeal left the opponents of the project confused. The source of the confusion was the announcement on March 5, 1992 of a ruling by the federal government's Standing Joint Committee for the Scrutiny of Regulations that the exemption amounted to a "usurpation of Parliament's sovereignty." In the judgment of that committee the federal government had acted illegally and unconstitutionally when it exempted the KCP from the EARP process. When announcing the committee's decision, Liberal MP Derek Lee, who co-chaired the committee with Conservative Senator Norman Grimard, described the appeal court judge's remarks as "at variance with our view of the law of Parliament and the general law of Canada." The report was introduced to the House of Commons on June 7, 1993 and subsequently passed without dissent or debate. But, as Bev Christensen complains, despite endorsing the report, the government was under no obligation to do anything about it, and to the dismay of those who had hoped the committee's ruling would prompt the federal government to act, the government did nothing.[33]

As if to add insult to injury the federal government continued to indulge its contempt for ethics and due process. In 1992, in response to concerns over the disappearance of hundreds of thousands of salmon in the Fraser River, and no doubt prompted as well by the persistent attempts of the Cheslatta Carrier Nation to inform other Canadians about the damage done to their lives by the Federal government and Alcan,[34] federal fisheries minister John Crosbie appointed Dr. Peter Pearce, a UBC Forestry Professor, to investigate these complaints. The Natives and other residents of the areas affected believed that the fish were dying as a direct result of the conditions in the river, which had resulted from the 1987 Settlement Agreement. This is precisely what the federal scientists attached to the task force had predicted in their report which was ignored. As reported by Christensen,[35] Pearce rejected this theory and, without even attempting to investigate the impact of Alcan's activities on the river ecology, he blamed the disappearance of the fish instead on overfishing (both inland and at sea), and on weather disturbances, such as successive El Nino occurrences in the Pacific Ocean which created unusually hot, dry weather in the interior of the Province and thus caused both the lower-than-usual water flows and the higher than usual temperatures in the Fraser River. He also blamed the breakdown of a fishing agreement with the United States which led to American and Canadian fisheries taking unusually large numbers of salmon at

the mouth of the Fraser River. Most of the blame, however, was placed with the Native fisheries on the Fraser River. It is interesting to note that Dr. Pearce was, at that time, also a member of Alcan's Board of Directors.

Needless to say, critics of the Alcan project questioned the propriety of appointing an Alcan director to investigate the disappearance of fish which they believed were dying as a direct result of the conditions of the river resulting from Alcan's activities following the 1987 Settlement Agreement. Critics also pointed out that since the federal government had failed to monitor the water temperatures in the 70 km stretch of the Nechako River through which all the sockeye migrate from the Fraser on their way to the Stuart River, the effect of higher temperatures in that river, induced by the reduced flows resulting from the 1987 agreement, were not considered in Pearce's report. Yet the known detrimental effects on Sockeye of temperatures higher than 17.5 C (63.5 F) were made abundantly clear, not only in the task-force report but in a technical report on the Nechako River prepared by Dr. Peter Larkin, and appended to Dr. Pearce's report.[36] Why then, if there was a known connection between water temperature and the health of the salmon, were the temperatures in the Nechako and Stuart Rivers, up which most of the sockeye swim on their way to their spawning grounds, not monitored?

Alcan has always claimed that the Kitimat/ Kimano project will serve the public interest. However, it has been pointed out by critics such as Richard Overstall, who was retained by local First Nations leaders to assess Alcan's economic performance, that, in truth, while Alcan has been profiting handsomely from Canadian resources it has been exporting the benefits. According to Overstall's analysis, as reported to David Suzuki for the CBC's *The Nature of Things* program "Trading Futures," Alcan pays just 1/3 of a cent per kilowatt hour for its energy, which is 1/8 of the world average. This is because of the very low water rentals it pays in British Columbia. Overstall estimates that over the past two decades Alcan paid about $1 million per year for energy. If they had been paying what B.C. Hydro pays, their cost would be closer to 20 or 25 million dollars. In other words, it seems that over the past decade the B.C. taxpayer has been subsidizing Alcan to the tune of 1/4 billion dollars.

Is there any justification for this, in the form of perceived benefits to Canada? Not according to Overstall. On the contrary, in the 1980's Alcan made nearly $3 billion of profit in Canada. It made just one half that amount in its overseas operation. But although Alcan has made most of its profits in Canada it has made most of its investments in its overseas operations. In the 1980's, for example, Alcan's asset growth in Canada declined 5 percent whereas overseas it has increased by 7 percent. Investment by public funds – which is what the 1987 Settlement Agreement amounted to – is meant to produce jobs, but jobs throughout the entire Alcan operation world-wide declined in the 1980's, and the decline was 20 percent greater in Canada than elsewhere.[37]

Why then was Alcan given "rights" to the Nechako at the expense of the fish and the livelihood of those whose livelihood depend on the river? For those who supported Alcan's activities it was believed that the 1987 Settlement Agreement would result in the creation of jobs. In fact, there is no evidence that this would have occurred. Apart from the ethical question of trading fish for jobs, there was never any basis for believing that the economic benefits promised by Alcan would compensate for the damage that would be done to the salmon fisheries whose estimated worth – before the effects of Alcan's activities were felt – was in the neighbourhood of $77 million.[38] If then the "rights" that were given to Alcan do not produce any societal benefits, and given the circumstances under which they were acquired, do the Canadian taxpayers have any moral obligation to compensate Alcan for the loss of the opportunity

to exercise their "rights" to the Nechako watershed?

Questions have also been raised by the growing suspicion that Alcan's real purpose behind the KCP was not to build more smelters that would employ more Canadians – the one they had promised to build in Vanderhoof of course depended upon finishing the KCP – but to produce surplus energy for sale elsewhere. Alcan had already, as early as 1978, tied its power lines into the B.C. power grid so that B.C. Hydro could sell its excess power to the U.S. Now, after securing the 1987 Settlement Agreement for itself, it seemed that the additional power to be generated at Kimano once the new generators were installed would be considered surplus to B.C's power needs and would therefore be permitted to flow through B.C. Hydro's power grid into Alberta and the U.S. As Christensen points out, this scenario seemed all the more likely since Alcan had cancelled its plan to build a smelter in Vanderhoof and had not announced plans to increase its smelting capacity at Kitimat, or anywhere else in B.C. for that matter. These fears were confirmed in May, 1991 when B.C. Hydro announced that, when the new generators were installed at Kimano, 285-megawatts of the electricity they generated would be purchased by Hydro for export to either Alberta or the U.S.[39] How does the opportunity for Alcan shareholders to become wealthy through the sale of hydro-electric power to Alberta and the U.S., at the expense of the B.C fisheries and Native communities, even begin to approach fulfilling Tom Siddon's and Alcan's promise that the KCP was in the public interest?

Like the Great Whale project, the Kimano Completion Project has been temporarily halted by the announcement on January 23, 1995 by British Columbia Premier, Mike Harcourt, that he was cancelling the project. However, in her recently published account of the circumstances leading up to this decision, Bev Christensen cautions against drawing the conclusion that the issue has been finally resolved. Commenting on Harcourt's surprise announcement, which she describes as "Too Good to be True," Christensen suggests that

> *There can be no doubt that the province-wide sense of relief and vindication expressed in the hours and days following ... Harcourt's ... announcement was entirely premature. It would be foolish indeed for anyone to believe that such a simple political statement had finally ended the long fight over who has the right to control the water flows in the Nechako River: Alcan; the Province of British Columbia; or the Government of Canada. Anyone harbouring such a naive belief has a lot to learn from the residents of the Nechako River Valley who have discovered – all too well – in their long struggle to prevent more water from being diverted out of this river, that you cannot always trust governments to act on, much less carry out, their promises.[40]*

The Alcan project controversy, writes Christensen, "is a case study of how the power of ordinary citizens, democratically vested in their governments, was voluntarily abrogated by those governments to the interests of a multinational company."[41]

Huckleberry Mine, Public Policy, and the Tyranny of the Corporate Agenda

In fact, if the Alcan story is any indication of things to come, the trend in Canada seems more and more to be favouring the interests of the corporate agenda. Among the more blatant examples of this trend is the decision of Environment Canada in March 1996 to allow the controversial Huckleberry copper and gold mine near Houston BC to go ahead without any further environmental assessment of the project. This decision was taken in total disregard of the welfare of the environment and the local Native community. The proposed mine, backed by Princeton Mining and a consortium of Japanese companies led by

Mitsubishi, is located on the traditional territory of the Cheslatta Carrier Nation, who have already been victimized by the Alcan project. As in the other case studies, it appears that once again the decison was influenced more by corporate pressure than by environmental and human welfare concerns; another example of government fast-tracking assessments and drawing conclusions about environmental safety based on inadequate data.[42] Nor would it be an exaggeration to suggest that, as with the treatment of the Cree in Quebec and the Innu in Labrador, government policies towards the Cheslatta have been suspiciously racist.

Notwithstanding the importance of developing policies that encourage responsible foreign investment in Canada, and with due recognition of the role of resource extraction for the Canadian economy and for maintaining a healthy and flourishing life-style, it is imperative that all such development be made to conform to the requirements of sustainability for both natural ecosytems and human communities. And sustainability should not be confused with economic growth. Such advice is clearly in keeping with the spirit of Canada's recently approved Environmental Assessment Act which was proclaimed into law in June 1995. What we have, however, is a sad record of governments at both federal and provincial levels failing to live up to the requirements of its own laws and policies. In her assessment of the Huckleberry Mine controversy, Joyce Nelson observes that Huckleberry Mine is the first of some 35 BC mining projects to undergo review under the new federal and provincial Environmental Assessment Acts.

> *As recent events indicate, some very powerful forces have a vested interest in the outcome of these processes. But the public has even more at stake, as mining disasters and expensive pollution clean-up from mining around the world indicate.[43]*

In the same report, Nelson reveals details of evidence made available by the Cheslatta of extraordinary corporate pressure to obtain approval for the proposed mine, which now appears to have succeeded.[44] Included among the documents was a letter dated February 7, 1996, from Canada's Ambassador to Japan, Donald W. Campbell, to Mel Cappe, Deputy Minister of Environment Canada, in which Campbell represents the concerns of prominent members of the Japanese Mining Community over "the nature and complexity of the environmental assessment process in Canada and its potential impact on the critical path of mining investment projects." In the same letter, Campbell advises Cappe that continuing Japanese mining investment in Canada may well hinge on "Canada's current handling of a number of ongoing projects, in particular the Huckleberry copper and gold mine development located in Northern British Columbia." The letter concludes with the warning that Japanese "participation in Huckleberry will be in question if the project does not receive Federal approval by mid-March."[45]

In a second letter released by the Cheslatta, dated February 13th, 1996, Princeton/Huckleberry Mines President J.C. O'Rourke warns federal environment Minister Sergio Marchi that "The future of the Huckleberry Mine hinges on receiving the Federal government's approvals immediately after the March 15 date." Finally, in a third letter released by the Cheslatta from Anne McLelland, Canada's Minister of Natural Resources, to Sergio Marchi and five other Ministers, McClelland urges a speedy decision on Huckleberry and repeats once again Campbell's warning that "Japanese investors are loosing patience given that initial plans called for the mine to be in production by early 1977."[46]

As in other cases previously discussed, such corporate pressure on the federal government compromises the federal environmental assessment process. It also provides an embarrassing example of the extent to which Canada's regulatory process is directed by foreign investment interests. According to the Cheslatta, the situation is no different at the provincial level. Among the Cheslatta's concerns with regard to the BC environmental assessment agency's approval of the mine in December 1995 are the apparant lack of technical evidence to support the Huckleberry proposal, concerns about the mine's structural integrity, the risks of contamination of fish-bearing water from acid rock drainage, and human health impacts.[47] And once again, as in the case of the Alcan project, the economic benefits derived from the mine will most likely be enjoyed chiefly by the consortium with very little benefits for the local community.

Technocracy, the Corporate Agenda, and the Betrayal of the Public Interest

How has it come to be that we live in a society that permits its governments to sacrifice the ecological integrity of the natural environment, upon which the safety and welfare of the public depend, for the sake of political and economic interests, and allows the biased reporting of these issues to be overlooked? As in Ibsen's play, we are confronted, so it seems, with conflicting perceptions of the "public interest" – one promoted by business and government, as reflected, for example, in the oft quoted remark by Charlie Wilson that "What is good for General Motors is good for America," and the one promoted by critics of industry and government who reflect a variety of social and moral concerns which challenge the equation of affluence and welfare, and who, like the Lorax in the story by Dr.Seuss, claim to "speak for the trees." Should these and other such related issues be left to public interest groups like Pollution Probe, Energy Probe, Friends of the Earth, Greenpeace, and so on, to deal with, or is there a role for the citizenry at large? Does the solution to the environmental crisis lie, as Aldo Leopold believed, in the achievement of universal ecological literacy? And to what extent do Canadians have a right to expect the kind of unbiased reporting from the media that will assist them in arriving at informed judgments on matters of public concern? How do we instruct and motivate Canadians to excercise consumer sovereignty by demanding more environmental protection and insisting on making the principle of ecological integrity take precedence over corporate profits? How, in other words, do we educate Canadians to adopt a life-style that will lead to a genuine "ecological society?" Of central importance for the agenda of environmentalism is to challenge and replace the technocratic attitude of industry and government with a more ecological outlook, such as that envisaged by Aldo Leopold.[48] As Michael W. Fox puts it

> [The] technocratic attitude is one of absolute indifference to the environment, except as a resource, and it sees environmental protection as a constraint to economic growth. The basic laws of nature, of ecology, are ignored. Technocrats have such arrogance and such faith in their technology that they firmly believe that they can improve upon nature without understanding her. . . . It is clear that without a total re-evaluation of values and ethics, technology will be misapplied and serious problems will arise. . . .[49]

Finally, it is imperative that the media learn to liberate itself from the influence that government and business seem to have over it so that it can perform its role more honestly as a trustee of the public interest, rather than allow itself to be used as an agent in what Noam Chomsky has called the "Manufacturing of Consent."[50]

In the examples previously cited environmental standards and public safety have been compromised for the sake of a corporate agenda that serves the political interests of those in power. Clearly there are no moral or even scientific grounds upon which such policies could be justified. Do we not detect in all of these instances precisely the same moral issue that is raised by

Ibsen in "An Enemy of the People?". And why is it that we must so often rely on the watchdog activities of public interest groups, NGO's, and investigative journalists, to defend those values associated with the respect for environmental standards that the citizens of a democracy like Canada have every reason to expect from their public officials, but which in practice is seldom exemplified?

In conclusion, it would thus appear that there is ample evidence that Canadian public policy and environmental legislation is directed more towards accommodating the corporate agenda than by the ethics of ecological citizenship and our obligations to posterity. As Harry Barton points out in his critique of the "Isle of Harris Superquarry," which is Scotland's version of mega-projects like Great Whale and the Kimano Completion project,

> Despite increasing doubts regarding the suitability and long term global sustainability of the traditional development paradigm, it refuses to lie down and die. The emphasis has been on dusting down and patching up the same ideas of an expanding market economy, raised material standards of living and the consumerist ideal. Meanwhile the concept of economic growth stubbornly remains as unilluminating and pervasive in the face of a bombardment of criticism as an intellectual black hole.[51]

Under the influence of this paradigm, citizens have been co-opted into a lifestyle of uncritical and anti-ecological consumerism which is gradually bringing about Garrett Hardin's scenario of "the tragedy of the commons."[52] The worst aspect of this scenario is the possibility that we may someday soon be forced by desperation to adopt something like Hardin's policy of "mutual coercion mutually agreed upon," when finally we have exceeded the limits of the natural carrying capacity of the biosphere and have reached as well the limits of our ability to manufacture technological fixes. And it is not clear whether at this point there will still be the seeds of hope with which to re-create the possibility of a future, as in the final scene of Dr. Seuss's story, "The Lorax." Would it not be better, therefore, to reach into our Orphic depths now in search of whatever combination of intelligence and imagination it will take to lead us into what Fritjof Capra calls "the Solar Age,"[53] and learn how to reduce our "ecological footprint" on the planet earth by seriously questioning the moral desirability of the life-style that has been imposed upon us by the corporate giants who con-trol our political economy?[54] This is not likely to happen so long as we subscribe to, and allow our politicians to define their standards of conduct by, Charlie Wilson's exhortation, previously cited, that "What is good for General Motors is good for America."

Perhaps we would be better advised to follow the advice of John Stuart Mill when he extolls the virtues of the stationary state and cautions us against allowing the ethic of growth and the pur-suit of wealth to overwhelm our quest for a politi-cal economy that will foster the improvement of mankind.

I cannot...regard the stationary state of capital and wealth with the unaffected aversion so generally manifested towards it by political economists of the old school. I am inclined to believe that it would be, on the whole, a very considerable improvement on our present condition. ...I know not why it should be a matter of congratulation that persons who are already richer than anyone needs to be, should have doubled their means of consuming things which give little or no pleasure except as representative of wealth. ... I confess I am not charmed with the ideal of life held out by those who think that the normal state of human beings is that of struggling to get on; that the trampling, crushing, elbowing, and treading on each other's heels which form the existing type of

social life, are the most desirable lot of humankind, or anything but the disagreeable symptoms of one of the phases of industrial progress. ...It is scarcely necessary to remark that a stationary condition of capital...implies no stationary state of human improvement. There would be as much scope as ever for all kinds of mental culture, and moral and social progress; as much room for improving the Art of Living and much more likelihood of its being improved, when minds cease to be engrossed by the art of getting on. Even the industrial arts might be as earnestly and as successfully cultivated, with this sole difference, that instead of serving no purpose but the increase of wealth, industrial improvements would produce their legitimate effect, that of abridging labour.[55]

ENDNOTES

[1] For example, E.F. Schumacher in *Small is Beautiful*, New York, Harper & Row, 1975, 1989 and E.J. Mishan in "The Rise of Affluence and the Decline of Welfare," H. Daly, ed., *Economics, Ecology, Ethics*, San Francisco, W.H. Free-man & Co., 1980. Some other discussions relevant to this issue are, D.H. Meadows, D.L. Meadows & J. Randers, *Be-yond the Limits*, Toronto, McClelland & Stewart, 1992, and H. Daly and John E. Cobb Jr. in *For the Common Good*, 2nd. ed., Boston, Beacon Press, 1994. According to Garrett Hardin the tragedy of the commons can be traced to the consequences of granting unrestricted access to the com-mons combined with the freedom to breed more livestock. ("The Tragedy of the Commons," *Science*, Vol. 162, Dec. 1968, and "Living on a Lifeboat," in James E. White, ed., *Contemporary Moral Problems*, West Publishing Co., 1985). What needs to be emphasized in this analysis is the seductive appeal of the power and wealth made possible by the conquest of nature and the exploitation of natural re-sources. Typical of the ideology that equates welfare with the domination of nature is the following statement by a former advisor to Franklin Delano Roosevelt. "A part of the conspicuous victory over nature on this continent has been the power which has been exhibited in subduing natu-ral materials and forces to a will for well being. Nature has been reduced to order, to regimentation. This is a process which should have freed men as it enslaved nature." (Rexford G. Tugwell, *The Battle for Democracy*, New York, Columbia University Press, 1935, p. 195). When this ide-

ology is coupled with the tendency of politicians to sacrifice the environment and environmental ethics for the sake of the power bestowed up them by the free-enterprise system, we have the ideal conditions for a tragedy of the commons.

Thus conceived, the scenario of the tragedy of the commons unfolds as follows. Picture a pasture open to all. It is expected that each herdsman will try to keep as many cattle as possible on the commons, since, as rational, self-interested beings, each herdsman seeks to maximize his gain. Explicitly or implicitly, more or less consciously, he asks himself, "What is the utility to me of ignoring the covenant by which the commons ought to be managed and adding one more animal to my herd?" Now this utility has one positive and one negative component. The positive component is a function of the increment of one animal. Since the herdsman receives all the proceeds from the sale of the additional animal, the positive utility is nearly +1. The negative component is a function of the additional overgrazing created by adding one more animal. Since, however, the effects of overgrazing are shared by all herdsmen, the negative utility for any particular decision-making herdsman is only a fraction of -1. Conscience tells him that adding one more animal to his herd is both unfair and ultimately self-defeating, since in the long-run, if everyone were to do so the commons would be overgrazed. But the self-interested part of him is not inclined to place any trust in the conscience of his fellow herdsman and this in the end will defeat even his own conscience.

The rational herdsman thus concludes that the only sensible course of action for him to pursue is to add another animal to his herd. And another; and another....But this is the conclusion reached by every rational herdsman sharing a commons, none of whom are prepared to trust the others – particularly when it is presupposed that all rational behaviour is self-interested and competitive behaviour. Therein lies the tragedy. Driven by a psychology of self-interest combined with a Hobbesian conviction that no one is trustworthy, each herdsman is locked into a system that compels him to increase his herd without limit. Because this occurs in a world with a limited carrying capacity which cannot be increased by means of a "technological fix," catastrophe is unavoidable. What the tragedy of the commons illustrates, for those who accept its assumptions, is the inescapable truth that the culture of consumerism, fuelled as it is by an ethic of growth and the competition for power, favours the forces of psychological denial rather than conscience and moral integrity. When faced with the double bind of remaining faithful to one's conscience or else pursuing one's own self-interest in a world in which it is believed that no one is to be trusted, and in which the rewards of power are more appealing than the prescriptions of conscience, self-interest will often take precedence over mo-

rality, and self-interested individuals will be prepared to benefit by denying the truth, even though society as a whole will suffer in the long run.

Pollution is the tragedy of the commons in reverse, with the actors adding something to the commons rather than removing something from it. Once again, the rational self-interested person finds that her share of the costs of the wastes (or externalities) that she discharges into the commons is less than the cost of purifying the wastes before releasing them. Since this is true for everyone we are once again locked into a system of "fouling our own nest," so long as we behave only as rational, independent, free-enterprisers and consumers. The foregoing analysis takes on added weight when considered in the context of Mark Sagoff's analysis of the consumer/citizen dichotomy in "At the Shrine of Our Lady of Fatima, Or Why Political Questions Are Not All Economic," in *Ethics and the Environment*, ed., by Donald Scherer and Thomas Attig, Prentice-Hall, 1983.

[2] See, for example, H. Johnson, *Man and His Environment*, British North American Committee, 1973; Julian Simon, *The Ultimate Resource*, Princeton, Princeton University Press, 1981, and *Population Matters*, New Brunswick, N.J., Transaction Publishers, 1990; M. Krieger, "What's Wrong with Plastic Trees?," *Science*, Vol. 179, 1973, Laurence Tribe, "Ways not to Think about Plastic Trees," *Yale Law Journal*, Vol. 83, No.7 (June 1974), and William Cronon, ed., *Uncommon Ground*, New York, W.W. Norton & Co., 1995.

[3] Cf., Herman Daly: "All groups assume that GNP measures something of importance to the economy and most assume that this is clearly bound up with human welfare....The tendency to forget that the GNP measures only some aspects of welfare and to treat it as a general index of national well-being is...a typical instance of the fallacy of misplaced concreteness [the fallacy of applying abstract theories and concepts to facts and experiences to which they do not apply, such as identifying the public good with wealth, abstracted from the sufferings of human beings who create it, and abstracted from the harm to both the human and non-human environments that results from the extraction of the natural resources that are converted into wealth]....The possibility that an increase in economic welfare would necessitate a larger increase in non-economic welfare and thus a net reduction in total welfare has not been taken seriously" (*For The Common Good*, Op. Cit., pp. 63, 146). Or, as E.F. Schumacher complained, "the idea that there could be pathological growth, unhealthy growth, disruptive or destructive growth, is to [the economist] a perverse idea which must not be allowed to surface." (*Small is Beautiful*, Op. Cit., p. 51)

[4] This is the argument put forward in his book, *Trashing the Economy*, Bellvue Wa., Free Enterprise Press, 1993. 2nd. ed., 1994. For further discussions of the significance of the

"Wise Use Movement" see A.L. Rawe and Rick Field, "Tug-O-War with the Wise Use Movement," *Z Magazine*, October, 1992, and Lorelei Hanson, "Turning Rivals into Allies: Understanding the Wise Use Movement," *Alternatives*, vol. 21, no.3, 1995. The Origins of the Share movement in B.C. have been explored in a documentary entitled "The Last Battlefield," which was prepared for the C.B.C.'s Fifth Estate and broadcast in 1993.

[5] *On Liberty*, ed. by Elizabeth Rapaport, Indianapolis, Hackett Publishing Co., 1978, ch. 2, p. 21

[6] Harry G. Johnson, *Man and His Environment*, Op. Cit., p. 5, and Eugene Rabinowitch who deplores that "many rationally unjustifiable things have been written in recent years – some by very reputable scientists – about the sacredness of natural ecological systems, their inherent stability and the danger of human interference with them." (*The Times*, 29 April, 1972)

[7] "What's Wrong with Plastic Trees," Op. Cit., p. 453

[8] Based on a CBC radio report by Jay Ingram on "Quirks and Quarks," Feb. 1991.

[9] "Quirks and Quarks," Op. Cit.

[10] See also Paul McKay, *Electric Empire: The Inside Story of Ontario Hydro*, Toronto, Between The Lines, 1983, and R. Paehlke's discussion of Amory Lovin's attack on the nuclear industry in *Environmentalism and the Future of Progressive Politics*, New Haven, Yale University Press, 1989.

[11] The following discussion is based on material taken from the CBC's *The Fifth Estate*, and *The Nature of Things* program entitled "Trading Futures," both of which were broadcast in 1994, as well as an article by John Goddard entitled "Sold down the River," published in *Harrowsmith*, Dec., 1993, and a recently published book by Bev Christensen entitled, *Too Good to be True*, Vancouver, Talon Press, 1995. Christensen's book has been particularly instructive.

[12] John Goddard, "Sold down the River," *Harrowsmith*, Op. Cit., p. 41

[13] Ibid.

[14] These figures are based on David Suzuki's special report for the CBC's *The Nature of Things*, "Trading Futures," broadcast in 1993, and the CBC's *The Fifth Estate* Report, also broadcast in 1993. Other sources include Bev Christenson's *Too Good to be True*, Op. Cit., and John Goddard's "Sold Down the River," Op. Cit.

[15] David Suzuki, "Trading Futures," Op. Cit.

[16] John Goddard, op. cit., p. 40

[17] Ibid.

[18] For a narrative account of the events associated with the fraudulent and forced re-location of the Cheslatta people from their traditional territory see Christensen, Op. Cit., pp. 83 ff. and Sheila Jordan's film, "No Surrender," which documents the conflict between Alcan and the Cheslatta Indian

nation over the damage caused to the environment by the diversion of the Nechako river and the subsequent confiscation of their traditional lands by Alcan for the purpose of completing the reconstruction of the Nechako watershed.

[19] Christensen, Op. Cit., p. 159

[20] Christensen, Op. Cit., p. 148-150; *Vancouver Sun*, 20 Dec. 1990

[21] Christensen, Op. Cit., 148 ff., the CBC's, *"Fifth Estate"* report broadcast in 1993 and a memo by H. Mundie written July 18, 1986, and reprinted below, p. 16 (Christensen, Op. Cit., pp. 194-5). In fact this represents an even greater concession by the DFO who had previously argued for a compromise position that would allow Alcan to divert 69 percent of the water flows—a figure which, as Mundie makes clear in his memo, was still too high and therefore unacceptable.

[22] John Goddard, "Sold down the River," Op. Cit., 45

[23] Vancouver, Talon Books, 1995

[24] The text of this memo also includes the statement "Staff were instructed to support the Minister's position while adhering to the evidence. I find it impossible to do both." (As reported on the CBC's *The Fifth Estate*.)

[25] Ibid., pp. 194-195

[26] Cited by Christensen, Op. Cit., p. 196

[27] Included in the recommendations is one stating that water temperatures should not exceed 63.5 degrees F between the dam and the Nautley River and 68 degrees F below the Nautley. The settlement Agreement requires Alcan to maintain the water in the Nechako at a temperature no higher than 71 degrees F. Christensen, Op. Cit., 196

[28] Ibid., pp. 196-197

[29] Ibid., p. 197

[30] Ibid., p. 198

[31] While this judgment was supported both by federal court justice Allison Walsh, who on May 16th, 1991 declared that the failure of the federal Cabinet to order a review of the project was "a failure to undertake a legal obligation," and by the federal government's all-party, Standing Joint Committee for the Scrutiny of Regulations (see Christensen, Op. Cit., pp. 165-178 and Goddard, Op. Cit., p. 47), it can be argued that it is open to question. In the first place, granting exemptions from Environmental Assessment proceedings is relatively common in Canada (See the discussion of the Huckleberry Mine controversy below). In the second place, while the Canadian Environmental Assessment Act requiring an Environmental Assessment Review Process (EARP) of all mega-projects had been passed prior to Oct. 12th 1990 when the federal Cabinet met and approved an order exempting the Kimano Completion Project from the EARP process, it did not actually come into force until June 1995 when it was proclaimed into law. It is therefore likely that

the exemption was not actually from statute law but only from a Cabinet policy (the EARP guidelines order) which did not yet have the status of law.

[32] Christensen, p. 166

[33] Ibid, p. 178

[34] In July, 1992, the band asked B.C.'s Attorney General to investigate laying criminal charges against Alcan under section 182 of Canada's Criminal Code which states that anyone who improperly interferes with or offers any indignity to a dead human body or human remains, whether buried or not, is guilty of an indictable offence and liable to imprisonment for a term not exceeding five years. This action was prompted by Alcan's decision to release larger than usual volumes of water from the Kenny Dam Reservoir, which resulted in raising the level of Cheslatta Lake more than 13 feet and flooding two graveyards on the shores of the lake. Christensen, Op. Cit., p. 198

[35] Ibid., pp. 200 ff. See also, John Goddard, Op. Cit., p. 47

[36] "Analysis of the Possible Causes of Shortfall in Sockeye Spawners," 1992. See Christensen, Op. Cit., p. 201.

[37] As reported by Overstall to David Suzuki during the making of "Trading Futures."

[38] Christensen, p. 173

[39] Ibid., p. 180

[40] Too Good to be True, Vancouver, Talon Books, 1995, p. 5

[41] Ibid, p. 10

[42] Such is the view of Karen Kristen, a lawyer with the Sierra Legal Defence Fund. See Joyce Nelson's report on the Huckleberry Mine controversy in Canadian Dimension, May-June, 1996, pp. 55-56.

[43] Op. Cit., p. 56. See also the featured article in the Insight section of the Toronto Star, Saturday, August 3, 1996 documenting the record of Canadian mining companies in the American West.

[44] Op.Cit.

[45] Ibib., p. 55

[46] Ibid., p. 56

[47] Ibid., p. 55

[48] See, "Aldo Leopold on Education," in J.B. Callicott, In Defense of the Land Ethic, Albany, State University of New York press, 1989, pp. 223-237. A land ethic, according to Leopold, was an evolutionary possibility and an ecological necessity. "There is no other way for land to survive the impact of mechanized man." (A Sand County Almanac, New York, Ballantine, 1970, p. 239, xix.) Commenting on Leopold's, vision Callicott writes: "When ecological understanding and awareness become generally distributed in our culture, then the land ethic will follow as a natural and psychologically necessary consequence. Evolution has endowed us with what we might call, following Hume, a set of moral sentiments which are, so to speak, triggered by the recognition of a fellow member of our sociey or community. The basic concept of ecology is that the myriad non-human natural beings – soils and waters, plants and animals – are functioning members of a single natural community to which we also belong and upon which we utterly depend for the means to life. When this basic concept of ecology is taught at all levels of education, from story and song in early childhood education to abtract, theoretical mathematics, science, and philosophy in higher education, the land ethic may be transformed from one man's dream to all mankind's reality." (Ibid., p. 237)

[49] Superpigs and Wondercorn, Op. Cit., pp. 82-83

[50] Cf., "Manufacturing of Consent: Noam Chomsky and the Media," Directed by Mark Achbar and Peter Wintonick, National Film Board of Canada, and Companion book to the film ed. by Mark Achbar, Montreal, Black Rose Books, 1994.

[51] Environmental Values, Vol. 5, Number 2, May, 1966, p. 119

[52] Science, Vol. 162, 13 December 1968, pp. 1243-1248. Reprinted together with "Second Thoughts on the Tragedy of the Commons" in H.Daly, ed., Economics, Ecology, Ethics, Op. Cit.

[53] The Turning Point, New York, Bantam Books, 1982, pp. 389ff.

[54] The ecological footprint is a measure of the 'load' imposed by a given population on nature. It represents the land area necessary to sustain current levels of resource consumption and waste discharge by that population. See, Mathis Wackernagel and W.E. Rees, Our Ecological Footprint, Gabriola Island BC, New Society Publishers, 1996, and W.E. Rees and Mathis Wackernagel, "Ecological Footprints and Appropriated Carrying Capacity: Measuring The Natural Capital Requirements of the Human Economy," in Jansson, Hammer, Folke and Costanza, eds., Investing in Natural Capital, Washington D.C., Island Press, 1994. A reduction of the human ecological footprint may be forced upon us by the kind of Draconian measures advocated by Garrett Hardin in his tragedy of the commons and Life-Boat ethic scenarios, or in the more thoughtful and humane ways advocated by E.F. Schumacher, Murray Bookchin, Herman Daly and William Rees and his associates on the task force on Healthy & Sustainable Communities Centre for Human Settlements at the University of British Columbia. For a systematic, in-depth discussion of the impact of population growth on the carrying capacity see Joel E. Cohen, How Many People Can the Earth Support?, New York, W.W.Norton & Co., 1995.

[55] Principles of Political Economy, Bk. IV, ch.6, Collected Works of John Stuart Mill, Vol. III Toronto, University of Toronto Press, 1965, pp. 753-754.

ANIMAL RIGHTS AND NATIVE HUNTERS
A CRITICAL ANALYSIS OF WENZEL'S DEFENCE[1]

9

by Wendy Donner

IN THIS PAPER I EXPLORE THE ETHICAL ISSUES IN THE animal rights debate. On one side are those who argue that animals are beings with moral standing or rights, and therefore it is wrong to hunt them, and on the other side are those who argue that hunting and trapping animals is morally permissible if this activity is part of, and sustains, a traditional and ecologically sound aboriginal culture. The perspective I adopt in attempting to grapple with some extremely complex and painful dilemmas is that of a moral agent who is located outside of two communities – aboriginal hunters and animals – but whose moral decision to buy, boycott, or attempt to ban the commercial products of the hunting activities has the potential to impact on both of these communities. In order to illuminate the issues at stake, I use the case study of the Clyde Inuit seal hunters of Baffin Island as described by George Wenzel in his book *Animal Rights, Human Rights*.[2]

Many philosophers mark the beginning of contemporary environmental ethics with the publication of works arguing that non-human animals have moral status. Two camps quickly developed: one consisting of those who were primarily concerned about the treatment of individual animals, and the other one who identified themselves with more radical environmental theories primarily concerned with holistic elements and the environment rather than individual animals. Fundamental questions remain about whether these two positions can be reconciled. There is already a great deal of philosophical literature on the moral status of non-human animals. According to those who defend moral standing for individuals, a criterion of moral

standing sets out the characteristics of what a being must have if its interests and well-being are to be taken into account in making moral decisions. Historically, the utilitarian Jeremy Bentham argued that sentience or the mere capacity to feel pleasure and pain is sufficient to confer moral status on a being. In arguing that sentient animals merit such consideration, Bentham says that "the question is not, Can they reason nor Can they talk? but, Can they suffer."[3] More recently, Tom Regan has made a similar point. He argues that "if a given theory considers human pain and suffering morally relevant, but denies the moral relevance of the pain and suffering of the black bear, then it seems to be rationally defective. For pain is pain, and pain is in itself undesirable, to whomsoever it may occur, whether beast or human."[4]

The two most prominent current defenders of strong status for animals are Tom Regan and Peter Singer, although they undertake this defence from two different theoretical perspectives, the perspective of rights theory in the case of Regan and of utilitarianism in the case of Singer.[5] Peter Singer's utilitarian argument appeals to a principle of equal consideration of the interests of sentient beings which are comparable to human interests. He claims that "similar interests must count equally regardless of the species being involved."[6] Alternatively, he claims that "if a being suffers there can be no moral justification for refusing to take that suffering into consideration."[7]

Tom Regan wants to ground animal status even more securely in rights. He claims that animals who are "subjects of a life" have inherent value. Inherent or intrinsic value is contrasted with instrumental value in many discussions of environmental ethics. Something has instrumental value if it is valuable in virtue of being a means to an end which is valuable in itself. In the context of environmental ethics, the view that non-human animals or the environment have only instrumental value means that they are valuable only insofar as they are useful for the well-being of humans. This attitude is soundly rejected by many animal rights supporters and environmentalists, who argue that animals and/or the environment have intrinsic or inherent value, that is, value in themselves, apart from their usefulness for human ends. Regan makes the inherent value of many animals, those who are subjects of a life, central to his argument. Animals are subjects of a life "if they have beliefs and desires; perception, memory, and a sense of the future, including their own future; an emotional life together with feelings of pleasure and pain; preference and welfare-interests; the ability to initiate action in pursuit of their desires and goals; a psychophysical identity over time, and an individual welfare in the sense that their experiential life fares well or ill for them, logically independently of their utility for others."[8] Such animals have rights.

According to both Regan and Singer, if beings are such that they can feel pleasure and pain or are subjects of a life, their experiences matter to them and thus moral agents must take account of them for their own sakes in moral deliberations. These deceptively simple but logically compelling arguments have persuaded many to radically change their views on the status and appropriate treatment of animals. It was recognized that logical consistency required that if humans have moral standing in virtue of their possession of consciousness, other animals with consciousness, especially those mammals at the higher end of the evolutionary scale with fairly developed consciousness also had such standing.

In this paper I will defend a more moderate position than those of Regan and Singer. The position I defend is, I believe, the weakest that can plausibly be maintained on the question, although even a stance as moderate as this has radical implications in the light of current human treatment of many non-human animals. This position, roughly put, is that at least those animals who have capacities more complex than sentience, i.e. those who have some degree of rationality, have some moral standing in their own right as individuals and not merely as members of species with a role in the functioning of ecosystems. Animals with some degree of rationality beyond mere sentience include all mammals such as chimpanzees, whales, dogs, dolphins and seals. But the criterion of possession of some degree of rationality beyond sentience would exclude reptiles, fish, crustaceans and molluscs.[9] According to this view, it is impermissible to sacrifice the basic interests of some individual animals, primarily interests in continuing to live and in not suffering, in order to promote unimportant or peripheral human interests. Or, alternatively put, it is permissible to sacrifice important interests of some animals only in order to promote important interests of humans. It is wrong to treat animals as mere means to human ends. This shifts the emphasis of the discussion to the question of what are important human interests.

A similar position is advanced by Donald VanDeVeer.[10] He defends Two Factor Egalitarianism which he explains "assumes the relevance of two matters: 1) level or importance of interests to each being in a conflict of interest, and 2) the psychological capacities of the parties whose interests conflict."[11] He expands this by advancing what he calls the Weighting Principle which maintains that "the interests of beings with more complex psychological capacities deserve greater weight than those with lesser capacities – up to a point."[12] The conclusion again is that basic interests of some animals ought not to be sacrificed unless important human interests are at stake. And, the more complex the psychological organization of an individual animal, the greater the weight that ought to be given to its interests.

This moderate position must be dealt with and responded to by defenders of native hunters and trappers. These defenders argue that hunting and trapping animals is morally permissible if this activity maintains traditional native society. One important element of the case of those who so argue is the claim that, while killing animals may be wrong in other contexts or circumstances, it is permissible in this context because of the important human interests which outweigh the interests in the life of the animals.

Traditional aboriginal cultures are so valuable that they merit efforts to preserve them. This gives members of these societies a moral advantage over their southern non-native counterparts who hunt animals to sell furs in a commercial market. I concur with the claim that it is important to protect and preserve aboriginal cultures and that members of these communities have a moral advantage in the matter of hunting and trapping. There is also a moral advantage derived from the past and continuing harms inflicted upon native people and their cultures by the impact of Euro-Canadian colonization and policies of resettlement of many native communities to pursue the ends of Canadian bureaucracies and institutions at the expense of native interests. The crucial question then is, how strong is this moral advantage and how does it manifest in different concrete situations? This debate is heavily context-dependant and our conclusions may vary from one case to another. But the same underlying factors and conditional principles should be brought in and appealed to in these varying cases.

As my discussion centres around one case study of a native hunting society, my first task is to provide some relevant background information on this particular case of the Clyde Inuit of Baffin Island.

In September 1985 the Council of the European Economic Community voted to extend the temporary two year ban which "forbade the importing of commercially hunted sealskins and products manufactured from them into any part of the European Community."[13] While this ban was primarily directed at the hunting of harp and hooded seals, especially seal pups off the coast of Newfoundland, it also destroyed the market for ringed seal furs hunted by Canadian Inuit such as the Clyde of Baffin Island. According to George Wenzel, the timing of the ban was disturbing because it occurred in the middle of the investigation of the Royal Commission on Seals and the Sealing industry in Canada into the "scientific, environmental, social and economic ramifications of sealing" and Wenzel believes that this investigation would have persuaded the EEC of "the environmental integrity and socioeconomic importance of at least some aspects of sealing."[14] In particular Wenzel notes the evidence given to this Commission by Inuit on the importance of seal hunting to their subsistence culture. But during this period the public was presented with "glossy photographs of protesters clutching baby seals amid scenes of pools of blood staining crystal-pure ice."[15] Wenzel counters that "sealskins, in a northern world colonized and ruled by Euro-Canadians, provide a small measure of independence from mines and oil wells, bureaucracy and good intentions."[16] As well, Inuit rights to hunt are grounded on their clearly demonstrated interest in the natural environment and their "consistent acknowledgment of the environment as an active element of their day-to-day lives."[17] Wenzel sums up the divisions in the debate:

> Inuit emphatically state that hunting is their means of subsistence, their history, their culture. In reply, opponents state that Inuit claims on seals for subsistence veil a commercial economy based on profit. History 'proves' that fur traders and government services have transformed Inuit from an independent aboriginal people to consumers in a cold climate, and that Inuit

opposition to the seal protest is proof of collusion with the fur industry and gives the lie to claims of subsistence and cultural need.[18]

Opponents claim that Inuit are now just like southerners. The artifacts central to a traditional culture, such as dogteams and snowhouses, harpoons and sealskin clothes, are gone and in their place are snowmobiles and rifles. Wenzel responds that the Inuit are traditional people in the modern world and so they do not need to live up to the caricatures of acceptable traditional life, depictions of which are highly romanticized and see humans living in traditional cultures as being like people living in a "natural state."

The harsh climate of Baffin Island is part of the context. Winter continues from October to May during which period the temperature averages -35 degrees C. The days are short; in December and January there is only an hour or so of twilight and the rest of the day is spent in darkness. Survival in such a climate requires the kind of awareness of the environment which has been lost by most members of southern industrial societies.

In contemporary resettled Inuit communities only about one-fifth of the adult population work for wages as clerks, truck drivers, labourers, interpreters, or teachers. The rest engage in traditional activities such as hunting or processing the products of hunting, or family and community activities. Hunters work in groups based on kinship ties. Usually they hunt seals within a day's distance of the village, but longer winter hunting trips for caribou and polar bears are carried out by groups of up to five hunters with supplies for a month. Inuit hunters use either traditional harpoons or modern rifles. While seal meat is the mainstay staple food in the traditional diet, other seasonal foods are consumed when available. The summer diet includes fish (arctic char), berries, caribou, small whales such as beluga, migratory birds such as ducks and geese, but the winter diet is primarily seals. Women process the meat, prepare the skins of seals, polar bear and caribou, and sew clothes and boots.

The activities of historical hunter-gatherer societies were of necessity tied to natural ecological cycles. Everything used was taken from the surrounding environment and there was little if any waste. These were subsistence cultures, but one of the issues in dispute is whether contemporary communities such as the Inuit can still accurately be so characterized, and if so which model of subsistence is the most appropriate. Wenzel claims that there are several different models of subsistence invoked by participants in the debate, and that often opponents of native hunters invoke models that unfairly affect the discussion. Shortly I take up these different models, but here it is important to emphasize according to Wenzel that "it is necessary to discuss Inuit subsistence today as an adaptive response not only to the exigencies of the natural environment, but also in regard to the social and economic constraints to which Inuit have been exposed."[19]

These constraints are tied to commercial relations between Inuit and Europeans and Canadians and go back for several hundred years. Accounts of these relations, which are at the heart of the dispute, lend themselves to opposing analysis of dependence-independence. Do these commercial contacts allow traditional Inuit cultures and Europeans to evolve in mutually beneficial ways; do they open the door to colonization, dependence and victimization which escalate with increasing Inuit involvement or entrapment in an international capitalist free market economy; or do commercial sales of some products of hunting provide a fighting chance for Inuit, a small means of countering European domination? Although this is one of the crucial questions that separates the two sides in the debate, it is difficult to resolve because the same historical and more current events and even the same information and statistical data can be used to support conflicting hypothesis and conclusions.

Wenzel claims that the Inuit needed to keep adaptive efficiency in a harsh environment and so incorporated European tools and materials into their culture. An important historical turning point for the Clyde Inuit community occurred around 1870 when economic contact around the fur trade intensified. The opponents of native trapping see decline and exploitation; Wenzel sees "environmental resilience that is an Inuit hallmark."[20] The opponents see only negative impact upon Inuit culture from the contact and the introduction of European hunting technologies, for "'modern' hunting tools led to...greater dependence on Europeans for food and clothing."[21] However, Wenzel claims that guns give a needed advantage to offset the devastating effects of resettlement.

The event that perhaps had the most dramatic impact upon the Clyde Inuit was the resettlement of their community from their traditional ecological niche, and the hunting areas they knew well, into planned and centralized communities that fit Canadian government policies.

These new communities were more distant from the more abundant food supplies. While there is a more than adequate supply of seals in the immediate area of the settlements, other animals are now only to be found at some distance from the community. Since resettlement, the Inuit now need to earn enough money to buy modern hunting equipment and snowmobiles so that they can travel long distances to hunt. The rationale of resettlement was efficient provision of Canadian educational, medical and social services, but the facts of life that followed were "money, satellite communications, compulsory education and social welfare, high-quality health care, airports and hotels."[22] The teachers, nurses and administrators were almost all white southerners. That the dogteam was given up for the snowmobile was a necessary adaptation to these imposed conditions. But the animal rights movement claims that these modern technological innovations and new eco-nomic relations have changed northern life to such an extent that Inuit hunting is no longer necessary or tied to cultural traditions.

The collapse of the market for seal fur has had serious consequences for the Clyde Inuit. In the period prior to the ban, "Inuit had a commodity for which they could receive a reasonable value in return; southern supplies of equipment, dry goods, and foodstuffs became once again accessible."[23] By the end of the 1970s, "imported equipment had become integral in all types of subsistence activities."[24] The impact of the seal product ban was dramatic. The Inuit now required money to finance their subsistence culture, and the source of this money was being cut off. "The immediate effect was a decline in all types of Inuit harvesting because the same equipment used for seal hunting was important to almost all wildlife harvesting."[25] For while seals are found close to the community, most other species require long hunting trips. Thus at first glance there seems to be a moral imperative to support native hunting by lifting the ban, and perhaps even to persuade consumers that they have an obligation to buy fur to preserve the community.

The claim that the Inuit remain a subsistence culture is clearly foundational and requires clarification and defence. Wenzel delineates three different notions of subsistence which are used in the debate.

The first two of these are the commonly accepted usages, but Wenzel rejects them as inappropriate to the context. These two senses are utilized by critics of trapping to argue that Inuit no longer meet the conditions of a subsistence lifestyle. Wenzel claims that "no aspect of aboriginal hunting cultures is treated so simplistically as the notion of subsistence."[26] He continues, saying that

"in everyday parlance, subsistence is used in one of two ways by us. One way is in a minimalist, often pejorative, sense, suggesting that human life is sustained at the barest possible margin. Newspapers daily describe

the urban homeless as living 'at the edge of subsistence'...

In the second, more sophisticated usage, subsistence describes a process by which an organism satisfies all its own needs and consumes all that it produces itself. Among anthropologists and economists, a subsistence economy is often characterized as a self-contained system... This perception...emphasizes material production, especially the production of food, for the producer's own use."[27]

Since subsistence involves a closed system of production and consumption and since changes had opened up the Inuit system to external forces and relations, the Inuit, according to critics' interpretations, are no longer subsistence hunters. Wenzel instead enunciates a third sense of subsistence which he feels more accurately fits the Inuit case.

Inuit live a subsistence life not merely because they have a detailed knowledge of their ecological niche and the species within it, but because their own community is organized around certain social principles and relations of kinship, cooperation and sharing. Hunting activities are organized cooperatively and based on the needs of the community as a whole. "For Inuit, the basis of secure, successful subsistence is the social relatedness of one person to another, rather than individual prowess or special equipment. And the only means of establishing these extended, long-lasting relations is through kinship. Social relatedness through kinship becomes a means of redressing the unpredictability of the environment."[28] Production is a social activity and the community members share economic output. So kinship relations shape economic activities.

One key element of this model is the relatedness of humans and animals in their environment. Hunters and animals are joined in one community. The social factors of kinship and sharing are the glue of the subsistence culture. "Harvesting involves the relating of society to the environment...All living things are part of one system of reciprocal rights and responsibilities. In this cultural system, harvesting is the point of articulation between hunter and animal, society and environment."[29]

Inuit relate to animals as co-residents of the same environment. They believe, according to Wenzel, in the co-equality between animals and humans, and Wenzel defines this equality as follows: "Just as Inuit share the products they harvest among themselves, so seals or caribou share themselves with Inuit. Inuit hunters reciprocate this generosity by sharing with others as animals have with them."[30] Or, "for Inuit subsistence is the result of a positive reciprocity that occurs when animals and men fulfill their obligations to one another."[31] Animal rights advocates would argue that according to Wenzel, Inuit believe that animals have an obligation to share themselves with Inuit, i.e., they have a duty to permit the Inuit to kill them. Contrast this with Regan's view that animals are subjects of a life, that they have "an individual welfare in the sense that their experiential life fares well or ill for them, logically independently of their utility for others, and logically independently of their being the object of anyone else's interests."[32] This view categorically rejects the characterization of an animal subject of a life's interests in terms of its usefulness to Inuit interests. And I think it rightly does so.

It is not true that animals voluntarily offer themselves up to be killed by Inuit (or by anyone else), or that they have duties to be killed. They have their own lives, their own well-being, their own mental and emotional experiences, their own social relations, and their own communities, and they have desires and interests to continue carrying out these lives unmolested. They do not desire to be killed any more than a human being would if the human were the hunted rather than the hunter. And if seals are killed for trivial or less than important reasons then they are wronged. Wenzel complains that "animal rightists seek to impose upon Inuit an atomistic form of anthropomorphism, in which animals are individually idealized as each having inherent moral worth. This view is in contradiction to that of Inuit for whom animals, through their meat and pelts, offer the means by which individual humans contribute to the collective security of the social group."[33]

Wenzel here cannot be complaining about the anthropomorphism in general, for he spends a good deal of time explaining the Inuit anthropomorphizing of seals. "Animals, too, react to the ungenerous hunter by withholding themselves from them."[34] He is complaining about the type of anthropomorphism which sees an individual animal as having worth in its own right, rather than the type of anthropomorphism which sees animals as agreeing to be used for human ends. This point, central to Wenzel's case, is an extremely vulnerable and damaging element of the case for native trappers. It too easily gets lost in all the shouting that while the legacy of Euro-Canadian colonization is one of massive harm to, and violation of, aboriginal people and communities, this particular issue is being fought, quite literally, on the backs of the innocent animal bystanders, and that justice is not done or harms undone by ignoring their well-being and interests. So the notion of subsistence at the foundation of the case is very much in need of repair. The objectionable anthropomorphising of animals must be removed. Inuit respect for animals must be measured by their behaviour and action, primarily a refusal to inflict unnecessary death and suffering on the animals in their environment.

J. Baird Callicott, in his defence of native environmental ethics, emphasizes just this behavioural component. He does this against the backdrop of a more general defence of native environmental ethics against those who would claim that this romanticizes traditional native cultures. He explains this objection, saying that "with few exceptions, however, professional ethnographers and anthropologists consider the American Indian-as-ecological-guru to be neo-romantic nonsense, a post-sixties edition of the Noble Savage with an environmental spin."[35] Callicott argues to the contrary that American native cultures "represented their natural environments by means of an essentially social model, which although mythic in substance, was identical in form to the ecological model of a biotic community."[36] In practice they espoused an environmental ethic. The line of argument that Callicott endorses, one that claims that this ethic in *practice* manifests respect for animals hunted by the Inuit, is a promising avenue of response to the objections of opponents. Whether this avenue will succeed, then, depends on whether an empirical case can be built up that establishes that native treatment of animals who are hunted is in fact respectful of these animals — the test being whether or not unnecessary suffering and death are inflicted.

Callicott also accepts the spiritual world view articulated by Wenzel, but his approach is more convincing because he supports it with arguments more likely to be acceptable to those who are sceptical of such spiritual claims. He says that "I have claimed that the typical traditional American Indian attitude was to regard all features of the environment as enspirited. These entities possessed a consciousness, reason, and volition no less intense and complete than a human being's. The Earth itself, the sky, the winds, rocks, streams, trees, insects, birds, and all other animals therefore had personalities and were thus as fully persons as other human beings."[37]

This pan-psychism goes far beyond the claims of defenders of animal rights and welfare in its attribution of an equal degree of consciousness to all elements of the environment, and is likely to be rejected by those, including animal rights supporters, who are sceptical of such general spiritual claims. However, other elements of the traditional native world view as described by Wenzel, provide a more plausible response to objections *if and only if* they can be shown to support and lead in practice to the very behavioural restraints that limit killing individual animals which are called for by defenders of the rights and moral standing of individual animals. But here some care must be taken to separate out those claims which do lead to such behavioural constraints from those claims which will not satisfy those sceptical of the spiritual world view associated with native environmental ethics.

As Callicott explains, some important implications can be teased out of this world view. He says "most American Indians lived in a world which was peopled not only by human persons and personalities associated with all natural phenomena. In one's practical dealings in such a world it is necessary to one's well-being and that of one's family and tribe to maintain good social relations not only with proximate human persons, one's immediate tribal neighbours, but also with the non-human persons abounding in the immediate environment."[38] There are conceptual connections between the concept of a person and behavioural constraints which exhibit respect. "Toward persons it is necessary, whether for genuinely ethical or purely prudential reasons, to act in a careful and circumspect manner."[39] He says that "some American Indian cultures...represented the plants and animals of their environment as engaged in social and economic intercourse with one another and with human beings. And such a social picture of human-environment interaction gave rise to correlative moral attitudes and behavioural restraints...A cardinal precept...is that non-human natural entities, both individually and as species, must be treated with respect and restraint."[40]

This direction of emphasizing the behavioural manifestations of respect is the appropriate route for defenders of native hunters to take. But some other stands of the argument are not as likely to quell complaints of animal rights defenders. For example, Callicott says that "the implicit overall metaphysic of American Indian cultures locates human beings in a larger social...environment...Existence in this larger society, just as exist-

ence in a family and tribal context, places people in an environment in which reciprocal responsibilities and mutual obligations are taken for granted...The world around...is bound together through bonds of kinship, mutuality, and reciprocity."[41]

Some sorting out of these connected claims is called for. From the perspective of animal rights defenders, claims of mutual obligations, if interpreted to mean that animals voluntarily agree to be killed by Inuit, are objectionable and unconvincing. However, if claims of kinship are interpreted as they are within a human context, to mean that respect calls for a refusal to endorse or inflict suffering and death or to sacrifice some members of the community, then the model of an extended community which includes the surrounding environment and the animals who inhabit it is acceptable and indeed welcome to animal rights defenders. But the problem is that both Wenzel and Callicott equivocate on the issue of the practical manifestations of respect and interpret respectful actions differently in the case of human and animal kin. Defenders of animal rights can respond to the invocation of mutual obligation and respect by pointing out that it is no more respectful to inflict unnecessary suffering and death on animal kin that it is to do so to human kin. If indeed all members of the community are equal, then no individuals should be sacrificed unnecessarily.

What then, do the defenders of native trappers' rights have to do to meet the legitimate concerns of those who argue for animal rights or status? I agree that because of the harshness of the climate and the proximity of abundant supplies of seals and caribou it is morally permissible for Inuit to hunt those animals they will fully use for their own immediate needs for food, clothing, and shelter. The question before us now, then, is whether it is permissible to sell the sealskins for money. One perplexing paradox is that when viewed as a consumer product, fur appears to be trivial and unimportant and certainly not the sort of commodity that would justify the death of an animal. A high fashion "status" fur coat worn on the streets of Toronto or New York seems to deserve the scornful comment of animal rights activists that "it looked better on its original owner." Holmes Rolston agrees. He says that "as these uses of animals pass from the essential through the serious into the merely desirable and finally to the trivial, the ecological pattern rapidly fades, and the justification collapses...The use of fur for status – a jaguar coat on an actress – is highly artificial. Status is a cultural artifact, as is the status symbol. The suffering traded for it is not justified by any naturalistic principle."[42]

However, viewed from the other end of the process, the perspective of the hunter, fur functions not as fashion object but as a means of maintaining an endangered way of life. There is a need for some sale of sealskins to obtain that amount of money necessary to buy equipment to maintain traditional life.

Part of the difficulty in resolving this, and indeed in sorting out the very issues and arguments, is that the two sides in the debate rely upon different underlying environmental theories. Wenzel implicitly relies upon holistic environmental principles such as those propounded by the land ethic or deep ecology to make his case.[43] According to these perspectives, what has value are wholes, or species as a whole, of functioning ecosystems. On this view, seals have value as part of an ecologically sound system. It is the species as a whole that has value, the species as it plays its role or has its relations in the ecosystem of Baffin Island. Individual seals have no value or status on their own. All is well as long as the species is not hunted to extinction. So Wenzel argues as though all that he has to establish are certain minimal claims. He believes that if he can show that in general it is permissible for Inuit to hunt seals and sell furs to obtain money to sustain their lifestyle, then as long as they do not hunt seals to extinction they are not acting wrongly. But in the end, this holistic argument will not withstand scrutiny as it stands.[44]

Holistic theorists such as Callicott and Naess maintain that the human species is not more or less valuable than any other. Consistency then requires that, if holism is acceptable, it must be acceptable when applied to the human species. The consequence of this – that humans should reduce our numbers by 90 percent, that famine, war and disease are natural methods of controlling human population – are harshly pointed out by critics who conclude that such holistic theories are morally unacceptable.[45] Individual humans, not just the human species, must matter. But if they matter then logic must lead us to extend this standing to individual members of other species. On this view each and every individual animal life has value, and each and every animal killed for unimportant purposes is wronged.

So we need to examine and scrutinize overall numbers and statistics in order to attempt to determine whether each and every animal killed is killed for an important or a trivial purpose. Important needs would include food, clothing and shelter. Recall that I have also accepted the need for Inuit to have some money from sale of furs to buy, maintain and replace hunting equipment and other necessities which are now required to overcome the barriers of resettlement. (However we must recall that seals are plentiful in the immediate environment of the new settlements.)

Unfortunately, I am left to speculate here, for Wenzel does not provide all of the key information and statistics to determine this. What needs to be determined is whether, beyond the numbers of seals killed in order to meet the legitimate needs above outlined, other seals are killed so their furs may be sold in exchange for money which is then spent on unimportant products, or on products which are part of a lifestyle which is indeed less and less traditional. For the Inuit lifestyle may still be traditional, but less traditional. The new elements introduced into the Inuit lifestyle may not further their adaptation to a changing physical and social environment, but may undermine it.

Wenzel argues as though, in principle, any change incorporated into the Inuit lifestyle becomes part of their traditional lifestyle as long as Inuit claim that this is the case. This is different from a related point. It would be unwarranted to claim that Inuit are not entitled to choose and change their lifestyle and cultural values. It is equally their right to choose to preserve a traditional way of life or to choose to integrate or assimilate this way of life into wider Canadian society. However, if they choose to change their way of life to one that is less traditional, then they begin to lose the moral advantage based upon the value of preserving such a traditional life. This is a conditional, if, then statement, and we need to establish the truth of the antecedent clause. Here we need some criterion for determining limits. There must be some limits or boundaries to changes to tradition beyond which it is not reasonable to maintain that it is still traditional. If we say that in principle any change is permitted, then no limits are set out. Wenzel does not discuss the question of what are the outer boundaries or edges beyond which he would concede that the traditional life was being undermined rather than promoted by fur sales. So we are left groping for the truth.

Certain information which would allow before and after boycott comparisons would be helpful, but Wenzel does not provide any figures after 1985, and most of the numbers only go up to 1983-4. But we want to know if numbers of seals killed dropped significantly after the boycott. If numbers did drop, then there is room for suspicion that some seals had been killed unnecessarily. There are some figures for the transition period of the early boycott. In 1981, 3,378 seals were killed and this number dropped to 2,678 by 1983. If we assume that subsistence hunters would return to their abundant food supply, then one hypothesis is that 700 seals were killed in 1981 to finance unimportant or nontraditional items. There is also some evidence that money was used to buy southern

food, including junk food, as a one-day sample menu from 1984 reveals.[46] There is not one item of "country food" or traditional local food on this menu. Instead, the menu lists eggs, canned ham and white bread for breakfast, processed cheese and white bread for lunch, T-bone beef steak for supper, and sodas, potato chips and candy bars for snacks. If money from the sale of fur is used to finance this diet, then the moral advantage is crumbling.

There are also other reasons to be wary, and perhaps it is instructive to look to the dangers illustrated by some analogous situations. Consider the case of small third world farmers who were persuaded or induced to grow cash crops for export. Such involvement in the international market in many cases has made these farmers extremely vulnerable to economic and political forces beyond their control as prices go on a roller coaster.

The history of the fur trade in Canada is also rife with examples of rapid market expansions and contractions, even collapses, as consumer tastes for these luxury items change. To rely on a high fashion product so open to such market fluctuations is a risky business at the best of times. However, the animal rights educational and activist program would not have had its dramatic effect if it had not touched some raw moral nerve in many consumers.

While some consumers may have been intimidated into refraining from buying furs, many others stopped buying furs because of moral qualms about what they came to view as an objectionable product. So Inuit cannot expect to find a secure and stable market for such an emotionally charged commodity. Some defenders of native hunters may even go as far as to argue that consumers ought to buy this product, to support this culture, despite their moral queasiness, but this is unlikely to succeed. So even from the perspective of enlightened self-interest it would seem wise not to depend on sales of this item to finance a traditional lifestyle.

This last point raises a whole series of questions about the value of preserving minority cultures and endangered ways of life such as those of farmers on land threatened by drought or maritime fishers who face a precarious future. Unfortunately, the deeper question of the general obligations of members of Canadian society to support such endangered ways of life is beyond the scope of this paper.[47]

In this paper I have attempted to clarify the positions at stake in the debate between the defenders of native hunters and of animal rights. Hopefully by clarifying the arguments which are at issue in this debate, arguments which opponents often ignore or misconstrue, it will be possible to shed some light rather than heat on these questions.

ENDNOTES

[1] I presented earlier versions of this paper at the Institute for Research on Environment and Economy (University of Ottawa), the Canadian Society for the Study of Practical Ethics, and the North American Society for Social Philosophy. I would like to thank the members of the audience on those occasions, and in particular Will Kymlicka, for the helpful questions and comments.

[2] George Wenzel; Animal Rights, Human Rights; Toronto, University of Toronto Press; 1991.

[3] Jeremy Bentham, quoted by Martin Benjamin in "Ethics and Animal Consciousness" in Thomas Mappes and Jane Zembaty, eds., Social Ethics, Third Edition; New York:McGraw-Hill; 1987; p. 481.

[4] Tom Regan; "Honey Dribbles Down Your Fur"; in Philip Hanson, ed., Environmental Ethics: Philosophy and Policy Perspectives; Burnaby, B.C., Simon Fraser University Publications; 1986; p.101.

[5] For defences of animal moral status, see Tom Regan, The Case for Animal Rights, Berkeley: University of California Press, 1983; and Peter Singer, Animal Liberation, New York: Avon Books, 1975. J. Baird Callicott provided one early challenge in "Animal Liberation: A Triangular Affair", in People, Penguins, and Plastic Trees, 2nd Edition, ed. Donald VanDeVeer and Christine Pierce, Belmont, California: Wadsworth, 1995, 237-53. Some prominent writings of radical environmentalists are: Arne Naess, Ecology, Community and Lifestyle, ed. and trans. David Rothenberg Cambridge: Cambridge University Press, 1989; Aldo Leopold,

A Sand County Almanac New York: Oxford University Press, 1989; J. Baird Callicott, In Defense of the Land Ethic: Essays in Environmental Philosophy, Albany: State University of New York Press, 1989; Bill Devall and George Sessions, Deep Ecology: Living as if Nature Mattered, Salt Lake City: Gibbs Smith, 1985. The divisions are summed up by Mark Sagoff in "Animal Liberation, Environmental Ethics: Bad Marriage, Quick Divorce", in Environmental Philosophy: From Animal Rights to Radical Ecology, ed. Michael Zimmerman, Englewood Cliffs, New Jersey: Prentice Hall, 1993, 84-94.

[6] Singer, 48.

[7] Ibid., 8.

[8] Regan, 243.

[9] For further discussion see Peter Singer, "Animals and the Value of Life", in Matters of Life and Death, Third Edition, ed. Tom Regan, New York: McGraw-Hill, 1993, 282-95.

[10] Donald VanDeVeer, "Interspecific Justice", in VanDeVeer and Pierce, 85-98.

[11] Ibid.,92.

[12] Ibid.,93.

[13] Wenzel,1.

[14] Ibid,2.

[15] Ibid.,3.

[16] Ibid.,3-4.

[17] Ibid.,4-5.

[18] Ibid.,5.

[19] Ibid.,25.

[20] Ibid.,29.

[21] Ibid.,29.

[22] Ibid.,34.

[23] Ibid.,51.

[24] Ibid.,53

[25] Ibid.,53.

[26] Ibid.,57.

[27] Ibid.,57-8.

[28] Ibid.,60.

[29] Ibid.,61.

[30] Ibid.,63.

[31] Ibid.

[32] Regan,243.

[33] Wenzel,182.

[34] Ibid.,63.

[35] J. Baird Callicott, In Defense of the Land Ethic,9.

[36] Ibid.

[37] Ibid.,189.

[38] Ibid.,189.

[39] Ibid.

[40]J. Baird Callicott, "The Search for an Environmental Ethic", in Tom Regan ed., Matters of Life and Death, 370.

[41]Callicott, "Indian and Western European Attitudes", 189-90.

[42]Holmes Rolston, III, Environmental Ethics, Philadelphia: Temple University Press, 1988, 85.

[43]For explorations of the land ethic see Aldo Leopold, A Sand County Almanac and J. Baird Callicott, In Defense of the Land Ethic: The founder of deep ecology is Arne Naess, who has written extensively on it. See, for example, Ecology, Community and Lifestyle.

[44]Callicott acknowledges this when he responds to objections that holistic theories are "ecofascist". He tempers this holism with a place for the value of individuals as well as holistic elements. See Callicott, 91-94.

[45]Ibid.,92.[46]Wenzel, 119.

[47]For a defence of minority cultures, including aboriginal cultures, with liberal societies, see Will Kymlicka, Liberalism, Community and Culture, Oxford: Oxford University Press, 1991 and Multicultural Citizenship, Oxford: Clarendon Press, 1995.

ARGUMENTS FOR VEGETARIANISM

10

by Michael Allen Fox

1. An Overview of the Issues

THE TOPIC OF VEGETARIANISM OCCUPIES AN IMPORTANT PLACE IN A COLLECTION of essays devoted to applied environmental ethics, for three reasons: 1) Animal agriculture is one of the oldest and today most significant ways in which humans impinge on and transform the environment, and many would argue that it has become unsustainable and destructive from an ecological standpoint. 2) The treatment of animals in intensive production facilities ("factory farms") – which has become the dominant trend in North America and elsewhere – raises disturbing and fundamental ethical questions about our relationship to nonhuman species. 3) Some environmental ethicists and feminists either don't see the use of animals for food as a moral problem or remain prepared to defend meat eating. The question may be raised whether they acknowledge certain connections between, and implications of, beliefs they purport to hold. It seems doubtful, in addition, whether they have adequately taken into account the very evident negative impact of the economy of animal agriculture, to which our society is so deeply committed. These issues will be addressed in the discussion that follows. In particular, I shall take a look at 1) and 2); with respect to 3), I have considered environmental ethicists' dietary choices elsewhere,[1] and will confine myself to a few reflections on feminism and vegetarianism.

There are many grounds that might be adduced in support of choosing to be a vegetarian. However, four principal ones seem to stand out:

a. assuring good health for ourselves;

b. alleviating animal suffering and preventing unnecessary animal deaths;

c. helping avoid environmental damage and depletion; and

d. addressing the world hunger problem, which is closely related to the problem of social injustice.

These grounds, and the arguments that spring from them, are linked together closely because, as will become evident, they are mutually reinforcing or interactive. They also have a cumulative or convergent force that no single argument has on its own. Not surprisingly, therefore, the case for vegetarianism has to be understood *holistically*, or as we might better say, *ecologically*. Let us now examine each argument in turn.

2. Arguments for Vegetarianism

Good health. It is easy to dismiss good health as an ethical argument for vegetarianism since one's health seems to be a matter of merely prudential concern. However on closer examination this is not so clear. It may make sense to assert that one has duties to oneself, and if this is so, then the duty to pursue good health might well be one of these. Kant argued, for example, that the "supreme practical principle," observance of which is obligatory for all rational beings, is to "Act in such a way that you always treat humanity, whether in your own person or in the person of any other, never simply as a means, but always at the same time as an end."[2] According to Kant each rational being is an end in itself, a being of intrinsic value, and this value is always to be respected and preserved. It would not be at all difficult to see aiming at good health as part of the process by which each person fulfils this duty. For if one neglects one's health, one treats oneself as a means, not an end, and without good health one will be unable to participate fully in the moral life because the powers of agency will be weakened and restricted.[3]

Another approach is Aristotelian in character. According to this view happiness is the goal of life for a human being. However, happiness is not to be equated with pleasure or even contentment. Rather, it is the overall quality of a life led as an attempt to realize fully that specific form of excellence which is characteristically human. For Aristotle this meant the right and able exercise of our rational powers, and a life led in this way is a virtuous life. To attain the life of virtue we are cautioned to avoid extreme states, such as self-indulgence and self-deprivation or excessive pleasure or pain.[4] Realizing happiness depends upon securing the optimum state of wellbeing for a member of our species, and this most certainly includes and is contingent upon good health.[5]

In like manner there are numerous non-Western traditions, such as Buddhism and Confucianism, according to which the key to the good life and/or the pathway to enlightenment encompass healthy living, self-discipline and the avoidance of extremes that might upset one's physical and mental equilibrium.[6]

Even apart from the foregoing positions, which stress in one manner or another a duty to oneself to be healthy, it is possible to develop an ethical argument that one has an obligation to others to maintain one's health. These others might be specific family members or dependants, but they might, in a utilitarian approach, include members of society at large, all of whom have an interest in productivity, controlling health care costs, etc.

Now it is well known that certain kinds of meat eating, at any rate, are unhealthy. The statistical correlation between high (fatty) meat consumption and increased probability of colon, breast and other cancers, heart disease and atherosclerosis – far and away the leading causes of death in North America – has been well established by many independent researchers.[7] These realizations prompted Health and Welfare Canada to issue a new version of "Canada's Food Guide to Healthy Eating," which appeared in 1992. Alternatives to meats (such as tofu and legumes) are accentuated, as well as 5-10 servings per day of vegetables and fruits, and 5-12 servings per day of grain products. Critics maintain that an even greater shift toward a vegetarian diet might have been endorsed had it not been for extraordinary lobbying efforts of the livestock industry.[8]

As evidence continues to mount in Canada and elsewhere linking meat eating with serious health problems, and vegetarian diets with better health and greater longevity, many have begun to accept that a shift in diet is not only prudent and self-interested, but also reflects a different world-view.[9] This includes an awareness that the good life for a human being entails good health, and that good health in turn rests on a carefully chosen diet. But beyond this, many are learning that the amount of meat we consume collectively has a profound impact on how we use and manage natural resources – forests, land, water, fossil fuels. To put it simply, the greater our dependence on meat and other animal products, the more we commit these resources to satisfying this demand; and if (as we shall see later on) this form of agro-industry abuses the environment in ways that are deleterious to our health, the more animal products we consume, the more our wellbeing will suffer.

Animal suffering and death. The modern agribusiness industry, with its tendency toward fewer and larger farms and its increasing reliance on intensive rearing methods, is the source of the greatest amount of animal suffering and death of any human activity involving species other than our own. The Government of Canada reports that "Total confinement of dairy cattle, pigs, and poultry is now common practice."[10] Excesses are well documented.[11] The scale on which animals are "processed" for food beggars the imagination. In Canada alone over half a billion food animals a year are slaughtered, or nearly 1.5 million per day.

An additional 29 million chicks annually are simply destroyed for various profit-related reasons.[12] For some people suffering is the central or only issue here; utilitarians typically regard animals as fully replaceable, and for them the special wrongfulness of factory farming consists in the brutal procedures characteristic of that activity: forced, life-long confinement in artificial and barren environments, forced impregnation, debeaking, separation of veal calves and piglets from their mothers in early infancy, crowded caging, social deprivation, suppression of grooming and other species-specific behaviours, and cruel transportation, holding and slaughtering methods. If the pain and suffering inherent in these practices could be eliminated, then for those whose sole preoccupation is with such things, no ethical issue would remain. Painless, instantaneous slaughter following a reasonably decent, if short, domesticated life would be an acceptable outcome. For others, who see animals as irreplaceable individuals or "subjects of a life" in Tom Regan's sense,[13] this is unacceptable because such individuals are bearers of rights, preeminent among these being the right to life.

It is not my purpose here to try to settle this dispute but rather to indicate that the problem of vast amounts of suffering contingent upon current food animal rearing and marketing practices is a real one that we cannot ignore, no matter what our philosophical persuasion. Some may subscribe to the view that animal suffering and death in colossal quantities does not matter morally, or that if it does matter, its ethical import is offset or neutralized by the human enjoyment of animal products and the various forms of economic gain generated by satisfaction of human wants that are dependent upon using animals for food. However, it would seem that only an alienated, desensitized form of consciousness could declare that human-caused animal suffering and death on a very great scale do not matter or are easily offset by other considerations. It is difficult to see how widely practiced, institutionalized cruelty of any kind can

be in the best interest of society. In any event, human enjoyment in eating meat and economic gains accruing to those whose livelihoods depend on the meat, egg and dairy industries could be realized just as well by the alternatives available in a vegetarian economy. Far less suffering would be generated, the overall utility of the latter system, one reasonably assumes, would be greater, and therefore the system itself would be morally preferable.

Now as judged by their attitudes and behaviour, most people apparently do not care very much, if at all, about these issues. However, this lack of caring may point to a self-serving, or self-protective blind spot in people's moral consciousness. For as Jeremy Bentham pointed out long ago, and many others since have reaffirmed, animal suffering should concern us because *all* forms of suffering should concern us – or at the very least suffering that is comparable in kind and degree to what we are familiar with at first hand. A diet that depends on massive mechanized carnage should at least give us pause to consider what we are doing to satisfy our palates. As Carol J. Adams has argued, "Meat eating is the most oppressive and extensive institutionalized violence against animals."[14] Even if we don't subscribe to the very strong view that "Meat is murder," we should still be appalled at the cruelty and death-dealing to which we acquiesce by being meat eaters. It is difficult to avoid drawing the conclusion that we must each face up to the fact that our choices as consumers materially affect the amount of animal suffering and death. We either opt in or we opt out of the animal agony system. If we do not think too carefully or too critically about our diets, we can easily overlook the consequences they have; but this is also a choice, namely, a choice of omission. We are no less responsible for it than for any other choice. If we *are* informed about the misery created by factory farming and related activities, yet still knowingly elect to eat meat, we are even more culpable.

An alternative way of understanding this form of neglect is that it springs from culturally conditioned perceptions of our food and the ways in which we as individuals choose, more or less consciously, to affirm them in our daily lives. That is, each of us sees animal flesh in a market or present before us cooked upon a plate as either "meat" (or some "cut" thereof), or else as body parts of a once living, now dead animal, perhaps even related to us as a natural kin. It is obvious that the former way of seeing tends to evoke thoughts and feelings of pleasure, comfort, hunger, nourishment, wellbeing, and the like, while the latter may be accompanied by thoughts and feelings of horror, disgust, displeasure, uneasiness, perhaps even guilt. The basis for either set of reactions is not "purely subjective": both are grounded in meaningful interactions with the world and shared attitudes toward it. The main point is simply that ethical responses here, as elsewhere, are contingent on how we (choose to) see the world and relevant items in it. If there is a significant sense in which we choose how we perceive animal flesh offered for food, or at any rate ought to become aware of how we perceive it and why, then it follows again that we are responsible for our actions that proceed from our way of seeing.

Kathryn Paxton George has argued recently, however, that a universalizable ethical commitment to vegetarianism cannot be grounded in traditional moral theories (in particular utilitarianism and rights theory) because these assume the normalizing standpoint of a privileged, young, Western, white, male subject.[15] In addition she adduces empirical support for the claim that the impact and risk factors of a strict vegetarian diet are much less likely to be borne by this class of individuals than they are by women, infants, children, adolescents, the elderly, some nonwhites, and many persons in developing countries. These differential effects are masked by treating the implied male subject of traditional ethical discourse as a stand-in for all of humanity, and his health requirements as correspondingly universal.

This is not the place to engage in a detailed examination of George's argument, and we must concede that she poses a serious challenge to the view that people in general are better off, from the perspective of health, consuming a vegetarian diet. The fundamental issue she raises is who the "we" is here, and who arrogates to him- or herself the right to speak on everyone's behalf. Ethics today, George affirms, must be capable of reflecting diverse standpoints, or in short of being formulated contextually. Her points are well taken that: a) vegetarianism cannot readily and unproblematically be absorbed into a feminist ethical framework; and b) an adequate ethical defence of vegetarianism, which is sensitive to the range of issues raised by both environmental ethics and feminist theory, still remains to be developed. Yet George "continue[s] to affirm that we have moral obligations to animals and that killing or harming any animal is an evil and is often wrong,"[16] and also "assume[s] that any feminist ethic will in some way incorporate a recognizable version of the equal worth of differently situated individuals, whether human or animal."[17] It seems clear, then, that these ethical commitments will have to be incorporated into any new theory about how humans ought and ought not to treat animals, and that their implications will have to be worked out somehow in the dietary choices of each of us, however different our standpoints and situations may be. As George would no doubt agree, we cannot simply pass on to animals the costs of whatever difficulties our individual life situation might be perceived to have. For far too long this has been the path of least resistance and compromise humans have followed because they have granted little or no moral status to animals. There is no question that the "equal worth of lives" criterion, cited earlier, requires sacrifices of us in order to be put into practice. Exactly how and which remain to be determined from the standpoint in question and cannot be dictated by a detached, global theory.

Having said all this, it should not go unmentioned that George's article, controversial and persuasive though it is, does not reach beyond the first two of our grounds for vegetarianism. That is, she does not take up the issue of the environmental impact of meat eating/meat production, nor that of meat diets and social injustice, the latter of which must certainly be weighed against the injustices she contends vegetarianism would create for those who are likely to suffer because of it from inadequate nutrition and from nutrition-related diseases. But without seeing the cumulative effect of all our arguments it would be premature to pronounce upon the adequacy of ethical vegetarianism.

Environmental impact of meat production. The eco-destructive consequences of the meat industry's operations have been summarized concisely, with ample documentation from both governmental and non-governmental sources, by John Robbins in *Diet for a New America*.[18] These include: toxic chemical residues in the food chain, pharmaceutical additives in feeds, polluting chemicals and animal wastes from feedlot runoff in waterways and underground aquifers, topsoil loss caused by patterns of relentless grazing, domestic and foreign deforestation and desertification owing to the clearing of land for grazing and for cultivating feed, threatened habitats of wild species of plants and animals, intensive exploitation of water and energy supplies, and finally ozone depletion owing to the extensive use of fossil fuels and to significant production of methane gas by cattle. Sharon Bloyd-Peshkin sums up this sorry state of affairs in these simple terms: "Meat production is a major source of environmental damage."[19]

Some Canadian data will help to put these complex problems in perspective. From the beginnings of white settlement until the present, expanding agriculture has been the major factor in an 85 percent reduction of wetlands in Canada.[20] Agricul-

tural acreage has increased fourfold since 1900, and the total area under irrigation has more than doubled between 1970 and 1988.[21] It must be assumed that the consumption of meat is a dominant force here, given that in North America some 95 percent of oats and 80 percent of corn produced ends up as livestock feed.[22] Canadian farm animals produce 322 million litres of manure *daily*, an overwhelming proportion of which comes from cattle. Each marketed kilogram of edible beef generates at least 40 kg of manure, and each of pork 15 kg. These wastes, as well as the runoff of water used to clean farm buildings and equipment, pesticide residues and other agricultural chemicals are often poorly handled and cause water and soil contamination, as well as air pollution.[23] Finally, it is estimated that between 400 and 2500 gallons of water are required in the overall process by which one pound of meat is produced;[24] a pound of wheat, by contrast, requires only 60 gals.[25]

Obviously not all of the environmentally damaging effects of today's unsound agricultural practices can be attributed to production of animals for food. It is clear that some of the abuses could be mitigated by, for example, a more dedicated approach to recycling manure into crop fertilizer, greater reliance on natural means of pest control instead of chemicals, and the like. It has been argued that the target of criticism should not be meat production per se, but rather the intensive rearing methods used by contemporary agribusiness. There is some point to this rejoinder, and surely those who obtain their meat from free-range animals and organic farms contribute in a lesser degree to the environmental toll exacted by human life. But vegetarians can live even more lightly in nature. It has been calculated that:

All the grain fed to livestock could feed five times as many people. *(Proponents of intensive animal agriculture claim that we only put animals on land that could not support plant production. But we could grow more than enough plant food*

for human consumption if we used even a frac-
tion of the land that is now used to grow plant
food for livestock consumption.)[26]

If one of the leading principles of ecologically
informed ethical thinking is that we ought to minimize the harmful impact of our lives – individually and collectively – on the planet, then it follows that we ought to make those lifestyle choices
that help to advance this objective. The principle
of nonmaleficence (minimizing harm) certainly
seems to be about as basic a moral guideline as
can be imagined. And even if we added the quali-
fier "all things being equal," I submit that the obligation to choose the vegetarian option would still
remain. It has been shown by many nutritionists
that a vegetarian diet lacks nothing that people
need (meat, in short, is not necessary); and it is
questionable whether reliance on free-range animals for meat would suffice to maintain the kind
of meat diet most of us have come to take for
granted, or even a fraction of this level of meat
consumption. It certainly could not sustain high
levels of meat consumption worldwide. Therefore
a commitment to vegetarianism appears clearly
to be the best way to reduce environmental harm
and degradation caused by the human need for
nourishment, and should for this reason be made
by each of us.

World hunger and injustice. Over twenty
years ago, in her book *Diet for a Small Planet,*
Frances Moore Lappé described the wasteful
feedlot process of rearing cattle for beef as "a protein factory in reverse" (16 units of protein input
for each one of output;[27] other estimates place the
ratio as high as 20 to one, and the ratio of caloric
input to caloric output for human consumption at
ten to one[28]). She also reported her "discovery that
in 1968 the amount of humanly edible protein fed
to American livestock and not returned for human
consumption approached the whole world's protein deficit!"[29] Lappé pointed out that the poor
countries of the world are often net exporters of
food to the more affluent countries (this, appar-

ently, remains the case today); that ruminants
could graze entirely on marginal rather than prime
agricultural lands because they produce protein
efficiently from cellulose; and that the North
American food production system basically feeds
animals, not people. The latter finding has received
confirmation recently from Alan Durning, senior
researcher at the Worldwatch Institute, who contends that nearly 40 percent of the world's grain
and 70 percent of American grain are fed to livestock.[30] Meanwhile, Oxfam estimates that 14.6
million hectares of often choice land in developing nations is dedicated to producing animal feeds
for European livestock.[31] Michael Redclift places
the figure much higher, at 21.6 million hectares.[32]
According to another report, "Worldwide over
one-third of all grain is grown to feed livestock,
whilst at least 500 million people are malnour-
ished."[33] These are scarcely rational uses of abundant but ever more precious planetary resources.

The average North American is overfed and
over proteinized; this is too well known to be debatable any longer. According to David Pimentel,
who has been studying the environmental impact
of modern agriculture for more than a decade, per
capita daily consumption of protein in the United
States is 102 grams (70 of which is of animal origin), while the United Nations Food and Agricultural Organization's recommended level is 41
grams.[34] As Robbins points out, people in the developing world "are copying us. They associate
meat eating with the economic status of the developed nations and strive to emulate it. The tiny
minority who can afford meat in those countries
eats it, even while many of their people go to bed
hungry at night, and mothers watch their children
starve."[35] He estimates that "a given acreage can
feed twenty times as many people eating a pure
vegetarian (or vegan) diet-style as it could people
eating the standard American diet-style." The
same acreage would feed between six and seven
lacto-ovo vegetarians.[36] Meanwhile, Lester Brown
of the Overseas Development Council calculates

that a mere ten percent reduction in American meat eating would free up enough grain to feed all of the 60 million humans who starve to death annually.[37] Robbins concludes that "Hunger is really a social disease caused by the unjust, inefficient and wasteful control of food."[38] Exploitation is clearly a principal feature of this "disease," as the poorest countries of the world find their traditional agricultural practices and diets increasingly undermined, their peoples increasingly undernourished, their lands deforested for grazing, their position in international markets deteriorating, and other negative effects of the international meat economy controlled by multinational corporations visited upon them.[39]

Production, distribution and control of the market are the complex, dynamic elements that reinforce and perpetuate these forms of exploitation. Their scope goes beyond what we have space for here. Suffice it to say, however, that everyone has a clear choice between abetting the conditions which enable the "social disease" of world hunger to flourish and saying "no" by means of her or his own dietary commitments.

The third and fourth grounds for vegetarianism illustrate, when considered together, just the sort of connection environmental thinkers should be making. When unsustainable meat production takes its toll on the environment and consumes an inordinate share of the earth's resources, everyone is impoverished, especially those who are already short of food. These cumulative effects of the preferred North American diet are concisely summarized by Keith Akers at the conclusion of a very detailed discussion of what he labels "vegetarian ecology":

In the long run, we are all going to be vegetarians. Doubtless through further exploitation of the environment, we can prolong the period in our history in which we think it necessary to kill animals for food. But the ecological limitations of this procedure will soon make manifest to all that a
vegetarian economy is both necessary and desirable.

Only a small minority of the world's citizens will ever be able to consume meat at current American levels: the resources to support a more intensive livestock agriculture simply don't exist. We will probably not feel the real effects of our present actions in the realm of agriculture for another twenty or thirty years. In the interim, things will merely become slightly less pleasant, year after year. To continue to maintain a meat economy can only make matters increasingly difficult for everyone, and can only adversely affect the goals of health for everyone and world peace.[40]

3. Conclusions

It has been shown that meat eating not only causes much suffering and death to sentient nonhuman animals, but also is inseparable from activities that are ecologically damaging and environmentally unsustainable. These activities, in addition, are antithetical to the aims of social justice and equality, which are part of the wider meaning of sustainability.[41] Meat eating is bound up with the oppression and exploitation of others elsewhere in the world who have less than we do of the basic necessities of life – in large measure because we have more than we need. Meat eating therefore contributes materially to the process whereby the poorer citizens of the world have their interest in a better life denied, while at the same time it promotes the identical interest of the more affluent.

Many persons – including some who identify themselves as environmental holists – fail to see connections that ought to be drawn between large-scale ethical issues which should concern us all. These issues make vegetarianism a moral imperative. Animal liberation theories stress sentience in their critique of the meat industry and judge that the suffering it causes to nonhuman animals makes meat eating immoral. Animal rights theories place emphasis on the possession of interests and rights by nonhuman animals and find herein the moral basis for opposing meat eating. One might expect that any ethical outlook which purports to be more overarching than these would bring the sorts of connections discussed earlier into even sharper focus. Examples of such an outlook are provided by ecocentric theories of environmental ethics (deep ecology, spiritual ecology, Gaiaism, the respect for nature view) and by anti-domination perspectives (ecofeminism, social ecology, Greenism, radical ecologies). Lori Gruen, an ecofeminist writer, explains the sort of standpoint these theories embody as follows:

Ecofeminists must ... attempt to establish a different system of values in which the normative category of "other" (animals, people of colour, "Third World" people, the lower classes, etc.) is reevaluated. By recognizing that the exploitation that occurs as a result of establishing power over one group is unlikely to be confined to that group only, ecofeminists are committed to a reexamination and rejection of all forms of domination.... Making connections, between the various ways in which oppression operates and between those individuals who suffer such oppression, will allow all beings to live healthier, more fulfilling, and freer lives.[42]

What this form of analysis helps us to see is that consistency in theorizing, and between theory and practice, is not just a purely "rational" value that philosophers cherish and that everyone should aim to realize; it is also a matter of seeing connections between what we believe, espouse, feel, and do, and that this in turn can lead us to a better understanding of what it means to minimize the harm that we cause by our choices and to live more lightly on the planet.

In bringing this discussion to a close it is also important to reflect briefly on just what has and

has not been established. Reasons have been provided in support of the proposition that eating copious quantities of meat, and meat that comes from factory farms, is immoral. It has been shown that vegetarianism is consistent with the overriding aims of environmental ethics, while meat eating is inconsistent with them; but it remains to be determined whether eating meat is wrong in itself and therefore in all cases. In addition we have not touched upon the question of whether veganism (refraining from dietary consumption of *any* animal products) is morally obligatory. These are only two of the issues that require to be addressed in a more comprehensive discussion than there is space for here. Perhaps enough has been said, however, to indicate that what we eat is a matter of how we choose to live, of our philosophy of life.[43]

ENDNOTES

[1] See Michael Allen Fox, "Environmental Ethics and the Ideology of Meat Eating," *Between the Species*, 9 (1993), pp.121-132.

[2] Immanuel Kant, *Groundwork of the Metaphysics of Morals*, trans. H.J. Paton (London: Hutchinson University Library, 3rd ed., 1956), p.96.

[3] Kant was not a vegetarian, nor did he ascribe any very significant moral status to animals. It is his way of arguing with which we are concerned here, and this may in fact lead to conclusions other than he might have thought. For discussions of Kant's views on animals, see A. Broadie and Elizabeth M. Pybus, "Kant's Treatment of Animals," *Philosophy*, 49 (1974), 375-383; Mary Midgley, *Animals and Why They Matter: A Journey Around the Species Barrier* (Harmondsworth, Middlesex: Penguin Books, 1983), pp. 51-61.

[4] See especially Aristotle's *Nicomachean Ethics*, Books I, II, VII, and X.

[5] Aristotle, like Kant, was not a vegetarian and argued that animals were quite different from and inferior to humans. But again we are concerned with his form of argument and how it might be developed. For a discussion of Aristotle's views on animals and vegetarianism, see Daniel A. Dombrowski, *The Philosophy of Vegetarianism* (Amherst: University of Massachusetts Press, 1984), pp. 63-73.

[6] See Gary E. Kessler, *Voices of Wisdom: A Multicultural Philosophy Reader* (Belmont, CA: Wadsworth, 2nd ed., 1995), Chap. 2.

[7] John Robbins, *Diet for a New America* (Walpole, NH :

Stillpoint Publishing, 1987; Neal D. Barnard, *The Power of Your Plate: A Plan for Better Living* (Summertown, TN: Book Publishing, 1990); Nick Fiddes, *Meat: A Natural Symbol* (New York: Routledge, Chapman & Hall, 1991).

[8] "Industry forced changes to food guide, papers show," *Toronto Star*, 15 January 1993, A2.

[9] Bhiku Jethalal, "Prescription for good health," *Toronto Star*, 3 December 1994, L1, 16: Vacanto Crawford, Brenda Davis and Victoria Harrison, *Becoming Vegetarian: The Complete Guide to Adopting a Healthy Vegetarian Diet* (Toronto: Macmillan Canada, 1994).

[10] Government of Canada, *The State of Canada's Environment* (Ottawa: Ministry of Supply and Services Canada, 1991), p. 9-26. According to the Ontario Egg Producers' Marketing Board ("Egg Farming in Ontario," n.d.), "well over 90 percent" of eggs in Canada are produced using confinement methods.

[11] See especially Jim Mason and Peter Singer, *Animal Factories* (New York: Harmony Books, rev. and updated ed., 1990); see also H. Gordon Green, "That bacon you're enjoying is from a pig penitentiary," *Toronto Star*, 12 October 1991, F2; Bob Hunter, "Warning: reading this may spoil your supper," *eye weekly* (Toronto) 25 August 1994, 11; Scott Kilman, "Animal farm's brave new world," *Globe and Mail*, 1 April 1994, A11; "Transportation Exposed: Truckers Speak Out," *Canadians for the Ethical Treatment of Food Animals Newsletter*, No. 13 (Summer 1994), pp.1-6.

[12] Source: Agriculture and Agri-Food Canada, 1995 statistics. Over 80 percent of these animals are chickens, three percent are pigs and fewer than one percent are cattle.

[13] Tom Regan, *The Case for Animal Rights* (Berkeley and Los Angeles: University of California Press, 1983), p. 243.

[14] Carol J. Adams, *The Sexual Politics of Meat: A Feminist-Vegetarian Critical Theory* (New York: Continuum, 1991), p. 70.

[15] Kathryn Paxton George, "Should Feminists Be Vegetarians?" *Signs: Journal of Women in Culture and Society,* 19 (1994), pp.405-434.

[16] George, "Should Feminists Be Vegetarians?", p.407.

[17] George, "Should Feminists Be Vegetarians?", p.408.

[18] See above, note 7.

[19] Sharon Bloyd-Peshkin, "Mumbling About Meat," *Vegetarian Times,* No. 170 (October 1991), p. 67.

[20] Government of Canada, *The State of Canada's Environment*, pp. 9-9, 9-15.

[21] Government of Canada, *The State of Canada's Environment*, pp. 26-6, 9-14.

[22] Animal Alliance of Canada, "Enviro Facts about livestock production" (compiled from Worldwatch Paper 103, Worldwatch Institute, 1991; Government of Canada, *The State of Canada's Environment*; Agriculture Canada, Livestock Market Review, 1993).

[23] Government of Canada, *The State of Canada's Environment*, p. 9-26.

[24] Animal Alliance of Canada, "Enviro Facts".

[25] Fiddes, *Meat: A Natural Symbol,* p. 215.

[26] Animal Alliance of Canada, "Enviro Facts" (italics in original).

[27] Frances Moore Lappé, *Diet for a Small Planet* (New York: Ballantine, rev. ed., 1975), p. 11.

[28] Fiddes, *Meat: A Natural Symbol*, p. 211.

[29] Lappé, *Diet for a Small Planet*, p. 3

[30] Alan Durning, "Fat of the Land: Livestock's Resource Gluttony," *World Watch*, 4/3 (May-June 1991), pp.11-17.

[31] Mark Gold, "On the Meat-Hook," *New Internationalist*, No. 215 (January 1991), pp.9-10.

[32] Michael Redclift, *Sustainable Development: Exploring the Contradictions* (London: Routledge, 1987), p. 93.

[33] Fiddes, *Meat: A Natural Symbol*, p. 211.

[34] David Pimentel, "Environmental and Social Implications of Waste in U.S. Agriculture and Food Sectors," *Journal of Agricultural Ethics*, 3 (1990), 5-20.

[35] Robbins, *Diet for a New America*, p. 351.

[36] Robbins, *Diet for a New America,* p. 352.

[37] Lester Brown, cited in Robbins, *Diet for a New America*, p. 352.

[38] Robbins, *Diet for a New America*, p. 353.

[39] For detailed discussion see Redclift, *Sustainable Development;* Gold, "On the Meat-Hook"; Fiddes, *Meat: A Natural Symbol.*

[40] Keith Akers, *A Vegetarian Sourcebook* (Arlington, VA: Vegetarian Press, 1983), p. 140.

[41] See Rajni Kothari, "Environment, Technology, and Ethics" and Stephen R. Sterling, "Towards an Ecological World View," in *Ethics of Environment and Development: Global Challenge, International Response*, ed. J. Ronald Engel and Joan Gibb Engel (London: Belhaven Press; Tuscon: University of Arizona Press, 1990), pp. 27-35, 77-86; Vandana Shiva, *Staying Alive: Women, Ecology and Development* (London: Zed Books, 1989).

[42] Lori Gruen, "Dismantling Oppression: An Analysis of the Connection Between Women and Animals," in *Ecofeminism: Women, Animals, Nature,* ed. Greta Gaard (Philadelphia: Temple University Press, 1993), pp. 80, 84.

[43] The author gratefully acknowledges the assistance of Andrea Maenza, Director, Animal Alliance of Canada, in providing essential research materials and helpful comments.

CATTLE AND PRAIRIE ECOLOGY
THE AGRICULTURAL AND ECOLOGICAL RELEVANCE OF CATTLE TO THE PRAIRIES

11
by R.D.H. Cohen

THE BEEF CATTLE INDUSTRY HAS RECEIVED A GREAT deal of negative attention from various sources and in recent years the consumption of beef in the developed world has declined markedly. The first wave of criticism was concerned with the health risk associated with consuming beef. The main issues were lipids and cholesterol, antibiotic resistance acquired through the meat and the use of hormones and hormone like anabolic agents to promote growth. These concerns have been addressed previously (Cohen 1991) but are summarized briefly here.

Beef is a rich source of protein and many other nutrients essential to human health. It is not an energy rich (high fat) food. In response to public pressure, the beef industry has reduced the amount of total fat in beef by as much as twenty percent in the ten years, 1979-1988 (Sahasrabudhe and Stewart 1989). Also, a 100g serving of roasted lean beef provides exactly the same amount of cholesterol as a 100g serving of light chicken meat without the skin, namely 85mg (National Cattleman's Association 1982). Yet the perception that beef is high and chicken is low in fat and cholesterol persists and the decline in beef consumption has been accompanied by a concomitant rise in the consumption of chicken meat. The association between red meat intake and coronary heart disease and atherosclerosis has not been demonstrated, though there is a well demonstrated association between high blood cholesterol and these diseases. Factors such as genetics, gender, obesity, exercise, cigarette smoking, alcohol consumption and total fat intake have a greater effect on blood cholesterol than cholesterol intake per se. The human body synthesizes five to six times as

much cholesterol as we eat and Brisson (1981) concluded in his book that "the intake of dietary cholesterol has no significant effect on the concentration of cholesterol in the blood of *healthy* persons in the general population" and that "the sustained fear of dietary cholesterol is not justified based on the scientific evidence available". These conclusions are still true in 1995. While reducing cholesterol intake can reduce blood levels in persons with a genetic predisposition for high blood cholesterol, it will never move them into the low blood cholesterol group. Reducing cholesterol intake has no effect on blood levels of persons with a genetic disposition for low blood cholesterol.

Antibiotics are used in feedlot rations to improve growth rate and feed efficiency as well as for the prevention of infectious diseases. This practice has raised concerns regarding the safety to human health by way of transfer of resistance to antibiotics through the meat. The evidence against this practice is entirely circumstantial (Cohen 1991). If antibiotic resistance has resulted from sub-therapeutic use in animal feeds it might be expected that the population most at risk would be the animals themselves. However, after forty years of sub-therapeutic use of antibiotics in animal feeds, animal performance is still improved by their use (Hays and Muir 1979). Furthermore, the use of antibiotics in the human population is approximately double that in all animals and natural selection for resistance is therefore more likely to have occurred in the human population. In one study, 45 percent of salmonella isolates from hospitals showed resistance to tetracycline while only eighteen percent of isolates from meat showed resistance (Guest 1976). In 1969, the Swan Report in the United Kingdom recommended that restrictions be placed on human medicinal antibiotics that were being used in animal feeds. These restrictions were enacted but did not reduce the incidence of disease or infections in the human population due to bacteria of animal origin (Guest 1976). Neither did they improve the efficacy of therapy of human or animal diseases due to a decrease in resistant bacteria nor has the bacterial contamination during the processing of food of animal origin been reduced (Guest 1976). In 1986, the use of antibiotics in human medicine was sixteen times greater than in veterinary medicine in the United Kingdom (Walton 1986). One might ask "In what sector is resistance caused by overuse more likely to be occurring?".

The use of agents such as estradiol –17b, testosterone, progesterone, trenbolone, zeranol and other estrogenic substances for the promotion of growth in cattle is widespread. The beneficial anabolic effects of these substances to the beef industry cannot be disputed. Yet there are still public concerns as to their safety. The fact is however, that 100g of beef, from a steer implanted with an estrogenic hormone to enhance growth and efficiency of feed conversion, contains 1.4 - 2.5 nanograms (ng) of estrogen and 100g of beef from a steer not implanted contains 1.2 – 2.0 ng of estrogen (1 ng = 10^{-9} g or 1 billionth of a gram). In comparison, 100g of peas and cabbage contain 400 and 2,400ng of estrogen respectively and 15ml (1 tablespoon) of wheat germ and soy bean oil contain 152 and 28,370ng of estrogen respectively. (These data are quoted from Agriculture Canada / Health and Welfare Canada / Inter-American Institute for Cooperation on Agriculture, Report on use of Hormonal Substances in Animals, 1986). Where then is the greater threat, if there is one, to human health? The Scientific Working Group on Anabolic Agents of the Council of the European Economic Community, which comprised of sixteen signatories from eight countries, concluded that anabolic compounds or their metabolites produced no residues of a significant genotoxic potential and that, provided accepted animal husbandry practices were followed, they did not present a harmful effect to health (Lamming 1987). Nevertheless, the EEC instigated a ban on these substances in a move that may have been more related to a need to reduce agricultural subsidy payments than to reduce a possible threat to human health. However, the ban has continued to fuel the fires of public speculation that those substances pose a threat to human health.

The latest attack on the beef industry has come from the animal rights movement, and in particular from Rifkin (1992), who have used the environmental movement and youth to advance their cause. For example, Rifkin (1992) states "cattle production and beef consumption now rank among the gravest threats to the future well-being of the earth and its human population." But his is not a lone voice. Pitts (1992) quotes Ryan Eliason, spokesman for Youth for Environmental Sanity (YES) as saying "Cattle and other livestock account for twice the amount of pollutants as come from all US. industrial sources" and "Livestock production is perhaps the most massive force behind the destruction of our planet" and "There is not a single major environmental problem today that would not be profoundly benefited by a reduction in meat consumption". While such protagonists have concentrated on the beef industry they also claim a domino effect ..... "The collapse of the global cattle complex will likely precipitate a chain reaction, resulting in the elimination of other grain-fed meats from the human diet" (Rifkin 1992).

This paper will examine the ethics of this 'environmental vegetarianism movement'. Using the Canadian prairies as the reference environment, it will be argued that the beef industry should expand and become a more integral part of agriculture, otherwise we are indeed headed for environmental disaster. It will be argued that, contrary to

Rifkin's beliefs, the prairie environment has been transformed not by cattle but by cropping; that cattle pose only a very minor threat to the so called 'greenhouse' effect, a threat that has in fact diminished with the demise of the bison, which occurred because of hunting practices and preceded the rise of cattle in western North America; that water use in cropping practices causes more environmental damage than does the beef industry; that cattle grazing is crucial to the ecology of the soil, preventing erosion and salinization, restoring carbon and conserving other nutrients essential to plant life and critical to the conservation of wildlife.

Transformation of the Prairie Environment

The need for an agricultural industry to feed the world's population is obvious and cereal crops should and will remain the staple of the world. However, the World Wildlife Fund (1988) stated "In only 100 years, the Canadian prairie grasslands and parklands have been so radically transformed by human activity that they have become one of the most endangered natural regions in Canada. Little native prairie remains in its native state, and what remains is rapidly disappearing. The diversity of prairie landscapes and of their wildlife is steadily being depleted...... The Canadian prairies have been transformed to produce food to feed the nation and to earn export dollars...... In the process agriculture, and to a lesser degree urbanization and industrialization, have transformed more than 80 percent of the native prairie landscape. Almost all of the remarkable tall-grass prairie is gone. Some 90 percent of the fescue grassland has been plowed...... Approximately 1.2 million ha (or 40 percent) of wetland habitat in the mixed prairie and aspen parkland regions have been converted to agricultural use...... Such quantitative data do not convey the full extent of the loss. Quality has also suffered, as the best and most fertile ecosystems were the first to disappear". Similar remarks undoubtedly apply to other agricultural regions of the world. On the Canadian prairies, it is not livestock grazing but the growing of cash crops, with the encouragement of provincial and federal government policies, that have been responsible for this transformation. In fact, apart from National, Provincial and District Parks and Wildlife Reserves, the only remaining native prairie is that which has been grazed by cattle for the past 100 years.

The beef industry has taken advantage of the cash crop industries by utilizing residues and grains unsuitable for human use or for which no other market can be found. The utilization of these grains is due to expediency rather than necessity since high quality grain-free beef is produced in many parts of the world, including North America. The fact is that beef cattle are the first to drop off the list of grain users when other markets for grain can be found.

It is true that cattle grazing has modified much of the native prairie landscape, but it is also true that the beef industry stands virtually alone among the agricultural industries on the prairies in its desire to protect and preserve the native landscape while still using it for food production. Much has and is still being learned about the sustainable management of grazed prairie rangelands despite a serious lack of funding for range research in Canada.

Rifkin (1992) claimed, with cavalier disregard for reality, that "The elimination of beef will be accompanied by an ecological renaissance. Cottonwood trees will shade the prairie once again [though they never did shade the grassland prairies], providing refuge for thousands of native birds. Streams and springs will come to life, bringing back freshwater trout and other native fish. The large mammals of the plains will repopulate the western range once again, their numbers spreading out to fill the millions of acres of restored grassland. Predator species will thrive." Paradoxically, he concludes "At the same time more agricultural land and more grain will be potentially available..." (Rifkin 1992). However, the truth is the reverse. If beef cattle are eliminated there will be little or no market for forage. If forage production is not increased on the Canadian prairies and made an integral part of crop rotations, soil organic matter content, already severely depleted, will be further reduced and grain production will become even more dependent on chemicals. Topsoil erosion, particularly on the more fragile soils, and salinization will increase. A return to favorable grain prices will result in more wetlands being drained and rangelands being broken to replace the destroyed land. More chemical fertilizers, herbicides and pesticides will be required to sustain production and add to the pollution of waterways. More fossil fuel will be converted to carbon dioxide by tractors.

The other common environmental criticisms of the beef industry are its contribution to the 'greenhouse' effect, its inefficient use of water, and environmental destruction caused by overgrazing. The remainder of this discussion will compare the impacts that cattle grazing and cropping have on these and other important environmental concerns and conclude that it is indefensible to maintain that the ethic of vegetarianism is environmentally friendly.

Crops, Animals and the Greenhouse Effect

There are many 'greenhouse' gases, ranging from water vapor to chlorofluorohydrocarbons. Agriculture contributes three 'greenhouse' gases in consequential amounts – carbon dioxide (CO_2), methane (CH_4) and oxides of nitrogen, particularly nitrous oxide (N_2O). Although CO_2 is the preeminent 'greenhouse' gas (Hanson 1991; Council For Agricultural Science And Technology 1992), the global warming potential of N_2O and CH_4 are respectively 290 and twenty-one times that of CO_2 and are therefore of concern when emitted into the atmosphere. Nitrous oxide emissions from soil occur as a consequence of disturbance by people, animals and fertilization, and are far greater on cropped than grazed soils. Robertson

(1993) concluded that row crop agriculture contributed most heavily to global N_2O fluxes, primarily through the effects of fertilizer inputs. Although soil emissions of nitric oxide (NO) have been shown to be greater from grazed than ungrazed soils (Davidson et al. 1993), they are far less than those from cultivated soils (Robertson 1993). The Council for Agricultural Science and Technology (1992) cited evidence that even no-till cropping increased the emission of N_2O in comparison to grazing.

There has been an over-emphasis on cattle as a source of CH_4 and their contribution to the 'greenhouse' effect. Methane is a product of the anaerobic decomposition of organic matter and the normal digestion process in the rumen is only one biological system in which this takes place. The rumen is the first and largest compartment of the stomach of ruminant animals and is primarily a fermentation vat. On a world basis, the largest contributors to methane gas production are the wetlands (26 percent), rice growing (20 percent), all domestic animals (15 percent), and the fossil fuel industry (14 percent). In Canada, wetlands account for 82.8 percent of methane production, humans for 6.6 percent, forest fires for 3.4 percent while all cattle account for only 2.9 percent of the national methane output (Hanson 1991, Figure 1, see graph on next page).

Methane emissions from Canadian cattle amount to less than 0.25 percent of global emissions. Similarly, Byers (1991) estimated that all cattle in the US contribute less than 1 percent to global methane. But methane is only one of the 'greenhouse' gasses and Drennen and Chapman (1991) estimated that the entire beef cattle population of the world contributed less than 1 percent of all 'greenhouse' gasses. Further, the carbon emitted as methane from cattle is recycled carbon from plants and soil. It is not new or fossil carbon such as that emitted from fossil fuels.

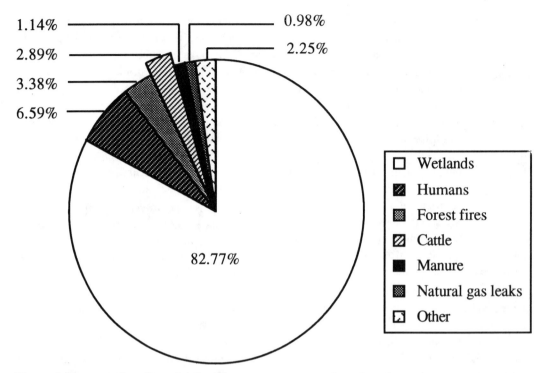

Figure 1. Sources of methane in Canada as a percentage of total methane emissions.

It should also be remembered that, before settlement, approximately sixty million bison (large ruminant animals similar to cattle) ranged the great plains of North America. This is close to twice the number of cattle on this part of the continent today. Thus, it is safe to assume that methane production from cattle in this region is less than it was before settlement for ranching took place. Finally, Hanson (1991) stated "The methane content of the gas from the Burn's Bog Landfill in Delta BC is equivalent to that produced from 374,000 cattle but the province of British Columbia only has 300,000 head of cattle distributed over millions of square miles (an exaggeration) while the Burn's Bog Landfill is concentrated on only two square miles and is only one of many landfills in BC. We appreciate the fact that man is creating a large amount of environmental damage but we believe that focusing on trivialities such as methane produced from cattle detracts from the efforts

which should be directed to important issues".

The contribution of agriculture in North America to global warming is in fact very small. For example, the Council for Agricultural Science And Technology (1992) reported that if all US farming was eliminated, the warming potential of CO_2, CH_4 and N_2O would be reduced only one percent globally.

Water Use in Crop and Animal Agriculture

It has frequently been claimed that beef production is a major user of the world's water supply. For example, statements given much media publicity include "The water that goes into a 1000lb steer would float a destroyer", "More than half of US water consumption goes to raising beef", "It takes twenty-five gallons to produce a pound of wheat but 2,500 for a pound of meat" and "To produce a day's food for one meat-eater takes 2,500 gallons; for a pure vegetarian only 300 gallons" (Robbins 1990). Such statements are not only inaccurate but they display a profound lack of understanding of ecology. Horton (unpublished data) calculated from research data the water balance (intake and output) of a steer entering the feedlot at 700 lb, finishing at 1,100 lb, on feed for 125 days, with a dry matter intake of 19.35 lb/day, at a ration dry matter of 71 percent with an average summer temperature of $73.7°F$ and average winter temperature of $34.2°F$. He measured body water in the fed steer at 227.8 lb, feed water consumed at 987.5 lb, and free water consumed at 8,481.25 lb for a total water intake of 9,696.55 lb. He also measured water output through the feces at 2,050 lb, urine at 5,506.25 lb, evaporative loss at 2,275 lb for a total output of 9,831.25 lb indicating that a steer returns 134.7 lb more water to the environment than it removes. The water that it creates is metabolic body water, that is water that is created as a product of the chemical reactions which take place in the body of the animal. Although these calculations do not account for water used in processing and packaging, meat is almost always dry cooked, thereby releasing water into the environment. In comparison, grains and pulses must be wet processed or cooked, thereby taking up water from the environment. In contrast to the numbers presented by Robbins (1990), data taken from Agriculture Canada, Environment Canada, and Statistics Canada and reproduced by the Canadian Cattleman's Association (undated) indicate that it takes 130L (29 gallons) of water to produce 1kg of beef and that most of this water is recycled to the soil in urine or treated and re-used. For example, they cite the Cargill beef processing plant at High River, Alberta, as treating the water used in the plant and using it to replenish Frank Lake, a major waterfowl nesting area. The Canadian Cattleman's Association (undated) also quotes the following Statistics Canada data: Processing one can of vegetables takes 35L of water; a barrel of beer takes 5,678L; flushing a toilet takes 32L and the manufacture of a car takes 147,971L.

Irrigation, which is used almost exclusively for crop production on the Canadian prairies, has, in addition to increasing food production, led to massive movements of salts from the lacustrine soils (soils formed by deposits in extinct lakes) of the Canadian prairies both to the surface and into the river and closed drainage fresh water systems (Johnson 1989). Sacred Aboriginal lands have been flooded, plant species have been lost, wildlife habitat has been destroyed and grazing lands for both wildlife and cattle have disappeared. This environmental destruction, which has not been confined to the Canadian prairies, eclipses the worst environmental effects which can be attributed to the effects of grazing by cattle. In addition, irrigation requires the increased burning of fossil fuel to pump the water onto the land, adding more CO_2 to the atmosphere. Further, irrigation increases the release of water vapor, an important 'greenhouse' gas, to the atmosphere. The movement of salts to the soil surface during the evaporation of moisture from the soil requires increased irrigation to flush the salts from the soil and ultimately into the waterways, thereby compounding the cycle.

The Council for Agricultural Science And Technology (1992) listed five environmental consequences of water use in agriculture:

1. Health effects of nitrates in ground water and effects of nitrogen and phosphorus fertilizers in stimulating eutrophication of lakes and reservoirs.

2. Effects of sediment from farmer's fields on the quality of water in streams, lakes and reservoirs.

3. Downstream effects of increasing salinity of return flows of irrigation water; effects of irrigation on instream flows needed to protect aquatic habitat.

4. Loss of wildlife habitat from drainage of wetlands for crop production.

5. Effects of animal wastes on the quality of ground and surface water, especially where confined animal feeding is concentrated.

Numbers one to four are exclusive consequences of cropping practices while five is related to confined rather than grazing animals, another good argument for finishing of beef on pasture rather than in the feedlot.

Environmental Impact of Grazing vs Cultivating

Overgrazing has occurred throughout the world and contributed to desertification. However, overgrazing has destroyed far less of the world's terrestrial environment than cultivation. "Almost all the original grasslands of the world have been cultivated, substantially reducing their organic matter contents .... they become susceptible to erosion; no longer productive, some have to be abandoned, or returned to managed animal pasture" (Stewart and Tiessen 1990). Even so, these authors echo the popular sentiment that animal pasture is an alternative only to the abandonment of destroyed crop land rather than something that should be an integral part of cropping systems. The real problem is that humankind is unsuccessfully attempting to defy the most basic law of ecology which is that sustainability rests on diversity. In the rush to tear up the land for the short term economic gain we have practiced a monoculture that is destroying the land. Monoculture requires the continual use of the land to produce a crop from a single species of plant. This requires continual plowing which destroys the physical characteristics of the soil, enhances the removal of moisture and important plant nutrients such as nitrogen from the soil to the atmosphere in the form of 'greenhouse' gasses such as nitrous oxide, encourages the upward and horizontal movement of salts through the soil eventually leaving it too saline to support plant growth, speeds the erosion of soil from the action of wind and rain, removes plant diversity either by mechanical

(plowing) or chemical (herbicides) means and ultimately requires the use of increasingly non-sustainable amounts of fertilizers and pesticides to maintain soil fertility and control pests and diseases. Meanwhile, cattle and wildlife have been relegated to the marginal lands, forced to compete for a scarce and fragile resource, blamed for overgrazing the land and then returned to the destroyed cultivated lands to reclaim them.

Saskatchewan alone is losing topsoil at a rate between 3 and 25 tonnes (t) / hectare (ha) / year (yr) (Johnson 1989). Salinization affects approximately 2 million ha to some degree and 240,000 ha are seriously affected (Hodgins 1991). Salinization is increasing at 5-10 percent per year (Johnson 1989). The organic matter content of soils in Saskatchewan has declined from between 4 and 8 percent to between 1.5 and 2.5 percent and even to less than 1 percent (Johnson 1989) on the marginal lands that have been cultivated. Between 20 and 50 percent of the organic matter is depleted after only seven years of cultivation, depending on the characteristics of the soil being cultivated (Hodgins 1991). All these problems have been caused by cultivation, not grazing. The answer to them lies in the wise use of perennial forage crops (crops used for animal feed such as alfalfa) and, in particular, perennial pastures as part of cash crop rotations. This means that cattle must become increasingly integrated into prairie agriculture since, only through cattle, can forage be converted to food for people and currency for the farmer who cannot be expected to labor without monetary return. Soil degradation is arrested by restoring the flow of carbon and nitrogen back to the soil with perennial forage crops, particularly legumes. By ignoring the use of perennial legumes in crop rotations, prairie farmers are ignoring the possibility of returning perhaps as much as 600-800 kg of biotic nitrogen (N) / ha / yr (Johnson 1989), without the cost of transport and machinery required for the application of chemical nitrogen and the pollution, both atmospheric and aquatic, with which chemical nitrogen is associated. In addition, perennial forages break the cycle of many of the diseases, pests and weeds that farmers currently must control with chemicals.

One common excuse for not using perennial forages in cash crop rotations is that they remove moisture from the soil and reduce yields of subsequent grain crops. However, the opposite is true. Droughty soils, those that do not retain moisture, are created by loss of organic matter and top soil erosion. Water use of forage crops is diverse and, depending on management, they can be the most energy efficient crops grown (Spedding 1988). But forage crops and perennial pasture require a market and that market is cattle. Cattle consume 83 percent of their feed as pasture and forage and derive their agricultural importance from the effective conversion of energy not usable by people into high-quality protein and other essential nutrients for human consumption. Altruistic farmers are moving voluntarily to an integrated holistic form of organic farming, that is to say a way of farming that relies on using the inherent biological diversity of the whole agricultural ecosystem. This form of farming will "maintain soil fertility to grow high quality crops and remain productive over long periods of time without the need to rely on large quantities of inputs from outside the system" (Lampkin 1992). However, the majority of farmers may need incentives to induce them to change.

Pastures, Crops
and the Global Carbon Balance

The world wide net CO_2 gain to the atmosphere is about 3 giga tonnes (Gt) /yr (1 Gt =1 billion tonnes) from burning fossil fuels and vegetation and this is the major human induced contribution to the 'greenhouse' effect (Bruce 1990). The world's carbon reservoir (Bruce 1990) consists of the oceans (36,000 Gt), fossil-fuel reserves (5,000 to 10,000 Gt), soils (1,500 Gt), atmosphere (735 Gt) and vegetation (560 Gt). t'Mannetje (1991) re-

ported that there was little difference between rain forests and rangelands as stores of carbon. He estimated the total carbon stores on rangelands to be between 52 and 58 t/ha and, with a total global estimate of five billion ha of rangeland, the amount of carbon stored would be 275 Gt or 13 percent of the total terrestrial non-fossil carbon. Rangeland carbon stores can also be calculated as 49.1 percent of vegetation carbon and 13.4 percent of non-fossil carbon from data presented by Bruce (1990). However, 72.8 percent of terrestrial non-fossil carbon is stored in the world's soils and it is this huge reservoir which is being destroyed by cultivation and cropping practices such as those used on the Canadian prairies. It is this destruction which requires the most urgent attention of agricultural environmentalists and which can be halted most effectively by the inclusion of forage, pasture and cattle in our cropping rotations.

There are 286 million ha of class one, two or three arable land in Canada[1], 82 percent located in the western provinces and 36 percent in Saskatchewan. If agricultural production and wildlife habitat is to be sustained, at least 50 percent of this area should be in perennial forage production at any point in time. This means permanent reclamation of the most fragile soils to perennial forage and the inclusion of forage in crop rotations on all other soils. Seeding much of the cropland to tame or indigenous species will relieve the pressure on the estimated 10 million ha of remaining native rangeland and pasture in the province, allowing rejuvenation of wildlife habitat, ensuring the preservation of native plants, increasing the size of the carbon sink and the extent of soil nitrification, thereby helping to alleviate the 'greenhouse' effect and reducing the extent of soil erosion, denitrification and salinization. However, the re-integration of cattle into prairie cropping rotations and a substantial increase in the production and consumption of beef are essential to this holistic approach.

Grazed Pastures,
Crops and Nutrient Recycling

Grazing animals return a large proportion of consumed plant nutrients to the soil (Table 1). Frame (1970) reported that manure patches on fertilized pastures in Britain have the equivalent of 112kg phosphorus (P) /ha and 224kg potassium (K) /ha and urine spots had fertilizer equivalents of 336kg nitrogen (N) /ha and 560kg K/ha. He also reported that urine spots and fecal deposits from a single cow may each cover 1 m^2/d and this can have a marked influence on plant productivity. For example, in Britain, Brockman (1971) showed that pasture yield increased from 10,000kg/ha for cut and removed pasture to 12,000kg/ha for grazed pasture with the same rates of fertilization.

Table 1. Nitrogen (N), phosphorus (P$_2$O$_5$*) and potassium (K$_2$O *) excretion in the feces and urine of cattle grazing native range in North America (adapted from Petersen 1956).

	N	P$_2$O$_5$	K$_2$O
In feces (%)	0.38	0.18	0.22
In urine (%)	1.10	0.01	1.15
Total (g/d)	194.00	46.00	159.00
Fertilizer equivalent (kg/ha) [†]	15.20	1.60	7.70

* The fertilizer value of phosphorus and potassium has conventionally been expressed as phosphorus pentoxide (P$_2$O$_5$) and potassium oxide (potash; K$_2$O) which contain 43.7 percent elemental phosphorus and 60.9 percent elemental potassium respectively.

† Assumes a 200 d grazing season at 2.5 ha (5 ac) per cow and calf pair but does not include any nitrogen, phosphorus or potassium excreted in the feces and urine of the calf and returned to the soil.

Plants take up the nutrients that they require for growth from the soil and herbivores (plant eating animals) obtain the nutrients that they require

for growth from the plants. Thus, if plants or plant parts are harvested (as for example in a grain or oilseed crop) or if herbivores are harvested (as for example the removal of cattle from a pasture to a feedlot or packing plant) then nutrients are removed from the soil. If the plants remain in the ecosystem they mature, senesce and decay and in the process liberate their nutrients back to the soil. Similarly, while a herbivore remains on pasture it returns those nutrients not used or required for maintenance and growth back to the soil via excreted urine and feces. The removal of five important nutrients from the soil in a crop of grain or calves per tonne of the nutrient taken up by plants in a wheat crop or grazed pasture (Table 2) is calculated from data presented by Pieper (1974), Owen (1976), Cohen (1980), Padbury and Marciniak (1986), Ensminger et al. (1990) and Saskatchewan Agriculture and Food (1991) and presented in Table 2.

Table 2. Amount of elements[†] removed in a crop of grain or calves (R kg) as a proportion of the elements taken up by spring wheat and pasture plants (V t).

	N	P	K	Ca	Mg
Wheat R/V (kg/t)	735	852	86	204	500
Calves R/V (kg/t)	39	36	4	71	1

† Calculated as elemental nitrogen (N), phosphorus (P), potassium (K), calcium (Ca) and magnesium (Mg).

It is obvious that the removal of nutrients from the soil is considerably greater for a crop of wheat than it is for a crop of beef calves. This, of course, is the reason why grain cropping cannot be sustained under current farming practices without substantial inputs of chemical fertilizers. The production and application of these fertilizers, together with the production and application of herbicides and pesticides which are also used in the grain, vegetable and fruit industries, and the tilling of the soil and harvesting of the crops requires large inputs of fossil fuel which is burnt and emitted to the atmosphere as CO_2. The fact that beef, wool and sheep meats can be produced from pasture without any additional inputs, apart from occasional medication to maintain the health of the animals, makes these industries the most sustainable of all agricultural enterprises.

Beef vs Crop Production and the Conservation of Wildlife

A list of rare native vascular plants in Saskatchewan has been compiled (Romo, personal communication). The list, available on request, consists of 454 different species which have become rare, not because of cattle grazing but because of crop production. Obviously, crop production is a necessary agricultural activity but much land has been broken that should have remained intact. This has resulted in the loss of plant and animal life that would not have occurred if grazed by beef cattle.

Cultivation destroys wildlife habitat. Cattle may also affect habitat by removal and/or trampling of vegetation that could otherwise be used for food and cover. However, cattle may also benefit wildlife by opening up dense stands of herbaceous or shrubby vegetation that retard wildlife movement (Holechek et al. 1989). Cattle largely fill the niche vacated by the demise of the bison. Moderate grazing, 30-50 percent of the current year's herbage production, which is the present recommendation for range management, can result in a mosaic of grazed and ungrazed vegetation with the heaviest use near the water sources. While uniform vegetation use may be desirable from the standpoint of maximizing livestock production, it can be undesirable for wildlife because of reduced habitat diversity and greater social interaction with livestock (Mackie 1978). In many instances, water development for livestock has been beneficial also to wildlife because it has permitted the use of areas from which wildlife were previously excluded due to lack of free water (Holechek et al. 1989). Heavy grazing by cattle reduces plant species diversity and the nutritive value of wild ungulates deteriorates because they are forced to become less selective (Holechek et al. 1989). However, in some ecosystems, ungrazed plant communities have less diversity of plant species than those that are heavily or moderately grazed (Holechek et al. 1989). In contrast, breaking and draining the land removes all the habitat.

Grazing of rangelands with only one species of animal causes a trend away from one vegetation type to another which is usually detrimental to the animal causing that trend. Therefore, common use (grazing the range by more than one type of animal) generally results in greater vegetation and animal productivity than single use (Bennett et al. 1970; Holechek et al. 1989). Ranchers understand this and welcome wildlife for their aesthetic, environmental and economic value. Pronghorn antelope and cattle are beneficial grazing companions, sharing the same habitats yet grazing different species (Holechek et al. 1989). White tailed and mule deer, bighorn sheep, moose and elk have some social aversion to cattle but, with the exception of bighorn sheep, this is of minor importance if stocking rates are moderate (Holechek et al. 1989). Elk are in most direct competition with cattle for plant species since the diets of these animals are more similar than for other species (Heady 1975) but both can be accommodated if stocking rates are moderate. In contrast, wildlife are not welcome on cropland, though farmers welcome their presence on pasture land. Pasture land therefore acts as a buffer between wildlife habitat and crops; a buffer which would not exist if crop land was adjacent to wild land.

Grazing opens perennial grassland vegetation and allows invasion by annual forbs (herbaceous plants that are not grasses) and grasses which are important foods for many species of rodents (mice, ground squirrels, prairie dogs etc.) and lagomorphs (rabbits, hares etc.) which in turn provide food for birds of prey such as Swainson's and Ferruginous Hawks and food and shelter for Burrowing Owls, all of which are threatened grassland species. In addition, virtually all gallinaceous game birds (prairie chickens, quail etc.) depend heavily on annuals and/or early successional forbs for food (Holechek *et al.* 1989). Grasshoppers, which provide a critical high-protein food for many game bird species, are more abundant on moderately or heavily grazed than ungrazed range and are killed with insecticides on cropland. Therefore, cultivation destroys both habitat and food supply for wild animals while beef cattle play a positive role in enhancing the wildlife environment. Nevertheless, moderation and good management are essential ingredients in this symbiotic relationship.

Crop and Animal Biotechnology and the Environment

Much of the current thrust in agricultural biotechnology is aimed at increasing the efficiency with which energy passing through the ecosystem from the sun and fossil fuels is captured to produce food and other agricultural products. In livestock production, one way in which this is achieved is by producing the same or more product while at the same time reducing, or holding constant, the amount of feed that animals eat. This will directly or indirectly reduce the impact of animals on the environment. Examples are the development of recombinant bovine somatotropin (BST) for dairy cattle (which increases the amount of milk a dairy cow will produce per unit of feed consumed); manipulation of the rumen fermentation process (for example feeding ionophore antibiotics not used in human medicine to increase the efficiency with which animal feed is digested in the rumen and as a consequence reduce the production of methane); development of somatostatin vaccines (which increase the production of growth hormone in the animal causing it to grow faster thereby producing more meat per unit of feed) and the induction of twinning in sheep and beef cattle (such as using inhibin vaccine technology which increases the number of viable ova shed at ovulation), embryo splitting (to produce two embryos

where there was only one at the time of fertilization), and genetic selection of lines of cattle in which twinning is common (to increase the rate of natural twinning). These developments are important since about 70 percent of the feed used in the production of beef is consumed by the breeding cow and 95 percent of this is pasture and forage (cultivated crops which cannot be eaten by humans and which are grown specifically for animal feed such as alfalfa). However, pasture and forage produce more methane as a product of digestion than does grain. The Council for Agricultural Science and Technology (1992) stated: "Extensively managed beef cows and their replacements produce about one half of all emissions by ruminant livestock". Interpreting such facts as justification to eliminate beef cattle (Rifkin 1992 and others) amounts to 'throwing the environmental baby out with the bath water'. It has already been argued that the total methane emissions from cattle make a very minor contribution to the 'greenhouse' effect. However, there are other ways of reducing this negative environmental impact while maintaining the environmental benefits of the beef cow. Increasing the efficiency of growth (such as with anabolic agents or somatostatin vaccines), manipulating rumen fermentation (to increase the efficiency of digestion and reduce methane production) and feeding one cow to produce two calves (as for example with the induction of twinning in the beef cow) will not only reduce the size of the national cow herd required to meet the demand for beef but will also reduce the environmental impact of grazing and emission of methane to the atmosphere. The Council for Agricultural Science and Technology (1992) calculated that genetic improvement plus adoption of BST (or somatostatin vaccine) technology will reduce methane emissions by up to 20 percent, agents that promote protein gains at the expense of fat could reduce emissions by 20 percent and improvements in feed formulations could reduce emissions by 3-4 percent .

In contrast, some research in crop biotechnology is directed towards increasing production, perhaps even at the expense of the environment. Yet this receives scant attention from the media, the Animal Rights or vegetarian movements. For example, Science (1992 vol. 257 p 1347) unashamedly reported that scientists "would like to engineer wheat so that it could prosper up to the 54th parallel, the latitude of the southernmost parts of Alaska and the northern Canadian prairies". This will surely only continue the cycle of land degradation and pollution resulting from the removal of native vegetation; drainage of wetlands; destruction of habitat; and the cultivation, erosion and pollution of soils and waterways with salts, fertilizers and herbicides. Is this extended plowing of fragile lands what Rifkin (1992) meant when he stated "....more agricultural land and grain will be potentially available"? Other examples of crop biotechnology that may well lead to increased environmental pollution are the patenting by scientists of an experimental line of salt-tolerant flax and the development of a transgenic cultivar of flax which will grow on herbicide polluted soils where no other crops will grow. Both are likely to increase environmental degradation because now farmers will be able to profit from pollution practices.

Conclusions

For too long now the beef industry has been the scapegoat for many of the ills of society. This paper has argued that beef is not a high fat food and that the amount of cholesterol synthesized by the human body exceeds that which is eaten by the average meat eating person by a factor of five to six. The link between beef consumption and coronary heart disease is, at best, extremely weak. The suggested link between human resistance to antibiotics having its foundation in the practice of feeding sub-therapeutic levels of antimicrobials to beef cattle is nothing short of circumstantial. The evidence shows that salmonella resistance to tetracycline in isolates taken from hospitals ex-

ceeds that in isolates from meat by a factor of 2.5 and that the ban on the addition of antibiotics used in human medicine to animal feeds in the European Community has not improved the efficacy of therapy of human or animal disease. The fear of hormonal disturbances in the human population being caused by the use of estrogenic hormonal substances in beef production are totally unfounded. The truth is that many foods of plant origin contain estrogens in concentrations that are many thousands of times greater than those in beef from cattle in which these products have been used.

Finally, this paper has discussed the misconceptions that beef production, and hence consumption, are a major cause of environmental destruction. Evidence has been presented that the contribution of beef cattle to the 'greenhouse' effect is minimal and that the production of methane from cattle is probably less now than it was before settlement, when the bison population was nearly twice the present population of cattle on the northern great plains of North America. Claims of excessive water use in beef production have been refuted and placed in context with non meat food products. This paper argues that far more serious environmental destruction, such as soil erosion, salinization and contamination of the soil and water systems with pesticides and fertilizers, has occurred from plowing the soil for the growing of cash crops on the Canadian prairies than that which has occurred in the production of beef. The paper argues that the planting of pasture and forage crops, such as alfalfa, should be an integral part of crop rotations giving new life to the soil by controlling erosion and salinization and helping with the restoration of the global carbon balance. However, it must be recognized that, for farmers to make a living, the agricultural practices that they use must provide an economic return and the only way that an economic return can be realized from the inclusion of pasture and forage crops in these rotations is through the production of beef and sheep meats and wool. Evidence is provided to show that the removal of nutrients from the soil is far greater when the soil is used to grow a cash crop in comparison to a crop of beef animals and that the grazing of beef cattle is much more compatible with the concept of biological biodiversity and agricultural sustainability than the growth of a cash crop.

Some may still argue that even if the growing of a forage crop or pasture is less environmentally harmful than the growing of a cash crop, the latter produces more food. But at what cost? Current mainstream cropping practices are not sustainable. In contrast, range beef and sheep production is the most sustainable agricultural practice. The constant heavy removal of nutrients from the soil when the crop is harvested has depleted the natural fertility of the soil to the point that in many instances a crop cannot even be grown without heavy application of chemical fertilizers. The build up and spread of pests and diseases as a result of the monocultural cropping practices is so rapid that in many instances it is not possible to grow a crop without the heavy application of chemical pesticides. The erosion and salinization of soils, as a result of constant plowing, has so destroyed many soils that it is no longer even possible to grow a crop.

Others may argue that most forage and pasture is grown on land unsuitable for grain and row crops and that the elimination of beef would result in those lands going back to natural vegetation. The truth of the first part of such a statement is as lamentable as the fallacy of the second part. The very sustainability of the arable land suitable for grain and row cropping is dependent on a rest phase during which forage crops and pasture should be grown to rejuvenate the soil. People do not function properly without rest and neither does soil. If the soil had not been plowed for grain and row cropping but had instead been used for beef ranching, the land would not need to go back to natural vegetation, it would never have left the state.

Others still may claim that, if beef was eliminated, the increased demand for grain needed to replace beef in the human diet could be easily supplied out of that presently going to supplement cattle feed. Grain is primarily a carbohydrate source, beef is primarily a protein source. Beef would therefore have to be replaced by a high protein legume crop such as soybeans, lentils, chick peas, otherwise there would be an increase in the incidence of kwashiokor, a disease primarily of children in third world countries caused by insufficient protein in the diet. Cattle are not fed these high protein crops. Protein supplements are fed only in very small amounts and mostly only for a short time to feedlot cattle. When fed, these supplements are in the form of protein meals such as soybean meal, canola meal, linseed meal, all of which are byproducts of the production of edible oils and are not consumed by humans. Beef can be and is, in many areas of the world, produced without any inputs of grain or protein supplements at all. Feeding grain to cattle is a modern phenomenon of world trade inequities. Western democracies are overproducing grain that the rest of the world cannot afford to buy. This drives the price of grain below the cost of production and this 'cheap' grain finds its way increasingly into beef production. On average, only about 17 percent of the feed consumed by cattle comes from grain, compared with 85 percent for swine and 94 percent for poultry (Cohen 1991), and almost all of that is classed as unsuitable for human consumption. That classification may not be relevant to people starving in third world or war torn countries but neither can it be blamed on the beef producer and consumer. These unfortunate people cannot afford to pay the price of a bushel of grain and the farmer cannot afford to grow the grain at a price that they can afford to pay. If the rich countries were prepared to subsidize grain export prices to make it economically viable for the farmers to grow the grain and economically non viable for feedlot operators to buy the grain, then the beef industry would and should still survive, though it would be a changed industry. But eliminating the beef industry will have absolutely no effect on the plight of the millions of starving people in the world today; it will simply drive many farmers out of existence. The irony is that, as Stewart and Tiessen (1990) point out, world starvation has occurred largely as a result of over-cultivation and over-cropping and unless we learn from that experience, the developed world will continue to head down the same path.

It has not been the intention of this paper to disregard the many and complex effects that beef production has on society and the environment or to suggest that the practices involved in the production of beef cannot be improved. Neither has it been intended to cast aspersions on the grain and row cropping practices of prairie farmers and researchers. Rather, the purpose of the paper has been to place beef production in its rightful context as an integral part of sustainable, holistic agriculture. While the Canadian prairies have been used as the reference region, many of the arguments advanced here can be applied, with minor modification, to other major agricultural areas of the world. There are many reasons for choosing to be a vegetarian (religion, culture, a dislike for the taste of meat, abhorrence at the thought of killing and eating animals etc.), but choosing and promoting this lifestyle for environmental motives is both misguided and unethical.

ENDNOTES

[1] The Canadian Land Classification System places land in the following classes: 1.Soils with no significant limitations that restrict their use for crops, high in productivity for a wide range of crops; 2.Soils with moderate restrictions that reduce the choice of crops, or require moderate conservation practices, moderately high in productivity for a fairly wide range of crops; 3.Soils with moderately severe limitations that reduce the choice of crops or require special conservation practices, medium to moderate in productivity for a moderate range of crops; 4.Soils with severe limitations that restrict the choice of crops; 5.Soils that are unsuited for the production of common field crops, capable only of producing perennial forage crops; 6. Soils which are capable only of producing native perennial forage crops; 7. Soils with no capability for arable agriculture or permanent pasture.

References

Bennett, D., Morley, F.H.W., Clark, K.W. and Dudzinski, M.L.; "The effect of grazing sheep and cattle together"; *Australian Journal of Experimental Agriculture and Animal Husbandry;* 1970; 10 : pp. 694-709.

Brisson, G.J.; "Lipids in Human Nutrition"; Jack K. Burgess Inc., Englewood, New Jersey; 1981.

Brockman, J.S.; "The difference in yield between cut and grazed swards"; *Journal of the British Grassland Society;* 1971 26 : p. 192.

Bruce, J.P.; "The Atmosphere of the Living Planet"; *World Meteorological Organization Publication No. 735;* Geneva; 1990.

Byers, F.M.; "Livestock – climate interactions in global warming and climate change"; *Journal of Animal Science;* 1991; 69 (supplement 1) :224.

Canadian Cattleman's Association; "Just Facts. The Canadian Cattle Industry and the Environment"; CCA, Calgary; Undated.

Council for Agricultural Science and Technology; "Preparing US agriculture for global climate change"; *Task Force Report No. 119*; Ames, Iowa; 1992.

Cohen, R.D.H.; "Phosphorus in rangeland ruminant nutrition : A review"; *Livestock Production Science*; 1980; 7 : pp. 25-37.

Cohen, R.D.H.; "The Beef Industry"; In (J.M. Naylor and S.L. Ralston, editors) *Large Animal Clinical Nutrition;* Mosby Year Books, St. Louis, Missouri; 1991.

Davidson, E.A., Herman, D.J., Schuster, A and Firestone, M.K.; "Cattle grazing and oak trees as factors affecting soil emissions of nitric oxide from an annual grassland"; In *ASA Special Publication number 55*; 1993; pp. 109-119.

Drennen,T. and Chapman, D.; *Greenhouse Gasses, Ecological Cycling and North-South Politics*; Cornell University, New York; 1991.

Ensminger, M.E., Oldfield, J.E. and Heinemann, W.W.; *Feeds and Nutrition*; Clovis: The Ensminger Publishing Co.; 1990.

Frame, J.; "Fundamentals of Grassland Management, Part 10: The Grazing Animal"; *Scottish Agriculture;* 1970; 50 : pp. 28-44.

Guest, G.B.; "Status of FDA's Program on the Use of Antibiotics in Animal Feeds"; *Journal of Animal Science*, 1976; 42: 1052-1057.

Hanson, E.H.; "Methane Gas and Its Sources"; *Paper presented to the Canadian Society of Animal Science*; Western Branch biennial meeting, Chilliwack, BC; 1991.

Hays, V.W. and Muir, W.M.; "Efficacy and Safety of Feed Additive Use of Antibacterial Drugs in Animal Production"; *Canadian Journal of Animal Science*; 1979; 59: pp. 447-456.

Heady, H.F.; *Rangeland Management*; McGraw-Hill Inc., New York; 1975.

Hodgins, G.; "Saskatchewan State of the Environment Report"; *Agriculture*; Saskatchewan Environment and Public Safety; 1991; pp. 37-42.

Holechek, J.L., Pieper, R.D. and Herbel, C.H.; *Range Management : Principles and Practices*; Prentice Hall , New Jersey; 1989.

Johnson, R.; "The Role of Forages in Sustainable Agriculture"; *Proceedings of the Saskatchewan Forage Council*, Saskatoon (D. Gayton, Editor); 1989.

Lampkin, N.; *Organic Farming*; Farming Press, Ipswich, United Kingdom; 1992.

Lamming, G.E.; "Scientific Report on Anabolic Agents in Animal Production"; *The Veterinary Record*; October 24, 1987.

Mackie, R.J.; "Impacts of Livestock Grazing on Wild Ungulates"; *Transactions of the North American Wildlife and Natural Resources Conference;* 1978; 43: pp. 462-476.

National Cattleman's Association; 191982; "Beef Cattle Research Needs and Priorities"; *Beef Business Bulletin*; National Cattleman's Association Englewood, CO.

Owen, E.; 1976. "Farm Wastes: Straw and Other Fibrous Materials"; In: A.N. Duckam, J.G.W. Jones and E.H. Roberts (Eds.) *Food Production and Consumption: The Efficiency of Human Food Chains and Nutrient Cycles*; North Holland Publishing. Co., Amsterdam.

Padbury, G.E. and Marciniak, J.P.; "Utilizing Chaff to Feed Beef Cows"; *Canadian Society of Agricultural Engineers Annual Conference Proceedings*, Saskatoon; 1986.

Petersen, R.G., Lucas, H.L. and Woodhouse, W.W.; "The Distribution of Excreta by Freely Grazing Cattle and Its Effect on Pasture Fertility: 1. Excretal Distribution"; *Agronomy Journal* ; 1956; 48: pp. 440-444.

Pieper, R.D.; "Effect of Herbivores on Nutrient Cycling and Distribution"; *Proceedings of the 2nd US-Australian Range Workshop*; 1974.

Pitts, Lee.; "Say NO to YES"; *Cattlemen / December*; 1992; pp. 36-38.

Rifkin, J.; *Beyond Beef, The Rise and Fall of the Cattle Culture*; Penguin Books Canada Ltd., Toronto; 1992.

Robbins, J.; *Diet for a New America*; Stillpoint Publishing, Walpole, New Hampshire; 1990.

Robertson, G. P.; In *Agricultural Ecosystem Effects on Trace Gases and Global Climate Change*; ASA Special Publication number 55; 1993; pp. 95-108.

Sahasrabudhe, M.R. and Stewart, L.; "Total Lipid and Cholesterol in Selected Retail Cuts of Canadian Beef"; *Canadian Institute of Food Science and Technology Journal*; 1989; 22: pp. 83-85.

Saskatchewan Agriculture and Food; Agricultural Statistics, 1991.

Spedding, C.R.W.; *An Introduction to Agricultural Systems*, 2nd edition; Elsevier Applied Science, London; 1988.

Stewart, J. and Tiessen H.; "Grasslands into deserts?"; In: (C. Mungall and D.J. McLaren, Eds.) *Planet Under Stress;* Oxford Press, Toronto; 1990.

t'Mannetje, L. "Global Issues of Range Management"; *Trail Boss News*; March 1991.

Walton, J.R.; "Impact of Antibiotic Restrictions in Animal Production on Public Health"; *Journal of Animal Science*. 62 (Supplement 3); 1986; pp. 74-85.

World Wildlife Fund Canada. 1988. Prairie Conservation Action Plan 1989-1994.

ENDANGERED SPECIES POLICY
ETHICS, POLITICS, SCIENCE AND LAW

12
by Alex Wellington

INTRODUCTION

EVER SINCE THE DEATH OF MARTHA, THE LAST remaining passenger pigeon, humans have become increasingly concerned about their role in the extinction of other species.[1] High levels of public concern have led to the passage of endangered species protection legislation in some jurisdictions. Canada has recently entered a period of protracted, and at times intense, discussion about the introduction of a proposed federal Endangered Species Act.[2] This proposed legal reform, as with all legal reform, occurs within a social context that includes the political climate, institutional structure, media coverage, public perception and a huge range of social actors.[3] In this paper, I would like to set the proposed legal reform in the context of debates about the preservation and protection of endangered species, debates that are occurring in many countries around the globe and that are heating up as the prospects for many species become more dire and as efforts to preserve them become increasingly expensive.

In this paper I examine several aspects to the policy debate over protection for endangered species.[4] I have focused on issues involving factual uncertainty and issues representing value disagreement. Both of these play a significant role in the policy debate. One can identify two extreme positions in the policy debate over endangered species. One extreme would advocate the protection and preservation of each and every endangered, threatened and vulnerable species and its habitat, to ensure that no species becomes endangered and particularly, that no species goes extinct. Species have a right to exist and humans are obligated to do whatever is in their power to ensure their continued existence. This position would not accept any balancing of interests, any weighting of goals, nor any tradeoffs.

The other extreme position would insist that it is almost never the case that the benefits of species preservation, such as they are, would be sufficient to offset the costs of preservation. These costs would include the indirect effects of reduction of economic growth and the frustration of human desires for development and growth. This position would ultimately downgrade the worth of species to such an extent that almost any trivial human interest could outweigh the survival interest of other species.

To construct the case for preservation involves several interlocking claims: that there is an extinction crisis; that humans are the cause of that crisis; and that extraordinary measures are needed to ward off the full effects of the crisis, namely ecocatastrophe. Further, the case for preservation also includes arguments about why we should care about species: that many species have direct utility, that most have indirect utility, that humans value species for aesthetic, cultural, moral and spiritual reasons as well, that all species may have intrinsic value, and that each species has a right to existence. The policy position that follows from the case for preservation is that legal measures should be enacted to protect species from endangerment and to prevent extinction. In particular, there must be provision made for habitat protection.

To construct the case for the anti-preservationist position also involves several interlocking claims: that there is no crisis; that humans are part of nature and thus whatever they do is natural, even causing extinction; and that special concern is not warranted regardless. The case against preservation insists that we need not undertake extraordinary efforts to preserve species, ultimately, since whatever value species have is value that is outweighed by (other) human interests. The corresponding policy position for the anti-preservation position is that legal measures to protect species which would interfere with human activity that is otherwise legitimate are not justifiable.

There are cases where conceptual and factual disagreements are neutral with respect to policy options. Further, agreements on policy can emerge even when there are disagreements on factual or value issues.[5] One of these instances of possible common ground, I would argue, is the need for full and accurate information about the status of species upon which to base decisions. It is necessary to have the facts at hand concerning which species are at risk and to what extent in order to engage in the irreducibly value driven debates about which species have what value and to what extent. Thus, I argue that while determining priorities in the allocation of resources has to be subject to the vagaries of the political process, the listing of endangered species must not be.

In the first section of this paper, "Philosophical Issues", I examine arguments for and against species preservation and grapple with the question, "why preserve species?".[6] Ultimately, I argue that the case in favour of species preservation is more defensible than the case against. In the second section, I outline the current situation in Canada, highlighting the distinctive features of the Canadian context and emphasizing the need for legislative reform. Then in the third section, "Practical Issues", I address the issues of recovery priorities and habitat protection, both of which have significant implications for any version of endangered species protection policy in Canada. The question which motivates the discussion in that

section is "which objectives should guide recovery efforts?"

I. PHILOSOPHICAL ISSUES

Arguments For and Against
Preserving Species: Facts and Values

In this section, I first outline the general structure of the arguments for and against preserving species, indicating the main points of disagreement and contention. Then I go on to discuss the disputed claims which I have set out in the form of Challenge and Response. The challenges are presented by those who wish to deny that any special measures are needed to preserve species and the responses are presented by those who wish to argue for extensive species preservation measures.

The debate over endangered species preservation can be presented in the first instance in terms of a disagreement over whether or not there actually is a global extinction crisis. Yet, it quickly branches out into a series of related issues. On one side are the so-called doomsday prophets who say: There is a global extinction crisis. Ecocatastophe looms. Extreme measures are necessary, since the potential consequences of the extinction crisis - namely, ecocatastrophe - are so serious. On the other side are the naysayers and sceptics who emphatically deny that there is a global extinction crisis. They say further that ecocatastophe does not loom, or as one book title put it: "Apocalypse Not".[7]

This debate relates to the questions about the role of human agency: the claim that there is a crisis implies that the current rates and levels of extinction are in some sense 'unnatural'. Those who deny that there is a crisis often collapse their position into the claim that extinction is natural, whether or not there is a "crisis". Defendants in law suits involving endangered species, for instance, typically try to "demonstrate that their alterations of the environment do not differ in kind, or in magnitude, from natural changes that have occurred in the relatively recent past".[8] The arguments against preserving species can thus be framed as arguments in favour of allowing or causing species to go extinct. Since the arguments in favour of preserving species are arguments against causing or allowing species to go extinct, the issue of human causation for extinction arises. Preservationists argue that the crisis is caused by human agency, or at the least that the extent of anthropogenic extinction is the problem.

The Nature of the Crisis and the Role of Human Agency

Challenge: There is no global extinction crisis, since there is no proof that extinction rates are climbing. Current rates will not lead to ecological collapse. **Response:** There is a global extinction crisis, since there is good reason to think the rates are climbing. We do not know how many extinctions are enough to cause ecological collapse, but we cannot afford to wait until we are over the threshold.

Discussion: It is somewhat of an understatement to say that this is an area fraught with scientific uncertainty. Even those who think there is a crisis acknowledge that the dimensions of the crisis are difficult to determine with information that is presently known. Estimates of current rates and predictions of future trends are based on highly speculative data. Here are some examples of extinction predictions found in the literature: one species an hour, five species a day or several hundred species a day; forty thousand species a year, one million species by the end of the century, or between fifteen and twenty percent of all species by the end of the century; twenty percent of all species by 2011, almost all species in the tropics by the year 2025, or twenty-five percent of all species on earth by 2041, and so on.[9]

Neither the number of species presently going extinct nor the number of species presently existing is known with any measure of certainty. Estimates of the number of species presently residing on earth range from three million to thirty million

or more.[10] If biologists are far from knowing how many species exist they are even farther from knowing how many populations exist.[11] As biologists have noted, the ability of a species to adapt to changing environmental conditions depends "in large measure on the genetic diversity within a species".[12] The existence and viability of genetically distinct subspecies and populations are thus crucial to the long-term adaptability of any species. The threat to biodiversity, then, comes not just from the loss of species, but also from the loss of subspecies and local populations.[13] Yet, many critics of endangered species protection resist protecting populations and subspecies, for fear that the expense of so doing would be overwhelming.

Many people are surprised to learn that the definition of species is subject to dispute. The dictionary defines species as "a category of biological classification...comprising related organisms or populations potentially capable of interbreeding".[14] However, among scientists and philosophers of science just what species are is not entirely clear.[15] Whether a species is entitled to protection depends on a determination that the species is a distinct species and is threatened with endangerment or imminent extinction. Thus, seemingly esoteric debates over what constitutes a species can have a bearing on real world practices, since the focus of protection is on species.[16] Critics of the so-called "bandwagon of the species extinction issue" point to the uncertainty over how species are defined to underscore points about the uncertainty of the rates of extinction.[17] Assuming that there can be general agreement on a working definition of species, there will continue to be debates about the number of individuals a species needs to be viable. Those who are sceptical about the need for preservation initiatives will tend to argue that the existing numbers of a given species are higher than estimated or that the numbers needed to prevent extinction are lower than projected.[18]

Those who wish to argue against preservation latch on to the uncertainty issues, and emphasize the speculative nature of the known data. They challenge the projected rates of extinction and contend that the scientific evidence does not support the high rates that are publicized. They also dispute the claims associated with the ecocatastophe model. In their book *Extinction*, Anne and Paul Ehrlich argue that we cannot simply go on causing species to go extinct, without at some point facing an ecocatastrophe. The Ehrlichs popularized the ecocatastrophe model by means of the image of "rivet popping".[19] If one keeps on taking rivets out of a machine, eventually there will be a breakdown, a collapse.[20] Other authors have used the image of an interconnected web of species which is progressively unravelled as species go extinct. Thomas Lovejoy stresses that the effects of each incremental loss may be imperceptible, but by the time the accumulated effects were to be noticed, the situation could be quite catastrophic.[21] The damage, once noticed, could be irreversible and life-threatening even for humans.[22]

There is some temptation for preservationists to respond each time a species is on the brink of extinction by predicting that collapse will follow the extinction of that species. When the species does go extinct, however, and collapse does not follow, then the argument loses some force. The critics of preservationist policies will point to the possibility of counterproof to undermine the general argument.[23] It is of course possible to delay the predicted catastrophe for indefinitely long periods of time, but this will eventually cause the approach to cease having much use as a rhetorical strategy. What it comes down to, ultimately, is a threshold problem. There will be some point at which the rate of extinction does pass over the line and surpass the threshold of safety. At that point, there will be a crisis of the sort represented by mass extinctions of previous eras.[24]

Although the current rates of extinction and future projections of expected extinctions are subject to debate there is nevertheless general agreement that the threat of widespread species extinction is real.[25] Even sceptics about the numbers thrown around admit that the threat to biodiversity is real, and that the predicted losses to biodiversity are "deeply dismaying".[26] People tend to accept the claim that at some point after continuous habitat loss, there will be an irreversible impoverishment of the biosphere. There is also general agreement that not enough is being done presently to avoid extinctions and that the vast majority of current endangerments are due to human causes.[27] Human activity may not always be the immediate cause of vulnerability, but human activities have a cumulative effect that compromises the ability of other species to adapt to changes in their environment.

Challenge: Extinction is natural, whether or not there is a crisis. Special concern for anthropogenic (human caused) extinction is not warranted. **Response:** Mass extinction is not 'normal', even if natural. Special concern for anthropogenic extinction is warranted.

Discussion: The story of evolution, it seems, is that the number of species extinctions is only slightly less than the number of species originations. Almost 90 percent of species that have ever existed have gone extinct, and thus, most species that have ever lived have gone extinct. The vast majority of these extinctions occurred before humans had even evolved. Further, since humans are part of nature, then whatever humans do is natural. Extinction is simply the result of the inability of some species to adapt to environmental change. Many of the same pressures that push a species toward extinction also make speciation more likely.

Extinction, according to the anti-preservationist argument, is inextricably part of the evolutionary process, and human activity presents just one more instance of selection pressure on species. It could be said to be natural for humans to undertake intentional, deliberate, and conscious action to modify their habitat for the benefit of their species. If this results in the loss of habitat and consequent extinction of other species, well that's natural. Moreover, useful information can be obtained from observing which species are able to adapt to the particular selection pressures represented by human activity. Special concern about the current rate or scale of extinction is unwarranted.

Advocates of species preservation initiatives have two replies. First, although extinction is a natural process, mass extinction is not a normal process. There appear to be different "rules", so to speak, for mass extinction than those that govern the phenomena of "normal" background extinction.[28] The significant thing about the change of "rules" is that it changes the kind of species that go extinct. It is increasingly the case that human-caused extinctions are "discontinuous in type and rate with non-human caused extinctions".[29] Humans may thus be setting in motion another mass extinction. Further, anthropogenic extinctions, as Norton points out, skew evolutionary trends, and may result in the progressive simplification of ecosystems in addition to species loss.[30]

The first response to the claim that even human-caused mass extinction could be "natural" is to deny that it is normal; the second is to assert that it is also "natural" for humans to avoid causing mass extinction. It could easily be seen to be just as 'natural' for humans to strive to continue in existence and to try to prevent mass extinction. To fail to do so would thus be unnatural. On this account, it would also be natural for humans to intentionally, deliberately and consciously decline to modify the habitat of other species so as not to jeopardize the continued existence of their own species. In order for humans to be motivated to actively try to prevent endangerment and avoid causing the extinction of other species, people need to be persuaded that there are good reasons for caring about species.

Reasons for Caring About Species and Weighting Those Reasons

In commonsense, everyday moral discourse we care about beings that matter, beings that are entitled to moral consideration, beings whom we should respect, beings that can claim rights against us or to whom we perceive that we have duties or obligations. In the more rarefied and explicitly analytical mode of discourse that constitutes moral philosophy, it is necessary to ask why we should care about any particular being. Likewise, we also need to ask whether we ought to accord rights to those beings we do recognize as rights-holders, and whether there are other beings that we should extend rights to. In other words, moral philosophy requires us to critically reflect upon our intuitions and to construct theories which can help to make sense of our intuitions or which may lead us to decide that we need to revise our intuitions to make them more coherent and consistent. The question which we need to ask for our present purposes is whether we should care about species, and if so, why should we care about them.

Preservationists claim that species have value, that they are valuable.[31] Most anti-preservationists would concede that many species have some kind of value. The recognition that species have value alone is not sufficient, however, to justify preservation programs. The problem is to show that all species have some value, if one wants to argue for preserving all species that currently exist. One needs also to show that certain species have a very high value, if one wants to argue for the allocation of resources in order to ensure the survival of those species. There are thus two dimensions: what value a species has and how much weight that value will carry in cases of conflict over values.

The discussion of values raises tricky and complex philosophical issues concerning the source of valuing and the proper characterization of values. For some philosophers, humans are the source of values and if something is not valued by some human (preferably a presently existing human) then that thing can not be said to be valuable. For other philosophers, humans are not the only source of values. Nature can be said to have value entirely independent of human assessment or recognition of that value. Another debate concerns the type of value that should be accorded to non-human nature. For some philosophers, nature can only be of instrumental value. If non-human nature is not valued instrumentally by humans, then it can not be said to be valuable, according to those philosophers. For other philosophers, nature can have intrinsic value, or inherent worth, ie., it can be valuable in itself. Often, the debate between these positions can be characterized as a debate between anthropocentric (human-centred) and non-anthropocentric ethical theories.[32]

Arguments for preserving species are typically of three types: (1) those based on the direct utility of certain species; (2) those based on the indirect utility, potentially, of any or even all species; (3) those based on the intrinsic value or inherent worth, or even the right to existence of all species.[33] The first two types of reasons are clearly anthropocentric and the third type of reason suggests non-anthropocentric reasons for saving species.

Challenge: The only legitimate way to assess the worth of species is in terms of direct utility to humans, preferably in economic terms. Species must be shown to have value in terms of human interests, and to serve human needs to be deemed worthy of protection. **Response:** Species do have value in terms of human interests, and they do serve human needs. Yet, they also have worth in other terms beyond utility.

Discussion: The challenge and the response assume the backdrop of economic analysis, which is an ethical framework based on a series of interlocking assumptions.[34] It is based on utilitarian-

ism, anthropocentrism, and the presumption of instrumental value for non-human nature.[35] The approach requires those who would argue for preservation to establish the value of species in terms of utility. The term utility refers to that which is useful, that which produces satisfaction, pleasure or fulfilment of human needs. The concept of utility is part of the moral theory of utilitarianism, yet its relevance extends far beyond the confines of that particular theory.[36] To talk about utility in the contemporary context is to talk about benefits and costs.[37] The economic analysis insists on taking into account the opportunity costs of any action or option, that is the value of what is forgone by choosing a particular alternative.

Utility can be evaluated in terms of direct benefit to humans, usually measured in economic terms, and in terms of indirect benefit to humans. Methods to measure direct benefit are fairly certain, but still contested; ways to measure indirect benefit are less clear. Utility is assessed in terms of how much one would be willing to pay for a good, or, conversely, how much compensation one would demand in return for giving up that good.[38] Market prices provide the clearest way to measure utility, but when dealing with unpriced goods it is necessary to rely on indirect pricing methods (surveys, inferences, shadow pricing) which may ultimately amount to little more than conjectures.[39] There are at least two different aspects of both the direct benefits and the indirect benefits of species. One aspect is the current benefit to presently existing humans, and the other aspect concerns potential benefit to future generations. I will briefly address the latter topic below once I have dealt with the issues of direct and indirect utility.

Environment Canada distinguishes two kinds of direct uses of the environment - extractive and non-extractive uses. Extractive uses of species are typically inputs of a commercial process. Examples include fishing, forestry, and agriculture. Some recreational uses (hunting and fishing) can be included in this category, while other recreational uses (eco-tourism) are also covered under the direct non-extractive use category. Wild species and wildlife-related recreation activities are a source of revenue. In Canada, for example, a Statistics Canada Survey, the "Importance of Wildlife to Canadians", found that nearly nineteen million Canadians spent over five billion dollars taking part in wildlife-related activities.[40] These benefit estimates relate to wildlife generally, and thus cannot be attributed fully to endangered species. It has been estimated that as much as forty million a year plus spinoff effects could be attributed to the contribution of endangered mammals and birds to the benefits of wildlife-related activity.[41]

Other ways in which species provide direct utility to humans in terms of economic benefit are as medicine and food. Examples of medicines that have been derived from wild species include aspirin (white willow), the anti-cancer drug taxol (Pacific yew tree), and other cancer treatments specifically for childhood leukaemia and Hodgkin's disease (rosy periwinkle).[42] Wild species are sometimes used as food, and more often to provide genetic resources to breed with the domesticated species which are eaten. Currently, less than 5 percent of plants have yet been screened for their medicinal value and less than 4 percent of plant species are used for food. Other plant species may thus prove to be valuable for drugs or food in the future. Some species also provide resources for other material needs (including building materials, fuels, oils, and waxes). The argument is basically that species should be preserved in order to ensure that the potential economic benefit they might provide can someday be realized.[43] Species should not be allowed to go extinct since some have already proven to be useful and many others could be discovered to be similarly useful in the future.

An argument for species preservation on the basis of ecological benefit to humans represents indirect utility. Species provide ecological benefit by their ecological functions and their contribution to biological diversity. They help to generate and maintain soils, dispose of wastes, recycle nutrients; they provide filtration and flood control, erosion protection, pest control, energy storage and climate regulation. Certain species function as keystone species, central to the functioning of a particular ecosystem, and other species are umbrella species, whose habitat requirements overlap with other species. These species have obvious value, and it is argued that while the role of most species is not known it is clear that interdependency is the rule. Humans are biological organisms and, as such, are thoroughly dependent upon the functioning of the ecosystem (understood very loosely) for their well being (health and life).

Those who argue for the preservation of species point to the irreversibility of mistakes and the foolhardiness of assuming abundant functional redundancy to argue that we cannot afford to take chances with our life support system. Species provide the basis for the services humans derive from the ecosystem. The extinction of a species represents a disruption in ecological services. Because species depend on each other, each additional loss makes other further losses more likely. It is therefore prudent for humans to attempt to save every species in the face of uncertainty and lack of full information about ecology. On the indirect utility argument, then, it is necessary to act as if the survival of all other species was about as important as the survival of the human species because doing so would better serve the interests of humans in long term survival.

Norman Myers has proposed the application of the "precautionary principle" to the biodiversity problem. He has argued that the burden of proof should rest with those whose activities would likely disrupt the environment, and threaten endangerment, to demonstrate that their actions will not result in unacceptable damage.[44] Many environmental economists have argued for the adoption of a "safe minimum standard" of conservation for biological diversity.[45] Such an approach would consist of a general rule to avoid extinction in day-to-day resource management decisions. There would be provision for exceptions, but only when "it is explicitly decided that costs of avoiding extinction are intolerably large or that other social objectives must take precedence".[46] The objective is to improve the well-being of future generations "by preserving some species that will prove useful and valuable in the future and that would otherwise have been lost".[47] The underlying argument is that meeting the goal of efficiency as set out by economic analysis may not be sufficient to assure a sustainable economy, particularly if sustainability includes the notion of not imposing large losses on future generations.

The topic of obligations to future generations has generated a vast literature. Environmentalists argue that we owe it to potentially existing future humans to preserve species. Future generations are the beneficiaries of keeping options open. One of the great difficulties for economic analysis in addressing the problem of extinction is that it is irreversible. If an area is preserved, it could always be developed later, but if it is developed it can not be subsequently transferred to preservation. Thus, future generations are deprived of option value significantly more with present development than with present preservation. Decisions to preserve species, then, become more defensible as greater weight is placed on obligations to future generations to protect their potential share of the earth's resources. But if one is going to take a purely anthropocentric approach, it will be difficult to justify the allocation of resources to save species for people who may or may not come to exist, who may or may not actually have a use for them, and who may or may not actually appreciate their existence.

The anti-preservationist may admit that a few species have direct utility and that many species potentially have indirect utility. They would insist, however, that the direct utility of preservation should be traded off against the direct utility of development. This is to compare short term economic benefit with short term economic benefit. Usually, the development option would provide greater direct utility, and typically, the benefits of development are easier to measure. It is hard to explain why we should save some species that may or may not come in handy sometime in the future, when value can be produced now by activities that cause their extinction (using them as a resource or taking over their habitat for other uses).

If indirect utility is brought into the picture, then we must compare the combined direct and indirect utility of development on the one hand, and the combined direct and indirect utility of preservation on the other hand. Environmentalists tend to compare the short term economic benefits of development with the long term ecological and other benefits of preservation, since that often does favour the preservation option. But as Simon and Wildavsky and others point out, there are costs associated with "the long-run indirect effects of reduction of economic growth on human health".[48] If one brings in the long term benefits, or the indirect utility, of the development option then things are not so clear cut.

To recap the difficulties for the preservationist position, it is easy to show that certain species, a few select ones, currently have direct utility. However, it is much harder to argue that each and every species will prove useful in terms of direct utility, no matter how long we wait. Even in terms of indirect utility, there are great uncertainties about how much biodiversity is required to maintain humanity's life support system. Detailed knowledge of ecosystem functioning is often lacking, and may be unavailable for the foreseeable future. It is an open question whether increments in biodiversity will actually increase the likelihood of utilitarian benefits. Some economists will argue that there should be a presumption of positive value for any species; other economists will dispute that presumption. Defenders of preservationist policies will then often try to bring in other values besides the economic and the ecological, such as aesthetic or cultural values.

Some species clearly have aesthetic and cultural value for some people. Indicators of the aesthetic value of endangered species, in particular, include the money spent on consumer goods containing the images or representations of endangered species. Examples of such goods are coffee table picture books, posters, t-shirts, calendars, mugs, toothbrushes and even postage stamps.[49] The money spent on admissions to zoos, particularly when the zoo has on display specimens of endangered species illustrates their perceived value. Another indication is the increasing popularity of birdwatching - reportedly the fastest growing recreational activity in present times - a pursuit in which the rarity of the bird significantly increases the value of sightings. Sightings of endangered, threatened and vulnerable bird species would thus be considered to be even more desirable than sightings of common, everyday bird species. The cultural significance of certain North American species, such as the Whooping Crane, the Peregrine Falcon, or the Bald Eagle, has been much remarked upon.[50] If people do go to view the bird, then it constitutes a direct non-extractive use. Otherwise, it is a passive use value and reflects a judgment of aesthetic or cultural significance.

It is sometimes difficult to separate out instances of the attribution of aesthetic value and instances of the attribution of existence value for endangered species. Existence value refers to satisfaction obtained from simply knowing that a species exists. To appreciate the existence value of a species it is not necessary to view or actually experience the existence of the species; it is sufficient simply to be aware of its presence in the world. Examples of indicators of perceived exist-

ence value would include money contributed to conservation programs for endangered species, and donations to environmental organizations which are earmarked for endangered species conservation.[51] Signatures on petitions, letters to the government and letters to newspapers can also indicate the level of public interest which may be based, at least in part, on perception of existence value. The discussion is still being framed in terms of value to humans, even if it is a rarefied kind of value such as existence value.

As for these other types of value attributed to species, they are susceptible to challenge as well. Not every species has aesthetic or cultural significance; further, some of the least significant ecologically are perceived to have the most aesthetic value and vice versa. Certain species may be perceived to embody great national cultural significance, for instance the beaver or the maple tree in Canada, but it is not necessarily the case that all endangered and threatened species will have such significance. Moreover, conservation biologists are frequently concerned about the prospects of reptiles and invertebrates (insects), which do not induce the same levels of public favour and thus are not afforded the same levels of protection as birds or mammals. The objective of protecting biodiversity through preserving species will likely need to rest on much more than aesthetic or cultural reasons.

The problems with taking the strong anthropocentric approach to justifying species preservation have led some philosophers to argue for a weak anthropocentric approach instead. Bryan Norton attempts to use the notion of transformative preferences to provide such an argument for preserving species. Norton claims that preservationists can rely on the "character-building transformative value of interactions with nature" to justify the allocation of resources for species preservation.[52] The transformative value is a form of indirect utility; species have utilitarian value not just in economic terms but also in psychological terms. He contends that evaluation of sets of consumption preferences can establish the superiority of "meaningful interactions with wild species and unspoiled ecosystems".[53] Yet, in order to say that some preferences are inferior they must be said to be inferior in relation to some value criteria prior to the preference transformation. Christopher Stone presents a similar notion of "morally corrected preferences", which faces a similar difficulty.[54] Unless morally corrected preferences are, by stipulation, coincident with environmental values, it is necessary for there to be some criteria to distinguish between good (in this case, preservationist) morally corrected preferences, and bad ones.

J. Baird Callicott claims that we care about other species because of bio-empathy.[55] He proposes that the capacity for sentiments that are other directed may have evolved as an adaptive strategy, or rather that moral sentiments may be naturally selected. He assumes then that we do care for other species due to our capacity for altruism and further, that we should continue to do so on the same basis. It is difficult to fit his approach into a policy perspective, since as it stands it seems to provide little more than a descriptive account of the possibility of other-regarding moral sentiments. It does not provide any way to argue for any particular account of the content of sentiments, nor to specifically justify the allocation of resources for the preservation of endangered species, for instance. If it is meant to be purely descriptive then it does not entail any specific prescriptions; to the extent that it is meant to be prescriptive, more needs to be said to fill in the missing parts.

Some people do acknowledge emotional ties to other species and would recognize the role of bio-empathy. However, many others would not acknowledge them and would emphasize instead the importance of moral sentiments in relation to members of our own species. Some people would acknowledge, and do appreciate, the role of experiences of nonhuman species in forming human ideals and aspirations but other people would argue that either they do not recognize the transformative value of species or that they recognize other, overriding transformative values associated with development and civilization. It comes down to the general challenge, why allocate resources to preservation options rather than to other options, options which are also productive of value? Why grant species moral standing?[56]

The most non-anthropocentric, or perhaps the least anthropocentric reason presented for saving species is the principle that all species should be deemed to have a right to exist. This principle is behind the "Noah Principle", which is based on the idea of stewardship for other species. Those who hold this view "find it arrogant for human beings, who have occupied the planet for only a tiny fraction of its history, to wipe out many other species simply to meet our own insatiable needs".[57] As David Ehrenfeld, who introduced the principle, explains, it should provide a justification for the "conservation of non-resources".[58] It should not be necessary to have to show that this particular species or this particular ecosystem is crucial to the long term well being of the planet, or to have to show that we should protect all species and ecosystems because we do not know which ones will cause catastrophe by their extinction or elimination. It should be enough simply to state that there is an obligation of stewardship falling on humans to ensure the well being and flourishing of all non-human species. Such ideas will not be foreign to those who are already adherents of the preservationist ethos, but they will not be readily acceptable to those who are not.

The critics, who do not share certain intuitions associated with the preservationist ethos, resent the allocation of social resources to ends which reflect those intuitions. For the anti-environmentalist, all that is at stake are preferences and the crucial issues concern whose preferences get counted, and what weight they are granted. What complicates the matter further is the distribution of costs and benefits. Critics of preservation complain that other people, who are not necessarily environmentalists or are even anti-environmentalists, end up effectively paying the costs of furthering the interests of environmentalists.[59] There is a concern about the fairness of the distribution of costs. It is not hard to see why there is concern that the costs of preservation are evenly distributed throughout the general population.

The problem can be encapsulated in the following quote: "Even if it is true that 'no food, no clothing, no shelter, no land, and certainly no luxury or technology is worth the irreplaceable loss of any species', it is not obvious that people who do not share that view of a threatened species should be forced to pay for it on behalf of those who do".[60] People need to be persuaded that the protection of species is a public good, which deserves cooperative effort, and that the burden of protection, particularly the costs, will be fairly distributed.[61] These concerns sharpen the focus on how best to pursue preservationist objectives.

II. THE SITUATION IN CANADA

Currently there is not yet any federal legislation in place, although there may be soon. Four provinces have already passed endangered species legislation - Manitoba, New Brunswick, Ontario and Quebec - and others are planning to follow suit. The scope of the problem, nevertheless, is national since few of Canada's endangered species are to be found in only one province. In addition to species which have been previously extirpated from the country or gone extinct worldwide, another 260 or so Canadian species are at varying degrees of risk of extinction.[62] The "Canadian Species At Risk" list is produced by COSEWIC (Committee on the Status of Endangered Wildlife in Canada)[63] which assesses scientific reports on species and assigns status in the following categories: Extinct, Extirpated, Endangered, Threatened and Vulnerable.[64] Once a species has been designated as en-

dangered, then RENEW (Recovery of Nationally Endangered Wildlife Committee)[65] has the authority to design a recovery plan.

A remarkably strong level of public support for federal legislation to protect endangered species has been reported. An Angus Reid Poll conducted in May 1995 found that an overwhelming majority of Canadians (94 percent) support the idea of federal legislation for endangered, threatened, and vulnerable species of animals and plants.[66] Significantly, even after being apprised of the possible cost of implementation of such legislation (estimated to be about thirty-three cents per person per year), support remained high (89 percent).[67] This amount is considerably more than is currently spent on endangered species, which is less than ten cents per capita.[68] Further, most Canadians (75 percent) believe that endangered species of plants and animals should be legally protected "wherever they live", and less than a quarter of those asked (21 percent) thought these species should only be protected on public land but not on private land.[69]

Other indications of the high level of public support for strong federal endangered species legislation include joint letters to the Environment Minister from Canadian scientists and artists and the Body Shop petition.[70] A federally-appointed Task Force on Endangered Species, consisting of representatives from a very wide range of groups and organizations, "jointly recommended that a federal endangered species protection act apply to the full extent of federal jurisdiction... and that it require habitat protection".[71] The Canadian Endangered Species Coalition has found support for their goal of "effective legislation to protect and recover endangered species and their habitats" among a broad and diverse range of professional organizations, labour organizations and businesses as well as environmental organizations.[72]

Canada has further motivation to pass legislation since becoming a signatory to the United

Nations Convention for the Protection of Biological Diversity in 1992. Canada committed itself to "develop and maintain necessary legislation and/ or regulatory provisions for the protection of threatened species and populations".[73] Canada is also a signatory to the Convention on International Trade in Endangered Species (CITIES) which provides for controls on the market to prevent trade in endangered species.[74]

It helps to contextualize the arguments about the benefits and costs of species preservation. All of the reasons for saving species listed above apply in some sense to Canada. Imperilled species in Canada do have some direct utility, in terms of the economic benefits of wildlife-related activities which would apply to certain endangered species as well. They may ultimately have other direct utility (in terms of medicine or food) which we are not yet aware of. Canadian species at risk do have indirect utility, in terms of their contribution to ecosystem health. There are aesthetic and cultural values associated with many of the listed species. Moreover, there are many Canadians who believe we have a moral obligation to preserve species - for future generations, or on spiritual or other ethical grounds. Some Canadians feel that species have a right to exist and that we are obliged to try to protect them from endangerment. There are thus obvious benefits to be attained from preserving species, yet there are clearly costs as well.

The human activities which threaten the survival of species are ones which also have direct and indirect utility; they provide benefits to humans in various ways. The types of activities that have led in the past and continue to lead to endangerment of species include the following: "overhunting for meat and feathers, impacts of feral herbivores and carnivores, predation by domestic pets, competition for food with introduced birds and insects, overambitious animal damage control, egg-eating by exotic mammals and non-native birds, extensive forest clearing, excessive tourist development, overcollecting by private hobbyists, ... [and] agriculture related and grazing related habitat destruction".[75] The latter is one of the most significant factors in present day endangerment. Much of the habitat destruction that occurs is the result of unintentional activities undertaken to satisfy ordinary human desires. Endangerment, then, often occurs due to "subtle forms of permissive and involuntary habitat degradation" in the course of everyday activities.[76]

To provide some specific examples from the contemporary Canadian context, intensive agriculture has affected the Eastern Cougar (now endangered); insecticide and herbicide use has contributed to the decline of the Sage Thrasher (now endangered); overcollecting for specimen collections has decimated the Eastern Prickly Pear Cactus (now endangered); fire control and draining of wet prairie for use as cropland has contributed to the decline of the Small White Lady's Slipper (now endangered); the Western Prairie White Fringed Orchid (now endangered) has been afflicted with the loss of pollinators; and poisoning, shooting, and trapping has beset the Black Tailed Prairie Dog (listed as vulnerable). Other species, such as the Slender Mouse-Ear Cress (now endangered) have been affected by the introduction of invasive non-native weeds. Habitat fragmentation and habitat loss are the most serious continuing problems. Habitat fragmentation refers to the isolation of natural areas due to roads and incursions of human development. Habitat loss has been particularly acute in the prairies, which have experienced a loss of almost all the tall grass prairie ecosystem. The area in Canada which has the highest concentration of endangered species is the Carolinian region of southern Ontario, which is also the most densely populated.

The preventive and protective measures that are needed to deal with the kinds of problems listed above include things like provision of migratory bird habitat for breeding and even stopover purposes (as for the whooping crane), the prevention of pollution of rivers and the reversal of acidification of lakes (for fish and other aquatic species). Restrictions on agricultural land uses and limitations on commercial developments will also be necessary. If an endangered species is found primarily on private land, as is often the case in the U.S., then the costs of protection will likely include purchase of land or compensation to landowners. A peat mine project was required to move to an alternative location in order to avoid development in the critical habitat of an endangered plant in Nova Scotia.[77] In the case of the burrowing owl, Health Canada has already instituted a partial ban on a common pesticide (carbofuran). The pesticide is used on fruits, vegetables and grains to kill insects, but tiny amounts of the substance are fatal to the burrowing owl. The new regulations restricting the use of the pesticide specifically prevent spraying on roadsides and its use to kill grasshoppers in wheat, which happens to be the most common use.[78] Many farmers in the Prairies objected to the ban, saying that farm costs would be increased from crop damage and more expensive alternatives.

It is difficult to estimate the costs of increased protection compared to the status quo. The U.S. federal government spent $72 million (US) in 1995 for the endangered species program. That amounts to approximately $50 thousand dollars (US) per species (given a total of 1451 species). In addition, the states also fund programs; the total spent in 1991 or 1992 was $131 million (US).[79] An estimate by the Office of the Inspector General, U.S. Department of the Interior, "suggested that the total cost for the full recovery of all listed species and all candidate species ... (about 4,000 species) would be close to $4.6 billion (US).[80] That amount may very well be an overestimate, since it is extrapolated from figures for animal species, the recovery for which costs more than for plants. The Canadian RENEW program for 1993-1994 was estimated to cost about $3 million, with slightly less than one million ($761 thousand) coming from the federal government, slightly more than one

million coming from provincial and territorial governments and about the same coming from other organizations. The total would represent an average of $99,724 for each of the 32 species that received funding.[81]

There is no chance that funding will be allocated if the species is not listed in the first place. All the existing provincial statutes and the most recent version of the proposed federal law effectively make the listing determination a political matter. The proposed Act provides for the listing decisions to be based on scientific advice, but the politicians are under no obligation to "explain or justify their choices".[82] It leaves open the possibility that politicians could choose not to list an imperilled species for political, social or economic reasons. This provision is deplorable, as the listing decision should only be based on scientific criteria. There needs to be accurate information made available to the public about which species are actually at risk; this is a matter of conservation biology. Once the full list is public, then decisions will have to be made about what resources will be available to take further action. Those subsequent decisions will clearly require broader stakeholder involvement, and entail consideration of social, economic and political issues.[83]

The proposed federal law, Bill C-65, will only apply to about 40 percent of Canada's endangered species, specifically aquatic species, certain migratory birds and species on federal lands. There has been criticism of the failure of the Bill to cover species that cross over national borders, and there is concern that the Bill may not cover the habitat of migratory birds. Further, even for those species that are covered, habitat protection is not required.[84] The Bill requires the preparation of recovery plans within one year of listing for endangered species and within two years for threatened species. The Bill does prohibit killing or harming an endangered species or harming the residence of an endangered species.[85] These provisions will only apply, however, if a species is listed. The

Act is intended to work in conjunction with provincial initiatives.[86] Of course, it is better for there to be a law than no law, but one hopes that the final law that is passed will be strengthened.[87]

III. PRACTICAL ISSUES
HOW SHOULD SPECIES BE PROTECTED?

Legal Protection for Species

The U.S. Endangered Species Act is often said to be an instance of "prohibitive policy", which is meant to prescribe behaviour by "outlawing actions beyond a certain standard".[88] The rationale behind legislation of this sort is to "disallow any balancing of the benefits of the policy against the costs of compliance".[89] Prohibitive policy has been criticised for seeming to rule out "balancing of social objectives" by the use of mandatory rules. When there is disagreement over the goals or objectives of the legislation, and activities it prohibits have other redeeming social features (such as producing utility) it is seen by many people to be a costly and unjustified form of government intervention. Critics of prohibitive policy prefer instead the use of legislative and policy instruments which are flexible and negotiated compromises accompanied by wide discretion.

It is common for environmental legislation to have absolute sounding prohibitions in the letter of the law accompanied by practical compromises in the implementation and enforcement of the law. Standards and regulations and other instruments to implement the objectives of the law are often found to lack "real bite" or to be effectively "toothless" in terms of efficacy. Governments are keen to "take credit" for passing strong legislation, for achieving symbolic victories over a problem but they are also keen to "avoid blame" for actually doing something about the problem.[90] Governments have incentives to try to appease the environmentalist lobby by passing "good law", laws which should help to achieve environmental protection, but they also have incentives to refrain from making the legal measures sufficiently effective that they risk alienating powerful and important sectors of the economy whose interests could be negatively affected.[91] Environmentalists thus complain that the impressions of strong legislative protection is misleading since effectiveness of protection depends on the resources made available for implementation and enforcement.[92]

It is thus not surprising that in places which have passed endangered species legislation, the absolute prohibitions contained in the enabling legislation bear little resemblance to the reality of enforcement. This kind of legislation does have symbolic value even when it is not adequately implemented or enforced, but it is not likely to be effective. Politicians, in the U.S. and elsewhere, speak highly of legislation like the U.S. Endangered Species Act as an expression of the "national conscience", but very little funding is actually allocated to implementation of the act, particularly to recovery plans. As many commentators have noted, the way the government deals with the endangered species issue reflects a general ambivalence on the part of the public. It is not that the public does not care about the preservation of species, it is that the public cares about a lot more than just the preservation of species. There is no easy way to provide a set of principles or criteria "on which to base decisions when the preservation of species conflicts with other pressing public interests", as Mark Sagoff puts it.[93]

Habitat Protection and Recovery Priorities

To have effective species preservation programs it is necessary for legislation to provide for: prohibition against "taking" (loosely speaking, harming) listed endangered species; preparation of recovery plans for listed species; and designation of critical habitat required for survival of endangered species.[94] Recovery plans or programs are crucial to the preservation of species. Recovery plans are intended to "restore the listed species to a point where they are viable, self-sustaining components of their ecosystem".[95] Recovery plans aim to identify tasks and activities necessary to "recover a species to a stage where it can be downlisted from endangered to threatened or removed from threatened status (delisted)".[96] Critical habitat consists of the area the loss of which would substantially diminish the prospects for survival, or recovery, of a species.[97] Critical habitat is the minimum amount of land which would be required to halt the decline of a species. Although hundreds of species have been listed in the United States, critical habitat has been established only for a few of those species.[98] Most species do not have recovery plans prepared for them either. The main reason for these lacunae is lack of resources.

Despite the rhetoric of anti-preservationists and the public misconceptions about the U.S. Endangered Species Act, there has apparently been little inhibitory effect on development.[99] Unfortunately for many vulnerable, threatened or endangered species, the areas they would need to have protected as their critical habitat are often in areas in which alternative land uses (primarily development or agriculture) are perceived to better serve human interests. It is particularly problematic if economic interests are granted a privileged status over other human interests, such as ecological diversity, or aesthetic satisfaction, or scientific knowledge.

It is increasingly the case that those who promote the goals of preservation are taking the criticisms of their critics seriously. More and more attention is being accorded to the need to create a climate of cooperation. On occasion, legal protection for endangered species has been perceived to create a perverse incentive to "shoot, shovel, and shut up", ie., to actually destroy the population of an endangered species found on private land slated for development.[100] Thus, advocates of preservation have come to appreciate the need for private sector involvement in the protection and management of endangered species. It is im-

portant to avoid relying exclusively on prohibitive policy, and to build in incentives to motivate landowners, farmers and ranchers to participate in endangered species habitat protection.

There are various proposals that could help to create a conducive atmosphere for protecting habitats: monetary incentives to landowners to compensate for benefit forgone or to cover costs of actively managing their land to meet the requirements of a protected species; exemptions on taxes for lands on which protected species are located or which provide habitat.[101] Other possible measures include financial and technical assistance for habitat restoration, tax penalties for those who take over untouched wildlife habitats, and tax credits for property owners who sign conservation and stewardship agreements.[102]

It is very difficult, for even the most ardent adherent of the preservationist ethos, to argue that all species can be saved. It may be thought to be desirable, taking a preservationist stance, for each and every species that is at risk to be protected from extinction. Yet, it can hardly be argued that the resources would exist to effect the kind of preservation that would be needed were every species to be saved from the threat of endangerment. Even assuming that there was general agreement that preservation is to be pursued "at any cost", which is unlikely, to ensure that no species goes extinct ever again would be an incredibly difficult and expensive proposition.

In Canada, it may be somewhat less expensive than elsewhere to stave off extinction, given that only one-fifth of species currently listed reside exclusively or mostly on private land.[103] It costs more to protect species on private land due to the expense of land acquisition and compensation for landowners. Also, there are not a huge number of species at risk in Canada in comparison to the United States, or particularly tropical countries.[104] Even in Canada, however, it is unlikely that the full complement of resources needed to preserve species properly would be available. Thus, the question has to be addressed: how should recovery priorities be set?

The listing of a species, ideally, should be based only on biological considerations. Any species which is demonstrably imperilled should be listed, and all such species should be listed. Unfortunately, only a fraction of such species actually do get listed. As Stephen Meyer has observed, "the quantity and quality of biological data deemed sufficient to make a case for listing a species or designating a habitat becomes captive to the degree of political controversy likely to be generated".[105] There are many reasons for this. The main one is that there is likely to be a concern that once a species gets listed, there will be an assumption that there should be funds made available to ensure protection, and there is also the prospect of citizen suits to force the government's hand.

There are vast differences in the amounts of resources allocated to particular endangered species. There is a noticeable difference between the resources allocated to the RENEW program for the wood bison and the peregrine falcon and those allocated to the Lake Erie water snake, for instance.[106] The Whooping Crane, for example, has been one of the "lucky" endangered species whose public popularity and high profile ensured their listing and funding for their protection. This species has been the recipient of extraordinary efforts of both American and Canadian governments and numerous non-governmental organizations and extensive media campaigns.[107] But many species simply are not listed - or even if they are, sufficient funds to ensure their survival are not made available.

In terms of public interest in endangered species, researchers have found an implicit ordering or hierarchy of categories of species as follows: "large mammals, large birds, most small mammals and birds, butterflies, amphibians, most reptiles and fish, snails, clams, crustaceans, harm-

less insects, plants and other invertebrates, harmful insects, bats and snakes".[108] A test involving Finnish students found that students exhibited greater willingness to pay for "species that are well-known, taxonomically close to humans, and actually endangered".[109] Reviews of attitude surveys and comparisons of amounts donated to programs for particular species indicate that there is a preference for "charismatic megafauna" which are mediagenic.[110] Thus, psychological and emotional as well as cultural factors will play a role in determining the popularity of species.

The popularity factor discussed above is clearly going to affect the political dimensions of listing, developing recovery plans and setting aside critical habitat. There are, of course, ecological factors which need to be considered as well. One such factor will be the amount of support for a species inside and outside the scientific community. Other factors to be considered for setting recovery priorities include the degree of threat faced by a species, the potential for successful recovery and the taxonomic status. Many observers of the endangered species listing process have talked about the relevance of the concept of triage, or "emergency room conservation".[111] If not all species can be saved, saving those with the best chance of recovery and long-term viability should be the priority.

Another issue for determining recovery priorities is whether the focus of preservation efforts should be on species or habitats. There have been situations where the focus of contemporary endangered species legislation on "a species teetering on the brink of extinction" can end up working against efforts to conserve overall biodiversity.[112] In the Florida Everglades, for example, efforts to recreate optimum nesting conditions for vulnerable populations of wading birds by drainage were temporarily blocked in the name of protecting habitat for the endangered snail kite.[113] In this case, it looked as if the needs of a single species was inhibiting conservation actions for the rest of the ecosystem. Commentators have pointed to other similar situations to underscore the need for a focus on whole ecosystems and multispecies protection.

There is widespread agreement among conservation biologists that the ultimate objective of endangered species protection should actually be preserving overall biological diversity. The goal, they propose, should be to preserve "the maximum number of healthy species in ecosystems that require a minimum of maintenance".[114] Habitat protection is crucial to preserving related species and life processes as well as the target species. Preserving even an expensive habitat could be supported if it would save an extraordinarily large number of life forms, say if it were a so-called "biodiversity hotspot".

Habitat protection, Norton argues, "protects more human values, serves wider human goals, and, ultimately, saves more species".[115] It may also be a more efficient allocation of resources. The focus on single species protection is likely to remain for some time to come, however, due to certain public relations aspects, such as the fact that some prominent species have broader public appeal than the more amorphous habitat. Further, it is the case that protecting a species in the wild will also protect the habitat, and other species in that habitat.[116]

It comes back to the question of why we want to preserve species, why we care about avoiding extinction and endangerment. If the reason to preserve species is simply to conserve genetic information for maintenance of the gene pool or production of raw materials, it may be considered sufficient to preserve species in managed environments. Managed environments include zoos, botanical gardens, seed banks and laboratories. It is sometimes thought that this might be a cheaper way of meeting preservation objectives, yet these ways of preserving species can be fairly expensive as well. Last ditch efforts to save species in

crisis situations, in particular, can be very expensive and may not be fully successful.[117] Some species that are deemed worthy of protection will be in such a vulnerable state that extraordinary measures will be needed, measures such as captive breeding and subsequent reintroduction.[118] In addition, techniques involving cryogenic processes, embryo transplants, and artificial insemination may be required to assist a particularly vulnerable population or species.[119]

If the reason for preserving species is to preserve ecological and evolutionary wildness, however, then preservation in managed environments will not suffice. Then, the "way to save species is to save the places where they live".[120] It would be necessary to preserve species in relatively undisturbed habitat if the objective is to maintain overall biological diversity and to preserve remnants and fragments of wildness.[121] The choice of preservation objectives would be guided either by non-anthropocentric, or perhaps by only weakly anthropocentric reasons. The latter include preserving wildness for its transformative value or due to morally corrected preferences, and the former consist of recognizing intrinsic value in species or respecting the right of species to exist. Insofar as these non-anthropocentric or weakly anthropocentric ideas shape endangered species protection programs, there will be less concern with choosing among species and setting priorities for recovery. All species will be made the recipients of preservation efforts to the utmost. Every species at risk will be protected in their "home", and helped towards recovery. Such programs are likely to be highly effective.

However, the more that endangered species protection programs are guided by objectives which are chosen and justified on strong anthropocentric grounds then the less effective they are likely to be overall. Insofar as the goal of protecting biodiversity and saving species from extinction or endangerment is disputed, or at least that the allocation of funds to realize such a goal is contested, then programs will remain mired in the need to achieve the minimal protection publicly palatable for the least expenditure of resources. In such a situation, the question of priorities and choosing the "lucky" species, those which attract public favour or prominent attention, to target for recovery efforts will be paramount.

Some species will ultimately remain as captive populations for the foreseeable future, due to the lack of conditions suitable for reintroduction. Pere David deer, for example, have only existed in captivity and zoos for over a century. Species existing only as genetic material in gene banks, species existing only in captivity, and species bred only through captive breeding programs represent a range of managed preservation initiatives. Such initiatives may be required for certain species, already on the brink of extinction, but they are last resort measures. Long term success in preservation depends on reintegrating a species into a functioning habitat.[122] It is to be hoped that for most threatened and endangered species it will still be possible to provide protection in relatively undisturbed habitat. It is also desirable that endangered species protection move from a species-by-species crisis management approach to a more holistic, preventative approach aimed at conserving overall biodiversity.

It is necessary, certainly in the global context within which biodiversity is an issue, that species protection initiatives be linked with the resolution of socioeconomic problems and that they be sensitive to cultural differences and political imperatives. Preservationist environmentalists are increasingly cognizant of the need to reconcile the demands of social justice, respect for human rights, attention to matters of human welfare and so on with the concerns of environmentalism, including species and wilderness preservation.

CONCLUSION

For many people, it is self-evident why we should care about species, and furthermore, why we should undertake extraordinary measures to avoid causing the extinction of other species. These people's moral intuitions coincide with the preservationist ethos -the belief that species do matter and that humans have obligations to avoid doing harm to species. Such obligations follow from the fact that we humans are uniquely responsible for environmental destruction and species endangerment. We humans therefore have an obligation to avoid causing the harm, or if that is not feasible, to make reparations or to attempt restoration.[123]

However, not everyone adheres to anything like the preservationist ethos. Many other people, and not just anti-environmentalists, do not share those moral intuitions and in fact are sceptical of the claims made by preservationists on behalf of species which require the allocation of sizable amounts of resources or result in the frustration of other human goals. It is to be hoped that people who do not yet fully accept the case for protecting species and preserving wildness can ultimately be persuaded to support preservationist policies.

The position in this paper is that at the least, all species that are endangered, threatened or vulnerable should get listed. There should not be any political influence on the listing process. Canadians are entitled to know the real situation, they are entitled to be properly informed about the actual state of affairs concerning the status of species. This issue is predominantly a factual issue; although it may be accompanied by scientific uncertainty it is still the case that the issue can be resolved by the acquisition of more accurate information. Ultimately, no further decisions can be made without this kind of information. Listing is primarily a matter of making a determination about the current status of each species and should not be too costly in the first instance. Thus, each species is entitled to a determination.

The other two stages in the protection process are the preparation of recovery plans and designation of critical habitat. These issues are perhaps not so clear cut. They are not primarily factual issues, rather they are inherently value issues. It is a matter of values - moral, political, social and economic - whether any particular species merits extraordinary or even ordinary efforts. These issues can only be settled through public debate. Public perception and public interest will play a much greater role at these stages than at the earlier listing stage. Much greater amounts of resources are required to develop and implement recovery plans and to purchase and/or regulate and monitor critical habitat. There need to be efforts made to raise the profile of the issue, through public education and consciousness raising about the seriousness of the current situation and the imperatives for preservation initiatives.

It will come down to a question of political will, whether governments, non-governmental organizations, and private citizens are motivated, or can be persuaded, to act on behalf of endangered species. We may have to wait until our fellow citizens are convinced to ensure that the resources can be allocated to ensure the survival of endangered species, but in the interim we can at least become aware of the magnitude of the situation. There may not yet be widespread and definitive agreement on the claim that species have a right to exist, which entails duties on the part of humans to save every species everywhere everytime. It must nevertheless be recognized that species certainly do have a right to have their passing noticed and mourned.[124]

ENDNOTES

[1] Martha, who was named after Martha Washington, "died in the Cincinnati Zoo on September 1, 1914". Although at one time it seemed as if about a quarter of the birds found in North America were passenger pigeons, the indiscriminate slaughter by hunters and resulting fragmentation of the colonies led to a rapid decline. Charles Mann and Mark Plummer, *Noah's Choice*, page 75. Other extinctions that were human-caused had occurred previously, but this one attracted a very high level of public attention.

[2] Bill C-65, *An Act Respecting the Protection of Wildlife Species in Canada from Extirpation or Extinction*, had First Reading on October 31, 1996. It was then referred to the

House of Commons Standing Committee on Environment and Sustainable Development. I have not undertaken to provide a detailed discussion and analysis of the provisions of the proposed legislation - that is the subject of another piece. I have focused instead on the general policy debates concerning the legal protection of endangered species, and emphasized the issues that are of relevance in the Canadian context.

[3] There are many dimensions to the proposed legal reform - the jurisdictional issues involving federal and provincial governments, the bureaucratic issues concerning the role of the *Committee on the Status of Endangered Wildlife in Canada* (COSEWIC), the adequacy of resources to prepare and carry out recovery plans under the *Recovery of Nationally Endangered Wildlife* (RENEW) program, and the opportunities for input and oversight provided to the *Canadian Endangered Species Coalition*.

[4] The form of the first section of the paper will make use of the challenge, response, and discussion structure, which is designed to try to set out the polarities of the debate and then to work around them. The preservationist in me wants always to simply assert the views and positions associated with the preservationist ethos, but the philosopher in me insists that I always take account of the other sides of the debate, that I give full attention to the contrary views and positions associated with anti-preservationism and anti-environmentalism. I use the term "preservationist ethos" to reflect the belief that nature has value in itself, value that is not merely derived from or reducible to human concerns, value which ultimately entitles nature to be respected, preserved, protected and revered for its own sake. The preservationist ethos assumes that there are duties to species, that humans are under an obligation to avoid causing extinction of other species, and to minimize the negative impact of human activity upon ecosystems and wilderness. I have written on this topic once before, for my Master of Environmental Studies degree. That piece was entitled: "The Meaning of Extinction for Justice Between Species: An Examination of Some Philosophical Problems Concerning Nature Preservation". Unpublished Thesis, September 1990. I have borrowed some passages here and there, and made use of some of the research upon which that work was based for this present piece.

[5] Bryan Norton makes these points in the "Epilogue" to *The Preservation of Species*.

[6] This question has been framed in many different ways: Robert Elliot asks, "Should We Preserve Species?", and Claudia Mills asks "Preserving Endangered Species: Why Should We Care?".

[7] This is the title of a book by Ben Bolch and Harold Lyons which is subtitled: *Science, Economics and Environmentalism*. Another suggestive title along the same lines is *Ecoscam: The False Prophets of Ecological Apocalypse* by

Ronald Bailey.

[8] Lawrence Slobodkin, "On the Susceptibility of Different Species to Extinction: Elementary Instructions for Owners of a World", page 241.

[9] These estimates are provided by Mann and Plummer in *Noah's Choice* on page 64. They cite the following: L.R. Brown et. al., *Saving the Planet: How to Shape an Environmentally Sustainable Global Economy*, p.28; I. Deshmukh, *Ecology and Tropical Biology*, p.322; P. Eastman and T. Bodde, "Endangered Species Act", *BioScience* 32, 1982, p.246; E. Eckholm, "The Age of Extinction", *The Futurist*, October 1978, p.289; K. Miller and L. Tangley, *Trees of Life: Saving Tropical Forests and Their Biological Wealth*, p.17; Norman Myers, *The Sinking Ark*, p.20; E.C. Wolf, *On The Brink of Extinction: Conserving the Diversity of Life*, p.6; Norman Myers, *A Wealth of Wild Species: Storehouse for Human Welfare*, p.9; P.H. Raven, "Our Diminishing Tropical Forests", in *Biodiversity*, ed. by E.O. Wilson, p.121. See Mann and Plummer, *Noah's Choice*, page 257 for the complete list of references.

[10] See Robert May's article, "How Many Species Inhabit the Earth?" for examination of the various projections and extrapolations and their starting points. He says that "[a]ccording to best estimates, taxonomists have identified 1.5 to 1.8 million species, but the list is far from complete". (page 44) May points out that there is no central repository of information on species, and present methods would not suffice to discover and catalogue the number of species predicted by the lowest estimates. He laments the fact that "our society has devoted so little money and effort toward quantifying and conserving the forms of life that define the earth's unique glory". (page 48)

[11] As Paul Ehrlich and Gretchen Dailey discuss in "Population Extinction and Saving Biodiversity".

[12] D.D. Murphy et. al., "On Reauthorization of the Endangered Species Act", page 1.

[13] As Ehrlich and Daily explain: "Population and species extinctions are, of course, related by definition. A species cannot go extinct unless all of its populations are extinct, and the extinction of component populations influences the probability of entire species disappearing". "Population Extinction and Saving Biodiversity", page 64. Subspecies fall between species and populations in the taxonomic continuum.

[14] Webster's Ninth New Collegiate Dictionary.

[15] Biologists and philosophers have developed a series of definitions of species, including a biological species concept, an evolutionary species concept and an ecological species concept. The Biological Species Concept: Species are groups of actually or potentially interbreeding natural populations which are reproductively isolated from other such groups. (Mayr) This was later modified to lead into the Ecological Species Concept: A species is a reproductive community of populations (reproductively isolated from others) that occupies a specific niche in nature. (Mayr) The Evolutionary Species Concept: An evolutionary species is a single lineage of ancestor-descendant populations which maintains its identity from other such lineages and which has its own evolutionary tendencies and historical fate. (Wiley) See the papers collected in *The Units of Evolution: Essays on the Nature of Species*, edited by Marc Ereshefsky. Each of the species concepts has been subject to scrutiny and found lacking in certain respects. For instance, the biological species concept cannot account for asexual species. The ecological species concept cannot say what a species is independently of knowing what a niche is and vice versa. The evolutionary species concept cannot explicitly identify at what point along a continuum something becomes a species. Alexander Rosenberg, in *The Structure of Biological Science*, has observed that: "there is at present no general agreement on the explicit definition of the term 'species'". (page 181) The passage continues by pointing out that there is no agreement on "what counts as a logically or causally sufficient condition for a set of organisms to constitute a species, or for that matter on a necessary condition for species membership". Philip Kitcher's response to the whole debate is the following comment: "The most accurate definition of 'species' is the cynic's. Species are those groups of organisms which are recognized as species by competent taxonomists. Competent taxonomists, of course, are those who can recognize the true species". Kitcher, "Species", in Ereshefsky, ed., *The Units of Evolution*, page 317.

[16] In "The Birds" Gregg Easterbrook illustrates how seemingly abstract points of ornithology concerning whether certain breeds of spotted owls are disjunct or not have a bearing on the controversy over proposed bans on old growth logging to preserve spotted owl habitat.

[17] Julian Simon and Aaron Wildavsky use the "bandwagon" phrase in "Species Loss Revisited". They argued in 1984 that the scientific evidence differed greatly from the "by-then conventional wisdom that species are dying off at a rate that is unprecedently high, and dangerous to humanity". They revisit the issue and find that their earlier conclusions "remain sound". (page 41)

[18] Gregg Easterbrook, in "The Birds", suggests that there are many more spotted owls than "was assumed when the extinction alarm sounded". Easterbrook goes on to say that the plan to shut down logging in Washington State and Oregon to save the owls "may not only be unnecessary; it may be resting on an illusion". (page 22)

[19] They present the analogy between passengers on a plane and humans residing on spaceship earth.

[20] The Ehrlichs put it this way: "extinction must be stopped before the living structure of our space craft is so weakened that at a moment of stress it fails and civilization falls apart".

Extinction, page xiv. It is interesting that the Ehrlichs use such a mechanistic image for organic interrelatedness, since it suggests designers, engineers and mechanics for which there are no comparable analogues in the case of species extinction. The image is, nevertheless, quite graphic and highly suggestive in terms of the role of human agency.

[21] Thomas Lovejoy, "Species Leave the Ark One by One", page 22.

[22] Bryan Norton talks about the same threat in terms of "zero infinity dilemmas", which present environmental risks with low probabilities and high consequences. Each extinction "increases, however slightly, the probability that the next will prove disastrous". Norton, "On The Inherent Danger of Undervaluing Species", p.127.

[23] The story of the "snail darter that stopped a dam" - as the media presented the case of the Tellico Dam project and the then endangered snail darter - is illustrative. The 100 million dollar project was halted by a jeopardy ruling on behalf of the snail darter (a fish), but only temporarily. Due to political machinations and state legislative fiat the project went ahead. After the dam was finally built the critics of the Endangered Species Act were quick to point out that ecocatastophe had not occurred despite the apparent extinction of that population. It later turned out the the species was more prevalent than had been realized and it was reclassified from endangered to threatened in 1984 (downlisted). It is interesting to note that the project was considered to be unjustifiable economically. See Mann and Plummer, *Noah's Choice*, pages 47-148 and 165-175, for a more complete account of the story. See also Zygmunt Plater, "In the Wake of the Snail Darter: An Environmental Law Paradigm and Its Consequences".

[24] See David Jablonski, "Mass Extinctions: New Answers, New Questions" and David Raup, "Death of Species". There are enormous difficulties interpreting the fossil evidence concerning extinction rates, and several different models have been proposed to account for the timing and causes of previous mass extinctions. There is some disagreement over whether there was a previous period of a cluster of human caused extinctions. This disagreement concerns the "overkill hypothesis", relating to the extinction of Pleistocene megafauna in the Americas about eleven thousand years ago. See Jablonski, "Mass Extinctions".

[25] As Norton points out in his "Epilogue" to *The Preservation of Species*, p.268.

[26] Mann and Plummer, *Noah's Choice*, page 66.

[27] Norton discusses these as points of agreement reached by the Working Group whose activities resulted in the collection of papers, *The Preservation of Species*. See "Epilogue", page 268.

[28] See David Jablonski, "Mass Extinctions: New Answers, New Questions" and David Raup, "Death of Species".

[29] Norton, "Epilogue", *The Preservation of Species*, page 271.

[30] Norton says the following: "Specialized species are more likely to have highly evolved relationships... with other species in their environment, and the loss of such species may cause further disruptions and can result in a cascading effect through ecosystems.... Selective extinction...may create a world with fewer highly adapted, specialist species that are useful and pleasant to humans and more members of a few opportunistic species. While such species may be familiar... their population patterns can thwart human goals." Norton, "Epilogue", *The Preservation of Species*, pages 271-272.

[31] Value can be defined as follows: something that is of value is the object of a preference or the object of a judgement of importance; values are classified into categories - moral, aesthetic, economic, religious, political, legal, etc.; a theory of value is a theory about what things in the world are good, desirable, and important.

[32] See the introductory essay to this volume for elaboration on the range of ethical theories or approaches found in the environmental ethics literature, and in particular, discussion of the distinction between anthropocentric and non-anthropocentric theories. The debates over theory choice and characterization of value, while fascinating and stimulating, are beyond the scope of this paper. See the papers by Callicott, Norton, and Regan in *The Preservation of Species* (edited by Norton), in particular, for elaboration of the application of those debates to the issue of endangered species and further references.

[33] There are other ways of characterizing the reasons for saving species, which usually consist of developing lists of reasons. The kinds of reasons given are: Direct Utility Resourcism, Indirect Utility Resourcism, Aesthetic and Cultural Value, Existence Value, or Moral Reasons (including Spiritual Reasons). See the list found in Sewart Elgie, "Protected Spaces and Endangered Species", page 468, and the typologies found in J. Baird Callicott's "On the Intrinsic Value of Nonhuman Species" and Christopher Stone's *"Should Trees Have Standing? Revisited"*.

[34] The discussion of economic analysis in this paper is, of necessity, simplified and watered down. For more elaborate treatments of the topic, see: Donald Brown, "Ethics, Science and Environmental Regulation"; Steven Kelman, "Cost-Benefit Analysis: An Ethical Critique"; Herman Leonard and Richard J. Zeckhauser, "Cost-Benefit Analysis Defended". These articles can be found in Allan Greenbaum, Alex Wellington and Ellen Baar, editors, *Social Conflict and Environmental Law*. Also see Mark Sagoff, *The Economy of the Earth*, Chapter 2, 3, 4, and 5; and Ted Schrecker, *Political Economy of Environmental Hazards*, Chapter 3. Also see the Editors' Notes on "Ethics and Economics" in Greenbaum, Wellington and Baar, *Social Con-*

flict and Environmental Law, Volume One, Section One for elaboration and further references.

[35] Alan Randall puts it this way: it is utilitarian in that things count to the extent that people want them; anthropocentric in that humans are assigning the values; and the biota is regarded as an instrument for human satisfaction. Further assumptions include resource scarcity and interpersonal conflict. "What Mainstream Economists Have to Say About the Value of Biodiversity", pages 217-218.

[36] The principle of utilitarianism is "maximize the greatest good or happiness for the greatest number". Utilitarianism can be further characterized as follows: The right action or policy is the one which will make as many people happy as possible; the requirement of utilitarianism is to choose the action or policy (from all the feasible alternatives) that will maximize the total net benefit (benefits minus costs: happiness minus unhappiness) for all those affected by the action; the utility of every individual is to count equally. Utility is to be summed across persons, and the distribution of utility among persons is not morally relevant. In this paper, I do not wish to get into the debates between supporters of utilitarianism and supporters of non-utilitarian, deontological or rights-based moral theories about which theory or which version of which type of theory is the best theory. I would argue that one can quite fruitfully talk about both utility and rights without having to choose sides concerning which, if any, of the conventional moral theories is to be applied, at least in the first instance.

[37] Simply put, a benefit is a "gain, monetary or otherwise, that accrues to people from the use of a good or service" and a cost is a "loss, monetary or otherwise, required to obtain a good or service". Resource Futures International, "Rare and Endangered Species Legislation Economic Analysis", pages 12-13.

[38] For elaboration of "willingness to pay" and "willingness to accept", see Alan Randall, "What Mainstream Economists Have to Say About the Value of Biodiversity", page 218.

[39] There is a vast literature on the economic aspects of conserving biological diversity. However, I can only touch very briefly on the general issues in this paper. For more elaboration see: Richard Bishop, "Economic Efficiency, Sustainability, and Biodiversity"; Richard Norgaard, "The Rise of the Global Exchange Economy and the Loss of Biological Diversity"; Bryan Norton, "Commodity, Amenity, and Morality: The Limits of Quantification in Valuing Biodiversity"; Bryan Norton, "On the Inherent Danger of Undervaluing Species"; David Pearce and Dominic Moran, *The Economic Value of Biodiversity*; Alan Randall, "Human Preferences, Economics and the Preservation of Species"; Alan Randall, "What Mainstream Economists Have to Say About the Value of Biodiversity".

[40] Resource Futures International report the following: "This

amount [almost $5.6 billion] contributed $10.2 billion to gross business production, $7.0 billion to the Gross Domestic Product (GDP), $3.8 billion to personal income from 126 thousand jobs, and $3.1 billion to government revenue from taxes". The amounts are higher when the amount that anglers spent on trip-related items and equipment and that American tourists spent while visiting Canada for fish-and wildlife-related activities are included. Then "the expenditure total rises to $8.4 billion, the increase in GDP is $10.2 billion, the increase in tax revenues is $4.6 billion, and the number of jobs is 188 thousand". RFI, "Rare and Endangered Species Legislation Economic Analysis", page 23. See P. Logan, *The Benefits of Wildlife*. Canadian Wildlife Service: Ottawa, 1995. See also F.L. Filion et. al., *The Importance of Wildlife to Canadians: The Economic Significance of Wildlife-Related Recreational Activities in 1991*. Canadian Wildlife Service: Ottawa, 1994.

[41] The estimate is calculated on the basis of the "proportion of birds and mammals on the COSEWIC lists compared to the total numbers in Canada". Approximately 15% of the total mammals in Canada are at risk and about 11% of the total bird species that breed in Canada are at risk. Using a figure of 10%, RFI say that "the estimated net benefit to Canadians of wildlife-related activities involving endangered mammals and birds" could be $40 million per year. Resource Futures International, "Rare and Endangered Species Legislation Economic Analysis", page 24.

[42] "Canada's Endangered Species: A Growing Problem", Information Sheet prepared by the Canadian Endangered Species Coalition. See Norman Myers, *A Wealth of Wild Species: Storehouse for Human Welfare*.

[43] These arguments are sometimes labelled the "junk drawer" type of argument, which may not quite capture their significance fully. The general idea is that we cannot predict where the cure for cancer might come from, or when we might need a wild strain to breed with a monoculture that has been struck by disease, fungus or pests. We should thus keep around anything that could potentially be valuable some day.

[44] Norman Myers says this about the precautionary principle: "In essence, the precautionary principle asserts that there is a premium on a cautious and conservative approach to human interventions in environmental sectors that are (a) unusually short of scientific understanding and (b) unusually susceptible to significant injury, especially irreversible injury". Myers, "Biodiversity and the Precautionary Principle", page 74.

[45] The Safe Minimum Standard of Conservation (SMS) was originally proposed by Ciriacy-Wantrup and then further developed by Richard Bishop and Alan Randall. See Richard Bishop, "Economic Efficiency, Sustainability, and Biodiversity" and Alan Randall, "What Mainstream Economists Have to Say About the Value of Biodiversity" for

elaboration.

[46] Richard Bishop, "Economic Efficiency, Sustainability, and Biodiversity", page 72.

[47] Richard Bishop, "Economic Efficiency, Sustainability, and Biodiversity", page 72.

[48] Julian Simon and Aaron Wildavsky, "Species Loss Revisited", page 46.

[49] The United States Postal Service recently brought out an "Endangered Species Collection" of photographic stamps. The advertisements include the slogan "We've Honored Them With a Stamp" and the exhortation to "Show You Care" by buying the stamps.

[50] See, for instance, Mark Sagoff, "On the Preservation of Species" and Thomas Dunlap, "Organization and Wildlife Preservation: The Case of the Whooping Crane in North America". See also Charles Bergman, *Wild Echoes: Encounters With the Most Endangered Animals in North America* and Diane Ackerman, *The Rarest of the Rare: Vanishing Animals, Timeless Worlds*.

[51] An example of the former is the Red Panda conservation program promoted by the Metropolitan Toronto Zoological Society. Many environmental organizations have set up fund-raising campaigns organized around the issue of preserving endangered species.

[52] Bryan Norton, "On the Inherent Danger of Undervaluing Species", page 11.

[53] Bryan Norton, "On the Inherent Danger of Undervaluing Species", page 11.

[54] See Christopher Stone, "Legal Rights and Moral Pluralism".

[55] See Callicott, "On the Intrinsic Value of Nonhuman Species".

[56] If a being or entity is deemed to have moral standing, the interests or well-being of that entity must be counted or considered in deciding what it is permissable to do. Moral standing is relevant to the determination of which beings or entities matter, and to the evaluation of action. The harm which would be suffered by any entity with moral standing counts against the moral worth of any action or policy which would cause the harm. That harm must then be justified, outweighed by a more important moral claim, or else avoided. The moral status of species is addressed at length in the following articles: R. Willis Flowers, "Ethics and the Hypermodern Species"' Alastair Gunn, "The Restoration of Species and Natural Environments"; Lawrence Johnson, "Toward the Moral Considerability of Species and Ecosystems"; Eric Katz, "Buffalo Killing and the Valuation of Species". Also see the papers by J. Baird Callicott, Bryan Norton, Donald Regan and Elliott Sober in *The Preservation of Species*, edited by Bryan Norton.

[57] The quote is from Stewart Elgie, "Protected Spaces and Endangered Species", page 468.

[58] See David Ehrenfeld, *The Arrogance of Humanism*, "Life in the Next Millennium: Who Will be Left in Earth's Community?" and "Why Put a Value on Biodiversity".

[59] As Robert Carlton has put it, "it is unfair that the burden of the political decision to preserve species should fall disproportionately upon property owners who discover, or are informed that the presence of endangered species on their lands restricts them from uses of their property".

[60] Editorial, *Oceans* 12, September 1979, page 8.

[61] Robert Carlton makes these points in "Property Rights and Incentives in the Preservation of Species", page 266.

[62] See the "1996 List of Species at Risk Designated by the *Committee on the Status of Endangered Wildlife in Canada*".

[63] COSEWIC is constituted by representatives of government (federal, provincial and territorial), wildlife agencies and wildlife organizations. It was formed in 1976.

[64] Extinct: Any species of fauna or flora formerly indigenous to Canada no longer known to exist anywhere. Extirpated: Any indigenous species of fauna or flora no longer known to exist in the wild in Canada but existing elsewhere. Endangered: Any indigenous species of fauna or flora whose existence in Canada is threatened with immediate extinction through all or a significant portion of its range, owing to the action of humans. Threatened: Any indigenous species of fauna or flora that is likely to become endangered in Canada if the factors affecting it do not become reversed. Vulnerable: Any indigenous species of fauna or flora that is particularly at risk because of low or declining numbers, occurrence at the fringe of its range or in restricted areas, or for some other reason, but is not a threatened species. Vulnerable species have characteristics that make them particularly sensitive to human activities.

[65] RENEW was formed in 1988 by the Council of Canadian Wildlife Ministers. It is charged with the establishment of a national strategy for the recovery of endangered species.

[66] See "Public Support for Endangered Species Legislation", Report Prepared for the Canadian Endangered Species Coalition by Angus Reid Group, Inc., June 1995. The study consisted of 1500 telephone interviews conducted "among a representative cross-section of Canadian adults". 74% said they "strongly support" such legislation and 20% "somewhat support" it. The support is "remarkably homogenous across demographic variables such as age, gender, education, income, and province of residence".

[67] The amount of thirty-three cents was derived from data on expenditures in other countries on endangered species programs. For example, the Australian government spends about thirty-two cents per capita per year, and the U.S. federal government allocated seventy-two million dollars in the fiscal year 1995 which amounts to just over thirty-eight cents (Canadian) per capita. See S.R. Jones, *Endangered*

Species Update 12(3). It is expected that costs in the U.S. would be higher than the costs for conserving the same species in Canada because the U.S. endangered species program has to spend more money on land acquisition and compensation to landowners. Half of the listed endangered and threatened species in the U.S. were found exclusively on private land in contrast to only about 20% of Canada's species at risk (1994 and 1993 lists, respectively). See "Economic Costs and Benefits of Endangered Species Legislation", Information Sheet prepared by the Canadian Endangered Species Coalition.

[68] The total is estimated to be less than two million dollars a year. See "Economic Costs and Benefits of Endangered Species Legislation", Information Sheet prepared by the Canadian Endangered Species Coalition.

[69] There were very slight differences in the results obtained from specifically asking Canadians living in farm/ small communities. The numbers were as follows: 90% of farm/small community residents support legislation, 85% support it even after being apprised of the possible cost of implementation, and 71% believe that endangered species should be protected wherever they live. The only other differences were: "Quebec respondents were less likely than the national average (69%) to believe that endangered species should be protected "wherever they live" and "younger respondents were more likely than older respondents to support protection "wherever they live". See "Public Support for Endangered Species Legislation", Prepared for the Canadian Endangered Species Coalition by the Angus Reid Group, Inc.

[70] An Information Sheet prepared by the Canadian Endangered Species Coalition reports that: "In November 1995, over 180 Canadian scientists signed a joint letter ...[requesting] legislation for the sake of the nation's biological health. In June 1996, over 60 Canadian artists signed a joint letter... asking for strong endangered species legislation for the sake of the nation's cultural identity... The Body Shop collected 75,000 signatures on a "There Otter be a Law" petition requesting effective federal endangered species legislation".

[71] The Task Force members included: Canadian Pulp and Paper Association, Canadian Association of Petroleum Producers, Mining Association of Canada, Canadian Federation of Agriculture, National Agriculture-Environment Committee, Fisheries Council of Canada, Sierra Legal Defence Fund, Animal Alliance of Canada, Canadian Wildlife Federation, Island Nature Trust, and Canadian biological scientists.

[72] The Canadian Endangered Species Coalition is composed of the Canadian Nature Federation, the Canadian Parks and Wilderness Society, the Sierra Club of Canada, the Sierra Legal Defence Fund, the Union Québécoise pour la Conservation de la Nature, and the World Wildlife Fund.

[73] "Endangered Species", Information Sheet prepared by the Sierra Club of Canada for the Canadian Endangered Species Coalition.

[74] See Dale Gibson, "Endangered Species and the Parliament of Canada" for elaboration of the implications of treaty implementation.

[75] The list is taken from Stephen Kellert, "Social and Perceptual Factors in the Preservation of Animal Species", pages 50-51. Feral animals are descendants of domesticated animals which are now living in the wild.

[76] The quote is from Richard Webster, "Habitat Conservation Plans Under the Endangered Species Act", page 269. Involuntary or unintentional in the sense that they are not intended to destroy the habitat of other species, or to bring about endangerment. This is the point that runs throughout the writings of Charles Mann and Mark Plummer on the subject. See *Noah's Choice* and "The Butterfly Effect".

[77] The plant was the thread-leaved sundew. Resource Futures International, "Rare and Endangered Species Legislation Economic Analysis", page 28.

[78] "Prairie Owl the Cause of Major Pesticide Ban", *Globe and Mail*, 1996.

[79] Resource Futures International, "Rare and Endangered Species Legislation Economic Analysis", page 30.

[80] This works out to about $20 (US) per capita. Resource Futures International, "Rare and Endangered Species Legislation Economic Analysis", page 30.

[81] Resource Futures International, "Rare and Endangered Species Legislation Economic Analysis", page 29. As RFI point out, the RENEW program "has focused resources on large, popular animals which will tend to have higher total costs". Thus, the "figure is probably not representative of average costs for all species". (page 29)

[82] COSEWIC will advise on listing but Cabinet will make the actual listing decision. See "December Update" and "One Page Summary of Key Points in Act" from the Canadian Endangered Species Coalition, which point out that the current Bill is actually step backwards from the 1995 draft legislative proposal in this respect.

[83] Similar points are made by the Canadian Endangered Species Coalition in their "Briefing Notes".

[84] As the Canadian Endangered Species Coalition point out, "where the scientific committee identifies that a species is facing imminent threats to its survival, the Minister may provide emergency protection to the species or its habitat". But the Minister is not required to do so. The Coalition also acknowledge that the Bill "allows citizens to bring private enforcement actions in court where the government is not enforcing the law". But such an action can only be brought after the government has completed an investigation of the matter, "even if there is an immediate threat to a species' survival". See "One Page Summary of Key Points in Act".

[85] See Canadian Endangered Species Coalition, "One Page Summary of Key Points in Act".

[86] Recently (October 1996), the federal and provincial wildlife Ministers signed a National Accord for the Protection of Species at Risk, which "commits all jurisdictions to legally protect endangered and threatened species, protect their habitat, and develop and implement recovery plans". Canadian Endangered Species Coalition, "December Update".

[87] It is beyond the scope of this paper to delve into the nitty-gritty examination of the provisions of the Bill and the various developments that have led up the most recent version. See the detailed "Analysis of Bill C-65, Canada Endangered Species Protection Act" from the Canadian Endangered Species Coalition. The analysis includes reference to the report of the federal Endangered Species Task Force ("Task Force Report") and the National Accord for the Protection of Species at Risk ("National Accord").

[88] Stephen Yaffee, *Prohibitive Policy*, page 1.

[89] Stephen Yaffee, *Prohibitive Policy*, page ix.

[90] Kathryn Harrison provides an analysis of the actions of the federal government in Canada in these terms in her piece, "Federalism, Environmental Protection, and Blame Avoidance". See also, "Canada and Environmental Protection" by David Van Der Zwaag and Linda Duncan, who argue along the same lines.

[91] See Ted Schrecker, "Resisting Environmental Regulation" for an elaboration of these tensions.

[92] Terry Leitzell makes this point about endangered species protection specifically in "Species Protection and Management Decisions in an Uncertain World", pages 248-249.

[93] Mark Sagoff, "On The Preservation of Species", page 47.

[94] As Resource Futures International point out, these are aspects of the U.S. Endangered Species Act, the "earliest and probably still the strongest piece of endangered species legislation in the world". "Rare and Endangered Species Legislation Economic Analysis", page 10.

[95] U.S. Fish and Wildlife Service, *Report to Congress: Endangered and Threatened Species Recovery Program*, Washington, D.C.: Government Printing Office, 1990, page v.

[96] Timothy H. Tear, J. Michael Scott, Patricia H. Hayward, Brad Griffith, "Status and Prospects for Success of the Endangered Species Act: A Look at Recovery Plans", page 976.

[97] See William Lemp, "Promise and Peril: A New Look at the Endangered Species Act of 1973". The Act has recently been up for reauthorization which elicited a flurry of commentary and debate on the merits and demerits of the particulars of that law. See the articles in *Balancing on the Brink of Extinction: The Endangered Species Act and Lessons for*

the Future, edited by K. Kohm and in *Endangered Species Recovery: Finding the Lessons, Improving the Process*, edited by Clark, Reading and Clarke.

[98] See Richard Webster, "Habitat Conservation Plans Under the Endangered Species Act".

[99] Resource Futures International report: "From 1987 to 1992, the Fish and Wildlife Service had conducted 94,113 informal consultations and 2,719 formal consultations under Section 7 of the Act. Of the completed formal consultations, development activities were blocked in only 54 cases (2% of the total)". "Rare and Endangered Species Legislation Economic Analysis", page 10.

[100] The phrase is from Resource Futures International, "Rare and Endangered Species Legislation Economic Analysis", page 35. Robert Carlton, in "Property Rights and Incentives in the Preservation of Species", discusses the destruction of one of the three remaining populations of the San Diego mesa mint found on land being developed by a private developer. The developer wanted to "ensure that subsequent requests for federal construction grants would not be delayed because of endangered species considerations". Carlton, page 261.

[101] Robert Carlton discusses these proposals in "Property Rights and Incentives in the Preservation of Species". See also "Farmers and Ranchers and Canadian Endangered Species Legislation: Common Questions and Answers", Information Sheet prepared by the Canadian Endangered Species Coalition.

[102] Stephen Meyer, "The Final Act", page 29.

[103] "Almost 50% of the 728 threatened and endangered species listed as of 1993 in the US were on private land, whereas only an estimated 20% of the Canadian species listed in Canada were exclusively or mostly on private land". Resource Futures International, "Rare and Endangered Species Legislation Economic Analysis", page 3.

[104] The United States had 1,451 species at risk in 1995 and Canada has between 260 and 270 species at risk presently. The numbers for the tropics are difficult to determine but by all estimates they are enormous. See E.O. Wilson, "The Current State of Biological Diversity" and Peter Raven, "Our Diminishing Tropical Forests", both found in *Biodiversity*, edited by E.O. Wilson.

[105] Stephen Meyer, "The Final Act", page 27.

[106] RENEW Report #3, 1993, recounts that "between fall 1989 and March 1993, the peregrine falcon ... received 25.66 person-years and $1.26 million of resources from 50 separate contributors. In contrast, the Lake Erie water snake (also a Priority 1 species) received 0.3 person-years and $2 thousand. The work was supported by only one donor, the provincial government". As for the wood bison, " in 1993-194 alone over $700 thousand was spent ... under the RENEW program". Resource Future International, "Rare and Endan-

gered Species Legislation Economic Analysis", page 21 and page 31. Similar patterns of skewed allocations also occur in the United States. See Mann and Plummer, "The Butterfly Problem" and *Noah's Choice*.

[107] See Thomas Dunlap's "Organization and Wildlife Preservation: The Case of the Whooping Crane in North America" for more elaboration.

[108] Douglas Linder, ""Are All Species Created Equal?" And Other Questions Shaping Wildlife Law", page 196. Stephen Kellert has described the findings of his attitude research this way: humans favour "species that are large, aesthetically attractive, phylogenetically similar to human beings, and regarded as possessing the capacities for feeling, thought, and pain". Kellert, "Social and Perceptual Factors in Endangered Species Management", page 533. See also Steven Kellert, "Social and Perceptual Factors in the Preservation of Animal Species".

[109] Resource Futures International, "Rare and Endangered Species Legislation Economic Analysis", page 21. The study results are reported in M. Kuitunen and T. Tormala, "Willingness of Students to Favor the Protection of Endangered Species in a Trade-off Conflict in Finland", *Journal of Environmental Management*, Volume 42(2).

[110] E.O. Wilson, the editor of *Biodiversity* and author of *Biophilia* is often credited with coining the term "charismatic megafauna".

[111] Daniel Rohlf uses the phrase "emergency room conservation" in "Six Biological Reasons Why the Endangered Species Act Doesn't Work - and What to Do About It", page 184. The dictionary defines triage as follows: "the sorting of and allocation of treatment to patients... according to a system of priorities designed to maximize the number of survivors". Webster's Ninth New Collegiate Dictionary. See Suzanne Winkler, "Stopgap Measures" and Daniel Bennett, "Triage as a Species Preservation Strategy".

[112] The phrase is from Suzanne Winkler, "Stopgap Measures", page 80.

[113] Joe Alper, in "Everglades Rebound from Andrew", explains that the snail kite feeds on apple snails which crawl onto sawgrass in areas of standing water. The proposal was to restore the natural hydrological conditions within the park to benefit nesting populations of wading birds. Draining the area to attempt to restore the original pattern of water flow would have threatened the snail kite's food supply in the interim. There was a jeopardy opinion in the name of the snail kite issued under the Endangered Species Act putting a halt to the plans to drain the area. The article says "The wetlands will recover from the hurricane, but threats from urbanization, from agriculture, and -ironically- from the Endangered Species Act pose tougher problems". Eventually, a report from an Audubon panel maintained that "while maintaining the status quo could produce short-term ben-

efits for the snail kite, it would probably cause serious problems in the long run". The report recommended that restoration proceed. The report emphasized the entire ecosystem and multispecies management, rather than a single species approach. (page 1854)

[114] Suzanne Winkler, "Stopgap Measures", page 78.

[115] Bryan Norton, "Epilogue", *The Preservation of Species*, page 283.

[116] See Daniel Rohlf, "Six Biological Reasons Why the Endangered Species Act Doesn't Work - and What to Do About It" and the response by Michael O'Connell for further discussion of the debate about species versus habitat protection. See also, Alan Randall, "Human Preferences, Economics, and the Preservation of Species", pages 100-101. See also Bryan Norton, "Epilogue", *The Preservation of Species*, pages 278-283.

[117] Lawrence Slobodkin discusses the reasons that remedial actions may not be viable: many organisms are developmentally integrated into their local environment and cannot be expected to survive as well after being displaced; the reintroduced or introduced species may not be genetically appropriate, since populations of particular species that have been subjected to different selective regions in different regimes may differ in gene frequency; and the initial elimination of the species or subspecies or population is likely to have provided an opportunity for competing species to occupy the ecological space the extinguished population originally occupied. (page 237)

[118] In some cases, such as the California condor, biologists have had to use "aversion therapy to teach birds how to survive in the modern world". The aversion therapy is designed to teach the birds to avoid people and power lines, two major threats to their survival. The last remaining members of the wild population were removed for captive breeding, and since then humans have had to feed and now socialize them. See the article by Heather Dewar in *The Toronto Star*, Tuesday December 24.

[119] See the following articles in *Biodiversity*, edited by E.O. Wilson: William Conway, "Can Technology Aid Species Preservation?"; Peter S. Ashton, "Conservation of Biological Diversity in Botanical Gardens"; Tom J. Cade, "Using Science and Technology to Reestablish Species Lost in Nature"; Ulysses S. Seal, "Intensive Technology in the Care of Ex Situ Populations of Vanishing Species"; and Betsy L. Dresser, "Cryobiology, Embryo Transfer, and Artificial Insemination in Ex Situ Animal Conservation Programs".

[120] Suzanne Winkler, "Stopgap Measures", page 78. She goes on to say: "By extension, the way to save the greatest number of species is to save the places that house the richest biological inventory". She discusses the use of gap analysis, which looks for unprotected landscapes that are rich in species.

[121] As Aldo Leopold put it many years ago, wilderness is "the raw material out of which man has hammered the artifact called civilization". Yet, in the contemporary world situation wilderness preservation can only amount to the protection of remnants in the face of the "exhaustion of wilderness in the more habitable portions of the globe". *A Sand County Almanac: With Essays on Conservation from Round River*, page 264.

[122] Bryan Norton, "Epilogue", *The Preservation of Species*, page 279.

[123] This is the argument that Alastair Gunn makes in "The Restoration of Species and Natural Environments".

[124] I would like to thank Catherine Austen, Campaign Coordinator for the Canadian Endangered Species Coalition and Bill Rapley, Executive Director of Biology and Conservation for the Metropolitan Toronto Zoo, for providing me with packages of materials which were invaluable in the preparation of this paper. Thanks to Peter Shepherd for helpful comments and suggestions on this paper. In addition, I would also like to thank Allan Greenbaum and Jeff Nadir for passing along materials which helped provide inspiration.

References

Alper, Joe. "Everglades Rebound From Andrew". *Science*, Volume 257, 25 September 1992, 1852-1854.

Angus Reid Group. "Public Support for Endangered Species Legislation: Final Report". June 1995. Report prepared for the Canadian Endangered Species Coalition.

Bennett, David H. "Triage as a Species Preservation Strategy". *Environmental Ethics*, Volume 8, Spring 1986, 47-58.

Bishop, Richard C. "Economic Efficiency, Sustainability, and Biodiversity". *Ambio*, Volume 22(2-3), May 1993, 69-73.

Callicott, J. Baird. "On the Intrinsic Value of Nonhuman Species". In Norton, ed., *The Preservation of Species*, 1986.

Canadian Wildlife Service. *Endangered Species in Canada*. (cat. no. CW69-4/76E) Ottawa: Environment Canada, 1989.

Carlton, Robert. "Property Rights and Incentives in the Preservation of Species". In Norton, ed., *The Preservation of Species*, 1986.

Cigman, Ruth. "Death, Misfortune and Species Inequality". *Philosophy and Public Affairs*, Volume 10, Winter 1981, 41-64.

Clark, Tim W., Richard P. Reading and Alice L. Clarke, editors. *Endangered Species Recovery: Finding the Lessons, Improving the Process*. Island Press, 1994.

Dunlap, Thomas R. "Organization and Wildlife Preservation: The Case of the Whooping Crane in North America". *Social Studies of Science*, Volume 21, 1991, 197-221.

Easterbrook, Gregg. "The Birds - The Spotted Owl: An Environmental Parable". *The New Republic*, March 28, 1994, 22-29.

Ehrenfeld, David. *The Arrogance of Humanism*. Oxford University Press, 1981.

Ehrenfeld, David. "Life in the Next Millennium: Who Will be Left in Earth's Community?" In Kaufman and Mallory, eds., *The Last Extinction*, 1986.

Ehrenfeld, David. "Why Put a Value on Biodiversity?" In Wilson, ed., *Biodiversity*, 1988.

Ehrlich, Paul. "Extinction: What is Happening Now and What Needs to be Done". In Elliott, ed., *Dynamics of Extinction*, 1986.

Ehrlich, Paul and Anne Ehrlich. *Extinction: The Causes and Consequences of the Disappearance of Species*. Random House, 1981.

Ehrlich, Paul R. and Gretchen C. Daily. "Population Extinction and Saving Biodiversity". *Ambio*, Volume 22(2-3), May 1993, 64-68.

Elgie, Stewart. "Protected Spaces and Endangered Species". In Hughes, Lucas and Tilleman, eds., *Environmental Law and Policy*, 1993.

Elliot, Robert. "Should We Preserve Species?" *Habitat Australia*, Volume 7(5), October 1979, 9-10.

Elliot, Robert. "Why Preserve Species". In Mannison, McRobbie and Routley, eds., *Environmental Philosophy*, 1980.

Elliott, David K., editor. *Dynamics of Extinction*. New York: John Wiley and Sons, 1986.

Ereshefsky, Marc, editor. *The Units of Evolution: Essays on the Nature of Selection*. MIT Press, 1992.

Feinberg, Joel. "Legal Moralism and Free Floating Evils". *Pacific Philosophical Quarterly*, Volume 61,

1980, 122-155.

Flowers, Willis. "Ethics and the Hypermodern Species". *Environmental Ethics*, Volume 8, Summer 1986, 185-188.

Gibson, Dale. "Endangered Species and the Parliament of Canada". September 1994. Analysis prepared for the Canadian Endangered Species Coalition.

Grumbine, R. Edward, editor. 1995. *Environmental Policy and Biodiversity*. Island Press.

Gunn, Alastair. "Why Should We Care About Rare Species". *Environmental Ethics*, Volume 2, Spring 1980, 17-37.

Gunn, Alastair S. "The Restoration of Species and Natural Environments". *Environmental Ethics*, Volume 13(4), Winter 1991, 291-310.

Hanemann, W. Michael. "Economics and the Preservation of Biodiversity". In Wilson, ed., *Biodiversity*, 1988.

Harrison, Kathryn. "Federalism, Environmental Protection, and Blame Avoidance". In *New Trends in Canadian Federalism*, edited by Francois Rocher and Miriam Smith. Broadview Press, 1995.

Hughes, Elaine L., Alastair R. Lucas and William A. Tilleman II. *Environmental Law and Policy*. Emond Montgomery Publications, 1993.

Jablonski, David. "Mass Extinctions: New Answers, New Questions". In Kaufman and Mallory, eds., *The Last Extinction*, 1986.

Johnson, Lawrence E. "Toward the Moral Considerability of Species and Ecosystems". *Environmental Ethics*, Volume 14(2), Summer 1992, 145-157.

Katz, Eric. "Buffalo-Killing and the Valuation of Species". In Sumner, Callen and Attig, eds., *Values and Moral Standing*, 1986.

Kaufman, Les and Kenneth Mallory. *The Last Extinction*. Cambridge, Mass.: MIT Press, 1986.

Kellert, Stephen. "Social and Perceptual Factors in Endangered Species Management". *Journal of Wildlife Management*, Volume 49(2), 528-536.

Kellert, Stephen. "Social and Perceptual Factors in the Preservation of Animal Species". In Norton, ed., *The Preservation of Species*, 1986.

Kohm, Kathryn A., editor. *Balancing on the Brink of Extinction: The Endangered Species Act and Lessons for the Future*. Island Press, 1991.

Kurdila, Julianne. "The Introduction of Exotic Species Into the United States: There Goes the Neighborhood!" *Boston College Environmental Affairs Law Review*, Volume 16, 1988, 95-118.

Leitzell, Terry. "Species Protection and Management Decisions in an Uncertain World". In Norton, ed., *The Preservation of Species*, 1986.

Lemp, William. "Promise and Peril: A New Look at the Endangered Species Act of 1973". *St. Louis University Law Journal*, Volume 27, 1983, 959-979.

Linder, Douglas. ""Are All Species Created Equal?" And Other Questions Shaping Wildlife Law". *Harvard Environmental Law Review*, Volume 12, 1988, 157-200.

Lovejoy, Thomas. "Species Leave the Ark One by One". In Norton, ed., *The Preservation of Species*, 1986.

Mann, Charles C. and Mark L. Plummer. "The Butterfly Problem". *The Atlantic*, Volume 269(1), January 1992, 47-70.

Mann, Charles C. and Mark L. Plummer. *Noah's Choice: The Future of Endangered Species*. Alfred A. Knopf, 1995.

Mannison, Don, Michael McRobbie and Richard Routley, editors. *Environmental Philosophy*. Monograph Series, No. 2. Department of Philosophy, Research School of the Social Sciences, Australian National University, 1980.

May, Robert M. "How Many Species Inhabit the Earth?" *Scientific American*, October 1992, 42-48.

Meyer, Stephen M. 1994. "The Final Act - In Defense of Endangered Species". *The New Republic*, August 15, 1994, 24-29.

Mills, Claudia. 1992. "Preserving Endangered Species: Why Should We Care?". In Mills, ed., *Values and Public Policy*.

Mills, Claudia, editor. 1992. *Values and Public Policy*. Harcourt Brace Jovanovich College Publishers.

Murphy, D.D., D. Wilcove, R. Noss, J. Harte, C. Safina, J. Lubchenco, T. Root, V. Sher, L. Kaufman,

M. Bean, and S. Pimm. "On Reauthorization of the Endangered Species Act". *Conservation Biology*, Volume 8(1), 1994, 1-3.

Myers, Norman. *The Sinking Ark: A New Look at the Problem of Disappearing Species*. Oxford: Pergamon Press, 1979.

Myers, Norman. *A Wealth of Wild Species: Storehouse for Human Welfare*. Boulder, Col.: Westview Press, 1983.

Myers, Norman. 1993. "Biodiversity and the Precautionary Principle". *Ambio*, Volume 22(2-3), May 1993, 74-79.

Nitecki, Matthew, editor. *Extinctions*. University of Chicago Press, 1984.

Norgaard, Richard B. 1988. "The Rise of the Global Exchange Economy and the Loss of Biological Diversity". In Wilson, ed., *Biodiversity*.

Norton, Bryan. "On the Inherent Danger of Undervaluing Species". In Norton, ed., *The Preservation of Species*, 1986.

Norton, Bryan, editor. 1986. *The Preservation of Species: The Value of Biological Diversity*. Princeton University Press.

Norton, Bryan. "Commodity, Amenity, and Morality: The Limits of Quantification in Valuing Biodiversity". In Wilson, ed., *Biodiversity*, 1988.

O'Connell, Michael. "Response to: "Six Biological Reasons Why the Endangered Species Act Doesn't Work - and What to Do About It". *Conservation Biology*, Volume 6(1), 1992. Reprinted in Grumbine, ed., *Environmental Policy and Biodiversity*.

Pearce, David and Dominic Moran. *The Economic Value of Biodiversity*. IUCN/ The World Conservation Union. Earthscan Publications Ltd., 1994.

Plater, Zygmunt. "In the Wake of the Snail Darter: An Environmental Law Paradigm and Its Consequences". *University of Michigan Journal of Law Reform*, Volume 19, Summer 1986, 805-862.

Randall, Alan. "Human Preferences, Economics and the Preservation of Species". In Norton, ed., *The Preservation of Species*, 1986.

Randall, Alan. "What Mainstream Economists Have to Say About the Value of Biodiversity". In Wilson, ed., *Biodiversity*, 1988.

Raup, David. "Death of Species". In Nitecki, ed., *Extinctions*, 1984.

Regan, Donald. "Duties of Preservation". In Norton, ed., *The Preservation of Species*, 1986.

Rescher, Nicholas. "Why Save Endangered Species?" In *Unpopular Essays on Technological Progress*. Pittsburgh: University of Pittsburgh Press, 1980.

Resource Futures International. "Rare and Endangered Species Legislation Economic Analysis". June 29, 1995. Draft for Discussion Prepared for the Canadian Endangered Species Coalition.

Rohlf, Daniel J. 1991. "Six Biological Reasons Why the Endangered Species Act Doesn't Work - and What to Do About It". *Conservation Biology*, Volume 5(3), 1991. Reprinted in Grumbine, ed., *Environmental Policy and Biodiversity*.

Rolston, Holmes III. *Philosophy Gone Wild: Essays in Environmental Ethics*. Buffalo: Promotheus Book, 1986.

Rosenberg, Alexander. *The Structure of Biological Science*. Cambridge University Press, 1985.

Russow, Lilly-Marlene. "Why Do Species Matter?" *Environmental Ethics*, Volume 3, Summer 1981, 101-112.

Sagoff, Mark. "On The Preservation of Species". *Columbia Journal of Environmental Law*, Volume 7, Fall 1980, 33-67.

Sagoff, Mark. "Can Environmentalists Be Liberals: Jurisprudential Foundations of Environmentalism". *Environmental Law*, Volume 16, 1986, 775-796.

Schrecker, Ted. "Resisting Environmental Regulation: The Cryptic Pattern of Business-Government Relations". In *Managing Leviathan: Environmental Politics and the Administrative State*, edited by Robert Paehlke and Douglas Torgerson. Broadview Press, 1990.

Simon, Julian L. and Aaron Wildavsky. "Species Loss Revisited". *Society*, Volume 30(1), November/ December 1992, 41-46.

Slobodkin, Lawrence. "On the Susceptibility of Different Species to Extinction: Elementary Instructions for Owners of a World". In Norton, ed., *The Preservation of Species*, 1986.

Smith, Edwin. "The Endangered Species Act and Biological Conservation". *Southern California Law Review*, Volume 57, 1984, 361-413.

Sober, Elliott. "Philosophical Problems for Environmentalism". In Norton, ed., *The Preservation of Species*, 1986.

Soule, Michael and B.E. Wilcox, editors. *Conservation Biology: An Evolutionary Ecological Perspective*. Sunderland, Mass.: Sinauer, 1980.

Stone, Christopher. *"Should Trees Have Standing?* Revisited: How Far Will Law and Morals Reach? A Pluralist Perspective". *Southern California Law Review*, Volume 59, 1985, 1-154.

Sumner, Wayne, Donald Callen and Thomas Attig, editors. *Values and Moral Standing*. Bowling Green Studies in Applied Philosophy, Volume VIII. Bowling Green, Ohio: Bowling Green State University, 1986.

Tear, Timothy H., J. Michael Scott, Patricia Hayward, Brad Griffith. "Status and Prospects for Success of the Endangered Species Act: A Look at Recovery Plans". *Science*, Volume 262, 12 November 1993, 976-977.

Vanderzwaag, David and Linda Duncan. "Canada and Environmental Protection: Confident Political Faces, Uncertain Legal Hands". In *Canadian Environmental Policy: Ecosystems, Politics and Process*, edited by Robert Boardman. Oxford University Press, 1992.

Varner, Gary E. "Do Species Have Standing". *Environmental Ethics*, Volume 9, Spring 1987, 57-72.

Vermeij, Geerat. "The Biology of Human-Caused Extinction". In Norton, ed., *The Preservation of Species*, 1986.

Versteeg, Hajo. "The Protection of Endangered Species: A Canadian Perspective". *Ecology Law Quarterly*, Volume 11, 1984, 267-303.

Webster, Richard. "Habitat Conservation Plans Under the Endangered Species Act". *San Diego Law Review*, Volume 24, 1987, 243-271.

Wilson, E.O., editor. *Biodiversity*. Washington Academy Press, 1988.

Winkler, Suzanne. "Stopgap Measures". *The Atlantic*, Volume 269(1), January 1992, 74-81.

Yaffee, Steven L. *Prohibitive Policy: Implementing the Federal Endangered Species Act*. Cambridge, Mass.: MIT Press, 1982.

PROTECTING THE TATSHENSHINI:
WILD NATURE AS RESOURCE?[1]

13

by Anne C. Bell

THE TATSHENSHINI RIVER IS PART OF A VAST AND practically undeveloped watershed extending through the Yukon, British Columbia and Alaska. In the last century, and likely for centuries before that, it was used for hunting and fishing and as a trade route by the ancestors of the Champagne-Aishihik and Tlingit peoples. More recently it has become a popular wilderness adventure destination, while Native people continue to fish at its mouth and headwaters. In the late 1980s conflict arose over a proposal to mine a copper deposit at Windy Craggy Mountain, near one of the tributaries of the river in the British Columbian section. At the instigation of commercial outfitters, over thirty environmental organizations in Canada and the United States lobbied to protect the area. After much public and heated debate, the British Columbia government decided to set it aside as a Class A Provincial Park in June 1993.[2]

For the most part, the Tatshenshini issue was represented by conservation groups and the media sympathetic to their cause as a classic struggle between good and evil: would the integrity of this wild and pristine place be safeguarded forever, or would it be sacrificed to the profit motive? Upon closer consideration, however, the battle lines appeared much less clearly defined. Stakeholders on both sides were using each other's arguments to defend their case. While conservationists undertook cost/benefit analyses of the river, the mining faction adopted an "environmental" outlook. Common to both groups was an underlying utilitarian philosophy: the Tatshenshini must be put to its best use – its value

must be maximized for the benefit of present and future generations.

Although opinions about the desired outcome differed, the parameters for discussion were, for the most part, agreed upon. It was accepted by conservationists, industrialists and government alike that economic (resource) and scientific (biological) value must be carefully weighed in reaching a decision. Although traditional preservationist arguments about the aesthetic and intrinsic value of nature were also invoked, these were often accompanied by or framed in terms of an economic or scientific rationale. How and why this was the case are the questions addressed in this paper.

Preservation as the Wisest Use

There is little evidence to show that conservationists opposing Windy Craggy disagreed, in principle, with society's need for large-scale development or continued economic growth. Indeed, groups like Tatshenshini International, the World Wildlife Fund and the B.C. Wildlife Federation made a concerted effort to reassure the mining industry and government that the protest over Windy Craggy was an exception, not the rule.[3] Their caution in this regard was a response, perhaps, to warnings from the pro-mining faction that killing the project would send "an extremely negative message to the mining industry about British Columbia."[4] Whatever the reason, conservationists did not want to be seen as opposing the otherwise justifiable "pursuit of productive labour."[5] Rather, they were searching for balance, and since idle mines and other large, more easily accessible copper deposits existed elsewhere,[6] it was held that these should be developed instead of Windy Craggy. In essence, the dispute was not over resource extraction *per se*, but over the location of the mine. Elsewhere business could proceed as usual, uncontested. Preservation could, in this instance, accommodate the best of both worlds.

When it was announced that the Tatshenshini – Windy Craggy issue would be referred to the Commission on Resources and Environment (CORE), the burden of proof in this regard was considerably lightened for conservationists. Until then, the review under the provincial Mine Development Assessment Process had focused exclusively on the best way to proceed with the project. From an environmental standpoint, this meant addressing technical concerns through studies, inventories, mitigation strategies, treatment technology, compensation packages, and so on.[7] The "do nothing" option, preservation, was not on the table for discussion. With the CORE referral, however, the context of the debate changed.

CORE's mandate was to establish a province-wide land use strategy whereby, among other things, representative wilderness areas were to be allocated for protection. It embodied a view long-held by many conservationists that true multiple use only makes sense for the public domain as a whole:

The reason for determining land use allocations at the regional level is that a regional perspective can provide more flexibility in achieving a balance between economic, social and environmental interests.[8]

Tatshenshini advocates could therefore step back from the single issue to consider the larger provincial picture. This shift from close-up to panorama meant, in effect, that their exclusively preservationist demands could fit a more diversified development agenda. Significantly, preservation of the Tatshenshini could be proposed, not as an *alternative* to use, but rather as one of two possible options for use. The task facing conserva-

tionists was then to prove that the "use" value of preserving the Tatshenshini outweighed the other option: carefully controlled mineral and resource development in 25 percent of the area and preservation of the remaining 75 percent.[9]

Even before the CORE referral, Tatshenshini advocates felt that their best line of defence was to establish the Tatshenshini's true worth as wilderness. True worth of course had to be presented in terms that people could understand: economic value. An initial attempt was made by the organization, Tatshenshini Wild. Taking into account the region's importance to recreation, tourism and preservation, the group estimated that the total value of maintaining the Tatshenshini-Alsek river corridor in its natural state was approximately $13.4 million per year.[10]

Calls for further investigation were answered when the provincial Tatshenshini-Alsek Wilderness Study Steering Committee commissioned J.S.Peepre and Associates "to review and evaluate existing knowledge on the wilderness resources of the region."[11] Asked originally to assess only recreation and tourism values, Peepre and Associates felt it was important to expand the scope of the study to include the natural, cultural, visual, and wilderness features of the Haines Triangle.[12] In so doing they intended to provide a more comprehensive account, specifically one that fully paid tribute to the region's unusual biological diversity. Indeed, the final report provided a powerful piece of evidence for the Tatshenshini defence. It gave the best possible ratings for the river whose features were said to include: outstanding examples of representative landscapes; habitat essential for the preservation of rare species; habitat essential for the survival of significant populations of terrestrial mammals, avifauna, and freshwater fish; areas and sites of significant cultural, archaeological, historical and traditional resource gathering value; examples at specific sites of outstanding or unique landforms or geological features; outstanding areas for public recreation, tourism and nature or culture apprecia-tion; and outstanding wilderness attributes as a composite of all of the above criteria.[13] The as-sessment concluded "that the many public state-ments made about the region's superlative biotic, abiotic and cultural features in a scenic wilder-ness setting are accurate."[14] In other words, con-servationists had not been exaggerating. If ever there were a place where preservation could be considered the best use, it was the Tatshenshini.

Resourcing[15]

Once conservationists agree to discuss an issue within a multiple use framework, it makes sense to speculate about the features of an area as po-tential resources. As they attempt to hold their own in the cost/benefit arena they are led logically and inevitably to rationalize their protectionist stance, for example in terms of "cultural heritage prod-ucts" and "wilderness related tourism products."[16] Conservationists should be wary, however, of the compromises inherent in arguing from this per-spective. To do so is to participate in a story which denies entities value except insofar as they serve human designs. John Livingston reminds us that "resources do not exist in and of themselves, they *become*."[17] They are a social creation, a category imposed by humans on any thing once it is deemed useful. Resourcing is the act of turning things into assets by discovering a use for them. It is an exer-cise in translation really.[18] Resources are under-stood within the expansionist, exploitive project of modern society. The value of, for instance, a hermit thrush or a chocolate lily in and of them-selves, is not. To legitimize their existence, and to allow us to weigh their value against that of another resource, their worth is expressed in a lan-guage that is shared by industry, government and society at large. That language defines "value" in terms of utility to humans.

The *Wilderness Study* is a masterful example of resourcing. Its stated purpose was "to define wilderness in its broadest sense, including all of the resources and uses that together define the re-gion's biological and cultural diversity."[19] Accord-ingly, the Tatshenshini's wildlife, vegetation and geological features, its interest to science, the cul-ture and history of its first human inhabitants, the tourist experience – all were couched in terms of the "uses" made and "benefits" arising to soci-ety.[20] While reflecting a high regard for the Tatshenshini on scientific grounds, the study also stressed its economic value, thus drawing atten-tion to considerations which would otherwise have been ignored by decision-makers in the CORE process. Under the broad categories of natural, cultural, tourism, visual and wilderness resources, the authors managed to demonstrate the utility of, literally, all that the eye could see. For example, the sweeping meadows of *Dryas*, a plant charac-teristic of the alluvial fans of the Tatshenshini and its tributaries, were listed as a "Wilderness Re-lated Tourism Resource."[21] Although they served no obvious human purpose in the traditional sense, they were nevertheless valued because they were on a scale "uncommon in the province" and "rarely as easily accessible."[22] In other words, since scale and accessibility matter primarily to tourists, their merit was established in terms of the viewing pleasure of passers-by.

No memory of the Tatshenshini would be com-plete without the off-white softness of *Dryas* gone to seed. This early colonizer of silt and rubble crowds the river banks and its significance to the Tatshenshini experience is undeniable. To suggest, however, that the human presence defines its worth and consequently justifies its existence is another idea entirely. The two notions imply radi-cally different attitudes to nature. Natural entities can be of benefit to us, obviously, but does that benefit constitute their reason for being? When asked what snakes were good for, John Muir an-swered that they were "good for themselves."[23] This insight has no place within a resourcist frame-work. It runs contrary to the driving assumption of that world view: that value is added on, external, a function of use. While such arguments may be expedient, they often lead conservationists to de-emphasize concerns that are central to their thinking or engagement.[24]

The Use Paradox

The *Wilderness Study* reported that, despite the minimum impact camping methods rigorously practised by commercial rafting parties, the fragile vegetation of the Tatshenshini was "almost certainly affected by use."[25] For those who touted the beauty of the river's wildflowers and sub-alpine meadows to gain support for its preservation, this situation presented a problem. The gist of the resourcist defence was that the Tatshenshini was one of the few places left offering a true wilderness experience. Unique and irreplaceable, it would be forever compromised were the Windy Craggy mine to proceed. Efforts to promote the Tatshenshini as a tourism resource, however, resulted in a sharp increase in use – the number of people visiting the area more than doubled between 1990 and 1992.[26]

The tourism resource argument is a fickle one. Obviously its validity is contingent upon the presence of tourists. "In our society, if a thing has value, then it *must be used*. Otherwise we could not put value to it."[27] If people did not or could not use the river, then it would not be a resource. Thus, Tatshenshini advocates who defended the river on the basis of its tourism potential fostered the expectation that this potential could be realized. Whether such a prospect was realistic or desirable however was questioned even by its proponents: Peepre and Associates were of the opinion that more use of the Tatshenshini "would reduce the quality of the wilderness experience."[28]

Commercial rafting companies, many of whom contributed considerable time and money to the conservation effort, were faced with the practical implications of this inherent paradox. Their clients were lured by the Tatshenshini's promise of pristine wilderness, yet their very presence jeop-

ardized the river's reputation, and thus the industry itself. For this reason, outfitters began working with the Parks Services in both Canada and the United States to limit further growth in river traffic: "The quality of the experience that people come here for must be assured," explained Johnny Mikes of Canadian River Expeditions.[29] Nevertheless, despite such intentions, demand for permits to run the river continued to rise. Vested economic interest dictates that as demand goes up so should supply, at least to the point where profits are maximized. It should come as no surprise then that in the 1992 season British Columbian and Yukon guides reportedly ran ten more trips than the allowed number of eighteen.[30]

A fundamental assumption of the resourcist story is that more use is better than less. More use means more benefit to more people. 'How much tourism can the river withstand?', we ask. 'What is the Tatshenshini's carrying capacity?'[31] So far the agreed-upon quota is seventy-two parties of twenty-five people per year: one group per day for the seventy-two day rafting season. This seemingly reasonable figure is in fact completely arbitrary. Since the region was virtually unstudied prior to the Windy Craggy proposal, the quota has little basis in precise knowledge of the river's biotic communities. If anything, the Tatshenshini's capacity to withstand tourism has been defined solely in terms of user perceptions. "Do you feel that recreational use is causing environmental problems on the river?"; "Did the number of people you encountered on the river detract at all from your enjoyment of the trip?"; "How many nights camping within sight of other parties would you *tolerate* before it is no longer your idea of a 'wilderness experience'?": these were the queries of resource managers as they attempted to determine the limits of acceptable environmental impacts.[32] The underlying imperative, not explicitly acknowledged, was to maximize utility.

This maximization rationale is perfectly suited of course to the designs of industry. The mining company, Geddes Resources, reasoned from precisely this premise for example, when describing potential spin-off benefits from the proposed Windy Craggy access road. Since lack of access was the "major limiting factor" to recreational use, it followed that tourism revenues would be "enhanced" were the road built: "availability of road access could provide for other recreational or tourism opportunities including shorter rafting trips, kayaking and hiking."[33] No longer should the Tatshenshini be the playground of the privileged few – "wealthy people who can afford $US 4000-a-shot commercial rafting trips"[34]; instead, it should be open to everyone.

Tatshenshini Wild countered that Geddes' claim, while valid, was "offset by the fact that such opportunities exist[ed] in abundance elsewhere in northwestern B.C. and southwestern Yukon."[35] Of note is the group's quiescence vis-a-vis the maximization principle. Disagreement was not about the propriety of expanding resource use *per se*, but again about location: the maximization imperative went unchallenged. The Tatshenshini was upheld as unique in the opportunities it offered for tourism – opportunities which were incompatible with roads, bridges, the dust and noise of ore trucks, and, of course, hordes of tourists.

Admittedly, the conservation argument was more complex and subtle than this, for stories other than mere resourcism came into play. These I have addressed elsewhere.[36] Here, my wish is simply to draw attention to the extent to which conservationists argued from, and thus legitimized, the very premise which drives industry.

The Economic Paradigm[37]

Opposition to Windy Craggy, and to the economic opportunities that it represented, was often portrayed as elitist – a move by the *haves* (outfitters, urban environmentalists) to deny employment and recreational opportunities to the *have-nots* (the unemployed, miners, "families on their summer vacations"[38]). Such accusations have plagued the conservation movement throughout its short history[39] and can be explained, in part, by the privileged backgrounds of nature advocates generally: people who take advantage of remote wilderness tend to be better-educated, better-employed and better-heeled than most.[40] More significantly, however, charges of elitism signal the unease and even outrage of those forced to defend a dear and unquestioned belief. Conservation – particularly the extreme preservationist variety of conservation – is threatening. It is perceived by many to undermine one of the axiomatic pillars of the industrial story: that resources should be allocated and used so as to maximize the net benefits to society.

Despite such perceptions, many conservationists are far from rejecting this maximization imperative. In fact, in many cases it becomes a *sine qua non* of their approach. The task – never an easy one – is to demonstrate that protection can rival development, even in terms of utility. The hope for conservation is that, in resorting to cost/benefit analyses, it will be possible to draw attention both to the "external costs" of development and to societal preferences which "often do not have any readily available market expression."[41] It is an attempt to compensate for the fact that ordinarily, development benefits are the subject of well-defined monetary estimates, whereas conservation benefits are not.[42]

The strength of the argument hinges on the interpretation given to *utility*. This concept, which derives its authority from economics, refers to the satisfaction of human desires or preferences. Maximizing utility means achieving the greatest possible human benefit from a given resource. For the proponents of Windy Craggy, utility could only be maximized if the Tatshenshini were opened up to mineral and recreational development. Conservationists, on the other hand, maintained that preservation could accommodate a wider range of preferences. For one thing, the majority of recreationists already had its roads and hotels elsewhere in Canada; wilderness lovers should also be allowed their corner of paradise.[43] Equally important, conservation would take into account the preferences of those who appreciated wilderness vicariously for its non-use "option," "bequest" and "existence" values.[44] From this perspective, it seemed that elitism more properly characterized the narrow, self-serving projects of industrialists than the broader aims of conservationists: "the profit-seeking motives of a few," should not be allowed to jeopardize "an irreplaceable international public resource."[45]

One of the difficulties facing decision-makers of course is to compare such disparate interests. Economists suggest that monetary valuation can and should be used to measure and weigh utility. Money is the "measuring rod" of choice, not because in itself it is necessarily desirable, but because "all of us express our preferences every day in terms of these units."[46] Money is an obvious common denominator. It is a readily available metaphor for value, which in turn is a function of utility yielded.

Misunderstandings can and do arise though when money as a unit of measurement is confused with profit – money in pocket. Such confusion tends to work to the advantage of industry which is able to base its benefit estimates on economic tangibles like employment opportunities, tax revenues and corporate profits. The Windy Craggy project was expected to result in a considerable flow of hard cash. In contrast, no such literal interpretation could be given to the estimated worth of the preservation option, and as a consequence, in the eyes of many it lost its appeal. "How useful is a wilderness that is locked in snow and ice for most of the year?" asked the critics. "Can wilderness recreation ever generate sufficient economic activity, considering the short season and limits on numbers, to offset the potential economic benefits of the mine proposal?"[47]

Faced with such daunting questions, conservationists had little choice but to respond in kind.

Because the debate was framed in terms of economic utility, it became a strategic necessity to raise doubts about the financial viability of the mine. Luckily, a world-wide slump in the copper market and Geddes' sloppy financial analyses worked in their favour. This advantage might have been lost, however, if the financial picture had changed or if Geddes had managed to convince decision-makers that the mine would "create too many jobs and too much wealth"[48] not to proceed. In that case, their position would have been that much the weaker for having agreed to discuss the issue on such terms in the first place – terms which were clearly set out in the following comments by the British Columbia Ministry of Parks:

An all-weather road will destroy a unique wilderness resource and will eliminate established wilderness tourism businesses. This is a very high price to pay and can only be justified when the company has firm long-term sales contracts which have an obvious net economic and social benefit to BC which outweighs the irreplaceable losses.[49]

It is important to consider what sort of expectations are engendered by economic reasoning. In adhering to the same mode of valuation as industry, conservationists implicitly, though perhaps unwittingly, encourage dollar-for-dollar, job-for-job comparisons. Through their use of economic metaphors they create the impression that nature protection can be not only profitable, but that it should compensate economically for foregone development opportunities. In referring to the Tatshenshini as both "resource" and "asset" they seemed to invite comments like the following:

If I were the BC finance minister, I might want to figure out how to tax grizzly bears. It will be tough to get any other kind of revenue from the wilderness through which the great Tatshenshini River flows in the most northerly corner of British Columbia.[50]

Language forces us into its patterns.[51] Monetary valuation is the language of exploitation and trade-offs. To adopt that language with the intention of countering the very values that it embodies – profit maximization, economic growth, the human domination of nature – seems problematic at best. It makes no sense really since the story itself excludes the possibility that value might mean something other than human preference or that human activity might be "motivated by factors other than maximizing utility."[52]

Neil Evernden calls resourcism the "Trojan horse of the industrial state."[53] While this remark might bring to mind the tactical risks outlined in the preceding analysis, Evernden is alluding in fact to something far more insidious than the pitfalls of strategic planning. He is drawing attention to the dangers, treacheries, lies and compromises inherent in a particular world-view. He is calling on nature advocates to reconsider the meaning of their engagement.

To reject resourcist arguments would likely put conservationists at an extreme tactical disadvantage, at least in the short term. They would be left with the proposition that natural entities should be protected for their own sakes, regardless of human benefit, and that idea, as Livingston maintains, is incomprehensible to most people.[54] It intimates a world beyond that of human concerns, a world in which the nonhuman exists and carries on independently of our stories and projected values. That world lies largely outside of our immediate ken and experience, which is precisely why it evades those who are not already open to entertain its possibility on the grounds of inference, intuition, feeling or faith.

Like it or not, conservationists are implicated in a fight for control over undeveloped areas like the Tatshenshini, and if they step back, the proponents of industry will simply step in. Were it not for the lobbying efforts of those advocating less consumptive uses of the river, what once seemed like a foregone conclusion in favour of the Windy Craggy mine would never have been overturned. And therein lies the dilemma. Resourcist approaches to conservation presume a human-centred agenda and fit squarely within the dominant economic paradigm. For that reason they make sense to many and thus bear at least some promise of persuading decision-makers. Yet in the long-term it will not suffice to accommodate the preservation of places like the Tatshenshini as exceptions to the rule; for it is precisely this rule – the relentless exploitation of nature for economic gain – which is pushing us and our nonhuman fellow beings to the brink of annihilation. Sooner or later we will have to account for that fact, and for our role in sustaining the belief that, with a few minor sacrifices, business can proceed as usual.

END NOTES

[1]The author gratefully acknowledges the financial support of the Northern Scientific Training Programme and the Social Sciences and Humanities Research Council of Canada. This paper has been adapted from a chapter of *Conservation Stories: Protecting the Tatshenshini*, a Major Paper submitted to the Faculty of Environmental Studies, York University, Toronto: 1993. Because it is an excerpt only, a detailed examination of other arguments resorted to by Tatshenshini advocates was not possible, specifically those centred on endangered species, endangered spaces and wilderness preservation.

[2] The Yukon and Alaska sections of the Tatshenshini - Alsek watershed were, to a large extent, already protected by Glacier Bay National Park and Preserve and Kluane National Park Reserve.

[3]World Wildlife Fund Canada, "Endangered Spaces," Toronto: Summer 1991, p.1; Mark Hume, "Government review of mine on hold", *The Vancouver Sun*, 04/10/92; Paul Chard, "Scientists hit the Tat to study wildlife", *Yukon News*, 07/08/92.

[4]Schreiner, John. "Windy Craggy battle may prove costly." *The Financial Post*, 04/14/92.

[5]The Sockeye Society of Haines Alaska, to Michael Dunn, Environment Canada, covering letter for *Response: Windy Craggy Project: Revised Mine Plan: Stage 1 Environmental and Socio-Economic Impact Assessment*, Haines, Alaska: February 1991, p.3.

[6]The Sierra Club, *Alaska Report*, 16:1, March 1990, p.4.

[7]Province of British Columbia. *Mine Development Assessment Process: Windy Craggy Copper/Gold/Silver Project, Geddes Resources Limited*, July 1992, pp.14,59,55.

[8]Commission on Resources and Environment, *Report on a Land Use Strategy for British Columbia*, Victoria: August 1992, p.19.

[9]Commission on Resources and Environment. *Interim Report on Tatshenshini/Alsek Land Use*, 1, Victoria: January 1993, p.24.

[10]Tatshenshini Wild, "Tatshenshini Issue Summary" (draft), 1989, p.14.

[11]J.S. Peepre and Associates, *Tatshenshini-Alsek Region Wilderness Study*, Victoria: July 1992, Foreword.

[12]The Tatshenshini flows through the Haines Triangle, an area lying south of the Yukon, east of Alaska and west of the Haines Highway.

[13]Peepre, p.II.

[14]*Ibid.*, p.II.

[15]See Donna Haraway's discussion of resourcing in "Situated Knowledges: The Science Question in Feminism and the Privilege of Partial Perspective," *Feminist Studies*, 14:3, Fall 1988, p.592.

[16]Peepre, pp.57,53.

[17]John A. Livingston, *The Fallacy of Wildlife Conservation*, Toronto: McLelland and Stewart, 1981, p.16.

[18]See Neil Evernden, "The Environmentalist's Dilemma", *The Paradox of Environmentalism*, Toronto: York University, 1984, p.10.

[19]Peepre, p.I.

[20]*Ibid.*, p.I.

[21]*Ibid.*, p.54.

[22]*Ibid.*, p.14.

[23]Roderick Nash, *Wilderness and the American Mind*, Third Edition, London: Yale University Press, 1982, p.128.

[24]See Jeff Culbert regarding "cross-reasoning" in "Green Politics and the Tyranny of the Thinker," *Undercurrents*, 5, Spring 1993, p.5.

[25]Peepre, p.52.

[26]Roger Toll, "A dozen days on the Tatshenshini," *New York Times*, 09/06/92. This increase was a clear indication of the effectiveness of the publicity campaign being waged by Tatshenshini International.

[27]Livingston, p.43. See also p.16.

[28]Peepre, p.52.

[29]Toll.

[30]"Too many rafting trips cause a rift," *Toronto Star*, 11/14/92.

[31]The expression "carrying capacity" was originally a term used by cattle ranchers to refer to the number of grazing cattle that a certain area could support. Two comments are necessary: first that the idea had a very narrow and precise application, which is hardly the case when one is talking about tourism impacts in a wilderness area; and second that parks have more in common with beef ranches than we might like to think. See Kaj Arhem who argues that in less developed countries, parks, like ranches, produce products for consumption by foreigners, and that the environmental and social consequences are equally devastating, "Two Sides of Development: Maasai Pastoralism and Wildlife Conservation in Ngorongoro, Tanzania," *Ethnos*, 3:4, 1984, p.206.

[32]Ethan Askey and Peter Williams, "Visitor Survey, Tatshenshini - Alsek River Use Study", Vancouver: Simon Fraser University, Summer 1992; see also Matthew S. Carroll and D.R. Johnson, *Tatshenshini - Alsek River Recreation Survey: Summary of Results*, National Park Service, University of Washington, 1985.

[33]Geddes Resources Limited, "Windy Craggy Project Public Information Meetings," report prepared for the Mine Development Steering Committee, Government of British Columbia, Vancouver, May 1990, p.18; See also Geddes Resources Limited, *Road Justification and Corridor Assessment, Windy Craggy Project*, Toronto, May 1989. The same argument is used by Len Mychasiw, Yukon Renewable Resources, Letter to Marg Crombie, Indian and Northern Affairs, Canada, Whitehorse, 09/02/88, p.3. Note that in a Marktrend survey, 69 percent of those polled considered the creation of access roads into previously unreachable areas to be an advantage (Marktrend Marketing Research Inc. *Attitudes to Mining in British Columbia: Summary Report*, 04/14/89, p.20). CORE (1993) considered increased access and the corresponding tourism opportunities to be one of the advantages of the mining option. In other words, the opinions of business, government and the general public reflected a common belief in the maximization imperative.

[34]Former Geddes president Gerald Harper, as quoted in Campbell Reid, "Wild rivers versus mountain of copper," *The Mercury*, Hobart, Tasmania: 05/30/90. Note that the mine-supporting BC Environmental Information Institute used the same argument, "Member's Bulletin," Vancouver, 12/13/91, pp.8,14.

[35]Tatshenshini Wild, p.11.

[36]Bell.

[37]A similar version of this section of the paper was previously published as "Cost-Benefit Analysis: A Conservation Caveat" in *The Trumpeter*, 11:2, Spring 1994, pp.93-94.

[38]Harper, as quoted in Reid.

[39]Nash, p.205; see also p.243.

[40]See Carroll and Johnson, p.3; and Askey and Williams, p.24. See also Nash, pp.60,364.

[41]David Pearce and R. Kerry Turner, *Economics of Natural Resources and the Environment*, Baltimore: Johns Hopkins University Press, 1990, p.321.

[42]*Ibid.*, p.313.

[43]See Nash, p.205.

[44]"Option value" expresses a preference to preserve wilderness in order to keep future options open; "bequest value" expresses a preference to preserve wilderness for future generations; "existence value" expresses the satisfaction we gain from knowing that wilderness exists.

[45]National Wildlife Federation, comments to Norm Ringstad, Mine Development Steering Committee, Anchorage, 02/13/91.

[46]Pearce and Turner, pp.10, 121.

[47]B.C. Environmental Information Institute, p.12.

[48]Sarah Davison, "Group intensifies river basin work", *The Whitehorse Star*, 07/23/92.

[49]Mike Murtha, Ministry of Parks, to Raymond Crook, Mine Development Steering Committee, Prince George, 09/12/88, p.4.

[50]Schreiner.

[51]Peter L. Berger and Thomas Luckmann, *The Social Construction of Reality: A Treatise in the Sociology of Knowledge*, New York: Anchor Books, 1967, p.38.

[52]Pearce and Turner, p.136.

[53]Evernden, *The Natural Alien*, Toronto: University of Toronto Press, 1985, p.24.

[54]Livingston, p.50.

References

Arhem, Kaj.; "Two Sides of Development: Maasai Pastoralism and Wildlife Conservation in Ngorongoro, Tanzania,"; *Ethnos*; 1984; 3:4.

Askey, Ethan and Williams, Peter; *Visitor Survey, Tatshenshini-Alsek River Use Study*; Simon Fraser University, Vancouver; Summer 1992.

B.C. Environmental Information Institute; *Members Bulletin*; Vancouver; 12/13/91.

Bell, Anne C.; "Conservation Stories: Protecting the Tatshenshini"; *a Major Paper submitted to the Faculty of Environmental Studies*; York University, Toronto; 1993.

Berger. Peter L. and Luckmann,Thomas; *The Social Construction of Reality: A Treatise in the Sociology of Knowledge;* Anchor Books, New York; 1967.

Carroll, Matthew S. and Johnson, D.R.; *Tatshenshini-Alsek River Recreation Survey*; National Park Service, University of Washington; 1985.

Chard, Paul; "Scientists hit the Tat to study wildlife"; *Yukon News*; 07/08/92.

Commission on Resources and Environment; *Report on a Land Use Strategy for British Columbia*; Victoria; August 1992.

Commission on Resources and Environment; *Interim Report on Tatshenshini/Alsek Land Use, 1*; Victoria; January, 1993.

Culbert, Jeff; "Green Politics and the Tyranny of the Thinker"; *Undercurrents, 5*; Spring ,1993; pp.4-8.

Davison, Sarah; "Group Intensifies Rriver Basin Work"; *The Whitehorse Star*; 07/23/92.

Evernden, Neil; "The Environmentalist's Dilemma"; in Neil Evernden ed. *The Paradox of Environmentalism*; York University, Toronto; 1984; pp.7-17.

Evernden, Neil; *The Natural Alien*; University of Toronto Press, Toronto; 1985.

Geddes Resources Limited; *Road Justification and Corridor Assessment, Windy Craggy Project;* Toronto; May, 1989.

Geddes Resources Limited; "Windy Craggy Project Public Information Meetings"; *report prepared for the Mine Development Steering Committee*; Government of British Columbia, Vancouver; May, 1990.

Haraway, Donna; "Situated Knowledges: The Science Question in Feminism and the Privilege of Partial Perspective"; *Feminist Studies, 14:3*; Fall, 1988; pp.575-599.

Hume, Mark; "Government Review of Mine on Hold"; *The Vancouver Sun*; 04/10/92.

Livingston, John A.; *The Fallacy of Wildlife Conservation;* McClelland and Stewart, Toronto; 1981.

Marktrend Marketing Research Inc.; *Attitudes to Mining in British Columbia: Summary Report*; 04/14/89.

Murtha, Mike (Ministry of Parks); *Letter to Raymond Crook*; Mine Development Steering Committee, Prince George; 09/12/88.

Mychasiw, Len (Yukon Renewable Resources); *Letter to Marg Crombie*; Indian and Northern Affairs, Canada, Whitehorse; 09/02/88.

Nash, Roderick; *Wilderness and the American Mind*; Third Edition, Yale University Press, London; 1982.

National Wildlife Federation; *Comments to Norman*

Ringstad; Mine Development Steering Committee, Anchorage; 02/13/91.

Pearce, David and Turner, R. Kerry; *Economics of Natural Resources and the Environment;* Johns Hopkins University Press, Baltimore; 1990.

Peepre, J.S. and Associates; *Tatshenshini-Alsek Region Wilderness Study*; Victoria; July 1992.

Province of British Columbia; *Mine Development Assessment Process: Windy Craggy Copper/Gold/ Silver Project*; Geddes Resources Limited; July 1992.

Reid, Campbell; "Wild Rivers Versus Mountain of Copper"; *The Mercury*; Hobart, Tasmania; 05/30/ 90.

Schreiner, John; "Windy Craggy Battle May Prove Costly"; *The Financial Post*; 04/14/92.

Sierra Club; *Alaska Report*; 16:1; March 1990.

The Sockeye Society of Haines Alaska; "Covering Letter to Michael Dunn, Environment Canada, for Response; *Windy Craggy Project: Revised Mine Plan*; Stage 1 Environmental and Socio-Economic Impact Assessment; Haines Alaska, February 1991.

Tatshenshini Wild; *Tatshenshini Issue Summary* (draft); 1989.

Toll, Roger; "A Dozen Days on the Tatshenshini"; *The New York Times*; 09/06/92.

World Wildlife Fund Canada; *Endangered Spaces*; Toronto; Summer 1991.

_____. "Too Many Rafting Trips Cause A Rift"; *The Toronto Star*; 11/14/92.

THE LONG AND THE SHORT OF ENVIRONMENTAL DEFENCE

14

by Jerry Valen DeMarco

"Will the defenders of nature please rise?"
                                    Arne Naess
*"I speak for the trees, for the trees
      have no tongues."*
                                    Dr. Seuss
*"The Master's tools will never dismantle
      the Master's house."*
                                    Audre Lorde

Introduction

A DESIRE TO PROTECT NATURE LIES DEEP WITHIN THE psyches of many who engage in the environmental debate. Many act out of concern for their own species, *Homo sapiens*, and for its future generations. Others seek to show that our present use of the environment is inefficient, sub-optimal – economically unsound. Another camp worries about cutting off future use options by forever transforming the planetary ecosystem. A final group seeks to protect nature for its own sake. While this list is both incomplete and oversimplified, it does show that being an environmentalist can mean a great many things. Although I find myself arguing according to all of the philosophies that underlie the above contentions depending on the issue and the forum, I would place my ideology firmly in the final category.[1]

This essay is intended to be practical in a sense. That is, I hope to demonstrate that one can practice environmental defence through intervention in the legal forum while being true to one's biocentric or ecocentric ideals.[2] The ethics that support legal doctrine are often purely anthropocentric (human-centred). A number of these ethical perspectives will be alluded to but the focus will be on those that support the legal doctrine, such as efficient use and rights-based arguments.

Their weaknesses as compared to approaches based on the intrinsic value of nature will be noted.

Examples of those arguments that succeed in protecting nature will be analyzed. Invariably, those that achieve the most in terms of short-term success are those that challenge the ethical *status quo* the least. The recurring question to keep in mind is this: will short-term successes achieved through today's dominant legal discourse compromise long-term hopes for a less ecologically destructive existence?

Environmental Ethics

A daunting number of relatively distinct ethical perspectives is appealed to in efforts to protect nature.[3] The most important differentiation to be made amongst them is the use/non-use distinction. Use-based arguments are generally couched in terms of nature's utility to humans. For the purposes of this paper, the concept of use is defined broadly such that use can mean everything from converting a wild river into hydroelectricity to hunting waterfowl to appreciating a scenic vista to consuming meat. Nature is understood as resource. Non-use arguments, on the other hand, generally speak of nature's right to exist for its own sake.

A similar but not completely analogous distinction is the difference between the anthropocentric view and non-anthropocentric perspectives such as deep ecology, biocentrism and ecocentrism. Arne Naess calls it the difference between deep and shallow ecology.[4] Shallow or reform arguments deal mainly with the health and well-being of people as opposed to deep ecology's focus on life, the Earth and the connections between them. Biocentrism is based on a reverence for all life as opposed to only human life or the lives of "higher" beings. Ecocentrism views humans as simple members of an ecosphere where other life-forms, species and communities are inter-related and inter-dependent. Conversely, anthropocentrism places humans at the centre of concern and justifies the protection of nature for purely human ends.[5] Since I have defined use broadly, little emphasis will be placed on the distinction between use-based arguments and anthropocentric arguments. They are both at odds with the protection of those aspects of nature that serve no apparent human end.

Ethical Relevancy

At the core of all ethics is the concept of relevancy. Relevant interests are those for which a duty or obligation is owed, according to the ethic. For illustrative purposes, Roderick Nash's progressive axis of "ethical extension" can be used to show units of ethical relevancy.[6] The categories of ethically relevant groups and individuals vary amongst ethical perspectives. The most limited ethic would be one concerned solely with the actions of the actor ("self"). An ethic which looked at the universe and all sub-categories would be the most all-encompassing. About halfway down the axis is the step from humans to non-human entities. This jump is a crucial one in terms of environmental ethics because it marks the dividing line between what is generally excluded and included from concern in an anthropocentric worldview.

SELF

FAMILY

TRIBE

REGION

NATION

RACE

HUMANS

ANIMALS

PLANTS

LIFE

ROCKS

ECOSYSTEMS

PLANET

UNIVERSE

FIGURE 1: Ethical Relevancy[7]

Nash has developed another axis of historical rights extension. This figure illustrates the expanding relevancy of certain groups via the inclusion of some of their rights in Western law.

Natural Rights

English Barons (Magna Carta, 1215)

American Colonists
(Declaration of Independence, 1776)

Slaves (Emancipation Proclamation, 1863)

Women (Nineteenth Amendment, 1920)

Native Americans
(Indian Citizenship Act, 1924)

Labourers (Fair Labor Standards Act, 1938)

Blacks (Civil Rights Act, 1957)

Nature (Endangered Species Act, 1973)

FIGURE 2: Rights Expansion[8]

When compared to the first axis, one can see that Western law has been slowly expanding its concept of ethically relevant groups through legal recognition. Nash sees the inclusion of a segment of nature as another step in the extension of rights in American liberalism.[9] Aldo Leopold calls it a process of "ecological evolution."[10]

As each group is afforded legal rights, recognition of their moral standing is, at least in part, achieved. It may be that nature (especially endangered species) is a relevant human concern, but is not possessed of legal rights *per se*. So long as nature protection legislation remains chiefly concerned with protecting nature for purely human ends, as opposed to intrinsic value, rights will be absent. In fact, given nature's limited legal and moral standing, it is not surprising that species extinctions are proceeding much more rapidly now than ever before.[11]

Many environmental ethics, to one degree or another, support environmental laws. What follows is a discussion of the main environmental ethics proposed in the literature. Note that there is overlap amongst categories. As well, more pluralistic ethics which incorporate portions of different ethical perspectives have been espoused by writers such as Christopher Stone.[12]

Sentience and Rights

The notion of the capacity to suffer as the measuring stick for ethical consideration is epitomised by the ideas of Jeremy Bentham. In this framework, "lower" animals are excluded from human concern. The dividing line is one limited by our interpretation of the ability of animals to experience pain. At the very least it excludes plants. This view is behind calls for the "humane" treatment of animals. It has spawned "Animal Welfare Acts" in many jurisdictions. These acts are often limited to domestic animals. For instance, a wild fox caught in a leg-hold trap would not find legal protection in an animal protection act aimed at domestic animals. As well, individual animals are the focus as opposed to species or natural communities. That is, concern is directed at the "rights" of the individual.[13]

Conferring rights, in a legal sense, on domestic animals may seem sensible to some degree as such animals are, in part, products of human interference. This is similar to the recognition of the legal standing of human constructions such as trusts and corporations. It is based on the understanding that domestic animals possess more of the characteristics of human property than do wild ones.

Some have called for the extension of rights to many other forms of nature. Stone's "Should Trees Have Standing?" popularized the issue of grounding the protection of nature in legal rights.[14] Stone argued for the expansion of standing doctrine to

the point of including non-human entities.[15] Speaking for the trees has its problems, however, according to John Livingston:

Taken to the extreme, the result of the extension of rights would be to "humanize", or domesticate the entire planet. All life would be a human farm [...]

If the domestication of the planet is thought desirable, the price of total conquest would be to confer rights on all species conquered, usable against everyone. But past evidence of the human conquest of nature displays massive extinctions, widespread suffering and disfigurement [...]

The need is not to invest endless time, energy and creativity in futile attempts to rationalize rights for non-humans within the existing belief structure, but rather to systematically address, with every intellectual tool at our disposal, the pathological species-chauvinist belief structure itself. The humanist tradition dictates that people have absolute rights against all things non-human, and that the human interest is the court of last resort.[16]

Rights language, by its very nature, cannot divest itself of its human-centred origins. The granting of individual rights, according to the sentience criterion or any other, would do little for nature as a whole. That is, an entire ecosystem could be dismantled (or euphemistically speaking: developed) regardless of the rights of its individual members if other rights, namely human rights, were deemed more important. As well, in balancing the rights of nature against the rights of humans and property, there is no assurance that nature would take precedence nor that an appropriate rights-guardian could be determined. Just as women and minorities are still faced with discrimination even though their rights have been legally recognised, so too could nature. Jennifer Caldwell says that Stone's theory, "in using concepts constructed by humans for their own benefit [...] suffers from the very weakness that Stone deplores."[17] That is, simply extending human guardianship to cover nature would fail to fundamentally challenge the human-centred perspective that, itself, ultimately leads to much ecological harm.[18]

At present, the existence of animal rights legislation does not limit our use of nature, but rather addresses the concerns of those who are offended by the cruel treatment of animals. Focus on the rights of the individual, however, often obscures larger problems of extinction and habitat destruction. This is evidenced by the protests of animal rights advocates vis-a-vis efforts to protect native flora and fauna by eradicating non-native mammals such as goats and pigs.[19] According to Mark Sagoff:

> [...] the moral obligation to preserve species is not an obligation to individual creatures. It cannot, then, be an obligation that rests on rights.[20]

Preserving nature as a whole requires a different approach rather than a refinement of the individual rights concept. Holmes Rolston III puts it this way:

> When we try to use culturally extended rights and psychologically based utilities to protect the flora or even the insentient fauna, to protect endangered species or ecosystems, we can only stammer.[21]

Individual animal rights, and animal liberation in general, are laudable goals for which to strive but they will not ensure the preservation of nature.

Interconnectedness

Reductionist thinking is challenged by holism. Holistic ethics seek to consider the larger picture rather than to simply distil general rules and theories from observation. Charlene Spretnak describes a holistic approach known as ecological postmodernism in this way:

> Ecological postmodernism [...] encourages us to expand the gestalt, our perception of the whole, in every situation so that we no longer collaborate in the modern project of fragmentation, with its championing of certain fragments above all else. Just as modern scientists discounted and ignored perturbations observed outside of the accepted model, so modern economists ignored the effects of unqualified economic growth on the "fragment" of the whole that is nature. Modern statesmanship proceeded by ignoring the sovereignty of native peoples, a "fragment" that was clearly outside the accepted model, and modern rationalists denied any spiritual perceptions as anomalous quirks not to be mentioned.[22]

A holistic approach would focus on the interactions of the community rather than the rights of the individual. As much of legal doctrine focuses on the individual, a shift to relational/ holistic thinking would indeed require profound changes to the atomistic workings of the legal system.[23]

Aspects of Leopold's "Land Ethic,"[24] and indeed many environmental ethics, stress the importance of connectivity. According to Leopold, "a thing is right when it tends to preserve the integrity, stability and beauty of the biotic community. It is wrong when it tends otherwise."[25] A focus limited to the community or ecosystem, however, can exclude some species. According to David Ehrenfeld, "Leopold leaves us with no justification for preserving those animals, plants and habitats that [...] are almost certainly not essential to the 'healthy functioning' of any large ecosystem."[26]

Holism lies behind legislation that requires the examination of cumulative environmental impacts and much government policy. While holistic ethics are not inherently anthropocentric, applied holism has been normally human focused. Emphasis is placed on humankind's dependency on the biosphere. Rolston notes:

Fortunately, it is often evident that human welfare depends on ecosystemic support, and in this sense all our legislation about clean air, clean water, soil conservation, national and state forest policies, pollution controls, renewable resources, and so forth is concerned about ecosystem-level processes.[27]

In the context of the *Great Lakes Water Quality Agreement*'s "ecosystem approach," Anne Bell notes that the anthropocentric "life-support system"[28] (what befalls the earth befalls humankind) view of interconnectedness can be problematic:

The current widespread support for the ecosystem approach masks a fundamental philosophical conflict between ecocentric and anthropocentric attitudes toward nature. Yet as the ecological crisis deepens and life-sustaining "resources" are further depleted, the latent contradiction is bound to surface. While businesses, government and private citizens seem prepared to act out of enlightened self-interest, more difficult choices lie ahead [...]

The currently predominant interpretation of the ecosystem approach fails to challenge in any fundamental sense, the way we live our lives – and therein lies much of its appeal.[29]

She notes, for example, that implementation of the ecosystem approach, as evidenced by an analysis of research funding allocation, has been biased in favour of economically significant species.

An additional problem with policy based on the "life-support system" notion is that it is at the mercy of the incompleteness of the knowledge of anthropogenic effects and the unpredictability of such effects. It is also exceedingly difficult to implement as ecosystem-level effects often cover many different jurisdictions.

Ethics and laws based on interconnectedness alone will not protect nature completely or equally.

Levels of interests are based on the individual's or species' role in the "web of life." "Keystone" species, those that are perceived to keep the ecosystem intact, are given special consideration. For those that contribute little to the maintenance of the functioning biosphere or for those at the mercy of our incomplete understanding, interconnectedness-based ethics offer little hope.[30]

Wise Use

Traditional conservation, normally associated with Gifford Pinchot, is concerned with the wise and efficient use of natural resources. Pinchot pointed out that "conservation did not mean protecting or preserving nature."[31] Rather, its goal is to "control nature and serve the material interests of humankind but with an eye to long-term needs" according to a "gospel of efficiency."[32] The movement is decidedly anthropocentric and utilitarian. Of all environmental ethics, efficient use is closest to the mainstream. It simply extends the ambit of concern farther into the future (sometimes including future human generations[33]).

Conservation lies behind much of forest management, soil management, energy policy, environmental impact assessment and export policy. Traditional conservation has been reincarnated under the rubric of "sustainable development" as defined by the World Commission on Environment and Development.[34] It does nothing to question our use of nature, but rather seeks to make our use more efficient in order to satisfy the maximum public good. It is arguably not so much a distinct environmental ethic but rather an extended utilitarian ethic. Paul Shepard went as far as calling it "the most insidious form of nature hating because it poses as a virtue, as prudent, foreseeing, and unselfish."[35]

According to traditional conservation, the preservation of landscapes is to serve a human demand – only the commodities are aesthetic landscapes[36] and recreational havens, not pulp and paper. According to Thomas Birch, nature has been placed "on the supermarket shelf of values, along with everything else."[37] Ramachandra Guha contends that nature, in the Western world, has been packaged and enjoyed like any other commodity.[38] In that sense, benefit for nature is merely incidental to landscape preservation for human ends.[39]

Aboriginal spokesperson Marie Wilson has this to say about environmentalists who support conservation-based preservationism:

[...] the Indian attitude toward the natural world is different from the environmentalists'. I have had the awful feeling that when we are finished dealing with the courts and our land claims, we will then have to battle the environmentalists. [...] I feel quite sick at this prospect because the environmentalists want these beautiful places kept in a state of perfection: to not touch them, rather to keep them pure. So that we can leave our jobs and for two weeks we can venture into the wilderness and enjoy this ship in a bottle.[40]

The chasm between the "humans apart from nature" view and the "humans as a part of nature" perspective is nowhere more evident than in the conflict between aboriginal peoples and park advocates. Preservation, however, is not simply limited to such an interpretation. Preservationist arguments can also be made according to both ecocentric and biocentric perspectives.

Intrinsic Rightness

The notion "that nature has intrinsic[41] value and consequently possesses at least the right to exist" is the cornerstone of the positions labelled "biocentrism," "ecocentrism," and "deep ecology."[42] The idea has been traced back to the seventeenth century.[43] Ehrenfeld calls it the recognition of the rights of non-resources, "including species that have no significance to people or even to the healthy functioning of the ecosystem."[44]

While biocentrism's focus on life and ecocentrism's concern aimed at the well-being of the whole ecosphere distinguish themselves from one another, their premise is based on the intrinsic value of nature. Deep ecology can be viewed as a philosophical movement that incorporates aspects of both biocentrism and ecocentrism.[45] Naess sums up the deep ecology position in seven precepts:

1. Rejection of the man-in-environment image in favour of the relational total-field image.

2. Biospherical (or ecological) egalitarianism in principle.

3. Principles of diversity and of symbiosis.

4. Anti-class posture.

5. Fight against pollution and resource depletion.

6. Complexity, not complication.

7. Local autonomy and decentralization.[46]

The first two points best demonstrate how deep ecology draws on both ecocentrism and biocentrism. Alongside the "intrinsic value" notion, the view of humans as part of nature rather than dominant over or apart from it characterizes these ethical approaches.[47] The purpose of wildlife and wilderness preservation according to the intrinsic value of nature, and not its resource value has been defined as follows:

The preservation of wildlife forms and groups of forms in perpetuity, for their own sakes, irrespective of any connotation of present or future human use.[48]

This view of preservation is clearly "antithetical to the self-interest position"[49] that lies behind wise use (conservation), many manifestations of environmental holism (life-support system) and Western society's National Parks systems.

Rolston takes issue with anthropocentric ethics in the following fashion:

There is something overspecialized about an ethic, held by the dominant class of Homo sapiens, *that regards the welfare of only one of several million species as an object and beneficiary of duty.*[50]

Ehrenfeld would probably substitute "arrogant" for "overspecialized" while Livingston would likely choose "chauvinistic." Either way, it is clear that the concept of the "intrinsic rightness" of nature without reference to humankind's preferences and uses separates this view from all resourcist and anthropocentric ethics.

Irreconcilable Differences

On one hand, there is clearly overlap between some ethical concepts. On the other hand, there is conflict even within a seemingly uniform perspective such as anthropocentrism. In reference to environmental debate, for instance, Neil Evernden makes the following observation regarding the extreme philosophical gap that exists between mainstream human-centred environmentalism and the equally human-centred goals of industrialism:

Environmentalists will assert that if the current action continues, our future well-being will be imperiled and our children will inherit a blighted planet. Cease, they say, and learn to live in a small-scale, cooperative society without the constant pressure for growth and transformation. Industrialists may reply that it is all very well for the impractical environmentalist to advocate such irresponsible action, but if their policies were ever to be put in place, our life-style would be in jeopardy, jobs would be lost, and food shortages would loom. To the environmentalists, what is at risk is the very possibility of leading a good life. To the industrialists, what is at risk is the very possibility of leading a good life. The debate, it appears, is actually about *what constitutes a good life*.[51]

Mutually exclusive worldviews have collided. Of course, the gap between non-anthropocentrists and resourcists is much wider still. Although in certain instances the same environmental policy can accommodate different perspectives, over time, values change and new information may be added to make the resourcist calculus shift from

protecting nature to using it.[52] As biodiversity plummets and consumption and human population increase, the ability of anthropocentric arguments to adequately protect nature approaches the vanishing point. Given that, can the adoption of human-centred legal argumentation be justified if the true goal is to effect change at the fundamental level of ethical obligations?

Defending Nature

Undoubtedly, the most suitable form of intervention will depend on the milieu in which the environmental debate is being played out. In the Canadian environmental context, Linda Duncan notes that:

Many have lost patience waiting for change. They are turning to increasingly desperate means to bring attention to the fate of the earth – endangered species, disappearing wildlands, contamination of air, water and the soils, and for some, a disappearing way of life.

Where dialogue or petitions have failed to generate government action, many have opted for more desperate measures – blockades, marches, tree-spiking and other forms of sabotage.

And, while generally thought of as less litigious than our neighbours to the south, Canadians are turning to the courts.[53]

Environmentalists generally view litigation as the last resort. Unfortunately, in a great many instances it does eventually come down to the last resort. Political lobbying, garnering media attention and participation in public consultation processes are all undertaken, but they do not always work in favour of nature. The industrialist's voice is often too strong to overcome in both the media and political forums. In public consultation exercises, the interests behind use and industrial development are well represented.

The high cost of litigation is enough to deter most environmentalists. Environmental groups often operate on shoestring budgets. Those that are more radical in nature are often denied charitable status (donations are not tax deductible). The narrow scope of debate also discourages would-be intervenors. Often, broad environmental issues can only be "hooked onto" one narrow aspect of the law – often involving administrative law. For instance, the main legal issue involved in British Columbia's recent Clayoquot Sound debate (aside from the arrests) was the rate of tree "harvest." There was law available which could be used to quarrel with the "sustainability" of logging but not the "appropriateness" of logging. Nevertheless, the use of the legal regime by environmental advocates is increasing. It is extremely valuable in expanding public awareness and can sometimes succeed in protecting nature.

The Ethical Bases for Existing Law

In efforts to defend nature through the legal system, it is virtually impossible to escape resourcism.[54] Whether the argument is made according to the public interest, the right to a healthy environment, sustainability or even the rights of endangered species, legal success almost invariably involves demonstrating an unwise human *use* of the environment. The *World Charter for Nature*, which has little legal weight, is one of the only environmental laws that refers to the intrinsic value of nature.[55] Even the United States Endangered Species Act's purpose is to preserve species that are "of aesthetic, ecological, educational, historical, recreational, and scientific value to the Nation and its people."[56] In general, "[l]egislation defines the environment as something to be used; a natural resource to be managed for human benefit. The Environment itself is a legal non entity."[57]

Another serious shortcoming is that, on simple anthropocentric grounds, the current state of environmental law fails to deliver. According to

James M. Olson:

The institutional framework served well for specific issues, particularly those involving procedural reform. But when the problems are large, multi-faceted, multi-jurisdictional, and involve scientific uncertainty, the framework is inadequate.[58]

The reality is that most environmental problems fall within the latter category.

Ten years ago, P.S. Elder, in response to Stone's "Should Trees Have Standing?", opined that environmental problems can be taken care of simply, without extending rights to nature. He said, in paradigmatic humanistic language, "it follows that we can identify any matter of concern and legislate about it, if we want to."[59] His suggestions included:

[...] legislate environmental criteria which must be considered by decision-makers and allow court challenges under broader rules of standing for failure to meet minimum standards of procedure or substance in decision-making, guarantee the rights to public interest groups or concerned citizens to participate in open hearings with full information and financial aid to intervenors; extend environmental impact assessment to include the social and economic environments, and mandate a more searching inquiry of broad alternatives to the proposed project.[60]

Elder proved prophetic. Virtually all of the above suggestions have been incorporated into the body of environmental law. We did identify the matter of concern and we did legislate about it, but unfortunately that has not translated into an improvement in the environmental state of affairs. The assumptions that underlay Elder's proposals were simply untenable. For instance: participation does not ensure the completeness of inquiry;[61] information is never full; and the predictability of impacts is imprecise at best. Marginal environmental law reform has done wonders, however, for the dockets of practising environmental lawyers. Ehrenfeld would not be surprised. In *The Arrogance of Humanism*, he successfully exposes the fallacy of humanism's principal assumption – that all problems are soluble by people.[62] This supreme faith in human reason is misguided. Most biocentrists, ecocentrists and deep ecologists would agree.

The Long and the Short

"The end result is what matters," say those concerned with practical environmentalism. Any argument that succeeds is a good argument to use according to this consequentialist perspective. More often than not such arguments will be phrased according to the "public interest." In using the courts as a means to protect nature, virtually all legal "hooks" necessitate the use of resourcist language. Quite often such arguments succeed in securing outcomes environmentalists desire. When governments fail to act according to the strict letter of the law or according to the public interest, legal intervention can be used to force them to carry out what they have been established to do.

Using the language of the legal system can indeed accomplish a great many laudable environmental goals. If the objectives are short-term and do not challenge the underlying assumptions of the legal system, there is little reason for concern. The legal system in such cases can be an appropriate forum for resolution. However, for a great many environmentalists, pressing issues are simply manifestations of underlying pathologies. Such pathologies can not be treated by the existing regime. Audre Lorde, in the feminism context, says that "[t]he Master's tools will never dismantle the Master's house."[63] Similarly, in protecting nature through resourcist argumentation, the pillars of resourcism will never be felled. All that will be challenged is "the efficiency in being what we

are."[64]

Evernden notes the problems of arguing strictly according to enlightened human self-interest:

In seizing arguments that would sound persuasive even to indifferent observers environmentalists have come to adopt the strategy and assumptions of their opponents. As Anthony Brandt has observed, the industrialist and environmentalist tacitly agree on one thing: that nature is for something. Nature is a conglomeration of natural resources, a storehouse of materials. 'The industrialist and the environmentalist are brothers in the same skin; they differ merely as to the best use the natural world ought to be put to.'[65] In their haste to persuade society of the significance of the non-human they have succumbed to the temptations of expediency. They have endorsed the search for subterfuges, for ways to encourage the behaviour they want, without having to contend with the attitudes embraced by the majority.[66]

Shallow arguments are doomed to failure whenever the public interest "can be perceived as lying elsewhere."[67] In other words:

Prudential, self-interested concerns do not...provide a comprehensive insurance policy for nature. They provide coverage only insofar as there is existing or potential harm to human health and welfare, and then only if that harm is perceived.[68]

Evernden points to the newspaper filler reports that say that "science had determined the current worth of the human body to be $12.98...by adding up the market value of the materials which make [it] up."[69] When environmental arguments are phrased strictly according to the resourcist terms that underlie much of economics and law, they "vastly underestimate" and "completely misunderstand" the value of nature, just as the $12.98

figure absurdly approximates the value of human life.[70]

Many, however, fall into this convenient trap. While scientist Edward O. Wilson, in *The Diversity of Life*, recognizes that if "a price can be put on something, that something can be devalued, sold, and discarded"[71], he stumbles into the resourcist hollow in his concluding plea for the preservation of biodiversity:

> We should judge every scrap of biodiversity as priceless while we learn to use it and come to understand what it means to humanity.[72]

While arguing according to self-interest is eminently natural for the anthropocentric environmentalist, to one who is not simply concerned with humankind, it can be perceived as selling one's soul. Bill Devall notes the practical dilemma that can be faced by the intervening deep ecologist:

> In practical political debates, arguments based on reform [anthropocentric] and deep perspectives are both appropriate in certain situations. But the weaknesses of reform arguments should also be noted. In particular I am concerned with the dilemma of environmental activists who feel they must use reform arguments in order to be understood by political decision-makers and who reject using deep arguments because they are seen as too subversive. In using reformist arguments, however, activists help to legitimate and reinforce the human-centered (anthropocentric) worldview of decision-makers.[73]

Livingston compares this dilemma to that faced by Aristotle's would-be politician:

> If you describe the nature of environmental problems as you truly understand and believe it to be, you will be labelled a misanthropist, the public will reject you, and you will be hoisted on the horn of futility. If,

on the other hand, you waffle on about manipulative techniques toward within-the-system solutions, you will have rejected both natural philosophy and yourself. You will be horned by your own set of personal deities. The dilemma: futility or self-deception.[74]

What of the non-anthropocentric lawyer *cum* defender of nature then? Devall, who is not a lawyer, feels that he "can bring forth a deep ecology position as well as work on the practical, sometimes anthropocentric, strategies."[75] Unfortunately, in law, anthropocentric strategies do not surface sometimes – they are the only game in town. Livingston warns that intervening is a risky business:

> Is it even remotely possible, then, for the deep ecologist to assume a public position that can begin to be useful, and without backfiring? I think it may be, but one must be very, very careful in both the conceptualization and the execution. We must check both our motives and our arguments every step of the way, lest we delude ourselves into believing in the purity of those motives and arguments. The pit of self-delusion is always close at hand.[76]

In *Deep Ecology*, Devall and George Sessions note that defending nature can take on many acceptable forms:

> Ecological resistance [...] means defending natural diversity through education, public speaking, and use of lawsuits; trying to convert public opinion to the cause; and informing politicians and decision makers. Resistance is another name for affirmation – joyful affirmation of the integrity of Nature, natural diversity, and minimum human impact on place.[77]

There may be a role for the non-anthropocentric lawyer who wishes "to participate in the rescue of at least some tattered remnants of non-human nature,"[78] but the duality of objectives must never be forgotten. One must do everything possible now, in the short term, to save what is left of natural diversity. If and when anthropocentrism is ever abandoned and the long term objective is finally achieved, it would be lamentable if most of the *bios* were already extinguished. In securing short-term victories, the resourcist horn must not be further sharpened. That is not easily avoided. One must be clear about intentions. This route must be recognized as but one arm of a strategy – a strategy for the meantime.

I have not attempted to show that anthropocentrism is an ethic that should logically be rejected. Regardless of reason, rationality and logic, my ethical stance ultimately comes from the heart and not the mind. While I hope that biocentrism and ecocentrism gain further acceptance, the reality of the present-day dominance of resourcist ethics must not be ignored. Resourcism underlies much of the law and political debate. Its tenets are enshrined in classical economics and humanism. For those who think biocentrically or ecocentrically but for reasons of short-term gains feel forced to argue according to the prevailing resourcist story, the dilemma is great. Both challenging from within and from without, however, are necessary to effect change. As well, "law may not create new realities, but it can mediate the debate between those who are satisfied with the *status quo* and those who are striving to visualize alternatives and put them into practice."[79] In essence, legal environmentalism can be the short-term means to ensure that the long-term dream remains a possibility.

A shift away from anthropocentrism, if it ever occurs, will take years and years. For the endangered species and places of today, there is no time to wait, for extinction is permanent.[80] In fact, using legal argument may be the only hope for much of threatened nature. We would be remiss if we did not use such means.

ENDNOTES

[1] I have not consciously been concerned with the intrinsic value of nature throughout my "environmental" life. As a boy, my original tendency to be concerned for nature stemmed from being an amateur naturalist. I was particularly interested in birds and was awed by the array of forms in which they had evolved. I am sure that one of the reasons I was saddened by stories of the extinctions of the Labrador Duck, the Great Auk, the Carolina Parakeet and the Passenger Pigeon was partly due to the fact that I knew that I would never be able to see a living "specimen." With endangered species such as the Whooping Crane or the Eskimo Curlew, a similar concern arose. This made seeing threatened birds all the more satisfying, for there was a chance that very few people would ever see one.

However, the perceived increased value of finding a rarity ate away at me slowly but surely. Why would I be less pleased to see the backyard commoners such as Blue Jays and American Robins than a Whooping Crane? I did not grasp the philosophical distinction that lay at the heart of this conundrum for many years. In the meantime, my bird list grew and grew. When I was old enough to drive, I sometimes ventured many miles to see a rarity that I heard about through the birders' grapevine.

As a student and traveller in Europe, I began to understand what was bothering me about rarity and "listing." At that time, my awareness of environmental degradation and its causes was developing at a rapid rate. In England, when I had the chance to go birding, it was a strange experience. Birding in Britain often means sitting in a blind patiently waiting for birds to avail themselves of a marsh constructed by the local naturalist club. On occasion I felt like Elmer Fudd, only my greatest joy would be "ticking" off a new species for my list rather than blowing it out of the sky. Aside from that one important distinction there was little to choose between weekend hunter and amateur ornithologist. I was peering through an expensive optical device, driving many miles to get there, and rarely thinking about the absurdity of the entire exercise. In another sense it was philately – only the items collected were just listed in a book rather than fastened to its pages.

One lunch time a White Stork flew in from the North Sea and graced us with its presence for a short time. Almost instantly there was a traffic jam of birders from all neighbouring towns. One of my colleagues in the blind had raced to the pay phone when the stork arrived. A few minutes later the telephone-tree worked its wonders and hundreds of cars clogged the lanes around the marsh. Not coincidentally the stork flew off at the outset of all of the commotion and only the first arrivals obtained this prized addition to their lists.

That evening, when I returned to the marsh for a dusky walk, the stork came back. This time there was no one there to alert the local birding constituency. As I sat there and watched it carefully wade through the estuarine reeds, I did some rough calculations of the impact of that noon-hour horde of well-intentioned birders. I extrapolated it by adding up all the similar incidents being played out elsewhere in the bird-loving world. While my conclusions were wrought with assumptions and untested methods, I was sure of one thing: if birding and like pursuits were everyone's idea of respecting nature, we would soon love the planet's inhabitants to death. I then decided that I was going to do my best to save nature from our actions, those well-intentioned but misguided and those not. I guessed that the most tangible of accomplishments could be won through the courts. It was time to go to law school.

Years after that stork-induced decision, I find myself immersed in a career in environmental defence. Fittingly, I am as troubled about using the court system to protect nature as I was the day I contemplated the environmental ramifications of a stork alighting in a marsh in Cley-next-the-Sea, East Anglia.

This time though the ethical considerations are quite different. While I was easily able to find less destructive manners in which to appreciate nature subsequent to the stork's visit, I am not at all sure that the concern for the intrinsic value of nature that underlies many of my actions has any place in successful legal argument. Will I only succeed in protecting nature by demonstrating its utility to humans, whether as game, primary resource, scenery or other useful commodity?

²Biocentrism is a life-centred perspective that reveres life itself and imputes inherent value to all individual living beings. Ecocentrism is also concerned with the intrinsic value of nature but adds a holistic and inter-connected view of the ecosphere that includes species, natural communities and the physical landscape. It is often termed Earth-centred but home-centred is also used.

³For an introduction to the field of environmental ethics, see Des Jardins, Joseph R., *Environmental Ethics: An Introduction to Environmental Philosophy*: Belmont, California: Wadsworth, 1993 and Pojman, Louis P., ed., *Environmental Ethics: Readings and Theory and Application*, Boston: Jones and Bartlett, 1994.

⁴Naess, Arne, "The Shallow and the Deep, Long-Range Ecology Movement: A Summary," *Inquiry* 16, Spring 1973, p. 96.

⁵Both philosopher John Passmore and conservationist Aldo Leopold moved away (at least in part) from anthropocentrism over the course of their lifetimes. After publishing *Man's Responsibility for Nature* (London: Duckworth, 1974), Passmore changed his resourcist view: "We do need a "new metaphysics" which is genuinely not anthropocentric... The working out of such a metaphysics is, in my judgement, the most important task which lies

ahead of philosophy." (Devall, Bill, and Sessions, George, *Deep Ecology*, Salt Lake City: Peregrine Smith Books, 1985, p. 53). See Passmore, "Attitudes Toward Nature," Peters, R.S., ed., *Nature and Conduct*, New York: St. Martin's Press, 1975. Similarly, Leopold "underwent a dramatic conversion from the 'stewardship' shallow ecology resource-management mentality of man-over-nature to announce that humans should see themselves as 'plain members' of the biotic community" (Seed, John, "Anthropocentrism," in Devall and Sessions, p. 245).

⁶Nash, Roderick, *The Rights of Nature: A History of Environmental Ethics*, Madison: The University of Wisconsin Press, 1989, p. 5.

⁷Nash, p. 5.

⁸Nash, p. 7.

⁹Nash, p. 12. See also Christopher Stone's discussion of the "unthinkable" in "Should Trees Have Standing?: Toward Legal Rights for Natural Objects," *Southern California Law Review* 45, 1972, pp. 450-501.

¹⁰Leopold, Aldo, *A Sand County Almanac and Sketches Here and There*, New York: Oxford University Press, 1989, p. 202 (originally published in 1949).

¹¹Edward O. Wilson is of the view that "[t]he sixth great extinction spasm of geologic time is upon us, grace of mankind. Earth has at last acquired a force that can break the crucible of biodiversity." The force, of course, is *Homo sapiens*. Wilson, Edward O., *The Diversity of Life*, New York: W. W. Norton & Company, 1993, p. 343.

¹²See Stone, Christopher D., "The Environment in Moral Thought," *Tennessee Law Review* 56, Fall 1988, pp. 1-11, and *Earth and Other Ethics: The Case for Moral Pluralism*, New York: Harper & Row, 1987. Stone sums up the problems of trying to resolve everything in a simple ethical statement: "[...] moral monism's ambitions [...] to unify all ethics within a single framework capable of yielding the One Right Answer to all our quandaries, collide with the variety of things whose considerableness commands some intuitive appeal: normal persons in a common moral community, persons remote in time and space, embryos and fetuses, nations and nightingales, beautiful things and sacred things. Some of these things we may value because of their intelligence (higher animals); with others, sentience seems the key (lower life). On the other hand, the moral standing of membership groups, such as nation-states, cultures, and species has to stand on some other footing, since the group itself (the species, as distinct from the individual whale) manifests no intelligence and experiences no pain. Other entities are genetically human, either capable of experiencing pain (advanced fetuses) or nonsentient (early embryos), but lack, at the time of our dealings with them, full human capacities. Trying to force all these diverse entities into a single mold – the One Big, Sparsely Principled Compre-

hensive Theory – forces us to disregard come of our moral intuitions, and to dilute our principles into unhelpfully bland generalities. The commitment is not only quixotic; it imposes strictures on thought that stifle the emergence of more valid approaches" (1988, p. 10).

[13]Rights-based arguments can be linked to both deontological ethics and utilitarianism. Deontological ethics are based on acting on principles or maxims (in Immanuel Kant's words). This can be contrasted with utilitarian ethics which are based on the consequences of a given course of action. See Des Jardins, pp. 29-35, 115-118 and Pojman, p. 25.

[14]Stone, 1972. See also Tribe, Laurence H., "Ways Not To Think About Plastic Trees: New Foundations for Environmental Law," *Yale Law Journal* 83:7, 1974, pp. 1315-1348.

[15]Corporations had already made the leap.

[16]Livingston, John, "Rightness or Rights?", *Osgoode Hall Law Journal* 22:2, Summer 1984a, pp. 320-321.

[17]Caldwell, Jennifer, An Ecological Approach to Environmental Law, Auckland, New Zealand: Legal Research Foundation Inc., 1988, p. 156.

[18]Some authors avoid traditional ethics language altogether because it carries with it so much humanist baggage: "...the current arguments about environmental ethics are incoherent because they use terms that only make sense in a system which has an agreed concept of human purpose and direction a *telos*. At present, such terms as rights, interests, utility and duty are all disguises for a determination to hold on to power" (Simmons, I.G., *Interpreting Nature: Cultural Constructions of the Environment*, London: Routledge, 1993, p. 121).

[19]The Galapagos and Hawaiian Islands are good examples.

[20]Sagoff, Mark, "Animal Liberation and Environmental Ethics: Bad Marriage, Quick Divorce," *Osgoode Hall Law Journal* 22:2, Summer 1984, p. 306.

[21]Rolston, Holmes III, "Environmental Ethics: Values in and Duties to the Natural World," in Bormann, F. Herbert, and Kellert, Stephen R., eds., *Ecology, Economics, Ethics: The Broken Circle*, New Haven: Yale University Press, 1991, p.74.

[22]Spretnak, Charlene, *States of Grace*, San Francisco: HarperSanFrancisco, 1991, pp.19-20.

[23]One incarnation of environmental holism is the Gaia hypothesis of James Lovelock (*Gaia: A New Look at Life on Earth*, Oxford: Oxford University Press, 1979). From the Gaia perspective "individual beings and species such as *Homo sapiens* [are] to the earth as cells and organs [are] to their own bodies – parts of indivisible wholes" (Nash, p. 157). The planet therefore possesses "the traditional requirements for ethical considerability: consciousness, the ability to feel pain, and an interest or capacity for what might be termed happiness" (Nash, p.157). The interests of the earth

are primary to those of the components according to this approach.

[24]Leopold, p. 201.

[25]Leopold, p. 225.

[26]Ehrenfeld, David, *The Arrogance of Humanism*, Oxford: Oxford University Press, 1978, p. 188. Aspects of the "Land Ethic", however, have inspired the development of ecocentric ethics.

[27]Rolston, 1991, p. 88.

[28]Rolston terms it "culture...tethered to the biosystem" (Rolston, Holmes III, *Environmental Ethics*, Philadelphia: Temple University Press, 1988, p. 3).

[29]Bell, Anne, "Non-human Nature and the Ecosystem Approach: The Limits of Anthropocentrism in Great Lakes Management," *Alternatives*, 20:3, July/August 1994, p. 24.

[30]"I am not so certain that (the interconnectedness argument) can protect the Houston toad, the cloud forests, and a vast host of other living things that deserve a chance to play out their evolution unhindered by the enactment of our humanistic fantasies" (Ehrenfeld, p. 192).

[31]Nash, p. 9.

[32]Nash, p. 9.

[33]See "The Rights of Future Generations" in Shrader-Frechette, K.S., *Environmental Ethics*, Pacific Grove, California: Boxwood Press, pp. 59-81.

[34]See World Commission on Environment and Development, *Our Common Future*, Oxford: Oxford University Press, 1987.

[35]Shepard, Paul, *Man in the Landscape*, New York: Alfred A. Knopf, 1967, p. 236.

[36]The aesthetics argument can render individual species commodities as well: "those like the big kangaroos that might be seen on safari, are zealously protected by conservationists [...] Yet the small, inconspicuous marsupials, such as the long-nosed bandicoot and the narrow-footed marsupial mouse, include a distressingly large number of seriously endangered or recently exterminated species" (Ehrenfeld, p. 180).

[37]Birch, Thomas, "The Incarceration of Wildness: Wilderness Areas as Prisons," *Environmental Ethics* 12:1, Spring 1990, p. 21.

[38]Guha, Ramachandra, "Radical American Environmentalism and Wilderness Preservation: a Third World Critique," *Environmental Ethics* 11:1, Spring 1989, pp. 78-79. His criticism of American wilderness preservation is, however, sometimes misdirected at deep ecology. The parks system in North America was substantially conceived out of pure human self-interest and not out of a wholly biocentric or ecocentric vision of nature.

[39]See Livingston, John, *The Fallacy of Wildlife Conservation*, Toronto: McClelland and Stewart, 1981, pp. 42-46.

"The standard self-interest argument, even at the aesthetic level, acknowledges no earthly role or place for wildlife beyond the human interest, no existence beyond the human purpose" (p. 45).

[40]Wilson, Marie, "Wings of the Eagle," in Plant, J., and Plant, C., eds., *Turtle Talk*, Philadelphia: New Society Publishers, 1990, pp. 82-83.

[41]Some authors distinguish between the terms inherent and intrinsic (see for example, Des Jardins, p. 146). I use intrinsic value in the sense that encompasses both goodness independent of human valuing (what Des Jardins calls "inherent worth") and worth that depends on humans who value (what Des Jardins terms "intrinsic value").

[42]Nash, p. 9.

[43]Not with certainty however. George Sessions points to Baruch Spinoza (1632-1677) "as the organicist who most closely anticipated both ecological consciousness and environmental ethics" (Nash, p. 20). Donald Worster contends that the seventeenth- and eighteenth-century organicists "remained convinced of the legitimacy of human control" (Nash, p. 22). See Devall and Sessions, pp. 236-242, and Worster, Donald, *Nature's Economy*, San Francisco: Cambridge University Press, 1977, pp. 47-50.

[44]Nash, p. 84.

[45]Deep ecology incorporates principles that appear similar to other perspectives including the "social ecology" approach of Murray Bookchin. The distinction between them is best highlighted by deep ecology's focus on the need for a new dominant philosophy as opposed to social ecology's emphasis on the need to change "patterns of social domination and hierarchy" (Des Jardins, p. 240). In this sense social ecology is akin to ecofeminist approaches. Ecofeminist authors such as Karen Warren draw attention to the similarities between the domination of non-human nature and the domination of women (see Warren, Karen J., "The Power and the Promise of Ecological Feminism," *Environmental Ethics* 12:2, pp. 125-146; and Gaard, Greta, ed., *Ecofeminism: Women, Animals, Nature*, Philadelphia: Temple University Press, 1993).

[46]Devall, Bill, *Simple in Means, Rich in Ends*, Salt Lake City: Peregrine Smith Books, 1988, pp. 21-22, and Naess, pp. 95-100. Another list, with slight variations depending on the source, is usually cited as the deep ecology "platform" (Des Jardins, p. 217):

1. The flourishing of human and nonhuman life on earth has intrinsic value. The value of nonhuman life-forms is independent of the usefulness these may have for narrow human purposes.

2. Richness and diversity of life-forms are values in themselves and contribute to the flourishing of human and nonhuman life on earth.

3. Humans have no right to reduce this richness and diversity except to satisfy vital needs.

4. Present human interference with the nonhuman world is excessive, and the situation is rapidly worsening.

5. The flourishing of human life and cultures is compatible with a substantial decrease of the human population. The flourishing of nonhuman life requires such a decrease.

6. Significant change of life conditions for the better requires change in policies. These affect basic economic, technological, and ideological structures.

7. The ideological change is mainly that of appreciating *life quality* (dwelling in situations of intrinsic value) rather than adhering to a high standard of living. There will be a profound awareness of the differences between big and great.

8. Those who subscribe to the foregoing points have an obligation directly or indirectly to participate in the attempt to implement the necessary changes.

[47]This point is, however, shared with some versions of interconnected-based ethics.

[48]Livingston, 1981, p. 17. Ehrenfeld's definition is: "they should be conserved because they exist and because this existence is itself but the present expression of a continuing historical process of immense antiquity and majesty" (pp. 207-208).

[49]Livingston, 1981, p. 44.

[50]Rolston, 1991, p. 96.

[51]Evernden, Neil, *The Social Creation of Nature*, Baltimore: The Johns Hopkins University Press, 1992, p. 5. Elsewhere (Evernden, Neil, *The Natural Alien*, Toronto: University of Toronto Press, 1985, p. 26), Evernden draws on E.F. Schumacher to demonstrate the conflict of worldviews: "All through school and university I had been given maps of life and knowledge on which there was hardly a trace of many of the things that I cared about and that seemed to me to be the greatest possible importance to the conduct of my life... [My perplexity] remained complete until I ceased to suspect the sanity of my perceptions and began, instead, to suspect the soundness of the maps" (Schumacher, E.F., *A Guide for the Perplexed*, New York: Harper Colophon, 1977, p. 1).

[52]See Ehrenfeld, pp. 200-204.

[53]Duncan, Linda F., *Enforcing Environmental Law: A Guide to Private Prosecution*, Edmonton: Environmental Law Centre, 1990, p. 1.

[54]Statute law often refers to the "efficient management" of natural resources. The common law normally views land as "property." For example, the "use and enjoyment of property" is often a key issue.

[55]Devall (p. 29) draws attention to this passage from the Charter: "Every form of life is unique, warranting respect regardless of its worth to man and to accord other organisms such recognition man must be guided by a moral code

of action." Another example is the preamble of the province of Ontario's "Environmental Bill of Rights, 1993," (*Statutes of Ontario*, 1993, Chapter 28) which states: "The people of Ontario recognize the inherent value of the natural environment."

[56]Nash, p. 176 (Public Law 93-205, 87 *U.S. Statutes at Large*, p. 884). Nature advocates fall into the language of resourcism even when the forum is theirs. In *Our Common Lands*, a guide to defending the National Parks system, the following heading can be found: "The Endangered Species Act: Protecting the Living Resources of the Parks" (Simon, David J., *Our Common Lands*, Washington: Island Press, 1988, p. 253).

[57]Caldwell, p. 156.

[58]Olson, James M., "Shifting the Burden of Proof: How the Common Law can Safeguard Nature and Promote an Earth Ethic," *Environmental Law* 20, 1990, p. 896.

[59]Elder, P.S., "Legal Rights for Nature – The Wrong Answer to the Right(s) Question," *Osgoode Hall Law Journal* 22:2, Summer 1984, p. 291.

[60]Elder, pp. 291-292.

[61]See Fiorino, D.J., "Environmental Risk and Democratic Process: A Critical Review," *Columbia Journal of Environmental Law* 14, 1989, pp. 501-547 regarding the participatory dilemma.

[62]Ehrenfeld's definition of humanism encompasses anthropocentrism, resourcism and faith in human reason. Edward Abbey, in *Desert Solitaire* (New York: Ballantine Books, 1968, p. 20), has another definition: "I'm a humanist; I'd rather kill a *man* than a snake."

[63]Lorde, Audre, "The Master's Tools Will Never Dismantle the Master's House," in *Sister Outsider: Essays and Speeches*, Trumansberg, New York: Crossing Press, 1984.

[64]Evernden, Neil, "The Environmentalist's Dilemma," in Evernden, Neil, ed., *The Paradox of Environmentalism*, Downsview, Ontario: York University, 1984, p. 15.

[65]Brandt, Anthony, "Views," *The Atlantic Monthly*, July 1977, p. 49.

[66]Evernden, 1985, p. 10.

[67]Evernden, 1985, p. 10.

[68]English, Mary R., "Introduction," *Tennessee Law Review* 56, Fall 1988, p. viii.

[69]Evernden, 1985, p. 10.

[70]Evernden, 1985, p. 10. We are often blind to this absurdity when we apply this thinking to nature. See also Bell, Anne, "Cost-Benefit Analysis: A Conservation Caveat," The Trumpeter: Journal of Ecosophy, 11:2, Spring 1994, pp. 93-94.

[71]Wilson, E.O., p. 348.

[72]Wilson, E.O., p. 351.

[73]Devall, p. 5.

[74]Livingston, John, "The Dilemma of the Deep Ecologist," in Evernden, Neil, ed., *The Paradox of Environmentalism*, Downsview, Ontario, 1984b, p. 63. Tribe (pp. 1330-1331) puts the dilemma this way: "What the environmentalist may not perceive is that, by couching his claims in terms of human self-interest – by articulating environmental goals wholly in terms of human needs and preferences – he may be helping to legitimate a system of discourse which so structures human thought and feeling as to erode, over the long run, the very sense of obligation which provided the initial impetus for his own protective efforts."

[75]Devall, p. 28.

[76]Livingston, 1984b, pp. 71-72.

[77]Devall and Sessions, p. 201.

[78]Livingston, 1984b, p. 61.

[79]Mickelsen, Karin, and Rees, William, "The Environment: Ecological and Ethical Dimensions," in Hughes, Elaine L., Lucas, Alastair R., and Tilleman, William A. II, eds., *Environmental Law and Policy*, Toronto: Emond Montgomery Publications Limited, 1993, p. 23.

[80]Livingston notes the short-term usefulness of the "rights of nature" argument even though he comes down hard on it conceptually: "[...] as a stratagem against the time when the hierarchal concept of our relationship with the nonhuman is done with, it may have utility" (1981, p. 54).

References

Abbey, Edward, *Desert Solitaire*, New York: Ballantine Books, 1968.

Bell, Anne, "Cost-Benefit Analysis: A Conservation Caveat," *The Trumpeter: Journal of Ecosophy*, 11:2, Spring 1994, pp. 93-94.

Bell, Anne, "Non-human Nature and the Ecosystem Approach: The Limits of Anthropocentrism in Great Lakes Management," *Alternatives* 20:3, July/August 1994, pp. 20-25.

Birch, Thomas, "The Incarceration of Wildness: Wilderness Areas as Prisons," *Environmental Ethics* 12:1, Spring 1990, pp. 3-26.

Brandt, Anthony, "Views," *The Atlantic Monthly*, July 1977, p. 49.

Caldwell, Jennifer, *An Ecological Approach to Environmental Law*, Auckland, New Zealand: Legal Research Foundation Inc., 1988.

Des Jardins, Joseph R., *Environmental Ethics: An Introduction to Environmental Philosophy*, Belmont, California: Wadsworth, 1993.

Devall, Bill, *Simple in Means, Rich in Ends*, Salt

Lake City: Peregrine Smith Books, 1988.

Devall, Bill, and Sessions, George, *Deep Ecology*, Salt Lake City: Peregrine Smith Books, 1985.

Duncan, Linda F., *Enforcing Environmental Law: A Guide to Private Prosecution*, Edmonton: Environmental Law Centre, 1990.

Ehrenfeld, David, *The Arrogance of Humanism*, Oxford: Oxford University Press, 1978.

Elder, P.S., "Legal Rights for Nature – The Wrong Answer to the Right(s) Question," *Osgoode Hall Law Journal* 22:2, Summer 1984, pp. 285-295.

English, Mary R., "Introduction," *Tennessee Law Review 56*, Fall 1988, p. vii-xiv.

Evernden, Neil, "The Environmentalist's Dilemma," in Evernden, Neil, ed., *The Paradox of Environmentalism*, Downsview, Ontario: York University, 1984, pp. 7-17.

Evernden, Neil, *The Natural Alien*, Toronto: University of Toronto Press, 1985.

Evernden, Neil, *The Social Creation of Nature*, Baltimore: The Johns Hopkins University Press, 1992.

Fiorino, D.J., "Environmental Risk and Democratic Process: A Critical Review," *Columbia Journal of Environmental Law 14*, 1989, pp. 501-547.

Gaard, Greta, ed., *Ecofeminism: Women, Animals, Nature*, Philadelphia: Temple University Press, 1993.

Guha, Ramachandra, "Radical American Environmentalism and Wilderness Preservation: a Third World Critique," *Environmental Ethics* 11:1, Spring 1989, pp. 71-83.

Leopold, Aldo, *A Sand County Almanac and Sketches Here and There,* New York: Oxford University Press, 1989 (originally published in 1949).

Livingston, John, "Rightness or Rights?", *Osgoode Hall Law Journal* 22:2, Summer 1984, pp. 309-321.

Livingston, John, "The Dilemma of the Deep Ecologist," in Evernden, Neil, ed., *The Paradox of Environmentalism*, Downsview, Ontario: York University, 1984, pp. 61-72.

Livingston, John, *The Fallacy of Wildlife Conservation*, Toronto: McClelland and Stewart, 1981.

Lorde, Audre, *Sister Outsider: Essays and Speeches*, Trumansberg, New York: Crossing Press, 1984.

Lovelock, James, *Gaia: A New Look at Life on Earth*, Oxford: Oxford University Press, 1979.

Mickelsen, Karin, and Rees, William, "The Environment: Ecological and Ethical Dimensions," in Hughes, Elaine L., Lucas, Alastair R., and Tilleman, William A. II, eds., *Environmental Law and Policy*, Toronto: Emond Montgomery Publications Limited, 1993, pp. 1-29.

Naess, Arne, "The Shallow and the Deep, Long-Range Ecology Movement: A Summary," *Inquiry 16*, Spring 1973, pp. 95-100.

Nash, Roderick, *The Rights of Nature: A History of Environmental Ethics*, Madison: The University of Wisconsin Press, 1989.

Olson, James M., "Shifting the Burden of Proof: How the Common Law can Safeguard Nature and Promote an Earth Ethic," *Environmental Law 20*, 1990, pp. 891-915.

Passmore, John, "Attitudes Toward Nature," in Peters, R.S., ed., *Nature and Conduct*, New York: St. Martin's Press, 1975.

Passmore, John, *Man's Responsibility for Nature*, London: Duckworth, 1974.

Pojman, Louis P., ed., *Environmental Ethics: Readings and Theory and Application,* Boston: Jones and Bartlett, 1994.

Rolston, Holmes III, *Environmental Ethics*, Philadelphia: Temple University Press, 1988.

Rolston, Holmes III, "Environmental Ethics: Values in and Duties to the Natural World," in Bormann, F. Herbert, and Kellert, Stephen R., eds., *Ecology, Economics, Ethics: The Broken Circle*, New Haven: Yale University Press, 1991, pp. 73-96.

Sagoff, Mark, "Animal Liberation and Environmental Ethics: Bad Marriage, Quick Divorce," *Osgoode Hall Law Journal 22:2*, Summer 1984, pp. 297-307.

Schumacher, E.F., *A Guide for the Perplexed*, New York: Harper Colophon, 1977.

Seed, John, "Anthropocentrism," in Devall, Bill, and Sessions, George, *Deep Ecology*, Salt Lake City: Peregrine Smith Books, 1985, pp. 243-246.

Shepard, Paul, *Man in the Landscape*, New York: Alfred A. Knopf, 1967.

Shrader-Frechette, K.S., *Environmental Ethics*, Pacific Grove, California: Boxwood Press, 1981.

Simmons, I.G., *Interpreting Nature: Cultural Constructions of the Environment*, London: Routledge, 1993.

Simon, David J., *Our Common Lands*, Washington: Island Press, 1988.

Spretnak, Charlene, *States of Grace*, San Francisco: HarperSanFrancisco, 1991.

Stone, Christopher, *Earth and Other Ethics: The Case for Moral Pluralism*, New York: Harper & Row, 1987.

Stone, Christopher, "Should Trees Have Standing?: Toward Legal Rights for Natural Objects," *Southern California Law Review 45*, 1972, p. 450-501.

Stone, Christopher, "The Environment in Moral Thought," *Tennessee Law Review 56*, Fall 1988, pp. 1-11.

Tribe, Laurence H., "Ways Not To Think About Plastic Trees: New Foundations for Environmental Law," *Yale Law Journal 83:7*, 1974, pp. 1315-1348.

Warren, Karen J., "The Power and the Promise of Ecological Feminism", *Environmental Ethics*, 12:2, Summer 1990, pp. 125-146.

Wilson, Edward O., *The Diversity of Life,* New York: W.W. Norton & Company, 1993.

Wilson, Marie, "Wings of the Eagle", in Plant, J. and Plant, C., eds., *Turtle Talk*, Philadelphia: New Society Publishers, 1990, pp. 76-84.

World Commission on Environment and Development, *Our Common Future*, Oxford: Oxford University Press, 1987.

Worster, Donald, *Nature's Economy*, San Francisco: Cambridge University Press, 1977.

_____, "Endangered Species Act", Public Law 93-205,87 US Statutes at Large p 884.

_____; "Environmental Bill of Rights, 1993", Statutes of Ontario, 1993, Chapter 28

ENCOURAGING ENVIRONMENTAL CARE

A CODE OF ETHICS FOR SHORT HILLS PARK

15
by Ingrid L. Stefanovic

IN 1991, FOLLOWING A LENGTHY PROCESS OF BROAD public consultation, the Ontario Ministry of Natural Resources (OMNR) published a Management Plan for Short Hills Provincial Park, a 688-hectare park located on the southwest edge of St. Catharines in the Regional Municipality of Niagara. The Ministry recognized on the one hand, that there was clear public support for preserving this park as a "wild, natural area, with only very basic facilities to support trail use."[1] On the other hand, it was equally clear that a wide variety of recreational uses of the park – ranging from hiking, horseback riding, sport fishing, cross country skiing, mountain biking, nature and heritage appreciation, as well as outdoor education – were to continue.[2]

The common ethical dilemma of how to reconcile ecocentric and anthropocentric needs surfaced in the Ministry's recommendations. The Plan concluded that there was a need to explore ways of satisfying both environmental and human needs. On the one hand, the park's significant natural features unique to the Niagara escarpment deserved to be protected. On the other hand, a variety of "high quality, day-use recreational and interpretive experiences" were also to be accommodated.[3] Due to the variety of uses of the park and because some conflict over trails had already been evident, the Ministry's goal was to seek ways to "minimize conflict between trail users" themselves.[4]

Traditional ways of minimizing social conflict and environmental disruption often amount to policing procedures, and to use of essentially *negative reinforcement* techniques and punishment of behaviour. So for example, fines may be admin-istered for littering, or for overnight camping within Short Hills; or with the new Management Plan, specific user groups (for example, snowmobilers and motorcyclists in this case) are now excluded from the park by law.

Planner Oscar Newman reminds us, however, that the root of the word "policing" is "polis," meaning community.[5] Certainly, assigning a Park Warden to control behaviour within Short Hills Provincial Park may be necessary, but it is not in itself a sufficient condition of ensuring acceptable behaviour within the park. Studies have shown that for many (perhaps the majority) of park users, prompts, cues, information dissemination and better education about behaviour expectations, naturally regulated by members of the community, also encourage constructive activities and help to restrict potential friction between park visitors.[6]

It is in this spirit of pursuing such methods of *positive reinforcement* of responsible behaviour that a Code of Ethics was drafted for visitors to Short Hills Provincial Park.[7] It has evolved in consultation with hikers, equestrians, bikers, and lovers of the park. At one of the workshops convened during the course of the study, a Friends of Short Hills group has been struck; they are currently investigating means of implementation and communication/dissemination of the code to park visitors.

To our knowledge, such park-centred codes of ethics are rare to the point of being nonexistent in Ontario, and even in Canada. (Some moral imperatives may find their way into general introductory visitor brochures, but not in a self-contained, unified format.) It is true, as David Johnson notes, that "unlike most other aspects of human existence, [enjoyment of outdoor activities] does not have a long-established, tight code of laws regulating it. Rules are still few and loose."[8] It is precisely on account of this degree of freedom, however, that there may be a need for a level of ethics "considerably higher" than in more naturally restrictive settings, and with more heavily socially or politically monitored activities. Perhaps the time is right to seek to encourage responsible behaviour and environmental care in our parks, with the guidance of codes of ethics. Indeed, this is the argument of the present paper.

What is a Code of Ethics?... (and Why Do We Need One?)

In very general terms, a code of ethics is a written articulation of moral guidelines, designed to lead to minimally acceptable standards of human conduct. A survey of the current literature on ethical codes suggests that, as an expression of general agreement on shared beliefs, a code should:

- serve to provide *a common vocabulary* about what is right and what is wrong;

- offer a thoughtful *framework for conflict resolution* and policy development;

- *clarify ethical issues* and help to resolve disagreement about moral dilemmas, thereby seeking to decrease, if not eliminate, unethical practices;

- *impose some constraints* on individual behaviour;

- *reduce uncertainty* as to ethical and unethical courses of action;

- *suggest some course of action* to follow up on charges of unethical conduct;

- *facilitate improved cooperation* among interested parties, by enhancing mutual ethical understanding of norms of action;

- *promote environmental awareness*, by sensi-

tizing the public to shared social and environmental values.[9]

There is some disagreement among academics, policy makers and practitioners, about the usefulness of codes of ethics. Some of the common complaints made about ethical codes include the following:

- they are little more than *"window-dressing"* and "public relations gimmicks" which are designed to impress outsiders but are not taken seriously by practitioners;

- they are *too abstract* – too broad, and difficult to apply in specific situations;

- if they manage to express consensus, then they end up being *too vague*, and too weak in their provisions; as a result, they provide little practical guidance;

- *they may be counterproductive,* if they formalize the very status quo which they are only apparently attempting to change;

- they are *difficult to enforce,* because they are often not covered by law;

- they are *unnecessarily restrictive* on individual rights and freedom of choice;

- they *unnecessarily complicate matters of management,* by introducing new rules and standards to be enforced;

- *they are ineffective* in handling systematic corruption.[10]

It is important to acknowledge that any code of ethics may be potentially subject to the above criticisms. Indeed, in this vein, even the most energetic defenders of codes of ethics recognize that codes are not a cure-all for every sort of unethical behaviour. Nevertheless, particularly in conjunction with other forms of environmental education, written standards can and do help to clarify and resolve ethical dilemmas. Many of the above dangers and complaints directed towards codes of ethics can be avoided through careful formulation and competent administration of codes. In this respect, the goal must be not to avoid formulating ethical codes, but on the contrary, to do so conscientiously, prudently, while remaining mindful of the potential pitfalls noted above.

In the case of Short Hills Provincial Park, we recognized that one way of avoiding the risk of constructing an abstract and ultimately irrelevant code was to maintain open lines of communication with the community. The initial stages of the study consisted of a dialogue with community members regarding the very issue of the feasibility of a moral code for encouraging ethical social and environmental interactions. A mail-out questionnaire to approximately 90 individuals collected information on whether organized groups already relied upon their own code of ethics, and whether they could identify sources of conflict in the park. In-depth, one-to-two-hour long interviews were scheduled with a select group of individuals, representing a cross-section of organized visitor groups identified in the park. A Workshop was held on June 12, 1993, at Brock University, in an effort to bring these groups together to discuss the potential of a common code of ethics to help to resolve issues relating to social and environmental conflicts within the park.

Individual codes of ethics were obtained from hiking, equestrian, cyclist, motorcyclist, ski-doo and naturalist associations. At the same time, there was overwhelming consensus in support of the need of a *common* code of ethics, directed specifically to integrating diverse activities, and regulating overall conduct within the park. Respondents agreed that such a common code would be helpful in addressing the *relations between* individual visitor groups, as well as special environmental considerations *of the park itself.*

While there was clear support for such a code, all groups did recognize the need of other means of regulating members' conduct, in addition to a code of ethics. Such means ranged from self-enforcement, group monitoring, pledges, education sessions, meetings and information manuals. This indicated to us that, according to those surveyed, a code of ethics should not be expected to operate in isolation from other means of regulating behaviour.

One question asked in our survey was whether there were "any identifiable groups with whom your own group might be expected to come into conflict within Short Hills Provincial Park." Hikers and naturalists did suggest that mountain bikers, motorized vehicles and equestrians could present potential sources of conflict with respect to their own objectives within the park. Representatives of a nature club suggested that they have found "trails crowded and eroded by passing horses, such that one member suffered significant leg injury after a fall."

Altogether, there was acknowledgment of the need to address the issue of *how best* to resolve actual and potential conflicts in the park. Dramatic headlines in a local newspaper at this time, read "Equestrians *vs.* Pedestrians", and "Short Hills battle a sign to planners of disaster ahead."[11] On the other hand, contrary to such headlines, emerging from our research was a clear indication overall by respondents of goodwill towards one another, and a genuinely conciliatory spirit towards resolving potential social conflicts.

On the issue of environmental preservation, there was some disagreement regarding the degree to which the park should be developed to support recreational and educational activities. One respondent wrote that the "Board of Education is most anxious to add Short Hills to their list of resources. However, in order to facilitate *school use,* we need access to the park, parking for a bus, and washrooms." While the Board representative was appreciative of the need to preserve the natural environment of the park, he was equally concerned that pupils from elementary grades would be unable to access educational trails, because of large distances required for walking from parking lots, and because public facilities were insufficiently available.

Others (like the Niagara Falls Nature Club) appeared to welcome the wildness of the park. They wrote: "The people of the Niagara Falls Nature Club value and appreciate the opportunities in Short Hills Park to observe and study the birds, trees and wildflowers in a significantly sized natural habitat." What emerged from such comments was a lack of consensus among various sectors of the public, as to what extent Short Hills – originally deemed to be a natural environment class park – could nevertheless be developed to accommodate human (e.g. including children's) use. In short, it was unresolved as to how to balance anthropocentric (human-centred) and ecocentric (wilderness-centred) visions of what the park should be.

The problem of how to reconcile these conflicting anthropocentric and ecocentric demands has riddled environmental ethics. On the one hand, philosophers such as Tom Regan have suggested that "the development of what can properly be called an environmental ethic requires that we postulate inherent value in nature."[12] Otherwise, he argues, we must resort to a "management ethic" for the "use of the environment," instead of a proper ethic of the environment itself.[13] Critics of the anthropocentric world-view contend that when we value humans above all else, inevitably the natural environment is seen to be less important and consequently we feel justified in degrading nature if it is to society's advantage. These critics maintain that it is such a human-centred world-view that is to blame for the environmental crisis in the first place. Instead of an anthropocentric ethic, what we need instead, they argue, is an ecocentric ethic to protect the earth as valuable in and of itself.[14]

On the other hand, critics of the opposite extreme – of ecocentric morality – have pointed out that to assume that the environment possesses value in and of itself is still to justify such value *on human grounds.*[15] To be sure, reconciling anthropocentric and ecocentric demands presents ongoing ethical challenges which continue to be addressed in the philosophical literature to this day.[16] Not surprisingly, although these general issues of how best to balance human and environmental needs were considered within the extensive public consultation process prior to development of the management plan, our study showed that the concerns had been incompletely resolved. That a code of ethics would need to address some of the difficulties in balancing these anthropocentric and ecocentric interests, was clear from the initial stages of our study.

Toward a Code of Ethics
for Short Hills Provincial Park

Before we discuss the code itself, a number of key philosophical assumptions which grounded our approach may warrant some discussion here. Presumably, a variety of methods might be employed to evolve a code of ethics, building on either anthropocentric or ecocentric theoretical foundations. We chose to rely however on the phenomenological method, inasmuch as phenomenology seeks to ally itself with neither a subjectivistic nor objectivist extreme but instead aims to uncover the essential belonging and interplay of the two. For the phenomenologist, neither nature in and of itself, nor humans are central.[17] Rather, firmly grounded in a description of human being-in-the-world, phenomenology will maintain that "the relation is more fundamental than what is related."[18]

Originally defined as the study of "phenomena", or of "that which appears" to human understanding, phenomenologists aim to describe things, events and processes as they show themselves, in and of themselves, rather than in terms of any preconceived theoretical filters.[19] Instead of imposing generalized, abstract hypotheses upon the lived world, the intention is to "lay bare" essential patterns of meaning through a careful see-ing and listening. The synergism and complexity of phenomena is thereby to be preserved, rather than manipulated into neat, static categories, ultimately disengaged from the phenomenon under study.[20]

Translating this approach to our research meant that instead of imposing a top-down, preconceived system of theoretical principles to instruct a code of ethics, we proceeded to evolve the code bottom-up, so to speak, through a careful listening to what community members had to tell us about their needs and perceptions. Questionnaires were designed, not in order to facilitate a quick quantitative compilation and survey of views; on the contrary, leading questions encouraged respondents to share their stories in a narrative format. (This meant, in some cases, that participants went to their computers, reprinted the questions, and literally went on for pages, sharing their ideas.) Interviews were structured in such a way as to encourage community members to share their thoughts with minimal interruption by the interviewers, allowing for a stream of dialogue to emerge as spontaneously as possible.[21]

Our aim in all cases was to be attentive to essential messages which emerged throughout the course of our data gathering stages. Even the final questionnaire, which elicited views on the contents of a code of ethics, initially gathered information from respondents not on what "ought" and "ought not" to happen in the park, but rather, on what aspects of the park they found to be valuable in and of themselves, inasmuch as they provided for a genuine *sense of place* in Short Hills.[22]

Edward Casey reminds us of the fundamental significance of place, as the condition of meaningful description of our way of being in the world. He writes that "to be is to be in place...[P]lace, by virtue of its unencompassability by anything other than itself, is at once the limit and the condition of all that exists."[23] A holistic sense of place provides the context for that which is meaningful

within a specific locale. What I find to be valuable about an environment is coloured by the interest which I take in it, which itself is elicited by a holistic perception of the environment's sense of place.

Such an understanding of the foundations of human values as grounded in an originary sense of place guided our research project in Short Hills Park. The research method aimed to elicit essential community values about the sense of place of the park as a whole, and to reflect those values in the code, rather than to impose any preconceived, abstract theoretical model of ethical rules of conduct upon park visitors. Such a phenomenological approach, it seemed to us, was warranted, if the code was indeed to bring to light ethical precepts which could be seen to be ultimately relevant to the very members of the community who cared for Short Hills Park.

To enlarge further upon these views, some words might be helpful about a second set of related philosophical assumptions that related to the need for an *ontological* grounding of an ethical code.[24] We should emphasize two points in this regard. First, phenomenological ontologists argue that a distinction has arisen between abstract value systems and concrete facts. This has resulted in ethical theories of free-floating ideals that seem to be detached from and irrelevant to the lived world of decision-making. Such a separation between facts and values, moreover, is seen to be possible only on the basis of a more primordial ontological rift that has developed between subject and object. Let us spend a moment to examine these two propositions and how they affected the development of a code of ethics for Short Hills Park.

In the modern epoch, we may be inclined to describe values as subjective, and facts as objective.[25] Values are apparently fuzzy opinions; facts reflect reality. Philosophy supposedly describes subjective value systems; science studies objective facts. Yet, as Don Marietta observes, gradually we have come to understand that the "notion of brute, theory-free facts is an obsolete concept, no longer useful in science or the philosophy of science."[26] Conrad Brunk and his colleagues provide a fascinating illustration in their book entitled *Value Assumptions in Risk Assessment*, of how the same set of scientific facts are differently interpreted by distinct individuals, because of hidden value systems affecting the interpretation of those facts.[27] In other words, facts are rarely if ever value-free because they are interpreted always within the context of taken-for-granted assumptions and beliefs. At the same time, values cannot afford to be divorced from facts; otherwise they become irrelevant and lack a proper "fit" with the lived world of our everyday existence.[28]

In assigning significance to a specific environment like Short Hills Park, I think it is fair to say that normally we would not seek to assemble a cumulative list of discreet, objective "facts" about it – that it provides specific natural science features or a particular terrain of trees and trails – and only then proceed to "value" the park. On the contrary, the process of moral awareness is more complex, and fundamentally other than one of linear, technical process.[29]

Joseph Kockelmans explains that "it is of the greatest importance to realize that a human being is not born a moral agent, but that he grows up and is educated to become a moral agent. The importance of this remark becomes clear when one realizes that the experiences in which ethical discourse must take its point of departure have already occurred in the life of an individual long before they received an explicit ethical meaning in the limited sense of this term...Thus it seems to me that reflections on the foundations of morality should begin at a level where the distinction between ontology, anthropology and ethics is not yet relevant."[30]

The point is here, that ethical beliefs are not just arbitrary, subjective opinions, nor are they abstract, technical constructions, but in order to be meaningful, they arise within the concreteness of lived experience. In this respect, the phenomenological task of evolving a code of ethics becomes more than a philosophical construction of abstract moral rules for the community to follow. Once again, the task becomes one of illumining taken-for-granted community values that sustain that community in their everyday experiences of the park prior to the evolution of the code.

To turn to our second, related point, we have suggested that the tendency to separate human values from the world of "facts" rests on a more fundamental dualism that has developed in modern metaphysics between subjects and objects themselves. The rift briefly described above, that has played a prominent role in environmental ethics between anthropocentric and ecocentric foundations, is merely a reflection of a more fundamental ontological dualism that has evolved between subjectivity and objectivity.[31]

To bridge this chasm, phenomenologists describe the ontological belonging of humans to their lived worlds, and they emphasize this belonging in the hyphenated description of human being-in-the-world.[32] Rather than grounding their thought either within a subjective idealism, or the alternative of an objective realism, phenomenologists seek to describe the ontological *relation between* humans and the environments within which they find themselves.[35]

How did such an ontological presupposition affect our work at Short Hills? First of all, it made us wary of subjectivistic, human-centred assumptions which would immediately assign ontological priority to humans over the natural environment. There has been much criticism in the field of environmental ethics, of *anthropocentrism*. From Deep Ecology to Leopold's Land Ethic, the arguments against assuming that humans come first – and that the environment is nothing more than a resource for the use of human beings – have been presented in many different forms.[32]

More specifically, consider by way of example the definitions coming out of the United States of "outdoor ethics" – a term signifying precisely the domain of our Short Hills project. At a conference in 1987, the Director of National Park Service in Washington stated that "outdoor ethics are a code of man's creation which governs his conduct in the use of the outdoors."[33] Similarly, the Assistant Deputy Minister for Parks and Wildlife in Manitoba defines outdoor ethics again as a "system of code morals which applies to man's use of the out-of-doors."[34]

Putting aside the gender critique of sexist language here (*viz.* women use outdoors too!), both of the above definitions clearly stipulate *the use of* the outdoors. Indeed, a commonly accepted term in the Short Hills Management Plan which we found somewhat problematic was of *user groups*. In all of these cases, the claim that the environment is there *for human use* may lead one to the conclusion that the world is there exclusively for human purposes; and it is precisely such a view of nature in terms of its purely instrumental value to humans that, according to many theorists, has provided the justification for the domination, manipulation and exploitation of the environment and the current unsustainable state of society.

Paul Eagles reminds us that even such a phrase as "natural resource management is value laden" – as is indeed the very concept of management.[35] "To manage is to guide or control," he explains. "Typically, management involves setting goals, marshalling resources and taking action to fulfil those goals. It is inherently manipulative. Some managers feel that they must interfere, must change the environment, or they are not properly fulfilling their management role."[36] Yet, as we all know, sometimes the best environmental policy may turn out to be non-interference with natural cycles.[37]

As much as phenomenologists avoid committing themselves to a subjectivistic ontological foundation, they similarly avoid an objectivist, eco-centric perspective which itself becomes ultimately naive. Douglas Torgerson explains that the paradox of the eco-centric move is that:

"it de-centers the human and, at the same time, places humanity at the center of things. As soon as humanity is expelled from its privileged position, it is readmitted, so to speak, by the back door. Human reason is divested of its pretensions, but placed in judgment of all being. It could not be otherwise, for environmental ethics depends, after all, on ethical discourse. Discourse presupposes rational participants, and the only natural beings we know to be potentially qualified participants happen to be human beings."[40]

Arguments for the "intrinsic value" of nature in and of itself, existing independently from human consciousness, assume the human understanding of that very statement of value – and to this extent, it becomes impossible to completely abandon the human standpoint.[39] Those who see the dangers of an *ego*-centric perspective may wish to opt instead for an *eco*-centric view, but Torgerson reminds us that in such a move, we cannot, in fact, avoid employing human parameters for the very purpose of assigning value to the environment itself. We cannot escape *being* human in the projection of value onto non-human entities.

How do the above considerations impact upon Short Hills Park? They serve to remind us of the recurring dialogue among those who wished to preserve the park's natural, wild features for their own sake, and those who sought to accommodate human needs and wants which inevitably impact upon the wildlife of the park. Inasmuch as phenomenology will opt for neither a pure subjectivism nor a pristine objectivism to ground an ethic, we sought ways to avoid grounding the ethical discussion on either a purely anthropocentric, or, on the other hand, a purely ecocentric foundation. What then was the alternative?

Recall our discussion above, that from the phenomenological perspective, one seeks to shed light on the *human-environment relation*. In this light, the challenge was not to evolve a code to exclusively support the human "use" of the environment, but neither was it to argue for the intrinsic value of the environment *separate from* human concerns. Instead, the aim was to remain sensitive to the reciprocal relation between humans and the environments within which they find their place. The phenomenological task was to see that Short Hills Park is not there merely for human utilization, yet it may benefit from human stewardship and care.[40] Such care though, as genuine, should be park-directed, for the good of the environment as a whole.[41]

In addition to these phenomenological assumptions of our study, there were some practical guidelines to which we adhered in the formulation of a code of ethics for Short Hills Park. Having contacted superintendents from every major national park in the United States, we were particularly moved by a code of ethics which is provided to visitors of Grand Canyon National Park as a bookmark. (See Appendix A)[42]. This code begins with some fundamental "understandings", on the basis of which an environmental "pledge" is then articulated. The code is concise, and powerful in its simplicity. It captures the essence of a caring attitude towards the park, as the foundation of responsible conduct. We decided to follow the example of including a general understanding of commonly accepted precepts as the context for a pledge of a personal, moral commitment to protect the environment.

Indeed, in our overview of other ethical codes in general, we saw the practical advantages of including both global guidelines as well as more specific codes of conduct in the park.[43] One of these advantages was the maximum flexibility in levels of communication of a code which could be conveyed either in a brief, immediate fashion, or in other arenas with a more detailed explanation. For instance, a short, to-the-point review of basic moral tenets could be posted in such strategic meeting points as feed stores for horses, or in sports stores for hikers and bikers. Another suggestions was that one-line prompts and cues, based on some of the more general precepts of the code of ethics, could be posted on wooden signs, carefully placed in appropriate areas of the park. A more detailed code of conduct could be useful to Boards of Education, who might seek some more specific and pragmatic direction of a code, to be communicated within a program of environmental education. The same could be said for organized visitor groups, keen on encouraging environmental awareness among their own group members.[44]

In the end, a code of ethics (including a code of conduct) was presented to community members at a Workshop at Brock University on September 30, 1994. Small, 4-5 member working groups deliberated over details of the draft proposal, and their valuable suggestions were incorporated into some modifications of a final code, found in Appendix B to this paper. The Friends of Short Hills Group, who held their first organizational meeting shortly after this Workshop, began the process of investigating appropriate ways and means of communicating the code to park visitors.[45] Board of Education members will be similarly considering ways in which the code might be integrated into current environmental education programmes for children in Niagara.[46]

Some Policy Recommendations

On the basis of this two-year study, we propose the following policy recommendations:

1. that the Ontario Ministry of Natural Resources, together with other Ministries and Departments with responsibility for human-environment relations, recognize the potential for *positive reinforcement* of responsible human behaviour within their programs. Concurrently, we en-

courage government support of community-cen-
tred initiatives, such as is found in the recently-
formed Friends of Short Hills Park.

2. that these same Ministries recognize the positive role that can be played by a carefully formulated code of ethics, within the broader framework
of a program of enhancing environmental awareness among the public. Such "recognition" could
range from explicit encouragement of the formulation of codes of ethics within Management Plans,
to education of public service employees of the
impact of philosophical and ethical assumptions
upon behaviour.

Clearly, formulating a code of ethics is not the
sole route to encouraging environmental care, nor
do we advocate blind obedience to any rigid set
of codified rules. (Chandler reminds us of Aristotle's warning that it is quite possible to obey laws
and regulations, while remaining unethical.[47]) It
may be true that ultimately, it is one's own conscience which is the genuine source of environmentally responsible behaviour.[48]

At the same time, however, it is in the sharing
of common paradigms that communities are
formed.[49] If shared paradigms, reflected in a code
of ethics, may help to increase environmental
awareness and resolve some conflicts among community members; if a code may broaden one's
environmental vision so that one's conscience is
better informed, then perhaps such a philosophical articulation of ethical guidelines does indeed
have some significant role to play in guiding the
future of our parks.

APPENDIX A

A model code of ethics from
Grand Canyon National Park
PO Box 129
Grand Canyon, AZ 86023. U.S.A.

CODE of ETHICS

As a member of the world
community, I understand that:

All life on earth – human, plant
and animal – is joined in one
world community. This is our
natural heritage.

Every person has a right to a safe
and healthy environment in
which to live. Plants and animals
share that right.

Our air, water and atmosphere
are replenished and maintained
by the diverse natural
communities of the world. I share
responsibility for protecting these
communities.

As a member of the world
community, I pledge:

To show respect for the world's
natural heritage by taking care
not to harm or degrade it through
ignorance, carelessness or misuse.

To continue to increase my
understanding about the diversity
of life and to share that
knowledge with others.

To express my opinion on issues
of concern that affect our natural
heritage, and to actively support
its protection.
Enjoy your visit to
Grand Canyon National Park.

APPENDIX B

A CODE OF ETHICS
FOR SHORT HILLS PROVINCIAL PARK
As a friend of Short Hills Park,
I understand that:

- ☙ The park is a unique, natural environment to be preserved for its own sake, as well as for future generations.
- ☙ My responsibility is of a care-taker, to actively seek to promote the ecological health and diversity of the park.

I pledge to:

- ☙ *show respect; tread lightly.*
- ☙ *pack out* at least what is packed in.
- ☙ *keep wildlife wild*, by observing from a safe and non-interfering distance.
- ☙ *observe, not disturb* natural features in the park. Memories outlast specimens.
- ☙ *preserve the peace* in the park. Be considerate of others.
- ☙ *protect the park from disruptive activities*, such as fires or vandalism.
- ☙ *become better informed* about the needs of Short Hills Park, and share my knowledge with others.

SOME GUIDELINES FOR CONDUCT

1. Show respect; tread lightly.

1.1 *Remain on established trails.*

1.2 *Respect the rules of multi-use trails.* Meet and pass with respect. Use caution and speak quietly in approaching, to pacify the horses. Cyclists will remain in single file to the right of trails, announcing themselves in advance of bends, and yielding to others.

1.3 *Avoid using trails when wet,* especially when cycling or horseback riding.

1.4 *Avoid trespassing* on private property.

2. Pack out at least what is packed in.

2.1 *Avoid all littering.*

2.2 If possible, *leave the park cleaner than you found it.*

3. Keep wildlife wild, by observing from a safe and non-interfering distance.

3.1 *Avoid feeding wildlife,* as it upsets the natural food chain.

3.2 *Control all pets* brought into the park.

4. Observe, but do not disturb natural features in the park.

4.1 *Preserve plants and flowers.*

4.2 *Natural systems, as well as cultural artifacts will remain duly undisturbed in the park.*

4.3 *Refrain from polluting* the environment in any way.

5. Preserve the peace in the park. Be considerate of others.

5.1 *Be courteous in sharing trails.*

5.2 *Use common sense in announcing yourself,* particularly on narrow trails with limited visibility.

5.3 *Curtail rowdiness.*

6. Protect the park from disruptive activities.

6.1 *Fires are prohibited* in the park.

6.2 *Report to the Park Superintendent, at the telephone number below, any vandalism* encountered within the park.

7. Become better informed and share your knowledge about Short Hills.

7.1 *Be aware of and sensitive to the needs of the park.* Be open to new knowledge about the park.

7.2 *Support environmental education* about Short Hills Park.

For further information, or to voice your views, please contact the Ontario Ministry of Natural Resources, PO Box 1070, Fonthill, Ont. LOS 1EO. Telephone: (905) 892-2656.

ENDNOTES

[1]Ontario Ministry of Natural Resources, *Short Hills Provincial Park Management Plan*, Fonthill, Ontario: OMNR, 1991, p. 2.

[2]*Ibid*, p. 7.

[3]*Ibid*, p. 4.

[4]*Ibid*, p. 21. Examples of conflicts between trail users included complaints by hikers of damage to trails by equestrians, mountain bikers startling horses and similar instances relating to the sharing of multi-use trails in particular.

[5]Newman, Oscar, *Defensible Space: Crime Prevention through Urban Design,* (New York: Macmillan Publishing Company, 1972), p. 3.

[6]For instance, studies by psychologists have shown that there was a significant reduction in the rate of destructive lawn-walking in areas of a new "mini-park", simply by erecting signs reading "University Mini-Park: Please Don't Trample the Grass." (Cf. Hayes, S.C. and Cone, J.D., "Decelerating environmentally destructive lawn-walking behaviour", in *Environment and Behaviour,* 9, pp. 91-101). Certainly, such prompts may not achieve such success under some conditions (for example, when the cost of obeying the cue is too high), but nevertheless, researchers have learned much about the power of positive prompts. Reich and Robertson have shown that the chances of success of written cues are much enhanced when they are positively worded: thus for example, people are less likely to obey an overly forceful sign, such as "You *must* not litter", and may even react in direct opposition to such an order; more effective would be a sign which read "Thank-you for not littering". (Cf. Reich, J.W. and Robertson, J.L. "Reactance and normal appeal in antilittering messages", in *Journal of Applied Social Psychology,* Vol. 9, pp. 91-101, 1979). Similarly, a prompt in the form of an acceptable alternative may prevent environmentally unfriendly acts: for instance, psychologists suggest a nearby sidewalk might serve as a prompt not to walk on newly planted grass, or a nearby garbage bin may offer a cue not to litter. (Cf. Bell, Paul A.; Baum, Andrew; Fisher, J.D.; Greene, Thomas E.; *Environmental Psychology,* (Fort Worth: Holt, Rinehart and Winston, Inc., 1990), p. 480; and "Methods to Control Negative Impacts of Recreation Use", by A.W. Magill, *River Recreation Management and Research Symposium*, Jan. 24-7 1977, 402-4.

[7]Research Assistants on this project were Marie Poirier, Institute of Environmental Policy, Brock University; David Sztybel, Department of Philosophy, University of Toronto; and Lynn Topp, Recreation and Leisure, Brock University. The researchers gratefully acknowledge the financial support for this project, provided through a Social Sciences and Humanities Research Council (SSHRC) General Research Grant; and a Grant-in-Aid, through the Department of Philosophy, University of Toronto. Thanks is also extended to Brock University's Institute of Environmental Policy, who hosted both workshops on the project.

[8]Johnson, David N., "Outdoor Ethics and Public Education in Africa", in Proceedings of the International Conference on Outdoor Ethics, November 8-11, 1987, Lake Ozark, Missouri. Sponsored by the Izaak Walton League of America. P. 22.

[9]Cf. for example Kernaghan, Kenneth, "Managing Ethics: Complementary approaches", *Canadian Public Administration,* Vol. 34, No. l, Spring, pp. 132-145; Lang, Reg and Hendler, Susan, "Ethics and Professional Planners", in D. MacNiven, *Moral Expertise,* (London, 1988); J.S. Beazley, "What is this Thing called Ethics and Sometimes, The Code of Ethics?", in *Photogrammetric Engineering and Remote Sensing,* Vol. 57, No. 5, May 1991, pp. 4970499; Schaefer, Jame, *Toward an Ethic for the Great Lakes Basic Ecosystem,* A discussion paper prepared for the Societal Committee of the Great Lakes Science Advisory Board, Windsor, Ontario. November, 1989; and Ralph Clark Chandler, "The Problem of Moral Reasoning in American Public Administration: The Case for a Code of Ethics", in *Public Administration Review,* 43, Jan/Feb. 1983, pp. 32-9.

[10]Cf. Kernaghan *Ibid,* p. 135; Lang and Hendler, *Ibid,* p. 61; and Ralph Clark Chandler, *Ibid*.

[11]Stories by Doug Draper in the St. Catharines *Standard.* June 26, 1993.

[12]Regan, Tom, "The Nature and Possibility of an Environmental Ethic," in *Environmental Ethics,* 3 (1981), p. 34.

[13]*Ibid.*

[14]See, for example, David Ehrenfeld, *The Arrogance of Humanism* (New York: Oxford University Press, 1978.)

[15]Torgerson, Douglas, "The Paradox of Environmental Ethics," in *Alternatives,* Vol. 12, No. 2, Winter 1985, pp. 26-36.

[16]See, for example, Leslie Paul Thiele, "Nature and Freedom: A Heideggerian Critique of Biocentric and Sociocentric Environmentalism" in *Environmental Ethics,* Summer 1995, Volume 17, Number 2, pp. 171-190.

[17]*Ibid.*

[18]Stambaugh, Joan, "Introduction" to Martin Heidegger's *On Time and Being,* (New York: Harper & Row, Publishers, 1972) p. x.

[19]Cf. Husserl, Edmund, *Ideas Pertaining to a Pure Phenomenology and to a Phenomenological Philosophy*. Translated by F. Kersten. (The Hague, Netherlands: Martinus Nijhoff Publishers, 1983); and Heidegger, Martin, *Being and Time*. Translated by John Macquarrie and Edward Robinson (New York: Harper and Row, 1962). For a layman's introduction to phenomenology, see "What is Phenomenology?" by I.L. Stefanovic, in *Brock Review*, Volume 3, Number 1, 1994, pp. 58-77.

[20]The term "synergism" builds on the notion that, on the strength of the interaction between discrete entities, the total effect is greater than the sum of the individual effects.

[21]A paper describing the phenomenological method as it impacts upon the interview process is in preparation. Some preliminary remarks are available in a paper describing a similar process of interviews on another project—the interdisciplinary "Ecowise" research study funded by the Tri-Council program of awards, and investigating the sustainability of the Hamilton Harbour Ecosystem. See "Interdisciplinarity and Wholeness: Lessons from Eco-research," by Ingrid Leman Stefanovic, *Environments: A Journal of Interdisciplinary Studies,* Vol. 23, No. 3, 1996.

[22]Some clues for this approach were provided to us by a particularly instructive article by Jim Cheney, entitled "Postmodern Environmental Ethics: Ethics as Bioregional Narrative", in *Environmental Ethics: Convergence and Divergence*, (McGraw-Hill, 1993).

[23]Casey, Edward, *Getting Back into Place: Toward a Renewed Understanding of the Place-World*, (Bloomington and Indianapolis: Indiana University Press, 1993), pp. 14-15.

[24]Ontology is the study of the meaning of Being itself. Instead of focussing merely on essents (things), ontology seeks to illumine the condition of the possibility of the appearance of things in the world. See Martin Heidegger, *Being and Time*.

[25]For a fascinating discussion of the belonging and overlapping of facts and values, see Don E. Marietta Jr., "Knowledge and Obligation in Environmental Ethics: A Phenomenological Analysis" in *Environmental Ethics,* Summer 1982, Volume 4, Number 2, pp. 153-162; also J. Baird Callicott, "Hume's Is/Ought Dichotomy and the Relation of Ecology to Leopold's Land Ethic," pp. 163-174 in the same issue of *Environmental Ethics.*

[26]Cited in Marietta, D. *Ibid,* p. 267-8.

[27]Brunk, Conrad G.; Lawrence Haworth and Brenda Lee, *Value Assumptions in Risk Assessment: A Case Study of the Alachlor Controversy,* (Waterloo, Ontario: Wilfrid Laurier University Press, 1991.) For a recent work on similar issues of how hidden value assumptions affect interpretations of risk, see William Leiss and Christina Chociolko, *Risk and Responsibility*, (Montreal: Mc-Gill-Queen's University Press, 1996.)

[28]On the notion of sustainable "fittingness", see Maurice Mandelbaum, *The Phenomenology of Moral Experience,* (Baltimore and London: Johns Hopkins Press, 1969), especially pp. 61ff.

[29]Cf. in this connection, Hans-Georg Gadamer, *Truth and Method*, (New York: Seabury Press, 1975, p. 284) who seeks to distinguish between the *techne* of the craftsman and the *phronesis* (practical knowledge) of the judge who seeks to interpret, in a morally justifiable sense, a specific law.

[30]Joseph J. Kockelmans, "The Foundations of Morality and the Human Sciences", in *Foundations of Morality, Human Rights and the Human Sciences*, edited by Anna-Teresa Tymieniecka, and Calvin O. Shrag, (Dordrecht, Holland: D. Reidel Publishing Company, 1983), pp. 381-2.

[31]On this point regarding the subjectivism and objectivism of the modern age, see Martin Heidegger, "The Age of the World Picture" in *The Question Concerning Technology and Other Essays*, translated with an introduction by William Lovitt, (New York: Harper & Row, Publishers, 1977.

[32]Cf. Heidegger, Martin, *Being and Time,* op.cit.

[33]A paper entitled "The Contribution of Phenomenology to Environmental Ethics" describes more fully the significance of the ontological ground of ethics, and is in preparation by the author.

[34]See for example, Walter O'Briant's "Man, Nature and the History of Philosophy", in Blackstone, William T. (ed.), *Philosophy and Environmental Crisis,* (Athens: University of Georgia Press, 1974); Aldo Leopold's *A Sand County Almanac with Essays on Conservation from Round River,* (New York: Oxford University Press, 1949); David Ehrenfeld, *The Arrogance of Humanism,* (New York: Oxford University Press, 1978); and Arne Naess, *Ecology, Community and Lifestyle,* (Cambridge, England: Cambridge University Press, 1989).

[35]Mott, William Penn Jr., "A National Park Service Perspective on Ethics", in *Proceedings of the International Conference on Outdoor Ethics,* November 8-11, 1987, Lake Ozark, Missouri. Sponsored by the Izaak Walton League of America, p. 39.

[36]Goulden, Richard, "Meeting the Outdoor Ethics Challenge in Canada", in *Ibid,* p. 80.

[37]"Is the squirrel that lives in the tree a natural resource? Not usually, unless someone wants to hunt it or eat it, or look at it. The concept of a natural resource, then, is inherently anthropocentric." Cf. Paul F.J. Eagles, "Environmental Management in Parks", in Philip Dearden and Rick Rollins, *Parks and Protected Areas in Canada: Planning and Management,* (Toronto: Oxford University Press, 1993), p. 154.

[38]Eagles, Paul, *Ibid,* p. 155.

[39]Planner Michael Hough advocates the design principle of "doing as little as possible". "The greatest diversity and identity in a place, whether a regenerating field or urban wetland, or a cohesive neighbourhood community, often comes with minimum, not maximum interference." For elaboration on this perspective, see *Out of Place: Restoring Identity to the Regional Landscape,* (New Haven and London: Yale University Press, 1990), pp. 190-1.

[40]Torgerson, Douglas, "The Paradox of Environmental Ethics", *op.cit.*, note 15, p. 27.

[41]Cf. J. Baird Callicott, *op.cit.*, note 25, who clearly shows the fallacy of seeking philosophical justification for the "intrinsic value" of nature, apart from human understanding.

[42]Leslie Paul Thiele shows how a Heideggerian phenomenological understanding of nature and freedom provides a significant impetus for fostering a new ethic of ecological stewardship and "care," distinct from both ecocentric identification with nature as well as from egocentric manipulations. See "Nature and Freedom: A Heideggerian Critique of Biocentric and Sociocentric Environmentalism" in *Environmental Ethics*, Summer 1995, Volume 17, Number 2, pp. 171-190.

[43]Interestingly, in their deliberations on the meaning of crimes against the environment, the Law Reform Commission of Canada has come to a similar conclusion. In reflecting upon "homocentric" and "ecocentric" ethics, they explain that "there remain some serious conceptual and practical obstacles to the provision of legal protection to the natural environment *for its own sake*, apart from considerations of human benefits, wishes, uses and health risks. It would amount to granting rights to nonhuman entities. From a practical standpoint, it is inconceivable that natural resources could ever be totally insulated from economic and political considerations. Nor is it evident that we cannot provide adequate protection for the natural environment itself by continuing to permit a homocentric ethic to underlie our environmental regulations and laws, but one which now gives more scope to the *quality* of human life, and to our responsibility of *stewardship* or trusteeship over the natural environment." (See "Crimes Against the Environment" by the Law Reform Commission of Canada, in *Ethical Issues: Perspectives for Canadians*, edited by Eldon Soifer, (Peterborough, Ontario: Broadview Press, 1992), pp. 217-218.

[44]We acknowledge with gratitude the detailed and extremely informative responses which we received from virtually every park superintendent contacted in the U.S.A.

[45]It was useful to compare, for example, the codes presented in *Codes of Ethics: Ethics Codes, Standards and Guidelines for Professionals Working in a Health Care Setting in Canada*, compiled by Francoise Baylis and Jocelyn Downie, Published by the Department of Bioethics, The Hospital for Sick Children, Toronto, Ontario, Canada. 1992.

[46]Sometimes these more detailed codes of conduct could include actual *examples* of ethical dilemmas, and routes for resolving such dilemmas. While we saw the advantages to this, at the same time we were concerned to keep the code of ethics, in its complete form, to a single typed page. We felt that anything longer might be seen to be vexatious and tedious to some.

[47]Further information about the Friends of Short Hills Group is available from Ms. Marie Poirier, at the Institute of Environmental Policy, Brock University, St. Catharines, Ontario.

[48]Contact, for example, Mr. Bert Murphy, Consultant in Environmental Education for the St. Johns Outdoor Studies Centre, Fonthill, Ontario.

[49]Chandler, Ralph Clark, *op.cit.*, p. 34.

[50]For a discussion of stages of moral development, see Daniel L. Dustin, "To Feed or Not Feed the Bears: the Moral Choices we Make", in *Parks and Recreation,* October 1985, pp. 54-57, 72.

[51]Cf. Chandler, Ralph Clark, *op.cit.,* for some further discussion of this notion.

MARKETS FOR NATURAL HERITAGE
PROSPECTS AND PERILS FOR PROTECTING BIODIVERSITY IN SETTLED LANDSCAPES

16   *by Allan Greenbaum*

THIS CHAPTER IS ABOUT SOME WAYS OF CONSERVing nature in those parts of the country where most of the land is privately owned. In it I discuss the potential of private market mechanisms based on innovative legal instruments such as conservation easements for achieving conservation goals. Market approaches to nature conservation might seem particularly attractive to two sorts of conservationists: first, advocates of "free market environmentalism"[1] who favour market solutions over government "intervention" as a matter of principle; and second, pragmatic conservationists who seek new avenues for private initiatives in addition to government action.

I sound a cautious note. These approaches do have some ethical advantages, at least if we grant the philosophical principles and assumptions that free market advocates tend to espouse. They cannot, however, be relied upon to provide a level of protection for nature that is adequate even according to the market advocates' own philosophical principles. I also suggest that, even as a supplementary measure, the widespread use of markets to protect natural heritage may have the effect of undermining the ethos of voluntary stewardship upon which conservation in settled regions will always to a large extent rely.

The specific examples I refer to in this chapter tend to relate to southern Ontario, because that is the place with which I am most familiar. The purpose of the chapter is not, however, to provide the reader with concrete information on natural heritage conservation issues, programs and policies in Ontario or elsewhere, but rather to explore some of the philosophical issues raised by certain ap-

proaches to conservation. The discussion should be relevant to anywhere that analogous situations arise.

Why the Interest in
Private Market Conservation Strategies

Governments have used two major tools to conserve natural heritage in the settled regions of Canada. One is to acquire lands with significant natural features and habitats through purchase, expropriation or other means. The other is to regulate what private landowners can do with lands that contain such features. In addition to these two means, governments have used various tax measures to encourage or reward the conservation of natural heritage. In the view of many conservationists, governments have seldom used the means at their disposal with sufficient vigour to arrest the erosion of biodiversity and the loss of representative natural communities in southern Canada.

Now, because of fiscal crises and the rising success of neoconservative movements and parties in Canada and elsewhere, we can expect that governments at all levels will be increasingly unwilling or unable to implement policies by means involving either generous spending or aggressive regulation of private property. This in turn means that efforts to protect biodiversity and natural heritage in settled regions will have increasingly to rely on various forms of "private stewardship".

In large measure, private stewardship can be advanced through informal channels of landowner education and moral suasion. In many cases, landowners are unaware of rare species or ecologically important features on their properties, and when informed about the significance of the natural heritage that they own they take great pride in protecting it. In some private stewardship programs, owners who agree to manage their lands in ways that protect heritage values receive tokens of appreciation such as "stewardship certificates". In Ontario, the Natural Heritage Stewardship Program produces a newsletter filled with information, advice and encouragement for owners of private lands with natural heritage value.

Notwithstanding the successes of some private stewardship programs, conservation may depend on ways of formally securing protection, especially in circumstances where protection of natural features would entail some economic sacrifice on the part of the landowner. Nature conservation organizations have always been involved to some extent in creating private nature reserves. Organizations such as the Royal Society for the Protection of Birds in Britain and the Nature Conservancy in the United States – forerunners of the conservation land trusts being created today – have amassed extensive land holdings for the purposes of nature preservation. In Canada, too, naturalist and conservationist organizations have frequently bought land in order to protect its natural heritage values. For example, several sites containing remarkable assemblages of rare species and unique habitats along the Lake Huron shoreline narrowly avoided being turned into cottage lots because they were purchased by the Federation of Ontario Naturalists.

In the absence of government action, conservation groups will be forced to rely all the more on private reserves and related private market mechanisms such as land trusts and conservation easements (discussed below) to achieve natural heritage and biodiversity conservation goals. Conservation easements have been called "potentially the best legal device for habitat protection that wildland proponents currently have at their disposal", because while laws aimed at habitat protection can be repealed, not implemented, or left unenforced whenever the political climate turns

against nature preservation, conservation easements are a kind of private property right held by the wildland proponents themselves.[2]

For naturalists and environmentalists, this turn to strategies within the framework of private property and the market is chiefly a pragmatic response to changing circumstances. It is seen as an expansion of the range of options available for the protection of natural areas, an exercise in "creative conservation.[3] At the same time, this strategy is consistent with an approach to environmental issues that prefers market based resolutions on philosophical grounds. In the next section, I will review some of the general concepts relevant to the philosophical arguments for a market based approach to nature conservation. In the sections to follow, I will discuss the mechanisms of the market based approach and then discuss and evaluate the arguments for this approach in greater detail.

The Conceptual Context:
Ethics, Economics and the Environment

For its philosophical and ideological advocates, the market based approach to environmental protection is preferred on the grounds of liberty, economic efficiency, and fairness or equity. All three may be regarded as ethical ideals or desiderata. Liberty and fairness are quite familiar as moral concepts, and will be discussed briefly. The moral concept of economic efficiency is a little more complicated, and will be examined at greater length.

Liberty is a widely shared moral and political value, but one that is interpreted in widely disparate ways. What market advocates mean by liberty is the freedom to dispose of one's property or labour as one sees fit, on the basis of contractual arrangements upon which one has freely agreed, without coercion by another person or by the state.[4] Clearly, liberty in this sense is better respected if environmentalists persuade or pay landowners to protect ecologically significant features than if they force landowners to do so by means of government regulations.

Economic efficiency as an ethical ideal is rooted in the common-sense view that it is better for people to be better off – that is, happier, more satisfied – than to be less well off. It is related to the ethical theory of utilitarianism, which states that the rightness or wrongness of an act or policy depends on whether the total amount of utility (happiness or pleasure) it produces outweighs the total amount of disutility (unhappiness or suffering) it produces. Given a choice between courses of action, utilitarianism states that we are obliged to take the path that will produce the most favourable balance of utility, taking into account everyone who is affected.

As long as no third party is affected, it is assumed that a free market transaction will necessarily lead to a situation of greater over-all happiness than would exist if the transaction did not occur. This is because unless both parties expected to benefit from the transaction, they would not have entered into it. Since each of the parties is better off and no one else is affected, the total amount of satisfaction in society can be said to have been increased. In the jargon of economics, this transaction satisfies the "Pareto criterion": that at least one person is made better off and nobody is made worse off.

Of course, few transactions in the real world can be expected to leave the welfare of everyone else unaffected. Nevertheless, a transaction that imposes negative effects on third parties (so called "external costs" or "negative externalities") may still contribute to the over-all good if the total benefits to those who benefit outweigh the total costs to those who suffer.[5]

The existence of externalities still poses a practical problem, however. If an activity or land use generates negative externalities, the parties responsible do not bear the full costs of their activity. In effect, the activity is subsidized by society, and so one would expect that more of the activity or land use will occur than would have occurred if the burdens were not partly shouldered by others. By the same token, if there are positive externalities – that is, if third parties benefit from the activity or land use – less of this socially beneficial activity will likely occur than would have if the responsible parties could cash in on this public windfall. Either way, the result is likely to be less efficient than it would have been in the absence of externalities. For these reasons, free market advocates generally endorse institutional frameworks (including regulations) that reduce externalities, provided that the social costs of reducing the externalities do not exceed the social costs attributable to the externalities themselves.[6]

In the absence of externalities or other "market failures", free market advocates tend to oppose government intervention in the form of regulation or expenditure both because it impairs liberty (as they understand it) and because it supposedly results in a less efficient outcome than would result from free market transactions. Markets, they argue, will put a resource to the use that maximizes its market value; in the absence of externalities, this tends to be the use that maximizes its value to society (as measured by people's aggregate willingness-to-pay). Government interventions, by contrast, are said to tend to allocate resources to uses that benefit those with political influence, regardless of whether those uses maximize social wealth.

Critics of economic efficiency as a basis for public policy are quick to point out that the notion of efficiency refers to the goal of maximizing the sum total balance of benefits minus harms, and says nothing about whether the benefits and disbenefits are equitably distributed.[7] Put another way, it is based on the ideal of maximizing the total wealth of society, irrespective of how that wealth is divided up. Market-ordered economies may be marked by great inequalities of wealth between rich and poor. These inequalities, in turn, feed back on the criterion of social welfare. Since the preferences of the rich are backed with greater ability (hence willingness) to pay, resource uses that satisfy the preferences of the rich will be deemed to contribute more to the "wellbeing of society" (as measured in these terms) than will resource uses that satisfy the preferences of the poor. Market society is represented by its advocates as the ultimate democracy in which everyone, by their spending decisions, "votes" with their dollars for the kinds of goods and services they want the society to provide, but of course some people have more "votes" than others. In reply, market advocates suggest that the political clout of the rich is even more disproportionate than their economic clout, and that therefore the results of government interventions are likely to be no more egalitarian than the results of market transactions.[8]

This brings us finally to the values of "equity" or "fairness". Fairness has to do with the distribution of benefits and burdens among members of society. According to some interpretations, fairness is associated with equality, and inequality is justified only to the extent that those on the bottom of the unequal arrangement would be better off than they would be under a more equal arrangement.[9] According to others, a particular policy is fair if it does not tend to impose burdens, costs or harms on members of some groups to the advantage of members of other groups. For still others, a distribution of benefits and burdens is fair if it reflects what people deserve or have earned.

Since there are many competing conceptions of equity or fairness, these are values that may be marshalled on both sides of this debate. Arguments for the market typically rely on liberty and efficiency arguments, and are frequently criticized for neglecting issues of fairness or equality. Efficiency, we have seen, concerns the aggregate welfare of society and is indifferent to the distribution of benefits and burdens among society's members. In particular, efficiency is compatible with a degree of social and economic inequality that would be viewed as socially unjust and mor-

ally unacceptable by those with a more or less egalitarian notion of fairness. Nevertheless, proponents of the market argue that regulatory approaches to natural heritage protection are also blind to the distribution of costs and benefits of regulation. In particular, they claim that regulations unfairly impose the costs of preservation on those who happen to own lands containing significant natural features or habitats. The benefits of protection accrue to society and nature generally, but the costs are borne by landowners who may be ill able to afford them.[10]

Those who are interested in preserving natural features are not necessarily interested in maximizing utility, protecting market liberty or ensuring social and economic equality. Nature conservationists give high priority to protecting those lands that provide vital ecological functions (such as critical habitat for wildlife populations); lands that contribute to the maintenance of biological and landscape diversity by virtue of their rare species, uncommon ecological communities or unique landscape features;[11] and lands that support uncommonly "high quality" examples of relatively common ecological communities, and which thereby have particular aesthetic, scientific or heritage value. These considerations have been incorporated into criteria for the application of various kinds of planning designations, such as "Environmentally Significant (or Sensitive) Area" ("ESA") used by many Ontario municipalities, and "Area of Natural and Scientific Interest" ("ANSI") used by the Ontario provincial government.[12] Areas may satisfy these criteria to a greater or lesser extent, so we may speak of them as having greater or lesser conservation value.

Why is conservation value a value? What, in other words, does conservation value consist in? This is a complex and controversial issue in environmental ethics, one that is beyond the scope of this chapter to canvas. One way of analyzing conservation value is as follows. In the first place, there are all the direct and indirect benefits that the features protected may confer on present and future humans. Let us refer to these values as "resource values". Some people also value such features for their own sakes, apart from any direct or indirect use made of them by humans. Those people derive satisfaction from just knowing that the features in question (continue to) exist. Let us refer to this satisfaction as "existence value". Finally, the feature may have value in its own right or value to nonhuman beings or systems that have value in their own right, independent of any satisfaction they may provide for humans. Let us call this last category of value "inherent" value.

Inherent value is philosophically controversial. To oversimplify the debates, those who hold to an anthropocentric (human-centred) value theory deny that there is any such thing as inherent value in nature, while proponents of a biocentric (life-centred) or ecocentric (ecosystem-centred) value theory insist that there is such value, and that this value must be taken into account in determining what is a morally proper way to treat the natural environment.

The economic analysis we have been discussing above is based on an anthropocentric value theory (namely "preference utilitarianism") according to which morally relevant value consists in the satisfaction of human preferences. According to this view, it does not really make sense to talk about inherent values in nature. When those of an ecocentric persuasion speak of such inherent values, the economist would say that they are expressing an existence value. That is, according to the economist, when the ecocentrist says that some natural feature has value in and for itself, all this means is that the very existence of that feature is a source of satisfaction to the ecocentrist. This satisfaction is a social good, a contributor to overall utility, but it must be weighed against the satisfactions that would be derived from the economic activities or land uses that threaten the existence of the feature in question. Were the ecocentrist to maintain that such a balance must

take into account an inherent value in the feature *over and above* the satisfaction its existence provides, the economist would accuse the ecocentrist of merely trying to tip the moral and political balance in favour of the latter's own minority preference for nature preservation.[13]

The argument of this paper does not stand or fall on whether conservation value is reducible, in one way or another, to human welfare or satisfaction. Since wild beings can't buy property, market-based approaches will, from an ecocentric point of view, always tend to under-protect nature. On the other hand, since wild beings also can't vote, lobby or pay taxes, it may be that nature will inevitably be under-protected by the existing alternative mechanisms as well. More significant for our purposes is the concern that since few of the long-term, indirect resource values – much less the existence values – of natural features can be made to accrue exclusively to their "owners", these values tend to constitute "positive externalities". Economic reasoning discloses that markets will tend to under-supply "goods" that provide positive externalities (just as they tend to oversupply those that impose negative externalities). This implies that market mechanisms will tend to under-protect nature, even from the point of view of the value theory (anthropocentric preference utilitarianism) that pro-market arguments often rest on.

Market Mechanisms for Nature Conservation

Before assessing the arguments for and against market mechanisms for nature conservation in greater detail, it is necessary to say a bit more about what these mechanisms are. There are two institutional building blocks to the system I am describing. The first is a system of alienable property rights – both of the familiar sort and, more particularly, of a special kind called "conservation easements", about which more shortly. The second is a system of private non-profit organizations whose mission is to acquire property rights in environmentally significant land for the purpose of preserving natural heritage, biodiversity and ecological functions. These organizations are referred to as "conservation land trusts".[14] Conservation trusts may be nature, conservation or environmental groups that engage in other activities as well, or they may be more specialized bodies. In economists' terms, individuals express their preference for nature conservation to the extent that they donate money to conservation land trusts rather than spending it on other goods and services.

In order for a market to exist there has to be something that can be bought and sold. The "commodities" in this case are natural features and processes associated with particular pieces of land. These features and processes are what have conservation value. One way for these features to be acquired by those who want to preserve them is to buy the land outright. This has indeed been the usual way that governments, non-governmental nature groups and conservation land trusts have acquired natural features in the past.

To own a parcel of land is, strictly speaking, to hold a "bundle of rights" with respect to that land. The bundle includes, for example, the right to exclusive use of the land. In many cases, governments and private conservation groups want to use the lands they acquire for purposes in addition to simply conserving natural features – purposes such as nature-related recreation and education for the public or for organization members. In such cases, it often makes sense to acquire the whole bundle of rights recognized by traditional property law.

However, if all we want is the right to stop or restrict destructive activities on a particular piece of land, it is not necessary to have the exclusive right to use the land, nor even the right to use the land ourselves at all. The bundle of rights that constitutes outright ownership is more extensive than that required to protect particular features from destruction due to development or resource extraction (it may be insufficiently extensive to protect them from threats such as long-range pol-lution or global warming, but that is another story). If our purpose were simply the conservation of the valuable features, it would be desirable if we could acquire from the landowner just those rights that entitle the owner to use the land in ways that might threaten or destroy the valued features. We could then leave in the landowner's hands the exclusive right to use the land in ways that would not threaten or destroy those features.

Suppose, for example, we want to protect a farm woodlot that provides habitat for rare plants, birds and salamanders. We might want to pay the farmer to relinquish the right to log, build or otherwise disturb habitat in the woodlot. This would not give us the right to enter the woodlot at will, nor would it stop the farmer from entering it, hunting common game animals in it in the fall, taking maple sap in the spring, and so on. The farmer would, however, no longer have the right to use the woodlot in a destructive way, and would be paid a market price for having given up that right. We would have acquired only a small part of the bundle of rights that makes up the "ownership" of the farm. But since the arrangement would be a kind of property acquisition rather than merely a personal agreement with the owner, it would "run with the land" – ie., be registered against title and be binding on all future owners of the farm.

The sort of legal arrangement described here is called a "conservation easement", because it is analogous to a common law easement. A familiar example of a common law easement is a right of way across one property to provide access to an adjacent property (say, for a driveway or for hydro lines). In that case, certain rights pertaining to the first property (called the "servient tenement") are, so to speak, moved into the bundle of rights belonging to the owner of the second property (the "dominant tenement").

The difference between a conservation easement and an easement at common law is that the former is held not by the owner of an adjacent property but by a governmental or non-governmental organization concerned with conserving some aspect of the land. The conservation easement does not give its holder a right of way over the owner's land, but rather gives the holder a right to require that the owner manage the land in accordance with the terms of the easement. Finally, while common law easements have a long history, the conservation easement is a novel legal instrument created by statute. In Ontario, for example, a 1995 amendment to the *Conservation Lands Act* allowed non-governmental organizations to acquire conservation easements, thus establishing in the province the kind of market mechanism with which this chapter is concerned.[15] Conservation easements are still something of a novelty in Canada, but in the United States they cover close to a million hectares of land.[16]

It is important to note in passing that conservation easements and related legal instruments can be used to protect values other than natural heritage. In several North American jurisdictions, conservation easements have been used to protect agricultural land from (sub)urban development. Moreover, legislation enabling the creation of conservation easements is not necessarily or exclusively oriented toward the establishment of private market mechanisms, since such easements may be (or in some cases may only be) acquired by governments or public agencies. For example, Ontario's "Niagara Tender Fruit Lands Program" was to have established a scheme whereby easements for the conservation of high-quality orchard land in the Niagara Peninsula would be jointly purchased by the provincial and regional municipal governments. The program was aborted by the Conservative government shortly after its election in 1995.[17] In the present analysis, however, I am confining my attention to the protection of natural heritage and biodiversity values by means not funded through taxation.

Would the kinds of market mechanism sketched above actually have the potential to contribute in a practical way to the conservation of

natural heritage and biodiversity? Advocates of environmental protection through private property rights, such as Elizabeth Brubaker of the Canadian group Environment Probe, insist that they would. "When other resource users can find satisfactory substitutes for unique environmental tracts, they will find it cheaper to turn elsewhere than to engage in a bidding war with conservationists" she argues. "Since many industries have grown accustomed to having access to virtually free resources, they may be unable to match even the modest bids of those hoping to preserve the resource."[18]

In this connection, a system of conservation easements has particular advantages over traditional forms of land acquisition. Conservationists might not be able to afford to outbid developers for *all* the rights to a parcel of land, but as we have seen they do not need all these rights. A conservation easement might be used not to stop development on a parcel of land, but to control how and where on that parcel it occurs. The affordability hurdle should thus be much lower for an easement than it would be for an outright (i.e., fee simple) purchase, especially if the legal framework for conservation easements were flexible enough to permit the parties to negotiate any terms and transfer any rights. Indeed, one source estimates the cost, on a per acre basis, of acquiring a conservation easement to be only about three to five percent of the cost of purchasing the same property in fee simple, though the basis of this estimate is not provided.[19]

Ultimately, the persuasiveness of Brubaker's argument depends to a large extent on the nature of the resource use against which the conservationists are bidding. A group interested in preserving the ecological integrity of a scenic wooded tract near a large city might be able to outbid a logging contractor, but would be much less likely to be able to outbid a developer of estate subdivisions. Nevertheless, the ecological impact of the subdivision might be much greater than that of logging, even if the developer enters into an easement protecting certain especially significant features. Because the price of rights in land is relative to the development value of the land, only features unlikely to be destroyed anyway will be affordable. If land has high development value, the price of the land or of any easement that would encompass the development rights to the land would be prohibitively expensive. Conservation easements would be inexpensive for land with low development value, but in most cases such land would not be developed anyway, so the purchase of such easements would result in few natural features being saved from development.

Serious doubts remain, therefore, about the potential effectiveness of market forces in protecting nature, even in jurisdictions with conservation easement legislation. For philosophical proponents of the market, however, it is by no means necessarily a bad thing that preserving nature on land with high development value is difficult and expensive. We will have occasion to consider why this is so in the next section. My point here is merely that the practical advantages of market mechanisms from the point of view of those for whom nature protection is a priority prove more modest than some have implied.

Liberty, Efficiency and Equity Arguments

We may now turn to a more detailed consideration of the advantages, disadvantages and implications of market based nature conservation mechanisms. As mentioned above, arguments for market ordering typically rest on the values of liberty, efficiency and some versions of fairness. How would these arguments apply in the case of nature conservation issues?

Let us start with the value of liberty. I would begin this discussion by noting that the existence value of any natural feature will vary widely among members of society. As the famous American conservationist Aldo Leopold put it, "[t]here are some who can live without wild things and

some who cannot".[20] For some people the protection of natural heritage is an important value, for others it is not. Market advocates might argue that non-market mechanisms for nature preservation violate the liberty of those who do not value nature, either by forcing them against their will to protect natural features on their own property, or by forcing them through taxation to pay for the acquisition of such features.

Of course, the liberty value upon which this argument rests is a wholly anthropocentric one. Nature preservationists might argue that government action to preserve inherent values in nature does not violate liberty of would-be developers and exploiters any more than government action to prevent and punish violence violates the liberty of would-be murderers and assaulters. Libertarians would themselves reject this analogy on the ground that the liberty value they espouse presupposes at least a minimal mutual respect among persons, but does not presuppose a respect for inherent values in nature.

Stopping people from murdering does not on their view offend the principle of liberty because it is necessary to protect the liberty of victims (i.e., their freedom from unwanted lethal assault); stopping people from paving over rare orchids is not so necessary to protect the freedom of persons and so does offend the principle of liberty. If the government is stopping people from paving over rare orchids then it is infringing on the liberty of the paver, either for the sake of those who value the orchids or for the sake of the (existence of) orchids themselves. In the former case, the government is using its power to impose the preferences of some people (those who value rare orchids) on others (those who don't value rare orchids). In the latter case, it is imposing the moral beliefs of some people (those who think we ought to protect rare orchids for their own sake) on others (those who don't think we can have moral obligations to plants).

Whether or not this imposition is justified depends upon the relative weights assigned to individual human liberty and to various competing environmental values. What counts in favour of the market approach is that if the landowner – the would-be rare orchid paver – voluntarily relinquishes the right to destroy the orchids, in return (if need be) for payment out of funds voluntarily contributed for such purposes to a conservation land trust, then the orchids are saved in a way that is consistent with the strictest adherence to the principle of liberty. This is good from the point of view of orchid-lovers, from the point of view of the erstwhile paver, and finally from the point of view (if one there be) of the orchids themselves and of the ecological community of which they are a part. Pragmatic conservationists, with no particular philosophical or ideological commitment to the priority of libertarian principles, may favour such an approach because it avoids spawning resentments among landowners and taxpayers which have the potential of turning immediate conservation victories into long-term political liabilities.

Next, let us consider the argument from the value of efficiency. Nature conservation through flexible contractual conservation easement arrangements would be economically efficient in the sense that natural features will be conserved when the "conservation value" of the site (as determined by conservationists' willingness to pay) exceeds the "development value" (as determined by willingness to pay for goods and services derived from the development of the site). This approach will therefore tend to maximize human consumer preferences, and result in the conservation of lands with high conservation value and/or low development value.

Our meadow of rare orchids, for example, has existence value as an instance of natural heritage and as a contributor to regional biodiversity. It also has value for uses, such as housing or agriculture, incompatible with the continued existence of the

orchids. Which (non)use, then, should prevail? From the point of view of economic efficiency, the use that should prevail is the one that provides the greatest net aggregate (human) preference satisfaction. This means that to answer the question we cannot look only at the natural features of the site, nor only at the prospective development values. According to an economic analysis, a natural feature ought, on the basis of its existence value, be preserved if competing uses are of lower value. This same feature ought not be preserved, however, if the value of the competing uses exceeds the conservation value of the feature.

In the absence of both regulation and a market for conservation values (such as a system of land trusts and conservation easements), natural features will tend to be preserved only when there are no competing uses – that is, under circumstances of benign neglect. Natural features will tend to be destroyed if there is any profit to be made thereby, even if the conservation value of the natural feature (were there a market in which such value could be expressed) would exceed the revenues obtainable from the destructive use. On the other hand, if a regulatory scheme is in place that prohibits the development of sites meeting certain criteria of environmental significance, then these sites cannot be developed even if the value to society of their development would far exceed that of their conservation.

From the perspective of economic theory, both of these outcomes are inefficient. It might be that the value to society of the meadow in its natural state, as reflected in the amount that nature-lovers are – through conservation trusts – willing to pay for its preservation, is greater than its value for agriculture, as reflected in the amount that consumers are willing to pay for the agricultural products it would generate. However, conservation trusts may not be willing or able to outbid developers who want to construct houses on the site. In the latter case the orchids will not be preserved, and that is as it should be, since if people are willing to pay developers more for houses than they are willing to pay conservation trusts for the existence of rare orchids it is (virtually by definition) because the housing is worth more to them.

If housing on this site provides more utility than rare orchids do, then, from an economic point of view, housing is the better use of the site. But if the same net housing values could be provided by the development of a less sensitive site, doing so would produce even more utility, since the utility of the orchids to plant buffs and biodiversity advocates would be retained. Because developers would not have to outbid conservationists to build on sites without rare orchids and the like, housing on such sites would be that much cheaper, and market forces would tend to encourage development away from environmentally significant areas. If a land trust had already acquired a conservation easement on the site, the prospective developer would have to buy the development rights from the conservationists. If the developer offered enough, and if the orchids were not all that rare, the conservationists might accept the offer and use the money to acquire more or more valuable lands elsewhere.

So far I have been canvassing arguments to the effect that a reliance on market mechanisms of the kinds proposed will spontaneously result in an economically efficient level of natural heritage conservation. Even if this were true, it does not follow that we should necessarily adopt a policy of relying on these mechanisms. Critics of economic efficiency as a criterion for evaluating environmental policy argue that environmental "goods" such as natural heritage are in principle unpriceable, and that the goals of public policy should be determined by ethical values other than aggregate human welfare.[21]

Moreover, there are reasons to think that a market in conservation easements would not automatically result in an economically efficient level of nature conservation. In the first place, to do so the mechanism would have to operate in a context where hidden subsidies and other externalities did not distort the market's allocation of land uses. Environmentalists argue that current government policies in Canada subsidize environmentally destructive activities in a plethora of direct and indirect ways.[22] Conservationists would therefore not face a "level playing field" in bidding for land rights against the proponents of such activities.

The second reason for supposing that the market in conservation easements would not protect enough natural land (even from the perspective of an economic analysis) is the so-called "free-rider problem". The only way that the market will provide a good is if those who consume or otherwise benefit from that good can be made to pay for it – that is, if they can be excluded from enjoying the good if they do not. Markets thus tend to under-produce public goods such as environmental quality, because it is difficult to restrict the enjoyment or "consumption" of these goods to "buyers". If the "good" in question is not the tangible enjoyment but the very existence of something, it becomes not merely a practical but a logical impossibility to exclude "free riders".

In this case the free riders are those who derive satisfaction from the continuing existence of natural features protected by conservation land trusts but who do not contribute financially to them. Conservation trusts cannot prevent those who fail to pay their share from taking satisfaction from the continued existence of those natural features the trusts protect. Conservation trusts will thus always be underfunded relative to the social benefits they provide. For this reason, too, they will be disadvantaged in bidding for land rights against industries whose products typically must be purchased in order to be consumed, and who are thus in a better position than conservation trusts are to obtain payment for the social benefits they generate. Unlike the first disadvantage, this latter one cannot be remedied by more even-handed government policies.

Let us now consider the issue of equity. As mentioned before, critics of the market often argue that even when market outcomes are efficient in economic terms, they are very likely to be inequitable, both because some people are able to appropriate a much larger share of social benefits than others, and because those who are able to appropriate more are able – by virtue of their greater purchasing power – to have a disproportionate say in what counts as "social benefit". To some extent these criticisms apply in the present context. The market in natural heritage could obviously produce windfalls for owners of sites with particularly high conservation value. Conservation value would in turn be disproportionately determined by the preferences of those with greater amounts of disposable wealth. This is because the conservation and spending priorities of land trusts would tend to reflect the tastes and values of those who contribute the most money to them.

On the other hand, a market-based approach to nature conservation could have some egalitarian distributive consequences as well. It is sometimes suggested that government decisions to halt or restrict development in order to protect natural heritage satisfy the preferences of relatively affluent, and mainly urban, environmentalist and nature lovers, at the expense of less affluent rural communities.[23] Moreover, rural landowners are inclined to regard nature protection regulations not merely as infringements on their liberty but as a form of expropriation without compensation that unfairly imposes economic hardships on them.[24] Under the market system, conservationists would purchase development rights rather than rely on governments to restrict or extinguish them by means of regulatory or planning instruments. Such a system might be expected to effect a modest transfer of wealth from urban regions (where the bulk of "demand" for conservation value originates) to rural regions where the conservation value exists and which bear the economic "burden" of conservation.

Perils and Paradoxes

The upshot of the discussion so far is that market mechanisms such as conservation easements are, on their own, unlikely to provide adequate levels of nature conservation even from an anthropocentric (much less an ecocentric) perspective, but that they have certain attractive qualities from the points of view of liberty, efficiency and equity. The implication of all this would appear to be that while conservationists would be unwise to advocate reliance on a pure market model, even if such a thing were possible, there would be nothing to lose and perhaps something to gain, socially, from the introduction of conservation easement laws and their vigorous use by conservation land trusts.

Since conservation value is chiefly an "existence value" rather than a consumption value, it is especially likely to constitute a "positive externality". In economic terms, the purpose of conservation easements and the like is to "internalize" this externality by compensating the provider. In theory, if we internalize a positive externality we should end up with more of the value in question (and if we internalize a negative externality we should end up with less of the bad).

However, natural heritage is a "commodity" with a peculiar combination of attributes such that creating a market for it may, I will argue, have just the opposite of this intended effect. First, if the land has little or no development value, providing a positive externality by protecting natural features whose existence is valued is effectively costless to the "provider". Second, since conservation value is an existence value, a pure positive externality, there is no way for the "provider" to "withhold" this commodity from its "consumers" pending payment. This is the free rider problem discussed above. Third, the existence value in question often attaches to unique, non-fungible aspects of the land. It is not just that we want to protect so many hectares of forest habitat (though that is important too). Often, we want especially to protect this particular tract of forest habitat, because of the particular combination of species, communities and physical features it harbours. The "consumers" in this instance, those who prefer the continued existence of this unique set of features and are willing to pay for it, cannot "go elsewhere" in the market to satisfy that preference. Moreover, no amount of economic incentive can increase the supply of these "existence goods", it can only slow their loss. The landowner is thus in a monopoly situation.

These three factors intersect in such a way that the market scheme under consideration here could create an incentive for owners of valuable natural features to make extortionate threats to destroy those features unless the right to destroy them is purchased. By "extortionate", I mean that there is no other economic reason to destroy the feature – indeed, destroying the feature might be costly to the owner and provide no return in itself. For example, the owner might threaten to hire a knowledgable person to seek out and destroy all specimens of rare species on the property unless a conservation easement is purchased. This destruction is gratuitous, and in the absence of a market in natural heritage is irrational. If a conservation easement scheme is in place, however, it can be seen as a rational strategy on the part of the owner to appropriate some or all of the surplus conservation value of the land. Of course, such gratuitous destruction is also self-interestedly rational – and is reputed sometimes to occur – in the face of regulations aimed at preserving significant natural features.

To help explain the next step in my argument, let me coin the term "conservation surplus". I define conservation surplus as the difference between the conservation value and development value of a feature when the conservation value is greater.[25] In economic terms, the "conservation value" of, say, our meadow of rare orchids is what conservationists (through land trusts or otherwise) would be willing to pay to preserve that meadow. The "development value" is the net economic value

to the owner of "developing" the site in a way that would destroy or degrade the orchids' habitat. The market price of a conservation easement will be somewhere between the development value and the conservation value, where both are understood in economic terms. The higher the price the owner is able to obtain – that is, the closer the price comes to the full conservation value – the greater a proportion of the potential conservation surplus the owner will have succeeded in appropriating.

If the development value of the site is significant (so that preserving the orchids' habitat is not costless), the conservation surplus will tend to be small. In that case, most of the price of a conservation easement would go to compensate the owner for forgone development revenues. If the development value were very low, the conservation surplus could be quite large. Much of the price of a conservation easement in that case would, if the owner succeeded in driving a hard bargain, come out of the conservation surplus. In the absence of a market this "surplus" is notional only, and constitutes free good to society. It cannot be appropriated as a private pecuniary asset. With the creation of a market in conservation values, the conservation surplus becomes a pecuniary stake. It is a stake that can be won by the owner who drives a hard bargain by making a credible threat to "withhold" the good in question.

There are other circumstances where someone in a monopoly situation is able to reap a windfall by withholding the commodity until a high price is offered. But, except perhaps in the case of perishable commodities, the value is not destroyed thereby. Where the "commodity" is a unique and irreplaceable good the mere existence (not possession) of which is valued, the good can be withheld only by being destroyed. A pattern of gratuitous destruction (if itself not too costly) would establish the credibility of the threat sufficient to exact compensation for that good. A framework (such as conservation easements) to allow that compensation may thus actually result in *less* of the "good" (in this case, intrinsically valuable natural features) being "provided".

Perhaps, then, the conservation easement framework should be accompanied by strong laws against the gratuitous destruction of nature. There are obvious difficulties involved in framing and enforcing such laws. How is the law to draw a boundary between destruction that is "gratuitous" and that which is motivated by "legitimate" self-interest? Practical drafting and enforcement difficulties aside, such a law would nullify one of the advantages of conservation through market mechanisms, which is minimal intrusion on landowners' liberty to do as they please with their property. Conservationists have long regarded this notion of liberty as ecologically ignorant and ethically benighted.[26] Nevertheless, particularly in rural areas, it is still the case that many landowners (including those who accept that ecological and ethical responsibilities go along with property rights) deeply resent government interference with private property. What is resented is likely to be resisted, and given the difficulties of enforcement such laws may prove counterproductive.

I would conclude this paper by returning to a point made at the beginning. "Private stewardship" has always been, for its proponents, much more a matter of ecological education and moral suasion than of land acquisition and market mechanisms. The experience of "grassroots" nature conservationists tends to be that rural landowners, once informed, greatly value the contributions made by the features on their land to natural heritage and biodiversity.[27] They value these features, moreover, for their own sakes and not for any market value that might attach to them by way of conservation easements and the like.

This raises a further concern about market mechanisms. According to a well-known argument by Richard Titmuss, the American practice of buying blood does not actually increase the

blood supply because, while turning blood into a market commodity creates a financial incentive to give, it simultaneously undermines the "moral incentive" for voluntary donation.[28] By the same token, it is possible that the widespread adoption of market mechanisms for nature conservation will have the effect of undermining the moral incentive for voluntary stewardship.

We are left with the following three-pronged dilemma (or "trilemma", rather). 1) Reliance on voluntary stewardship is likely to result in inadequate levels of protection for very valuable natural features in circumstances where the opportunity cost to landowners of protection is significant. 2) Market mechanisms may tend to undermine voluntary (or merely passive) protection in circumstances where the opportunity cost of protection is low. Further, because existence value is the epitome of a public good from which none can be excluded, private funds for preservation will always tend to be scarce and, as a result, such mechanisms will also tend to result in inadequate protection in circumstances where the opportunity cost of protection is high. 3) Government action, to the extent that it is coercive, will undermine voluntary stewardship by fostering in the minds of rural landowners an association between nature conservation and oppressive bureaucracy. To the extent that government action is expensive, it will run afoul of fiscal constraints.

The way ahead is thus not clear. What is clear is that pure market mechanisms will provide inadequate levels of protection for natural heritage and biodiversity. This is so even if "adequacy" is judged according to criteria derived from a philosophical perspective – preference utilitarianism – within which arguments for market ordering are typically framed. Innovative and creative market-based approaches may provide new ways for nature conservation to proceed in a laissez-faire context, but even so may carry risks of their own.

ENDNOTES

[1] T. Anderson and D. Leal, *Free Market Environmentalism* (San Francisco: Westview, 1991).

[2] Brian Dunkiel, "Using conservation easements in creating regional reserve systems", *Wild Earth* 5(3):62-65.

[3] Stewart Hilts and Ron Reid, *Creative Conservation: A Handbook for Ontario Land Trusts* (Toronto: Federation of Ontario Naturalists, 1993).

[4] See Robert Nozick, *Anarchy, State and Utopia* (N.Y.: Basic Books, 1974). One may, of course, be "forced" by circumstances such as poverty or a weak bargaining position into disposing of one's property or labour under unsatisfactory terms, but this is not deemed by libertarians to be "coercion" in a morally relevant sense.

[5] In this case it is said to be efficient according to the less stringent "potential Pareto criterion". The costs and benefits are measured in terms of the dollar values that the beneficiaries and victims would themselves put on them. We could, for example, attempt to discover how much those who are negatively affected would be willing to pay to change the situation they dislike or, alternatively, how much they would demand in compensation for being willing to put up with it. In this way everyone's satisfactions and dissatisfactions could in principle be measured in the common currency of money, making it theoretically possible to add up all the satisfaction produced by (say) a particular land use, to subtract all the dissatisfaction produced, and to determine whether on balance the land use does or does not contribute to over-all welfare – in other words, whether it is or is not "economically efficient".

[6] Gordon Tullock, "The social cost of reducing social cost," in Garrett Hardin and John Baden, eds., *Managing the Commons* (San Francisco: W. H. Freeman & Co., 1977)

[7] See, for example, Ted Schrecker, *The Political Economy of Environmental Hazards* (Ottawa: Law Reform Commission of Canada, 1984) ch. 3.

[8] See Tullock (note 7 above); see also Charles Lindblom, *Politics and Markets* (N.Y.: Basic Books, 1977).

[9] John Rawls, *A Theory of Justice*, (London: Oxford University Press, 1971).

[10] Wallace Kaufman, *No Turning Back: Dismantling the Fantasies of Environmental Thinking* (N.Y.: Basic Books, 1992:116-132).

[11] Conservationists have come increasingly to define their goals in terms of the protection of "biodiversity". Biodiversity refers to the total range of biological diversity from the genetic level (the amount of genetic variation within species) through the species level (the number of species and other taxa) through to the ecological level (the variety of different ecological community types and ecological relations that exist. For a brief discussion of the various reasons given for valuing biodiversity, see, for example, E.O. Wilson, "Biophilia and the Conservation Ethic", in E.O Wilson and S. Kellert, editors, *The Biophilia Hypothesis* (Washington: Island Press, 1993).

[12] See, eg., Paul F. J. Eagles, "Criteria for the designation of Environmentally Sensitive Areas," in Suzanne Barrett and John Riley, eds., *Protection of Natural Areas in Ontario: Proceedings of a Conference* (North York: York University Faculty of Environmental Studies Working Paper No. 3, 1980); Catherine Dunster "Stewardship," *Wildflower* 6 (Spring 1990):31-36; John Riley and Pat Mohr, *Review of Conservation and Restoration Ecology for Land-Use and Landscape Planning* (Aurora, Ont.: Ontario Ministry of Natural Resources, 1994).

[13] Ecocentrists reply that economists, by treating statements of ethical principle as expressions of personal preference, are undermining the logic of their own argument as well. The economists' position is, after all, itself a matter of principle, but they do not seem to regard economic analysis as a mere personal preference to be weighed against others'. Rather, they regard it as a rational and ethical way of making policy decisions. As Mark Sagoff points out, to be consistent, economists would have to ask themselves how much they would be willing to pay to have policy decisions made on the basis of willingness-to-pay. See Mark Sagoff, At the Shrine of Our Lady of Fatima, or, Why Political Questions are Not All Economic," *Arizona Law Review* 23(1982):1292-95; and "We Have Met the Enemy and He is Us: Conflict and Contradiction in Environmental Law", *Environmental Law* 12(1982):291-92.

[14] See Hilts and Reid *Creative Conservation: A Handbook for Ontario Land Trusts*, cited above.

[15] Prior to the amendment (Bill 175) conservation easements could be held only by certain Ontario government agencies, and were little used. For more information on conservation easements, see: Ian Attridge, Thea Silver, Maria McRae and Kenneth Cox, *Canadian Legislation for Conservation Covenants, Easements and Servitudes: The Current Situation* (Ottawa: North American Wetlands Conservation Council, 1995), and Thomas Barret and Janet Diehl, *The Conservation Easement Handbook* (San Francisco: Trust for Public Land, 1988).

[16] Hilts and Reid, *Creative Conservation* pp. 125f.

[17] Michael Valpy, "An axe to the fruit trees", *The Globe & Mail* 14 July 1995 A15.

[18] Elizabeth Brubaker, *Property Rights in the Defense of Nature* (Toronto: Earthscan, 1995): 195.

[19] Neida Gonzalez, *A Citizen's Guide to Protecting Wetlands and Woodlands* (Don Mills, Ont.: Federation of Ontario Naturalists, 1996):53-54.

[20] Aldo Leopold, *A Sand County Almanac* (N.Y.:Ballantyne, 1966 [1949]), p. xvii.

[21] See, eg., Steven Kelman, "Cost-benefit analysis – an ethical critique", *Regulation* (Jan./Feb. 1981) pp.74-82, and the articles by Mark Sagoff cited above in note 11.

[22] Wayne Roberts, John Bacher and Brian Nelson, *Get A Life! A Green Cure for Canada's Economic Blues* (Toronto: Get A Life Publishing, 1993).

[23] Ted Schrecker, "Resisting Environmental Regulation: The Cryptic Pattern of Business-Government Relations", in R. Paehlke and D. Torgerson (eds.), *Managing Leviathan: Environmental Politics and the Administrative State* (Peterborough: Broadview, 1990).

[24] Kaufman (above note 5) pp. 116-132; Elizabeth Brubaker, *Property Rights in the Defense of Nature* (Toronto: Earthscan, 1995) pp.190-192.

[25] The concept is analogous to that of "consumer surplus" in economics.

[26] See, for example, Aldo Leopold's famous essay "The Land Ethic", in *A Sand County Almanac*, cited above.

[27] Sally Lerner, *Environmental Stewardship: Studies in Active Earthkeeping* (Waterloo: University of Waterloo Department of Geography, 1993).

[28] Richard Titmuss, *The Gift Relationship: From Human Blood to Social Policy* (N.Y.: George Allen and Unwin, 1971).

TERRORISM AT OKA
ENVIRONMENTAL RACISM AND THE FIRST NATIONS OF CANADA

17
by Laura Westra

THIS IS A CASE STUDY ABOUT ENVIRONMENTAL RACism, recently emerging as a "new" issue, in the United States and in Less Developed Countries. Environmental racism is a form of discrimination against minority groups and countries in the Third World, practiced in and through the environment. It involves such practices as the siting of hazardous or toxic waste dumps in areas inhabited primarily by people of colour, or hiring blacks or Native Americans to work in hazardous industries, or even exporting toxic waste to impoverished countries (Westra and Wenz, 1995). However, the problem acquires a new "face" when it affects the Aboriginal people of Canada. In their case, questions about environmental racism cannot be separated from issues of sovereignty and treaty rights, and this is clearly not the case for either urban or rural African-Americans, nor is it true of American Indian people. In the United States, Indians are "regarded in law as 'domestic dependent nations' with some residual sovereign powers. In Canada the majority of First Nations people seek recognition under the Constitution of Canada of an inherent right to self-government" (Fifth Report of the Standing Committee on Aboriginal Affairs, House of Commons, Canada, May 1991; henceforth cited as FR).

This difference is extremely significant as it injects an additional component of violence, repression and state-terrorism which is largely absent from cases affecting visible minorities in the United States, where even violence takes on quite different connotations and has no component of national self-defense (Westra, 1995a). This additional component will emerge clearly as the Oka confrontation is discussed in order to show this

Canadian "difference" in Section 3.

Environmental racism is not a new phenomenon, but it is a new issue to some extent as it has been targeted by the Clinton administration; Clinton signed an "Executive Order" on February 11, 1994 to make environmental justice for minorities a specific concern for the Environmental Protection Agency (Bullard, 1995).

1. The Mohawks at Kahnawake and Kanesatake, and the Confrontation at Oka, Québec, Summer 1990

In order to understand the events culminating in the Summer of 1990, several complex issues underlying the conflict must be understood. These are, a) the position of the Mohawks and their forms of government as well as that of the Canadian government; b) the environmental issue and he demands of the Township of Oka; c) the chronology of the actual events and confrontation. All three will be discussed in turn.

a) The Federal Government, the "Indian Act" and Mohawks' Governance

Mohawk communities in Canada total 39,263 persons, including Kanesatake, Kahnawake, Akwesasne, and another four. The Kanesatake community totals 1,591 persons and the department of Indian Affairs funds their budget for education costs. Status Indians are eligible to attend both elementary and secondary schools off the reserve (FR. 1991). Nevertheless the "status of Kanesatake with respect to the land does not fit within the usual pattern of Indian reserve lands in Canada": they are Indians within the meaning of the term under the Indian Act, live on Crown Lands (since 1945), reserved for their use (within the meaning of s.91 (24) of the Constitution Act of 1867), but they do not live on lands clearly having status as an Indian Act Reserve (FR, 1991).

The reason for this anomaly can be traced to the 1717 Land Grant by the King of France, and the "seigneurial grant at Lac des Deux Montagnes", given to the "Ecclesiasticals of the Seminary of St. Sulpice". The Sulpicians' mandate was "the purpose of protecting and instructing the indigenous people (a policy reflecting the ethnocentrism and paternalism of that time)" (FR, 1991). This led to continuous disputes between the Mohawks at Kanesatake and the Sulpicians over land sales and management. In fact the Sulpicians asked France's King for a second land grant, "to provide a greater land base for the Indians", and this, too, was granted in 1735. The Indians were told that the land would revert to the Sulpicians only in the event that the Indians would decide to leave. But the Sulpician's "tutelage" and paternalism quickly turned to tough-minded abuse. The Indians were allowed to build houses and grow crops, but they could neither sell land nor wood or hay, without explicit permission. They could be brought to trial for cutting wood for snowshoes, house-repairs or firewood and, despite the Indians' repeated petitions to the King of France and, after his defeat by the British, to all those in power, their miserable conditions and the exploitation of their lands continued unabated. The Sulpicians explained their position by saying that, without strict controls, the "Savages" would return to their "natural laziness" (Pindera and York, 1991).

A French native of the region turned Methodist missionary records many instances of inhumane cruelty and mistreatment of Indians on the part of the priests. When Amand Parent returned to establish a small Methodist Church at Oka in 1872, the Sulpicians felt he taught the Indians to behave "above their station", and he too encountered ill-treatment and hostility. In 1875, the Church was torn down by Crown order, because it had been erected without permission, with wood from the Seigneury (A. Parent, 1887). In 1936 the Sulpicians, blatantly disregarding the original French mandate, sold much of the land to a rich Belgian, Baron Empain, who in turn resold it in 1950.

The Canadian government records note the continuing disputes which at times led to confrontations in the area. In 1912, a decree of the Privy Council (then the highest Court of Appeal for Canadian cases), officially deprived the Mohawks of any rights in respect to the lands, "by virtue of aboriginal title" (Corinthe v. Seminary of St. Sulpice). As the Seminary continued to sell off lands, the Federal Government attempted to put a stop to the controversies by purchasing the rest of the Sulpicians' lands, in 1945, without consulting the Mohawks. These lands, however, were interspersed with "blocks" privately owned by the municipality of Oka (Begin, Moss & Miemczak, 1990).

The Mohawks, on the other hand, continued to advance their claims, on separate, but related, legal grounds:

1) territorial sovereignty flowing from status as a sovereign nation;

2) treaty rights;

3) the Royal Proclamation of 1763;

4) unextinguished aboriginal title under common law;

5) land rights flowing from the obligations imposed on the Sulpicians in the 18th century land grants by the King of France; (Pindera and York, 1991).

The Federal Government instead believed that a) the issues were settled by the Privy Council Order of 1912; b) that the claims were weakened by the fact the Mohawks have not been continuously in possession of the land since time immemorial, as "land use by natives and non-natives is also recorded". These land users included some white settlers, as well as other native tribes. However, the Federal Department also described the Mohawks at Oka as descendants of some of these other groups who had been in possession, that is the Iroquois, Algonquians and Nipissings (Information Sheet, July 1990, "Mohawk Band government"). In fact the Federal Government attempted to purchase additional land to give the Mohawks at Kanesatake a "unified land base", from 1985, up to the time of the Oka conflict.

Additionally, the Canadian Government requires certain specific forms of Indian government, in order to recognize Indians' sovereign nation status. The Mohawks at Oka have a long history of debate about their own forms of governance. They belong to the Six Nations of the "Iroquois confederacy (the other five are Oneida, Onondaga, Cayuga, Seneca and Tuscarora), governed by the "Great Law of Peace" (Kayanerakowa), or the "Longhouse System". But the department of Indian Affairs (under the Indian Act), supports the Act's election system of band councils, instead. Chief Samson Gabriel wrote in 1967 that the Longhouse was the only form of legitimate Mohawk governance. As Chief Gabriel put it,

We recognize no power to establish peacefully, or by the use of force or violence, a competitive political administration. Transactions of such groups in political and international affairs is very disturbing to the Six Nations "Iroquois Confederacy Chiefs" (Pindera and York, 1991).

In essence, there is a direct connection between any possible progress on land rights, native sovereignty or self-determination, and progress on the issue of Mohawk leadership or governance. The Department of Indian Affairs may permit the application of the Indian Act, "on an interim basis", until some appropriate alternative local form of government policy can be established. If the Mohawks could not agree on the forms of leadership and governance appropriate to their tribe, then the Department of Indian Affairs could refuse to

consider their claims, because no local (Native) governance policy was firmly established, as required.[1]

(b) The Environmental Issues and the Demands of the Oka Township in 1990

The previous section details the political and ideological controversies that led to the violence at Oka. "The controversies included conflicts over divergent Native ideologies about self-government and about the historical residence of other tribes in the disputed area, which was viewed by some to invalidate any native land claim on the part of the Mohawks." Before turning to a narrative of the events of the Summer of 1990, it is necessary to show the role environmental issues played in the racism and the violence of the events that followed the dispute.

The municipality of Oka, "legally owns the clearing in the Pines and calls it a municipal park", but the Mohawks argue that the land is theirs, and that they never sold it or gave it away, hence they do not recognize that ownership claim. The Pines have been part of the Kanesatake territory for over 270 years. About one hundred years ago, the fine and sandy soil of the crest of the hill overlooking Oka, was severely affected by deforestation, and in danger of being washed away by the rains. The Mohawks, together with the Sulpician fathers, planted "tens of thousands of trees in the shifting sand". That area is now known as "the commons", at the very heart of the eight hundred hectares of Mohawk settlement.

Thus the Mohawks' approach to dealing with the Pines was ecologically sound, and it is easy to understand their dismay at the later turn of events. They believed that the original "Lake of Two Mountains" seigneury (including the parish and the town of Oka), was their property. Yet they had to watch powerlessly as housing and recreational developments, including a golf course, continued to erode what they took to be Mohawk lands, in order to benefit the rich newcomers.

A small graveyard, the Pine Hill Cemetery, holds the bones of dead Mohawks at Kanesatake, the parents and grandparents of the warriors who were to fight for the Pines in 1990. It is placed between the Oka Golf Club's driveway and its parking lot.

The Mohawks have cherished the Pines since they were planted, and they organize a careful clean-up of the area every year. But in March, 1989, Oka's Mayor, Jean Ouellette, unveiled his plans for the expansion of the Golf Club. A strip of eighteen hectares of forest and swampland near the clearing in the Pines was to be bought and leased to the Oka Golf Club, in order to add nine holes to the present golf course. The Mayor did not consult the Mohawks as he believed he had the law on his side: the government had "consistently denied the Mohawk land claims for 150 years" (Pindera and York, 1991). When an angry citizen demanded to know a) why the township had been faced with a "fait accompli", instead of being consulted before the fact; and b) why the Indians had not been consulted, Ouellette responded with a shrug and said, "You know you can't talk to the Indians" (Pindera and York, 1991). Many citizens were outraged by the Mayor's attitude: nine hundred signed a petition opposing the project which was perceived not to be in the interest of the general public as well as being environmentally unsound.

This is basic to the argument of this paper. The Pines' soil is sandy, so erosion and shifting sands on the hillside would again become a continuing threat, if the painstakingly planted and nurtured trees were to be cut. At one time, in the nineteenth century, the sands had threatened to bury the town, and that formed the rationale for the planting of the pines themselves, to reforest the area. Moreover, there are two additional environmental problems that are not even mentioned in the literature describing the Oka incident: 1) the Indian "worldview" about land and their respect for natural entities and laws; and 2) the particularly haz-

ardous nature of the envisioned project.

First, Native Worldviews (basic to all Indian groups in North America) involve respect for nature and all the creatures with whom we share a habitat. Disrespect and wasteful use of anything on Earth are unacceptable to Indians as a people, totally aside from personal preferences or even personal or group advantage (M. Sagoff, 1989). This represents a basic belief, a value akin to a religious one, and not to be confused with political beliefs about sovereignty or self-governance.

Further, even aside from the issue of shifting sands and deforestation, or of religious and traditional beliefs, the enterprise, namely a golf course, for which deforestation was planned, is often a significant source of environmental contamination in spite of its benign green appearance (D. Pimentel, 1993). Lise Bacon, environmental minister at the time, could neither help nor intervene because the law did not require an environmental impact study for a recreational project in the municipality. But although "golf courses" are much in demand when they are adjacent to better housing developments, as well as for the sport for which they are created, their perfect manicured appearance depends heavily on fungicides, pesticides and other chemicals that are hazardous to wild life, ecosystems and human health (Pimentel, 1992; Pimentel, 1991).

Hence, aside from the question of Mohawks' rights in regard to First Nations' Sovereignty, the People of the Pines were correct in their opposition to the development, and so were the other objectors who protested on environmental grounds based on the value of life-support systems and the inappropriateness of siting a hazardous, chemically dependent operation near a fragile ecosystem on which the Mohawks depended (Westra, 1994a; Westra, 1994b). The Mohawks' life-style requires a healthy, unpolluted habitat even more conspicuously than other Canadians because their worldview entails particularly close ties to the land, and their traditional reliance on hunting and fishing self-sufficiency demands it. As a people, and as a separate Nation, they have the right to live according to their religious beliefs, without being second-guessed or overruled by others. Even if they were not viewed as a separate nation and a separate people, according to the Canadian Constitution, but simply as any other Canadians, they would have the right to live according to their own convictions. But the respect due and normally accorded separate ethno-cultural or religious groups was not accorded to the Mohawks.

Hence, they were treated in a way which did not accord them either the respect due them as free and equal citizens, or the respect due to citizens of a separate sovereign nation (that is, as people who were not subject to Canadian laws on their own territories). The lack of understanding and respect led to the ongoing hostility and the racism demonstrated through the events of the Summer of 1990.

In this case, the racism was and is perpetrated in and through the land; it manifested itself in the careless attempt to impose environmental degradation and ecological disintegrity, hence it can be termed appropriately a form of environmental racism, but one which showed a unique specifically Canadian "face".

c) The Chronology of the Events
and the Confrontation at Oka (Summer 1990)
In early March 1990 the Township Council pressed for proceeding with plans for the Golf Club expansion, against a background of vacillations from Ottawa about appropriate forms of governance. The Mohawks, although disagreeing among themselves on the part of the Mohawks, were united in their opposition to the Council and the Mayor of Oka. In essence, although the Mohawks had always maintained that even the blocks that had been sold off to the township were part of their territory, there was a lot of disagreement on the question of compliance with the Indian Act. The Department of Indian Affairs demanded that "traditional or band custom councils"

be used to pass band resolutions and to administer funds from Ottawa, and that some sort of democratic elections be used.

The Longhouse form of Government was the Mohawks' traditional way, involving clan mothers whose role was "to listen to the people of their clans and counsel the Longhouse chiefs" (Pindera and York, 1991). When word spread about a possible early start to the project, a camp was set up in the clearing in the Pines to alert band members through an "early warning system": this was the start of the occupation on March 10, 1990. As word spread through the Kanasatake, more and more people came to see what was happening, then decided to stay. Signs were erected near the edge of the golf course in French and English, saying "Are you aware that this is Mohawk land?" (Pindera and York, 1991).

Although many Mohawks did not take the occupation seriously, others started to spend more time at the camp each day as they returned from work or from school, and some initiated nightshift armed with sticks, branches and ax handles for protection. After Earth Day, April 22, 1990, when the Mohawks traditionally cleaned up the forest area of garbage and debris, more and more Mohawks joined the camp. They were armed and erected the Warrior Flag and set up barricades of cement blocks a few meters back from Highway 344, and pushed a large fallen log across the northern entrance of the Pines (Pindera and York, 1991).

In May, the Akwesasne War Chief, Francis Boots, made his first trip to the Pines, in response to requests from the Longhouse Chief's son for a patrol vehicle, a supply of two-way radios and $200.00 for gas and groceries (Pindera and York, 1991).

Although not everybody was in favour of being armed, eventually a consensus was reached for resistance. On May 7, a Mohawk representative was allowed to address the council of Oka citizens; he pleaded for peace rather than confrontation, but the Mayor insisted there was no room for negotiations or discussion: the land belonged to the township. Premier Robert Bourassa and the Québec Public Security minister were approached by the Mayor, who asked them to send the police to dismantle the barricades. Bourassa responded: "I don't want to send anyone to play cowboy over the question of a golf course." The Minister of Indian Affairs, John Ciaccia, was sent to negotiate, but he was not given the power to affect significantly the outcome of the discussions, beyond initiating a dialogue.

On June 5, the Municipality adopted a resolution: they proposed a moratorium on construction, but only if the barricades were lifted. The Mohawks refused, and Curtis Nelson of the Longhouse met with the Hon. Tom Siddon (Federal Minister of Indian Affairs) in Parliament in Ottawa, June 21. Nelson and other Mohawk representatives intended to press their land claims, but they were informed that, at best, they could hope for some "limited jurisdiction", hence they refused to discuss the barricades, and left (FR, 1991, Footnote 1).

The Municipality decided to seek an injunction against the Mohawks; at their meeting with the Hon. Tom Siddon on June 28, they compared the barricades to "a state of anarchy" (FR, 1991). Further, when the municipality sought the help of the Sureté de Québec on July 10, 1990, their request read, in part:

> . . . we ask you therefore to put a stop to the various criminal activities currently taking place...and to arrest the authors of the crimes, so that we can proceed with reestablishing the recreational use of the occupied land . . . (FR, 1991).

On July 11, the Police decided to intervene and, although before that date, "the use of arms by First Nation people" was unprecedented, this time an armed conflict developed. The police had backed

away from confrontation up to that time. When the police attacked and opened fire, the warriors who had been quietly joining the resistance for the past several months retaliated and gunfire was exchanged. Corporal Marcel Lemay of the police was fatally wounded and rushed to hospital. To this day, it is unclear who hit him, as the recovered bullet, could have come either from a police gun or from a warrior's gun. Eventually an inquest decided that it had been a Mohawk gun that had killed him but, since the only evidence submitted and accepted at the inquest was that of the police themselves, the result must remain uncertain (Pindera and York, 1991).

When a lawyer for the Kanasatake band in Montreal was told by the Mohawks that the police were getting ready to attack again, and he made "forty-five calls in four hours" trying to reach someone with the power to stop the attacks. He finally reached Premier Bourassa who, when told of the police officer's death, cancelled the second raid (Pindera and York, 1991).

From July 13th on a new strategy was initiated: the police would not permit supplies, food or medicine to enter the occupied lands, and even the Red Cross had to wait twenty-four hours before being permitted to enter. Indian women who attempted to go to the town to shop for groceries, were jeered at, jostled. On one occasion the police arrived barely in time to prevent a beating by the angry crowd. They had to leave without the food they had purchased. A Human Rights Commission official attempted to enter the roadblock to observe conditions at the camp, but he was refused, in glaring violation of the Québec Charter of Right and Freedoms. The Indians' survival was in fact dependent on the cooperation of other bands who brought in food and other necessities by canoe, under the cover of night, and across the dense bush. Attempted negotiations continued to be stalled and the Mohawks issued a revised list of demands on July 18th. That list read:

Title to the lands slated for the golf club expansion and the rest of the historic Commons; the withdrawal of all police forces from all Mohawk territories, including Ganienkeh in New York State and Akwesasne, on the Quebec, Ontario and New York borders; a forty-eight hours time period in which everyone leaving Kanesatake or Kahnawake would not be subject to search or arrest; and the referral of all disputes arising from the conflict to the World Court at the Hague (Pindera and York, 1991).

Their demands also listed three "preconditions" before further negotiation : 1) free access to food and other provisions; 2) free access to clan mothers and spiritual advisors; 3) "posting of independent international observers in Kanesatake and Kahnawake to monitor the actions of the police" (Pindera and York, 1991). Eventually talks were arranged in a Trappist monastery, la Trappe, at Oka, where the monks had been supportive of the Mohawks, and had sent food and supplies for the warriors and their families. At this time the Mohawks argued for their position on sovereignty: Loran Thompson, a Mohawk representative, showed his Iroquois Confederation passport, "complete with Canadian customs stamps from occasions when (he) had crossed the Canadian/ American border", hence he had proof that Canadian officials had accepted them as a separate nation. The Mohawks also explained the major political principles which governed them. They were (and are) "The Two Row Wampum" Treaty (originally a treaty with the Dutch, in 1717), and the "Great Law of Peace". The former supported peaceful but separate coexistence with non-Indians, as a canoe and a boat can both travel down the same river, provided each crew rowed their own boat only and did not attempt to straddle both. According to this Treaty, any Mohawk who would submit to any other government, would be treated as a traitor. The latter also supported separate sovereign status and non-submission, and it recom-

mended not bearing arms and preferring peace.

Unfortunately, although the Mohawks were perceived as patriots whose cause was valid even by some of the soldiers who eventually replaced police at the barricades, their situation placed them in a "vicious circle". If they were not recognized as a separate nation, they could not bear arms in their own defence or in support of their territorial claims. But without arms, "they will not be able to affirm their rights as a nation" (Pindera and York, 1991) or to protect disputed territories, until negotiations and peaceful talks could help rectify the problem.

At the Mohawks' request, international observers were allowed into the Pines, and it is very important to hear their comments:

"The only persons who have treated me in a civilized way in this matter here in Canada are the Mohawks", said Finn Lyng Hjem, a Norwegian Judge. "The army and the police do nothing. It's very degrading . . . degrading to us, and perhaps more degrading to the government who can't give us access."
(Pindera and York, 1991)

When Premier Bourassa asked the international observers to leave, they warned Québec and Canada of the "dangerous precedent" that had been set by arbitrarily breaking off talks.After many fruitless weeks of barricades and occupation, while the Mohawks' case became the cause for all First Nation People, no progress was made on any of their demands. Eventually the Warriors decided to "disengage", and accept the word of the Canadian Government that their land claims would be seriously considered. The warriors were taken off in police vehicles, each with several plastic handcuffs, as they showed they could easily break one handcuff with their bare hands. As a last gesture of defiance, a Mohawk Warrior Society Flag was smuggled onto the bus, and waived at onlookers as the police bus took them away.

This, unfortunately, was not the end of either

violence or racism. Many of the warriors were badly beaten by the police, during "interrogations." Some were roughed up as they were arrested and charged with "rioting and obstruction of justice." As well as Corporal Lemay, two Mohawks died. One, an elderly man, died of heart failure after a stone-throwing mob attacked him at the outskirts of town; the other was poisoned by tear gas and died later.

It is noteworthy that the Canadian Army (which eventually replaced the police) had only been used once before in Canadian history against domestic rebels: in the 1970 FLQ Crisis. The crisis at Oka was described in the Canadian Press as "the greatest ever witnessed in Quebec, Canada, even North America" (Pindera and York, 1991). Finally, more than ten months after the end of the conflict, disciplinary hearings were held "to examine the conduct of eight senior officers of the Quebec police, and of 31 junior officers, during the Oka crisis," (no information is available about the outcome of these hearings) and neither Quebec nor Canada showed any desire to improve relations with the people of the First Nation of Canada, even after the conflict.

2. Environmental Racism, Environmental Justice and Terrorism, The Canadian Difference

In this section, I will a) define and describe environmental racism in general; b) relate the specific position of the Indians of Canada's First Nation to environmental racism so that the difference in their case will become clear; and c) discuss the interconnectedness of the land issue and the environmental questions in relation to territorial rights. I will argue that their position required them to take a stand and even to take arms, and that the response of the Federal Government could be fairly characterized as State terrorism.

a) Environmental Racism

Environmental Racism can be defined as racism practiced in and through the environment. It re-

fers to environmental injustice whereby, for instance, toxic and hazardous waste facilities and business operations are sited with disproportionate frequency in or near poor, non-white communities. Speaking of the United States, Robert Bullard says:

If a community is poor or inhabited largely by people of colour there is a good chance that it receives less protection than a community that is affluent or white (R. Bullard, 1995).

This is a recurring situation because in the United States, environmental policies "distribute the costs in a regressive pattern, while providing disproportionate benefits for the educated and the wealthy" (R. Bullard, 1995). One will not find "municipal fills and incinerators; abandoned toxic waste dumps; lead poisoning in children; and contaminated fish consumption"(R. Bullard, 1995) in wealthy white neighbourhoods. This disparity has been institutionalized, and has lead to disregard and ultimately to ecological violence perpetrated against people and communities of colour.

Further, although both class and race appear to be significant indicators of the problems outlined, "the race correlation is even stronger than the class correlation" (B. Bryant and P. Mohai, 1990; M. Gelobter, 1988; United Church of Christ Commission, 1987). What is particularly disturbing about this trend, is that the ecological violence that is amply documented and which targets vulnerable and often trapped minorities, is not a random act perpetrated by a few profit-seeking operations that could perhaps be isolated and curtailed or eliminated, but that it is an accepted, institutionalized form of "doing business", taken for granted by most and ignored by all.

This institutionalized pattern of discrimination is an anomaly in a world which is committed to "political correctness", at least officially and in the so-called "free world" (M. Freedman and J. Narveson, 1994). For instance, both in Canada and the United States, neither Government Institutions nor corporate bodies would deliberately promote or practice hiring in an openly discriminatory manner, or explicitly advocate segregation in housing or education. Although both women and minorities often feel that either covertly discriminatory practices or "glass ceilings" exist both in business and government, which prevent them from achieving their full potential, still these difficulties are not openly fostered by institutions.[2]

Yet the practice of placing hazardous business operations such as dumpsites and other waste facilities in the "backyards" of minority groups is practiced regularly, with no apology. It is described as a purely economic decision with no consideration for the unjust burdens it may place on individuals and affected communities who are often too poor and weak to fight back (R. Rawls, 1993; A. Gewirth, 1983). Similarly, when the United States Environmental Protection Agency uses Superfund and other means to ameliorate acute problems in white neighbourhoods long before it even acknowledges or attempts to respond to environmental emergencies in black ones, then it appears that environmental racism is practiced almost by rote, with little fear of retribution. Bullard says:

> The current environmental protection paradigm has institutionalized unequal enforcement; traded human health for profit; placed the burden of proof on the "victims" rather than on the polluting industry; legitimated human exposure to harmful substances; promoted "risky" technologies such as incinerators; exploited the vulnerability of communities of color ... (Bullard, 1994).

The same practice of ecological destruction happens overseas, by the countries of the North and the West in relation to the countries of the South and the East. Toxic dumping and other unfair burdens are routinely imposed on Less Developed Countries whose leaders are often all too willing to trade off safety for their uninformed and unconsenting disempowered citizens for Western hard currencies. Those who may respond that no racism is involved, as the hazardous transactions simply reflect economic advantage and "good business sense", ignore the fact that most often the perpetuation of "brownfields" is founded on various forms of earlier segregation and racism. (Brownfields are areas that have been used for dumps or unsafe business operations. They are deemed to be appropriate locations for more of the same practices than are wealthier and relatively cleaner neighbourhoods.)

In the global marketplace, this approach has been termed the practice of "Isolationist Strategy" (K. Shrader-Frechette, 1991). In this case, the restraints and controls that businesses may employ in their home countries are not carried on in interaction with South East countries abroad. Relying on several arguments such as "The Countervailing Benefit Argument", "The Consent Argument", "The Social Progress Argument" and "The Reasonable Possibility Argument", the isolationist strategy replicates many "segregation" arguments and thus cannot be acceptable from the moral standpoint (K. Shrader-Frechette, 1991).

Unfortunately, often poor communities cannot fight off the harm that threatens them insidiously, through environmental contamination. When they actually try to do so, however, especially in present times and in the better educated and organized countries in North America (rather than in impoverished Third World Nations), they may reach a favourable outcome. For instance, in a recent ongoing case in Titusville, Alabama, a neighbourhood in Birmingham, a community group decided to fight Browning-Ferris Industries, who intended to site a waste-transfer station in their neighbourhood. The area was already legally the site of "heavy industry", legally, but garbage was to be excluded, according to the township ordinance. It was also one of the few areas where African-

Americans had been able to buy property in the city of Birmingham, so that the whole community was and is one of colour. In this case, the community was exposed to a lengthy legal battle, and even police violence as they demonstrated in the park between Birmingham's City Hall and its Civil Rights Institute. In the end, the city won against BFI, and the infamous facility, already built, stood empty as late as November 1994, when I visited at the invitation of the community leader, Ms. Whitlyn Battle, and the lawyer, Mr. David Sullivan. In this case, the perpetuation of "brownfields" in one specific area indicates the institutionalized intent to burden disproportionately citizens of colour with society's hazards, without consent or compensation (Westra, 1995; cp. Greenpeace, "Not in Anyone's Backyard! The Grassroots Victory over Browning-Ferris Industries", 1995 Video).

Examples of this kind of problem could be multiplied, although citizens' victories are rare indeed. From toxins in Altgeld Gardens in Chicago (Gaylord, 1995), to radioactive waste in Louisiana (K. Shrader-Frechette, 1995) and predominantly in the Southern United States (Bullard, 1994), the story can be repeated again and again with slight variations, and with the black communities regularly the losers. But it is not only the urban minorities that are so targeted; their rural counterparts fare no better. "Geographic equity" does not exist in North America any more than it does in Less Developed Countries.

b) Environmental Racism and The First Nation: Human, Religious Rights to Self-Defense

Recently there has been growing support for the defense of minority groups against the ecological violence perpetrated against them. The "First National People of Colour Environmental Leadership Summit" was held in October 1991 in Washington, DC. It united many grassroot groups and inspired them to seek governmental and national support for strategies to eliminate the rampant environmental racism practiced against them. (People of Color, p. 3). In this section, I will argue that the case of Canadian Indians is quite different in several senses from what has been described, although it remains environmental racism. Their case is unique because health and safety are not their only concern. Natives require high levels of environmental quality to meet both physical and spiritual needs. They need the land they inhabit to be free of toxic and chemical hazards so that various species of animal and fish, which are part of their traditional diet, do not suffer or disappear; but they also need spiritually, to be able to live in a way that is consonant with their worldview. The latter is grounded on respect for all living things with whom they share a habitat.

It can also be argued that the Native traditional world-view is so much a part of their deeply held values and beliefs, that it can be considered a religion common to most Indians in North America. Quite aside from the issue of status as a separate nation discussed in Section 2(b) above, the Mohawks' respect for their own ecologically inspired lifestyle should be treated as a matter of constitutionally protected right to freedom of religion under the Canadian Charter of Rights and Freedoms. In fact, the "Great Law of Peace", which forms the basis for the Oka Warriors' ideology, does not separate "church" and "state":

> . . . it provides a complex combination of spiritual and political rules . . . It is the rule book of an entire way of life . . . It forms the thesis of a modern theocracy (Pindera and York, 1991).

Hence the rights of the Mohawks to their traditional ways can be supported on the basis of freedom of religion, even before considering their separate National status. Unlike other minorities, these religious rights and freedoms are inseparable from environmental protection. Finally, this approach to ecological protection for large areas of wilderness is necessary for global sustainability and the Indian traditional way is closer to the mandate to "restore ecosystem integrity" which forms the basis of Environment Canada's "vision" statement, and a host of other regulations and mission statements, globally (Westra, 1994a; Westra, 1995b).

In sum, ecological concern is everyone's responsibility, but traditional American Indian "attitudes" toward nature appear to be particularly apt to support an environmental ethic (B. Callicott, 1989; D. Rabb, 1995). These attitudes also provide yet another reason why the Indians ought to have been permitted the peaceful enjoyment of their territory, and why their wishes in relation to the land ought to have been respected. The priests at St. Sulpice were granted lands twice on behalf of the Indians, with express instructions to administer it for them. In fact their second request explicitly cited the Indians' needs and lifestyle, to request larger areas from the King of France. The priests' needs, or their economic advantage was never considered. Their role was not that of owners, but that of caretakers and managers of the granted territories. Hence it would be unfair to penalize the Mohawks for the repeated sale of lands which were meant for their sole use and enjoyment. The lands were exploited, mismanaged and sold inappropriately, illegally, and in clear violation of the mandate from either the King of France or that of England (Pindera and York, 1991).

c) Land, Environment, Territorial Rights and Native Identity

I have argued that the Police of Québec, the Federal Government's officials, and the residents and bureaucrats of Oka, all can be charged with environmental racism. To prove this, it is not necessary to demonstrate specific intent on the part of any one person or group, as environmental racism may be perpetrated through carelessness, self-interest or greed. It is sufficient to show that the practice is accepted and even institutionalized in a way that does ecological violence to a specific community or group of colour. I have also argued that in this case the Indians' historical and legal claim to independent Nationhood as well as their traditional life-style, culture and religious belief all contribute significantly to their right to take a stance against environmental racism. The same combination of factors renders their resistance, their unshakable position and even their bearing arms, potentially justifiable on moral grounds.Moreover, if their position is morally defensible, then their activities should not be viewed as crimes against the law, but as self-defense, conscientious objections, and affirmation of religious and cultural self-identity. That in turn makes the actions of both police and government in support of ecological violence and repression possible forms of state terrorism. It is this particular situation and combination that makes environmental racism distinctly Canadian in this case, as I will argue below.

As the cultural self-identity argument is based on the understanding of the Indians as a people, one might ask, what makes a "people" other than law or custom? Do citizens voluntarily form associations, and is it their choice that makes them a community or a nation? Or is it the case that common allegiance to a state constitutes a nation or people? On what grounds, then is national identity to be grounded? According to Henry Sidgwick (1891), legitimate government rests upon the consent of the governed, hence the "voluntarist" model of what constitutes a nation, "derives from the rights of individuals to associate politically as they chose" (P. Gilbert, 1994). But it is hard to understand what makes a specific association worthy of recognition, other than the exercise of the citizens' collective will, as people willingly form associations that may be less than worthy of respect (e.g., the Ku Klux Klan). Another approach may be to appeal to a national character, emphasizing shared characteristics that might constitute a national identity. Paul Gilbert (1994) terms this "the ethnic model of nationality". But to view nations as species of "natural kinds", is to subscribe to a racist theory whose pitfalls we have all learned in Nazi and Fascist times (P. Gilbert, 1994). But there are other, better ways of conceiving of national identity: "culturalism", for instance, provides a useful model. This approach cannot rely exclusively on religion, which usually transcends national borders, hence language, common practices and aspirations, possibly even territory are required as well.(P. Gilbert, 1994). Even someone's upbringing is constitutive of the national identity of individuals. Will Kymlicka (1990) also discusses the parallel conception of "communitarianism", that is, viewing nations as groups living a common life in accordance with their own rules, hence this "community" view or "cultural view" (Gilbert), is also relevant to establish national identity. As Kymlicka points out,

Cultural membership affects our very sense
of personal identity and capacity
(W. Kymlicka, 1991).

First Nation people in general and Mohawks at Oka in particular can claim national identity, based on what Gilbert terms "culturalism", as well as their biological heritage and Kymlicka speaks of a "cultural heritage" for all Indians in Canada. This supports the Indians' claim that they are a "people", and that they can therefore demand to be treated as such:

"All peoples have the right to self-determination" declares the first article of the United Nations International Covenant on human rights. That is to say, they have the right to independent statehood (P. Gilbert, 1994).

If this is the case, then certain other rights follow from it; for example: "their right to throw off alien occupation, colonial status or absorption into some other state" (P. Gilbert, 1994). Further, at Oka, it seems that not only were the Mohawks treated unfairly, so that "some suffer harm as the cost of increased benefits to others" (an immoral

position); but also they were treated unjustly (an illegal action, additionally), because they were wronged through discrimination:

*Discrimination mistreats individuals because they are part of a certain group, so that the primary object of mistreatment is **the group of which they are a part (my italics)** (P. Gilbert, 1994).*

But Gilbert's discussion, which is primarily about possible explanation and justification for terrorism in certain circumstances, is intended to deal with the situation between Israel and Palestine and that between Ireland and England. Hence, it cannot apply precisely to our case, although, as we have seen, many parallels can be drawn.

What is required then, is to understand the specific way in which racism and discrimination is practiced against Indians in Canada which distinguishes their situation completely from that of African Americans in the United States and of Africans and other Less Developed Countries. As was argued earlier, the intent of the Executive Order by which President Clinton established an Office of Environmental Justice, was to eventually eliminate all practices excluding Black communities from the environmental protection and concern which favoured white communities and grant them not only defense against environmental threats, to some extent, but also redress in case of problems or accidents, both of which were not equally available to communities of colour.

African-Americans want to be included within the larger community. They want to avoid the de facto segregation to which exclusionary practices condemn them. They can argue that, neither in housing, job seeking, schooling, is segregation legally permitted at this time; thus, as I suggested earlier, environmental racism constitutes a "last frontier", or the only area within which racism is not only tolerated, but neither criticized nor discouraged or punished as such by the law.

The interest in avoiding this form of racism is equally true for Indians as it is for Blacks. But the forms of "discrimination", aside from those which involve the environment, are quite different for Canadian Indians; they are in fact opposite to those which affect Blacks. Any "colour-blind" interpretation of the law, is inappropriate for Indians: it is integration that is viewed as a "badge of inferiority" by Indians, not segregation. As Michael Gross puts it, in talking about education, for instance:

Where blacks have been forcibly excluded (segregated) from white society by law, Indians-aboriginal people with their own cultures, languages, religions and territories-have been forcibly included (integrated) into that society by law. That is what the Senate (sub-committee on Indian Education) meant by coercive assimilation the practice of compelling, through submersion, an ethnic, cultural and linguistic minority to shed its uniqueness and identify and mingle with the rest of society (Gross, 1973).

Hence, simply granting Indians the same rights as all Canadians is not only insufficient, but essentially wrong. Kymlicka says:

the viability of Indian communities depends on coercively restricting the mobility, residence, and political right of both Indians and non-Indians (W. Kymlicka, 1991).

It is therefore a necessary component of the Indians' rights and liberties, to deny "non-Indians the right to purchase or reside on Indian lands..." A fortiori then, the right to adversely affect and pollute or otherwise ecologically affect these lands should be equally impermissible. Hence the activities of non-Indians in lands adjacent to Indian lands, must be consonant with a "buffer zone" (as it is for instance in MAB (Man and the Biosphere) areas surrounding a wild "core" zone (see L. Westra, 1995b).

In the concluding Section, I will defend the Mohawks' actions as morally defensible and discuss the government's interventions as motivated by environmental racism supported by terrorist attacks.

3. Conclusion-National Identity, Environmental Racism and State Terrorism

On the account presented in the last section, the cause of the Mohawks at Oka can be defended as just on moral grounds: Environmentally and culturally they were clearly under attack. Those responsible for the circumstances in which they found themselves were guilty not only of racism but of environmental racism. The final question that must be asked at this point is whether the Mohawks were justified in taking up arms, and whether the police and the army were justified in the way they handled the Warriors after the "disengagement". The Mohawks are not the first or even the only people who have resorted to civil resistance and even violence in defense of the environment. What makes their acts different and in fact unique, has been described in the discussion presented in the previous sections.

In contrast, those chaining themselves to trees at Clayoquot Sound in B.C. came from all over Canada, and could have in fact come from anywhere in the world in defense of the common cause: protecting the environment in general. The Indians also shared this generalized concern, as I have shown, through their concern for the forest in relation to the township. The Mohawks were also motivated by other, specific reasons. These were: 1) the way their identity as a people is dependent on a certain place, so that any attack on either its size or its environmental quality and integrity, must be construed as an attack on their identity; and 2) the spiritual and religious components of their need for the land, which go beyond our own acknowledged need for wild places for various reasons (Westra, 1994a).

Hence, for the Indians, defense goes beyond ecological concern in a general sense. It becomes a case of self-preservation. That makes bearing arms for that purpose more than a simple criminal act, as some claimed. Hence, the paradigm or model according to which the Mohawks activities must be viewed, is not that of breaking the law or that of committing crimes. The closest model is that which fits other binational territorial disputes, such as those between Ireland and Britain, or between Israel and Palestine where, as Gilbert has argued, border disputes are not open to democratic decisions based on votes. Neither Israelis nor Palestinians can democratically decide on the location of a specific border affecting their two nations. The only avenues open to these national groups, as to the Irish in their territorial dispute, is either to declare war, or to attack or respond to violence through terrorist attacks, outside a formal war situation.

Therefore these acts cannot be simply defined as "random violence" or as crime, because significant differences exist: the perpetrators announce their intention to stand their ground or to fight, and publicize their political motives explicitly, in contrast with the hidden and furtive activities of criminals. Hence , the Mohawks' use of force must be viewed, and perhaps justified, in terms of terrorism, not random violence.[3] It is important to note that they resisted and defended, but did not launch violent attacks beyond their own territories: in fact all their interactions and negotiations with the representatives of the Canadian Government or the township were characterized by reasoned arguments, and the repetition of their claims and the reasons for those claims, coupled with the sincere desire to achieve and maintain peace. They bore arms for self-defense, not attack.

I have argued elsewhere that often even terrorist aggressive violence may be defensible in principle, though not in its practical expression, and I have called defensible violence of this sort, a form of "whistle blowing", as it calls attention to some grave injustice (Westra, 1990). The extent of the injustice and the discriminatory treatment, neither

of which were random occurrences but rather formed a historical pattern on the part of the Canadians, has been discussed previously. Their perpetration justifies, I believe, resistance on grounds of self-determination. Their resistance then becomes analogous to that intended to throw off foreign occupation (P. Gilbert, 1994).

The events may be described, using Gilbert's felicitous expression, as an "ethical revolution". Such a revolution is typically based on a "different conception of the state and the community." It is an "inspirational aspect of violent change", which might be of two kinds. It might be "ethically conservative", or "ethically radical". The former appeals to values which the resisting group shares with the majority, including its opponents, but which are not properly implemented. The latter, "makes its case on the basis of a change in the values themselves", and is persuasive because it demands a change of values. The Mohawks' case seems to fit the second model. They can be seen as "ethical revolutionaries", as people who "seek to change the criteria for membership of the political community" (P. Gilbert, 1994).

They were criticized for not using democratic means to state their grievances and get redress, but their grievances were not of the sort that can easily be settled by democratic means. This is because the very core of their complaint was that the Mohawk nation was not viewed as an equal, viable political community, responsible for decisions affecting their people and their land. It is here that the parallel with terrorism becomes even clearer.

International terrorism is most often concerned with a) territory, and b) political equality. But claims to self-determination should be "made within existing borders", an impossibility when the very extent of the territory within those borders is at issue (as argued earlier), and when the dissenting and protesting group is in a clear minority position. But in that case, the group seeking redress that is, as in this case, at the same time environmental, territorial and concerned with national independence, has no democratic recourse, no peaceful voice through which to make its claim other than perhaps attempting a "sit in" to gain national and international attention. It seems as though it must resist, even while seeking peace. And if its arguments and claims are not heard and respected, it seems as though its only recourse is to resist attack, and bear arms. Note that they were indeed resisting peacefully, and only turned violent, when violently attacked.

What is the State to do in response to such a position? Should it respond with force and attack? But then can we not charge it with hypocrisy and view its actions as open to a tu quoque argument (P. Gilbert, 1994). It is not sufficient, as we have seen, to say that government force must intervene to "punish crime", as the Indians are not breaking a law to which they are legitimately subjected. On the contrary, their claim is that that law is not their law, that state is not their state, and its values are not theirs. In this, the Canadian Constitution appears to support their position. When weighing the forms of violence (that is the Indians' and the State's), there seems to be little cause to view the former as "wrong", the latter as "right", from the moral standpoint.

The stronger the moral case for the Mohawks, the weaker, morally, the case for the "legal" repression and violence they had to endure. While the reasons for supporting the Indians' position at Oka are many, and defensible, only one possible reason can be given in support of the Army's intervention (P. Gilbert, 1994). The state has the authority to enforce the law and to punish crimes. But is the State's violence against those who are not subject to its laws (or whose major claim for resistance is that they are not), morally better than their opponents' resistance? When we compare even terrorists' action "seeking to gain power, and those of the agents of the State in seeking to retain it", there may be no moral reason to term the former "criminal" and the latter "punishment of crime". This is particularly the case, when a) there was no violent attack on the part of the Mohawks; and b) the main reason for the latter's resistance was to protest the assumption that they were in fact subject to those laws.

It is also clear that the other alternative, that is the presumption that while the Mohawks belonged to a separate, sovereign nation, Canada could bear arms against them as a form of warfare, is not appropriate. Rules of war demand that if violence is to be part of a just war, then the war should be first openly declared. This is the reason why terrorism is not precisely warfare, whether it is practiced by dissenting groups or by the State itself. State terrorism, therefore, refers to violent responses to terrorism on the part of a government. It is often the alternative preferred to simply treating terrorists as criminals (that is, as innocent until proven guilty, using restraints but not violence against them, and so on). But although a violent response is often employed, this use of state power is hard to justify as anything other than retaliation.

State terrorism involves warlike intentions which are impeded by constraints from issuing in open war. These constraints are characteristically political rather than military, reflecting . . . political inhibition resorting to (war) . . . (P. Gilbert, 1994).

However Gilbert adds that normally, "internal State terrorism" does not have the "warlike aims" of "acquisition and control of territory". It seems that the Oka situation instead manifested precisely this aim; perhaps then it represents an atypical form of state terrorism as it has this added component while manifesting many of the usual ones as well.

On the other hand, as Gilbert outlines and defines state terrorism, the Federal Government's intervention through the police and, particularly through the army appears to fit under this heading. The state, of course, purports to be operating "within the framework of the law, which it presents itself as upholding" (P. Gilbert, 1994). But if its legal framework is "unable to resist terrorism", then the state may simply "resort to the covertly warlike operations which constitute state terrorism." Yet, lacking an openly declared war, "the ordinary rules of civil life" should guide the state's acceptable intervention. Armed attacks on dissenting citizens of another country (or even of one's own), or beatings as part of "interrogation" or "capture", are not the way the state ought to deal even with hardened criminals or serial killers, before or after sentencing. Hence the state denounced the Mohawks as criminals during the crisis but only belatedly treated them as such after their case came to court. Throughout the crisis, a state of war appeared to prevail, giving additional credence to the Mohawks' claim to sovereignty and national independence, something that is already legally true in Canada for people of the First Nation in general.

It is clear that the Federal Government cannot have it both ways: either their attack on resisting Mohawks is war, in which case 1) a proper declaration of war, 2) the recognition of their independent nationhood, and 3) adherence to the rules of war, are mandatory, or it is not. Further, over and above these formal requirements, from the moral standpoint, only a war of self-defense (from an actual attack, not from dissent), may be viewed as a just war (Westra, 1990). Or, we might accept the other alternative, that the state is viewing their resistance as criminal. It has been shown that this does not appropriately describe the government's response: unless a criminal is presently attacking a police officer, for instance, drawing fire against him is not a permissible, legal response. As explained earlier, the Mohawks were standing their ground, not even fleeing from the law; and

If terrorists are denied due process of law, then the same acts are criminal . . .
(P. Gilbert, 1994).

To start shooting prior to trial and conviction of specific individuals, is to deny them due process. Had they even been convicted criminals, killers, retaliation in kind is not appropriate, particularly in a country with no capital punishment. And, it must be kept in mind, no one was ever found guilty of murder. Those who were considered the "worst offenders" were perhaps Ronald Cross (nicknamed "Lasagne") and Gordon Lazore. Helene Sévigny reports on the actual sentencing:

Sentence "Sa Majesté la Reine vs. Ronald Cross et Gordon Lazore" Province of Quebec, District of Terrebonne, No.700-01-000009-913;Judge B.J. Greenberg, Superior Court, Criminal Division, St. Jerome, Feb. 19,1992. The two were found guilty of half of their charges, primarily attacks with "arms" such as baseball bats. The case was appealed Feb. 20, 1992. On July 3, 1992, the other 39 Mohawks that were originally taken from the barricades and detained, were acquitted (H. Sévigny, 1993: 229-288) (L.W. tr. from French).

The Mohawks' well-founded message and their fight against racism in all its forms, including its environmental aspect, has been around for a long time, as has the Indians' effort to have their cause and their reasons heard. Gilles Boileau's indictment of the "lords wearing cassocks" ("les seigneurs en soutane"), presents a detailed historical account of the difficulties the Mohawks had to endure (G. Boileau, 1991).

Boileau's final exhortation to the "seigneurs" is one which should be taken to heart by all Canadians:

The "Messieurs" and all others must recognize that the Mohawks have a right to "their dignity and our respect," and it is high time that Oka should be recognized primarily as Indian Land (G. Boileau, 1991).

In conclusion, the Oka case combines several unique features specific to the Canadian political scene. It manifests aspects of environmental racism, as the ecologically inappropriate choices of a non-Indian majority were to be imposed on the Mohawks, without regard for their traditional lifestyles. At the same time, this imposition infringed their right to self-determination and their constitutional status as a First Nation. Finally, the case shows the inappropriate use of force and the employment of state terrorism in response to the Mohawks' position, one that, I have argued, is defensible on moral, environmental and legal grounds.

ENDNOTES

[1] All information in this section is taken from the Background Paper "The Land Claim Dispute at Oka"; Library of Parliament; BP-235E; 1990).

[2] Velasquez, M.; Business Ethics, Concepts and Cases; Prentice Hall; Englewood Cliffs, N.J.; 1991; see ch. 5 for a discussion of "institutional discrimination".

[3] Terrorism may be viewed as having the characteristics of both war and crime. It can be said that it "essentially means a method of war which consists of intentionally attacking those who ought not to be attacked (Teichman, 1986). Paul Gilbert terms this the "unjust war model" and contrasts it with the "defensive war model", which would permit a more open-minded view of terrorism, linking it to such potentially justifiable acts as "tyrannized" or other forms of self-defense. This view would also permit one to distinguish it from criminality, in cases dealing with terrorism for national reasons. See Gilbert, Terrorism and Nationality, especially chapters 2 and 3).

References

Begin, P., Moss, W., Miemczak; "The Land Claim Dispute at Oka"; *Background Paper*; Research branch, Library of Parliament, BP-235E; 1990.

Boileau, Gilles; *Oka, Terre Indienne*; Méridien; Montreal; 1991; *Le Silence des Messieurs*.

Bullard, R.; *Dumping in Dixie*; Westview Press; Boulder, Co.; 1994.

Bullard, R.; "Overcoming Racism in Environmental Decisionmaking"; in *Faces of Environmental Racism-Confronting Global Equity Issues*; Rowman Littlefield; Lanham, MD. 1995, pp.3-28.

Gaylord, C. and Bell, E.; *Faces of Environmental Racism*, Westra, L. & Wenz, P., eds.; Rowman Littlefield; Landham, MD; 1995; pp.29-40.

Gewirth, Alan; "Human Rights and The Prevention of Cancer"; in *Human Rights*; University of Chicago Press; Chicago, Illinois; 1983; pp. 181-217.

Gilbert, Paul; *Terrorism, Security and Nationality*; Routledge; London, UK; 1994.

Hornung, Rick; *One Nation Under the Gun*; Stoddard Publishing Co.; Toronto, Ont.; 1991.

House of Commons, Canada; "The Summer of 1990"; *Fifth Report of the Standing Committee on Aboriginal Affairs*, K. Hughes, M.P. Chair; May 1991 (Second Session of the Thirty-fourth Parliament, 1989-90-91.)

"Impact of the People of Color Summit"; in *People of Color, Environmental Groups, 1994-95 Directory*; R. Bullard, Charles Stewart Mott Foundation; Flint, MI.

Kymlicka, Will; *Liberalism, Community and Culture*; Clarendon Paperbacks; Oxford University Press; Oxford, UK; 1991.

Kymlicka, Will; 1990; *Contemporary Political Philosophy: An Introduction*; Oxford University Press; Oxford.

Narveson, J. and Freedman, M.; *Political Correctness For and Against*; Rowman Littlefield; Lanham, MD.; 1994.

Parent, Amand; *The Life of Rev. Amand Parent, Forty-seven Years Experience in Evangelical Work in Canada; Eight Years Among the Oka Indians*; Briggs Publishing; Toronto; 1887.

Pimentel, D. et al; "Environmental and Economic Effects of Reducing Pesticide Use"; in *Bioscience*, Vol. 41, No. 6, 1991.

Pimentel, D. et al; 1992; "Conserving Biological Diversity in Agricultural/Forestry Systems"; in *Bioscience*, Vol. 42, No. 5.

Pimentel, D. et al; "The Relationship between 'Cosmetic Standards' for Food and Pesticide Use"; in D. Pimentel and H. Lehman, eds., *The Pesticide Question: Environment Economics and Ethics*; Chapman and Hall; New York; 1993; pp. 85-105.

Pindera, Geoffrey and York, Loreen; *People of the*

Pines, The Warriors and The Legacy of Oka; Little, Brown and Co. (Canada) Ltd.; 1991.

Rabb, D.; 1995; "Is There an Amerindian Philosophy"; paper presented at the Ontario Philosophical Society meeting; University of Windsor; October 28.

Rawls, J.; 1993; "The Law of Peoples"; in *On Human Rights*; Basic Books, Harper Collins; New York, NY; pp. 41-82.

Sagoff, Mark; *The Economy of the Earth*; Cambridge University Press; 1989.

Sévigny, Helène; *Lasagne – L'Homme derriere le masque*; Editions Sedes; St. Lambert, Québec; 1993.

Shrader-Frechette, K.; *Risk and Rationality*; University of California Press; Berkeley, CA.; 1991.

Shrader-Frechette, K. and Wigley, D.; 1995; "Environmental Racism: A Louisiana Case Study"; in Westra, L. and Wenz, P., eds., *Faces of Environmental Racism-Confronting Global Equity Issues*; Rowman Littlefield; Lanham, MD.; pp. 135-162.

Sidgwick, H.; *The Elements of Politics*; Macmillan Publishing; London, U.K.; 1991.

Teichman, J.; *Pacifism and the Just War*; Oxford University Press (Blackwell); Oxford, U.K.; 1986.

Westra, L.; (a). *An Environmental Proposal for Ethics: The Principle of Integrity*; Rowman, Littlefield; Lanham, MD; 1994.

Westra, L.; (b). "On Risky Business – Corporate Responsibility and Hazardous Products"; *Business Ethics Quarterly*; January 1994, Vol. 4, No. 1; pp. 97-110.

Westra, L.; *Faces of Environmental Racism: Facing Global Equity Issues;* "The Faces of Environmental Racism – Titusville, Al. and BFI", eds. L. Westra and P. Wenz; Rowman, Littlefield; 1995; pp. 113-134.

Westra, L.; "The Foundational Value of Wilderness"; in *Perspectives on Ecosystem Integrity*; Kluwer Publishers; 1995; Dordrecht, The Netherlands; pp. 12-33.

Westra, L.; "Terrorism, Self-Defense and Whistleblowing"; *Journal of Social Philosophy*, 1990; Spring Issue, Vol. 20, No. 3; pp.46-58.

ETHICS AND THE ENVIRONMENTAL IMPACT STATEMENT
LOW-LEVEL FLIGHTS OVER INNU* TERRITORY

18
by Ronald Pushchak

Introduction

AN EMERGING AND OPTIMISTIC VIEW OF ENVIRONMEN-tal ethics is that public decisions are moving away from traditional utilitarian methods that seek the greatest good for the greatest number and toward a social justice ethic that recognizes individual rights. Recent decisions that reflect a social justice ethic have been celebrated as examples where people and communities were allowed to exercise their right to protect environments and cultures, and where opportunities were made available for people to have their voices heard.

From a southern Canadian vantage point, there is some evidence that recent environmental decisions have reached higher levels of social justice. This is particularly true where federal or provincial governments have failed to impose unwanted hazardous waste facilities, nuclear plants and municipal waste sites on unwilling communities in Canada and the United States (Rabe, 1994; Gerrard, 1994). It is increasingly considered unjust to force communities to accept the impacts of such facilities without their consent or reasonable compensation.

For projects affecting aboriginal peoples, however, decisions have not generally kept pace in recognizing their rights to protect environments and traditional ways of life. In many instances, it is apparent that social justice is not yet the ethical basis for resolving environmental disputes. A key example is the federal government's decision to significantly increase the number of military training missions flown at low altitudes and high speeds over native lands in Labrador and Quebec, despite the opposition of the Innu people.

From an aboriginal vantage point, the search for social justice in dealing with military flying activities in the region has followed a long and winding road. In the process, native communities that depend on the natural environment for their living have increasingly come into conflict with non-native governments, their economic goals and political methods. Fair decisions have been hard to achieve when governments fail to see the intrinsic value of the native economy, one that is valued for itself and not for its usefulness to non-native interests. Fairness has been elusive when the significance of a native culture in maintaining the health of its people is not recognized.

This paper examines two dimensions of the decision to increase low-level military flights in Labrador; the first is the role of the Environmental Impact Statement and its failure to reveal the social and economic impacts of low-level flights on native communities. The second is the Environmental Assessment Panel's failure to provide a fair hearing process or to use reasonable standards of fairness in deciding that Labrador should be the host for military flights.

The Military Proposal

In May, 1995, the Canadian government decided to accept the recommendations of the Environmental Assessment Panel on Military Flying Activities in Labrador and Quebec to expand low-level training flights from 7,000 to 15,000 flights a year over lands traditionally occupied by the Innu and other aboriginal peoples. The Department of National Defence (DND), which proposed expanding its military flying activites in the region in its 1994 Environmental Impact Statement (EIS),

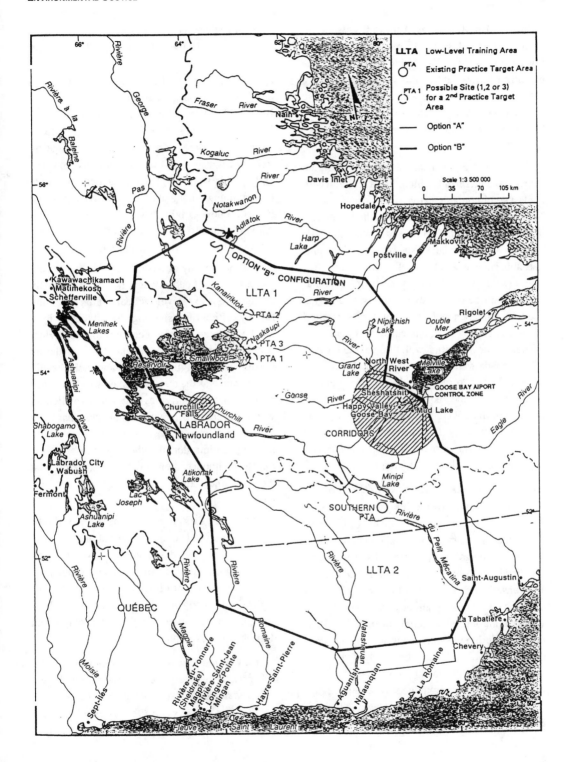

estimated that 90 percent of these flights would be at 500 feet or less and 15 percent would be as low as 100 feet. The DND planned to extend the existing twenty-eight to thirty-one week flying season to thirty-nine weeks a year and to increase the area to be overflown to cover 130,000 square kilometers of central Labrador and eastern Quebec.

This area of Canada has traditionally been the aboriginal domain of the Innu. It is a region where the last semi-nomadic native hunting activities in North America still continue over the better part of the year with native groups following the caribou, moose and smaller species that support a limited subsistence economy. The Innu have frequently said they want to continue their traditional way of life free of low-level military overflights and without dependence on a military-supported economy. However, in this case, the interests of the Innu came in conflict with those of the government. Canada wanted to use central Labrador and eastern Quebec to meet its NATO commitments and, ultimately, the choice was simple: either the interests of the government or the Innu would be met. The fate of the Innu was decided when the Environmental Assessment Panel accepted the EIS and expanded low-level flight training.

History of Military Activities in Labrador

Military overflights of the Innu and impacts on the social and economic life of the aboriginal peoples of the region are not recent phenomena, rather they have been going on for more than fifty years. The airfield at Goose Bay was established in 1941 as a transatlantic transfer point for both American and Canadian military aircraft in World War II. The base introduced wage labour in central Labrador and during the war, a long sequence of economic and social changes began, fueled by the strong attraction of jobs in Goose Bay. Workers were drawn not only from the surrounding region but also from Newfoundland and beyond to work at the base.

After the war, the base was used as a "cold war" strategic airfield by both the United States and Canada although most of the investment was made by the US. This lasted until the mid-1970s when the US ended its large scale involvement at Goose Bay. At that time, Goose Bay and its surroundings began to be used for flight training. The Canadian Air Force started low-level navigation training flights in 1954 which continued up to the early 1980s when large scale, tactical low-level flight training became the central activity at Goose Bay. Low-level flights began with the Canadian Air Force but the German Air Force joined in 1981 followed by the Netherlands in 1987.

The Goose Bay airbase, created as part of the war effort a half century ago, has been gradually changed to a low-level tactical military training facility without considering the effects of low-level flights and a new economy on aboriginal peoples that have lived on the land or considering the effect on aboriginal physical and social health. At no point was the question asked whether it was right to continue activities that were expedient in war, but were causing significant social hardship and cultural change in peace. Low-level flight training was introduced without the consent of the Innu and without settlement of the land claims that they and other native groups have made in the region.[1]

Over the years there have been many high-speed, low-altitude overflights of aboriginal people that have startled and stressed those hunting and living on the land. Subsonic and supersonic overflights have disturbed sleep, disrupted hunting activities and caused anxiety for both adults and children.[2] Sebastian Pastichit, one of the Innu described the experience this way:

"They fly too low over our marshes and forests. They spread death on our land. They fly unbelievably fast, making an unbelievable noise. The animals can't feed properly. They have to feed at night when the jets aren't

*flying...When they go over, it's like an
explosion. You feel the ground shake. They
scare the life out of me."[3]*

The Innu community feared that the noise and
stress would affect the psychological health and
ultimately the physical health of its people. They
believed it would discourage people from continuing to live on the land and would increase dependence on the non-native wage economy.

The Innu people were also concerned about the
effects of noise on natural systems; the caribou,
moose and waterfowl species that are part of their
native economy. However, beyond noise impacts,
the Innu expected that the expansion of the non-
native economy and the presence of a larger
number of transient military personnel in Goose
Bay would result in an increase in social costs
including substance abuse, sexual abuse and com-
municable diseases that are presently severe problems in the region's native communities.

At the end of the process, the Innu feared that
the cumulative effects of the low-level flight training proposal, together with the impacts of other
non-native projects in the region (mining, highway development, tourism) would cause substantial social and economic change and put an end to
the native economy. Once this has occurred, the
Innu would be vulnerable to the "boom and bust"
pattern commonly observed in northern development since there would be no guarantee that the
base would be supported by the government in
the future. Withdrawal of the base would devas-
tate the community if self-reliance were no longer
an option.

The Environmental Impact Statement (EIS)

Given the long sequence of military developments
in Labrador, the EIS that the DND had to produce
in order to win approval for expanding low-level
flight training was extremely important. It was in
fact the focal point of the Innu struggle because it
was the only restraint on the government's military plans. The EIS required that a rational deci-

sion be made about the acceptability of the project,
a decision which took into account the social and
economic as well as the natural impacts of the
military flight proposal.

The EIS was also the only opportunity native
people had to voice their concerns about the decision. Ironically, the culture and way of life of the
Innu depended on the fairness of a process that
was entirely outside their experience. Once the
EIS was approved, their chances to change what
had been done would end. It was obvious that the
only opportunity for an ethical outcome lay in the
EIS process.

The question whether to expand or put an end
to low-level military flights in this region brought
into sharp focus the ethical impact of the proposal
because the outcome would indicate how Canadians valued the environment of the region and
the way of life of the Innu compared to other non-
Innu cultures and economies. It would also reveal
whether imposing flight noise, human health
changes and stress on the Innu rather than other
Canadians or Europeans was fair. As in many other
environmental conflicts, the burden of fairness lay
squarely on the EIS process and ultimately on the
panel making the decision to accept or reject the
proposal.

The EIS History

The 1994 EIS of potential impacts from low-level
military flights over Labrador and eastern Quebec was not the first EIS study of the proposal.
An earlier EIS in 1989 documented the impacts
of a much larger number of proposed flights
(40,000) together with other impact-generating
components that included live weapons use, a
coastal target and flight area and expansion of
ground facilities at Goose Bay. The 1989 EIS was
reviewed by an environmental assessment panel
which had a mandate to examine the environmental, social and economic impacts of both the existing and proposed military activities. The panel
found the 1989 EIS to be deficient in thirty-eight

major aspects and sent it back to DND without holding hearings.[4] It was assumed at that time, given the failure of the EIS, that the low-level military flying proposal was dead. Prime Minister Mulroney, in the spring of 1990, announced that the project would not proceed. It seemed as if the outcome might favour the Innu to some extent since low-level flights would only be permitted at the 1987 rate of 7,000 a year.

However, as John Livingston, one of Canada's foremost environmental theorists has said regarding environmental conflicts, "every gain is temporary, every loss is permanent". The federal government needed the low-level flight training proposal to keep its commitment to NATO to provide training opportunities for allied pilots. Because the agreement under which NATO nations participated in the training program, called the Multinational Memorandum of Understanding (MMOU), had to be renewed in 1996, the project had to receive approval through the environmental assessment process by 1995 at the latest.

Undeterred by the failure of the first (1989) EIS, the federal government decided to try again. It created a new environmental assessment panel to review the project, one that in practice was more responsive to the interests of the government. The DND, having spent six million dollars on the first EIS, now began a second one using new consultants. The second EIS was submitted in 1994 and cost more than twice as much as the first.

In the new proposal, the DND scaled down the project by reducing the maximum number of flights each year from 40,000 to 18,000, and by eliminating both live ammunition use and the coastal target range. However, it also increased the number of night flights from fifty to a maximum of 1,400 and expanded the training area by 30,000 square kilometers.

The new EIS, submitted in April 1994, required rapid approval by 1995 to meet the signing deadline for the MMOU in the following year. Thus

began a review process that moved quickly from initial responses to hearings within five months, a period that is unconscionably short given the document's 4,000 page length (published in five volumes) and technical content.

The EIS Process

There were two parts in the EIS process that were critical in deciding to proceed with low-level flight training. The first was the EIS document in which the DND was required to:

- explain the need and rationale for the project
- examine reasonable alternatives to the undertaking
- describe the environments to be affected
- predict the impacts of low-level flights.

The second part was the set of hearings held to review the EIS. In this case, as in many other environmental conflicts, environmental assessment hearings were the final protection against an EIS that failed to reveal all the impacts or that did not judge their significance fairly. As Justice Berger said, "when the interests of government and business coincide, a hearing is necessary to present the alternative view."

If the choice were left to the federal or provincial governments or to the residents of Happy Valley-Goose Bay who depend on the base for their livelihood, the project would be approved without question. Because the hearings were the last opportunity for the Innu to be heard, they had to be both accessible to the participants and fairly conducted. However, as the Innu feared, the hearing process raised questions about the impartiality of the panel and whether the hearings were conducted fairly.

The EIS Document

1. Need For the Project

The central question in the EIS process was whether the DND needed to increase the number of low-level flights. Establishing need is an essential component of the EIS process because it prevents proponents like DND from implementing projects simply because they want to or because there is enough money to start them. Establishing the need for a project is a strong protection for both natural and human environments because it prevents impacts from being generated unless there is a clear and well-supported reason to create them.

The question of need for the project was raised in the 1989 EIS review and it was suggested at that time that the DND had not established that the flights were needed. Although the DND suggested in 1989 that low-level flight training in Labrador and Quebec was:

"necessary as an 'effective counterweight' to Eastern bloc countries and their formidable collective military power, "

by the time the first EIS was published, the extensive political restructuring that occurred in Eastern Europe following the dismantling of the Soviet Union meant there was no Eastern Bloc. That alone required a rethinking of the need for the project.

The 1994 EIS did no better in explaining the need for the project. For example, from 1989 to 1994, the DND reduced the number of low-level flights by more than 50 percent from 38,000 to 18,000 sorties without an explanation. If the flights were necessary before, were they not necessary now? A reduction in flights by more than half indicated that what the military originally said it needed was not firm and this cast doubt on the new demand for 18,000 flights.

Throughout the process, the DND had a difficult time explaining how the number of flights was determined. Rather, it explained that need was derived from defence policy. However, most people were frustrated to learn that, in a "Catch 22" fashion, the EIS was not required to explain defence policy that determined the number of flights.

One aspect of the need for the project that was clear was Canada's commitment to NATO. As the EIS stated:

"The military activities taking place at CFB Goose Bay therefore help Canada to be strong supporters (sic) of the NATO concept of peace and freedom through solidarity and adequate collective military defence."[5]

and further that:

"by allowing allied fighter pilots to train at CFB Goose Bay, the government of Canada is signalling its commitment to our Allies and to the world."[6]

This indicated that the motivation for low-level military flights was primarily support for NATO and the keeping of international commitments rather than meeting an actual need. Furthermore, although NATO has been declining in importance, the EIS did not discuss the general reduction in NATO activities and the present formation of new European alliances with the likely reduction of Canadian involvement in European security affairs.[7] It neglected the impact of the Maastricht treaty which provided for a European security and defence identity, a fact that casts the long-term NATO role in some doubt. Without a credible threat that calls for a collective defence, the need for the project was questionable.

2. Need For A Labrador Site

The DND proposal suggested that:

"No practical alternative currently exists for Allied flight training in Europe or North America or is likely to be developed in the near future."[8]

The EIS took this position without a search for other sites or an analysis of existing flight training opportunities in Europe or North America, despite the fact that air bases have been closed across Canada. Further, the EIS acknowledged that there are only three out of thirteen NATO nations presently participating in the DND proposal. The other ten nations have met their needs at home by flying 600,000 to 800,000 flights a year in Europe. Evidently, there is a substantial capacity for training flights in Europe, more than thirty times that of the DND proposal in Labrador. Furthermore, the DND admitted that it was looking for a fourth NATO nation to raise the demand at CFB Goose Bay to the full 18,000 sorties.[9] If demand was high, why couldn't the DND find another partner? The answer may be that the demand for flight training was more perceived than real. It was also not clear why missions were being flown in Canada when an increase of 2.5 percent of the average number of European flights would meet the entire DND demand, unless the purpose was to provide relief from low-level flights for Europeans by imposing those impacts on the Innu.

This is a moral choice the DND was not entitled to make. **As Robert Nozick said:**

"No moral balancing act can take place among us; there is no moral outweighing of one of our lives by others so as to lead to a greater overall social good. There is no justified sacrifice of some of us for others."[10]

The EIS did, however, indicate that the LLFT area is large in extent and sparsely populated with no permanent settlements. Apparently, the absence of a permanent settlement was an important criterion in choosing the Labrador-eastern Quebec location for LLFT. As noted in the 1989 EIS and its critiques, the proposal had the effect of transferring physical and human impacts from densely populated areas of Europe and Canada to the sparsely populated Labrador region and that the significant criterion was the absence of a permanent settlement, not the absence of effects on aboriginal Canadian people and their culture.

In the 1989 EIS Critique, the DND was told to demonstrate that the proposal:

"is not simply a means of transferring noise impact from European settlements to Canadian aboriginal populations. That would suggest the values guiding this EIS place greater weight on the well-being of

residents in European communities than on the well-being of native Canadian populations."[11]

The 1994 EIS failed to address this issue other than to state that European airspace was too congested. It did not explain that people affected by low-level flights in the UK, the Netherlands and Germany were actively opposing additional environmental impacts from low-level flight training.

3. Rationale

The rationale in an EIS requires the proponent to explain why the proposed undertaking is the most reasonable method of achieving the project objectives, in this case the training of Allied and Canadian pilots, and that the project has been sited in the most reasonable location. This time, rather than providing a purely military rationale, the DND in its new EIS, suggested the project should be approved to keep the base operating and provide economic development for the region. It argued that military flying played a key role in the growth and stability of the economy of central Labrador and that it wanted to avoid jeopardizing the existence of the base. The EIS suggested additional investment was needed in the Labrador economy, however, it was not clear how the need for further investment was established for Goose Bay nor was there a reasonable explanation why military investment was preferred to other economic investment options for the region.

It appeared the DND was no longer solely a military concern, instead, it had become an agency for economic development. The expansion of low-level flights was now necessary to support the non-native economy created by fifty years of military development in the region, in effect to justify the environmental, economic and social changes to date.

4. Alternatives

The generation and analysis of reasonable alternatives is a key element of the EIS process, one that ensures the greatest protection for environmental and human resources. Without adequate alternatives, it might be assumed the DND's proposal was the only opportunity to provide low-level flight training. In reality, there were many other alternatives. To meet current environmental assessment standards, the DND should have examined several alternatives to the project such as:

- Distributing the projected flights among a number of bases in Canada including bases that are closed or in the process of being closed.

- Allocating all of the flights to another base in Canada such as Cold Lake, Alberta.

- Redistributing European flights within the larger European flight capacity.

The EIS indicated in its discussion of alternatives that all bases in the region already had major operational roles that limited the amount of extra air traffic they could handle.[12] In their brief discussion, neither existing bases or training area alternatives were identified, nor were capacities to fly more missions examined. The DND did not examine other bases far from Labrador in central or western Canada and their capacities for flight training. In the end, alternatives to the proposal were not seriously investigated in the EIS. The DND's reasoning seemed to be that the regions of central Labrador and eastern Quebec were good locations for military flights because the human population is sparsely distributed and there are no permanent settlements. The assumption was that there would be little of human value to fly over.

5. Predicting Environmental Impacts

Predicting impacts on both natural and human environments was a problematic part of the environmental assessment for DND. Impacts must be predicted in order that the severity of each change can be judged and a decision made about how much impact is acceptable. In the 1994 EIS, impacts on each part of the natural environment were estimated based on extensive scientific studies.

Both the degree of impact and its likelihood were indicated. However, for the human environment, a similar level of investigation was not provided for assessing social impacts and in many instances it was assumed that DND activities have had and would continue to have no effect on the social and cultural activities of the Innu.

Two instances of this reasoning were evident. First, the EIS suggested that the decline of subsistence practices in the region was not the fault of DND activities since there has been a general decline of traditional economic sectors as a result of lumbering, mining, forestry and other practices.[13] Second, the EIS suggested that present social and public health problems found in Goose Bay and local communities were not a result of DND activities, rather they reflect community health and social problems found throughout northern Canadian communities. The DND carefully studied the impacts on the natural environment but paid little attention to social problems assuming they would occur anyway.

The DND assumed their operations at Goose Bay have had no appreciable effect on aboriginal peoples, their economy or social life, despite the fact that the CFB Goose Bay facility is the single largest facility for economic and social change in the region and has admittedly been the most significant force for the past fifty years. This assumption reveals a punishing asymmetry in the impacts predicted by DND. The base was described as the most important facility for the present and future economic well-being of the region but it was assumed not to be the single largest source of social and cultural change. It generated the greatest increases in employment and income but it was assumed not to cause social stress or lead to dependence on the wage economy. In the end, few social impacts were attributed to the CFB Goose Bay facility and few public health impacts were predicted. Clearly, the rigor applied in predicting biological impacts was not equally applied to social and cultural change.

6. Failure to Predict Impacts on Human Health

The failure to predict social impacts or to estimate their significance is most apparent in the assessment of impacts on human health in the communities near the base (14). A number of impacts were noted as minor or negligible. This was the case for sexually transmitted diseases (STDs), prostitution, drug use, sexual assault and violence against women.

6.1 Sexually Transmitted Diseases

The EIS predicted that a 25 percent increase in transient personnel at CFB Goose Bay would have little effect on sexual disease transmission, however, the DND did not estimate the number of additional cases that would be transmitted through personnel contacts with civilian and aboriginal people. It was assumed that base personnel are not STD carriers and that Canadian personnel are medically screened and not sent to CFB Goose Bay if they have a serious medical problem. Whether serious medical problems include STDs is unknown. The EIS stated rates of STDs among military personnel are low, but the rates were not reported.

6.2 Frequency of Sexual Contact

The DND said the frequency of sexual contact between base personnel and civilian and aboriginal people was low but did not provide estimates or comparisons between CFB Goose Bay and other bases in Canada or the United States regarding sexual contact. The DND argued that pilots and crews would be too busy with military activities to be involved in sexual contacts. There were no estimates offered of existing sexual contact or prostitution rates, even though sex is known to be traded for money and other material benefits (clothing and alcohol) in Goose Bay. The DND did not predict increased incidence rates if more pilots and crews were assigned to the base.

6.3 Alcohol, Drug and Substance Abuse

The rates of illegal drug use or alcoholism in the armed forces or in base personnel were not re-

ported and impacts were assumed to be negligible. Although alcoholism is prevalent in Labrador communities, information on how much is consumed through the base or the number of 'sign-in' visits of aboriginal people to base drinking facilities was not reported. Given that rates of use are unknown, the DND concluded the impact would be negligible.

6.4 Sexual Assault and Violence Against Women

Although there was substantial disagreement between estimates of sexual assault and violence against women (the RCMP estimated two in 100 assaults were committed by military personnel while the Mokami Status of Women Centre's estimate was eight in 100), the DND did not provide an investigation of existing rates or predict the increase in sexual assaults against women that would occur following a 25 percent increase in personnel at the base.

7. Assessing the Impacts

Natural and human impacts were assessed differently and they were judged dfferently. Natural impacts were predicted scientifically with some degree of confidence whereas the impacts on people were arrived at by guessing. In many cases they were poorly studied and not based on comparisons with the experiences at other military bases in the developing world.

In the end, it is ironic that severe and immediate impacts on the natural environment could not be directly attributed to low-level flights. If they had been, the Environmental Assessment Panel might have found it difficult to accept the EIS depite the political urgency to sign the agreement by 1996. Unfortunately for the Innu, the most important impacts were clearly social; the indirect and long-term changes to their subsistence economy through dependence on the base, the changes to human health, and the long-term social changes that would inevitably occur following expansion of activities at CFB Goose Bay.

Because there were no large, immediate natural environment impacts that were likely to occur because of low-level flights, it was critical for the Innu to have the Panel recognize the indirect and cumulative social impacts that aboriginal people would experience if the project were approved. This placed enormous importance on the Environmental Assessment Panel and its ability to reach a fair decision. The Panel would have to recognize the major changes in the way of life of the Innu caused by years of military flying activities and by other mining, transportation, hydroelectric and economic developments in the region. It was up to the panel to investigate the long-term social changes the proposal would produce.

The Environmental Assessment Panel Hearings

The value of the hearings for the Innu depended on the fairness of the Panel. An impartial and independent Panel was essential to examine the questions about long-term economic and social changes that were not addressed in the EIS. It was an ill omen, however, that the members of the Panel had been changed since the first EIS and that a new panel appointed in the waning years of the Mulroney administration was prepared to act quickly to meet the government's pressing deadline.

From the beginning, the new Panel failed to keep an "arm's length" relationship with the DND. The Panel's science advisor held extraordinary meetings with DND staff to resolve problems with the EIS and responded to requests by the DND and the government not to have land claims issues included in the EIS, something the first Panel had wanted addressed. Given the haste the Panel was willing to take to move the EIS along, one of the Panel members, Dr. Paul Wilkinson, resigned in April 1992. He felt the meetings held with DND had compromised the integrity and credibility of the Panel and he expressed doubts about the Panel's ability to conduct a thorough and impartial review.

When the EIS was published in April 1994, the Panel again showed its willingness to expedite the process. The 4,000 page EIS was to be reviewed in ninety days and following the review, hearings were held quickly in a six week period from September to October 1994. The Panel futher reduced the opportunity for the Innu to attend by scheduling hearings in the traditional moose hunting season. This reduced confidence in the Panel's impartiality, particularly since the Innu had asked that the harvest season be avoided because many people, particularly those engaged in the subsistence economy, would be out on the land. Requests to postpone the hearings were denied by the panel.

The Panel was also asked to hold hearings in Ottawa and other Canadian cities to permit the opinions of many Canadians to be heard. This was also rejected by the Panel. The effect was to isolate the hearings in Labrador and eastern Quebec away from the scrutiny of the larger population and to limit intervenors to those in areas where aboriginal people were outnumbered three to one.

Faced with an unfair process, the Innu decided not to attend the hearings because the apparent bias of the Panel and actions taken to limit participation meant that the outcome was foregone. The Innu did not want to condone the decision by their presence.

As expected, the outcome reflected the views of the non-native majority who depend on the military economy. Of the 131 intervenors, thirty-seven were aboriginal and more than two-thirds of them were opposed to expanding low-level flights. However, the majority of intervenors (government, business and non-native people) supported the project. Also, as one might guess, those living in communities near Happy Valley-Goose Bay where military employment is significant supported the proposal. People living in commmunities far from the base tended to oppose it. The farther the hearings were from the base, the more opposition there was to low-level flying. This was particularly true of the sessions in Quebec where two-thirds of the participants opposed it, one-third remained neutral, and no one supported the project.[15] Nevertheless, more hearings were held in the Happy Valley-Goose Bay area than anywhere else and the views of their residents were heard most often. In two-thirds of the non-technical hearings, the DND stated that the project was needed to create long-term jobs and economic development in the region and warned that failure to approve would mean the base would close and an economic collapse would follow, a form of economic blackmail which proved successful. The panel approved the proposal and rapidly published its decision in February, 1995.

Equity in the EIS Process

The final question is whether the outcome was fair to those who were affected by low-level flying in Labrador and eastern Quebec. Was it fair to expand low-level flying in a region without permanent settlements while avoiding the more densely populated areas of Canada? Was it equitable to continue a process of economic and social change in a region with a declining subsistence economy that was already experiencing considerable upheaval?

The question of equity is ultimately the central question. A fair outcome is one that distributes burdens equitably in location, in time and to each culture. If one group has been arbitrarily chosen to receive all the impacts without serious public discussion about the distribution of burdens, the outcome is unlikely to be fair.

To determine whether the outcome of the EIS process was fair to the Innu, four criteria of fairness should be met:

1. Temporal fairness
2. Geographic fairness
3. Economic fairness
4. Cultural fairness

1. Temporal Fairness

It is unfair to expose a community to the impacts of a project repeatedly or over a long period of time where other communities have not been similarly affected. In the DND proposal, the history of the military presence in Labrador makes it clear that resource-harvesting communities have repeatedly and over many years experienced low-level overflights when other Canadian communities have not. A history of overflight impacts on a single set of communities should exclude it from additional exposures if the outcome of the EIS is to be fair. Recent decisions in provincial environmental assessments indicate that continuing an existing impact should be considered an impact in its own right and not a justification for continuing to affect the same community.

2. Geographic Fairness

To be fair geographically, any impact including overflight activities should not be concentrated in one geographic area when other locations remain free of impacts. In the DND proposal, LLFT activities were to be concentrated in central Labrador and eastern Quebec. Many alternative locations were not seriously considered in the EIS, consequently, the outcome was not equitable geographically.

3. Economic Fairness

A project is unfair if the economic costs of the proposed undertaking fall on a community that is economically disadvantaged or that has not voluntarily agreed to accept compensating benefits. In the DND proposal, the economic costs were borne largely by the subsistence (old) economy that relies on resource harvesting. There was little recognition of the unfair distribution of economic benefits, which primarily go to the non-aboriginal wage economy, and the costs which affect the native economy. Further, there was no discussion of compensation for the economic burdens imposed nor was there a suggestion that impact management steps would be taken in the event the proposal is approved.

4. Cultural Fairness

It is unfair to impose impacts on one cultural group and avoid another without justification. Arbitrarily selecting one cultural group to bear the noise and stress of low-level flights fails the test of cultural fairness. The DND's justification for imposing low-level flights on the Innu was that population densities in Europe were high and permanent settlements in Canada ought to be avoided. It was clear both in the EIS and the Panel's decision that permanent settlements were valued more highly than native non-permanent communities.

Conclusion

Should the Environmental Impact Statement process have taken into consideration the ethical outcomes of the military's low-level flight training program? The answer to this question lies in how the environment is defined. If the environment includes the economy and culture of a community, then the views of the communities most affected by the project should guide the decision. This is particularly true for native communities because their values were substantially different from non-native groups in this case.

The EIS failed to reach a fair decision because the long-term impacts on the social and economic lives of the Innu were not fully disclosed. Because all the impacts were not clearly stated, the choice made could not be an informed choice. It is also apparent that the Panel's bias in favour of the proposal meant the EIS process was also unfair. In the end, the outcome was inequitable in all respects; time, location, economy and culture because the project was conceived and judged from a perspective outside the Innu community.

Addendum

Given the DND claim in the 1994 EIS that no practical alternative existed for Allied flight training in Europe or North America and that none would likely be developed in the near future, a surprising announcement was made in May, 1996 that the Cold Lake air base in Alberta was proposing to host additional NATO military flight training missions that were then being flown in Texas.[16] The proposal was enthusiastically supported by the provincial and local governments with promises of 4,000 square miles of unrestricted air space and financial support for roads and buildings needed to expand flight activities. How was it possible that a substantial capacity for flights, which did not exist for the EIS in 1995, suddenly materialized in Alberta in 1996 after the Labrador project had been approved?

Clearly, the DND did not admit in its 1994 EIS study that the capacity for more flights existed at the Cold Lake base. While it is not surprising that the military committed this sin of omission, it is the EIS process that failed the Innu because the Environmental Assessment Panel did not hold the military's EIS to the most basic requirement, that alternatives to the project be fully examined. Instead, it allowed the DND statements of limited flight capacity to pass without evidence even though that deficiency had been pointed out by Innu representatives in both the 1989 and 1994 EIS reviews. In the end, it was the Panel and its failure to demand reasonable EIS methods or to apply principles of fairness to its decision that allowed more low-level military flights to come to Labrador.

END NOTES

[1]Morris, Rose, Ledgett; "Critique of the Impacts of the Project on Innu Aboriginal Rights, Negotiation and Settlement of Innu Land Rights and Innu Human Rights"; in Peter Armitage, editor, *The Compendium of Critiques of the EIS: Military Flight Training*; Nitassinan; 1994.

[2]Berglund, M. Birgitta; "Impact of Noise on Human Health: a Review of the Goose Bay   EIS on Military Flight Training"; in Peter Armitage, editor, *The Compendium of Critiques of the EIS: Military Flight Training*; Nitassinan; 1994.

[3]National Film Board of Canada; *Hunters and Bombers*; NFB, Montreal; 1990.

[4]Environmental Assessment Panel Reviewing Military Flying Activities in Labrador and Quebec; *Deficiency Statement Respecting the Goose Bay EIS: an Environmental Impact Statement on Military Flying Activities in Labrador*

and Quebec; May 1990.

[5]Department of National Defence; *EIS: Military Flight Training*; Ottawa; 1994; p.3.4.2.

[6]Department of National Defence; *EIS: Military Flight Training;* Ottawa; 1994; p. 5.1.1.

[7]Spaven, Malcom; "Technical Review of the Adequacy of the Revised Goose Bay EIS"; in Peter Armitage, editor, *Compendium of Critiques of the EIS: Military Flight Training;* Nitassinan; 1994.

[8]Department of National Defence; *EIS: Military Flight Training;* Ottawa; 1994; p.5.1.2.

[9]Department of National Defence; *EIS: Military Flight Training;* Ottawa; 1994; p.5-32.

[10]Nozick, Robert; *Anarchy, State and Utopia New York*; Basic Books; 1973; p.33.

[11]Pushchak, Ronald; "Review of the Goose Bay EIS: an Environmental Impact Statement on Military flying Activities in Labrador and Quebec"; in Peter Armitage, editor, *The Compendium of Critiques of the Goose Bay EIS Nitassinan*; 1990; Sec. VIII, p.5.

[12]Department of National Defence; *EIS: Military Flight Training;* Ottawa; 1994; p.5.1.2.2.

[13]Department of National Defence; *EIS: Military Flight Training;* Ottawa; 1994; p.2.7.3.3.

[14]Department of National Defence; *EIS: Military Flight Training;* Ottawa; 1994; p.11.5.3.1.

[15]Heisey, Ariane and Ronald Pushchak; "Review of the FEARO Hearings, EIS: Military Flight Training" report to the Innu Nation; Toronto 1995; p.10.

[16]Holubitsky, J.; "Cold Lake Turns Up the Heat"; *Calgary Herald*; May 3, 1996; p.A4.

References

Armour, A. B., Bowron, B., Miller, E., and Miloff, M.; "A Framework for Community Impact Assessment"; In *Methodology of Social Impact Assessment*; Finsterbush, K., and Wolf, C.P.(eds.); Stroudsberg, Pa.; Hutchinson, Ross; 1982.

Armour, A.; *Facility Siting Processes: A State-of-the-art Review*; Atomic Energy Canada Limited, Toronto; 1990.

Armour, A.; *The Cooperative Process: Facility Siting the Democratic Way*; Plan Canada; March 1992.

Bardecki, M. J.; "Coping with Cumulative Impacts: an Assessment of Legislative and Administrative Mechanisms"; *Impact Assessment Bulletin, Vol. 8 (1 & 2)*; 1989.

Beanlands, G. and Duinker P.; *An Ecological Frame-work for Environmental Impact Assessment in Canada*; Ottawa, Federal Environmental Assessment and Review Office; 1983.

Blishen, B. R., Lockhart, A., Craib, P., and Lockhart, E.; *Socio-economic Impact Model for Northern Development*; Canada, Department of Indian and Northern Affairs; 1979.

Bowles, R. T.; *Social Impact Assessment in Small Communities*; Toronto, Butterworths; 1981.

Branch, K., Hooper, D. A., Thompson, J. B., and Creighton, J.; *Guide to Social Impact Assessment: A Framework for Assessing Social Change*; Boulder, Col., Westview Press; 1981.

Branch, K. et al; *Guide to Social Impact Assessment: a Framework for Assessing Social Change*; Boulder, Col., Westview Press; 1984.

Buckley, R.; "Perspectives in Environmental Management", Ch.6; *National Audit of Environmental Impact Predictions*; NY, Springer-Verlag; 1991; pp. 93-120.

Burdge, R.; "Utilizing Social Impact Assessment Variables in the Planning Model"; *Impact Assessment Bulletin, Vol. 8 (1 & 2)*; 1989.

Carley, M. J. and Bustelo, E. S.; *Social Impact Assessment and Monitoring: A Guide to the Literature*; Boulder, Col., Westview Press; 1984.

Dirschl, H. J., et al; "Evolution of Environmental Impact Assessment As Applied to Watershed Modification Projects in Canada; *Environmental Management, 17 (4)*; 1993.

Duinker, P.; "Ecological Effects Monitoring in EIA: What Can It Accomplish?"; *Environmental Management, 13 (6);*1989.

Gerrard, M.; *Whose Backyard, Whose Risk: Fear and Fairness in Toxic and Nuclear Waste Siting*; Cambridge, MIT Press; 1994.

Gibson, R. and Savan, B.; *Environmental Assessment in Ontario*; Toronto, Can., Envir. Law Research Foundation; 1986.

Gibson, R.; "Environmental Assessment Design: Lessons from the Canadian Experience"; *Environmental Professional, 15 (1)*; 1993.

Holubitsky, J.; "Cold Lake Turns Up the Heat"; *Calgary Herald*; May 3, 1996; p. A4.

Kennedy, A. and Ross, Wm.; "An Approach to Integrate Impact Scoping With Environmental Impact Assessment"; *Environmental Management, 16 (4)*; 1992.

Krawetz, N., et al; *A Framework for Effective Monitoring*; CEARC, Ottawa; 1987.

McDonald, G. T.; "Regional Economic and Social Impact Assessment"; *EIA Review, Vol. 10 (1 & 2)*; 1990.

Meredith, T.; "Environmental Impact Assessment and Monitoring"; in B. Mitchell, ed., *Resource Management and Development*; Toronto, Oxford U. Press; 1991.

Monahan, P. J.; *Social Equity and Waste Management: A Legal Perspective*; Director, York University Centre for Public Law and Public Policy; 1993.

National Research Council; *Improving Risk Communication*; National Academy Press, Washington DC; 1989.

O'Hare, M.; "Not On My Block You Don't: Facility Siting and the Strategic Importance of Compensation"; *Public Policy 25*; Fall 1977.

Peterson, E. B. et al; *Cumulative Effects Assessment in Canada: and Agenda for Action and Research*; CEARC, Ottawa, Min. Supply & Services; 1987.

Pushchak, R.; "Methods of Treating Benefits in Risk Evaluation"; In Grima, A. et al, eds. *Risk Perspectives on Environmental Impact Assessment*; Institute for Environmental Studies, Env. Mon. No. 9; 1989.

Pushchak, R. and Burton, I.; "Risk and Prior Compensation in Siting Low-Level Nuclear Waste Facilities: Dealing with NIMBY Syndrome"; *Plan Canada 23 (3);* 1983.

Rabe, B.; *Beyond NIMBY: Hazardous Waste Siting in Canada and the United States*; Washington DC, Brookings Institute; 1994.

Ross, H.; "Community SIA: A Cumulative Study in the Turkey Creek Area, Western Australia"; *Eastern Kimberly Working Paper no 27*; Canberra Centre for Resource and Environmental Studies, Australian National University; 1989.

Ross, H.; "Community Social Impact Assessment: A Framework for Indigenous Peoples"; *Environmental Impact Assessment Review*; 1990; 10: pp. 185-193.

Sadler, B.; "Impact Assessment in Transition: a Framework for Redeployment"; In Lang, R. (ed.), *Integrated Approaches to Resource Planning and Management*; Banff, Alta., School of Management, The Banff Centre, 1990.

Sandman, P. M.; *The Facility Siting Process of the Ontario Provincial Government and Interim Waste Authority: An Extended Critique and Alternative Proposal*; Training and Research in Risk Communication; 1993.

Schmeidler, E.; *Voluntary Site Selection: Five Case Studies*; Centre for Urban Policy Research, Rutgers University; 1993.

Spaling, H. and Smit, B.; "Cumulative Environmental Change: Conceptual Frameworks, Evaluation Approaches, and Institutional Perspectives"; *Environmental Management, 17 (5)*; 1993.

Wolfe, L.; *Methods for Scoping Environmental Impact Assessments: A Review of Literature and Experience*; Vancouver, FEARO; 1987.

LESSONS FROM THE MOOSE RIVER BASIN[1]
SUSTAINABILITY AND HISTORICAL INJUSTICE

19

by Wesley Cragg and Mark Schwartz [2]

Introduction

SUSTAINABLE DEVELOPMENT IS ABOUT ENVIRONMENtally friendly economic growth and the elimination of poverty through equitable distribution of economic wealth. Thought of this way, sustainable development is about the future. It is also about the past – or perhaps more accurately about escaping a past in which economic growth was more often than not environmentally destructive and distributively unjust. Finally, the idea of sustainability, as articulated by the Brundtland Commission and the increasingly converted business community, is inherently optimistic.

It is this optimism that sustainable economic growth remains a genuine possibility at this stage of human economic history that is most frequently questioned by critics. Can we find in nature the resources and the capacity to support the growth that will be required if the grinding poverty in which much of the world now lives is to be overcome? And can we find in ourselves the political and moral resources required to ensure that wealth is fairly distributed?

These questions offer profound challenges in their own right. Yet they appear to leave unaddressed some central environmental and social problems whose focus is not so much the future as the past. Indeed much of the current sustainable development rhetoric implicitly suggests a posture popularized by Prime Minister Trudeau in his first term of office when he argued, faced with aboriginal discontent, that a political system could only be held responsible for its own actions. It should not be asked to correct historical injustices for two reasons. First, history could not be changed and those harmed could not be compensated. Second, to require those now living to bear costs for which they are not responsible would be unfair.

Trudeau's position on this question was subsequently rejected by his government. It is now widely recognized that creating the conditions in which poverty and social inequity can be addressed requires that we face not just the future, but also the historical grievance-generating events which have shaped the present.[3]

Is there a lesson here for discussions of sustainable development? If so, what attention should be paid to historical injustices in the pursuit of sustainable development? Looked at globally, the legacy of injustice seems so complex that it defies analysis, let alone resolution. Discrete examples, on the other hand, may not have that character. A good example is Ontario Hydro's proposal for restructuring and developing the hydroelectric potential of the Mattagami River in northeastern Ontario.

The Mattagami River north of Kapuskasing was first harnessed in 1928 to provide power for a pulp mill which in turn gave life to the northern community of Kapuskasing. The same part of the river was redeveloped in the 1960's by Ontario Hydro to assist in meeting peak power demands of a rapidly growing industrial economy. Those developments had a significantly positive impact on the developing economy of the north and a significantly negative impact on the river itself and the subsistence economies of the original inhabitants of the river basin.

In the last decade, faced with what were then

thought to be accelerating demands for energy, Ontario Hydro proposed a redevelopment of what has come to be known as the Mattagami Complex. Although most other aspects of Hydro planning have been shelved in response to greatly reduced growth in Ontario's economy, this particular proposal is still under active study. Blocking the development have been Native grievances linked directly to the environmentally damaging impacts of the original development.

What is at issue then is the meaning of sustainability in a setting in which there is strong support for resource development juxtaposed with deeply felt historically grounded grievances connected with previous exploitation of natural resources. Added to this are serious concerns about the environmental impacts of both the current complex and its redevelopment for the river and the river basin.

This article will look at the Mattagami project from an economic and ethical perspective. In particular, we will examine three approaches to resolving both past and present issues raised by the project. The first was developed by Ontario Hydro in the context of its now shelved twenty-five year plan, which aimed at what might be called compensatory justice based on economic analysis. The First Nations in the area are calling for a recognition of their right to self-government, followed by co-planning and co-management of resource development. The Ontario Government is advocating a process-oriented solution based on equitable participation in the decision making process.

We begin with the case itself. The second section of the article examines the case from the perspective of distributive justice and sustainable development. We turn in section three to a description and evaluation of the three alternatives outlined in the preceeding paragraph, and then draw some lessons on the moral stucture of the concept of sustainability. We conclude with some

observations about the nature of the exercise and a postscript describing how the case has evolved over the period of our study.

Part One – The Case[4]

The Moose River Basin is an area larger in size than Ireland. The Mattagami is one of three rivers that empty into James Bay via the Moose River. The ecosystems of the region, in common with other boreal and sub-arctic areas, are fragile and easily damaged. The Ontario Hydro complex which is the focus of our study consists of four dams on the Mattagami River 60 to 100 km north of Kapuskasing. Vegetation in the vicinity of the four dams consists mainly of boreal forests. The Basin's wildlife population includes moose, bear, beaver, fox, otter and numerous species of birds, amphibians, and fish.

Aboriginal settlement would appear to date back as much as 5,000 years. European settlement dates to 1776 when the Hudson's Bay Company opened a post on Moose Factory Island. In the early 1900's railway lines opened up the area to agriculture, mining, and lumbering. In the following years, private hydroelectric developments were established in the Basin to provide power to new resource industries.

In 1922, the "model" town of Kapuskasing was built around a pulp and paper mill which was operated by the Spruce Falls Pulp and Paper Company and owned by Kimberly Clark and The New York Times. The first of four dams in the complex, the Smoky Falls station, was built by Spruce Falls in 1928 to supply inexpensive hydroelectric power to the mill. This dam destroyed a beautiful natural water fall and did cause long term environmental damage, but not on the scale of later hydroelectric developments. In the 1960's Ontario Hydro added three more dams: Little Long (1963), Harmon (1965), and Kipling (1966). Unlike the Smoky Falls station, however, these were "peaking" stations, operating only 5 hours per day and requiring "headponds" whose water levels were to fluctuate up to 3 metres each day. Also required was a spillway which would operate during the spring runoff. The spillway was created by diverting water into Adam Creek, a small natural water course adjacent to the river itself. The resulting erosion has created river banks 20 to 30 metres in height and washed millions of cubic metres of soil down the river.

The hydroelectric developments of the 1960's have had a significant impact on the Basin's ecology and its aboriginal inhabitants. Construction of the dams provided employment for some aboriginals. Connecting the communities of Moose Factory and Moosonee to the Ontario power grid has resulted in important improvements for the communities affected. These developments have also been accompanied by deterioration in water quality; fluctuating water levels leading to trapped fish, sandbars, and silted-over spawning beds; erosion; significant flooding; a loss of food and habitat for beavers and other animals; and the destruction of historic Cree settlement sites, historic portages, fur trade sites, and cemeteries. Aboriginal inhabitants have also linked noise from generators to declining birds, otter, mink, and fox in the area of the dams and complained of deterioration in the quality of the fur from beaver, muskrat, and otter. The dams' construction roads have improved access for non-native hunters generating competition for resources, and provided greater access for logging companies whose cutting activities have also had a negative impact on fur-bearing mammals and fish. Finally, the use of the rivers for transportation has been seriously affected by the fluctuating river levels.

All of these impacts have taken a toll on the traditional way of life of the Basin's aboriginal inhabitants and appear to have been accompanied throughout by an absence of consultation, mitigation, or compensation by Ontario Hydro.

In 1990, Ontario Hydro submitted to the Ontario government an environmental assessment calling for a redevelopment of the four dams to increase the hydroelectric generation capacity of the Mattagami River. Additional generating units were proposed for the Little Long, Harmon, and Kipling stations. The base load Smoky Falls station was to be retired, and a new peaking power station constructed adjacent to it. The goal was to optimize energy production from the river by building a new "in-step" operation which Ontario Hydro projected would provide enough new energy to suppy the demand of electricity for 150,000 homes. In its environmental assessment, Ontario Hydro predicted that the redevelopment would cause little new damage while reducing environmental impacts on the part of the existing operations.

In 1991, the owners of Spruce Falls Pulp and Paper Company, having failed to find a buyer for an increasingly uneconomic operation, announced their decision to shut down most of the Kapuskasing mill operation with the possible loss of 1,200 direct and 6,200 indirect jobs in a town of 11,000. The resulting political crisis caused the Ontario government to intervene. As a result, the company was sold by Kimberly Clark and The New York Times to its employees. As part of the package, the Smoky Falls station was sold to Ontario Hydro on the condition that the environmental assessment process found the redevelopment proposal acceptable. Alternatively, the Ontario government would be required to pay Ontario Hydro $247 million.[5] The focus of this article is the debates and proposals generated by the ensuing environmental assessment process. The project's stakeholders include:

Ontario Hydro, the proponent of the Mattagami extension proposal. Although the urgency for finding new sources of power has now vanished, the project has until recently been regarded as an efficient way of providing inexpensive hydro electric power to the Ontario grid.

The aboriginal people now living in the Moose River Basin. Most affected by the dams in question are the aboriginal residents of Moosonee, about 900 in number, and Moose Factory, a community of about 2,200 aboriginal inhabitants. In total there are about 10,000 aboriginal inhabitants in the Basin area. For these people, on-going land claims and their traditional way of life is of deep significance.

The Ontario government with political, economic and financial interests in discussions and negotiations that have accompanied the environmental assessment process.

The non-aboriginal residents of surrounding communities where unemployment is high and opportunities for economic development have been warmly welcomed. Other stakeholders include the more distant municipalities, labour unions, independent power producers, tourist operators, and environmental groups.

Part Two: The Structure of Injustice
1) Distributive Justice and the concept of sustainable development
Ontario Hydro's proposed Mattagami Complex extension poses a complex challenge to the application of the notion of sustainable development. That complexity derives in large measure from the nature of the environmental impacts of earlier developments set against the likely benefits of further development. Economic analysis suggests, as we have already pointed out, that redevelopment of the complex would bring substantial benefits to the town of Kapuskasing, to the economy of the northeastern region of the province and to Ontario Hydro consumers. Analysis also suggests that the proposed development would have beneficial environmental impacts. This of course is a significant component of Ontario Hydro's case for development. If we focus exclusively on the future, the proposal might therefore seem to be sustainable. Nevertheless, it has generated considerable controversy and deep opposition, particularly from the Native population. It is virtually impossible to understand that opposition without exploring the links between sustainability and distributive justice.

The idea of sustainable development has been reformulated by critics of the Brundtland Commission definition in numerous ways. Criticism, however, has not managed to undermine the importance of the role the idea continues to have in the thinking of those concerned with the impact of modern industrial development on the world's environment. It has continued to play this role in part, we suggest, because of the way in which the idea of sustainable development has helped to bring environmental concerns into dialogue with economic ones.

Under-riding that dialogue is a set of moral imperatives. This is evidenced by two things. First, sustainable development is at its most fundamental level about sharing the planet's resources with the future in equitable ways. Second, underlying the concept is a conviction that unsustainable development carries with it morally significant costs that are cumulative and will be passed as costs to future generations. The harnessing of the great rivers draining the Canadian Shield illustrates these points; discussions of future developments unavoidably confront them.

What then is the moral structure of sustainable development?[6] We propose that it must include the principle that: *The costs of resource development should be born by those who will reap its benefits.*[7] This principle is clearly a principle of distributive justice. Failure to respect it, we propose, must unavoidably lead to injustice, the imposition of morally significant costs unbalanced by benefits to those on whom they are imposed. We shall argue that sustainable resource development which is insensitive to this principle may be possible. However, in those cases where it occurs it will be by accident and not design.

2) Cost benefit analysis and the problem of externalities
For much of the century, Ontario Hydro, a publicly owned provincial public utility, has studied and exploited the hydraulic potential of the great rivers draining the Canadian Shield. The Province

of Ontario has been the direct beneficiary of hydroelectric development undertaken by Ontario Hydro in pursuit of this mandate.

Even a cursory survey of the evidence shows that hydroelectric development in the north has not been constrained or guided by principles of sustainable development in the past. The dams constructed on northern rivers have diverted and altered the flow of rivers in environmentally significant ways, resulting in the creation of huge new reservoirs needed to ensure reliable energy delivery over long time periods in response to fluctuating demand. The resulting energy has been delivered at relatively low monetary cost to the residents of Ontario with considerable economic benefit. On the other hand, substantial costs have been imposed on Native communities in the absence of meaningful consultation and countervailing benefits recognizable as such by those affected.

The legacy of these developments is reflected in an acute sense of grievance which now dominates discussion of northern Ontario resource use. It is reflected as well in substantial environmental problems that now confront Native and non-Native communities in the north.[8]

What is the source or origin of the injustice that has been imposed on Native communities in the north? A first clear candidate is moral insensitivity on the part of planners, developers and the Crown corporation itself. The histories that are now being collected and the accounts of the Native people that are now being assembled in defence of self-government claims suggest that much of the development has taken place in an environment in which the fact that the land was occupied and under use by an indigenous population was simply ignored.[9] A second candidate is the Friedmanite character of modern economic activity. The task of business, Friedman has argued, is to operate as profitably as possible within the constraints set by law. So long as they work within the law, managers are not responsible for monitoring or compensating costs that have no direct

impact on profits. Responding to inequities resulting from economic activities is more properly the responsibility of governments.[10] Finally, it might be argued that the injustice resulting from northern hydro development is a direct consequence of the structure of the planning process that guided the development of the hydraulic potential of the north of Ontario.

It is this third explanation that holds the key to the problems of injustice on the one hand and unsustainability on the other. Ontario Hydro's mandate is an economic one. Ontario Hydro is directed by law to maximize economic benefits and minimize costs which must be passed on to consumers. In the past, where hydroelectric installations were concerned, the costs Ontario Hydro could not avoid passing on to consumers were those costs resulting from construction, transmission and maintenance of its northern generating facilities as well as whatever compensation the law required be paid to those with a legal right to compensation, private property owners for example. Legally speaking, Ontario Hydro was entitled to regard all other costs as externalities and therefore not its responsibility. For the most part, this was the path Ontario Hydro chose to follow. Given its mandate, the approach taken is hardly surprising.

Ontario Hydro's past approach to the development of Ontario's northern rivers is best characterized as "least cost" planning. It is an approach to planning that Litchfield argues has dominated energy planning by utilities throughout North America until very recently.[11] It reflects a Friedmanite approach to the issue of corporate social responsibility. Finally, it is an approach which taken by itself, in the absence of alternative non corporate responses to environmental and human impacts, is obviously open to the charge of moral insensitivity. In the case under consideration, no adequate strategies for dealing with external (to Ontario Hydro) costs were put in place by the government. As a consequence, the full burden of carrying those costs was shifted to the indigenous residents of the north and their communities.

It is this legacy which underlies the conflicts which Ontario Hydro's proposals for the redevelopment of the Mattagami Complex have generated. It remains a legacy in spite of the fact that all of the parties to the conflict acknowledge the inadequacies of past planning and development and have committed themselves to the idea of sustainable development in planning and assessing new projects. The central dilemma is to determine what role that legacy should play in creating a sustainable development strategy for the Mattagami River.

Part Three:
The Structure of Environmental Conflict
1) Economic analysis and compensatory justice

Ontario Hydro's proposal for redeveloping the Mattagami Complex derives from its mandate "to provide a reliable supply of electrical power and energy to the people of Ontario, at the lowest long-term feasible cost."[12] Its proposal is designed to assist it to meet its obligations by expanding the four existing sites so as to extract the greatest possible energy potential of the river with the least possible adverse environmental effects.

It is clear from both the *Environmental Assessment Summary* and *The Demand Supply Plan Report* that the proposed extensions are designed to increase the peak energy capacity of Ontario Hydro. Its case for the project rests on "least-cost" planning that incorporate all (but only) those costs to be "borne directly by Hydro."[13] Ontario Hydro acknowledges that "(c)osts and benefits for the Ontario community beyond these direct costs are not factored into cost comparisons."[14] In this respect the approach used in developing the current proposal is no different from that which Hydro has used in developing all its hydraulic sites in northern Ontario in this century.

In spite of the similarities with past planning methods, however, the approach used to plan the Mattagami extension represents important differences. Among other things, it incorporates a commitment to take into account social and environmental as well as the economic impacts in the planning process. This change is clearly significant. Given a commitment to "least cost" planning, how is it to be accounted for?

The answer lies in two places. First Ontario's *Environmental Assessment Act*[15] which aims at "the betterment of the people of Ontario by providing for the protection, conservation and wise management in Ontario of the environment".[16] That act defines the environment broadly to include the natural environment as well as "the social, economic and cultural conditions that influence the life of man or a community".[17] This Act has meant significant changes to the regulatory environment in which energy planning must now take place in Ontario. As a result, in planning the Mattagami extension, Ontario Hydro has been required by law to take into account costs which previously it had externalized.

It is clear from the *DSP Environmental Analysis* offered in justification of the Mattagami extension, however, that not only the law but also Ontario Hydro's own thinking has undergone significant changes since the 1960's. Respect for principles of sustainable development is now Ontario Hydro policy.[18] This has been interpreted to mean that project planning must consider environmental protection and conservation, regional economic stability, recreation, health, heritage protection and aboriginal concerns. More striking for our purposes, however, is recognition that sustainable development carries the moral implication that:

Generally, it is preferable that those who bear the risks also share equitably in the benefits.[19] To be committed to sustainable development is thus understood to require qualified respect for the principle of distributive justice already identified.

The planning and internal environmental assessment process which appears to have emerged as a result of these changes can be summarized in the following way:

1) Meet the electrical power needs of the province in the most sustainable manner possible;

2) Integrate environmental as well as economic costs in all cost calculations;

3) Inform and consult with the public in identifying benefits and costs;

4) Mitigate all adverse impacts where economically feasible;

5) For all residual impacts, provide substitute off-setting benefits for losses where economically feasible;

6) Compensate fairly for all adverse residual impacts where mitigation or substitution is not possible.

Ontario Hydro's own assessment has led it to conclude that, tested against these criteria, the Mattagami Extension represents the lowest cost option available to it and that the criteria constitute a fair basis for responding to the concerns of all those likely to benefit or suffer as a result of the development. The redevelopment will allow a more efficient and productive use of the hydraulic potential of the river than the present installations allow. The construction phase will provide jobs. Permitting the redevelopment will justify the purchase of the Smoky Falls station from the Spruce Falls Pulp and Paper Company, saving tax dollars and indirectly strengthening the economic viability of the mill and consequently of Kapuskasing, by contributing to the continued provision of low cost power through the Ontario grid. These economic benefits are to be accompanied by minimal environmental damage and the potential for certain environmental improvements.[20] For example, there will be little impact on soil, vegetation, wildlife, and aquatic habitat. There will be a reduction in shoreline erosion in headponds, downstream erosion in Adam Creek, and in the passage of fish through the Adam Creek control structure.

Ontario Hydro does acknowledge that negative environmental impacts may occur as a result of the redevelopment that it is proposing. However, those that do occur will be mitigated. For example, although there may be additional angling and hunting pressure on fish and wildlife populations from the construction workforce, measures will be taken to both restrict and discourage excessive hunting and angling activities during the construction period.[21] Although the peaking operations will increase the water level fluctuation downstream of the Kipling station, Hydro proposes to maintain minimal water levels to prevent the dewatering of aquatic habitat. A new spawning habitat will be created in the Smoky Falls' tailrace[22] to compensate for the loss of spawning grounds as a result of the redevelopment.[23] Ontario Hydro's environmental assessment also acknowledges that there will be some residual impacts. For example, Hydro proposes to "co-operate with trappers to identify yields before the project and compensate financial losses resulting from project activities".[24] It has also offered to compensate for impacts on aboriginal harvesting activities. Thus:

...Ontario Hydro will seek to provide fair compensation for all subsistence users and licensed trappers in the project area, for any losses that may result from the undertaking. With their co-operation, funding will be provided to area First Nations to define both pre- and post-development levels of aboriginal harvesting.[25]

Furthermore:

Should impacts be identified, options such as financial compensation, replacement of losses in kind (eg., provision of fish, fowl, etc. from other sources) or other equivalent impact management measures (e.g., to establish new trap lines, relocate cabins, etc.) will be offered.[26]

The commitment to inform and consult is reflected in "public information and feedback" which "were the cornerstones of the public involvement program for the Mattagami River Extensions Environmental Assessment Study".[27] And although Hydro's relationship with the Nishnawbe-Aski First Nations is acknowledged as strained,[28] attempts have been made to rectify the situation including the appointment of a Corporate Aboriginal Affairs Coordinator.[29]

Finally, Ontario Hydro has undertaken to deal with the grievances to which the earlier developments on the river have given rise. However, at the time of the original environmental assessment, it rejected the view that settling those grievances is or should be an element in any environmental assessment carried out under the Environmental Assessment Act.

Ontario Hydro's position on the Mattagami Extension represents an attempt to achieve important economic goals within a sustainable development framework. However, the resulting development model has failed to win agreement particularly on the part of Native stakeholders. Seen from a Native perspective, Ontario Hydro's approach which Ontario Hydro acknowledges, was implemented without substantial Native input on consultation, has two defects. First is its fundamentally utilitarian structure. The overriding objective is the provision of adequate supplies of reliable, low cost electricity for the people of Ontario. The key to the exercise is identifying low cost or lowest cost options. Achieving this goal, however, becomes extremely difficult unless the monetary value of costs and benefits can be accurately determined.

Herein lies the difficulty for many of the participants.[30] For example, Hydro's environmental assessment identifies as priorities: low cost reliable electric power, efficient use of water resources, environmental protection, conservation, regional economic stability, recreation, health, heritage protection and aboriginal concerns. If we probe the documents assembled in response to the *Demand/Supply Plan*, we discover as aboriginal concerns: a deep sense of obligation to the land or "mother earth"; treaty rights; control over those land areas on which they have relied for subsistence, and finally a profound sense of obligation to the Creator, their traditional way of life, and aboriginal rights. It is not at all clear how one would seek to cost environmental impacts from the perspective of this set of concerns.[31]

The importance of the ability to cost impacts is further emphasized by the way this approach to planning relies on substitution of off-setting benefits for costs incurred and, failing that, on compensation. Values readily quantified can be easily assimilated to this approach. The risk, however, is that values that cannot be quantified will be ignored just because the methodology has no way of dealing with them.[32] In short, the problem in using a mitigation and compensation approach is that it appears to call for what has been described as the commodification of values. It is perhaps not surprising that the methodology and its application have given rise to both offence and criticism. Aboriginal reaction to Ontario Hydro's plans reflects that kind of judgment. To propose financial compensation for polluted water, or poisoned fish, or the loss of traditional hunting grounds, or flooded grave sites is, from a Native perspective, to misunderstand in a profound way the nature of the losses for which compensation is being offered.

Second, lying at the heart of the First Nations' refusal to cooperate is a deep sense of historical grievance, grounded not simply in the costs that have been imposed as a result of hydro electric development. Rather it is a reaction to the contempt for Native values, and the way of life in which they have traditionally been enshrined, implied by the way development in the north has typically taken place. It is unlikely that a planning and assessment process, which assumes that adequate mitigation, substitution and compensation are in principle available for all unavoidable negative impacts could respond to that sense of injustice. These sentiments are captured by the alternative solution to the conflict proposed by First Nation leaders.

2) Respecting rights:
the self-government option

The First Nations' response to the Mattagami extension proposal has three components. First is a commitment to sustainable development, which the Native People's Circle on Environment and Development suggests has always has been a guiding concept for Native people. This commitment, they go on to say, is reflected in the view that "the land and its resources be preserved for the benefit of past, present, and future generations".[33]

As with Ontario Hydro, sustainability is closely linked to economic well-being. What separates the two views, however, is how best to achieve that goal. As Randy Kapashesit, Chief of the Mocreebec First Nation, points out:

Ontario Hydro's notion of economic development is not supportive of the kind of economy that is reflective of our own culture, values, traditions and environment.[34]

For Hydro, the land is a resource to be used. From a Native perspective, the land is something deserving great respect, a source of cultural, aesthetic, spiritual as well as economic values. The land is seen as of great value in its own right. Its health is viewed as directly linked to their well-being.[35]

The implications of these two perspectives for dealing with the concept of sustainability are striking. What for Ontario Hydro are impacts properly discussed with a view to substitution and providing financial compensation raise questions for the aboriginal people about their capacity to sustain a way of life.In short, from an aboriginal perspec-

tive, sustainability is impossible in the absence of respect for the land. Unavoidably, therefore, sustainability raises the issue of historical grievances, the second component in the aboriginal perspective on the Mattagami extensions.

Why is this so? The aboriginal position on grievances is succinctly set out by Chief Kapashesit in a statement to the Environmental Assessment Board which was created to evaluate Ontario Hydro's twenty-five year *Demand/Supply Plan* who argues that:

Justice requires that...past grievances be settled before future projects are even considered. It is immoral for Ontario Hydro to be talking about future projects when they have not entered settlements to compensate for the damage they inflicted by past projects.[36]

At first glance this stance may appear paradoxical. If, as we have been suggesting, the objectionable character of Ontario Hydro's proposal for resolving conflicts over the Mattagami Extension rest in part in the suggestion that the way to deal with residual impacts of the development it is proposing is through compensation, how is it possible that Native leaders should propose that serious grievances be resolved through compensation?

The question is important. It is also relatively easily answered. Those historical grievances now hold enormous symbolic value for the Native people of the north. They represent the failure on the part of an alien and insensitive culture to give to the land slated for development, as well as the life dependent on it, the profound respect which is its due. The Native inhabitants response to this failure is analogous to the outrage which would greet a proposal to burn the contents of Canada's libraries to heat the city of Toronto, or the art hanging on the walls of the Louvre to light the city of Paris.

To understand the analogy requires seeing books and paintings as renewable resources, which in a sense they are. There is no shortage of either authors or painters to renew our libraries or art galleries. But to see books and paintings in this light would be clearly unacceptable, indeed offensive for many people raised in a European culture. Native people regard the western response to water as a renewable natural resource in a similar way. At issue in both cases is an implied disrespect for things of great value and, by implication, for the people who value them.

What then could count as compensation? Or more properly, what is the role of compensation in cases such as this? Compensation cannot replace valued items with things of equal value. What compensation can do is restore a sense of respect or acknowledge in a significant way the nature of the offence which has been given.[37] It is unlikely that a people so offended could accept as sincere a commitment to change that offered nothing by way of restitution for activities said now to be regretted and not to be repeated.

The third component of the aboriginal position on the proposed Mattagami Extension is the demand that there be no further development until the rights of the First Nation communities to self-government have been recognized. Recognition is to include control over the development of natural resources in areas of Native jurisdiction. The logic of this demand flows directly from the importance of sustainability to the traditional native way of life and the failure on the part of those developing the north to respect values of central importance to the Native communities affected. Control over the land and uses imposed would ensure that future development was appropriately responsive to those values.

As with the Ontario Hydro proposal for the Mattagami Complex, this solution to the current impasse has clear strengths. If we accept that sustainability is a fundamental value in aboriginal culture, as Native leaders have claimed, it would move environmental values to a much more significant place in the evaluation of development

proposals than has been the case previously. It would ensure respect for the interests of a minority who have been required historically to carry substantially more than their fair share of the costs of development.

The idea of a veto for aboriginal or local communities over development proposals in areas like northern Ontario has been advanced in a number of formats and contexts and is not unique to the aboriginal people of northeastern Ontario. For example, the environmental assessment *Guidelines for the Great Whale River Hydroelectric Project* require that "the proposed (Great Whale) project must...respect the rights of local communities to determine their future and their own societal objectives".[38] But is this proposal consistent with the moral principle that those who benefit from an activity should carry the costs it generates? To satisfy this principle requires a careful accounting of the interests of all those who have a stake in any decisions about the future of, for example, the Mattagami Complex. What is being proposed would appear simply to shift control over development from one stakeholder, Ontario Hydro, to another. It is not obvious that the effect of such a shift would be a fair sharing of the costs and benefits of decisions affecting the use of nature's resources.

There are two immediate objections to this interpretation of this second option, seen from a northeastern Ontario aboriginal perspective. What First Nation stakeholders are calling for in this case is co-planning and co-management of resources.[39] Surely a demand of this nature is not inconsistent with principles of distributive justice. Further, the demand for self-government is a rights claim. It is not based on an appeal to principles of distributive justice or sustainable development. As such it might well be argued that it is immune to moral arguments seeking to balance costs and benefits of actions and policy decision for those affected.

These are important considerations. What they

seem to point to is a weakness in the analysis of the moral underpinnings of the idea of sustainable development. The principle that those who reap the benefits of a development project should bear the costs can be operationalized acceptably only where there is substantial agreement on what is to count as a cost or a benefit. However the concepts of cost and benefit are culturally sensitive. One form of moral insensitivity is insensitivity to this fact. Historical injustice is frequently the result. When it occurs, it undermines trust on the part of its victims in the willingness of its perpetrators to change their ways. The demand for self-government can be seen as a response to that breakdown in trust.

Whether the idea of self-government, accompanied as it almost always is with a desire to exercise control over natural resources, is an acceptable response to the fact of historical injustice is too large a question for this paper.[40] Seen from the perspective of sustainable development and its moral underpinnings, however, it raises an instructive point. If we accept that individuals themselves are usually the best judges of their own interests, then it is unlikely that a principle like the one we have highlighted will find morally acceptable implementation in the absence of equitable participation in decision making by those likely to be affected.[41] And while acknowledging this point does raise significant difficulties for shaping decision making so that it reflects adequately the interests of future generations, it does point to the need to add a principle of equitable participation as a practical requirement for sustainable development.

It is considerations of this sort which lead to the third option presented by stakeholders for resolving the conflict generated by the Mattagami extension proposal.

3) Operationalizing the principle of equitable participation

As the stakeholder analysis in Part One indicates, the Ontario Government had a substantial finan-

cial, economic and political interest in resolving the conflict that emerged in response to the Mattagami Extention proposal. In response to a report it commissioned in July 1991 and extensive informal negotiations with First nation representatives, the provincial government undertook to create two consultative processes. Both were designed to resolve conflict over the Mattagami Extension proposal while laying the framework for constructive resolution of the longer term resource use planning issues. Both processes reflected an acknowledgement that the short term and longer term issues could not be resolved unless both non-Native concerns about the economic future of the region and aboriginal concerns about the right to equitable participation in resource development and resource management were addressed.

First, the Ontario government undertook to create a "technical group" whose mandate was to review "how the design and/or operation of the (Mattagami Complex) Project could be modified to achieve the primary objective of environmental enhancement as well as the production of energy." The government proposed that the group have four members, two appointed by the government and two by the Moose River James Bay (Aboriginal) Coalition and/or its members, on behalf of Moose Factory, New Post, and MoCreebec First Nations. In proposing this group, the government committed itself to providing the financial and technical resources the group would need to assess the Mattagami extension project, consult broadly and report back to the government and the elected chiefs and councils of the New Post, Moose Factory and MoCreebec First Nations.[42]

The intention was to bring the environmental assessment process to a successful conclusion while recognizing the importance of First Nation self-government concerns by appointing an advisory group with an equal number of Native and non-Native members. Further, the technical group was to be given a mandate to report with recommendations to the appropriate bodies on any issues of concern identified in the consultative process. In proposing the committee, the Minister implied a willingness to be guided in his decisions on the project by a consensus report that won First Nation approval.

The second element in the government proposal was the creation of a baseline data collection project which was given the task of describing the existing biophysical, social, cultural and economic environmental conditions in the Moose River Basin. These data could then be used to identify a base line against which the cumulative impacts of resource development in the basin could be measured.[43] The government also proposed that "traditional knowledge" as well as data gathered using the techniques of modern science should be included in the data base.

Here the government was responding to a fundamental Native environmental concern, namely, that the environment should be looked at holistically. In responding to resource development proposals, Native spokespeople argued that what matters is not the aggregate environmental impact of any particular development looked at in isolation but the cumulative impact of resource development in the Moose River Basin looked at together. Native groups also argued that cumulative impacts could only be calculated against pre-established environmental benchmarks. Identifying such benchmarks for the Moose River Basin before further development was approved was therefore a fundamental First Nation demand.

The proposals advanced by the Ontario government, which were accepted by the Moose Cree First Nation as a single package, focus on matters of process. They assume that, if a fair dispute resolution process can be established, sound environmental and economic decisions will be forthcoming. As such, the Ontario government proposals are not derived directly from a commitment to

sustainable development or to the equitable sharing of the costs and the benefits of resource development. The option proposed does seem to rest on a moral principle however, namely the principle of equitable participation.[44] Are there important connections between these two principles? As a matter of practice, the answer is surely yes.

We have already suggested that the deep sense of grievance that Native leaders have carried into the Mattagami extension debate can be understood as a legitimate moral response to the lack of respect exhibited in the past for their peoples' values by resource developments. It is at least arguable that the Native people of northern Ontario would not have been treated as they were had they been granted the right to equitable participation. It is equally difficult to see how, in practice, distributive justice or sustainable development could be guiding principles of resource development where equitable participation on the part of those likely to be adversely affected was denied.

Part Four: The Moral Structure of Substainability

What lessons can be learned from the debate that has been generated by Ontario Hydro's Mattagami Extension proposals? There would seem to be several.

1. Commitment to sustainable development by itself is not likely to lead to consensus on environmentally acceptable development unless we are able to unpack carefully the moral structure of that idea. This need may not be obvious in morally homogeneous cultural settings. But where the moral underpinnings of the idea are not carefully considered, consensus may reflect little more than a pervasive cultural bias. It was not the presence of Native people in northern Ontario that made hydraulic development of northern rivers unsustainable. What their presence has done, though all too slowly and at great cost, is to make the

unsustainable character of that development visible.

2. Distributive justice is an important component of sustainable development. The relevant principle of distributive justice is that those who benefit from resource development should bear the costs it generates. Injustice results when significant costs are externalized. Hence, externalizing costs is simply incompatible with a commitment to distributive justice and hence to sustainable development.[45]

3. The identification, measurement and sharing of costs and benefits of development is a key element in assessing sustainability. This process, however, is culturally sensitive. That is to say, what counts as a cost and a benefit will be a function of the values and patterns of life of those affected. Because of this, moral insensitivity is both a significant obstacle to assessments of sustainability and a source of injustice.

4. One form of moral insensitivity to which least cost planning seems particularly prone is the monetization of costs. Monetizing all costs assumes the homogeneity of values. But more importantly, it assumes that everything valued, particularly anything which is a part of the natural environment, can be instrumentalized in monetary terms. What our study suggests is that this view clashes with the need for cultural sensitivity in identifying, assessing and sharing costs and benefits. The issue here is not whether in some cultures at least there are things which are so valuable they cannot be given up whatever the circumstances. Rather the issue is how the cost or perhaps the loss of things of that sort is to be assessed.

5. In practice, ensuring equitable participation in processes which are directed toward the identification, measurement or sharing of costs is a requirement of sustainable development. This is not because it is in principle impossible for people to identify and measure impacts from the perspective of those with a different cultural background. Rather it is because: first, it is reasonable to assume that adults are the best judges of the value of things seen from their own perspective; and second, overcoming moral insensitivity in practice is a difficult challenge and one which is likely to be met only imperfectly much of the time in the absence of the active cooperation and participation of those whose perspective is in question.

6. Finally, while historical injustice is not an infallible indicator of unsustainability, it does stand as a powerful symbol of moral insensitivity. Moral sensitivity is not a necessary condition of sustainable development. However, where it is absent, sustainability can only be realized by accident, not by design.

Part Five: Final Observations and a Concluding Postscript

This paper is an exercise in applied ethics. Our purpose in writing it has been to identify the moral values that underpin the pursuit of sustainability, values that must be respected if it is to be achieved. The argument of this paper is designed to support two conclusions in this regard. First, sustainable development does indeed have a moral structure. Second, the moral structure of sustainability has three components. The first two are principles of distributive justice: *those who benefit from resource development should bear all its costs*; *costs and benefits of resource development should be distributed fairly*. The third is a practical corollary of the first two: *equitable participation in planning and management of resource developments on the part of those on whom a particular development is likely to have an impact is in practice necessary if moral insensitivity in identifying and "costing" costs and benefits likely to accrue from development and injustice in the distribution of costs and benefits is to be avoided.*

Our analysis has not outlined a strategy for eradicating historical injustice in this or any of its many manifestations, although the article does purport to identify the political, legal, economic, or social roots of historical injustice. Neither does it make substantive recommendations about policies, procedures or initiatives required if sustainable development is to be achieved in social environments in which historical injustice is a seriously complicating factor. Ethical analysis alone cannot provide answers to these questions. It can help to expose the moral structure of historical grievances. It can also help to identify morally necessary conditions for their resolution. However, the task of rectifying those injustices requires a depth and breadth of practical wisdom, only one part of which is moral insight. Also needed will be depth of cultural knowledge, practical political skills, political and economic analysis and so on.

For some, this conclusion will appear a counsel of despair. In our view, however, it is a simple acknowledgement that moral values are only one of the keys to unlocking sustainable futures.

A Concluding Postscript

In 1994, the Ontario government gave approval for the Mattagami Complex project, thus avoiding the $247 million payment. A condition of that approval, however, is a proviso that any future Mattagami complex redevelopment will be overseen by a "Mattagami Extensions Coordinating Council" consisting of equal representation from the First Nations and the Ontario government. This uniting of aboriginal and provincial interests appears to be unprecedented for Ontario's environmental assessment process.

Whether the complex will be redeveloped in the future is now a moot point. However, in 1995, Ontario Hydro signed an agreement for the settlement of past grievances with one aboriginal First

Nation, and is currently in negotiations with several others. Such actions appear to reflect a new direction for Ontario Hydro, based on recommendations made by its Task Force on Sustainable Energy Development, such as, securing greater stakeholder involvement and strengthening partnerships with First Nation and aboriginal communities.[46] Also in 1995, the Ministry of Natural Resources launched the "Environmental Information Partnership" for the Moose River Basin consisting of First Nations, the federal government, and the Ontario government, a continuation of the original Baseline Data Collection Project. The goal of the partnership is to develop an information management system for the Moose River Basin that will assist in the identification and evaluation of potential cumulative effects of any planned developments within the Basin. Integral to that information management agreement is recognition that aboriginal environmental knowledge has a legitimate place along with modern science in that identification process.

Meanwhile discussions on aboriginal self-government are still pending amongst the First Nation, federal and Ontario governments.[47] Based on these recent developments, it appears to be the case that several of the "lessons" to be learned from the conflict are beginning to be put into practice. Whether or not a complete resolution to the conflict will emerge which is morally satisfactory to the major stakeholders, remains to be seen.

ENDNOTES

[1] The authors acknowledge funding support for this research on the part of the Social Sciences and Humanities Research Council (Strategic Grants Program), York University's Haub Program in Business and the Environment and York University's Faculty of Administrative Studies Small Research Grants Program.

[2] This paper is a product of an interdisciplinary environmental ethics research project which is studying four resource use proposals for northeastern Ontario and northern British Columbia. We wish to acknowledge the contribution of Maria Radford, who did much of the original document research. David Pearson, a project coinvestigator, Ralph Wheeler of the Ministry of Natural Resources who are

project partners, Mario Durepos from Ontario Hydro who are project partners, and Paul Wilkinson and Associates all have provided assistance at various stages in our research. The Ontario Aboriginal Research Coalition, created to direct research into the effects on Ontario's First Nations of Ontario Hydro's Twenty-five Year Plan, financed the collection of oral histories assembled to which we refer in a number of places. Chief Ernest Beck and David Fletcher of the Moosecree Factory First Nation, Chief Randy Kapashesit of the Mocreebec First Nation, and John Turner of the Mushkegowuk Tribal Council provided guidance and site visit assistance. David Fletcher has been of continuing assistance throughout the research process. Ontario Hydro arranged a site visit to the Mattagami Complex. Without the assistance of all of these people, this research would not have been possible.

[3]For a statement of Trudeau's position and a discussion of the issues raised by it, see A.W. Cragg, *Contemporary Moral Issues* — Third Edition (Toronto: McGraw-Hill, 1992), Chapter 5, "Native Rights".

[4] The information in the following case is based on Ontario Hydro's *Environmental Assessment,* Aboriginal Witness Statements (Adams, Conway, Roderique, J.Sutherland, P.Sutherland), and an exhibit from J. Morrison used during the DSP Environmental Assessment Hearing.

[5]Noble, K. "Kapuskasing Deal Best for Everybody," *The Globe and Mail*, B4.

[6]For an attempt to identify cross-cultural moral principles appropriate for resource development decisions, which goes beyond a discussion of the moral principles imbedded in the concept of sustainable development, see Michael McDonald, Jack T. Stevenson and Wesley Cragg, "Finding a Balance of Values: An Ethical Assessment of Ontario Hydro's Demand/Supply Plan" Report to the Aboriginal Research Coalition of Ontario (1992), and Wesley Cragg, Michael McDonald and Jack T. Stevenson, "The Demand/Supply Plan and the Moose River Basin" (unpublished). These reports are complementary ethical analyses of the Ontario Hydro 25 Year Demand/Supply Plan. The analysis is a direct moral evaluation which alludes to the concept of sustainable development but is not based on it. For a discussion that illustrates the need for value based analysis see Litchfield et al., "Integrated Resource Planning and the Great Whale Public Review" Background Paper, No. 7, Great Whale Environmental Assessment (Great Whale Environmental Public Review Office, 1994. Further references will be made to these reports in what follows.

[7]It might be argued that a fuller and wider application of this principle than what we propose here might require that it be qualified by phrases like: "In the absence of genuinely voluntary agreement to the contrary, the costs, etc." This caveat is ignored in this study since it is clear that introducing it would not modify the argument which we propose to

advance in what follows. The principle itself is defended by Andy Brook in "Obligations to Future Generations: A case study," *Contemporary Moral Issues*, e.d. A.W. Cragg (Toronto: McGraw/Hill Ryerson, 1993), 359. Brook ties this principle to two others:

Liberty: Our actions must not result in preventable and foreseeable restriction of others' opportunities (which disease, pain, mutation or costs of avoiding these would do).

Freedom from pain: Our actions must not result in preventable and foreseeable pain (or discomfort or diminution of ability) in others.

Brook ties these three principles in turn to a fourth which he claims under-rides all three:

Prior to considerations of individual distinguishing qualities of moral relevance, each person has the same value as any other.

For the purposes of the discussion in this paper, the distributive justice principle is the key one. What Brook's account offers is a defence of the use of that principle and proposals for others that a full examination of the ethics of resource extraction would want to explore.

[8]For the purpose of this discussion we propose to use as our definition of the term "environment", the meaning set out in by Ontario statute in the *Environmental Assessment Act:*

i) air, land or water,

ii) plant and animal life, including man,

iii) the social, economic and cultural conditions that influence the life of man or a community,

iv) any building, structure, machine or other device or thing made by man,

v) any solid, liquid, gas, odour, heat, sound, vibration or radiation resulting directly or indirectly from the activities of man, or

vi) any part or combination of the foregoing and the interrelationships between any two or more or them.

(Revised Statutes of Ontario, 1980, s.1(c))

[9]See Aboriginal Witness Statements, DSP Environmental Assessment Hearing, Exhibits: 829-886, 947-951, 1018-1019.

[10]See for example M. Friedman, "The Social Responsibility of Business is to Increase its Profits," *The New York Times Magazine*, September, 1970.

[11]Litchfield et al., "Integrating Resource Planning...," 1994.

[12]Ontario Hydro, *Environmental Assessment: Hydroelectric Generation Station Extensions Mattagami River*, October 1990, 2-1.

[13]Litchfield et al., "Integrated Resource Planning...," 4, describe this as the traditional planning model for utilities in North America in this century.

[14]Ontario Hydro, *Demand/Supply Plan Report*, DSP Envi-

ronmental Assessment Hearing, Exhibit #3, December 1989, 6-13.

[15]Presently the *Environmental Assessment Act* R.S.O. 1990, c.E.18.

[16]Ibid., s.2.

[17]Ibid. s.1(c).

[18]Ontario Hydro, *Demand Supply Plan Environmental Analysis*, DSP Environmental Assessment Hearing, Exhibit #4, December 1989, 3-3.

[19]Ibid., 3-5.

[20]Ontario Hydro, *Environmental Assessment Summary: Hydroelectric Generation Station Extensions Mattagami River*, October 1990, 18.

[21]Ibid., 23.

[22]A channel which carries away water which has passed through the generating station.

[23]Ontario Hydro, *Environmental Assessment Summary*, 24-25.

[24]Ibid., 6-13.

[25]Ibid., 6-48.

[26]Ibid., 6-48.

[27]Ibid., 8-11.

[28]The First Nations in the Moose River Basin refused to cooperate with Ontario Hydro's environmental assessment.

[29]Ontario Hydro, *Environmental Assessment Summary*, 8-11.

[30]These difficulties are the subject of ongoing debate among economists and others. An accessible (to the lay person) discussion is offered in Litchfield et al., "Integrated Resource Planning...". For a more detailed examination of the limitations of cost/benefit analysis from the perspective of distributive justice see McDonald, Stevenson and Cragg, "Finding a Balance of Values".

[31]This conclusion is not unique to the authors of this paper. Two recent attempts by major utilities, Ontario Hydro in its Twenty-five Year Plan and Quebec Hydro with regard to the Great Whale project, at costing impacts relevant to these concerns seem to have led to the same conclusion. Ontario Hydro put off assessing these costs to the formal environmental assessment process which of course was never completed. What they appear to have concluded was that costing would have to be arrived at through some process of negotiation after the developments they were seeking had been approved in principle. Quebec Hydro's environmental assessment from "Grande-Baleine Complex: Feasability Study", Hydro Québec, August 1993, is worth quoting in this regard:

The financial evaluation of sociocultural impacts is ... difficult. Many believe economists do not have the right to put a price tag on goods or values for which it is difficult, if not impossible, to imagine a market. Such people may find it reprehensible that economists perform economic assessments of certain aspects of Native culture.

Further: In the case of other externalities, which are generally social or cultural, an approach aimed at establishing an economic value appears neither appropriate nor possible. (Part 2, Book 8, p. 37)

[32]For a discussion of this point see Litchfield et al., "Integrated Resource Planning...".

[33]Native People's Circle on Environment and Development report prepared for the Ontario Round Table on Environment and Economy, 1992, 4.

[34]R. Kapashesit, "Evidence in Chief," DSP Environmental Assessment Hearing, Exhibit #1019, January 4, 1993, 7.

[35] Native People's Circle, Report, 4.

[36]Kapashesit, "Evidence in Chief," 7.

[37]There are no relevant studies that we know of in environmental ethics that probes this perspective. However, there are relevant studies in other areas. Philosophy of law and punishment is a good example. Punishment of offenders is often seen as a form of compensation for offensive actions. This theme is explored at length by Jean Hampton and Jeffrey Murphy in their book *Forgiveness and Mercy* (Cambridge: Cambridge University Press, 1988). H.L.A Hart explores a similar theme in *Punishment and Responsibility* (Oxford: Claredon Press, 1963), particularly "Punishment and the Elimination of Responsibility", 183. See also A.W. Cragg, *The Practice of Punishment: Toward a Theory of Restorative Justice* (London: Routledge, 1993).

A further note is appropriate here. Paul Wilkenson whose contribution to this paper is acknowledged elsewhere, has pointed out in private correspondence that compensation of the sort to which Chief Kapashesit refers need not be thought of in purely financial terms. He points out that "compensation might take a symbolic form such as the erection of a monument, a public apology, environmental remediation, economic development to replace lost opportunities, or many other forms." He also points out that acceptance of financial compensation should not be construed as a recognition by concerned First Nations of its appropriateness given the nature of the harms experienced.

[38]*Guidelines for the Great Whale River Hydroelectric Project*, #113.

[39]D. DeLauney, "Report of the Provincial Representative: Moose River Basin Consultations," prepared for the Ministry of Natural Resources, April 1992, 7.

[40]Will Kymlicka goes some distance in that direction in a recent article (unpublished) entitled "Concepts of Community and Social Justice" prepared for a conference on "Global Environmental Change and Social Justice" at Cornell University, September 1993. In that paper, Kymlicka ex-

plores the interplay of the right to self-determination of minorities with principles of distributive justice concerned with a fair distribution and use of natural resources.

[41]The idea of equitable participation has been most carefully examined in the context of medical ethics where it is now widely accepted that it is the competent patient's judgement of his or her own interests which should guide treatment and not that of the health care provider, Beauchamp T. and Childress, J., *Principles of Biomedical Ethics* (New York: Oxford University Press, 1979), p. 62 and p. 153, and Edmund Pellegrino, "Trust and Distrust in Professional Ethics," *Trust and the Professions: Philosophical and Cultural Aspects* (Washington, DC: Georgetown University Press, date) 81.

[42]Ministry of Natural Resources, "Draft Terms of Reference/ Work Plan for the Technical Group," July 28, 1993, 1.

[43]Ministry of Natural Resources, "Moose River Basin Baseline Data Collection Project, Background Report," August 1993, 2.

[44]Cragg, McDonald, and Stevenson, "Finding a Balance...," 20.

[45]It does not follow, of course, that any project with externalized costs is unsustainable. It does follow, on the other hand, that to externalize costs for which there are inadequate compensating benefits, recognizable as such by those on whom the costs are imposed, is unjust.

[46]Ontario Hydro, *Report of the Task Force on Sustainable Energy Development: A Strategy for Sustainable Energy Development and Use for Ontario Hydro*, October 18, 1993, 32-35.

[47]The members of the research team of which this project is a part were: Wesley Cragg, Principal Investigator, and co-investigators John Lewko, David Pearson and Craig Summers (Laurentian University). For further information about the project please write: Wesley Cragg, Faculty of Administrative Studies, York University, 4700 Keele St., North York, Ontario (M3J 1P3); E-mail wcragg@mail.fas.yorku.ca.

References

Adams, T.; "Witness Statement"; *DSP Environmental Assessment Hearing, Exhibit #855;* December, 1992.

Allen, G.; "Ontario Backs Mill Buyout Plan"; *The Globe and Mail;* June 20, 1991; a.4.

Bay and Basin Bulletin; *The Moose River Basin Project Newsletter, Vol.1, No.2*; January, 1995.

Beauchamp, T. and Childress, J.; *Principles of Biomedical Ethics*; New York; Oxford University Press; 1979.

Bennett, Kearon; "Small Hydro Research Summary Report"; *Appendix G, DSP Environmental Assessment Hearing, Exhibit #926*; November, 1992.

Brook, A.; "Obligations to Future Generations: A Case Study"; *Contemporary Moral Issues;* Toronto; McGraw/Hill Ryerson; 1993; p. 359.

Brundtland Commission; *Our Common Future*; Oxford; Oxford University Press; 1987.

Cheena, G.; "Witness Statement"; *DSP Environmental Assessment Hearing, Exhibit #883*; December, 1992.

Conway, T.; "Impacts of Prior Development"; *DSP Environmental Assessment Hearing, Exhibit #890*; December, 1992.

Cragg, A.W.; *Contemporary Moral Issues*; Toronto; McGraw-Hill Ryerson; 1992.

Cragg, A.W.; *The Practice of Punishment: Toward a Theory of Restorative Justice;* London; Routledge; 1993.

Cragg, A.W., McDonald and Stevenson; *Finding a Balance of Values: An Ethical Assessment of Ontario Hydro's Demand/Supply Plan*; November, 1992.

DeLauney, D.; *Report of the Provincial Representative: Moose River Basin Consultations;* prepared for the Ministry of Natural Resources; April, 1992.

Environmental Assessment Act; R.S.O.; 1980; c.140.

Environmental Assessment Act; R.S.O.; 1990; c.E.18.

ESSA (Environmental and Social Systems Analysts Ltd.); "Hypotheses of Effects of Development in the Moose River Basin Workshop Summary – Final Report"; *DSP Environmental Assessment Hearing, Exhibit #719*; March, 1992.

Faries, B.; "Witness Statement"; *DSP Environmental Assessment Hearing, Exhibit #876;* December, 1992.

Fowlie, L.; "Town That Refused To Die"; *Financial Post*; December 28-30, 1991; p.16.

Friedman, M.; "The Social Responsibility of Business is to Increase Its Profits"; *The New York Times Magazine*; September 13, 1970.

"Guidelines: Environmental Impact Statement for the Proposed Great Whale River Hydroelectric

Project"; *Evaluating Committee, Kativik Environmental Quality Commission, Federal Review Committee North of the 55th Parallel, Federal Environmental Assessment Review Panel*; published by Great Whale Public Review Support Office; 1155 Sherbrooke St. West, Suite 1603, Montreal, Quebec H3A 2N3.

Hampton, J. and Murphy, J.; *Forgiveness and Mercy;* Cambridge; Cambridge University Press; 1988.

Hart, H.L.A.; *Punishment and Responsibility*; Oxford; Clarendon Press; 1963.

Jones, I.; "Witness Statement"; *DSP Environmental Assessment Hearing, Exhibit #950*; December, 1992.

Kapashesit, R.; "Evidence in Chief"; *DSP Environmental Assessment Hearing, Exhibit #1019.*

Keir, A.; "Socio-Economic Impact Assessment: Reference Document of Hydroelectric Generating Station Extensions Mattagami River"; prepared for *Ontario Hydro Corporate Relations Branch, Volumes 1 &2*; January, 1991.

Kymlicka, W.; "Concepts of Community and Social Justice"; Unpublished; Presented at "Global Environmental Change and Social Justice" conference at Cornell University; September, 1993.

Linklater, M.; "Witness Statement"; *DSP Environmental Assessment Hearing, Exhibit #877*; December, 1992.

Litchfield, James, Hemmingway, Leroy and Raphals, Philip; "Integrated Resource Planning and the Great Whale Public Review"; *Background Paper No. 7, Great Whale Environmental Assessment;* Great Whale Public Review Office; 1994.

MacDonald, R.; "Witness Statement"; *DSP Environmental Assessment Hearing, Exhibit #852*; December, 1992.

Mackie, R.; "Can't Afford Mill Bailout, Premier Says"; *Globe and Mail;* July 15, 1991; Section A, p. 8.

Ministry of Natural Resources; "Draft Terms of Reference/Work Plan for the Technical Group"; July 28, 1993.

Ministry of Natural Resources; "Moose River Basin Baseline Data Collection Project, Background Report"; August, 1993.

Mittelstaedt, M.; "Hydro Looking To End Environmental Hearing"; *Globe and Mail*; November 13, 1992; a.5.

Mittelstaedt, M.; "Ontario Gives Hydro Project Go-Ahead"; *Globe and Mail*; October 6, 1994; b.10.

Morrison, J.; "Colonization, Resource Extraction and Hydroelectric Development in the Moose River Basin: A Preliminary History of the Implications For Aboriginal People"; *DSP Environmental Assessment Hearing, Exhibit #869;* November, 1992.

Mugiskan, Chief W.; "Witness Statement"; *DSP Environmental Assessment Hearing, Exhibit #866*; December, 1992.

Nation, K. and Noble, K.; "U.S. Firm Rejects Newsprint Mill Deal"; *Globe and Mail*; June 29, 1991; b.1 & b.4.

Native People's Circle on Environment and Development; *a report prepared for the Ontario Round Table on Environment and Economy*; 1992.

Noble, K.; "Kapuskasing Deal Best For Everybody"; *Globe and Mail*; August 15, 1991; Section B 1 & 4.

Ontario Hydro; "Demand/Supply Plan Report"; *DSP Environmental Assessment Hearing, Exhibit #3*; December, 1989.

Ontario Hydro; "Demand Supply Plan Environmental Analysis"; *DSP Environmental Assessment Hearing, Exhibit #4*; December, 1989.

Ontario Hydro; *Environmental Assessment: Hydroelectric Generating Station Extensions Mattagami River*; October, 1990.

Ontario Hydro; *Environmental Assessment Summary: Hydroelectric Generating Station Extensions Mattagami River*; February, 1991.

Ontario Hydro; *Report of the Task Force on Sustainable Energy Development: A Strategy For Sustainable Energy Development and Use For Ontario Hydro*; October 18, 1993.

Pellegrino, Edmund; "Trust and Distrust in Professional Ethics"; *Ethics, Trust and the Professions: Philosophical and Cultural Aspects*; Washington D.C.; Georgetown University Press.

Philp, M.; "Spruce Falls Mill May Close"; *Globe and Mail*; March 20, 1991; b.3.

Roderique, J.; "Witness Statement"; *DSP Environmental Assessment Hearing, Exhibit #875*; December, 1992.

Sears, S.K. and Paterson, M.; "Integrated Ecosystem – Based Planning for Hydroelectric Generation Development in a Remote Northern Ontario River Basin"; *DSP Environmental Assessment Hearing, Exhibit #382*; May, 1991.

Submission Letters re: Review of Environmental Assessment for the Proposed Hydroelectric Generating Station Extensions on the Mattagami River; Ministry of the Environment; Environmental Assessment Branch; 1992.

Sutherland, J.; "Witness Statement"; *DSP Environmental Assessment Hearing, Exhibit #873*; December, 1992.

Sutherland, P.; "Witness Statement"; *DSP Environmental Assessment Hearing, Exhibit #874*; December, 1992.

THE ROLE OF STEREOTYPES

EXPLORING ABORIGINAL ENVIRONMENTAL ETHICS

20

by Deborah McGregor

Introduction

ABORIGINAL ENVIRONMENTAL ETHICS ARE AN integral component of aboriginal traditional environmental knowledge, and as such, constitute what is recognized as an increasingly important area of research. Information about this type of knowledge is being widely pursued, both for intellectual and philosophical reasons, as well for more utilitarian purposes concerning the development of sustainable systems of resource use.

The potential for the latter has received international recognition in such documents as the Brundtland Report (WCED 1987, 14), which states that indigenous communities "are the repositories of a vast accumulation of traditional knowledge and experience that links humanity with its ancient origins." Such knowledge has been touted by many as a potentially vital contributor to solutions to the global environmental crisis (Berry 1988, Churchill 1994, Deloria 1995, Johnson 1992, Knudtson and Suzuki 1992, LaDuke 1995, Mander 1991). As the Brundtland Report states, society could "learn a great deal" from indigenous people "in sustainably managing very complex ecosystems" (WCED 1987, 115). In Canada, aboriginal environmental knowledge has already made contributions in such areas as natural resource management, environmental assessment, conservation policy, and sustainable development (Notzke 1994). The documentation of such knowledge is consequently emerging as a "burgeoning field of research" (Notzke 1994, 5).

Perhaps the greatest difficulty facing aboriginal environmental ethics research concerns stereotyping, a problem that has plagued the relationship between indigenous and colonial cultures since contact. Depending on one's own viewpoint, a person's stereotypes regarding aboriginal people may vary from one extreme to another. Among those who take a "pro-Native" standpoint, Native people tend to be portrayed as the "noble savage" or the "peaceful, mystical, spiritual guardian of the land" (Bird 1996, 3). For those who favour an "anti-Native" view, Native people are seen as everything from "eco-destroyers" (Deloria 1995) to "marauding, hellish savages" and "dissolute, pathetic drunks and misfits" (Bird 1996; 3,4). As Bird (1996, 4) states:

However they are depicted, Indians are the quintessential Other, whose role is to be the object of the White, colonialist gaze. Once Indians were no longer a threat, they became colourful and quaint...when Indians refuse to be quaint, White culture's imagery condemns them.

This paper argues that until the perpetual stereotyping that plagues Native/non-Native relations is sufficiently overcome, it will not be possible for non-Native researchers to gain a meaningful understanding of aboriginal environmental ethics. Two main reasons for this position are presented. The first is what Francis (1992) calls the problem of "The Imaginary Indian". Simply put, much of what non-Native society supposedly "knows" about Native people is based on images created by non-Native people. The existing body of misinformation clouds and biases research into aboriginal issues. Such misinformation must be deconstructed before non-Native people can begin to truly learn from aboriginal people.

The second reason is perhaps simply an extension of the first. The false images that exist of Native people lead to a variety of unrealistic expectations which Native people continually fail to meet in the eyes of non-Natives. This disappointment is compounded by the fact that Native people have over the last few decades asserted an ever-increasing voice over matters which concern them. The rise of this largely unknown, or at least misunderstood, entity in such areas as the debate over control of resource use is perceived as a significant threat by many non-Natives who are affected by such issues. Non-Native society is often reluctant at best to return any form of control over resources to what for them is an unknown party.

These issues are discussed further in the following pages.

The Imaginary Indian

The title of this section is borrowed from Francis' (1992) book of the same name. Francis' central idea is that, "Indians, as we think we know them, do not exist" (Francis 1992, 4). Rather, the concept of "Indian" "is the invention of the European" (Francis 1992, 4). This is as true today as in earlier times. As Francis (1992, 6) states:

> *Much public discourse about Native people still deals in stereotypes. Our views of what constitutes an Indian today are as much bound up with myth, prejudice and ideology as earlier versions were.*

Thus, what most non-Native people conceive of or think they know about Indians is imaginary (Berkhofer 1979, Bird 1996, Churchill 1994, Francis 1992). Tragically, some of these stereotypes have been supported by members of the scientific community, making them even harder to supplant (Deloria 1995).

The presence of these stereotypes can produce varied effects. One that is particularly troubling is the silencing or discrediting of the opinions of Native peoples. Currently, when non-Native interests proceed with the study of aboriginal people, they are carrying with them a great many preconceived notions. Whether they realize it or not, they hold a set of preconceptions which act as a framework within which to fit any new information or as a set of criteria to use in either accepting or rejecting new information.

Researchers employ a set of preconceived notions, which they often do not realize they hold, to sort and classify new information regarding aboriginal people. This leads to the distortion and even rejection of originally valid information. Non-Natives often have a hard time simply accepting information about aboriginal people as it is presented to them. This is because often no framework exists in their thinking which can consistently accommodate the ideas of aboriginal culture. Information gained from research is frequently distorted, and parts even discarded, so as to maintain the previously formed views of the researcher.

These types of problems were presented as significant issues by the 1993 Royal Commission on Aboriginal Peoples (RCAP 1993). The Commission felt these issues to be of such concern that it conducted a separate inquiry into the nature of aboriginal research. A research advisory committee was struck, part of whose mandate it was to develop ethical guidelines for aboriginal research (RCAP 1993, 37-40). A number of themes worth noting emerged from the Royal Commission report. Among these were:

1. the difficulty of representing aboriginal reality authentically in research

2. the role of stereotypes and attitudes that operate which influence research approaches, interpretations, and results

3. the omission of aboriginal concepts from research findings

4. the fundamental differences between Native and non-Native concepts and ideologies.

Because the already established (and stereotype-based) frame of reference held by researchers is so different from that of the Native people they are learning about, the aboriginal voice is frequently discredited, distorted, or ignored. Since information provided by aboriginal voices often does not fit into the stereotype-based ideological frameworks of non-Native researchers, aboriginal people are routinely seen as less valid sources of information than other non-Native researchers. In this way, stereotypes act as a major barrier to learning about aboriginal peoples.

Anti-Indian Sentiment and Aboriginal Control Over Resource Use

The issues surrounding stereotypes and the "unknown" nature of real aboriginal people become particularly intense in debates regarding control over resource use. The aspirations of Native and non-Native people, including environmentalists, often clash around the "thorny" issues of aboriginal and treaty rights and their relationship to resource use (Erasmus 1989). As Bird (1996) describes, Native people, far from having disappeared as many Europeans in the past predicted and hoped for, are very much alive and are asserting their identities and rights. Assertion of rights by Native people often threatens non-Natives and thus "Indians" have once again become threatening.

This conflict is not new. As Swartz (1987, 292) points out:

[a] long-standing problem in Indian/White relations [is] the freedom of most Indians from the restrictions of most federal and state game laws. There has always been a certain amount of animosity toward Indians from non-Indian sportsmen because of the "favouritism" which allows Indians to ignore hunting seasons, bag limits and other regulations that hamper non-Indian hunting and fisherfolk.

In recent years, as the aspirations of Aboriginal people and environmentalists have come into

conflict, the debate has intensified. Bird (1996, 4) writes that:

In Minnesota and Wisconsin, for example, Ojibway people have in recent years begun to reclaim their treaty rights to spearfish on lakes. Some White anglers became incensed, and the conflict unleashed a flood of virulent racism against Indians, or "timber niggers," as protest signs often dubbed them.

Bird (1996, 5) cites recent instances offering intimidation for the Wisconsin Ojibway, such as a sign posted in a local bar sporting the headline "1st Annual Indian Shoot". Contestants are invited to collect points for shooting various categories of Indians. Bird (1996, 4) writes that, "White culture seems to feel angry at Indians who do not fit the romantic mold."

Incidents such as these are not limited to the United States, but occur in Canada as well. One example is the backlash First Nations in British Columbia are suffering as a result of the Salmon fishing industry crisis. First Nations people are blamed for the decline in salmon stock. More recently, Algonquins in Ontario who are pursuing their land claim and treaty rights are complaining of racist harassment, similar to that experienced by the Ojibway in Minnesota and Wisconsin. In the business world, a move by some aboriginal groups to expand traditional activities into commercial enterprises, "has given rise to charges of unfair competition from non-Indian commercial interests" (Swartz 1987, 292). Environmentalists have also accused First Nations of planning to develop resources with a lack of environmental commitment (Notzke 1994, 100). Swartz (1987, 292) observes this apparent downfall of the image of the "ecological Indian", stating that:

it has become almost fashionable to repudiate the high regard for Aboriginal Indians that has been so characteristic of the movement in the past. Indeed some writers have gone so far as to castigate Indians for their apparent lack of environmental awareness.

Such a backlash of anti-Indian sentiment, at a time when Native people are asserting more than ever their rights to a distinct and meaningful role in mainstream society, makes cross-cultural communication between Native and non-Native parties all the more difficult. Researchers attempting to learn from aboriginal people will face even greater mistrust from First Nations communities. The amount of information that Native people will be willing to share with those outside of their communities will diminish. In the manner of a downward spiral, previous stereotyping (based on a lack of understanding) has resulted in a backlash of anti-Indian sentiment, which will decrease communication and result in further stereotyping. This negative trend must be reversed before positive research into aboriginal environmental ethics and other knowledge can occur.

Conclusion

Meaningful research into aboriginal environmental ethics requires open and honest communication among all parties. In order to achieve such communication and produce results that all sides consider positive, existing stereotypes of Native people must be deconstructed. All of us involved in such research need to examine our own assumptions. Brown and Vibert (1996) offer some important thoughts on this matter. They state (p. x) that we must understand that we are consumers of "facts that are socially constructed, molded by the social and cultural forces in place when the texts were created": a lesson that many environmental philosophers, activists and educators can learn from. It is important to remember that "none of us are free of the social and cultural contexts in which we are embedded" (Brown and Vibert 1996, xi), however easy it is to convince ourselves otherwise. In order to be critical in a meaningful way, we must be self-critical. We must realize that we never approach an issue or problem "with a blank slate". Brown and Vibert (1996, x) continue that:

We all carry a host of assumptions and expectations informed by Hollywood westerns and television, by the novels of James Fenimore Cooper, by childhood cowboy-and-Indian games, or by the "council rings" we joined at summer camp. Already in our minds are deep-seated if ill-defined images of "Indians", be they in savage red or dusky, romantic brown.

We cannot begin from a "neutral point", but "about ten steps back" (Brown and Vibert 1996, ix). There really is no neutral point. Where we stand on aboriginal issues may be revealed to us if we understand ourselves and why we think the way we do.

This does not mean that we can simply dismiss existing texts or ideas. Existing texts and ideas can, with critical analysis, reveal to us information about the underlying assumptions and attitudes that frame the questions asked, how the questions are answered, and what is considered valid and why.

This intellectual and often emotional exercise of self-appraisal and introspection is an essential element of cross cultural learning. It serves to enable us!

References

Berkhofer, R. Jr. 1979. The White Man's Indian: Images of the American Indian from Columbus to the Present. Vintage Books, New York, NY. p.261.

Berry, T. 1988. The Dream of the Earth. Sierra Club Books, San Francisco, CA. p. 247.

Bird, S. 1996. Introduction: constructing the Indian 1830s-1990s. In: Bird, S. (ed.). 1996. Dressing in Feathers: The Construction of the Indian in American Popular Culture. Westview Press, Boulder, CO. pp. 1-12.

Brown, J., and Vibert E. 1996. Introduction. In: Brown, J., and Vibert, E. (eds.). 1996. Reading Beyond Words: Contexts for Native History. Broadview Press, Peterborough, ON. pp. ix-xxvii.

Churchill, W. 1994. Indians Are Us?: Culture and Genocide in Native North America. Between the Lines, Toronto, ON. p. 382.

Deloria, V. 1995. Red Earth, White Lies: Native Americans and the Myth of Scientific Fact. Scribner, New York, NY. p. 286.

Erasmus, G. 1989. A native viewpoint. In: Hummel, M. (ed.). 1989. Endangered Spaces: The Future for Canada's Wilderness. Key Porter Books Ltd., Toronto: ON. pp. 92-98.

Francis, F. 1992. The Imaginary Indian: The Image of the Indian in Canadian Culture. Arsenal Pulp Press, Vancouver B.C. p. 258.

Johnson, M. (ed.). 1992. Lore: Capturing Traditional Environmental Knowledge. Dene Cultural Institute and International Development Research Centre. Hay River, NWT. p. 190.

Knudtson, P., and Suzuki, D. 1992. Wisdom of the Elders. Stoddard Publishing Co., Toronto, ON.

LaDuke, W. 1995. Traditional ecological knowledge and environmental futures. In: Endangered Peoples: Indigenous Rights and the Environment. Special Issue of the Colorado Journal of International Environmental Law and Politics. University Press of Colorado, Niwot, CO. pp. 126-230.

Mander, J. 1991. In the Absence of the Sacred: the Failure of Technology and the Survival of the Indian Nations. Sierra Club Books, San Francisco, CA. p. 446.

Notzke, C. 1994. Aboriginal Peoples and Resource Management in Canada. Cactus University Publications, North York, ON.

Royal Commission on Aboriginal Peoples (RCAP). 1993. Integrated Research Plan. Minister of Supply and Services, Ottawa, ON.

Swartz, D. 1987. Indian Rights and Environmental Ethics: Changing Perspectives, and a modest proposal. Environmental Ethics, Winter 1987. Vol 9. pp. 291-302.

World Commission on the Environment and Development (WCED). 1987. Our Common Future. Oxford University Press, New York, N.Y. p. 400.

AN OVERVIEW OF ECOFEMINISM

21
by Annie Booth

Eco-feminism is about connectedness and wholeness of theory and practice. It asserts the special strength and integrity of every thing ...We see the devastation of the earth and her beings by the corporate warriors, and the threat of nuclear annihilation by the military warriors, as feminist concerns. It is the same masculinist mentality which would deny us our right to our own bodies and our own sexuality, and which depends on multiple systems of dominance and state power to have its way. Ynestra King, ecofeminist, 1981.[1]

IN THE 1970S, FEMINISTS FIGHTING FOR WOMEN'S RIGHTS BEGAN TO FIND COMMON ground with environmentalists fighting for the protection and preservation of the natural world. Women concerned with both causes began making connections between the abuse heaped upon the physical environment and the abuse heaped upon women's minds and bodies. This chapter examines some key tenets of ecofeminist theory and summarizes some of the debates amongst ecofeminists. The chapter concludes with a discussion on the contributions ecofeminism makes to a new way of seeing and our place within the natural world.

In the Beginning

The term "ecofeminism" was coined by French feminist Francoise d'Eaubonne in 1974. D'Eaubonne wished women to believe in their ability to bring about an ecological revolution.[2] The term has been adopted and expanded far beyond what d'Eaubonne probably envisioned. Ecofeminism reflects efforts to develop a "feminist" consciousness, hence the focus on "liberating" women from their oppression, a concomitant interest in "feminist" spirituality, and linkages with the environmental movement of the 1960s and early 1970s. The main threads of ecofeminism developed during the late 1970s and early 1980s. Key proponents to pick up on d'Eaubonne's term include Susan Griffith (poet and author), Ynestra King (activist), Elizabeth Dodson Gray (theologian), Hazel Henderson (economist), Carolyn Merchant (academic), and Rosemary Radford Ruether (theologian). Karen Warren, Charlene Spretnak, Jim Cheney, and Michael Zimmerman arrived in the field in the late 1980s as ecofeminism became a legitimate academic topic.

As a philosophy, ecofeminism is still in its formative stages and subject to much discussion and debate. Ecofeminism claims to respect the concept of diversity, both natural and philosophical. There is no one single teaching or belief that solely characterizes ecofeminism. There are some generally agreed upon and interrelated beliefs in ecofeminism which are the roots from which theory and debate is developing:

1. Whether by nature or by socialization, women hold the potential for different ways of seeing and relating which offer unique insights on interactions between humans and the natural world;

2. These female insights (tendencies rather than absolutes) have been ignored, devalued or suppressed in societies dominated by masculine values (referred to as patriarchies), as women have been devalued;

3. The suppression and domination of women and of the natural world (with subsequent harm to both) are intimately connected. Women are controlled because they are

thought to be closer to nature, and the control of nature is justified by its personification as female;

4. By understanding and re-valuing female ways of seeing and relating, both women and men can discover more positive ways of interacting with the natural world and with each other.[3]

Do We Live in a Patriarchal Society?

Ecofeminists (and feminists) work towards dismantling a worldview they label "patriarchy." When ecofeminists talk about a patriarchy they are talking about a culture or society in which men, and male experiences and activities, are paramount. If the experiences or activities are part of female life only, such as child-bearing or female work tasks, those experiences will be considered less valuable and important. In a patriarchy, women automatically hold lesser positions in society, in politics and in cultural events. Patriarchy is, essentially, a way of seeing the world and others in which "good" is substituted for "male" and "bad" for "female." Male experience is projected outward on to society and its institutions and, as Hazel Henderson says, it is "universalized...as if it were *human* experience. Of course it is not...(emphasis in original)."[4]

If patriarchies emphasize a masculine perception of the world, what does that perceptual world consist of? Ecofeminists argue that masculine experiences are those of disconnection, separation, individuation, and isolation from others, from the self, and from the body. The source of this need to separate and divide may originate from biological or psychological needs, or it may be a socially conditioned behavior pattern. While the ability to discriminate between things is necessary for personal development, ecofeminists such as Stephanie Leland argue that the overemphasis on this activity in patriarchal society eventually becomes destructive:

The masculine drive to discriminate can

result in extremism and conflict. Life is viewed as a battleground of irreconcilable opposites, such as masculine/feminine, subject/object, body/mind, good/evil, feeling/ intellect, black/white.

By conceptualizing everything into conflicting mental images, a dichotomy of opposites is established which emphasizes differences rather than relationships... .[5]

The ecological consequences of patriarchy might be profound. One group of ecofeminists, including Eisler, Gray, Griffin, and Ruether, locates our ecological crisis in this emphasis on hierarchical rankings of gender differences. At the point that we first treated male as superior to female, we started our ecological/social crisis, as that initial ranking led to other rankings: human over animal, culture over nature, European over non-European. But that first male over female ranking, androcentrism, was the key.[6] The subsequent oppression of women was the justification for the oppression of the rest of nature, as the female and the natural were linked. Thus, according to these ecofeminists, androcentrism preceded and led to the anthropocentrism upon which many ecophilosophers focus.[7] Griffin describes the connection between the two ideas graphically:

One of the most profound ways through which we fragment wholeness is through the categories of masculine and feminine. We assign to the masculine the provence of the soul, of spirit, or the transcendent, and we read feminine as representing nature and the Earth. To some degree it's a system that functions because if you don't have somebody who is earthly, who's going to make the dinner?[8]

Vandana Shiva, sees similar concerns at work in the long history of "maldevelopment" in the developing countries which is devastating so many indigenous human cultures and ecosystems.[9]

The appearance of the phenomenon of androcentrism has been located at two different points in human history. One group of ecofeminists, led by Riane Eisler, draws upon archaeological data to suggest that during the Neolithic period there was a concerted attack on peaceful, female respecting cultures by patriarchal, warring cultures. This attack eventually succeeded in destroying the female-respecting cultures.[10] A second group focuses around the theories of Carolyn Merchant, that the crucial change occurred during the advent of the Scientific Revolution in the seventeenth century. Merchant argues,

The female earth was central to the organic cosmology that was undermined by the Scientific Revolution and the rise of a market-oriented culture in early modern Europe.[11]

Undermining the sanctity of nature also undermined the position of women and minorities. Hallen points out that this period was also the time of the largest pogrom against women in Europe, the sixteenth and seventeenth century witch hunts, which resulted in the burning of thousands of women. It was also a time of decreased tolerance for Jews, gypsies, and others perceived as being less than fully human.[12]

Ecofeminism and Feminism: Sisters Under the Skin?

The feminist movement has had great influence on the ecofeminist worldview. Many women have found their way into ecofeminism through the feminist movement. Feminists have shared both key theories and goals and internal divisions with ecofeminists. Feminists and ecofeminists share a concern for bettering the lot of women everywhere and gaining for them rights and privileges at least equal to those of men. Ecofeminism shares the feminist analysis of patriarchal culture. Ecofeminism has, however, taken the unique step of tying the oppression of women into the oppression of nature and argues that wherever the natural environment is degraded it is usually women and their children who suffer most immediately. Ecofeminism has also critiqued traditional feminist theories.

Drawing upon earlier analysis by feminist Alison Jagger, Karen Warren defines four distinct schools of thought in feminist theory: liberal feminism, marxist feminism, socialist feminism, and radical/cultural feminism.[13] Each school has made some attempt to examine women's connections to the natural world, however it is from the radical/cultural feminist traditions that most ecofeminist theories and practitioners have come.

To feminist theory, ecofeminism has contributed its ideas concerning the key debate over whether masculine and feminine identities are taught or are innate. Ecofeminists have also contributed to the dialogue on the appropriate choice of strategy: should individuals work for the betterment of women (or children, men, or nature) through a focus on changing the social conditions and politics, or through raising and changing individual consciousness? It is through the examination of these questions, argues Ynestra King, that ecofeminism can provide an analysis which in missing in most feminist theory: a non-dualistic examination of human relations with nature.

Each major contemporary feminist theory – liberal, social and cultural – has taken up the issue of the relationship between women and nature. Each in its own way has capitulated to dualistic thinking, theoretically conflating a reconciliation with nature by surrendering to some form of natural determinism. The same positions have appeared again and again in extending the natural into the social (cultural feminism), or in severing the social from the natural (socialist feminism). Each of these directions are two sides of the same dualism, and from an ecofeminist perspective both are wrong in that they have made a choice between culture and nature.[14]

King argues that the narrow analyses that each feminist perspective espouses could benefit from the ideas that other schools of feminism develop. Socialist feminists can benefit from radical feminists' idealism and from its valuing of the individual's perspective. Radical feminism can humanize feminist and ecofeminist perspectives. Conversely, radical feminists can benefit from a social feminist's lessons in historical and social causes of women's (and nature's) oppression and from their interest in practical work. Ecofeminism's strength is in contemplating a blurring of the either/or debate found in most feminist circles.

Other Influences

In addition, ecofeminism has benefited from its participation in larger environmental ethics or ecophilosophical debates. Much of the dialogue has occurred between ecofeminists and deep ecologists. In addition, bioregionalism, social ecology and other perspectives have also taken an interest in ecofeminist ideas. As deep ecology has had the most to say regarding ecofeminism, a quick synopsis is presented.

Earlier in deep ecology's history, its adherents shared a sense of the futility of "shallow" environmentalism. While such activities as fighting pollution or working to conserve wilderness and wildlife were important, they failed to address the root causes of such problems. While there are still minor skirmishes on the distinctions between shallow and deep, as a basis for internal identification the distinction is only a start. The focus of a great deal of deep ecological debate is now on a few key principles, including the principles of biospheric egalitarianism, and an ecological consciousness that locates humanity within the natural world.

Warwick Fox describes deep ecology's interest in biospheric egalitarianism as follows:

Deep ecology is concerned with encouraging an egalitarian attitude on the part of humans not only toward all members of the *ecosphere, but even towards all identifiable* **entities** *or* **forms** *in the ecosphere...the kind of egalitarian attitude they advocate is simply meant to indicate an attitude that, within obvious kinds of practical limits, allows all entities (including humans)* **the freedom to unfold in their own way unhindered by the various forms of human domination** *(emphasis in the original).*[15]

Biospheric egalitarianism is not an argument that is logically derived. Bill Devall and George Sessions describe it as an "intuition" that all things have an equal right to live and develop in their own way.[16] Or, in other words, humans have no higher intrinsic worth than the rest of nature, and so are not justified in subduing the earth to their own limited ends. Essentially biospheric egalitarianism removes humanity from the top of the value pyramid.[17] Therefore, the concept suggests that we treat the living beings we are forced to use (to meet requirements of food, shelter, etc.) with care and respect.

Attempting to facilitate a biospheric egalitarianism leads naturally into the process of developing an ecological consciousness, a process which most deep ecologists subscribe to. Devall and Sessions describe it this way:

This process involves becoming more aware *of the actuality of rocks, wolves, trees, and rivers – the cultivation of the insight that everything is connected...It is learning to be more receptive, trusting, holistic in perception, and is grounded in a vision of nonexploitive science and technology.*[18]

The cultivation of an ecological consciousness, suggest several deep ecologists, begins to lead into a new understanding of humans as part of the natural process, a sense of ourselves as embedded in the "matrix" of life.[19] This recognition of self-in-relationship draws clearly from principles of ecological science; as eating, breathing animals we are dependent on our ecosystems to physically support us. However, the concept goes beyond a recognition of pure physical reliance to suggest that there is an essential mental/emotional/spiritual connection that needs to be made as well. This connection has been variously described as acknowledging a sense of identification with the rest of the world, finding spiritual oneness, or finding/cultivating the self within the Self.

Such identification derives from a number of sources. The experiential source is important. Personal involvements and knowledge often drive home to us how close we are to others and how tight our connection to the earth truly is. To behave ecologically correctly, one must care for the world. To care for the world, one must know it.

Another source of the deep ecological sense of identification is spiritual. Deep ecologists point to a variety of influential spiritual traditions, including Native American beliefs, many eastern traditions (Buddhism, Taoism), and some Christian traditions among others. These traditions share certain elements, such as the loss of the narrowly defined egoistic sense of self into a greater reality.[20]

Deep ecology and ecofeminism will likely continue to influence the other's philosophical development into the future. Both philosophies need the other's practitioners to continue to question and challenge assumptions and ideas so that each can continue to develop, or at least cannot fall into philosophic complacency.

The Importance of Gender

A key debate in ecofeminist circles comes out of one critique of patriarchy. Ecofeminists have persistently argued for the need to recover and respect women's contributions to society's problems. The heart of their argument has largely been based on the perceived devaluing of the feminine, and the linkages between the domination of women and the domination of the earth. As Ynestra King first argued,

Why women? Because our present patriarchy enshrines together the hatred of women

and the hatred of nature. In defying this patriarchy we are loyal to future generations and to life and this planet itself. We have a deep and particular understanding of this both through our natures and through our life experience as women.[21]

King argues that there are important, and divisive, questions on the nature of gender that ecofeminists must address. The first is whether the women/nature connection, noted by many ecofeminists, is liberating or a rationale for the continued subordination of women. Other questions arise from the first. Is there a separate female "culture" in industrial society? If there is, is female culture a contrived ghetto forcibly constructed long ago by oppressive male regimes? Or does a female culture provide a necessary critique of patriarchy? Ecofeminists must ask themselves what are the implications of gender difference? Should we or can we do away with gender difference? Or can we recognize "difference" without legitimating domination based on difference?[22]

The validity of questioning gender roles goes unchallenged in ecofeminist circles. Even ecofeminism's severest critic, Janet Biehl, agrees with the belief that the simple integration of women into existing structures in society, including resource management institutions without questioning those institutions takes society nowhere.[23] Yet integration, or tokenism, has been the focus of much traditional "liberal" and "socialist" feminism.

A second issue was raised by an early social critic, Ruether, who argued that trying to solve the ecological crises by validating a patriarchal vision of "womanhood" would be equally futile:

The (current) concern with ecology could repeat the mistakes of nineteenth century romanticism with its renewed emphasis on the opposite, "complementary natures" of men and women. Women will again be asked to be the "natural" wood-nymph and earth mother and to create places of escape from the destructive patterns of the dominant culture. Women will be told that their "highest calling" is to service this type of male need for sex, rest, emotionality, and escape from reality in a simulated grassy flower Eden. But the real power structures that are creating the crisis will be unaffected by such leisure time games.[24]

Perhaps not so oddly, this "earth mother" role is one many male deep ecologists accord to women, a role they claim to seek in their own psyches, although they frame it more respectfully. The earth mother role is also the crux of a critical disagreement within ecofeminist circles. Ecofeminists such as Spretnak, Starhawk, and others have ignored Ruether's warning and thrown themselves into the reclamation of "feminine" virtues, without recognizing the problematic nature of such action in a patriarchal society.

Different Genders, Different Realities?

There is considerable, and crucial, related debate over whether or not men and women have qualitatively different perceptions. Is the world a different place for those of different gender? Or are these differences culturally created by patriarchal culture? Are these differences something that should be valued?

Connected to this debate is a controversial question: do women participate with nature in a fundamentally different way from men? This question is dangerous, says Ynestra King, for it can be "potentially liberating or simply a rationale for the continued subordination of women?"[25] Relatedness and connection are precisely what deep ecologists profess to envy in women, and are ideas that many ecofeminists such as Spretnak and Gray attempt to recover and revalue as well, an effort that angers ecofeminists like Ruether and Biehl. In later work Biehl argued that women cannot be said to have a biologically or even cultur-

ally inculcated "nature," as escaping this "nature" is the only way to liberate women from life-roles which limit options and potentials.[26] The difficulty Biehl and others have with the argument that women are closer to nature is that the same reasoning has been used to justify female oppression.

A number of ecofeminists argue that men and women have different experiences and perceptions. Hazel Henderson states that two anatomically different forms will result in two very different ways of living in the world. With such biological processes as menstruation and childbirth going on in their bodies, it is argued, women never have the chance to forget or ignore their deep connections to the natural world. They are therefore unlikely to try and transcend or escape that world as do males.[27] One clear rebuttal to this line of reasoning is made by Griscom:

First, simply because women are able to bear children does not mean that doing so is essential to our nature...Second, I find it difficult to assert that men are "further" from nature because they neither menstruate nor bear children. They also eat, breathe, excrete, sleep and die; and all of these, like menstruation, are experiences of bodily limits. Like any organism, they are involved in constant biological exchange with their environment and they have built in biological clocks complete with cycles.[28]

Another group of ecofeminists chose to locate the female/nature connection in psychological processes rather than biological processes. Gray's assumption of a "feminine" experience draws in part on Nancy Chodorow's theory that men are forced to separate themselves psychologically from their mothers as they seek a male role model. This early push to separate from the mother leads to an adult masculine personality that, as Rubin argues, "comes to be defined more in terms of denial of connection and relations."[29] Females have no need to seek such early separation and so develop no intense feelings of self as distinct from an other. Instead, they are more apt to see themselves in terms of their relationships with others rather than as wholly separated.[30] Interestingly, Chodorow does not seem to deal much with early father-daughter connections that can be so important for many women.

Spretnak argues that the gender differences go back as far as infancy. She writes,

When experimental psychologists study the sexes' functioning in the area of senses and attention, as well as in the traditional area of study, cognitive skills, they conclude that man is a "manipulative animal" who tends to express himself in actions, while woman is a "communicative animal," who prefers to remember, share, and transmit signs and symbols to others. From infancy, males are fascinated by objects, females with human faces, voices and music; later females are more empathic and socially responsive.[31]

While vacillating on the question of whether such gender differences are innate or socially constructed, many ecofeminists agree that the consequences, as reflected in male tendencies, are unfortunate. Leland argues specifically that the urge to "separate, to divide, to individuate" is a masculine urge, and that there are significant consequences.

For many women, the consequences of their tendency towards relationship and connection are problematic. Catherine Roach, for example, points out that women's ability to connect enables them to more easily identify with nature, but it also limits their personal development of self:

In patriarchal culture the cost of this sense of connection is that women do not to the same degree and with the same ease of men perceive themselves as capable, powerful individuals able to bring about change, to get angry, or to assert will.[32]

Even Biehl, in an early piece, argued that feminist psychoanalytic work had demonstrated that women develop "soft ego boundaries." The personal development of women becomes a struggle against an overwhelming sense of connectedness.[33]

All but the most vehement ecological feminists point out that such critiques address a societal inclination, rather than serve as an individual indictment. Many men in patriarchal society, says Spretnak, are as victimized as women, and in no way share patriarchal values.[34] The problem, as Gray sees it, is not that men experience life as men, but that masculine values on a societal level have come to dominate our way of seeing and being.[35]

Ecofeminists have also spent considerable time discussing the idea of self. Ecofeminists such as French, King and Leland would agree with deep ecologists that alienation and the separation between human and nature are significant causes of ecological degradation. They are, however, hostile towards the deep ecological solution of dissolving individual self within a larger world Self. The hostility is perhaps understandable. As Biehl rather sarcastically notes, when women are asked to become "one" with something, as in traditional marriages, it often means losing their self.[36]

A good part of ecofeminist critique seems to stem from confusions that the deep ecologists themselves have created by not making clear the role of the individual within the larger whole. Subsuming the self to serve the whole is clearly an unpleasant alternative to many women (and other marginalized beings as well) who have not profited from this strategy in the past. Further, such a view can often rationalize and justify horrendous treatments of the individual, so long as the whole is not threatened.[37] Deep ecologists, however, often gloss over the importance of the individual in their quest for more permeable individual boundaries. One male ecofeminist, Jim Cheney, identifies this tendency as one peculiar to male theorists. This is, Cheney suggests, because they themselves are uncomfortable with their own strong individuality.[38]

Cheney, Biehl and Plumwood also identify a more sinister, if unconscious, motive underlying the expansion of self into Self. As Cheney describes it, there is no need to respect the other as a distinct individual if the other is simply absorbed and thereby contained and controlled.[39] Plumwood points out that an assumption that the rainforest's needs are our own can lead to an assumption that our needs (such as cheap beef) are also the rainforest's.[40] Who is to say that the redwood tree does *not* wish to serve humanity's needs as a picnic table?

Ecofeminists claim the question is not one of the either/or variety: *either* the isolated, alienated individual *or* the self lost in a whole. A more useful variation would be to put the stress onto the relationship between beings.[41] To acknowledge the relationship, rather than an impersonal "cosmological" connection, gives back the uniqueness and value of the individual as well as the larger whole. It validates the individual-within-community attachment to lands and beings that is, for example, at the basis of Native American worldviews[42] or Aldo Leopold's Land Ethic.[43] Unfortunately, there is also considerable legitimacy to the concern articulated by Fox, Biehl and others: personal attachments make a fragile platform on which to base environmental and social changes.[44]

Ecofeminists, then, are left with a confusing problem. Do they acknowledge and embrace a tendency shared by many women (and men) to see themselves in connection with others through relational ties? If so, how then do they work to ensure that they do not become absorbed by the other, particularly when they are told that "connection" is an ecologically sound state? No clear consensus has really emerged among ecofeminists, although it is quite clear few ecofeminists have much interest in being told by

deep ecologists to subsume their personal individuality for the greater ecological good.

Ecofeminist approaches to the idea of relationship have also been mixed. Starhawk, for example, joins the deep ecologists in using metaphors based on western/rational images drawn from the new physics, which hark back to older understandings of how things are interconnected:

Modern physics no longer speaks of separate, discrete atoms of dead matter, but of waves of energy, probabilities, patterns that change as they are observed, and recognizes what shamans and Witches have always known: Matter and energy are not separate forces, but different forms of the same thing...Nature is seen as having its own, inherent order, of which human beings are a part.[45]

Similarly, Marti Kheel writes of discovering the concept of holism (a term that deep ecologists have also flirted with) which describes a nature made up of "individual beings that are part of a dynamic web of interconnections in which feelings, emotions, and inclinations (or energy) play an integral role."[46] Both metaphors have also been used by Gray and Spretnak.[47] Like the deep ecologists, ecofeminists use the metaphors to demonstrate that humans cannot artificially divide themselves from the rest of the world, but must acknowledge an intimate interconnection with it. However, for ecofeminists like Biehl, these metaphors are connected too closely with current questions concerning "female" nature. Recently, another description of appropriate relations has come to be preferred by these ecofeminists. This new description, interestingly, takes ecofeminists closer to what Native Americans have been describing and further from the deep ecologists.

At the heart of this new approach is the ecofeminist's early need to reclaim subjectivity, feeling, emotion, and caring as legitimate sources of knowledge, precisely because they were disregarded as feminine values. Whether seeking to reclaim them as "feminine" ways of knowing (i.e. ways particularly associated with or possibly unique to women) or merely arguing that such ways need to be re-valued, ecofeminists seek ways of knowing that, says Hilary Rose,

> *transcend dichotomies, insists on the scientific validity of the subjective, on the need to unite cognitive and affective domains; it emphasizes holism, harmony, and complexity rather than reductionism, domination and linearity.*[48]

Finally, ecofeminist knowledge stresses the importance of understanding which is found through personal connection and caring.[49] An excellent example of such a connection is the animal rights movement. Whatever one thinks of such ideas, the concerns are clearly felt by those involved: the animal rights activists are often motivated by a personal love of individual animals or by experiences with abused domesticated or captive animals.

Ecofeminists such as French, Harrison, and Kheel argue that it is these feelings which we must recover as legitimate sources of knowledge. It is feeling and personal experiences which lead us to care, one solution to the techno-industrial worldview. Both Lahar and Kheel argue that without a sense of personal connection and caring about an object or event we will not be able to act in an ethically sound manner. Abstract ethical principles (such as traditional philosophy and often deep ecology construct) are insufficient as they fail to evoke any true commitment and can easily be manipulated to meet other ends.[50]

Thus, ecofeminists are beginning to describe relationships with the natural world that have as their basis, caring, or even "love." Exercising this "loving" relationship can take many different forms. Warren argues for the use of the first person narrative in writing or speaking nature. This use of "I" gives back to the discussion a felt sen-

sitivity towards subjects as it specifically locates the writer within a relationship with the subject. Further, it acknowledges the relationship process as an essential component.[51] Such a loving perception celebrates differences, a critical concern of ecofeminists.

Loving perception is in contrast to environmental (or other) ethics which focus on identifying similarities or a "unity in sameness." Thus, in traditional environmental ethics, other animals, plants, or ecosystems become recognizably moral actors, to whom we owe rights and duties, only because of identifiable similarities to humans. Based on this criteria some people might grant moral consideration to higher mammals but draw the line at the lower invertebrates such as mussels.[52] Warren's "loving perception" would allow an individual to embrace a considerably larger community of morally relevant beings.

Other ecofeminists have advanced the idea of an ethic of love. Mary Daly grounded her 1973 theory (her more recent work takes a significantly different direction) on an idea of intimate relationship that bears considerable resemblance to Native American ideas of family relations (although there is also an early echo of Warren's emphasis on the first person narrative):

> *In the refusal of our own objectification, those who find the covenant [of sisterhood] find something like what [Martin] Buber called I – Thou. This happens first among women, as sisters... the covenant embraces our sister the Earth and all of her nonhuman inhabitants and elements. It embraces, too, our sisters the moon, the sun and her planets, and all the farthest stars of the farthest galaxies. For since they are, they are our sisters in the community of being (emphasis in original).*[53]

Starhawk and Carol P. Christ have joined Daly in working out an ethic of love that embraces women, men and non-human nature.[54] However, an ethic of love or care can have limitations in application.

The emphasis on emotion and on caring raises troubling questions. Biehl in particular sees this growing focus as a rejection of the benefits and value of rationality, a dangerous trend. Biehl argues it is the ecofeminists' focus on holism that leads them to embrace a personal, experiential subjectivity as a feminine value. Yet there is nothing liberating for either women or men in a complete embrace of subjectivity or of experiential caring as a basis for improving our relations with each other or the natural world:

Not only is 'caring' compatible with hierarchy, if it is grounded in any way in 'women's nature' – or men's for that matter – let alone in social constructions, it lacks any institutional form. It simply rests on the tenuous prayer that individuals will be motivated to 'care.' But individuals may easily start or stop caring. They may care at their whim. They may not care enough. They may care about some but not others. Lacking an institutional form and dependent on individual whim, 'caring' is a slender thread on which to base an emancipatory political life.[55]

To embrace experience, feeling, and subjectivity as legitimate ways of knowing is, according to Biehl and other critics, to reject rationality, and a necessary objectivity. It is to throw away the best in western cultures along with the worst of its rational excesses. Yet, for all their enthusiastic reclamation of emotion and subjectivity, few ecofeminists appear to take that step. Most are legitimately wary of moving from one extreme to another: from hyper-rationality to hyper-emotionality. As Plumwood points out, to focus on emotion and subjectivity to the exclusion of other forms of knowledge is to fall into the old dualistic trap ecofeminists set out to criticize.[56] King is also critical of such mental habits:

According to the false dichotomy between subjective and objective – one legacy of male western philosophy to feminist thought – we must root our movement either *in a rationalist-materialist humanism* or *in a metaphysical-feminist naturalism...However, we do not need to make such choices (emphasis in original).[57]*

What goes unnoticed by many ecofeminists is that, in their arguments, they replicate the situation they argue against: polarities and dualities. It is King who may be most accurate when she states that women's (and men's) nature is neither fully biological nor fully cultural. It is both. Further, any such "nature" in and of itself is neither oppressive or liberating; that depends on the cultural context.[58] Yet, for all of its unresolved questioning ecofeminism does recapture values that, whether "female" or not, have been long undervalued. In asserting a more relational, female way of experiencing the world, some ecofeminists hope to create a more balanced worldview, one that values both genders as well as the natural world. In stressing relationship, the ecofeminists make a valuable contribution to ecophilosophical debate.

Ecofeminists and Spirit

Ecofeminists seem split on the question of spirituality, part of the baggage inherited from the feminist movement. Socialist feminists are still denouncing the cultural feminists for being fools lost in a spiritual fantasy. Cultural feminists are accusing the socialists of being unsympathetic to the human need for spiritual comfort. For every wicca priestess Starhawk, speaking of the value of the Goddess and her link to nature, there is a social ecologist like Janet Biehl, arguing that animistic beliefs will never free humanity. However, critical questioning of spirituality by ecofeminists has emerged only in the last few years. The earliest ecofeminists were seeking to reclaim and restructure spirituality to reflect women's experiences as well as men's.

As with some Native American writers, early ecofeminists approached the question of spirituality by criticizing what they saw as failures in conventional western "patriarchal" religions. Theologian Rosemary Radford Ruether was among the first to so do. She argued that mainstream religions sought to deny essential "natural" cycles in favour of spiritual transcendence, in the process denying both the female and the fleshy body:

> Patriarchal religion split apart the dialectical unities of mother religion into absolute dualism, elevating a male-identified consciousness to transcendent apriority. Fundamentally this is rooted in an effort to deny one's own mortality, to identify essential (male) humanity with a transcendent divine sphere beyond the matrix of coming-to-be-and-passing-away. By the same token woman became identified with the sphere of finitude that one must deny in order to negate one's own origin and inclusion in this realm. The woman, the body, and the world were the lower half of a dualism that must be declared posterior to, created by, subject to, and ultimately alien to the nature of (male) consciousness, in whose image man made his God.[59]

This denial of the feminine and the natural is the essence of almost all ecofeminist critiques of western religion. This discussion, however, will focus more on positive constructs by ecofeminists rather than on their deconstruction of the Judeo-Christian religion.[60] The important point is that many ecofeminists seek alternatives that include the practice of Wicca, goddess worship, paganism and pantheism.

Nontraditional spirituality has been a significant influence on the development of ecofeminist theory, particularly nature based spirituality. Spretnak, in particular, celebrates nature spirituality for its contributions to a re-valuing of things female:

> What was cosmologically wholesome and healing was the discovery of the divine as immanent in and around us. What was intriguing was the sacred link of the Goddess in her many guises with totemic animals and plants, sacred groves, womblike caves, the moon-rhythm blood of menses, the ecstatic dance – the experience of knowing Gaia, Her voluptuous contours and fertile plains, Her flowing waters that give life, Her animals as teachers...(emphasis in original).[61]

Goddess and nature based religions, such as Wicca (witchcraft) and other pagan variations, are the most common paths discussed by ecofeminists. Ecofeminists like Spretnak and Starhawk believe that such traditions offer valuable ways of seeing the world. In part, they argue, such spirituality gives back to women (and men) a sense that women could be strong, decisive, fully functioning beings, rather than a weaker vessel constructed from Adam's rib. Starhawk also argues that goddess spirituality (and all nature based spirituality) finds divinity in nature, in life, in humans and in other living beings. The focus is on life here and now as it is lived on the existing earth. It respects both male and female elements and values them as necessary complements (although there are groups which recognize only the female deity and ignore the male). She believes that the Goddess is a powerful symbol, representing life, the cyclical patterns of life, death, and life, and other natural cycles.[62]

Riane Eisler, in support of Goddess worship, argues that patriarchal religions encourage a dominator mode in human-human and human-nature interactions. Such a model, such as many transcendent eastern religions, permits an indifference to suffering. Or, as in many western religions, it permits dualisms: culture versus nature; man versus woman; spiritual leaders versus common followers.[63] Eisler, in particular, characterizes goddess worship as a return to a better, more peaceful life. Drawing on archaeological work by Marija Gimbutas, Eisler has argued for the historical existence in the Neolithic era of peaceful, earth-respecting cultures which were goddess-worshippers. Invading Indo-European cultures brought a male god, instruments of war, and finally destruction to the peaceful goddess-worshippers. Eisler's thesis is that goddess worship necessarily led to a harmonic state of existence. To reclaim the goddess today, is to reclaim this way of life.[64]

Carolyn Merchant has also argued that the loss of the idea of a living, sacred earth in the fifteenth and sixteenth centuries led to the beginning of earthly degradation:

The image of the earth as a living organism and nurturing mother has served as a cultural constraint restricting the actions of human beings. One does not readily slay a mother, dig into her entrails for gold or mutilate her body...As long as the earth was considered to be alive and sensitive, it could be considered a breach of human ethical behavior to carry out destructive acts against it.[65]

Goddess spirituality has a connection to the growing interest among feminists in demonstrating that some early political entities were actually matriarchal (based on the female perspective) rather than patriarchal, and that the earliest power in the spiritual universe was female. Scholars are still arguing over whether there is sufficient archaeological evidence to suggest that there were once actual matriarchies and whether Goddess worship was truly the celebration of all things female that modern interpreters make of it.[66] Eisler's theories and her sources, for example, have come under heavy criticism by, among others, ecofeminists concerned over the dearth of solid archeological work to back up such ideas.[67] Yet, the "historical" evidence offered by Merchant and Eisler has been used by ecofeminists such as Spretnak and Starhawk to demonstrate the impor-

tance of thinking of the earth as a living being, and of recovering the importance of the feminine.

However, for many ecofeminists the important thing is not necessarily the history of the idea but rather the idea itself. As feminist Monique Wittig writes:

There was a time when you were not a slave, remember that...You say you have lost all recollection of it, remember...you say there are no words to describe it, you say it does not exist. But remember. Make an effort to remember. **Or failing that, invent** *(emphasis added).*[68]

It is in the remembering, however incomplete, and in the current process of invention, that Goddess spirituality offers ecofeminists a chance to draw connections between themselves, others and the natural world. However, there are others, such as Gray and Biehl, who are disturbed by the question of spirituality in general and in the focus of goddess worship in particular in ecofeminist circles. Critics of ecofeminism are concerned over the interest in spirituality as an issue, regardless of its particular manifestations. Such critics deride spiritually oriented ecofeminists as being devoid of any practical inclination and lacking understanding of the historical and social causes of oppression. Catriona Sandilands, for example, argues that the emphasis on developing a personal spiritual connection with the earth elevates such spiritual and "natural" knowledge above anything that is merely "cultural" and profane. This simply sets up yet another divisive dualism.[69] Other persuasive criticisms are leveled by Janet Biehl, who has been particularly vehement in her critique.[70]

Like most Marxist influenced scholars, Biehl appears to believe that rationality and spirituality are mutually exclusive. One cannot possess both.[71] Myths, such as religion, are dangerously cooptable because they do not demand analysis or critical thinking. Instead it requires only the leap of faith spiritually-inclined individuals must make:

"I believe." In contrast, logic, scientific discovery and other "rational" explorations of the world appear not to be co-optable. In distinct contrast to Merchant, Biehl argues that the "death of nature," the move to seeing nature as a mechanistic, dead pile of resources, was the liberation of humanity rather than the beginnings of its downfall. Biehl particularly derides the concept of "hylozoism," the belief in a living world, as historically it was associated with cultures which were particularly lacking in the ideas of equity and democracy. Referring to ancient China, Greece and Rome, Biehl points out that a living earth negated the values of individual humans, giving them a fatalistic outlook and a willingness to be led by tyrannical leaders. Having dominion over a no longer watchful earth, led to gains in political freedoms: it made revolts against injustice possible as people were fighting only against human tyrants.

As a historian, Biehl might have been expected to know better, for as much evil has been committed in the name of scientific rationality as has under the rubric of religion. Nor does rationality necessarily lead to critical or comprehensive thinking, as generations of scientists who cannot see past the limitations of their own disciplines testify. Biehl's arguments ignore the large number of tyrants and fatalistic followers that have existed in non-earth worshipping cultures. Or the lack of personal freedoms and social justice in such pseudo-scientifically and rationally organized entities as Nazi Germany. And it ignores cultures that reflect a sense of a "living, aware" earth and a sense of individual freedoms, as epitomized by some traditional indigenous South Sea Island and North American cultures. Are these, too, problematic and to be discarded? Or will they be somehow exempted, in the name of cultural and racial plurality, while non-native spiritualists are castigated for succumbing to mind-numbing superstition? On the other side, there is also a great deal that is uncritical in some of the arguments presented by Spretnak or Starhawk.

Clearly, neither the ecofeminist spiritual practitioners nor their critics have reached a consensus. Interestingly, ecofeminist spirituality, particularly goddess worship, does share some common elements with Native American spirituality. It has an earth-centered focus. It recognizes a life-force in nature and some aspect of divinity there as well. It honours and respects the feminine as well as the masculine. It starts to suggest, as for Native Americans, that spirituality should be so much a part of life that it is inseparable from that life. However, there are crucial differences, differences which Native Americans recognize. Marie Wilson, of the Gitksan writes:

When I read about ecofeminism, I find that the attitudes towards women and the feelings inside myself are different. It's difficult to explain, but it's as if women are separate. Though I agree with the analysis, the differences must be because of where I come from. In my mind, when I speak about women, I speak about humanity because there is equality in the Gitksan belief: the human is one species broken into two necessary parts, and they are equal. One is impotent without the other.[72]

Ecofeminist spirituality also lacks grounding, for the most part, in the simple, common, everyday thoughts and actions of life. It is too deliberate and still too self-conscious for most people. And for some people, it can serve as an escape, as a way to avoid coming to grips with some of the fundamental problems facing human societies. Biehl is correct here, although Starhawk is emphatic that true feminist spirituality requires an engagement with life:

...True spirituality, based on a spirit that is not separated from life but manifest in matter and the world, may require us to paddle upstream, and require effort, work and anguish instead of beatific bliss, if we are to have any hope of preserving the balance of life on the planet.[73]

This is a realization not limited to the far-out goddess-worshippers, but one that many people recognize. Even critics of spirituality are looking for an organizing myth that directs them towards action designed to better the world. For many ecofeminists, the question of spirituality and myth and metaphor will be troubling for some time to come.

Ain't Nothing Perfect: Critiques of Ecofeminism

Ecofeminism, for the moment, is such an internally riven, convoluted set of ideas that it can be difficult to point out critical gaps. A problem for one ecofeminist theorist will likely be repudiated and re-addressed by another ecofeminist. Perhaps this is its largest flaw: so many theories and theorists label themselves "ecofeminist" that it becomes difficult to describe what ecofeminism is. A tolerance for diversity is a good thing, in general, in contrast to one hard and fast dogma, but as Janet Biehl has been moved to comment, "dogmatism is clearly not the same thing as coherence, clarity, and at least a minimum level of consistency."[74]

One of the greatest criticisms of ecofeminist theory, and one that might not be resolved quickly, is the tendency of ecofeminists to argue dualisms. *Either* female experience and nature is a biologically based reality *or* it is a social construction. *Either* we focus on the construction of social and political alternatives *or* we work on spiritual issues, including personal redemption. *Either* men are wholly responsible for any number of patriarchal crises, including the ecological crisis, *or*, ... well there is no "or" here. Men, collectively, in western patriarchy are, often, simply the "bad guys"; there are few non-trivial efforts to find any redeeming quality in men, nor to acknowledge that women might have been equally complicit in social and ecological oppression. In fact, this is a key criticism of ecofeminist theory; it has so little place or consideration for men, or for less flattering views of women.

Feminism has been from the start justly critical of patriarchy. Part and parcel of a feminist critique has often been a critique of men, as men make up the largest part of the ruling structure of patriarchy. Yet patriarchy often disenfranchises men as well as women. Men might well participate, knowingly or not, yet so too do women, knowingly or not. Grounding a critique of politics only in the (possibly) unique experiences of one gender is no less reactionary or bigoted because that experience is female than it is when the only validating experience is male. As Merchant has commented, ecofeminists run the risk of becoming as hierarchical as the patriarchy they seek to overthrow.[75]

There is no dualism either in the fact that many ecofeminists are white and middle-class, and it has been difficult to include people of colour or to engage with issues of concern to people of colour. This is not to suggest that there are no people of colour writing, names on articles rarely indicate anything, or even that there is a deliberate attempt to ignore the concerns of women of colour. However the number of women writing explicitly about ecofeminism as it affects women of colour are so few that the same individuals often show up time and again in collections of readings on ecofeminism: Vandana Shiva (India), and Cynthia Hamilton and Rachel Bagby (African American).[76] Thus, ecofeminists talk of "women's" issues or "women's" reality without always acknowledging the fact that the issues and reality for a white, economically comfortable academic in North America might be very different from issues of concern to a woman of colour in the inner-city or a woman in famine-ridden Ethiopia, or even a rural farmer trying to achieve the North American dream. This insularity is changing, but most slowly. As King and Warren have recognized,

Feminism must be a 'solidarity movement' based on shared beliefs and interests rather than a 'unity in sameness' movement based

on shared experiences and shared victimiza-tion.[77]

However, ecofeminism has spent much of its time arguing that all women are oppressed by patriarchy, as is nature, and both are exploited for the same reasons. In other words, the ecofeminists' focus has been on sameness, or similar experience. But avoiding sameness should not result in dualisms, as it often seems to in ecofeminism.

The dualism between spiritual ecofeminists and political or social ecofeminists is particularly troubling. What is spirituality if it cannot be translated into greater social involvement? Even in the "patriarchal" religions there is a strong tradition of social and political activism that had a grounding in spiritual beliefs: Christ, Gandhi, Martin Luther King, Jeanne d'Arc, the Christian families and churches that hid Jews during the Holocaust, there are uncountable examples. But at the same time, what is social life without some sort of sense of a broader set of ideas and values? It does not have to be spirituality that provides this, but it often is. Rationality and logic take us so far; eventually there comes a need for a great emotional leap of intuition. Spirituality often provides the lift for just such a leap.[78]

True, social and political activism and religion do not always lead to positive results, for example National Socialism in 1930s Germany. Is this a valid reason, however, for declaring one or the other to be dangerous or useless? Great things have been accomplished using social activism or spirituality and often both. To insist on rigid distinctions, as some ecofeminists, as well as other philosophers, are inclined to do, is to believe that black and white is an appropriate colouring of the world. But most often the decisions and the issues are painted in shades of gray. Why not the responses?

The bitter, personal exchanges that this dualism has occasioned are equally problematic. Agreeing to disagree while working together and respecting each other's opinions often seems a secondary goal for some ecofeminists, especially when debating with other philosophers. And yet, these are people who should have a commitment to attempted cooperation. They have after all a similarly stated goal: a socially and ecologically sound world. For all their discussion of cooperation, the importance of relationships and loving care, some ecofeminists seem to be as willing as the next patriarch to treat others as objects with nothing of value to contribute. There is a lingering and regrettable flavour of turf-wars, one-upping the other critic, and self-righteousness in much ecofeminist writing. This wrangling points to two difficulties. First is the difficulty, and not only amongst ecofeminists, of translating between value and action. Humanity has always confronted the dilemma of contradictory needs and outside pressures. Second is the problem of attempting to make change while being forced to operate in a system that functions in a completely different way.

Finally, ecofeminists often do themselves a great disservice in how they use ideas in their rush towards legitimacy. Often there seems a willingness to play fast, loose, and careless with history, with science, or with religion. For example, some ecofeminists have tried to demonstrate legitimate, historically based grounds for the idea of ancient women who had high status and were fully functional social and political beings. It is an understandable goal but to fulfill it, ocasionally data is used that is no where near as incontrovertible as is presented. Arguing that women's domination began with the fall of the Neolithic women-centered cultures by using only one, contested source of information leaves them open to the sort of criticism that the Biehls are only too happy to give.[79]

Further, it is important that ecofeminists avoid the trap of seeking so hard to legitimize themselves that they come to believe their ideas are best expressed in obscure academic journals in language that requires at minimum a post-doctorate in philosophy. Ecofeminism, along with other ecophilosophies, can only succeed when it reaches and captivates as many people as possible, especially outside of academe. Otherwise, the people most in need of finding new ways of thinking, or new words that express what they have already felt but couldn't communicate, are going to dismiss ecofeminism. And that would be everyone's loss.

Visions Of New/Old Realities

For all its flaws and definitional slipperiness, ecofeminism makes a positive contribution to ecophilosophy. Its practitioners were the first to raise the question of women's social status as an important consideration in the environmental movement, and put women's issues and ideas into the agendas of the other ecophilosophies, including deep ecology and bioregionalism. Ecofeminists raised questions that made both women and men take a hard look at the way they operated and at means as well as ends. Most importantly, it gave back to fifty-two percent of the human race a sense that they can contribute to the search for a better world without having to play the unsuccessful game already in place.

There is a legitimate question of whether ecofeminism offers any truly unique visions of different realities. Perhaps it is the rediscovery of old visions. Or perhaps it is the creation of new visions with a grounding in possible realities. Ecofeminists such as Barbara Starrett believe in the idea of vision itself, for thought can translate into concrete action:

It has...been noted that power/passion resides in the mind. Intensity begins with thought, and to experience intensity is to experience power. But power always finds a form...Thought can alter reality; thought can create reality.[80]

What kind of reality would ecofeminists think into existence? French suggests that it is a reality that has as its central doctrine something other than the use of power to control others, which is so central to patriarchal society:

The only true revolution against patriarchy is one which removes the idea of power from its central position, and replaces it with the idea of pleasure...To restore pleasure to centrality requires restoring the body, and therefore nature, to value...The restoration of body and nature to value would preclude the treatment of both body and nature that pervades our world – the torture and deprivation of the one, the erosion and pollution of the other.[81]

Finally, says Starhawk, ecofeminism offers a reality which offers new roles for the individual, including responsibility and awareness. Most importantly, ecofeminism brings to the social-ecological debate the emotion of love, caring, as a significant justification for action:

Life, being sacred, demands our full participation...Life demands honesty...It demands integrity—being integrated, having brought together and recognized our conflicting internal forces, and being integrated into a larger community of selves and life-forms. Life demands courage and vulnerability, because without them there can be no openness and no connection; and it requires responsibility and discipline, to make choices and face the consequences, to carry out what we undertake. And finally, life demands love...love, of self and of others, erotic love, transforming love, affectionate love, delighted love for the myriad forms of life evolving and changing, for the redwood and the mayfly, for the blue whale and the snail darter, for wind and sun and the waxing and waning moon, caring love for the Cambodian child and the restless ghetto teenager, love of the eternally self-creating world, love of the light and the mysterious darkness, and raging love against all that would diminish the unspeakable beauty of the world... .[82]

It is in the challenging of old visions and in the provision of new possibilities that ecofeminism perhaps reaches its greatest potential. The ability and willingness to place the difficult questions of equity and natural resources onto the social agenda is no mean feat in and of itself. To further the discussion into the realm of practical solutions, as is the hope, I believe, for ecofeminists everywhere, is to make a profound difference in the world. In all these areas, ecofeminism promises much.

ENDNOTES

[1]Ynestra King. 1981a. "The Eco-Feminist Imperative." In Leonie Caldecott and Stephanie Leland (eds.). 1983. *Reclaim the Earth.* London, England: The Women's Press. pp. 9-14, p. 10.

[2]Francoise d'Eaubonne. 1974. *Le Feminisme ou la Mort.* Paris, France: Pierre Horay. p. 204.

[3]These principles are largely derived from the following works: Ynestra King. 1983. "Towards an Ecological Feminism and a Feminist Ecology." In Joan Rothschild (ed.). 1983. *Machina Ex Dea.* New York, NY: Pergamon Press. Pp. 118-129; Ynestra King. 1988. "Ecofeminism: On the Necessity of History and Mystery." *Women of Power* 9(Spring): 42-44; Charlene Spretnak. 1988. "Ecofeminism: Our Roots and Flowering." *Women of Power* 9(Spring): 6-10; and Karen J. Warren. 1987. "Feminism and Ecology: Making Connections." *Environmental Ethics* 9(1): pp. 3-20.

[4]Hazel Henderson. 1983. "The Warp and Weft: The Coming Synthesis of Eco-philosophy and Eco-feminism." In Leonie Caldecott and Stephanie Leland (eds.). 1983. *Reclaim the Earth.* London, England: The Women's Press. pp. 203-214. p. 207.

[5]Stephanie Leland. 1983. "Feminism and Ecology: Theoretical Connections." In Leonie Caldecott and Stephanie Leland (eds.). 1983. *Reclaim the Earth.* London, England: The Women's Press. pp. 67-72. pp. 68-69.

[6]See Riane Eisler. 1987. *The Chalice and the Blade – Our History, Our Future.* San Francisco, CA: Harper and Row; Elizabeth Dodson Gray. 1981. *Green Paradise Lost.* Wellesley, MA: Roundtable Press; Susan Griffin. 1990. "Curves Along the Road." In Irene Diamond and Gloria Feman Orenstein (eds.). 1990. *Reweaving the World: The Emergence of Ecofeminism.* San Francisco, CA: Sierra Club Books. Pp. 87-99; Henderson, 1983; Rosemary Radford

Ruether. 1975. *New Woman New Earth: Sexist Ideologies and Human Liberation.* New York, NY: The Seabury Press; Vandana Shiva. 1990. "Development as a New Project of Western Patriarchy." In Irene Diamond and Gloria Feman Orenstein (eds.). 1990. *Reweaving the World: The Emergence of Ecofeminism.* San Francisco, CA: Sierra Club Books. pp. 189-200; and Starhawk. 1982a. *Dreaming The Dark: Magic, Sex and Politics.* Boston, MA: Beacon Press.

[7]Andree Collard with Joyce Contrucci. 1989. *Rape of the Wild, Man's Violence Against Animals and the Earth.* Bloomington, IN: Indiana University Press. p. 5.

[8]Griffin 1990: pp. 88.

[9]Shiva 1990: pp. 192-193.

[10]Eisler 1987; and Riane Eisler. 1990. "The Gaia Tradition and the Partnership Future: An Ecofeminist Manifesto." In Irene Diamond and Gloria Feman Orenstein (eds.). 1990. *Reweaving the World: The Emergence of Ecofeminism.* San Francisco, CA: Sierra Club Books. pp. 23 – 34.

[11]Carolyn Merchant. 1980. *The Death of Nature.* San Francisco, CA: Harper and Row. p. xvi.

[12]Patsy Hallen. 1987. "Making Peace with Nature: Why Ecology Needs Feminism." *The Trumpeter* 4(3): pp. 3-14. p. 9.

[13] Warren 1987. It should be noted that many of these "schools" have modified themselves over the years, but in brief, liberal feminism argues for maximum freedom in which individuals pursue their own interests. All ecological interests must be grounded in human interests since humans are the basis of all value. Therefore there can be no appeals to "intrinsic values of other beings," for instance, unless they are morally equivalent to humans i.e. rational, or sentient. Since few humans grant other beings any sort of moral equality with humans, liberal feminism has several drawbacks for ecofeminist theory.

Marxist feminism states that the oppression of women is linked to the oppression of classes and the institution of private property. Knowledge is a social construct. Both of these beliefs have contributed to ecofeminist theory. However, the Marxist belief that the transformation of the material world is necessary to meet human needs presents serious difficulties for those arguing for a less domineering relationship with the earth. A true Marxist would have few qualms over modifications of the earth if benefits were shared equally among all humans.

Radical/cultural feminism locates women's oppression in their reproductive biology and in the sex-gender system of most cultures. The control of female reproduction capabilities and sexuality, and the disavowal of body-mind connections, are problems which radical feminists confront. They advocate the integration of spirituality into the rest of life and turning felt experiences into theory. Critics note that radical feminists ignore history and the material basis of oppression. They also ignore social structures and locate women closer to nature than they do men (as do some ecofeminists).

Socialist feminism links both class domination and gender to women's oppression. Humans are thought to be created both historically and culturally through the interaction of physical biology, environment and society. Socialist feminists are deeply suspicious of spiritual radicals, who argue women's close connections to nature. This essentially reflects the second major camp in ecofeminist theory. (It should be noted that socialist and Marxist feminism are often lumped together by ecofeminists.)

[14]King 1988: p.42.

[15]Warwick Fox. "The Deep Ecology-Ecofeminism Debate and Its Parallels." *Environmental Ethics* 11 no. 1 (1989): pp.5-25. p. 6.

[16]Bill Devall and George Sessions. 1985. *Deep Ecology*. Salt Lake City: Peregrine Smith Books. p. 67.

[17]Alan R. Drengson. *The Trumpeter* 1 no. 4 (Summer 1984a): p. 11.

[18]Devall and Sessions 1985: p.8.

[19]Alan Drengson. "Introduction: Process, Relationships and Ecosophy." *The Trumpeter* 8 no. 1 (1991): pp.1-2.

[20]Devall and Sessions 1985: p. 67.

[21] King 1981a: p. 11.

[22]Ynestra King. 1981b. "Feminism and the Revolt of Nature." *Heresies* # 13 4(1): pp.12-16. p. 12.

[23]Janet Biehl. 1991. *Finding Our Way: Rethinking Ecofeminist Politics*. Montreal, Que: Black Rose Books. p. 11.

[24] Ruether 1975: pp. 203-204.

[25] King 1981b: p. 12.

[26]Biehl 1991: p. 9.

[27]Henderson 1983: p. 207.

[28]Joan L. Griscom. 1981. "On Healing the Nature/History Split in Feminist Thought." *Heresies* # 13 4(1): pp.4-9. p. 8.

[29]Lillian Brelow Rubin. 1976. *Worlds of Pain: Life in the Working-Class Family*. New York, NY: Basic Books. pp. 118-119. Cited in Gray 1982: p. 115.

[30]Nancy Chodorow. 1978. *The Reproduction of Mothering: Psychoanalysis and the Sociology of Gender*. Berkeley, CA: University of California Press. Cited in Gray 1982: p. 115.

[31]Charlene Spretnak. 1982. "Introduction." In Charlene Spretnak (ed.). 1982. *The Politics of Women's Spirituality: Essays on the Rise of Spiritual Power Within the Feminist Movement*. Garden City, NY: Doubleday & Co., Inc. p. xiv.

[32]Catherine Roach. 1991. "Loving Your Mother: On the Woman-Nature Relation." *Hypatia* 6(1)(Spring): pp. 46-59. p. 53.

[33]Janet Biehl. 1988. "Ecofeminism and Deep Ecology:

Unresolvable Conflict?" *Our Generation* 19(2): pp. 19-31. p. 4.

[34]Spretnak 1982: p. xiv.

[35] Gray 1981: p. 116.

[36]Biehl 1988: p. 29.

[37] Marti Kheel. 1990. "Ecofeminism and Deep Ecology: Reflections on Identity and Difference." In Irene Diamond and Gloria Feman Orenstein (eds.). 1990. *Reweaving the World: The Emergence of Ecofeminism*. San Francisco, CA: Sierra Club Books. pp. 128-137. p. 136.

[38]Jim Cheney. 1987. "Eco-Feminism and Deep Ecology." *Environmental Ethics* 9(2): pp.115-145. p. 120-121.

[39]Biehl 1988; Cheney 1987: 124; Jim Cheney. 1989. "The Neo-Stoicism of Radical Environmentalism." *Environmental Ethics* 11(4): pp. 293-325. p. 302.

[40]Val Plumwood. 1991. "Nature, Self, and Gender: Feminism, Environmental Philosophy, and the Critique of Rationalism." *Hypatia* 6(1)(Spring): pp. 3-27. p.13.

[41]Plumwood 1991: 20; Michael E. Zimmerman. 1990. "Deep Ecology and Ecofeminism: The Emerging Dialogue." In Irene Diamond and Gloria Feman Orenstein (eds.). 1990. *Reweaving the World: The Emergence of Ecofeminism*. San Francisco, CA: Sierra Club Books. pp. 138-154. p. 149.

[42] See for example Annie L. Booth and Harvey M. Jacobs. 1990. "Ties That Bind: Native American Beliefs as a Foundation for Environmental Consciousness." *Environmental Ethics* 12(1): pp. 27-43;

_____. 1988. *Environmental Consciousness – Native American Worldviews and Natural Resource Management: An Annotated Bibliography*. Chicago, IL: Council of Planning Librarians, Bibliography No. 214; and D.M. Dooling and Paul Jordan-Smith (eds.). 1989. *I Become Part Of It: Sacred Dimensions in Native American Life*. New York, NY: Parabola Books.

[43] Aldo Leopold. [1949] 1966. *A Sand County Almanac*. New York, NY: Oxford University Press. See also J. Baird Callicott. 1987. *Companion to a Sand County Almanac*. Madison, WI: University of Wisconsin Press.

[44] Warwick, Fox. 1990. *Toward a Transpersonal Ecology. Developing New Foundations for Environmentalism*. Boston, MA: Shambhala Publications, Inc.; Biehl 1991; Deanne Curtin. 1991. "Towards an Ecological Ethic of Care." *Hypatia* 6(1)(Spring): pp. 60-74; Roger J.H. King. 1991. "Caring About Nature: Feminist Ethics and the Environment." Hypatia 6(1)(Spring): pp. 75-89.

[45]Starhawk 1982b: pp. 178-179.

[46]Marti Kheel. 1985. "The Liberation of Nature: A Circular Affair." *Environmental Ethics* 7(Summer): pp. 135-149. p. 140.

[47]Gray 1982: p. 44; Spretnak 1982: p. xv.

[48]Hilary Rose. 1984. "Beyond Masculinist Realities: A Femi-

nist Epistemology for the Sciences." In Ruth Bleier (ed.). 1984. *Science and Gender: A Critique of Biology and Its Theories on Women.* New York, NY: Pergamon Press. pp. 57-76. p. 72.

[49]See Judith Plaskow and Carol P. Christ. 1989. "Introduction." In Judith Plaskow and Carol P. Christ (eds.). 1989. *Weaving the Visions: New Patterns in Feminist Spirituality.* San Francisco, CA: Harper and Row. pp. 1-13; Stephanie Lahar. 1991. "Ecofeminist Theory and Grassroots Politics." *Hypatia* 6(1)(Spring): pp. 28-45; and Kheel 1985.

[50]Kheel 1985: p. 144; Lahar 1990.

[51]Karen J. Warren. 1990. "The Power and the Promise of Ecological Feminism." *Environmental Ethics* 12(2): pp. 125-146. p. 135.

[52]For an example of this approach see Peter Singer. 1975. *Animal Liberation: A New Ethics for Our Treatment of Animals.* New York, NY: Avon Books.

[53]Mary Daly. 1982. "Sisterhood as Cosmic Covenant." In Charlene Spretnak (ed.). 1982. *The Politics of Women's Spirituality: Essays on the Rise of Spiritual Power Within the Feminist Movement.* Garden City, NY: Doubleday & Co., Inc. pp. 351-361. p. 360.

[54]Starhawk 1982a; Carol P. Christ. 1990. "Rethinking Theology and Nature." In Irene Diamond and Gloria Feman Orenstein (eds.). 1990. *Reweaving the World: The Emergence of Ecofeminism.* San Francisco, CA: Sierra Club Books. pp. 58-69.

[55] Ibid: p. 150.

[56] Plumwood 1991: p. 7.

[57]King 1981a: pp. 13-14.

[58]King 1981b.

[59]Ruether 1975: 194-195. See also Naomi Goldenberg. 1979. *Changing of the Gods: Feminism and the End of Traditional Religions.* Boston, MA: Beacon Press; and Gray 1981.

[60]See in particular Christ 1990; Mary Daly. 1990. *Gyn/Ecology.* Boston, MA: Beacon Press; Gray 1981; Judith Plaskow and Carol P. Christ (eds.). 1989. *Weaving the Visions: New Patterns in Feminist Spirituality.* San Francisco, CA: Harper and Row; Ruether 1975; and Charlene Spretnak (ed.). 1982. *The Politics of Women's Spirituality: Essays on the Rise of Spiritual Power Within the Feminist Movement.* Garden City, NY: Doubleday & Co., Inc.

[61]Spretnak 1988: p. 7.

[62]Starhawk. 1982a: p. 9.

[63]Eisler 1990.

[64]Eisler 1987. She draws heavily on the following: Marija Gimbutas. 1982. *The Goddesses and Gods of Old Europe 7000-3500 BC.* Berkeley, CA: University of California Press; Marija Gimbutas. 1980. *The Early Civilization of Europe.* Los Angeles, CA: University of California. Mono-graph for Indo-European Studies No. 131; and Marija Gimbutas. 1987. *The Language of the Goddess: Images and Symbols of Old Europe.* New York, NY: Van der Marck.

[65]Eisler 1987: p. 3.

[66]For a good presentation of existing evidence for matriarchies and Goddess worship see Merlin Stone. 1976. *When God Was A Woman.* New York, NY: Dial Press. See also the exchange between Sally R. Binford, Merlin Stone, and Charlene Spretnak in Charlene Spretnak (ed.). 1982. *The Politics of Women's Spirituality: Essays on the Rise of Spiritual Power Within the Feminist Movement.* Garden City, NY: Doubleday & Co., Inc. pp. 541-561, for key elements of this debate. More recent contributions can be found in Eisler 1987 and in Biehl 1991.

[67]Biehl 1991; and Janet Biehl. 1989. "Goddess Mythology in Ecological Politics." *New Politics* 2(2): pp. 84-105.

[68] Monique Wittig. 1971. *Les Guerilleres.* New York, NY: Avon Books. Cited in Carol P. Christ. 1982. "Why Women Need the Goddess: Phenomenological, Psychological and Political Reflections." In Charlene Spretnak (ed.). 1982. *The Politics of Women's Spirituality: Essays on the Rise of Spiritual Power Within the Feminist Movement.* Garden City, NY: Doubleday & Co., Inc. pp. 71-86.

[69]Cate Sandilands. 1991. "Ecofeminism and Its Discontents: Notes Toward a Politics of Diversity." *The Trumpeter* 8(2)(Spring): pp. 90-96. pp. 93-94.

[70] See for example the particularly vehement response to Goddess worshippers in Biehl 1989.

[71]Biehl 1991: p. 88.

[72]Marie Wilson. 1990. "Wings of the Eagle." In Christopher Plant and Judith Plant (eds.). 1990. *Turtle Talk: Voices For A Sustainable Future.* Philadelphia, PA: New Society Publishers. pp. 76-84. p. 77.

[73]Starhawk 1982b: pp.181-182.

[74] Biehl 1991: p. 3.

[75]Carolyn Merchant. 1990. "Ecofeminism and Feminist Theory." In Irene Diamond and Gloria Feman Orenstein (eds.). 1990. *Reweaving the World: The Emergence of Ecofeminism.* San Francisco, CA: Sierra Club Books. pp. 100 -105. p. 102.

[76]See for example Ann Spanel. 1988. "Indian Women and the Chipko Movement: An Interview with Vandana Shiva." *Woman of Power* 9(Spring): pp. 26-31; Vandana Shiva. 1989. "Development, Ecology and Women." In Judith Plant (ed.). 1989. *Healing the Wounds: The Promise of Ecofeminism.* Toronto, ONT: Between the Lines, pp. 80-90; Vandana Shiva. 1990. "Development as a New Project of Western Patriarchy." In Irene Diamond and Gloria Feman Orenstein (eds.). 1990. *Reweaving the World: The Emergence of Ecofeminism.* San Francisco, CA: Sierra Club Books, pp. 189-200; Rachel L. Bagby. 1988. "Building the

Green Movement." *Woman of Power* 9(Spring): pp. 11-17; Rachel L. Bagby. 1989. "A Power of Numbers." In Judith Plant (ed.). 1989. *Healing the Wounds: The Promise of Ecofeminism.* Toronto, ONT: Between the Lines, pp. 91-95; Rachel L. Bagby. 1990. "Daughters of Growing Things." In Irene Diamond and Gloria Feman Orenstein (eds.). 1990. *Reweaving the World: The Emergence of Ecofeminism.* San Francisco, CA: Sierra Club Books, pp. 231-248; Cynthia Hamilton. 1991. "Women, Home and Community." *Woman of Power* 20(Spring): pp. 42-53; Cynthia Hamilton. 1990. "Women, Home, and Community: The Struggle in an Urban Environment." In Irene Diamond and Gloria Feman Orenstein (eds.). 1990. *Reweaving the World: The Emergence of Ecofeminism.* San Francisco, CA: Sierra Club Books, pp. 215-222.

[77] Warren 1990: 131. See also Ynestra King. 1990. "Healing the Wounds: Feminism, Ecology, and the Nature/Culture Dualism." In Irene Diamond and Gloria Feman Orenstein (eds.). 1990. *Reweaving the World: The Emergence of Ecofeminism.* San Francisco, CA: Sierra Club Books. pp. 106-121. p. 113.

[78] See especially King 1990.

[79] See Eisler 1987; and Biehl 1991.

[80] Barbara Starrett. 1976. "The Metaphors of Power." In Charlene Spretnak (ed.). 1982. *The Politics of Women's Spirituality: Essays on the Rise of Spiritual Power Within the Feminist Movement.* Garden City, NY: Doubleday & Co., Inc. pp. 185-193. p. 190.

[81] French 1985: p. 444.

[82] Starhawk. 1982b. "Ethics and Justice in Goddess Religion." In Charlene Spretnak (ed.). 1982. *The Politics of Women's Spirituality: Essays on the Rise of Spiritual Power Within the Feminist Movement.* Garden City, NY: Doubleday & Co., Inc. pp. 415-422. p. 421.

References

Biehl, Janet.; 1991; *Finding Our Way: Rethinking Ecofeminist Politics*; Montreal, Que: Black Rose Books.

_____; 1989; "Goddess Mythology in Ecological Politics"; *New Politics* 2(2): pp. 84-105.

_____; 1988; "Ecofeminism and Deep Ecology: Unresolvable Conflict?"; *Our Generation* 19(2): pp. 19-31.

Booth, Annie L. and Jacobs, Harvey M.; 1990; "Ties That Bind: Native American Beliefs as a Foundation for Environmental Consciousness"; *Environmental Ethics* 12(1): pp. 27-43

Cheney, Jim; 1989; "The Neo-Stoicism of Radical Environmentalism"; *Environmental Ethics* 11(4): pp. 293-325.

_____; 1987; "Eco-Feminism and Deep Ecology"; *Environmental Ethics* 9(2): pp. 115-145.

Christ, Carol P.; 1990; "Rethinking Theology and Nature"; In Irene Diamond and Gloria Feman Orenstein (eds.), *Reweaving the World: The Emergence of Ecofeminism*; 1990; San Francisco, CA: Sierra Club Books; pp. 58-69.

Collard, Andree with Contrucci, Joyce; 1989; *Rape of the Wild, Man's Violence Against Animals and the Earth;* Bloomington, IN: Indiana University Press.

Curtin, Deanne; 1991; "Towards an Ecological Ethic of Care"; *Hypatia* 6(1)(Spring): pp. 60-74

Daly, Mary; 1982; "Sisterhood as Cosmic Covenant"; In Charlene Spretnak (ed.), *The Politics of Women's Spirituality: Essays on the Rise of Spiritual Power Within the Feminist Movement;* 1982; Garden City, NY: Doubleday & Co., Inc.; pp. 351-361.

Devall, Bill and Sessions, George; 1985; *Deep Ecology;* Salt Lake City: Peregrine Smith Books.

Drengson, Alan; "Introduction: Process, Relationships and Ecosophy"; *The Trumpeter* 8 no. 1 (1991): pp. 1-2.

_____; *The Trumpeter* 1 no. 4 (Summer 1984a): p. 11.

Eisler, Riane; 1990; "The Gaia Tradition and the Partnership Future: An Ecofeminist Manifesto"; In Irene Diamond and Gloria Feman Orenstein (eds.), *Reweaving the World: The Emergence of Ecofeminism*; 1990; San Francisco, CA: Sierra Club Books; pp. 23 - 34.

_____; 1987; *The Chalice and the Blade - Our History, Our Future*; San Francisco, CA: Harper and Row.

Fox, Warwick; 1990; *Toward a Transpersonal Ecology; Developing New Foundations for Environmentalism*; Boston, MA: Shambhala Publications, Inc.

_____; "The Deep Ecology-Ecofeminism Debate and Its Parallels"; *Environmental Ethics* 11 no. 1 (1989): pp. 5-25.

French, Marilyn; 1985; *Beyond Power: On Women, Men, and Morals;* New York: Ballentine Books.

Gray, Elizabeth Dodson; 1981; *Green Paradise Lost*; Wellesley, MA: Roundtable Press.

Griffin, Susan; 1990; "Curves Along the Road"; In Irene Diamond and Gloria Feman Orenstein (eds.), *Reweaving the World: The Emergence of Ecofeminism*; 1990; San Francisco, CA: Sierra Club Books; Pp. 87-99.

Griscom, Joan L; 1981; "On Healing the Nature/History Split in Feminist Thought"; *Heresies* # 13 4(1): pp. 4-9.

Hallen, Patsy; 1987; "Making Peace with Nature: Why Ecology Needs Feminism"; *The Trumpeter* 4(3): pp. 3-14.

Henderson, Hazel; 1983; "The Warp and Weft: The Coming Synthesis of Eco-philosophy and Eco-feminism"; In Leonie Caldecott and Stephanie Leland (eds.), *Reclaim the Earth*; 1983; London, England: The Women's Press; pp. 203-214.

Kheel, Marti; 1990; "Ecofeminism and Deep Ecology: Reflections on Identity and Difference"; In Irene Diamond and Gloria Feman Orenstein (eds.), *Reweaving the World: The Emergence of Ecofeminism*; 1990; San Francisco, CA: Sierra Club Books; Pp. 128-137.

_____; 1985; "The Liberation of Nature: A Circular Affair"; *Environmental Ethics* 7(Summer): pp. 135-149.

King, Ynestra; 1990; "Healing the Wounds: Feminism, Ecology, and the Nature/Culture Dualism"; In Irene Diamond and Gloria Feman Orenstein (eds.), *Reweaving the World: The Emergence of Ecofeminism*; 1990; San Francisco, CA: Sierra Club Books; pp. 106-121.

_____; 1988; "Ecofeminism: On the Necessity of History and Mystery"; *Women of Power* 9(Spring): pp. 42-44.

_____; 1983; "Towards an Ecological Feminism and a Feminist Ecology"; In Joan Rothschild (ed.), *Machina Ex Dea;* 1983; New York, NY: Pergamon Press; pp. 118-129.

_____; 1981; "The Eco-Feminist Imperative"; In Leonie Caldecott and Stephanie Leland (eds.), *Reclaim the Earth;* 1983; London, England: The Women's Press; pp. 9-14.

_____; 1981; "Feminism and the Revolt of Nature"; *Heresies* # 13 4(1): pp. 12-16.

King, Roger J.H. 1991; "Caring About Nature: Feminist Ethics and the Environment"; *Hypatia* 6(1)(Spring): pp. 75-89.

Lahar, Stephanie; 1991; "Ecofeminist Theory and Grassroots Politics"; *Hypatia* 6(1)(Spring): pp. 28-45

Leland, Stephanie; 1983; "Feminism and Ecology: Theoretical Connections"; In Leonie Caldecott and Stephanie Leland (eds.), *Reclaim the Earth*; 1983;London, England: The Women's Press; pp. 67-72.

Merchant, Carolyn; 1990; "Ecofeminism and Feminist Theory"; In Irene Diamond and Gloria Feman Orenstein (eds.), *Reweaving the World: The Emergence of Ecofeminism*; 1990; San Francisco, CA: Sierra Club Books; pp. 100 -105.

_____; 1980; *The Death of Nature*; San Francisco, CA: Harper and Row.

Plaskow, Judith and Christ, Carol P.; 1989; "Introduction"; In Judith Plaskow and Carol P. Christ (eds.), *Weaving the Visions: New Patterns in Feminist Spirituality*; 1989; San Francisco, CA: Harper and Row; pp. 1-13.

Plumwood, Val; 1991; "Nature, Self, and Gender: Feminism, Environmental Philosophy, and the Critique of Rationalism"; *Hypatia* 6(1)(Spring): pp. 3-27.

Roach, Catherine; 1991; "Loving Your Mother: On the Woman-Nature Relation"; *Hypatia* 6(1)(Spring): pp. 46-59.

Rose, Hilary; 1984; "Beyond Masculinist Realities: A Feminist Epistemology for the Sciences"; In Ruth Bleier (ed.), *Science and Gender: A Critique of Biology and Its Theories on Women*; 1984; New York, NY: Pergamon Press; pp. 57-76.

Sandilands, Cate; 1991; "Ecofeminism and Its Discontents: Notes Toward a Politics of Diversity"; *The Trumpeter* 8(2)(Spring): pp. 90-96.

Spretnak, Charlene; 1988; "Ecofeminism: Our Roots and Flowering"; *Women of Power* 9(Spring): pp. 6-10.

_____; 1982; "Introduction"; In

Charlene Spretnak (ed.), *The Politics of Women's Spirituality: Essays on the Rise of Spiritual Power Within the Feminist Movement*; 1982; Garden City, NY: Doubleday & Co., Inc.

Starhawk; 1982; *Dreaming The Dark: Magic, Sex and Politics*; Boston, MA: Beacon Press.

_____; 1982; "Ethics and Justice in Goddess Religion"; In Charlene Spretnak (ed.), *The Politics of Women's Spirituality: Essays on the Rise of Spiritual Power Within the Feminist Movement;* 1982; Garden City, NY: Doubleday & Co., Inc.; pp. 415-422.

Starrett, Barbara; 1976; "The Metaphors of Power"; In Charlene Spretnak (ed.), *The Politics of Women's Spirituality: Essays on the Rise of Spiritual Power Within the Feminist Movement*; 1982; Garden City, NY: Doubleday & Co., Inc.; pp. 185-193.

Warren, Karen J; 1990; "The Power and the Promise of Ecological Feminism"; *Environmental Ethics* 12(2): pp.125-146.

_____; 1987; "Feminism and Ecology: Making Connections"; *Environmental Ethics* 9(1): pp. 3-20.

Wilson, Marie; 1990; "Wings of the Eagle"; In Christopher Plant and Judith Plant (eds.), *Turtle Talk: Voices For A Sustainable Future;* 1990; Philadelphia, PA: New Society Publishers; pp. 76-84.

Zimmerman, Michael E.; 1990; "Deep Ecology and Ecofeminism: The Emerging Dialogue"; In Irene Diamond and Gloria Feman Orenstein (eds.), *Reweaving the World: The Emergence of Ecofeminism*; 1990; San Francisco, CA: Sierra Club Books; pp. 138-154.

ALLIES IN AGRICULTURE
FARM WOMEN AND THE ECOSYSTEM

22   *by Karen Krug*

A SOCIAL, FEMINIST LIBERATION ETHIC – INFLUENCED by theoretical principles from Latin American liberation theology – underpins the analysis contained within this paper. Both the feminist and the liberationist components are social in the sense that they depend upon social analysis to identify farm women and the ecosystem as oppressed. Because women are viewed as an oppressed group, and actions of solidarity with women and other oppressed groups are advocated, the paper reflects a liberationist feminist stance.

Liberation theology assumes a world of conflict in which power is systemically concentrated among a few so that unless one acts explicitly on behalf of the poor and oppressed, one acts against them. Thus, a fundamental principle in liberation theologies is "the preferential option for the oppressed". Latin American liberation theologians label as "oppression" the inequities and injustices that result from the very way society is structured to benefit the wealthy and to further impoverish or isolate the marginalized. In liberationist perspectives, the groups or entities disempowered by structured oppression are characterised as "the oppressed".[1]

Given the extreme conditions of poverty and violent repression in much of Latin America, identifying the poor and oppressed in that setting is a straightforward process. In North America, doing so is more difficult. Through social analysis, however, feminists have shown that inequalities are structured into capitalist patriarchal society on the basis of factors such as race, gender, class[2] and sexual orientation. More specifically, farm women in Canada have documented the structural in-

equalities that lead to the marginalization of women in agricultural and rural settings, thereby suggesting that farm and rural women are one group of the oppressed.[3] Members of various ecology and environmental movements have pointed to the ways in which the Ecosphere and its associated complex of ecosystems are damaged by the existing agriculture system, indicating that the planetary ecosystem[4] itself is an oppressed entity.

In keeping with the liberationist emphasis on the preferential option for the oppressed, this paper reflects a deliberate attempt to privilege the viewpoints of farm and rural women as well as of ecophilosophers and environmental activists. In addition, it emphasizes another dimension of liberationist perspectives – namely, the centrality of solidarity between groups of the oppressed. The primary objective of this reflection is to balance the expressed interests of rural and farm women with the interests of the ecosystem and its subunits, in order to identify the type of agriculture most able to serve their combined best interests.

Identifying the Oppressed

Farm women have noted various factors leading to their vulnerability in relation to farmers as a group. Most importantly, gender stereotypes continue to negatively affect rural women.[5] Women's knowledge about their farm operations is often not acknowledged.[6] Because so much of farm women's work is also ignored or undervalued, many farm women end up carrying a disproportionate amount of the total workload; working double and triple days; doing on-farm and off-farm work, domestic labour and childcare.[7] Thus gender stereotypes, and the consequent devaluation of farm women's contributions, often lead to unequal workloads between farm men and women.

Gender stereotyping perpetuates additional structural inequalities. Most mainstream farm groups are male dominated.[8] Partially because farm women's contributions and knowledge are undervalued, there is unequal participation by women in agricultural organizations. Since farm women's voices are not clearly heard, farm women do not influence farm policy as much as they could.[9] However, farm policy influences women. Unfair Matrimonial Property Acts and other unjust legislation,[10] combined with a lack of respect for farm women's contributions, result in farm women having limited ownership and control of resources.[11] These structural inequities lead directly to farm women's lower socio-economic status and increased vulnerability to poverty and economic insecurity – in short, to their oppression.[12]

Various ecofeminist and feminist ecological writers have argued that the environment has been intentionally and systematically mistreated in much the same way as women have been.[13] Specifically in reference to agriculture, similar claims have been made about human attempts to master and subdue nature.[14] In this literature, nature (often referred to in current writing as the ecosystem) is characterized as a victim of systemic injustice or, in liberationist terms, of oppression.

Paying special attention to rural women's voices, and to the perspectives of environmental activists, ecophilosophers, and others sensitive to the welfare of the ecosphere, reveals how the existing agricultural system produces and sustains various forms of oppression. In addition, it provides clues as to the most appropriate alternatives.

Styles of Agriculture

Three basic styles of agriculture emerge from the writings of rural and farm women and of members of the ecology and environmental movement who are concerned about agriculture. One form – referred to in this paper as "intensive agriculture" – encourages the use of large, technologically-advanced equipment, along with high levels of herbicides, pesticides and fertilizers, to obtain maximum yields in order that the greatest possible amount of product will be available for export. Organic agriculture is a second farming style. Although there are variations of organic agriculture, all are based on the general principle that farming practices should cause as little disruption to the natural environment as possible.[15] The third style of agriculture is characterised as "moderate agriculture" because it involves the use of moderate levels of fertilizers, pesticides, and herbicides to produce moderate volumes of product, primarily for domestic use rather than for export.

Virtually everyone agrees that the prevailing system is that of high-technology, high-productivity, high-input, export-oriented agriculture. Furthermore, there is general consensus that farmers face increasing pressure to farm in this intensive way. For example, the researchers of one segment of a radio show produced by Canadian farm women cite the words of Dr. Don Rennie, who is the Dean Emeritus of the University of Saskatchewan's College of Agriculture. Rennie maintains that:

> Agriculture must be more high-tech and science based in comparison to low-tech and driven by customer habit. We cannot afford that kind of agriculture any more. No longer can an industry like agriculture depend upon unskilled farm managers.[16]

Rennie, and others in government and industry who gain status, prestige or wealth from their involvement with and support of the agricultural industry, advocates intensification of the current system.[17] However, as discussed in detail below, others who are not benefiting from the dominant system disagree with the intensive agricultural approach.

Farm Women's Criticisms of Intensive Agriculture

Canadian farm women have documented how the

economic theory upon which the current system of intensive agriculture is premised leads indirectly to health problems and directly to poverty and stress among farmers, the decline of rural communities, and environmental degradation. Canadian farm women's analysis shows that in the intensive agriculture system global business elites control who grows, what is grown, how it is grown, how much it is worth, who gets it, and where it is grown. The criterion that determines who grows is competitiveness – defined as the ability to produce the desired product most cheaply.[18] Since labour is the factor over which primary producers have most control, it becomes the variable determining competitiveness.[19] Farm labour, particularly that of women, children, ethnic and foreign workers, is exploited.[20] As a result of the emphasis on competitiveness, farm families lose such "luxuries" as leisure time and holidays[21] and farmers feel forced to treat farming purely as a business rather than as a whole way of life.[22]

In keeping with the criterion of competitiveness, cash crops which provide the highest possible profits for corporations are grown rather than what is needed for local consumption.[23] Because the five major trading companies that control the grain supply are able to affect various factors in the global marketplace, the world grain price is set largely by them. Generally, crops are grown wherever it is most profitable for them to be produced.[24] Crops are also grown so as to maximize production,[25] which means continuous, monoculture cropping,[26] using high technology equipment[27] and incorporating large quantities of fertilizers, pesticides, and herbicides.[28] This style of farming encourages the overuse of costly inputs and expensive machinery.[29] It also leads to surplus production, the consequence of which is lower commodity prices.[30]

Government policies are generally consistent with the demands of global business elites. Competitive, export-oriented agendas are predominant.[31] Ironically, however, many Canadian farmers are not able to survive in the world competition because the low levels of government support they receive (in relation to that received by farmers in the United States and the European Economic Community) leave them with low or negative profit margins.[32] In addition, farmers are affected negatively by the Canadian cheap food policy[33] which is supported by government partially because it wins votes in more densely-populated urban regions.

Consumers benefit from the government supported cheap food policy at the expense of farm families. Because farm families' underpaid and unpaid labour serves as an unacknowledged subsidy[34], consumers do not have to pay the real costs for their food.[35] Most consumers fail to realize that corporations rather than farmers profit from food sales. Furthermore, since their primary concern is the cost of food, consumers tend to buy cheaper, imported products rather than domestic ones.[36] In this way, consumers tacitly support the agenda of global business elites.

Primary producers are at the bottom of the economic system, holding it up. Yet, farmers have no control over energy costs, inflation, interest rates, land prices and freight rates.[37] They must be responsive to regular and futures markets, labour costs, banks and multinationals, government policy and consumer demands. In the system as it is structured, middlemen, speculators and trading companies profit while primary producers are exploited.[38] Because there is an ever-increasing gap between cost of production and return on products,[39] farmers are forced to supplement their incomes with off-farm jobs.[40] Many are required to rent or leave their land.[41] Thus, there is no longer any assurance that farms can be passed on from generation to generation.[42]

Global business elites' encouragement of large-scale, competitive agriculture also threatens the viability of small rural communities. The demise of such communities is accelerated as the land of an increasing number of small farmers who have been squeezed out is concentrated in the hands of fewer larger farmers.[43] Centralization in agriculture leads to the depopulation and decline of rural communities.

Centralization also has negative ecological ramifications. As rural populations shrink and urban populations grow, the demand for land in cities increases. A direct and negative consequence for the natural environment is that farmland is lost to cities.[44] An indirect negative ecological impact of centralization is that farmers who believe they are eventually going to lose their land to cities are unwilling to pay the costs of conserving the soil.[45]

The push toward centralization is only one of the features of intensive agriculture that violently disrupts social and ecological systems. Because of the cost-price squeeze resulting from intense competition, some farmers simply cannot afford to go a year without a cash crop.[46] Continuous cash cropping leads to decreased soil fertility. It also requires increased chemical and fertilizer application levels, which contribute directly to environmental pollution[47] as well as to both long and short term health problems.[48] Monoculture farming (which is also an integral feature of intensive agriculture) has become normal,[49] although it damages the soil[50] and disrupts ecological balance.

Finally, in addition to the negative ecological consequences of the prevailing agriculture system, there is burgeoning evidence of detrimental effects in both individual and social spheres caused by the high level stress experienced over extended periods of time by rural and farm people.[51] Rural people experience health problems which result from stress – conditions derived from chronic stress, accidents which occur because farmers are working under stress, emotional and bodily harm inflicted because of a failure to cope with stress, and suicides which too frequently seem the only way to escape stress. High stress levels within farm families stem primarily from financial concerns.[52] Pressure to remain competitive in a system in which cost of production is higher than the

return on the product is necessarily stress-inducing.[53] So, too, is losing the family farm, or fearing that one may lose one's land and livelihood because of debt.[54] Being unable to afford the time or money required for a holiday,[55] and knowing that longer and longer work days are required in order to stay afloat ensures that there is no reprieve from stress. Seeing businesses close, job opportunities dissolve and local services disappear in small towns extends the stress to the entire rural community.

By reflecting on the impact of the current intensive agriculture system on themselves, their families and the communities of which they are a part, farm women have identified a complex of economic, health and social problems. Farm women's writing suggests that the intensive agriculture system is contributing to, rather than alleviating, the agriculture-related problems.

Environmentalist Critiques of Intensive Agriculture

Farm women who are sensitive to women's welfare have raised serious concerns about the intensive agriculture style of farming. Representatives of various ecophilosophies are equally critical of intensive agriculture.

While some ecophilosophers place particular emphasis on the negative consequences for the natural environment, most members of ecology/environmental groups who deal with agriculture are concerned about a range of social issues. For example, from a deep ecology perspective, Stan Rowe points to the irony in the fact that:

> *Society is moving heaven and earth to save and maintain an exploitative, industrial, export-based agricultural system that has poorly served a large sector of the farming population, while at the same time running down the soils, diminishing surface and subsurface water, destroying natural landscapes and decimating native flora and fauna.*[56]

Similarly, Starhawk, an ecofeminist, is highly critical of economic pressures that encourage the use of technologically advanced equipment to produce large quantities of products for export. Instead of intensive agriculture, she advocates small farms, subsistence food production, and the use of appropriate technology as means of creating rewarding and meaningful work.[57] From a perspective which comes close to that of social ecology, Brewster Kneen critically examines the food system; pointing to the negative social and ecological effects of a linear system that leads to distancing and requires uniformity. Kneen articulates an alternative based on self-reliance and the guiding principles of proximity, diversity and balance.[58] All three ecophilosophers reject intensive agriculture, and support more organic farming styles as means to resolve ecological as well as social problems.

Possibilities for Solidarity

More than a decade ago, Sarah Ebenreck championed a partnership farmland ethic that supported a cooperative approach to solving social and ecological problems. The ethic she advanced, which was rooted in feminist theory, advocated equal acknowledgment of the needs (economic, social and other) of farmers and the needs of the land.[59]

This same kind of cooperative endeavour is still being promulgated by others seeking to establish sustainable agriculture. Stuart Hill, who taught entomology and directed ecological agricultural projects at McGill University has argued that:

We have to stop viewing agriculture through such a narrow window and begin to take into account the relationship between food, health, social justice and the environment. We have to start measuring how many resources we use to produce and distribute our food, the environmental impact of pollutants, the working conditions of people involved in every stage of the process, and the nutritional quality of food.[60]

A very similar perspective is advanced by JoAnn Jaffe, who teaches at the University of Regina. She maintains that, "As we seek to find solutions to ecological problems, we must also talk about sustainable social systems and communities."[61] In Jaffe's opinion, environmental sustainability cannot be achieved unless basic issues of justice and fairness between and within nations are addressed. Both Hill and Jaffe share with Ebenreck and many ecophilosophers an understanding that ecological problems are related to other social problems, and cannot be addressed in isolation.

Points of Conflict Between Ecophilosophers and Farm Women

Although farm women are concerned not only with women's well-being but also with the health and integrity of the ecosystem, and ecophilosophers addressing agricultural issues are concerned with human social problems as well as ecological ones, there are conflicts over which action strategies to support. Many farm women concerned about women's collective well-being and members of environmental and ecology groups agree that the current system of intensive agriculture should be abandoned. However, between ecophilosophers and farm women there are points of disagreement over which alternative to intensive agriculture is most appropriate. The tensions between farm women and members of environmental/ecology movements reflect different views of sustainability.

One level of dispute concerns the setting of priorities – specifically, determining whether farm women and their families or the natural environment ought to be the first target for sustainability. In sharp contrast to some farm "women in Saskatchewan who express the very practical point of view that the first issue of sustainability is to keep the family on the farm,"[62] Rowe insists that "maintenance of the Earth is humanity's first priority."[63] Ecofeminist Catherine Keller agrees with Rowe that the natural environment must be protected since everyone's future depends upon it, and insists that small gains for the poor at the expense of the soil, water and air cannot be condoned.[64] In contrast, some farm women maintain that it is only when farm families feel economically secure that they will be able to think about the long-term needs of the natural environment and their communities. Related to this is the conviction that if family farms are not preserved, control will shift to corporate agribusiness and even worse environmental consequences will ensue.[65] The root of the disagreement is whether the natural environment should be protected in the short-term and farm families secondarily, or whether protecting farm families first will lead to the protection of the natural environment.

A second level of dispute centres on the question of who will pay the costs of a sudden move toward organic forms of sustainable agriculture. Some farm women have expressed concern that without initial changes affecting all farmers, it will be the most economically vulnerable ones who will be harmed by pressures to farm ecologically. For instance, one farm woman reported that in her local community several farmers who chose to act on principles consistent with organic agriculture (by farming less land and avoiding chemical use) lost their farms to others operating on the philosophy of intensive agriculture.[66] Since farm women are sensitive to human costs, they want assurances that they and their families will not bear the burdens of the transition to more sustainable forms of agriculture.

A third area of contention relates to feasibility. Farm women have questioned whether it is not too idealistic to assume that it is possible to move directly into a sustainable agriculture system that attains community well-being, environmental soundness, and just treatment of individuals.[67] Assessing where farmers and those who wield most power in society stand now, it does not seem that the mass revolution required for the realization of Rowe and other ecologists' visions is im-

minent. Without first re-educating people and finding means of enabling farmers to farm more ecologically while ensuring that those who can least afford to do so do not pay the costs, the utopian goals of organic agriculture will not be achieved. Neither will they be attained unless the economic climate is transformed so that all farmers can afford to farm in right relation with the earth.[68] Laudable as they may be, such objectives cannot be achieved overnight. The option for moderate agriculture would entail the development and implementation of strategies to begin to reverse the trends dictated by the intensive agricultural system. For instance, it would involve using the existing political structures to produce legislation capable of reducing the control wielded by global power elites and of producing greater financial equality among farmers.[69]

Forging Alliances

In some ways, supporters of organic agriculture and advocates of moderate agriculture disagree about what is the most effective way to move towards the shared commitments to justice and sustainability. However, despite their different thrusts, the two movements can be compatible. It *is* possible to reject the current approach to agriculture and to affirm the other two options (moderate and organic forms of agriculture) as principled directions. Both seek to reverse the dominant trends, and together they can reinforce one another. The organic option can set the long term visions and goals. The low-input, medium-productivity option can establish interim steps directed toward achieving these ideals.

If they are not perceived to be working at cross-purposes, organic and moderate agriculture can co-exist in the short term. Those who are able to farm organically can "pave" the way, as they are now, for others to do the same. However, the number of farmers committed to farming organically, and financially and practically able to do so, is limited. Transformation to organic agriculture on a large scale will not be possible until other farmers are financially secure enough, consumer demand and support is sufficiently strong, and equitable structures are established. Given the prevailing climate and attitudes, it seems reasonable to expect that arriving at this point will involve incremental stages of transformation – that is, an initial move to low-input, medium-productivity agriculture, followed by a gradual progression towards organic agriculture. Thus, there remains a need to introduce legislation capable of creating a climate in which it is in the best interests of all producers to farm in ways consistent with moderate agriculture. However, rather than being the final goal, this should be the means to accomplish the objectives of organic agriculture.

Understanding the two forms of agriculture to be complementary requires setting two kinds of priorities – those that relate to what is of greater and lesser value or importance, and those that relate to what actions ought to be taken when. It is necessary to distinguish between short-term and long-range goals, but chronological order does not necessarily correspond with relative value. What ought to be done first is not necessarily the same as what is more important in the overall scheme.

Affirming low-input, medium-productivity agriculture, while both providing space for organic producers to continue their innovative program and keeping sight of the long-range goal of creating a climate in which organic agriculture and egalitarian communities flourish, will not conflict with the ultimate objectives of farm women or of members of the ecology/environmental movement. This option is consistent with farm women's desire that the family farm be sustained and that environmental issues be addressed.[70] Combining the two streams of organic and moderate agriculture accommodates both farm women's and ecophilosopher's concerns in a way that the immediate adoption of either an organic or a moderate agriculture model alone would not.

In seeking solutions to the agricultural crisis, it is important neither to impose actions on farm women (and men) which are against their own best interests, nor to focus on human concerns to the exclusion of the environment. Both ecophilosophers and farm women have noted how the intensive agriculture system, which is shaped by the structures of patriarchy and capitalism, distorts human relationships with the rest of the world. An important argument from a social, feminist liberationist perspective is that because farm women have generally been more removed from the power and privileges of capitalist patriarchy[71], they tend to derive fewer direct benefits from the agricultural system and are thus more able to see ways that capitalist patriarchy might be transformed. However, due to the pervasiveness of the structures of patriarchy and capitalism, both farm women and men are trapped into participating in an agricultural system which prevents them from responding appropriately to the natural world. Addressing the ways that capitalism and patriarchy produce various types of oppression will free more farm women and men to see how alternative structures can produce a climate in which ecologically sound agricultural practices do not conflict with their own interests. Thus, one important step in moving *everyone* toward a form of agriculture capable of sustaining the ecosystem as well as just human communities (namely organic agriculture) is to develop policies which address the oppression created by patriarchy and capitalism.

Summary

On the basis of perspectives advanced by farm women and ecologists, in this paper the conclusion is drawn that taking seriously the needs of farm women (and small farm families) and of the ecosystem requires supporting both alternatives to the prevailing, high-production, export-oriented form of agriculture. While the first line of action must be to transform industrial, export-oriented agriculture into a more moderate form of agriculture which limits production and reduces export-dependency, this movement should support the long-term goal of making organic agriculture a viable option for all producers. Well-targeted policy revisions that address the effects of capitalist patriarchy must be made if a shift towards just, sustainable, ecological agriculture is ever to be realized.

ENDNOTES

[1] For an introduction to liberation perspectives, see: Gustavo Gutierrez, A Theology of Liberation, (Maryknoll, New York: Orbis, 1973).

[2] Sheila D. Collins, A Different Heaven and Earth, (Valley Forge: Judson Press, 1974), 161.

[3] As agricultural and farm women describe the problems in their context, they name not only themselves but others as victims. They broaden the identity of the oppressed to include rural and farm men and children, the poor in other parts of the world, and the natural environment.

[4] In this paper I use the term "ecosystem", favoured by Stan Rowe, to emphasize that "Nature" or the "Ecosphere" is an ecological system. See his Home Place: Essays on Ecology, (Edmonton: NeWest, 1990), 76.

[5] Ella Haley, "Getting Our Act Together: The Ontario Farm Woman's Movement" in Women and Social Change: Feminist Activism in Canada, eds. Jeri Dawn Wine and Janice L. Ristock, (Toronto: James Lorimer and Company, 1991), 177.

[6] Nettie Wiebe, Weaving New Ways: Farm Women Organizing, (Saskatoon: National Farmers Union, 1987), 29. Hereafter, this work will be designated as Wiebe, Weaving.

[7] Susan Watkins, What Are You Worth: A Study of the Economic Contribution of Eastern Ontario Farm Women to the Family Farm Enterprise, (produced by Women for the Survival of Agriculture, 1985), 7-21.

[8] Haley, 171-175, 177; 169.

[9] Wiebe, Weaving, 16.

[10] Gisele Ireland, The Farmer Takes A Wife: A Study by Concerned Farm Women, (produced by Concerned Farm Women, 1983), 49. Also see, Watkins, 18.

[11] Jean E. Keet, "Matrimonial Property Legislation: Are Farm Women Equal Partners?", The Political Economy of Agriculture in Western Canada, eds. G.S. Basran and D.A. Hay (Toronto: Garamond Press, 1988), 177-82.

[12] Because rural women have traditionally exerted influence in rural communities, the decline of such communities leads to a loss of their primary means of asserting control. Angela Miles, "Reflections on Integrative Feminism and Rural Women: The Case of Antigonish Town and Country" in Women and Social Change: Feminist Activism in Canada,

eds. Jeri Dawn Wine and Janice L. Ristock (Toronto: James Lorimer and Company, 1991), 60-61. Women are also especially vulnerable to battering and abuse and therefore suffer most from the lack of support facilities for victims of violence. Since rural women are the primary child-caregivers, they are particularly affected by inadequate day care options.

[13] Sherry B. Ortner, "Is Female to Male as Nature is to Culture?" in Women, Culture and Society, ed. M. Z. Rosaldo and L. Lamphere (Stanford: Stanford University Press, 1974), 67-87. Carolyn Merchant, The Death of Nature (San Francisco: Harper and Row, 1989). Rosemary Radford Ruether, Sexism and God-Talk, (Boston: Beacon Press, 1983), 72-92.

[14] Susan Griffin, Woman and Nature, (New York: Harper and Row, 1978), 52-54; Rowe, 163-185.

[15] For some, this means simply that chemicals and fabricated fertilizers ought not to be used. For others, it means using only natural, non-polluting energy sources, emulating natural ecosystems, and designing systems which require minimal intervention. As the degree of comprehensiveness and strictness in adhering to the basic operating principles vary, so too do the techniques involved.

[16] Don Rennie quoted in: Helen Barkley, Wendy Manson and Carol Kernan, "Farm Women: Farm Women and Sustainable Agriculture," part three of Rural Women's Radio Show, aired on Saskatoon Cooperative Radio Station (FM-CFCR), 24 August 1992.

[17] For example, the principles outlined in the Agriculture Canada document, Growing Together: A Vision for Canada's Agri-food Industry, reinforce the direction of intensive agriculture.

[18] Nettie Wiebe, "Cultivating Hope," Briarpatch, February 1991, 21. Hereafter this work will be designated as Wiebe, Cultivating.

[19] Ibid., 21.

[20] Watkins, p. 19, and others point to the exploitation of women and children's labour. Lois Ross notes the exploitation of ethnic and immigrant labourers in her Prairie Lives: The Changing Face of Farming, (Toronto: Between the Lines, 1984), 156-9. Hereafter this book is designated as Ross, Prairie.

[21] Ireland, 56. Womanist, II (Summer 1991), p. 18. Hereafter this work is designated as, Wiebe, Sowing.

[22] Wiebe, Weaving, 29.

[23] Wiebe, Cultivating, 21.

[24] Carole Giangrande, Down to Earth: The Crisis in Canadian Farming, (Toronto: Anansi, 1985), 122; 107-109.

[25] Wiebe, Cultivating, 21.

[26] Giangrande, 109.

[27] Ibid., 109.

[28]Wiebe, Cultivating, 20.

[29]Giangrande, 134.

[30]Vicki Dutton, "Farming in Saskatchewan: The End of a Way of Life", The Womanist, Summer 1991, 15.

[31]Nettie Wiebe, "Sowing Disunity: Canada's Federal Agriculture Policy", The Womanist, II (Summer 1991), p.18. Hereafter this work is designated as, Wiebe, Sowing.

[32]Dutton, 15.

[33]Watkins, 20, 48.

[34]Giangrande, 33-34, 132-134.

[35]Ibid., 102. While farmers generally cite dissatisfaction with Canada's cheap food policy, some also imply that the real issue is that farmers do not receive a fair share of the retail price paid by consumers for food. For example, see Ross's interview of Arlette Gaudet in Prairie, 104-105.

[36]Giangrande, 22.

[37]Giangrande, 28, 72, 68-69.

[38]Wiebe, Weaving, 23.

[39]Ireland, 51.

[40]Giangrande, 100. Also see Wiebe, Sowing, 18 and Watkins, 4.

[41]Dutton, 15.

[42]Giangrande, 39.

[43]Ross, Prairie, 139. Ross notes that prairie farmers who believe in agriculture argue that the loss of small farmers destroys communities, but points out that those in favour of agribusiness believe that bigger is better. In a separate article Ross herself argues that it is "probably impossible to develop sustainable rural communities if we accept the direction of fewer farmers and larger farms . . . [and that] rural communities need more people, not fewer." Lois Ross, "Rural Development," Briarpatch, October 1991, 22.

[44]Giangrande, 71-2.

[45]Ibid., 21.

[46]Ibid., 32, 42.

[47]Wiebe, Cultivating, 20.

[48]Diane Harkin, "Agricultural Chemicals Poisoning our Soil, and Human Water Supply," The Farmgate, November 1987. Also, Miller, 20.

[49]Wiebe, Cultivating, 21.

[50]Giangrande, 109.

[51]Ollie Miller, Sowing Circles of Hope: Support Groups for Older Farm Women in Saskatchewan, (Toronto: Women's Inter-Church Council of Canada, 1990), 20, 30, 37-38; Dutton, 15; Ireland, 28, 52-57.

[52]Watkins, 21 and Ireland, 51.

[53]Ireland, 51.

[54]Giangrande, 43.

[55]Ireland, 51.

[56]Rowe, 89.

[57]Starhawk, "Feminist, Earth-based Spirituality and Ecofeminism" in Healing the Wounds, ed. Judith Plant (Toronto: Between the Lines, 1989), 182-3.

[58]Brewster Kneen, From Land to Mouth: Understanding the Food System, (Toronto: NC Press, 1989), 136.

[59]Sara Ebenreck, "A Partnership Farmland Ethic" in Environmental Ethics, 5 (Spring 1983), 42.

[60]Stuart Hill quoted in Barkley, et al. For a fuller elaboration of his position see: Stuart B. Hill, "Ecological and Psychological Prerequisites for the Establishment of Sustainable Prairie Agricultural Communities" in Alternative Futures for Prairie Agricultural Communities, ed. Jerome Martin (Edmonton: University of Alberta Faculty of Extension, 1991), 197-230.

[61]JoAnn Jaffe, "Sustainable Agriculture in the Third World" in Barriers to Sustainable Agriculture, a publication of the International Agricultural Network [Saskatoon]: Perki's, [1991]), 11.

[62]Barkley, et al.

[63]Rowe does not fault farmers for seeking to survive, but rather the system of agriculture that perpetuates abuse of the ecosystem. Rowe, 171.

[64]Catherine Keller, "Women Against Wasting the World: Notes on Eschatology and Ecology" in Reweaving the World, eds. Irene Diamond and Gloria Feman Orenstein (San Francisco: Sierra Club, 1990), 262.

[65]Questionnaire data documented in Karen L. Krug, "Farm Women's Perspectives on the Agricultural Crisis, Ecological Issues, and United Church of Canada Social Teaching", (Th.D. diss., Emmanuel College and the University of Toronto, 1995), 74-75.

[66]Ibid., 75.

[67]For instance, Barkley, et al point out that inhabitants of farm communities wonder, "Is it possible to have a cleaner environment and chemical free food while farmers face increasing pressure to produce cheaper and cheaper food?"

[68]Currently, even if a large number of farmers could take the risk and move to organic farming, the existing system is not geared to it. Right now, organic foods are part of a specialty market and the trade system does not handle them. Because they have limited competition, most organic companies are able to set their own distribution and marketing structures. However, if more organic products flooded the market, organic producers would simply end up competing against one another in much the same way as other farmers do now.

[69]While space prohibits full exploration of this theme, one example of the kinds of strategies required involves placing caps, based on an upper limit of the number of acres per farmer, on subsidies to farmers. Capping would not only

limit production levels, but could also encourage smaller farm size, and ensure more equitable distribution of government funds. Encouraging limited production would reduce, rather than enhance, the rate of environmental degradation. By reducing the competitive edge of large-scale farmers, it would provide a measure of financial security to small-scale farmers. This would reduce stress generated by financial worries and, in turn, stress-related health problems. It would also stabilize rural communities by maintaining a population base of medium and small-scale farmers.

[70]Moderate agriculture could also correct some forms of racial injustice. By decreasing the North's export dependency, the exploitation (resulting from capitalist imperialism) of indigenous peoples in the South would be reduced. In addition, moderate agriculture would aim to increase the total number of producers, making land accessible to more people and creating possibilities for settling native land claims. Ideally, such interim measures would set the stage for community-based, labour-intensive organic agriculture where unequal access to land would not be tolerated.

[71]The term "capitalist patriarchy" refers to the complex of systemic power imbalances resulting from capitalism and patriarchy.

References

Agriculture Canada; *Growing Together: A Vision for Canada's Agri-food Industry*; Ottawa, Agriculture Canada; 1989.

Barkley, Helen, Manson, Wendy and Kernan, Carol; "Farm Women: Farm Women and Sustainable Agriculture"; Part 3 of *Rural Women's Radio Show*; aired on Saskatoon Cooperative Radio Station (FM-CFCR), 24 August 1992.

Collins, Sheila; *A Different Heaven and Earth*; Valley Forge, Judson Press; 1974.

Diamond, Irene and Orenstein, Gloria Feman,eds.; *Reweaving the World: The Emergence of Ecofeminism*; San Francisco, Sierra Club; 1990.

Dutton, Vicki; "Farming in Saskatchewan: The End of a Way of Life"; *The Womanist*; Summer 1991; 15.

Ebenreck, Sara; "A Partnership Farmland Ethic"; *Environmental Ethics*; 5 Spring 1983; 42.

Giangrande, Carole; *Down to Earth: The Crisis in Canadian Farming*; Toronto, Anansi; 1985.

Griffin, Susan; *Women and Nature*; New York, Harper and Row; 1978.

Gutierrez, Gustavo; *A Theology of Liberation*; Orbis, Maryknoll, New York; 1973.

Harkin, Diane; "Agriculture Chemicals Poisoning Our Soil, and Human Water Supply"; *The Farmgate*; November 1987.

Hill, Stuart B.; "Ecological and Psychological Prerequisites for the Establishment of Sustainable Prairie Agricultural Communities"; In *Alternative Futures for Prairie Agricultural Communities*, ed. Jerome Martin; Edmonton, University of Alberta Faculty of Extension; 1991; pp.197-230.

Ireland, Gisele; *The Farmer Takes a Wife: A Study by Concerned Farm Women*; Introduction by Susan Glover; Concerned Farm Women; 1983.

Jaffe, JoAnn; "Sustainable Agriculture in the Third World"; In *Barriers to Sustainable Agriculture*; A publication of the International Agricultural Network; 11; Saskatoon, Perki's; 1991.

Krug, Karen L.; *Farm Women's Perspectives on the Agricultural Crisis, Ecological Issues, and United Church of Canada Social Teaching*; Th.D. diss., Emmanuel College and the University of Toronto; 1995.

Keet, Jean E.; "Matrimonial Property Legislation: Are Farm Women Equal Partners?"; In *The Political Economy of Agriculture in Western Canada*, eds. Basran, G.S. and Hay, D.A.; Toronto, Garamond Press; 1988; pp.175-184.

Kneen, Brewster; *From Land to Mouth: Understanding the Food System*; Toronto, NC Press; 1989.

Merchant, Carolyn; *The Death of Nature: Women, Ecology and the Scientific Revolution*; San Francisco, Harper and Row; 1989.

Miller, Ollie; *Sowing Circles of Hope: Support Groups for Older Farm Women in Saskatchewan*; Toronto, Women's Inter-Church Council of Canada; 1990.

Ortner, Sherry B.; "Is Female as to Male as Nature is to Culture?"; In *Women, Culture and Society*, eds. Rizaldo, M. Z. and Lamphere, L.; Stanford, Stanford University Press; 1974.

Plant, Judith, ed.; *Healing the Wounds: The Promise of Ecofeminism*; Toronto, Between the Lines; 1989.

Ross, Lois; *Prairie Lives: The Changing Face of Farming*; Toronto, Between the Lines; 1984.

_____; *Rural Development*; Briarpatch; February 1991; pp. 22-23.

Rowe, Stan; *Home Place: Essays on Ecology*; Edmonton, NeWest; 1990.

Ruether, Rosemary Radford; *Sexism and God-Talk: Toward a Feminist Theology*; Boston, Beacon Press; 1983.

Watkins, Susan; *What Are You Worth? A Study of the Economic Contribution of Eastern Ontario Farm Women to the Family Farm Enterprise;* Women for the Survival of Agriculture; 1985.

Wiebe, Nettie; *Cultivating Hope*; Briarpatch; February 1991; pp.20-21.

_____; "Sowing Disunity: Canada's Federal Agriculture Policy." *The Womanist*; Summer 1991; p.18.

_____; *Weaving New Ways: Farm Women Organizing*; Saskatoon, National Farmers Union; 1987.

Wine, Jeri Dawne, and Ristock, Janice L., eds.; *Women and Social Change: Feminist Activism in Canada*; ed. Toronto, James Lorimer; 1991.

ENVIRONMENTAL EDUCATION IN A DEMOCRATIC SOCIETY[1]

23

by Pamela Courtenay Hall

SCHOOLING IS AN IMMENSELY IMPORTANT SITE FOR ethical inquiry, IN PART because schools can profoundly help or harm the human beings who enter them. Inside schools, people are placed in social structures which make them vulnerable to powerful influences in ways both planned and accidental. Schools are <u>designed</u> to make students subject to the influence of educators and administrators (who themselves are subject to the networks of power in which they must operate). And schools <u>tend also</u> to make students subject to peer pressure of a uniquely powerful sort, this by virtue of the large number of often similarly aged students grouped together under the guidance of typically just one adult, usually in ratios exceeding 25 to one. The ethical significance of schooling is heightened in all its dimensions by the fact that most western societies are meritocracies organized around *performance in schools* as a central index of merit; that is to say, people who perform well in schools are likely to have a greater future share in the social and material goods of their society than are people who leave school early or who fare less well in schools. Questions of educational policy and practice thus lead inexorably into questions of distributive justice.

There are deeper moral and cultural significances in schooling as well, which arise not least because schooling occupies a good part of most peoples' so impressionable early lives before they head out into other theatres of social action. The dominant images, values and practices upon which a society rests are sustained by cultural message systems – language, protocols, patterns of reception and response – which must be transmitted from one generation to the next.[2] This transmission begins at birth of course, and pro-

ceeds with great variation. But in schools, it continues with substantially less variation and on a mass scale. Thus, schools are one of the key sites where the transmission can be influenced on a mass scale – where the dominant images, values and practices can be brought to widespread critical awareness at the same time that they are being learned.[3] At the individual level, whatever is or isn't learned in school – whatever is or isn't developed – is carried along by former students as enlightenment, as burden, or as work yet to be done. Schooling experiences thus impact the moral development of students. Even in the worst cases, where schooling registers with students as a nightmare or as a waste of their time, schooling is likely to impact their moral development by damaging it, by inhibiting it, or by accidentally contributing to its taking one path rather than another – even sometimes by accident, a wonderful path. Finally, in the interactions students have with those whose lives they touch – now and in the future – the effects of schooling ripple on.

Taking as a starting point this recognition that schooling matters, I will explore in this chapter some of the ethical issues of schooling related particularly to environmental education. My purpose will be to help stake out what it takes for environmental education to be effective, well-grounded, and democratically justifiable. My focus will be on public elementary and secondary education, but the framework I develop will have many points of application to private, post-secondary and nonformal education as well.

My operating assumptions will include these. First, that the environmental problems of our time are serious.[4] Second, that we all want children to be educated in ways that help them to be intelligent and responsible in their interactions with nature (though we might disagree wildly as to what this consists in). And third, that we all want (or should want) schooling to proceed in ways which will not accommodate anyone's efforts or agenda to indoctrinate students, whether the goal of their indoctrination would be to turn students into corporate apologists, into radical environmentalists, or into dedicated happy consumers. I shall argue that the key step needed for this – the key step needed for environmental education to be and to be appreciated as effective, well-grounded and democratically justifiable – is for all of us – teachers, students, parents, administrators, education critics, concerned citizens, ministry of education officials, frustrated taxpayers – to reckon frankly and critically with the moral education dimensions of environmental education.

'Moral education' is a term that hasn't been very popular in the past two decades, except in discourses calling for a return to "family values" and to pre-Earth Day "three R's". It is a term that many educators try to avoid (using 'values education' instead), and a reality that many people try to pretend away. I think this happens because we in Canada are a society grown up under the janus-faced gift/distortion of liberal individualism. Our long immersion in the rhetoric of individual freedom leads many of us to want to insist that the educational ideals and methods we embrace are the antithesis of social conditioning. But (as I shall argue below) they are not and could not be. Moral education is an inescapable practice in a society of creatures whose lives include moral agency. And social conditioning (better expressed as social cultivation) is inescapably a part of moral education. I will explore these issues in a later section.

Understanding environmental education as moral education will help us to explore the power and limits of environmental education. It will also place us in a better position to understand the ethical issues of class, race, culture, gender and glo-

bal justice that ought to permeate environmental education curriculum and pedagogy, but which are presently too often ignored or unrecognized. These are the issues signified in such questions as: Whose knowledge and whose perspectives are chosen for inclusion in the curriculum of environmental education? Whose are excluded? Which learning styles are assumed? Which are ignored? Whose background learning and interests are given central place? Whose are marginalized? How are classroom problems of race, gender or socio-economic disadvantage dealt with? Does the curriculum include the environmental issues that arise in connection with gender, class, race, culture, justice for indigenous peoples, and justice for less industrialized nations?

These questions of inclusion and exclusion arise in part because they are basic to education, and in part because they come flooding in by related issues of class, race, culture, gender and justice which arise in environmental regulatory policy and practice. (An example of this is the host of ethical and structural issues involved in the fact that people who are poor, working class, or marginalized by race are more likely to be exposed to serious environmental contamination at home and in the workplace than people who are white and middle class.) However, my focus in the present chapter is on making clear the moral education dimensions of environmental education as a first step on the way to locating and dealing with these issues of inclusion and exclusion. The larger project I attempt elsewhere.[5]

In what follows, I will explore the particular importance of environmental education, then turn to an exploration of some of the moral, social and educational issues that make "doing" environmental education as ethically challenging as it is important. To be honest, my hope is not only to get environmental education onto the agenda of environmental ethics, and (conversely) to contribute to explorations of ethics among environmental educators. My hope is also to communicate to any interested and uninitiated reader some of the joys of doing volunteer environmental education in public schools. My current position in this field lies at the intersection of ongoing inquiry in philosophy and environmental thought, many years of lived environmentalism, and a collection of experiences teaching environmental education – as a high school math and physics teacher, as a volunteer educator and storyteller in elementary schools, as a mother, and now, as a teacher of environmental education (and other things) at the University of British Columbia. In what follows, I will be sharing some of my experiences, and some of the many things I have learned from my colleagues in education. But first, a few words on ...

The Importance of Environmental Education

I will begin this section by describing enviromental education as sometimes almost a blind spot in the literature of environmental philosophy. In the next section, I will turn to the work of environmental education theorist David Orr to show that even when environmental education is the focus of theorizing, a related problem of oversight can remain.

Most environmental philosophers believe in the necessity of deep reform. That is, most environmental philosophers believe that there will be no end to present patterns of ecological destruction without fundamental and widespread reform in the beliefs and practices that dominate industrialized societies.[6] Since it usually takes big educational initiatives to help bring such changes about, one might expect strategic and ethical issues in environmental education to loom large in the literature of environmental philosophy. But they don't. Outside of the circles of professional and volunteer environmental educators, one hears little about the strategies, ethical issues, present practices and funding needs of environmental education.[7]

Yet education (effective education) is crucial to the reforms which most environmental philoso-

phers call for – changes in the rates, methods, patterns and assumptions involved in human uses of nature (i.e., in extraction, production, distribution, consumption, disposal and storage). Why is effective education crucial to such reforms? For two reasons. First, these reforms require life changes that are profound for many people in industrialized societies, and counter to the goals instilled in us by that other vast educational system, television and advertising.[8] Second, the reforms require structural changes that take energy, knowhow, and political will to effect. In sum, they involve altered expectations, altered daily life practices, altered work practices, altered regulatory and enforcement practices, altered infrastructures, altered understandings of responsibilities and rights, greater citizen involvement in decision-making and implementation, and even altered taxation systems.

Such changes don't come easily, and in societies based on respect for the individual and respect for majority will, they cannot be imposed on people. So, if the view that deep reform is needed is correct, then education is the primary way to help make it happen ... education in the broadest sense: education in the schools at all levels, education in nonformal settings (e.g., parks, community centres, nature centres), education in adult settings (e.g., community groups, workplaces), education through the news media, education through popular literature, films, theatre, art, even dance and music. But especially in the case of publicly funded schooling, there are questions we need to ask, questions like: Education of what kind? Taught by whom? Who is to be in charge of the curriculum?

David Orr, Professor of Environmental Studies at Oberlin College in Ohio, argues that "It is not education that will save us, but education of a certain kind." He notes that environmental degradation "is not the work of ignorant people. It is rather largely the results of work by people with BAs, BSs, LLBs, MBAs, and PhDs."[9] Using words that Eli Wiesel directed against German education of the early 20th century, Orr argues that U.S. educational institutions (and we could add, many Canadian ones) emphasize "theories, not values, abstraction rather than consciousness, neat answers instead of questions, and technical efficiency over conscience."[10] In place of these, Orr recommends the following as central goals for an adequate environmental education.[11]

1) To help students develop the ecological literacy to 'distinguish between health and disease, development and growth, …, and *should do* from *can do*.'[12]

2) To help students achieve intellectual growth integrated with emotional growth, manual competence, and practical experience.

3) To overcome subject area fragmentation, exploring "life in all its manifestations" by connecting knowledge to its larger context.[13]

4) To provide "a sober view of the world, but without inducing despair" – this against the illusions fostered by a $120 billion advertising industry.[14]

5) To help students unlearn indifference to place and learn to "live well in a place" – to inhabit as caring stewards, rather than merely to reside as user-consumers or as "itinerant professional vandals".[15]

One of the chief practical recommendations Orr makes to accomplish the above goals is to incorporate the full-bodied study of school or campus resource flows (food, energy, water, materials, and waste) as part of the curriculum. Such projects are both pedagogic as well as practical – and indeed, their practicality is an important part of their pedagogic value, encouraging students to develop the awareness, skills and confidence needed to be responsible agents in the places they inhabit.[16]

Democratic Concerns...
According to Orr, education defined around goals

like these is the kind of education that is needed to help us work our way out of the loop of environmental crisis. There is much to be said for such goals, and I share them personally; they are at the core of my own environmental education practices, alongside my concern to help students to sustain and cultivate their sense of wonder.[17] But I wish at this point to focus on the underlying rationale that is often given to explain and justify such goals. It is that deep reform is needed, and that education is the primary way to get us there.

In the context of public schooling, this rationale leaves me feeling a little uneasy. Its starting point – that deep reform is needed – is <u>not</u> one that is shared by the majority of Canadians. This problem can probably be made clearer by using the term 'radical reform'. It doesn't matter that <u>I</u> happen to share the belief that deep or radical reform is needed.[18] Most of my fellow citizens do <u>not</u> share this belief, and so to try to build an educational program around it is to seek to privilege my own convictions over the views of those with whom I supposedly live in democratic cooperation. To be directed by the ideological convictions of a minority of the population … this is not a path that most of us would like to see educational reform take. In particular, those of us on the socialist-antiracist-feminist-environmentalist sides of class, race, gender and environmental issues have much to fear from such a dynamic. It more often serves the interests of the market than the interests of equality. It is also not likely to be effective. Nothing promotes backlash more quickly than launching into the classroom a program whose driving premise the majority of parents reject and may even find threatening. One needs only to teach in a community where resource industries predominate – e.g., a mining or farming or logging community – to understand the potential for this dynamic.

But the fact that environmental problems are serious and the <u>question</u> of whether deep reform is needed to deal with them – <u>this</u> is a more promising beginning. As the starting point of an environmental education program, it admits as controversial that which is controversial in our society, and guides students and teachers to explore it as such. The same learning in ecology, economics, ethics, sociology (etc.) can be pursued with such a starting point, but pursued without requiring a curriculum built upon premises that most Canadians don't accept. Posed as a question rather than an ideological commitment, the issue of radical reform becomes a starting point that asks all of us – environmentalists and environmental skeptics alike, no less than those in between – to approach open-mindedly. And this is the hallmark, I think, of a democratically justifiable starting point for environmental education.

Radical Reform through Public Schooling? Paradoxes and Possibilities

But now another politically charged question about education must be faced: Are public schools places where such radical rethinking of social practices and beliefs <u>can</u> come about? After all, as generations of Marxist and post-Marxist educational analyses have revealed, schools are sites of social reproduction.[19] Just as farms and factories produce the <u>material</u> goods that a society needs for its continued existence, so schools tend to produce the <u>social</u> "resources" and conditions necessary for the society's continued existence. Schools accomplish this by reproducing in students the language, knowledge, skills, work habits, attitudes, values and image-responsiveness necessary to carry on existing social patterns and practices. And so the skeptical question arises. In a society like ours whose "patterns and practices" are based largely on objectifying and exploiting nature, what hope could there be to find effective resources for critiquing environmental practices *within public schooling* – i.e., within the very institution that typically serves to *reproduce* existing patterns and practices?

Social reproduction theorists pose similar questions to those who look to public schools as po-

tential sites for social transformation in other regards – against sexism, racism, classism, homophobia, able-ism, etc. In each case, the question is: How can schools serve the goal of social transformation when studies have revealed the extent to which they serve the goal of reproduction of existing beliefs and practices?[20] Public school critics concerned about environmental education add to this challenge these particular constituent details: How can public schools serve as effective sites for environmental education when so much of what goes on in public schools separates children from nature, teaches them to treat nature as a collection of objects, dampens their curiosity, disengages their senses, and privileges the reading of texts over other more environmentally connected modes of learning?[21]

These are important questions for any of us seeking to understand the large-scale dynamics that make educational reform (and reform through education) so difficult. But in each case, I believe the answer lies in attending more closely to the fine grain of what actually does go on or can go on inside particular schools and particular classrooms, including inside teacher education and professional development programs.

In answer to the criticism that schools are inherently unsuited for environmental education, I think it is important *indeed* to acknowledge the structural limitations that public schools typically impose: standardized curriculum requirements, large student-teacher ratios, textbook and deskwork habits, etc. At the same time, it is unfair not to recognize the efforts teachers have made to move beyond these limits. Indoor and outdoor gardening, nature study and sketching, students writing about their own experiences of place, student-directed research and modeling of animal habitats, student participation in schoolground tree-planting or recycling programs ... these are features which are becoming increasingly more familiar in elementary and secondary schools. And they are features encouraged by recent curriculum developments at provincial levels. There is much room for more, but it is a mistake to think that schools have made no progress in the direction of "environmentalizing" education in the past 20 years.[22]

Key to this progress have been the efforts of particular individuals – teachers, volunteers, consultants and coordinators, often students too – working to make environmental education happen in particular classrooms, particular schools, or across particular school systems. Recognizing these efforts and the possibility for more of their kind is key to averting the dismal forecast which would otherwise press in upon us. Indeed, Osborne, like many others, criticizes social reproduction theory for stressing "the structure of the social and educational system and the constraints it places on people" while neglecting or underestimating "the scope and power of human agency, of the ability of people to resist and even transform the structures within which they live."[23] One of the things we need to do, then, is to make more visible the effects of the agency and resistance that particular people, teachers and others, have exerted for the cause of environmental education – make more visible their local successes against "the social machine". Indeed, there have always been inspired people who have made special things happen in schools. And I think that even in the driest of times in any particular school, the "social machine" is not utterly free to reproduce what it needs in the bodies and minds of our children, because many children are able to sense the contradictions of a badly ordered society in the contradictions they experience in uninspired classrooms. The seeds of emancipatory thinking are sometimes sown by human hands, but other times they rise up through cracks in the flooring ... or drift in through open windows.

Some Examples of Environmental ed. "agency and resistance"
One example of environmental ed. agency grown large and strong is the Colquitz River Watershed

Stewardship Project on southern Vancouver Island. The project began with the work of Leonard Ross, a grade 5 teacher at Strawberry Vale Elementary School who was interested in the idea of the watershed as a unifying theme for environmental education. Ross wanted to confront in his teaching the fact that "We all live in watersheds; we're just not aware of them." And so the path to awareness for his students has come to involve measuring stream water quality and water velocity, studying large invertebrates, birds and trees in the watershed area, and exploring the dangers to streams posed by culverts, ditching and vegetation removal. As it has evolved, students in the project have also participated in tree-planting projects, the removal of invasive species near streams, and salmon incubation projects. In 1996, in its second year of operation, the project involved 26 elementary and secondary schools, enlisting the participation of a few thousand students, 75 teachers, and many parents. It also involved all levels of government and more than 18 community group partners.[24]

But agency and resistance don't have to grow large to have their effects. I have seen children in my own neighbourhood come home from school brimming with excitement about special visits from teachers or volunteers who had shared with them their understanding of trees, of weather patterns, of aquatic life, of gardening. One of my warmest memories is of a young mother whose environmental education contributions centred around teaching young children nature songs. I will never forget how attuned the children seemed learning and singing these songs, which they still sing spontaneously every once in a while, now three years later.[25]

I have also seen the effectiveness of even short classroom visits in my own environmental education efforts in elementary schools. I typically tell stories about events in the lives of plants, insects or animals local to the region. My purpose with these stories is to help children see that these creatures – so different from themselves – nevertheless have needs, efforts, frustrations and flourishings as recognizable as our own. It would be difficult to gauge the effectiveness of nature stories amidst all the other factors of good nurturance and lucky intersections that help children grow to have respect for life.[26] But I see such connection and light in the children's faces during these storytelling times, and I witness such good questions and activities springing out from their hearings and tellings of stories, that as a practitioner, I have all the evidence I need. The capacity that children have for attunement and spontaneous care is one of the greatest sources of the grounded hopefulness that keeps me going, living as I do – *living as we all do* – in a society still configured to set economic power and environmental respect at odds with each other.

Efforts of volunteers to engage students in environmental education are common in schools today, in part due to the increasing emphasis which teachers, school boards and education ministries place on parent and community involvement. [27] Some efforts are even part of the mandate of government and non-profit organizations. For example, Bill McCuaig, a community forester for the District of West Vancouver, visits classes to teach students about the ecology of local trees. Denise Philippe, a Vancouver environmental educator, works for the nonprofit organization "City Farmer," visiting primary classrooms to teach children about composting with worms.

In between large-scale stewardship programs and short-term class visits, there are a host of other promising things happening in environmental education at schools across Canada. School resource flow studies are becoming an increasingly visible enterprise at all grade levels. The most popular version in elementary schools seems to be in the area of paper recycling and lunch waste reduction. Such projects, when done well, serve all five of the goals Orr identifies as crucial to effective education (see above). They provide students with

the opportunity to do interdisciplinary study of things happening right in their own school (goal 3) for the sake of assessing the ecological state of their school's operations (goal 1), and doing something about it if they discover problems (goals 2,4 and 5).

There are critical concerns to keep in mind, however. First, these projects need to sustain student commitment if they are to avoid becoming a mere translation of student environmental concern into more work for school maintenance staff. Second, they need to be well thought out if they are to challenge rather than augment problems of class, race and gender bias; similarly, if they are to educate rather than divert environmental concern.

For example, home and school greening initiatives conceived too narrowly (e.g., limited to lunch waste reduction) can end up focusing critical attention on the activities of homemakers and away from ecologically problematic ideologies, social relations and economic and political structures. The problems here are threefold. First, as Catriona Sandilands has observed, if environmental responsibility is seen as focusing on household behaviour, "then it is women's lives that come under the most intense scrutiny."[28] Second, as Sandilands notes, such a focus on individual behaviour can impede the development of broader critical social awareness; "it turns politics into actions such as squashing tin cans, morality into not buying overpackaged muffins, and environmentalism into taking our own cloth bag to the grocery store." That environmental reform might require collective action and deep structural change is not a part of this picture. Finally, the green consumer focus that is often part of such an individualistic, lifestyle-focused environmental morality is class-biased. As Sandiland notes, "Try telling a woman on welfare with three children to 'consume less,' let alone to 'buy green'."[29] The educational point of all these concerns is that students should be encouraged to direct their critical attention to the full range of likely contributing sources of environmental problems, neither restricting it to problems of individual behaviour, nor deflecting it from social and global structures that may privilege us by disadvantaging others.

But it's definitely a good idea in general to reduce lunch waste! And even better if the students take responsibility for it.

Environmental Education as Moral Education

I want to turn now to explore an ethical problem more endemic in environmental education, and in some ways deeply related to problems of class, race, culture and gender bias. This is the problem of *education vs. indoctrination,* which I will get at by way of some general observations about curriculum.

One of the central lessons of curriculum inquiry is that the overt curriculum is only one source and not always the major source of the learning that students do in schools. Much of what they learn comes via "the hidden curriculum" (or, "the implicit curriculum"); i.e., from the ways in which classrooms are structured and school buildings designed; the ways in which teachers interact with students; the ways students are expected to interact (or not interact) with each other; the ways in which the school day is organized; the emphasis placed on competition or cooperation, obedience to authority or independent thinking, artistic efforts, team sports or community volunteering, working with texts or working with people and projects; etc. In short, much of the learning that students do in schools comes not from the overt curriculum which teachers, textbooks and class exercises aim to develop, but rather, from the various school and classroom policies and traditions that shape the schooling experiences of young people ... policies and traditions involving how to eat, talk, sit, how to be (behave) in the classroom, how to be (behave) in the playground, how to locate oneself in the school community. These policies and traditions are no less about gender,

race, class and culture. And they *percolate* with issues of separation or integration, equity or disparity, marginalization or affirmation.[30]

The reality of non-overt teaching is now so widely recognized (even in sites so supposedly value-free as math classes and typing classes) that it has become commonplace among educational theorists to claim that all education involves moral education. Bowers 1995 goes even further. Bowers argues that the very learning of a language involves the transmission of the worldview and moral distinctions embedded in the language.[31] He concludes that all education is moral education. I find this conclusion tempting for this further reason: I think that for human beings of functioning levels of consciousness and mental abilities, *all experience is moral experience* (whether we admit it or not). From this it would follow that all arrangement of experience is arrangement of moral experience, a point crucial to this argument since education is the arrangement of students' experiences to achieve certain ends of learning. And I think that the arrangement of moral experience is most certainly a moral undertaking (indeed, since arranging things is itself an experience, hence, a moral experience). Thus we have it that all education is moral education ... both from the vantage point of the teacher and from the vantage point of the student ... if you accept the challenging assumption that all experience is moral experience!

Whatever the case at these outer limits, in its more careful articulations, the conclusion that all education involves moral education is difficult to resist. It has similarly been argued that all education involves environmental education.[32] I will scurry us over this terrain to bring us to the main concern of this section: how to deal with the moral education dimensions of environmental education, and the ethical issues that arise from them.[33] First then, the notion that all education involves environmental education, which I will get at by way of (again) some general observations on curriculum … this time, the explicit curriculum.

Yes, the *explicit* curriculum also does its share of *invisible* teaching. As educational theorists have long established, students learn not only by what is included in the curriculum, but also by what is left out.[34] Our omissions communicate to our students either (A) where the boundaries of Reality lie, or (B) where the boundaries of Knowledge worth bothering about lie, or (C) where the boundaries of their teachers' mandate, freedom, awareness, or energy lie. Students tend to advance from A to B to C as they rise from primary to elementary to secondary school, but sadly, this doesn't happen for everyone. Thus, in classrooms where nature is never discussed as anything more than *background of human action, object for human study* or *resource for human use*, some students may not graduate beyond this limited view. And when, outside the classroom or later in life, these students come to encounter hints or rumours that nature is something more than just *background, object* or *resource*, there is a good chance that the weight of educational authority will press these rumours away as unReal or not worth bothering about. The general point to be gathered here is that even educational programs and curricula that never raise a question about human-nature relations end up doing environmental education – by omission, as it were.

In short, all education involves environmental education, because all education either explores notions of human-nature interactions, or leaves prevailing notions unexplored or even unmentioned, hence quite likely reinforcing them via the *im*plicit curriculum. Regarding the latter case, there is clearly an educational loss in this environmental-education-by-omission. It involves a closing off of tremendous opportunities to help young humans find meaning in nature beyond what they readily find inscribed there by the patterns of human use that are dominant in their society. Does this loss of meaning entail larger consequences too? In particular, can we claim that

the cost of such lessons by omission is likely to register as a loss of potential environmental responsibility on the part of these students?

I don't think we can claim this, at least not easily. That is, I think many considerations have to be taken into account in order to support the claim that the loss extends that far. The question of what kind of value needs to be ascribed to nature in order to ground environmental concern is a question that has been debated for two decades in the literature of environmental ethics. Some argue that only an ethic attributing *intrinsic value* to nature (i.e., value in itself, apart from its usefulness to humans) is adequate to safeguard the range of environmental concerns that comprise the overlapping consensus of environmentalists. Others argue that enlightened but nevertheless human-centred views of nature are adequate to these concerns. Even beyond these philosophical issues, there are the psychological issues of human motivation to consider. So no quick conclusions about potential environmental responsibility are in order here.[35]

Nevertheless, environmental-education-by-omission clearly involves a loss of a chance to find more meaningfulness in the world than can be found in worldviews that recognize nature only as object. And this is a loss that public schools are neither obliged nor entitled to exact upon students. And so the question arises: What are the contours of the public school's responsibility in these most acutely moral dimensions of environmental education?

Some Problematic Approaches to Environmental Education

It may help at the outset to note a few problems that arise from efforts to overlook or to avoid the moral dimensions of environmental education. I have discussed these issues over the past four years with roughly 400 pre-service and in-service teachers whom I have met in UBC programs or in my visits to schools in Vancouver and in southwestern Ontario. Some of these teachers (a small but significant minority) [36] feel convinced that the science of ecology gives such strong warrant to a holistic understanding of nature that they believe the claims of radical environmentalism to have scientific authority behind them.[37] They thus feel justified in doing environmental education that is decidedly environmentalist, their goals being to change attitudes and to promote environmentally friendly behaviour. Their lesson plans thus involve little exploration of conflicting views.

This approach is found among environmental education researchers as well. As Robottom and Hart have shown (1993), the promotion of attitudinal and behavioural change (coming from various ideological viewpoints) has been a dominant and often unquestioned theme in several prominent forums for environmental education research. They note its steady presence in the *Journal of Environmental Education* from its inception, with such a lack of consideration of critical, interpretive and participatory understandings of education and research that they describe this research orientation as behaviouristic.

It is important to note that the subset of teachers and researchers who embrace this "ecology as warrant" strategy is not coterminous with the subset of teachers and researchers whose views are radically environmentalist. Some teachers who are themselves committed environmentalists neither try to push their beliefs onto their students nor think of the sciences of ecology as giving anyone warrant to do so. And on the other hand, I have met up with teachers and researchers who seem to follow the "ecology as warrant" strategy yet who are committed only to the mildest of environmental reforms, and who believe that no consideration of competing views needs to be built into their environmental education lesson plans or research – not only because their environmentalist teaching goals are so mild in degree, but also because to whatever extent their goals are not mild, ecology has anyway given them the go-ahead.

At the other side of the spectrum, some of the teachers I have met (again, only a minority, but again, a significant minority) are so convinced that environmentalism is detrimental to economic prosperity and human progress that they similarly feel that their views about environmental issues have the weight of some kind of authority behind them – in this case, the authority of common sense and economic necessity. As a result, their lesson plans are similarly geared more towards attitude promotion rather than toward (a) exploration of students' views and (b) fair and critical consideration of competing views.

In both cases – i.e., both for teachers who adopt the ecology-as-warrant approach and for teachers who adopt the economics-as-warrant approach – there are problematic risks along several fronts. First, both sides overlook the fact of conflicting perspectives within each of their respective, presumed-authoritative sciences. (There are many different research programs, and many different ideological orientations, to be found in the sciences of ecology. Ditto in economics.) Second, both sides overlook the complex interrelationships between science and values. (Values cannot be read out of science as if they exist out there in the world and are merely discovered by scientists through neutral observation. As decades of feminist and critical inquiry into science has shown, the values built into scientific practices reflect the cultural and ideological orientations of the people who have chosen for various reasons to devote a part of their lives to those practices.[38]) Third, both sides overlook the moral education dimensions of environmental education. Before delineating these dimensions, I will describe a similarly problematic approach, the "avoidance approach", which I have found to be fairly common, indeed more common than the "warrant" approaches.[39]

The "avoidance approach" to environmental issues and values is taken by teachers who think it best to avoid dealing with value issues in the classroom. For some, this arises because they haven't had the chance to do much pre-service or in-service exploration of ways of dealing with value issues, which indeed is a difficult task, as anyone who has ever tried it knows. The avoidance approach is typically sustained by the conviction that learning is more often sidetracked or interrupted by controversy than enhanced by it. And this view is particularly strong in communities hot in the midst of environmental disputes. In communities not embroiled by environmental conflict, most of the teachers I have met who take the avoidance approach also have the conviction that their own environmental values are sufficiently in line with majority views, and majority views sufficiently nonproblematic, that there is little danger of unwittingly influencing students' beliefs in ways that could be characterized as indoctrinating. To the extent that their classes are involved in environmental education via omission and via hidden curriculum, their operating assumption seems to be that whatever students happen to learn in their classes would be nothing but common sense anyway.

Teaching strategies characteristic of the avoidance approach include exploring only the simplest and least controversial of environmental matters with students (e.g., exploring "Why should we recycle?"), or exploring issues distant from the school community (e.g., the preservation of species on distant continents). A major problem with both of these strategies lies in the area of educational potential lost. Children and young adults have much to learn and much to gain in the exploration of their own and others' views on complex and controversial issues. Learning how to deal with value differences is essential to healthy human communion and democratic social processes. Further, to deal with issues close to home is to help students understand the community they live in – even the family or neighbourhood disputes they might be troubled by – and it can provide opportunities for students to learn about taking responsible action in their community.[40]

The Moral Education Dimensions of "Reflective Environmental Education"

Dealing with values and local environmental issues in the classroom isn't easy, and the dangers of slipping into classroom chaos, or of slipping from environmental education to environmental advocacy of a problematic sort, or of being unfairly accused of doing so, are enough to make many teachers want to avoid the slope altogether. I think it helps in dealing with these problems to have a clear view of the full range of moral education that teachers already actively engage in simply by teaching anything at all. For example, all teachers come to the classroom with an array of expectations (more or less clearly thought out) regarding student behaviours, attitudes and values, and the methods which they as teachers will use to communicate (and negotiate) these expectations. In environmental education, teachers similarly have some idea of the kinds of behaviours, attitudes and values which they believe they ought to help students cultivate, ranging from those standard to good education (e.g., cooperating with others, open-mindedness, respect for other people) to those particular to environmental education (which I hope we will someday think of as part of "good education" in general): e.g., avoiding wastefulness, awareness of environment, appreciation of place, and respect for all forms of life.[41]

The idea that teachers ought to try to help students cultivate certain habits and values (and overcome certain others) fell dramatically out of fashion in the 1970's amongst teachers trying to live up to the demands for freedom from authority characteristic of the era. But even these teachers had a moral education agenda: they clearly tried to encourage independent thinking in their classes. In other words, they were concerned to help their students cultivate the virtues requisite to independent thinking. In short, the reality of moral education persisted even when the rhetoric was against it.

Since that period, an educational movement known as 'Character Education' has developed. Embracing the fact of life that teaching involves moral education, the Character Education movement focuses on developing and sharing strategies to help young students cultivate the attitudes and values that are basic to democratic citizenship.[42] Of course, there are controversies in defining what these are. But it is possible to identify some basically agreed upon values, such as:

♦ respect for others

♦ care for others

♦ concern for community interests

♦ open-mindedness

♦ commitment to reflection and dialogue

♦ commitment to responsible action

♦ courage to express one's views on important issues.

These give us at least a widely agreed-upon core to constitute a basis for teaching practice and further discussion.

Of course, the problem at the heart of the democratic justifiability concern reveals itself in the very words I have used. I include on this list, 'respect for others'. The question immediately arises, is 'others' to include more than just people? In discussing values particular to environmental education a paragraph earlier, I had included 'respect for all life forms' on my list of examples. Here the tension between my concern for democratic justifiability and my commitment to deeper understandings of human/nature relations becomes acutely evident, because many people in Canadian society resist or reject the view that all forms of life should be respected. And this goes far beyond the complication of people having different conceptions of what respect entails. Some people draw the line of moral considerability to include only people, some go beyond that to include "higher" animals, some would include all animals, and some would even include forests,

plants and rivers.

Democracy-education tensions of this sort arise whenever societies become permeated by problematic structures and practices and there are individuals around in teaching positions who recognize the problems and want to help deal with them. But my believing my society to be badly ordered is no guarantee that it is, and my having an alternative vision for it is no guarantee that my vision is a good one. This is why democratic constraints on educational practice are so important. The great value of recognizing the cultivation approach is that it at least brings these democracy-education tensions into view. It directs us to *think* and *care* about whether the particular values and virtues that we do try to help our students cultivate are those which we are entitled to promote in our positions as teachers placed by public trust into positions of potentially coercive authority over students in a society[43] committed to democratic principles. Are there standards to appeal to outside of those internal to our society and to which we should hold our own society's values accountable? Yes, I would argue. These would include reckoning with the effects of our societies' values and practices *on other societies* and *on the earth*. This is often the source of the moral grounds for engaging on the radical education side of democracy-education tensions in environmental education. It's important to note that this pedagogical problem can often be avoided by using critical thinking "paths of escape" – i.e., asking students to subject likely problematic dominant values to their own scrutiny. But these paths may not be possible in every situation where teachers have to decide which values and virtues they should be helping students to cultivate. When they are not available, we can at least acknowledge this democracy-education tension and commit ourselves to the ongoing task of dealing reflectively with it. My own work on this task, both in theory and in practice, is still in progress.

There are, I think, four dimensions of moral education which are crucial to effective and democratically justifiable environmental education. The cultivation approach described above is one such dimension. Another, the clarification approach, focuses on connecting with students' experiences and concerns, and helping them to explore their own beliefs and values. This is the approach that came to dominate in the 1970's and 80's when many teachers were deeply concerned to avoid the blatant moral and political indoctrination that had been common in education in preceding decades. Known as the "values clarification movement", this approach was inspired by the work of American philosopher John Dewey, who noted almost a hundred years ago that effective teaching had to begin where the student is at, linking the curriculum to be learned to the students' experiences and interests.[44] Dedicated no less than Dewey to promoting critical reflection, the movement's founder, Louis Raths, believed that this was best achieved by asking reflective questions of students.[45] But the movement came to lose the critical perspective that had prompted it, and came eventually not only to reflect but also to fuel the naïve sort of relativism that became widespread in the 1970's, a relativism that Dewey and Raths alike would have abhorred.

As the critical purposes that inspired the program became lost in much of the practice, the values clarification movement combined with the general permissiveness of the era to leave many teachers feeling powerless to influence the moral development of their students. In the absence of a right to tell students what they should think, it was concluded that the only thing they could legitimately do was to encourage students to express their opinions. This was intended at least to give students a chance to get clear about what they actually do happen to think, and to hear about what other students think. The motto of the era could have been: "Everyone is entitled to their own opinion." (The grammar of this motto, which I fear we

may come to accept, may, in this context, have a ring of ironic truth to it.)[46]

But many educators rejected this motto. After all, they reasoned, some opinions simply are better founded than others. And some opinions are downright immoral (e.g., it's okay for me to steal from my classmates as long as I don't get caught). So we are not all equally entitled to our opinions. Some of us need to have them challenged. Again, this was supposed to happen in values clarification programs, both through the teacher's astute asking of open-ended questions (e.g., "What would happen if everyone took that approach to life?") and through dialogue with peers. But too often, it didn't.

Awareness of these facts was a large part of the concern that led to the critical thinking approach to moral education. This approach arose most directly out of the recognition that a considerable range of moral experience involves the consideration of reasons for the various moral choices and commitments that might be possible for us. A critical thinking approach encourages students to explore such reasons in the context of exploring general issues, case studies, and particular issues facing them in everyday life. Its methods include the kinds of questioning and dialogue found in the clarification approach, but it keeps evaluative goals central, helping students to reason about moral issues and to evaluate their own and others' views critically and open-mindedly.[47]

But moral experience does not depend entirely upon reason. There may, in fact, be regions of moral experience that are beyond the reach of rational discourse. In any case, recent work in moral philosophy, psychology and feminist theory has made it clear that one's moral judgement in any particular situation is tremendously dependent on how one perceives the situation, including how well one can empathize with the individuals involved. Further, perception and empathy depend upon a range of attunements which are deeply influenced by social location and which develop over time. Yet the role played by perception and empathy in moral experience has been vanishingly underestimated in mainstream western moral theorizing, registering strongly only in the streams of naturalistic moral philosophy that flowed against the dominant current.[48] And this philosophical neglect has been repeated in an educational neglect of moral perception and empathy as important pedagogical aims. Trying to turn this trend around, feminist and other educators have explored strategies for helping students to develop their perceptual and empathic capacities through in-depth learning about the experiences of others through such teaching strategies and resources as: small- and large-group sharing of experiences; guest speakers; documentaries; biographies and novels; etc.

I call this approach the moral perception approach. It is particularly exciting in the context of environmental education because of the important questions it highlights regarding human knowing, perception, human-nature relations, and educational possibilities. Much educational practice in western societies has been formed around the assumption that knowledge is the result of a human individual appropriately processing the chaotic array of perceptions that experience brings to him. If, however, perception is a much more preattuned and trained capacity than this account acknowledges, then it may be that education can be greatly improved by adequately focusing on helping students develop their perceptual capacities. An exciting array of research programs flows together in this concern: feminist reconceptualizations of epistemology and moral experience, ecological theories of perception developed in psychology, eco-philosophical explorations of perception and moral experience, and ecological theories of education. [49]

Yet to seek to expand students' empathic understanding of life without first exploring with them their present understandings would be odd

and presumptuous. Hence the importance of the second approach mentioned above, the clarification approach. Indeed, none of these approaches would get off the ground effectively were students not early on personally engaged with the curriculum which the teacher wishes to develop. The clarification approach does this by connecting with students' backgrounds and understandings right from the start. (See the examples in Appendix A.) I should add that for the teacher to exclude herself from consideration as someone who also has some expansion to do would be to commit the sin of pedagogical arrogance.

In sum, these four dimensions of moral education are: cultivation, clarification, critical thinking, and moral perception. Clearly, any one of these approaches, conducted well and with democratic and emancipatory goals in mind, will inevitably involve the other three. In particular, the cultivation approach could clearly comprehend the other three approaches simply by a full enough accounting of the virtues to be encouraged among students and the means needed to accomplish this. But each approach highlights aspects of moral experience and features of effective teaching not given central place in the others. Hence they are worth identifying separately. (These approaches and the methods they spur are summarized in the chart in Appendix B.)

The point of this mapping of moral education is to illuminate the dimensions of moral education which are clearly and justifiably part of good teaching, part of helping children and young people grow well. The call for environmental education to avoid the boundary between 'education' and 'indoctrination' must be informed by a realistic sense of the ways in which the teacher's job rightly requires that certain virtues, values, attitudes and habits be marked out as those which students ought to be helped to develop. But as the earlier history of Canadian education sharply illustrates, "training in the virtues" can go too far. This is where the clarification and critical thinking approaches to moral education are crucial. They contain inventories of ways for teachers to engage moral issues (including environmental ones) with their students *without* falling into miseducative forms of relativism (e.g., "Okay, that's your opinion. Now let's hear from someone else") and *without* falling into unwitting exercises in moral indoctrination.[50]

'Bad' Environmental Education ... and 'Good'

As I noted earlier, whether by inclusion or by omission, curriculum and teaching typically involve lessons about human-nature relations, and so it has widely been claimed that all education is environmental education. It has also been claimed by many environmental educators that all education which reinforces human/nature dualism and nature instrumentalism is bad environmental education.[51] I think this is a claim that needs some visiting – not that I think it is wrong, but I think it is important to state the problem more precisely, so that our cure for it is not simply to reverse the poles.

What makes environmental education that reinforces instrumentalism bad is not exactly that it teaches the wrong view. It's not as if environmental education should be aiming for indoctrination, only in this case, it has unfortunately chosen the wrong ideology. Education should not be in the position of teaching any particular environmental ideology on such terms; i.e., for the sake of producing converts. It should rather be in the business of exploring the many different views of human/nature relations that populate our world, examining both the wisdom and the contradictions, the values and the problems, to be found in all of them. The questions of ethics, ecology, anthropology, psychology, economics, political science, history, geography, art, literature, epistemology and ontology that are part of environmental philosophy are important questions for students to engage with. Answers to them ought not be taught via the questions never being raised (i.e., teaching by omission, reinforcing the status quo through

silence). But neither ought answers to these questions be taught as *revelations*. The questions of environmental philosophy as they are experienced by each student are not something that the teacher or the education ministry has the answers to. Recognition of this lies at the heart of ecological approaches to education.[52]

This is a point missed by some environmental education theorists, who are understandably eager to make change happen. But live issues have to be presented as live issues if schools are to live up to the requirements of democratic education. The outer lineaments of appropriate human/nature relations may be settled in the minds of many environmentalists and many pro-industrialists, but they are not settled issues in most democratic societies today. They are rather characterized by the same degree of pluralism that we see on abortion, on free trade, and on other fronts. Public schools are thus obliged to present these issues as issues to be explored responsibly and open-mindedly. This includes ensuring that all perspectives on an issue get a fair representation in curricular sources, a fair hearing in classroom discussions, etc.

There are also pragmatic reasons for environmental education teachers to be careful to give exploration of human-nature relations as open and balanced a format as can be done. These include the more obvious considerations of not upsetting colleagues, administrators or parents or students with lesson plans that could be interpreted as unfairly biased. But they also include end-goal considerations. For example, those students most in need of reflecting on human-nature relations – those who are caught up in consumerism and dismissive of environmental concern – are not likely to encounter the promotion of environmentalist values in the classroom as beckoning. But if the questions could be raised as the open and compelling questions that they are, then real learning becomes possible even for students who are environmental skeptics. Not, "Listen, class, here's what's wrong with thinking that nature is just a collection of objects to serve human needs," but rather, "What is nature? How is nature represented in the books you have read, in the television programs and films you see, in the music you listen to? Do you know of anyone whose attitude to nature is similar to yours? Do you know of anyone whose attitude to nature is very different from yours? Interview this person to find out what reasons or experiences has led this person to hold attitudes so different from your own." Appendix A lists some particular examples to help students enter into these questions. These examples provide a quick profile of what we get when we bring environmental education "beyond the three R's" – "Reduce, Reuse, Recycle" – to include this important fourth: Reflect.

The challenges of educating without indoctrinating won't go away for environmental educators – myself included.[53] They mandate constant attention to curriculum and teaching method in terms of fairness, accuracy or appropriateness, inclusiveness, and maintaining a healthy balance between (A) the forthrightness needed for modeling such democratic virtues as standing up for one's beliefs and subjecting them to scrutiny, and (B) the functioning neutrality needed to avoid abusing the power of the teaching position.[54] Even if our practices could be perfect (which I doubt), there would remain the constant challenge of responding to problems of perceived bias.

And here, I must say that there have been several times in my own teaching career when I have been confronted by students with problems of perceived bias in some part of my teaching. On most of these occasions I have searched and (much to my unsettlement) I have discovered correlative problems of unrecognized bias in some part of my *thinking*. It's not that I'm a bad person. It's just that I'm not omniscient. Such moments of criticism and consequent growth are hard to adjust to at first, but they can seem, a year or two later, like *gifts*. This is one of the most profound ways in which teachers learn from students no less than students learn from teachers.

Appendix A

SOME EXAMPLES OF REFLECTIVE ENVIRONMENTAL EDUCATION ACTIVITIES

Example 1 (For students at all levels, including post-secondary; even pre-school children can accomplish parts of this project): (1) First, ask students what particular places mean to them (their home, the schoolyard, a nearby field or forest or river). They could explore these meanings through journal writing, poetry, stories, letters to their mother, father, a distant relative or a friend, or through sketching, painting, photographic installations, sculpture, etc. (2) Have students share their different experiences with each other, in pairs, small groups, or with the whole class. (3) Then have students explore a wide range of media and literature – from environmentalist to resourcist, perhaps even including local planning proposals, real estate brochures, home gardening and redecorating magazines, documentaries and films – so that they can hear different perspectives on the significance of place. (5) Have students evaluate these perspectives in terms of criteria collectively developed by them in collaboration with you for this purpose.

Example 2 (For students in grades 3 to post-secondary): Have students interview a wide variety of local people, especially including elderly people, to find out what a particular local field, park, forest, river, or their backyard (etc.) means to them. Next: Compare the various perspectives which students have drawn together, identify recurrent themes, and evaluate the significance of such perspectives to the welfare of the community, first or simultaneously exploring what the factors of community welfare might be. (A question to raise: Should the land be considered part of the community?)

Example 3 (For students in grades 3 to 7): Have students create stories, poems or plays focusing on the life of a particular local animal or insect in its interaction with a human being who doesn't understand the creature or who doesn't value its life or who is engaged in projects that identify the insect as a problem – a child frightened by it, or a child wanting to catch it for some reason, or a gardener or picnic-goer annoyed by it, or a farmer having to deal with an infestation of its kind. The story or play is to include the perspective of the creature (as imagined by the student) as well as the perspective of the human being. Next step: Ask students to do some research on the creature of the story to teach the rest of the class some interesting things about it. Next step: After students read their stories or poems or perform their plays, have them compare the various perspectives they have collectively portrayed. Are any of the perspectives clearly right? Clearly wrong? Which are in need of rethinking or better understanding? Are there important considerations left out of some of them?

Other kinds of examples:
Studies of school resource flows and schoolground and regional ecology are briefly discussed in the preceding pages. For details, see Beer 1996 and my "Beyond the Three R's: Dealing with values and issues of class, race, culture, gender and global justice in environmental education" (manuscript in progress).

Some examples of more traditional critical thinking approaches to environmental education involve student research on particular environmental issues in preparation for classroom debate, or for role-playing in a pretend city council meeting, or for role-playing in a pretend environmental review board hearing, etc. For a detailed discussion of these approaches, including some criticisms to keep in mind, see Courtenay Hall, "A critical thinking approach to environmental education … and its limits" (in preparation for *the Canadian Journal of Environmental Education*).

Appendix B
DIMENSIONS OF MORAL EDUCATION

The Dimension or Approach	The Aim	Methods (All involve teacher & peer role modelling)
CLARIFICATION ("Values Clarific'n Movement" 1960's/70's; Links to constructivist approaches to education 1980's/90's)	To help students to clarify and reflect on the values which they hold, by articulating them, sharing them with others, and listening to the views of others.	Open-ended questions, activities and group discussions to: 1) Elicit views and values. 2) Encourage listening, comparison & reflection. 3) Encourage clearer understanding of the contours and limits of one's own views.
CULTIVATION (Spectrum from ed'n for democratic citizenship to ... indoctrination) {Links with Virtue theory, communitarianism}	To help students develop the values, beliefs and virtues they will need as members of a democratic society. **To what end? ...** i) To get ahead in the world? ii) To become cooperative and productive workers? iii) To grow as intelligent and caring social beings?	Encouragement, praise, questioning. Extrinsic rewards, enforcement & consequences. Teacher & peer examples. Stories & films with role-model value (incl. critical). Cooperative group, team or class projects. Community work. Experiential education. Situations encouraging the exercise of virtues.
CRITICAL THINKING {Emphasis on the role of reasoning and judgement in moral experience}	To help students learn to make and to act on reflective and responsible decisions. To help students appreciate the role of reason in moral experience.	List of reasons for/against. Research, discussion & role-playing to explore the reasons behind differing points of view. Learning critical concepts. Evaluating one's own and others' reasons; e.g., "Principle Testing" (see Coombs 1980)
MORAL PERCEPTION {Links with feminist, hermeneutic and ecological rethinkings of self, knowledge, and moral experience}	To help students develop their capacities to recognize and appropriately respond to the moral features of situations. *In other words:* To help students develop their capacities for **moral perception, caring, and imaginative empathy.**	Small, supportive group discussion of life experiences, of particular issues, and of ... ... stories, speakers, films, documentaries, plays, art, interviews, field trips, community work... GOAL: Exploration of one's own standpoint, own present limitations of empathy, & the hopes and struggles of others.

{An earlier version of this chart appears in Courtenay Hall 1996.}

ENDNOTES

[1] I am grateful to my colleagues and graduate students in the Department of Educational Studies at UBC and elsewhere, from whom I have learned a great deal about educational issues. I would especially like to thank: Jerrold Coombs and Ian Robottom for the valuable influence their work has had on my understanding; Alex Wellington and Allan Greenbaum for their insightful editorial advice and for encouragement that was *sine qua non* to this chapter; Don Kerr for constructive criticisms that helped me to improve the essay; and Denise Philippe for all of the above plus research assistance too. I have had to write this paper while recovering from a long-term illness; I regret any shortcuts or problems that have been beyond my present ability to repair. Financial support for part of the work on this paper was provided by a UBC Hampton Grant. Ethical analysis of this is ongoing.

[2] Bowers 1995, p.1.

[3] This can occur in early childcare as well, though to a lesser extent. A complex story needs telling here about the transmission of cultural message systems, and the role of these systems in enabling adults and children to resist dominant values and images. I explore this in my ongoing work on "the colonization of children," which includes exploring distinctions between colonization, socialization, and education.

[4] See note 18 below.

[5] I explore these issues in "Beyond the Three R's: Dealing with values and issues of class, race, culture, gender and global justice in environmental education" (manuscript in progress).

[6] For the sake of saving syllables, I will leave out the more precise designation, 'industrialized and post-industrialized societies'.

[7] The literature of environmental ethics and philosophy devotes surprisingly little space to strategies and issues in environmental education. For example, see the journal *Environmental Ethics* from its beginning in 1979 to the present day, or survey popular anthologies such as VanDeVeer and Pierce 1994, Pojman 1994, Armstrong and Botzler 1993, VanDeVeer and Pierce 1986, Scherer and Attig 1983, etc. It was a central purpose of the colloquium on "Environment, ethics and education" held at Yukon College, Whitehorse in July 1995 to help to turn this limited attention around. See Jickling 1996.

[8] Alan Thein Durning reports that "American companies spent $500 million marketing to kids in 1990, five times more than they spent a decade earlier." Further: "Total global advertising expenditures multiplied nearly sevenfold from 1950 to 1990; they grew one-third faster than the world economy and three times faster than world population. They rose – in real, inflation adjusted terms – from $39 billion in 1950 to $256 billion in 1990. (For comparison, the gross national product of India, the world's second most populous state, was just $253 billion in 1990.)" That's $48 for each person on the planet in 1990 [Durning 1994, pp.485-486].

[9] Orr 1991: 99. I have to register my disagreement with what I find to be a surprising degree of individualist social analysis in Orr's account. He writes: "We may infer from the mismanagement of the environment throughout most of this century that most [school graduates] emerged from [their] various educational institutions as ecological illiterates, with little knowledge of how their subsequent actions would disrupt the earth. ...[T]he ecological crisis represents, in large measure, a failure of education" [Orr 1992, p.x]. This analysis offers no mention of the structures and practices which these educated individuals are immersed in ... as if merely having a university education is enough to empower an individual to change entrenched social practices. Nevertheless, thinking of the power for change that might be possible if people could learn in schools that which Orr wishes them to learn, I have to recognize his point. Yet I am concerned that his criteria for educational success – i.e., what it would take for an educational institution to be exhonerated from Orr's criticism – requires not only enlightened teachers, enlightened administrators and enlightened school boards, but also students who are free from the kinds of personal and family problems which make learning difficult. I address these issues further in "Mint Roots: Notes on Despair, Faith, and the Perennial Nature of Social Movements" (manuscript in progress).

[10] Eli Weisel, as quoted in Orr 1991: 99.

[11] I should note that I have distilled these goals into an enumerated list for the sake of providing a condensed introduction to his analysis. Orr does not give these issues so simplistic a treatment. This list is loosely derived from Orr 1992, pp.101-105 and Orr 1991. A point of criticism: Orr couches his educational critique in the problematic discourse of 'literacy', identifying the goal as 'ecological literacy'. This handy term unfortunately paves the way for environmental education to be incorporated within existing programs to achieve 'scientific literacy' rather than vice versa. It also misrepresents as a skill what is really a complex set of understandings, abilities, knowledge, virtues and attachments (and skills too). (Some would argue that literacy itself is misunderstood when taken to be merely a skill. I concur; nevertheless, I think environmental education has enough hurdles to overcome that it does not need to have this terminological complication added to its track.)

[12] From Orr 1991: 102; italics added.

[13] Quotation from Whitehead 1967 (1929), as cited in Orr 1992, p.101.

[14] Orr 1992, pp.101-2.

[15]The phrase is from Wendell Berry, as quoted in Orr 1991: 101.

[16] Orr co-piloted such a program in the Meadowbrook Project (Hendrix College, Arkansas, and Oberlin College, Ohio). In the Hendrix study, students discovered that despite being located in an agricultural region, the college was buying only 9 percent of its food supplies from within the state. Following upon the students' recommendations, in-state purchases doubled the following year [Orr 1992, p.106].

[17]With thanks to the inspiration and insight of Harry Nielsen.

[18]Nor does it matter that my vision differs significantly from the catastrophic view. (I discuss this in "Mint Roots: Notes on Despair, Faith and the Perennial Nature of Social Movements" (manuscript in progress).

[19] Ken Osborne's brief summary of Marxist educational analysis makes clear the power of the dynamics involved in schooling's reproduction of social conditions: "In a society characterized by political and economic inequality schooling plays a key role in maintaining and legitimizing that inequality." The educational system is "a sorting machine, selecting youngsters for different slots in the economic and political system. Some do not complete high school; some end their formal education with a high school diploma; others go on to college or university, and even to graduate school." While on most accounts this seems noncontroversial and "just the way life is," Marxist and socialist analysis has amassed evidence to show that "students are assigned to differing levels of education not by ability but by social class; or, more subtly, that the particular definition of ability that schools use works to the disadvantage of large groups of students. Thus [e.g.,] middle-class children are more likely to be found in academic programs in high school and to go on to university than are working class children" [Osborne 1991: 46]. Feminist and antiracist analyses have extended this critique beyond class to gender, race and ethnicity. Explaining the persistence of inequality, Osborne writes:

"This system of structured inequality is integral to capitalism, and its strength and stability rest upon the fact that most people see it as natural and inevitable. The victims of the system tend to blame not the system for its inequalities, but themselves for their failure to 'make it.' In this way, the dominant groups in society maintain their hegemony. They do not have to use coercion or physical force. They persuade those they dominate that this is simply the way the world works. Indeed, they probably believe it quite sincerely. As a result, awkward questions are not asked. The status quo is maintained" [Osborne 1991: 46-47].

[20] Readers unfamiliar with social reproduction theory might find Anyon 1985 to be a particularly clear and vivid illustration (though arguably thin on evidential support or anticipation of objections to interpretation). See also Curtis et al. 1992 and Osborne 1992.

[21] See e.g. Weston 1996 and Orr 1992, pp.90-92.

[22] See e.g. Hart 1990 for an overview of recent curriculum developments in Saskatchewan and Alberta.

[23] Osborne 1991: 49. This underestimation of the scope for human agency is at the other extreme of the overestimation which I attribute to Orr in note 7 above.

[24] This description is summarized from Beers 1996: 1,4.

[25] Of course, children always sing spontaneously. Does it make a difference what the songs are about? I think it does, but this is a complex and controversial issue. Whatever the significance of learning songs and sounds of environments and nature, the importance of music education (and education in art, dance, storytelling, drama etc.) to environmental education – and vice versa – goes far beyond the sharing of themes. Our connections to our environments are not just of life support but of meaning too. Our capacity to perceive, to understand, to articulate, to rejoice, to mourn and to endure are enhanced by these forms. Similarly, our understandings of music, art, dance, storytelling, drama etc. are enhanced by exploring the interconnections of self and environment, art and place. (– Also, of course, by exploring the social, historical and technological context of music, art, dance, etc.) For more on the interdisciplinarity of life and the importance of curriculum integration, see Orr 1992 and Coombs 1991.

[26] This is the subject of my current research project, "Beyond the three R's: Ethics and narrative in primary environmental education".

[27] I should note that class, race and gender have their influence in the matter of volunteer environmental education no less than in other areas. Many people locked into shift work or rigid 9-5 work schedules don't have the freedom to take an hour or two off work to volunteer in schools. Some people without university degrees may feel less certain that their expertise will be recognized and appreciated in schools than people whose education is "university certified"—even if they actually might have more knowledge and talents to offer. People who have to deal with racial discrimination and language differences often face barriers (sometimes of racism, sometimes of language differences) that white anglo (or in Quebec, franco) volunteer environmental educators don't have to worry about (other than on behalf of the minority children in the class). And it remains the case (though things are getting better all the time) that gender can occasionally have an influence on how seriously a volunteer's efforts are taken by some teachers and some children. I'll leave it to your imagination to guess which is the privileged gender in these respects: which the gender more readily given authority when gender bias is existent in the classroom; which the gender whose efforts are more likely to be welcomed in such classrooms as extraordinarily generous; and in contrast, which the gender whose efforts are more likely to be received as simply "nice of you to come". But

my personal experience of such problems has been minimal.

28 Sandilands 1993: 46. Certainly, it is not only women's lives that come under scrutiny; men are taking on an increasing share in household duties. But on average, men haven't reached equality yet, and the distance yet to go tends to be even higher at lower socio-economic levels [see e.g. McMahon 1995]. Further, insofar as affluent families can afford to hire housekeepers to do "3R's" work for them, they can buy out of the responsibilities mandated by an individualistic, lifestyle-focused environmental morality. Thus it is that such a morality is class-biased as well as gender-biased.

29 Sandilands 1993, p.47n.2.

30 See e.g. Apple 1990; Goodlad 1984.

31 See Bowers 1995, ch.s 5 and 6. Norma Kassi noted at a conference in Whitehorse in 1995 that a lot of the difficulty involved in trying to understand an indigenous culture occurs because "a lot of our traditions are within our language." Kassi contrasts her situation with that of aboriginal children raised from early childhood in two languages: "I know from how I was raised, and being taught one language in the beginning of my life has now made it easier for me to understand a lot of things. Understand the indigenous beliefs and shamanism and things like that ..." (comments recorded in Kassi et al., 1996, p.40. Kassi (Gwatla Ashi) is of the Vuntut Gwitchin (Caribou People of the Lakes)). The embeddedness of culture and values in language is explored vividly in the personal reflections recorded in Kassi et al. 1996.

32 See e.g. Orr 1992, p.90.

33 It may seem that on Bowers' (1993) claim that "all education is moral education," and Orr's (1992) claim that "all education is environmental education," I risk having this main concern reinterpreted as "how to deal with the educational dimensions of education." But please note, I am operating only on the more moderate claim that all education involves moral education and environmental education.

34 Some widely noted examples include the omission of reproductive labour, human costs, and natural destruction from economics, and the omission of women's agency, of labour movements, and of racial discrimination from history texts and history teaching.

35 For overviews of these issues, see e.g. Norton 1986 and Courtenay Hall 1995 ch.s 2 and 9.

36 It will be interesting to find out the distribution of these various views across teaching populations. This is part of my ongoing research.

37 For problems with both of these views (i.e., (1) that the science of ecology is singular, holistic and supportive of holistic thinking, and (2) that we ought to seek scientific authority for moral views) see Courtenay Hall 1995, chapters 7-9.

38 Thus, the values found in science neither begin nor end with the handy five of predictability, fertility, simplicity, internal consistency, and external coherence. For discussion of values in science, see e.g. Longino 1990.

39 I hope the reader will forgive my vagueness on these questions of numbers (i.e., how many is a significant minority? How many a common group? I am currently involved in research to establish some clearer understanding of how teachers in various regions and at various levels divide on these issues. The casual sample of 400 from whom I have drawn the present sketches is too dispersed to warrant anything more than setting forth the patterns I have observed thus far.

40 But such goals may reach their limits in communities where environmental conflict is raging. I am in the beginning stages of exploring this issue in connection with the communities directly involved in the dispute over logging in Clayoquot Sound on Vancouver Island in 1993-95.

41 I recognize that including 'respect for all forms of life' here raises problems of democratic justifiability, given the prevalence of instrumentalist attitudes toward nature in our society. It would be running away from the heart of the problem to hope that the range of interpretations possible for 'respect for all forms of life' avoids this problem of democratically justifiability. I discuss this further along in the main text—in fact, next paragraph. See also note 45 below. This remains a tension I need to explore further.

42 See e.g. Berman and LaFarge, eds. 1993.

43 Some education critics would want to insert 'otherwise' here.

44 Dewey 1902. Explored more fully in Dewey 1965 (1938), pp.23-52.

45 In fact, Raths was a student of Dewey's philosophy, working from Dewey's book *Theory of Valuation* in developing his values clarification strategies [Simon and deSherbinin 1975].

46 The grammatical problem is using a plural pronoun-adjective ('their') to stand for a singular pronoun-subject ('everyone') The ironic truth is that an opinion about which I haven't really yet thought reflectively might sometimes be simply something I have absorbed from the people around me ... hence, it is "theirs", just as the motto says, and not really yet mine. But ah! ... this question of "When are my ideas genuinely mine?" is a complex one! (and not profoundly answered on individualist assumptions, I suspect).

47 See e.g. Coombs 1980. Critical thinking approaches have been criticized (as has traditional anglo-American philosophy itself) for cultivating adversarial approaches to inquiry over cooperative approaches, for commitment to positivist understandings of knowledge, and for obliviousness to critiques of mind/body and reason/emotion dualisms that would yield a richer understanding of human knowing and

moral experience. This is true of some critical thinking approaches, but not all. For example, it is remarkable how much Jerrold Coombs' early work contains resources to deal with some of these concerns – concerns that weren't even widely articulated at the time. I discuss this in "A critical thinking approach to environmental education ... and its limits" (manuscript in preparation for the *Canadian Journal of Environmental Education*).

[48] E.g., the work of David Hume.

[49] For further discussion, see e.g. Baier 1995, Nussbaum 1990, Gibson 1979, Abrams 1994 and Gough 1989.

[50] It's worth noting the strategic dubiousness of intended efforts to indoctrinate students. As Simon and deSherbinin note, moralizing—telling children what they should believe and value or "trying to shape and manipulate people into accepting a given set of values—is doomed to failure. The problem is that if a student has not been taught to examine and weigh his own values, he is prey to the next fast-talking moralizer who comes down the road. The next one might, in fact, be hustling drugs" [Simon and deSherbinin 1975, p.682]. I'll add one correction. Moral indoctrination efforts are not "doomed" to fail, at least in terms of the perspective of the skilled and unreflective indoctrinator; the student may in fact absorb her teacher's teachings so entirely that she never subsequently allows them to be exposed to questioning.

[51] Human/nature dualism is the set of beliefs and practices associated with the core notion that humans are essentially separate from nature, and that human societies are separate from ecological systems. Nature instrumentalism is the set of beliefs and practices associated with the view that nature is nothing more than a stock of resources for human use. For fuller discussion of these ideologies, see e.g. Leiss 1972, Evernden 1993 (1985), Plumwood 1996.

[52] See Gough 1989.

[53] It is clear that I have to attend as carefully as any teacher to making sure that my own environmentalist commitment does not lead me to cross the marshlands from education to indoctrination. My efforts in this regard are, and need to be, even more intense than you might guess. For I also believe that the social malaise inherent in environmental degradation is far deeper and less tractable than my discussion above has indicated. The deepest problem, I think, lies in the poverty of a dominant society and culture not yet capable of supporting and nurturing widespread respect for life and for natural systems in its members and its governance systems. Yet this is a concern that will not hold water with those not antecedently convinced of the importance of respect for nature. And so I feel bound by democratic considerations as well as by educational ones to try to ensure that my teaching respects *human and philosophical* diversity no less than *natural* diversity.

[54] By "functioning neutrality," I mean the practice of refraining from expressing one's own view on the topic being explored for the sake of facilitating student exploration rather than leading it coercively. This is not meant to preclude the asking of important questions that need asking nor the sharing of important information that needs sharing. But the teacher's first goal should generally be to have these questions and sharings come from students first (unless there are good particular reasons for doing otherwise).

References

Abram, David. 1996. *The spell of the sensuous: Perception and language in a more than human world*. New York: Pantheon Books.

Anyon, Jean. 1981. "Social class and school knowledge," *Curriculum Inquiry* 11, no.1 (spring): 3-42.

Apple, Michael. 1990. *Ideology and curriculum* (2nd ed.). New York: Routledge.

Armstrong, Susan J. and Richard G. Botzler. 1993. *Environmental ethics: Divergence and convergence*. New York: McGraw-Hill Inc.

Baier, Annette. 1995. *Moral prejudices: Essays on ethics*. Cambridge: Harvard University Press.

Beer, Teresa. 1996. "Public choice public schools," *Teacher: Newsmagazine of the B.C. Teachers' Federation* 9:2 (October).

Berman, Sheldon and Phyllis LaFarge, eds. 1993. *Promising practices in teaching social responsibility*. Albany, NY: State University of New York Press.

Bowers, C.A. 1993. *Education, cultural myths and the ecological crisis: Towards deep changes*. Albany, NY: State University of New York Press.

Bowers, C.A. 1995. *Educating for an ecologically sustainable culture: Rethinking moral education, creativity, intelligence, and other modern orthodoxies*. Albany, NY: State University of New York Press.

Bullard, Robert. 1994. "Environmental racism and the environmental justice movement," in *Ecology (Key concepts in critical theory)*, ed. Carolyn Merchant. Atlantic Highlands, N.J.: Humanities Press International.

Coombs, Jerrold. 1980. "Validating moral judgements by principle testing," ch.2 of *The development of moral reasoning*, ed. Donald Cochrane and

m. Manley-Casimir. New York: Prager.

Coombs, Jerrold. 1991. "Thinking seriously about curriculum integration," *Foci: Forum on curriculum integration.* Tri-University Integration Project (UBC, Simon Fraser University, the University of Victoria), Occasional Paper #4.

Courtenay Hall, Pamela. 1995. "Ecoholism and its critics: A critical exploration of holism in environmental ethics and the science of ecology." Unpublished Ph.D. thesis, University of Toronto, Department of Philosophy.

Courtenay Hall, Pamela. 1996. "Environmental education as values education: A critical framework," in *A colloquium on environment, ethics and education*, ed. Bob Jickling. Whitehorse: Yukon College.

Curtis, Bruce, D.W. Livingstone, and Harry Smaller. 1992. *Stacking the deck: The streaming of woking-class kids in Ontario schools.* Toronto: Our Schools/Our Selves.

Dewey, John. 1902. *The child and the curriculum.* Chicago: University of Chicago Press.

Dewey, John. 1965 (1938). Experience and education. New York: Macmillan Co.

Durning, Alan Thein. 1994. "An ecological critique of global advertising," in Pojman, ed.

Evernden, Neil. 1993 (1985). *The natural alien: Humankind and environment*, 2nd ed. Toronto: University of Toronto Press.

Gibson, J.J. 1979. *Ecological approach to visual perception.* Boston: Houghton Mifflin.

Goodlad, J. 1984. *A place called school.* New York: McGraw-Hill.

Gough, Noel. 1989. "From epistemology to ecopolitics," *Journal of Curriculum Studies* 21.

Hart, Paul. 1990. 'Environmental eduation in Canada: Contemporary issues and future possibilities," *Australian Journal of Environmental Education* 6: 45-63.

Jickling, Bob, ed. 1996. *A colloquium on environment, ethics and education.* Whitehorse: Yukon College.

Kassi, Norma (Gwatla Ashi) et al. 1996. "First Nations perspectives," in Jickling, ed., pp.32-48.

Leiss, William. 1972. *The domination of nature.*

New York: G. Brazillier.

Longino, Helen. 1990. *Science as social knowledge: Values and objectivity in scientific inquiry.* Princeton, N.J.: Princeton University Press.

McMahon, Martha. 1995. *Engendering motherhood: Identity and self-transformation in women's lives.* New York: The Guildford Press.

Norton, Bryan G. 1986. *Why preserve natural variety?* Princeton, N.J.: Princeton University Press.

Nussbaum, M. 1990. *Love's knowledge: Essays on philosophy and literature.* New York: Oxford University Press.

Osborne, Ken. 1992. "Critical Pedagogy," in *Teaching for a democratic citizenship.* Toronto: Our Schools/Our Selves. pp.45-63.

Orr, David W. 1991. "What is Education For?" *Trumpeter* 8:3 (Summer).

Orr, David W. 1992. *Ecological literacy: Education and the transition to a postmodern world.* Albany, NY: State University of New York Press.

Owram, Douglas. 1996. "Safe in the hands of mother suburbia: Home and community, 1950-1965," Ch.3 of *Born at the right time: A history of the baby-boom generation.* Toronto: University of Toronto Press.

Plumwood, Val. 1996. "Environmental education, liberatory education and place-sensitive narrative," in Jickling, ed., pp.76-89.

Pojman, Louis P., ed. 1994. *Environmental ethics: Readings in theory and application.* Sudbury, MA: Jones and Bartlett Publishers.

Robottom, Ian, and Paul Hart. 1993. *Research in environmental education: Engaging the debate.* Geelong, Australia: Deakin University Press.

Sandilands, Catriona. 1993. "On 'green' consumerism: Environmental privatization and 'family values'," *Canadian Woman Studies* 13:3 (Spring): 45-47.

Scherer, Donald and Thomas Attig. 1983. *Ethics and the environment.* Englewood Cliffs, N.J.: Prentic-Hall, Inc.

Simon, S.B. and P. deSherbinin. 1975. "Values clarification: It can start gently and grow deep," *Phi Delta Kappan* 56:10, pp.679-683.

Ungerleider, Charles. 1993. "Testing: Fine-tuning the politics of inequality," in *Contemporary educational issues: The Canadian mosaic*. 2nd ed. Toronto: Copp Clark Pittman.

VanDeVeer, Donald and Christine Pierce, eds. 1994. *The environmental ethics and policy book: Philosophy, ecology, economics*. Belmont, CA: Wadsworth.

VanDeVeer, Donald and Christine Pierce, eds. 1986. *People, penguins and plastic trees: Basic issues in environmental ethics*. Belmont, CA: Wadsworth.

Weston, Anthony. 1996. "Deschooling environmental education," *Canadian Journal of Environmental Education* 1 (Spring): 35-46.

INTERNATIONAL ENVIRONMENTAL JUSTICE
THE GLOBAL ENVIRONMENT AND RICH-COUNTRY OBLIGATIONS

24

by Peter Penz

Introduction

THAT THE ENVIRONMENTAL HERITAGE WHICH humanity shares globally is being threatened at this point
in history has rapidly been gaining universal acceptance. The appearance of the ozone hole, the
threat of global warming, the reduction of
biodiversity, the depletion of certain natural resources, such as tropical forests – all these are
developments that have entered general public
consciousness and are the objects of active international negotiations and of treaty-making. While
it is true that protecting the corresponding elements
of the global commons is for the common good
of humanity, there are nevertheless issues of international distributive justice involved. Not all
people suffer equally from the different forms of
global ecological damage. The geographic incidence varies (coasts and delta regions are particularly vulnerable to any sea-level rise), and the extent of injury varies with the degree of dependence of people on the land and with the (lack of)
resources that people have to protect themselves
from and adjust to ecological changes. The poor
are especially exposed to victimization by environmental hazards. At the same time, the responsibility for global environmental degradation and
the capacity for corrective action are also un-
equally distributed. It is the highly industrialized
countries to which, for example, the intensification of the planet's greenhouse effect and its injurious consequences must be attributed. Thus, the
pursuit of humanity's common environmental
good involves the issues of the distribution of both
the sources and the incidence of environmental
harm as well as of the benefits and costs of corrective action.

Distributive justice is a major concern in normative ethics and a pivotal component of social
justice. Although not all social justice is a matter
of distribution – e.g. the violation of basic human
rights is unjust not because the violations are unfairly distributed but because they violate non-distributive norms – questions of distribution are,
nevertheless, central to social justice. In this article, two approaches to distributive justice will be
explored. One is based on the principle that harming others is unjust and, if it occurs, it must be
compensated for. The other rests on the principle
of sharing, namely that the benefits and burdens
of social life within our collective habitat should
be shared equally. The first might appear not to
be a distributive principle. When A harms B and
B receives restitution from A, it might seem that
a non-distributive norm is applied. However, it
does involve distribution between A and B.
Moreover, the matter becomes more clearly and
broadly distributive when both the sources and the
impacts of harm are scattered. Given a certain assessment of the extent of the harm, responsibility
for paying the compensation has to be
distributively assigned, as does entitlement to
compensation. The second approach to be covered, that of equal sharing, is clearly distributive;
it refers to a particular distribution of certain benefits and burdens of the natural environment and
of social cooperation. It is in terms of these two
approaches, i.e. those of harm-and-compensation
and of sharing, that the question of distributive
justice will be explored here.

Given the global environmental issues with

which this article is concerned, **international** distributive justice is involved. We must address the question of distributive justice between different countries. More specifically, Canada's distributive obligations will be considered as part of this assessment of the distributive-justice implications of global environmental problems. Canada is not insignificant in this context. Our territory consists of a major part of the surface of the earth; our population is large enough to have a significant effect on global environmental problems; and our state is an important enough player in international environmental politics to be a member of the G7 elite of international oligarchs. In this context, what are Canada's moral obligations? More generally, what are the implications for a rich country like Canada?

These and related questions motivate this article. It analyzes the requirements for internationally just solutions to global environmental problems – solutions for which the North cannot validly be accused of "eco-imperialism". In particular, it will consider what this implies for the obligations of rich countries, such as Canada. To do this, I analyze and develop the concept of international justice with respect to the global environment. In fleshing it out substantively, I attempt to show that we need to go beyond the principles of non-interference and compensation for harm (which are related to the prevailing ethics of state sovereignty in the international domain) and bring in an ethic of sharing. Nevertheless, the principles of non-interference and compensation for harm remain important and can have quite radical implications for the justice obligations of rich countries. Because this is relatively unexplored terrain, the emphasis here is in the first instance on the general principles, with their application presented for the purpose of illustration. However, the focus on the implications for Canada's obligations at the end is entirely within the applied domain.

The article consists of eight sections. Following 1) the present introductory section, 2) it addresses the question of what international justice with respect to the global environment means. 3) The two principles of distributive justice, those of harm-and-compensation and of equal sharing, are then located in relation to standard normative theories in social ethics and in the more recent field of international ethics. 4) Next, the implications of the harm principle for international justice regarding the global environment are explored and the limitations of this approach made apparent. The complexity of interdependence and of the patterns of harm brought out by this analysis reveals a serious weakness of the harm principle and suggests the need to shift to a principle of equal sharing. 5) Equality is, first of all, required with respect to entitlements to the global commons, such as the atmosphere and the oceans. 6) This applies, in principle, also to land, the erstwhile terrestrial global commons, now appropriated by states. The justice of such appropriation is questioned, and this argument leads to a general case for egalitarianism. 7) Following a brief recapitulation of the conclusions of the argument about the general principles, 8) the obligations of a rich country like Canada are considered specifically in relation to global warming. It is argued that international environmental justice requires something like a tradable-emission-rights scheme rather than the 1992 Climate Change Convention.

The Notion of International Justice Regarding the Global Environment

What is international justice with respect to the global environment? Before answering this specific question, let me pose the more general one of justice concerning the environment. Environmental justice is social justice with respect to access to the natural environment, with respect to its quality, and with respect to public policies to protect or rehabilitate it. The interests of humans with respect to the natural environment is the only concern here. These interests are to draw on nature for personal sustenance, health and enjoyment (e.g. oxygen, protection against ultraviolet radiation, forests), for production (e.g. fish, sunshine and rain for agriculture), as well as to use it as "sinks" for waste gases and materials.[1]

Of course, human beings are not the only ones whose interests are at stake in decision-making with respect to the environment. There are also animals, species and ecosystems. Why are these excluded from the conception of environmental justice? A number of writers have, in fact, argued that their interests can be made part of the notion of environmental justice.[2] Without denying either that animals, species and ecosystems are entitled to moral consideration or that such consideration can be formulated in terms of rights, e.g. animal rights, this aspect will not be dealt with here. One reason is that I still have doubts that the environmental ethics of protecting nature for its own sake is appropriately formulated in terms of environmental **justice**. More importantly, the focus here is on international relations and thus on a particular set of relations between human beings. Instead of including nature as one or more right-holders under a conception of justice, it will simply be assumed that environmental ethics requires certain limits on the human use of nature and that these limits are respected. Where these limits lie is not addressed here. When I later use the language of "natural resources," this is not to assert that it is justifiable to treat all of nature instrumentally, but merely to indicate that I am dealing only with those instrumental uses of nature by humans which are not ruled out by environmental ethics. To the extent that environmental ethics requires particular restraints on human action, and thus requires political action to enforce such restraints, this will constitute social burdens which have distributive implications. Prohibiting logging to preserve the habitat of an endangered bird species is a particular burden for local loggers; protecting tigers in India involves special hazards to the local population, not the rest of the world. Thus, even when we deal with the protection of an environment that is deemed to have in-

trinsic value, there are implications for justice in social relations.

To return now to the question of the meaning of international justice regarding the global environment, let me distinguish this notion from two others, international environmental justice and global environmental justice. In our state-centred global political system, international environmental justice refers in the first instance to relations between territorial states. This need not be global, in that it may involve only the environmental relations between a pair of neighbouring states or among the states of a particular region in the world. On the other hand, global environmental justice concerns environmental justice in the world as a whole and need not be confined to justice between states. It may refer to environmental justice for all people in the world, as individuals rather than as nations. Ideally, global environmental justice should be the concern of this article. However, since the relations between states and their citizens also involve justice issues, i.e. intra-national justice issues, and these interact with notions of justice that go beyond states, global justice becomes too complicated to address within the confines of this article.[3] Intra-national complications are side-stepped here. For the sake of simplicity, the concerns will be limited to justice in inter-state relations. This topic offers enough challenges on its own. It will thus in effect be assumed, rather unrealistically, that states appropriately represent the interests of the people within their territories and that the states do not permit environmental injustice within their borders. For this reason, international rather than global justice is referred to. It represents only a first step of a more complete analysis.

Moreover, the focus will be specifically on the global environment. In particular, the global commons, such as the atmosphere and the oceans, are of central concern here. It is not so much bilateral or regional international environmental justice, but international justice with respect to the global environment that is emphasized.

Avoiding Harm and Sharing: Two Notions of Justice in Relation to Competing Theories

There is no established body of theory specifically on international environmental justice. Given that moral consideration for nature is not pursued in this analysis and is treated simply as a constraint, the approach here is to focus on social justice and international ethics. The intent here is not to provide a comprehensive review of specific and well elaborated theories, but merely to explore the implications of two widely understood and accepted social and moral norms. These are a) the principles of non-interference and of the avoidance of and compensation for harm and b) the norm of sharing. They also represent two polar notions in relation to which theories of social justice within countries as well as between countries can be located. Within countries, the focus on harm is represented by libertarianism, while the focus on sharing is represented by egalitarian or socialist theories of social justice. Utilitarianism and contractarianism represent more hybrid positions in relation to these polar positions.[4] In international relations, the autonomy of countries, which is closely linked to the principle of harm, is emphasized by those theories that stress the negative duty not to interfere (moral international-relations realism and the "morality of states"), while sharing between countries is advocated by cosmopolitan egalitarianism. In this section, I will briefly elaborate on these relationships between the polar positions identified and mainstream theoretical positions and, in the process, also identify some questions regarding the polar positions.

The central value of libertarianism is freedom, interpreted negatively as freedom from interference by others, including in particular interference by the state. This is to be distinguished from positive freedom, i.e. the ability to choose between options. A basic feature of the libertarian notion of freedom is that of property rights. Property represents an extension of the self into the material world and provides essential security for continued personal existence and self-realization. Harm to either person or property violates freedom from interference. Environmental harm can be interpreted as such a violation, although there is disagreement within libertarianism as to whether such harm is a more serious interference than that involved in prohibiting such harm and requiring its rectification. That is to say, requiring that pollution be stopped and be compensated for interferes with the polluter's freedom to produce and consume as she sees fit. The fact that two freedoms can be in conflict in this way indicates that freedoms have to be priorized. Environmental libertarianism certainly requires that environmental harm be treated as a basic violation of freedom.[5] The emphasis on sharing and equality in egalitarian and socialist ethics derives from the idea that as human beings we are all entitled to equal consideration. Related to this is a second consideration, that the burden of justification falls on those who advocate social relations resulting in inequality. A further basis of equal sharing is the argument that many or most inequalities are not such that we can be held responsible for them; we did not choose our genetic, financial and socio-familial inheritance nor (at least initially) our geographic, cultural, economic and political context. To be equally free to make choices about earning one's living and contributing to society's production (i.e. positive freedom) requires equality of opportunity in a broad sense.[6]

Two important theoretical positions regarding distributive justice are utilitarianism and contractarianism. Utilitarianism simply requires that the well-being of all human beings (in the relevant community) be maximized. This basic principle does not refer to an appropriate distribution. All that it requires is that distribution which maximizes total well-being. That is such an indirect a principle of distributive justice that it is often not accepted as being a principle of distributive justice at all. Yet quite egalitarian conclusions can be derived from it if the proposition that the well-being derived by the poor from given material resources (e.g. amount of money) is much greater than the well-being derived by the rich from the same resources. With respect to harm and sharing, this means that harm (including environmental harm) has to be counted in terms of its well-being effects, but only as part of an overall calculation, and sharing is to be pushed as far as the maximization of total well-being requires. One major consideration that stops it from being pushed to completely equal sharing is the damage that might be done to incentives to contribute to the social production that is available for distribution.

Critics of utilitarianism consider this still too indirect an approach to distributive justice. Contemporary contractarians propose, instead, a more direct approach to the determination of distributive justice. Impartiality in this determination is to be achieved through a thought experiment in which the members of the relevant community formulate a consensual social contract, without reference to, or even knowledge of, any features of their individuality; they only know about human nature in general and the way societies of humans function. In this thought-experimental situation, the participants are to formulate a social contract consisting of principles of justice and they are to do it recognizing that they could find themselves anywhere in the social structure governed by the proposed principles of justice. As in utilitarianism, incentives are taken into account. Different contractarians flesh out this basic framework differently. Egalitarian contractarians emphasize the natural aversion of participants to risk finding themselves in the worst possible social situations, and therefore include as a principle of justice the requirement that inequalities are to be tolerated only to the extent that they benefit the worst-off in society (e.g. by providing incentives for services or products that benefit the worst-off). This then combines a concern for harm and for

incentives with a concern for sharing; complete equality in sharing is sacrificed, but such that it serves the interests of the worst-off.[7]

When it comes to international relations there has been a tendency to either view them as beyond the realm of moral relations (the moral skepticism of international-relations realism) or to see international morality to be essentially one of non-interference, i.e. a form of libertarianism at the level of state-to-state relations (a moral version of international-relations realism or the "morality of states"). If we accept the propositions that we now live either in a global society or that the system of state relations itself consists of a certain kind of "society" and that all societies involve morality in intra-society relations, then we can reject moral skepticism regarding international relations. The question then is what does morality in international relations require. This is precisely the question that is here explored with respect to global environmental issues. The approach will be to begin with the idea that international relations require non-interference, including the avoidance of interference in the form of environmental damage, and the requirement to compensate for any such damage. It will follow an immanent critique, where the sharing approach is introduced in response to difficulties of an approach focused on non-interference and harm. An international sharing approach reflects cosmopolitan egalitarianism, including the cosmopolitan contractarianism in which the social-contract thought experiment is applied across nations.[8] The focus is thus on two schools of thought in international ethics, the ethics of state sovereignty and cosmopolitanism.[9]

The preceding discussion relating the two broad normative positions to specific ethical theories has the limited purpose of locating the analysis of this article in relation to these theories. There will be no attempt to continue to systematically relate the following analysis to these theories. Instead, the focus will be on the two broad moral norms, their practical implications, and their plausibility in terms of these practical implications.

International Environmental Harm: Problems of Assessment

As stated, the principle of non-interference is central to libertarianism as well as to the doctrine of state sovereignty. Given that the focus in this article is in the first instance on the relations between countries, state sovereignty rather than libertarianism will be the focus. The discussion, however, will at times draw on the kinds of rationale that are used in libertarianism, as in the conceptual exploration of non-interference with respect to the global commons. Moreover, the concern will be with the international rather than intra-national features of sovereignty, i.e. with the autonomy of the state vis-à-vis other states, rather than with the supreme legitimate authority of the state in relation to the society for which it is the governing structure. What this discussion will lead up to is the conclusion that the extent of environmental interdependence internationally makes it both difficult to assign responsibility for harm and inappropriate to make it the exclusive or even primary principle of international environmental justice.

Non-interference requires not only avoidance of acts of deliberate interference, but also avoidance of acts involving incidental harm to others. When others are harmed, they are entitled to compensation. This is clear when such harm, even though unintended, is predictable. Less obvious is the case of harm that is not readily predictable. At the very least, when the actors benefit from such action, then even unpredictable harm requires compensation, at least to the extent that compensation can be covered by the benefits. An example is the possible benefits from global warming that might accrue to farming on the Canadian prairies.[10] Canada can thus be deemed to benefit from its own earlier pollution, when the problem of global warming was still unknown, and can thus be held liable for damages out of its gains. But, more

directly, pollution involves direct benefits to polluters because it represents cheap disposal. Being harmed thus entitles the victims to compensation, at least when the harm is foreseeable or the party responsible for the harm benefits from it.

Concerning the global environment, the first moral obligation that arises from this non-interference perspective of justice is that all countries are required to **refrain from imposing foreseeable international environmental harm** on others. However, harm does occur, whether out of inconsiderateness, neglect, failure of internal control (such as a state's incapacity to prevent pollution by its own businesses or citizens) or accident. Therefore, justice requires also that culpability and entitlement to compensation be determined. In the following discussion of a) the depletion of the global commons and b) its degradation, I will assess to what extent it is possible to identify entitlements to and obligations for restitution.

a) Take the case of oceans. Industrialized countries can deprive poor countries of traditional ocean-fishing opportunities by using mechanized methods of fishing that are not available to the poor countries. By depleting fish stocks through technologically advanced fishing, the yield from fishing by traditional methods will be reduced. Similarly, by mining the ocean floor of minerals such as magnesium, technologically advanced countries deprive late developers of the opportunity to engage in such ocean mining at some later time. In either case, it is not clear who is to be held liable for the depletion of the resource. Are the late-comers in large-scale fishing whose arrival, let us say, overloads the system of fish survival and reproduction to be blamed and required to pay compensation, or should this be shared among all those involved in large-scale fishing? In the case of mining, are the latecomers harming the pioneers and early developers or have the latter harmed everyone else's opportunities. The harm principle itself does not provide a criterion for the assignment of responsibility when the harm is due to the accumulation of actions by different parties. More fundamentally, it does not indicate what the entitlement with respect to the resources of the global commons ought to be.

b) The degradation of the global environment is exemplified by global warming and upper-atmosphere ozone depletion. The responsible parties are those who pollute the air. The victims include the following: those whose land is flooded by a rising sea level; those who suffer loss and injury from storms due to increased atmospheric turbulence; those who get skin cancer from increased solar radiation; and those whose land is made less productive due to changes in temperature and in precipitation. In addition, there are those who, even though not worse off in the very long run, have to make costly adjustments in response to the environmental changes. Such costs are involved in changing crops and farming methods and in changing the production of agricultural supplies to suit the new farming. Determining which countries are harmed and by how much is clearly very difficult. Part of the difficulty is that it is not easy to isolate the extent of skin cancer, storm losses and changes in agricultural productivity due to human-produced pollutants, from what would have occurred in any case. The other half of the difficulty lies in assigning culpability. I have already mentioned the case where the damage is due to cumulative action. The problem of attribution applies also to synergistic pollution effects, as when two different emitted chemicals, each of which is harmless on its own, interact to form an injurious pollutant.

Introducing international economic relations further complicates the harm principle. The world has become globally interconnected not merely because of ecological interdependencies, but also because of international economic relations. Thus the purchasers (consumers and businesses) of the goods produced with the polluting technology will benefit from new or cheaper goods. In fact, if the production occurs under competitive conditions,

the benefits will not show up in exceptional producer profits, but in lower prices for buyers, so that the buyers, rather than the producers, are the major beneficiaries. To the extent that cross-border trade is involved, non-polluting countries can thus benefit from pollution-generating production. Moreover, to the extent that such polluting production is in response to the demand of importing countries, it would not occur if it were not for their willingness to buy the products. The causal role of the importing countries and the benefits they reap can be reasonably considered to make them partly liable for the environmental harm.

Another way in which rich countries become in effect internationally complicitous in environmental harm is through the provision of credit. A poor country's debt load, as a result of the international financial system, may be such that it creates a dilemma between protecting the natural environment and ensuring the survival of the rural population. Then creditor countries are implicated in the environmental harm committed in the poor country in the process of protecting the population in the short run. Such environmental harm involves international environmental justice, even though the natural environment whose protection is at stake is not global. International environmental justice is involved because the causal pressure is international.

Recognizing international interdependence not only in ecological processes but also in the economic relations that underlie them requires that we extend the definition of international environmental justice. In addition to justice with respect to access to the global environmental commons and with respect to its maintenance (where economic relations may implicate countries in the environmental degradation of others), international environmental justice needs to encompass justice with respect to the environmental consequences of international economic relations.

The high degree of environmental and economic interdependence between territorial states makes it extremely difficult to assign culpability for environmental harm and entitlement to compensation. This interdependence is now so developed that we should really consider the international system as a global society (and not merely as a society of states). This is reinforced by much more information about different countries among the general public than was the case **within** national societies only a century or two ago, by the extensive global networks that are being formed by business and voluntary organizations, and by the incipient formation of a world government in the United Nations and other transnational agencies. The idea of a global society is also strengthened by the fact that economic globalization is leading to popular reactions that are becoming connected with each other through advocacy networks. Once we think of all the countries in the world as forming one society, even if it is a heterogeneous mega-society, we have to employ principles of justice that emerged for application within rather than between societies. In that context, the principles of non-intervention and compensation for harm are certainly not the only principles of justice. In fact, the degree to which people affect each other and depend on each other suggests a quite different approach to justice, namely that of sharing.

Sharing Access to the Global Commons

Sharing becomes an obvious orientation to justice simply because a high degree of social interdependence makes other principles of distributive justice problematic and sharing is what we then naturally do, assuming we are being cooperative. Sharing normally means equal sharing, in the absence of persuasive arguments that justify deviation from the principle of equality. Such sharing is the approach that characterized the earliest societal units, namely the bands of hunter-gatherers that our ancestors lived in for all but the last minute of human evolution, so to speak. It is a notion understood and applied in all cultures, al-

though the spheres of social life in which it is deemed applicable varies, and the historical emergence of the hierarchical organization of society has pitted competing moral principles against it and has, in various historical periods, suppressed ideas about duties to share. As was indicated above, a more or less qualified form of equal sharing is also what certain versions of the contractarian theory of social justice generate and is also approximated by the form of utilitarianism that accepts that the equivalent resources generally provide higher well-being to the poor than the rich.

This means neither that equal sharing is unambiguous in its meaning nor that it is the only principle of justice that applies. It does not replace the principle of harm, but rather restricts its application. To some extent, the two principles are complementary. If there is initially an equal distribution and then one party enriches itself by harming another party, e.g. through pollution that makes cheap production possible, compensating for the harm also contributes to rectifying the resulting inequality. On the other hand, the principle of sharing stands in continual tension with the ideal of self-determination and its requirement of non-interference that underlie the harm principle. Egalitarian redistribution, to the extent that it is coercive, interferes with the realm of self-determination of the party being taxed. Moreover, equality does not obviate the need for productivity and incentives for such productivity. Incentives, therefore, either have to be made **part** of the notion of justice (as utilitarianism and contractarianism do) or have to receive sufficient moral consideration to justify **concessions** in the pursuit of justice (conceptualized free of incentives). Both self-determination and incentives are at least as applicable to international justice as to intra-national social justice. Nevertheless, equal sharing is the appropriate starting point when people are so interdependent that they can be deemed to be part of the same society, even if it is highly diverse and contains many political units.

Regarding international environmental justice specifically, the first question concerns entitlement with respect to the global environmental commons. To the extent that we are dealing with that part of the global commons which has not been appropriated by anyone, e.g. the atmosphere, we have, in the first instance, a collective entitlement that is not subject to distribution. The distribution of air to breathe is not at issue. Nevertheless, unappropriated global commons have a distributive dimension to the extent that scarcity prevails. No distribution issue arises as long as fish stocks are plentiful, but when fish catches negatively affect each other abundance has ended and distributive conflict appears. Similarly, in the case of the use of the environment as an emission "sink," scarcity with respect to absorptive capacity arises when other people are harmed either directly or through an ecological chain reaction. Harm is involved in both the depletion and the pollution of the global commons. However, as mentioned before, the harm principle does not solve the problem here because it is not clear what the entitlement of different countries is with respect to the global commons. Restricting uses of the global commons to the level where scarcity and mutual harm are completely avoided will often not be in the common global interest because maximum sustainable yield (e.g. of fish) can frequently and even typically involve some degree of scarcity and mutual harm. In the case of pollution, some harm may be accepted if the activities are sufficiently beneficial (e.g. growing rice even though it generates methane, a powerful greenhouse gas). In other words, simply prohibiting environmental uses involving mutual harm in the global commons is not the answer; some of these uses are simply essential, or important enough, to human existence to warrent the harm. The earlier issue of environmental harm now changes from that of a prohibition on harm and compensation for harm to a different issue, that of the proper distribution of rights whose exercise can harm others.

A principle of first-come-first-served in harvesting or mining resources in the global commons (for a long time the position of the U.S. government with respect to ocean minerals, for example), while a common distributive norm, is highly dubious as a principle of justice. While first-come-first-served might be justified on the grounds of providing an incentive for productive extraction as well as security of possession, it is devoid of a **justice** rationale. Why should access to resources in the global commons be determined by economic endowment or technological sophistication? Here is a clear case where sharing is the natural distributive solution. This does not mean that whatever is harvested or mined has to be equally distributed. That would ignore the costs of such harvesting or mining and the need for adequate incentives. But equal sharing does require that entitlements to such harvesting and mining is equally distributed and that, if a corporation or a fishing cooperative wants to tap those resources, it has to pay royalties to the holders of the rights. In the case of mobile resources, such as fish stocks, the only way that this can be done equitably is probably by having a global authority selling licences and distributing the proceeds from such sales on a per capita basis (apart from the costs required to maintain and police the global commons).

With respect to emission rights, the issue of distribution has led to the "greenhouse equity" controversy. In order to contain the degradation of the atmosphere and the resulting climate change, efforts are being made to limit the greenhouse-gas emissions of different countries. What should be the limits for particular countries, if the arrangement is to be fair? There is a tendency to advocate a capping of current emission levels, but this merely rewards those countries which have reached high emission levels and those which have so far not exerted themselves to reduce their emission levels. Schemes that require the reduction of the overall level of emission normally recognize this in that they do not require such reductions on the part of currently low polluters, but this is an ad hoc adaptation. A principled alternative would be to assign emission levels on the basis of population. This means equal per capita emission rights.[11]

If industrial capacity was entirely malleable and could be changed to clean technology from one year to the next, such rights might be enforceable without further provisions. However, industrial capacity currently in place is such that it is already committed to certain emission levels (with some, but limited, room for improvements). Globally, it is probably much easier to adopt clean technology where completely new factories are being developed and where obsolete machinery is being replaced. Industrial newcomers may be in a better position to adopt clean technology quickly than industrial oldtimers. In any case, the change to clean technology will be more rapid if it is promoted wherever it is easiest to accomplish. This is also a more efficient approach in that dirty technology is first eliminated wherever it is cheapest to do so. This means that emission rights need to be **tradable.** The big polluters will have to purchase emission rights from those poorer countries that have not yet developed to the point of being major polluters. Tradability then supports not only efficiency, but moves in the direction of distributive justice in that the kinds of transfers of resources and technology to the poorer countries that the rich countries have largely resisted (other than through investments that create external debts and later obligations of repayment and the quite minimal flows of international assistance) will now have to be made as a matter of obligation.

However, how the excess emissions, for which the rights have to be purchased, are calculated also involves an issue of justice. The approach of the World Resources Institute in the late 1980s was to calculate emissions to the atmosphere, not counting what is absorbed by oceans. But this implicitly means that entitlement to the absorptive capacity of the oceans (as opposed to the absorptive capacity of the atmosphere) is assigned, not on a per capita basis, but in proportion to how much pollution a country actually generates. This has been pointed out and severely criticized by Agarwal and Narain.[12] Clearly, the principle of equal sharing has to apply as much to the oceans' absorptive capacity as to the atmosphere's.

Equal Sharing and the Natural Resources of States

So far I have applied the principle of equal sharing only to what we now consider to be the global commons. But this principle really is applicable to all natural resources, including land. It is true that this runs counter to the idea of state sovereignty and, more specifically, the principle (frequently reiterated nowadays) of sovereignty over the environmental resources within the state's territory.[13] However, it is one thing to argue that a country is entitled to what its citizens have produced, and quite another to argue that it is morally entitled to those natural resources that it is endowed with. Why should these natural resources not be equally shared? Three arguments against the sharing principle, all of them related to historical processes, will be briefly considered: a) that justice is a matter of historical acquisition; b) that some countries have used up their natural resources and converted them into industrial wealth; and c) that human well-being and environmental protection depend on security of tenure. I will argue that the first position is self-defeating, but that the second and third should be accepted and can be accommodated in a sharing approach.

a) Libertarianism provides a historicist approach to the justification of the current distribution of natural resources. It is the argument that elements of nature, such as pieces of land, may be appropriated by mixing them with human labour, such as ploughing, seeding and harvesting. This has been offered as a justification for the initial privatization of parts of what was originally simply an all-encompassing global commons. Once such original appropriation has occurred, rightful ownership is a matter of voluntary exchange. Transfers through force or fraud violate the requirements of voluntary exchange.[14] At the state level, a further argument is required: the state must be the legimate governing authority of the people who are the rightful owners of the land.

The main problem with this approach to the justification of the existing distribution of natural resources between states is that, even if the original acquisition was justifiable,[15] the transfers of land through the course of history is unlikely to have followed the requirements of voluntary exchange. Surely, land that has not been coercively transferred at some time in the past and whose chain of transfers is thus morally unencumbered is a historical oddity. If coercive transfers had occurred strictly within eternally fixed state boundaries, then this issue would merely involve intra-national injustices. However, coercive land transfers have frequently been connected with changes in governance authority accomplished by military force or false promises. This certainly applies to Canada, where the transfer of land, to the extent that it occurred formally, was achieved under the pressure of European military superiority and at times fraudulent negotiations. (The claims of European colonists that the occupancy of hunter-gatherers did not constitute actual appropriation and therefore could justifiably be displaced by agriculturalists surely was a threadbare rationalization of coercive land transfers.) But the problem is not confined to settler-colonialist states. Conquest, subjugation and displacement have been central characteristics of human history long before the era of global European hegemony. These processes have been decisive in the distribution of natural resources between states.

One conceivable response is to persist with the libertarian-historicist approach and to work out all the distributive rectifications that are required by combining the principle of equal entitlement to

the global commons with the principles of non-intervention and compensation for harm. If such rectification is overwhelmingly demanding in the assessment of harm suffered in the present (as I argued above), it is impossibly complicated and contentious when rectification is taken far back in history. Quite simply, it has little plausibility as a comprehensive approach to distributive justice. That is not to say that the historical injustices underlying the current distribution of natural resources should be ignored. Rather, general rectification of the pervasive pattern of historical injustices can be accomplished only through egalitarianism in the present. The historicist approach thus can be taken as supplementing the support for equal sharing that comes from the earlier argument in terms of the contemporary interdependence among countries. (This argument by no means rules out more specific and limited rectifications of relatively recent and obvious historical injustices, especially as long as global egalitarianism remains an unrealized ideal.)

b) A second objection to international natural-resource egalitarianism is that some countries have, in the process of economic development, depleted their natural resources, such as forests and mineral and fossil-fuel deposits. Even if a claim to an equal share in the originally global commons is accepted, it can be objected that such countries were well endowed in an earlier historical period, but then either squandered this endowment or converted it into industrial capacity such that they are now less dependent on natural resources. The alternative cases of squandered resources and of industrialization require different replies. In the first case, those who were responsible for the depletion are now long dead and their heirs (or others living there now) cannot be held responsible for what happened long ago. This historical argument does not undermine the case for egalitarianism. (That incentives and responsibility for current conservation require that egalitarianism be appropriately qualified is, of course, a different argument.) The second case, that of industrialization, makes it clear that global sharing cannot be limited to natural resources. Otherwise, there would have to be redistribution from countries that are well endowed in terms of natural resources, but poorly endowed in industrial capacity, to countries with the reverse pattern of endowment. What is required is a sharing applied to productive capacity more generally, including not only natural resources, but also inherited industrial endowments. It is not land as such that needs to be redistributed, but the ability to acquire productive capacity, which can be accomplished by the transfer of purchasing power.[16] The principle of equal sharing is thus broadened. It is no longer merely environmental justice.

c) Incumbent occupancy in itself has some moral significance. The fact that a whole way of living, an elaborate culture, a collective identity, and personal expectations and "life plans" (to use Rawls's phrase) have emerged within a particular land with its natural-resource endowments is morally important. In particular, it has consequentialist significance, i.e. it has important consequences for human well-being. Well-being is advanced by security of tenure (from the personal to the macro-collective level). However, this does not mean that the current international distribution of endowments is just. These considerations merely justify constraints on the extent and rapidity of redistribution in the pursuit of international distributive justice. Unconstrained egalitarianism would require a sudden and massive redistribution, whose dislocations could well cause more misery than benefits to those currently disadvantaged. (In fact, these considerations apply as much to the rectification of historical injustices as to egalitarian redistribution.) Instead of a sudden equalization of productive endowments, a more gradual approach is warranted. (Of course, this must not be allowed to become a pretext for the subversion of equalization.) On-going redistribution has the further advantage of allowing rectification of inequalities

that emerge as a result of developments for which particular countries cannot be deemed to be responsible, such as changes in the value of natural resources due to changing patterns of demand and supply. As mentioned before, continuous redistribution must be such that incentives are protected while equality of opportunity is pursued in a radical form.

Conclusion: the Harm and Sharing Principles in International Environmental Justice

The harm principle of international justice, while initially appealing, especially with respect to environmental matters, is much too difficult to implement comprehensively, given the extensive interdependence of the global society today. This conclusion is sharply reinforced when historical harm is included. The harm principle fails completely with respect to the global commons, where the question is one of the distribution of use rights. The principle of equal sharing must fill the moral void left by the limitations of the harm principle. Even in the case of the natural resources within state territories, an argument for equal sharing can be made, on the ground that land consisted originally of a terrestrial global commons and its distribution through historical processes cannot be deemed to have been just by any stretch of the imagination. The harm principle does not become irrelevant, but it must be applied within a generally egalitarian framework. Various qualifications apply to this egalitarian framework. Equal sharing, however, remains central.

Rich-Country Obligations: The Case of Canada and Global Warming

This whole discussion of international environmental justice may sound very utopian. Globally privileged Canadians, it will be argued, will never voluntarily adopt all the measures required by international environmental justice. This is probably true, even though a substantial number of Canadians are actively working for international justice and making sacrifices for it. However, justice discourse has social functions other than to induce the kind of altruism, or what might better be called "equitism" (neither egoism nor altruism but a commitment to justice), that would make Canada act alone to reduce international injustices. First of all, while the Canadian government might not be willing to take corrective action alone, it might, under appropriate circumstances, be willing to collaborate with other countries to collectively bring about a just international environmental regime, if the public has become familiar with the justice arguments and has come to accept their validity. Even if the public and the government did resist the implications for appropriate action, a widely shared recognition of the validity of the justice claims can weaken such resistance. Weakened resistance may then allow poor countries to use whatever leverage is available to them, e.g. refusal to cooperate in unjust international environmental management schemes, in order to win the concessions from rich countries like Canada that are necessary to make international environmental regimes more just. This brief sketch obviously underestimates the obstacles. The point here is merely to indicate that the analysis of international justice and its introduction into public discourse is not simply futile.

Although I earlier argued that the harm principle, when pursued fully, becomes impossibly complex, it is worthwhile showing here that even quite obvious and relatively uncontentious understandings of environmental harm have demanding implications for the obligations of rich countries. I will take the case of global warming, with specific reference to Canada. In 1986 Canada's carbon emissions were 4.1 tons/capita, compared to 0.5 for China, 0.2 for India and only 0.03 for Bangladesh.[17] The average Canadian used the world's carbon sink over 100 times more than the average Bangladeshi. When and if global warming does occur, it is well possible that at least some Canadians, e.g. prairie farmers will actually benefit, while a sea level rise due to global warming

will have a devastating effect on agricultural and residential land in southern Bangladesh.

In the light of this situation, the Climate Change Convention adopted at the 1992 Earth Summit represented little movement in the direction of international environmental justice (except with respect to future generations undifferentiated in terms of countries). First of all, the US successfully insisted on the deletion of targets, contrary to what was advocated by most of the highly industrialized countires, including Canada, an early advocate of emission stabilization.[18] Secondly, the goal was simply to stabilize greenhouse-gas emissions at a sufficiently low level to protect food production, "allow ecosystems to adapt naturally to climate change" and enable the sustainable continuation of economic development.[19] Justice was not articulated as a concern. What was acknowledged was the need for assistance in the form of financing and technology transfer for pollution reduction, administered by the Global Environment Facility of the World Bank, as well as extra assistance for countries particularly vulnerable to climate change.[20] But no principles for allocating emission entitlements or the costs of restraints and of future protective and remedial actions were articulated.[21] Instead, the Convention seemed designed to merely offer poorer countries what was deemed to be sufficient incentive for them to collaborate.

In fact, following the Earth Summit, the poorer countries held back from making commitments to emission reductions, ostensibly waiting for the rich countries to take the lead in action, but probably also waiting for a more favourable deal with respect to financing and technology.[22] Fortunately, at the Berlin Conference of the Parties to the Rio Climate Change Convention, held in April 1995, it was the developing countries, many of which had in the meantime conducted studies of the impact of climate change on their development, that successfully exerted pressure for a strong emission-reduction mandate, against the opposition of the United States and its "carbon-club" allies (including Canada in what seems to have been a turnabout in policy). This shift by the stronger among the poorer countries has made prospects for the 1997 Kyoto Protocol on climate change much more promising.[23] That assumes, though, that the resistance of the carbon club is relatively soft. It may mean that the poorer countries will be able to force a movement towards greater international justice within an emission-control regime.

One approach that would represent international environmental justice, in the form of the harm principle combined with the principle of equal access to the global commons and requiring restitution to poor countries, would be the tradable-emission-rights scheme. If Canada were to support such a scheme, that would represent a serious move towards international environmental justice, unlike the 1992 Climate Change Convention. It would still not represent the kind of international environmental egalitarianism that follows from considerations raised in this paper: the distinction between "necessity emissions" (e.g. methane gas from rice cultivation) and "luxury emissions"; the recognition that international economic relations have involved environmental damage to poor countries; the overwhelming complications for the harm principle resulting from the way in which land, originally the terrestrial global commons, was appropriated in the historical past; and finally, the entanglement of unjustified inequalities in access to the environment with other kinds of unjustified economic inequalities. Nevertheless, Canadian support for a tradable-emissions-rights scheme would represent a major advance towards international environmental justice. In the absence of a commitment of this kind by the Canadian government, international environmental justice could be promoted by environmental and development-education organizations mobilizing for such a commitment.

ENDNOTES

[1] Environmental justice has been articulated by Peter Wenz as the application of principles of justice to environmental public policies. See Peter S. Wenz, *Environmental Justice* (Albany, NY: State University of New York Press, 1988), p. 21. A somewhat more restrictive conception is that of Dale Jamieson: environmental justice is the pursuit of social justice "in ways that are environment-preserving." See Dale Jamieson, "Global environmental justice," in *Philosophy and the Natural Environment*, eds. Robin Attfield and Andrew Belsey (Cambridge: Cambridge University Press, 1994), pp. 199-210.

[2] E.g. Wenz, *Environmental Justice*, ch. 13, and Jamieson, "Global environmental justice," p. 202.

[3] For example, what does global environmental justice require when compensation or redistribution is owed to a state with a poor population, but when that country's elite will use such payments to further enrich itself rather than to help those who have been harmed or whose poverty is the basis of the claim for redistribution? The issue also arises where such transfers do in fact go to the harmed or disadvantaged, but this is done in lieu of rectifying the intra-national injustices. An example might be the use of foreign funds for the colonization of frontier areas, such as Amazonia, to reduce the pressure for environmental justice in the form of land reform. On the other side of the international transaction, the states which are required to make the payments may use internally unfair systems to raise the necessary revenues.

[4] For a classification see e.g. David M. Smith, *Geography and Social Justice* (Oxford: Blackwell, 1994), ch. 3.

[5] See Wenz, *Environmental Justice*, pp. 65-6 for the position of libertarians like Murray Rothbard.

[6] For an articulation of this broad meaning, see G. Peter Penz, "Equality of opportunity: common ground for opposing ideologies," in *Moral Expertise: Studies in Practical and Professional Ethics*, ed. Don MacNiven (London: Routledge, 1989), pp. 117-21.

[7] The principles of justice of John Rawls, the foremost proponent of the contractarian approach, are more extensive and involve further constraints, including relatively libertarian ones. See John Rawls, *A Theory of Justice* (London: Oxford University Press, 1971). This means that his own approach is not wholly at the egalitarian end of the contractarian spectrum. For a more radically egalitarian version, see Rodney G. Peffer, *Marxism, Morality, and Social Justice* (Princeton, NJ: Princeton University Press, 1990), ch. 10.

[8] See e.g. Charles R. Beitz, *Political theory and International Relations* (Princeton, NJ: Princeton University Press, 1979), part III.

[9] For classifications of international ethics to which the above roughly conforms, see Beitz, *Political Theory and Interna-*

tional Relations, and Rachel McCleary, ed., *Seeking Justice: Ethics and International Affairs* (Boulder, CO: Westview), "Introduction," pp. 1-20. For a discussion of international ethics in terms of the perspectives of libertarianism, utilitarianism, and contractarianism, as well as Kantian deontology, see Steven Luper-Foy, ed., *Problems of International Justice* (Boulder, CO: Westview), "Introduction: global distributive justice", pp. 1-24. Classifications that cut across the above two are those of Janna Thompson, *Justice and World Order: A Philosophical Inquiry* (London: Routledge, 1992) and of the wide-ranging anthology by Terry Nardin and David R. Mapel, eds., *Traditions of International Ethics* (Cambridge: Cambridge University Press, 1992.) Both McCleary and Thompson also include communitarianism, and Thompson presents her own approach as communitarian. Communitarianism takes a variety of forms and, in its implications for international ethics, can range from the ethics of state sovereignty and non-interference to a cosmopolitanism anchored in the empirical claim that a global society with particular moral values is emerging. These complexities, however, will not be pursued in this article.

[10] Harvey A. Buckmaster, "The Arctic – a Canadian Case Study," in *Ethics and Climate Change: the Greenhouse Effect*, eds. Harold Coward and Thomas Hurka (Waterloo, ON: Wilfrid Laurier University Press, 1993), pp. 61-80.

[11] For a range of options, see Nigel Bankes, "International Responsibility," in *Ethics and Climate Change: the Greenhouse Effect*, eds. Coward and Hurka (Waterloo, ON: Wilfrid Laurier University Press, 1993), pp. 115-32.

[12] Anil Agarwal and Sunita Narain, *Global Warming in an Unequal World* (New Delhi: Centre for Science and Environment, 1991).

[13] See e.g. Bankes "International responsibility," in *Ethics and Climate Change*, pp. 130, n. 4.

[14] Robert Nozick, *Anarchy, State, and Utopia* (New York: Basic Books, 1974), pp. 167-82.

[15] For a critique of the original-acquisition argument, see G. Peter Penz, "Development refugees and distributive justice: indigenous peoples, land, and the developmentalist state," *Public Affairs Quarterly* 6 (1992, no. 1), pp. 111-113.

[16] This argument is developed somewhat more fully in Penz, "Development Refugees and Distributive Justice," p. 119.

[17] Kirk R. Smith, "The basics of greenhouse gas indices," in *The Global Greenhouse Regime: Who Pays? Science, Economics and North-South Politics in the Climate Change Convention,* eds. Peter Hayes and Kirk R. Smith (Tokyo: United Nations University Press, 1993), pp. 37-8. The data are mainly from G. Marland, T.A. Boden, R.C. Griffin, et al., *Estimates of CO_2 Emissions from Fossil Fuels Burning and Cement Manufacturing* (ORNL/CDIAC-25, Oak Ridge, TN: Oak Ridge National Laboratory, 1988).

[18] G. Bruce Doern, *Green Diplomacy: How Environmental Decisions are Made* (Toronto: C.D. Howe Institute, 1993), pp. 72-6.

[19] Peter Hayes and Kirk R. Smith, eds., *The Global Greenhouse Regime: Who Pays? Science, Economics and North-South Politics in the Climate Change Convention* (Tokyo: United Nations University Press, 1993), "Introduction," p.7. The quotation is from the Convention. Cf. Nigel Bankes, "International responsibility," in *Ethics and Climate Change: the Greenhouse Effect,* eds. Coward and Hurka, pp. 119-21.

[20] Hayes and Smith, eds., *The Global Greenhouse Regime*, "Introduction," p. 8-9; Bankes, "International responsibility," in *Ethics and Climate Change*, p. 124.

[21] Bankes, p. 129.

[22] Ravi Sharma, "Gasbagging the North," *Down to Earth* 3 (1994 Oct. 15): 17-8; Christopher Flavin and Odil Tunali, "Getting warmer: looking for a way out of the climate impasse," *World Watch* 8 (1995, no. 2), pp. 16-7.

[23] Christopher Flavin, "Climate policy: showdown in Berlin," *World Watch* 8 (1995, no. 4), pp. 8-9.

Notes on Contributors

Anne Bell

Anne Bell is a graduate student in the Faculty of Environmental Studies at York University, Toronto. She is also actively engaged in conservation, ecological restoration, and environmental education initiatives. Her current research focuses on the discursive dimensions of school-based habitat restoration.

Annie Booth

Annie Booth is an Assistant Professor in the Faculty of Natural Resources and Environmental Studies, University of Northern British Columbia.

Andrew Brook

Andrew Brook is Professor of Philosophy and Director of the Institute for Interdisciplinary Studies at Carleton University, Ottawa, Ontario. At various times, he has been a member of the Atomic Energy Control Board Panel on the Long Range Management of Uranium Tailings and consultant to Ontario Hydro, Atomic Energy of Canada, the Ministry of Natural Resources of Ontario and various consulting firms on ethical issues in resource and waste management. He was an expert witness before the *Canadian Environmental Assessment Agency* panel on the *AECL* proposal for a deep disposal facility for high level nuclear wastes in northern Ontario.

Roger Cohen

Roger Cohen grew up in New South Wales, Australia and obtained his Bachelor of Rural Science and Doctor of Philosophy degrees from the University of New England, Armidale. He worked for the New South Wales Department of Agriculture from 1967 to 1980 as a Livestock Research Officer before accepting a position as Assistant Professor in the Department of Animal Science at the University of British Columbia. In 1982, he moved to the University of Saskatchewan where he currently holds the rank of Professor in the Department of Animal and Poultry Science. His teaching and research interests are in sustainable beef cattle management, production and nutrition, range management and the development of computer decision support systems to help direct research and farm management practices towards the goal of agricultural sustainability. Since 1982, he has supervised 17 post-graduate students (10 M.Sc. and 7 Ph.D.) and has been a member of the supervising committees of a further 21 post-graduate students. Dr. Cohen has published 55 papers in refereed scientific journals, 2 scientific review papers, 1 book chapter, 64 conference papers and 50 technical reports. From 1982 to 1991 he was Director of the University of Saskatchewan Termuende Research Station, Lanigan; the University Beef Cattle Research Centre, Saskatoon; and the Saskatoon Record of Performance Bull Test Station.

James Cooney

Jim Cooney is Director of International and Public Affairs for Placer Dome Inc., a Canadian multinational gold mining company. He is active in a number of international industry and trade organizations and is a frequent speaker on ethics and social responsibility in the mining industry.

Wesley Cragg

Dr. Cragg is the George R. Gardiner Professor of Business Ethics in York University's Schulich School of Business where he is responsible for encouraging and coordinating research and curriculum development in business ethics. He is the author of a number of books and articles in business, environmental and applied ethics and is currently the President of the Canadian Philosophical Association. Dr. Cragg is coordinating planning for the creation of a Canadian Chapter of Transparency International.

Jerry Valen DeMarco

Jerry Valen DeMarco holds degrees in geography (Bachelor of Arts, University of Windsor), environmental planning (Master in Environmental Studies, York University), and law (Bachelor of Laws, University of Toronto). He is a staff lawyer with the Sierra Legal Defence Fund's Toronto office. He is also a Director of the Wildlands League and a Trustee of the Canadian Parks and Wilderness Society.

Wendy Donner

Wendy Donner is Associate Professor of Philosophy at Carleton University. She is the author of *The Liberal Self: John Stuart Mill's Moral and Political Philosophy* (Cornell, 1991) as well as the chapter on Mill's utilitarianism in the forthcoming *Cambridge Companion to Mill*. She has published several articles on environmental ethics, feminist ethics and political philosophy and is currently editing an anthology on principled identities.

Alan Drengson

Dr. Alan Rike Drengson is retired from the University of Victoria, Victoria, British Columbia. He is author of many poems, articles, books and a novel. He is a university philosophy and environmental studies teacher of over thirty-five years, a Nidan in Aikido - the Japanese nonviolent martial art, a mountaineer, skiier, stainglass craftsman, a devotee of natural farming, and folk musician. His recent books include: *The Deep Ecology Movement: An Introductory Anthology*, co-edited with Yuichi Inoue (North Atlantic Books, 1995) and *The Practice of Technology* (SUNY Press, 1995). He is the founding editor of two quarterlies, *The Trumpeter: Journal Of Ecosophy*, and the *International Journal of Ecoforestry*, as well as a founder of the Ecoforestry Institute.

Michael Allen Fox

Michael Allen Fox teaches environmental ethics, nineteenth-century philosophy, existentialism, and other subjects in the Department of Philosophy, Queen's University. He has published on a wide range of issues, including books on Schopenhauer, nuclear war, and animal experimentation. He is currently writing on the philosophy of vegetarianism.

Robert Gibson

Robert Gibson is an associate professor of environment and resource studies at the University of Waterloo and editor of *Alternatives Journal: Environmental Thought, Policy and Action*.

Allan Greenbaum

Allan Greenbaum is a Ph.D. candidate in sociology at York University, where, with Alex Wellington and Ellen Baar, he co-designed and co-taught a course on social conflict and environmental law in the Division of Social Science. He has degrees in philosophy, law and environmental studies. His research interests include environmental thought, the sociology of environmental aesthetics, and the role of values, beliefs and culture in environmental conflict. He is president of the Toronto Field Naturalists and is a founding member of the Environmental Studies Association of Canada.

Pamela Courtenay Hall

Pamela Courtenay Hall teaches philosophy of education, feminist theory and environmental education at the University of British Columbia. A former math and physics teacher, she completed her Ph.D. in philosophy at the University of Toronto with her thesis, "Ecoholism and its Critics: A Critical Exploration of Holism in Environmental Ethics and the Science of Ecology". She is the mother of two young children, Matthew and Stefan, and a frequent teller of original nature stories at local elementary schools.

Karen Krug

Karen Krug grew up on a family farm in Saskatchewan and is currently an assistant professor in the Environmental Policy Institute at Brock University. She teaches courses on agriculture and sustainability, gender and environment, environmental ethics, human settlement systems and human services planning. As a member of the Niagara Community Land Stewardship Council, she is involved in community liaison work on stewardship issues. She is on the Board of Directors of Niagara Peninsula Homes, which has undertaken two community economic development projects related to the food system - The Good Food Box and Niagara Presents. She also supports the work of the Preservation of Agricultural Lands Society, which aims to protect valuable tender fruit land in the Niagara region.

Deborah McGregor

Deborah McGregor is Anishnawbe and a member of the Whitefish River First Nation. Deborah works at First Nations House at the University of Toronto and is a part-time faculty member at York University. She holds a Bachelor of Science in Psychology (U of T) and a Master in Environmental Studies (York University). She is now completing her Ph.D. dissertation at the University of Toronto on Traditional Environmental Knowledge and Forest Management. She has worked as an educator, policy analyst, environmental and community planner, researcher, counsellor and curriculum developer.

Thomas Meredith

Thomas Meredith was born in Montreal, and lived and worked in Invermere, B.C. with Parks Canada for several years. He then studied environmental studies at the University of Waterloo, ecological conservation at the University of London, and biology at Cambridge University. He is now a professor of geography at McGill University where his research interests are in ecological research management and community empowerment for environmental protection.

Peter Miller

Peter Miller (Ph.D., Yale University, 1967) is former Chair of Philosophy at the University of

Winnipeg and an Adjunct Professor at the Natural Resources Institute, University of Manitoba. Dr. Miller pursues research in Environmental Ethics and is Co-Investigator in a SSHRC-funded project on Global Ecological Integrity. He participates in forest issues as Vice-President of T.R.E.E. (Time to Respect Earth's Ecosystems – a coalition of Manitoba environmental groups) and is co-leader of the Integrated Resource Management and Policy Working Group of the Manitoba Model Forest. Dr. Miller also serves on the Manitoba Environmental Council (which is advisory to Manitoba's Environment Minister) and is Past-President of the Canadian Society for the Study of Practical Ethics. He helped to establish Child Care Training programs at the University of Winnipeg and is currently Acting Director of Developmental Studies.

David Oppenheim

David Oppenheim is a recent graduate from the Faculty of Environmental Studies at the University of Waterloo, Waterloo, Ontario.

David Pearson

David Pearson is a geologist by training and environmental activist by persuasion. He is currently head of the Earth Sciences program at Laurentian University. He was the founding Director of Science North in Sudbury. For several years he has hosted a widely watched MCTV program called "Down to Earth" which is focused on environmental issues.

Peter Penz

Peter Penz is Associate Professor in the Faculty of Environmental Studies at York University, Toronto, and a Research Fellow of that university's Centre for Refugee Studies and its Centre for Practical Ethics. He studied economics at the University of British Columbia, later received his doctorate in normative economic philosophy from the University of Oxford, and then built on this area to adopt a thoroughly interdisciplinary approach with a primary focus on normative concerns. His books include *The Real Poverty Report* (Edmonton: Hurtig, 1971, co-authored) and *Consumer Sovereignty and Human Interests* (Cambridge University Press, 1986). His more recent research has been on the theory of basic needs, on development ethics, on conflicts between states and tribal peoples in Asia, and on land-rights mobilization in India. His current work is on global environmental justice and on development-induced population displacement. He also teaches on the latter two topics, as well as on theoretical perspectives in the social sciences.

Ron Pushchak

Ron Pushchak received his masters degree in Environmental Studies from York University and his doctorate in Urban Planning from Princeton University. He is a professor in the School of Environmental Health with a joint appointment in the School of Urban and Regional Planning at Ryerson Polytechnic University. He teaches courses in environmental planning and environmental assessment and his research interests are: environmental impact assessment, risk assessment and hazardous facility siting. Dr. Pushchak has been involved in a number of environmental planning cases including the Canadian concept for disposal of nuclear fuel waste, the Ontario Waste Management Corporation proposal to site a hazardous waste facility, and recent proposals for municipal solid waste disposal. Dr. Pushchak is a member of the board of directors of the Canadian Environmental Defence Fund, a national organization that deals directly with Canadian legal cases where national environmental resources are threatened.

Raymond Rogers

Raymond A. Rogers is an Assistant Professor in the Faculty of Environmental Studies, York University, Toronto. He is author of two books: *Nature and the Crisis of Modernity* (1994) and *The Oceans Are Emptying: Fish Wars and Sustainability* (1995). He also spent twelve years as a commercial fisherman on the south shore of Nova Scotia.

Lionel Rubinoff

Lionel Rubinoff is Professor Emeritus of Philosophy and Environmental Studies at Trent University, Peterborough, Ontario. In addition to numerous articles in scholarly journals and chapters in edited books, his publications include a critical edition of F.H. Bradley's *Presuppositions of Critical History*, *The Pornography of Power*, *Faith and Reason*, *Tradition and Revolution*, *Collingwood and the Reform of Metaphysics*. He is currently completing a book on the moral foundations of environmentalism to be entitled, *From the Domination to the Celebration of Nature*.

Mark Schwartz

Mark S. Schwartz is currently a Ph.D. Candidate in Business Ethics at the Schulich School of Business, York University. He holds a B.A. (York University), M.B.A. (Schulich School of Business) and L.L.B. (Osgoode Hall), and is a barrister and solicitor for the province of Ontario. He has taught both business ethics and business law at the Schulich School of Business. He is a Research Fellow for the Center for Business Ethics, Bentley College and a Director of the Ethics Practitioners' Association of Canada. His publications include: "Corporate Compliance and Ethical Decision Making in Canada" in *Corporate Conduct Quarterly* (1996) and *Business Ethics: A Primer* by the Center for Business Ethics, Bentley College (1996). His research interests include corporate codes of ethics and corporate social responsibility.

Elisa Shenkier

Elisa Shenkier has a Bachelor's degree in Philosophy from McGill University. Her Master's degree in Geography, also from McGill University, focused upon the ethical implications of resource conservation and exploitation. She is now working with various ethnic communities in Montreal where she lives with her son, Sacha-Leo.

Ingrid Leman Stefanovic

Ingrid Leman Stefanovic is Associate Professor and Associate Chair in the Department of Philosophy, University of Toronto. Her teaching and research interests are in the area of Phenomenology and Environmental Philosophy.

Duncan Taylor

Duncan Taylor is a faculty member in the Environmental Studies Program at the University of Victoria in Victoria, British Columbia. He is the author of numerous articles and has recently published a book on the environmental crisis in Canada called *Off Course*. He is an active bagpipe musician and wilderness treker. He teaches courses in the philosophical and valuational dimension of environmental problems and also leads wilderness and other experiential education journeys. He is a founder of the Ecoforestry Institute.

Alex Wellington

Alex Wellington is a Ph.D. candidate in philosophy at York University. She has previous degrees in law (LLB) and environmental studies (MES). Her research interests include political theory, intellectual property, and applied ethics. She co-edited *Social Conflict and Environmental Law* with Allan Greenbaum and Ellen Baar, a book which was developed for use in a team taught course in the Division of Social Science at York University. She has published articles on biotechnology patents and feminism and vegetarianism. She is an avid hiker and amateur nature photographer.

Laura Westra

Laura Westra is Associate Professor at the University of Windsor. She received her doctorate from the University of Toronto in 1983. Using her background in ancient Greek philosophy, her recent work deals primarily with environmental ethics, the philosophy of ecology and issues in environmental racism. Her published books include *An Environmental Proposal for Ethics: The Principle of Integrity* (1994); *Faces of Environmental Racism* (1995), co-edited with P. Wenz; and *Perspectives on Ecological Integrity* (1995), co-edited with J. Lemons. In press are *Consumption: Perspectives from Environmental Ethics and Business Ethics* (1997), co-edited with P. Werhane; *The Greeks and the Environment* (1997), co-edited with T.M. Robinson; and *Environment and Sustainability* (1997), co-edited with J. Lemons. She has also published about 60 articles and chapters in books. She has received two SSHRC grants (1992-95 and 1996-99) for her work on "integrity". She has worked with WHO, IUCN and other professional associations, on ethics and codes of ethics.